INTERNATIONAL MARKETING STRATEGY

Analysis, development and implementation

FOURTH EDITION

ISOBEL DOOLE AND ROBIN LOWE

THOMSON

Australia • Canada • Mexico • Singapore • Spain • United Kingdom • United States

International Marketing Strategy: Analysis, Development and Implementation 4th Edition

Copyright © 2004 Thomson Learning

The Thomson logo is a registered trademark used herein under licence.

For more information, contact Thomson Learning, High Holborn House, 50–51 Bedford Row, London, WC1R 4LR or visit us on the World Wide Web at:
http://www.thomsonlearning.co.uk

British Library Cataloguing-in-Publication Data
A catalogue record for this book is available from the British Library

ISBN 1-84480-025-3
First edition published 1994 by Routledge, London
Reprinted 1996 by International Thomson Business Press

Second Edition published 1999
Reprinted 2000 by Thomson Learning
Third edition published 2001
Reprinted 2002 and 2003 by Thomson Learning
This edition published 2004 by Thomson Learnng

Typeset by Photoprint, Torquay

Printed in Italy by G. Canale and Co.

To our children;
Robert, Libby and William,
Catherine and Jonathan

Contents

PART 2 STRATEGY DEVELOPMENT 139

List of figures, tables, illustrations and dilemmas

Figures

Dilemmas

Preface

Introduction

Markets and marketing are becoming ever more international in their nature and managers around the world ignore this fact at their peril. To achieve sustainable growth in markets that are becoming increasingly global or merely to survive in domestic markets that are increasingly attacked by international players, it is essential for organisations to understand the complexity and diversity of international marketing and for their managers to develop the skills, aptitudes and knowledge that are necessary in order to compete effectively.

This new and completely revised edition ensures the best-selling textbook *International Marketing Strategy* continues to meet the needs of the international marketing student and practitioner in an up-to-date and innovative manner. It recognises the increasing time pressures of both students and managers and so strives to maintain the readability and clarity of the previous editions as well as providing a straightforward and logical structure that will enable them to apply their learning to the tasks ahead.

The book continues to incorporate new, significant and relevant material with learning innovations that ensure its continued status as the best-selling UK text on international marketing strategy.

Structure of the book

As in previous editions, the book is divided into three main subject areas, analysis, strategy development and implementation, each incorporating four chapters. For each chapter the learning outcomes for the reader are identified and these lead to the key themes of the chapter that are explored in the text. Illustrations of the key issues are provided along with examples of the kind of practical dilemmas that are faced by international marketing managers.

Success in international marketing is achieved through being able to integrate and appreciate the interaction between the various elements of the international marketing strategy development process and so this is addressed in two ways. At the end of each chapter a case study is included. Whilst the main focus of the chapter case study is on integrating a number of the themes of the chapter the reader should also draw upon the learning from the chapters that have gone before to give a complete answer.

At the end of each part there is a more comprehensive integrative learning activity for the reader that focuses on international marketing planning. At the end of Part 1 the activity is concerned with analysis, at the end of Part 2 the activity is concerned with strategy development and at the end of Part 3 the activity is concerned with implementation. The format for these learning activities is similar so that the three integrative learning activities, when added together, integrate all the learning from the book and provide for the reader a practical and comprehensive exercise in international marketing planning.

New to this edition

A number of chapters have been revised and updated to ensure the inclusion of the latest developments in international marketing. Each chapter now has a case study that encourages further reflection and discussion on the key themes of the chapter.

The chapters (5 and 6) on international marketing in SMEs and global firms have been expanded to include the management and planning implications of the strategy development issues highlighted within the chapter.

In this new edition a new chapter (12) is included that focuses on how technology supports and enables the international marketing process in areas such as customer relationship management, value and supply chain management. It specifically addresses the impact of e-commerce on the way that business is being done in the business-to-consumer and business-to-business markets and the implications that this has for the future strategies of the organisations in those markets.

The majority of the case studies, illustrations and dilemmas are new or updated. Material is used from around the world and especially includes a number of cases and illustrations from the emerging markets of Asia, Latin America and Eastern Europe. The authors have endeavoured to cater for the needs of readers who are developing their international marketing skills in Europe, the Americas, Asia, Australasia or other parts of the world. Each illustration and dilemma has a question that highlights a specific issue that should be considered.

The Integrative Learning Activity is an innovative new section at the end of each part that has the objective of encouraging readers to integrate their learning from the chapters and the parts. By obtaining and analysing data through secondary sources, typically through the Internet, the reader is able to proceed through the steps of the international marketing strategy process and thus acquire further knowledge and have the opportunity to practise a number of their international marketing skills.

How to study using this book

The aim of the book is for readers to have an accessible and readable resource for use both as a course book and for revision. The text also incorporates the syllabus of the Chartered Institute of Marketing and so is essential reading for students of the CIM qualifications.

It has a clear structure which is easy to use and easy for the reader to follow, thus making it ideal for incorporation into a course delivered in a twelve-week teaching semester. Its geocentric view of international marketing with examples of good practice in competing internationally from around the globe makes it ideal for use with courses with multi-cultural students.

International Marketing Strategy has been developed to help the reader learn, understand and practise a number of elements of the international marketing strategy process. The process involves the analysis of a situation, development of a strategy against a background of a number of strategic options and the implementation of the chosen option. It is important to recognise that there is not one 'right' strategy, because success is ultimately determined by many factors and, besides, it will usually take a number of years before the strategy can be seen finally as a success or failure. Therefore, this book provides a framework, within the parts and chapter structure, in which to understand and evaluate the factors that should be taken into account (and which should be dismissed too).

Structure of the book

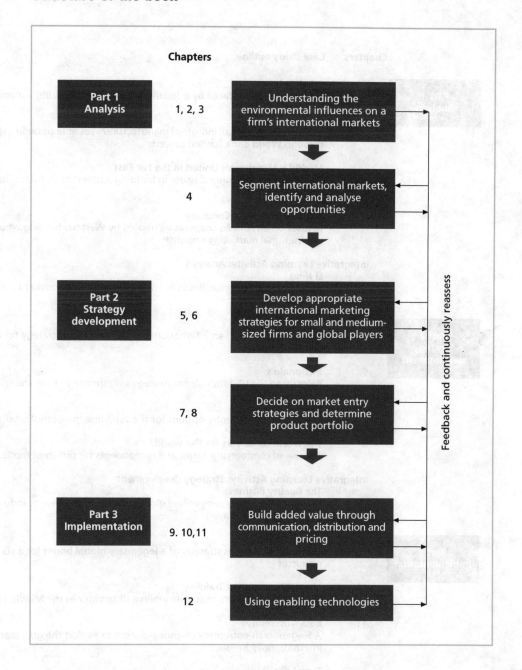

Case studies at the end of each chapter

Chapters	Case study outline

Part 1 Analysis

1   **Tokai Guitars**
Explores the issues faced by a Japanese guitar manufacturer expanding into Europe

2   **B F Rail**
Examines how a small industrial manufacturer was able to build exports in third world countries through World Bank funded projects

3   **Madrid v Manchester United in the Far East**
Debates the socio/cultural issues in building a brand in SE Asia. What is the brand? Is it the player or the club?

4   **The Day Chocolate Company**
Focuses on an African cooperative backed by Western funding who are trying to build their international marketing presence

Integrative Learning Activity: Analysis
Li Ning
Analysis of the opportunities in the domestic and global market for the leading sports goods supplier in China

Part 2 Strategy development

5   **Indeco**
The development of an international niche marketing strategy for an Indian firm targeting an emerging market

6   **McDonald's**
Refocusing the US firm's global strategy in response to their changing global market environment

7   **Muji**
Evaluating market entry options for the Japanese 'no-brand' retailer

8   **The world car or cars for the world?**
The use of common platforms and components for different models and brands of cars

Integrative Learning Activity: Strategy development
The Beauty Business
Examines the highly competitive global market of the beauty industry and the strategic challenges facing the global players

Part 3 Implementation

9   **Harley Davidson**
The communications strategy of a legendary global brand for a US firm with limited financial resources

10   **Merry Management Training**
Debates the problems that arise when a distributor in the Middle East did not perform as expected

11   **Beta Automotive**
A Singaporean entrepreneur endeavouring to exploit the grey market in auto parts to expand internationally in Asia

12   **Travel distribution**
The impact of technology innovations on the global distribution of travel products, such as flights and hotel rooms

Integrative Learning Activity: Implementation
ISS
Implementing the international marketing strategy of the ISS group, the leading global player in the cleaning services and facilities management market

Parts

The three parts focus on the topics of analysis, strategy development and implementation. Each part contains an introduction to the four chapters that have been grouped together.

Part 1 Analysis

Part 1 focuses on analysing the international marketing environment. It provides an introduction to how the international marketing environment influences how firms operate. It explores the changing nature of the environment and explains the structures that support and control international trade. Also considered are the social and cultural influences on customer buying behaviour in international markets.

Frameworks and processes are explained that provide the means to systematically identify and evaluate marketing opportunities and carry out market research across the world.

Part 2 Strategy development

Part 2 explains the international marketing strategy options available for small and medium-sized firms and also the largest organisations that will enable them to compete effectively in global markets. The factors that affect the choice of strategy are considered as well as the challenges that are posed to the managers of these strategies.

A key decision for most organisations is which market entry method to use to exploit the market opportunities from the many options available. This is then followed by the selection and development of the products and service strategy that determine the portfolio that will be offered to customers.

Part 3 Implementation

Part 3 deals with the international communication, distribution and pricing strategies that support the introduction and development of the business in the various worldwide markets. The different local market factors that affect implementation are considered. These factors may allow the associated implementation programmes and processes to be standardised across different markets but, frequently, it is necessary to adapt the strategies to suit local needs.

Finally, technology plays a key enabling role in international marketing strategy implementation. It supports the programme and process delivery and also provides opportunities for creativity that allow innovative firms to gain competitive advantage.

Readers should realise that these groupings of chapter topics within parts are primarily to provide a clear structure and layout for the book. In practice, however, there is considerable overlap between analysis, strategy development and implementation topics. For example, product strategy and market entry are considered by organisations is some situations to be implementation issues, and technology might be used to support analysis, set the overall international marketing strategy or support implementation.

Chapters

After the introduction to the chapters the learning objectives for the chapter are set out and these should provide the focus for study. To help to reinforce the learning and encourage the reader to explore the issues more fully the chapters contain a number of additional aids to learning.

Illustrations

The illustrations that have been provided are intended not just to reinforce a key issue or learning point that has been discussed within the chapter, but the questions that have been added are intended to enable the reader to reflect upon the deeper and broader implications too and thus provide a further opportunity for discussion. The aim has been for the settings for the illustrations to be as diverse as possible, geographically, culturally, by business sector, size and type of organisation in order to try to help the reader consider the situations described from alternative perspectives.

Dilemmas

The dilemmas included emphasise the point that there are few simple and straightforward management decisions in international marketing. Organisations and managers often face difficult dilemmas that require a decision. The dilemmas within a chapter provide the opportunity for the reader to identify the factors that should be taken into account in coming to the decision and, hopefully, consider rather more creative ideas that lead to decisions and solutions that add greater value.

Case studies

The case studies provide the opportunity for the reader to carry out more comprehensive analysis on key chapter topics before deciding what strategic decisions or plans should be made. These short cases provide only limited information and, where possible, readers should obtain more information on the case study subject from appropriate Web sites in order to complete the tasks. The reader should start with the questions that have been supplied in order to help guide the analysis or discussion. After this, however, the reader should think more broadly around the issues raised and decide whether these are indeed the right questions to ask and answer. International markets change fast and continuously and new factors that have recently emerged may completely alter the situation.

Integrative learning activities

At the end of each of the three parts of the book, new to this edition we have included an *Integrative Learning Activity*. The purpose of the integrated learning activities is to integrate the four chapters that make up each of the parts. More importantly, however, is that as a whole, the three activities provide a framework for planning an international marketing strategy and give the opportunity for readers to consider the practical issues involved in developing, planning and implementing an outline international marketing strategy. The objective of these activities is to provide a vehicle through which the reader is able to develop practical skills in research, analysis, evaluation and strategy development. In completing these activities you will need to synthesise the various strands and themes explored throughout the book and apply them to a practical situation.

Web support

The textbook is fully supported by the accompanying Web site that can be found at www.thomsonlearning.co.uk. This enables students and lecturers to access a number of resources in order to explore the subject further. Lecturers can use the site to access valuable online teaching resources, including a full set of PowerPoint slides to accompany the text and hints and tips on how to use the case studies, illustrations etc. in a classroom situation. Students are able to access learning resources to accompany the textbook and hot-links to other Web sites which may be useful in exploring the cases and illustrations in the text.

ID, RL, February 2004

ACCOMPANYING WEB SITE

Visit the *International Marketing Strategy* accompanying website at www.thomsonlearning.co.uk/marketing/doole4/ to find further teaching and learning material including:

For Students

- Internet Projects
- Multiple Choice Questions for each chapter
- Additional Cases with accompanying questions
- Related weblinks

For Lecturers

- Instructors Manual – including teaching notes, how to use the text and answers to the questions within the text
- Downloadable PowerPoint slides
- Case Study Teaching Notes to accompany cases within the text
- Dilemmas from the fourth edition with full commentaries to use as a teaching aid – ideal for classroom and tutorial discussion
- Cases from third edition with suggested outcomes

Acknowledgements

We would like to acknowledge the generous support of the Chartered Institute of Marketing in permitting the use of the CIM mini-cases taken from past examination papers of International Marketing from the Diploma in Marketing and also the use of examination questions, which form some of the discussion questions used at the end of each chapter.

Inevitably, in the task of writing this textbook we have had help, support and valuable contributions from many people. We would especially like to thank our colleagues from Sheffield Hallam University and other univerisities who have contributed a number of case studies and illustrations.

We are indebted to our students from many countries, the managers of many businesses in South Yorkshire, who have freely given their time to share their expert knowledge of international niche marketing, and managers in many larger companies, including IBM and Shell, who have discussed with us the challenges they face in global marketing. Over the years they have all helped to shape and influence our view of international marketing strategy.

The team at Thomson Learning have always encouraged us and we are grateful for their professionalism in turning the manuscript into its finished form.

Every effort has been made to obtain permission from the copyright holders for material reproduced in this book. Any rights not acknowledged here will be acknowledged in subsequent printings if due notice is given to the publisher.

ID, RL, February 2004

Walk-through tour

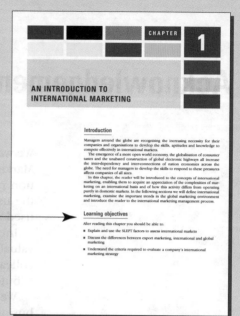

Learning objectives
Listed at the start of each chapter, highlighting the key concepts covered in each chapter.

Illustrations
Illustrations are provided throughout the text, showing international companies' marketing strategies, accompanied by a question.

Summary

Bulleted list at the end of each chapter briefly reviewing the main concepts and key points covered in the chapter.

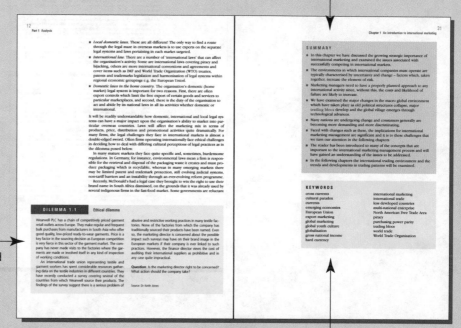

Dilemmas

International marketing dilemmas and associated questions are located throughout the text and provide a forum for classroom and tutorial discussion.

Keywords

Highlighted throughout the text where they first appear, alerting the student to the core concepts and techniques. Listed at the end of each chapter and emboldened within the index.

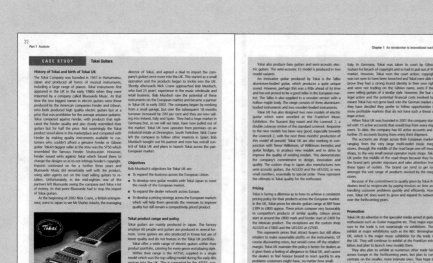

Case studies

Cases are provided at the end of each chapter. They draw upon real-world companies and help to demonstrate the theory in practice. Each case is accompanied by questions to test the readers' understanding.

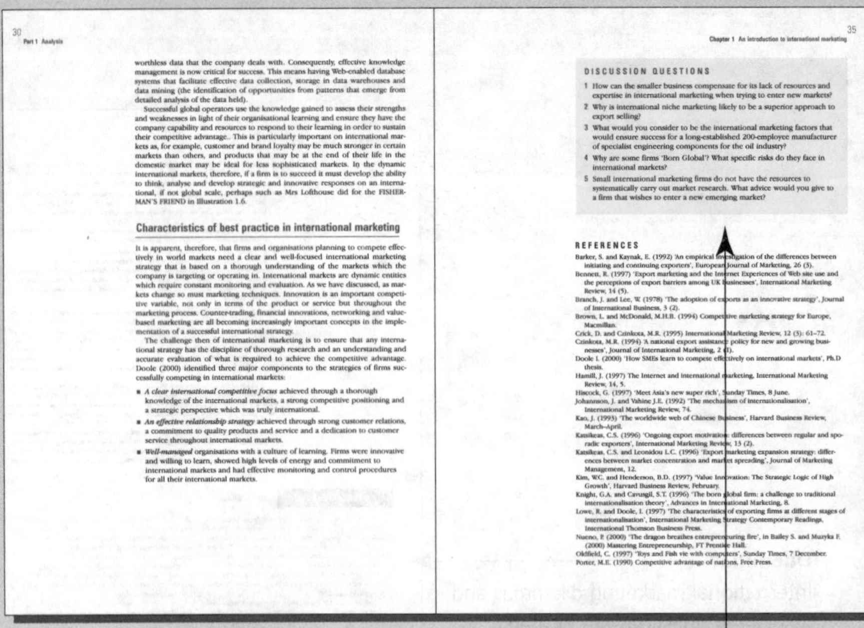

worthless data that the company deals with. Consequently, effective knowledge management is now critical for success. This means having Web-enabled database systems that facilitate effective data collection, storage in data warehouses and data mining (the identification of opportunities from patterns that emerge from detailed analysis of the data held).

Successful global operators use the knowledge gained to assess their strengths and weaknesses in light of their organisational learning and ensure they have the company capability and resources to respond to their learning in order to sustain their competitive advantage. This is particularly important on international markets as, for example, customer and brand loyalty may be much stronger in certain markets than others, and products that may be at the end of their life in the domestic market may be ideal for less sophisticated markets. In the dynamic international markets, therefore, if a firm is to succeed it must develop the ability to think, analyse and develop strategic and innovative responses on an international, if not global scale, perhaps such as Mrs Lofthouse did for the FISHERMAN'S FRIEND in Illustration 1.6.

Characteristics of best practice in international marketing

It is apparent, therefore, that firms and organisations planning to compete effectively in world markets need a clear and well-focused international marketing strategy that is based on a thorough understanding of the markets which the company is targeting or operating in. International markets are dynamic entities which require constant monitoring and evaluation. As we have discussed, as markets change so must marketing techniques. Innovation is an important competitive variable, not only in terms of the product or service but throughout the marketing process. Counter-trading, financial innovations, networking and value-based marketing are all becoming increasingly important concepts in the implementation of a successful international strategy.

The challenge then of international marketing is to ensure that any international strategy has the discipline of thorough research and an understanding and accurate evaluation of what is required to achieve the competitive advantage. Doole (2000) identified three major components to the strategies of firms successfully competing in international markets:

- *A clear international competitive focus* achieved through a thorough knowledge of the international markets, a strong competitive positioning and a strategic perspective which was truly international.
- *An effective relationship strategy* achieved through strong customer relations, a commitment to quality products and service and a dedication to customer service throughout international markets.
- *Well-managed* organisations with a culture of learning. Firms were innovative and willing to learn, showed high levels of energy and commitment to international markets and had effective monitoring and control procedures for all their international markets.

REFERENCES

Barker, S. and Kaynak, E. (1992) 'An empirical investigation of the differences between initiating and continuing exporters', European Journal of Marketing, 26 (5).

Bennett, R. (1997) 'Export marketing and the Internet Experiences of Web site use and the perceptions of export barriers among UK Businesses', International Marketing Review, 14 (5).

Branch, J. and Lee, W. (1978) 'The adoption of exports as an innovative strategy', Journal of International Business, 3 (2).

Brown, L. and McDonald, M.H.B. (1994) Competitive marketing strategy for Europe, Macmillan.

Crick, D. and Czinkota, M.R. (1995) International Marketing Review, 12 (3): 61–72.

Czinkota, M.R. (1994) A national export assistance policy for new and growing businesses', Journal of International Marketing, 2 (1).

Doole I. (2000) 'How SMEs learn to compete effectively on international markets', Ph.D thesis.

Hamill, J. (1997) The Internet and international marketing, International Marketing Review, 14, 5.

Hiscock, G. (1997) 'Meet Asia's new super rich', Sunday Times, 8 June.

Johannson, J. and Vahine J.E. (1992) 'The mechanism of internationalisation', International Marketing Review, 74.

Kao, J. (1993) 'The worldwide web of Chinese Business', Harvard Business Review, March–April.

Katsikeas, C.S. (1996) 'Ongoing export motivations: differences between regular and sporadic exporters', International Marketing Review, 13 (2).

Katsikeas, C.S. and Leonidou L.C. (1996) 'Export marketing expansion strategy: differences between market concentration and market spreading', Journal of Marketing Management, 12.

Kim, W.C. and Henderson, B.D. (1997) 'Value Innovation: The Strategic Logic of High Growth', Harvard Business Review, February.

Knight, G.A. and Cavusgil, S.T. (1996) 'The born global firm, a challenge to traditional internationalisation theory', Advances in International Marketing, 8.

Lowe, R. and Doole, I. (1997) 'The characteristics of exporting firms at different stages of internationalisation', International Marketing Strategy Contemporary Readings, International Thomson Business Press.

Nueno, P. (2000) 'The dragon breathes entrepreneuring fire', in Bailey S. and Muzyka P. (2000) Mastering Entrepreneurship, FT Prentice Hall.

Oldfield, C. (1997) 'Toys and Fish vie with computers', Sunday Times, 7 December.

Porter, M.E. (1990) Competitive advantage of nations, Free Press.

Discussion questions

Short questions, which encourage you to review and/or critically discuss your understanding of the main topics and issues.

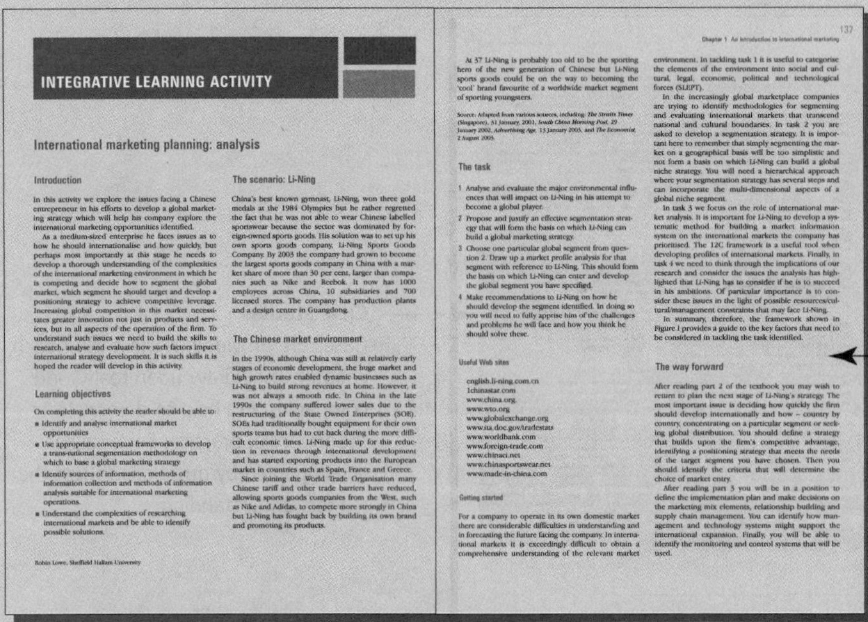

INTEGRATIVE LEARNING ACTIVITY

International marketing planning: analysis

Introduction

In this activity we explore the issues facing a Chinese entrepreneur in his efforts to develop a global marketing strategy which will help his company explore the international marketing opportunities identified.

As a medium-sized enterprise he faces issues as to how he should internationalise and how quickly, but perhaps most importantly at this stage he needs to develop a thorough understanding of the complexities of the international marketing environment in which he is competing and decide how to segment the global market, which segment he should target and develop a positioning strategy to achieve competitive leverage. Increasing global competition in this market necessitates greater innovation not just in products and services, but in all aspects of the operation of the firm. To understand such issues we need to build the skills to research, analyse and evaluate how such factors impact international strategy development. It is such skills it is hoped the reader will develop in this activity.

Learning objectives

On completing this activity the reader should be able to:

- Identify and analyse international market opportunities
- Use appropriate conceptual frameworks to develop a trans-national segmentation methodology on which to base a global marketing strategy
- Identify sources of information, methods of information collection and methods of information analysis suitable for international marketing operations.
- Understand the complexities of researching international markets and be able to identify possible solutions.

Robin Lowe, Sheffield Hallam University

The scenario: Li-Ning

China's best known gymnast, Li-Ning, won three gold medals at the 1984 Olympic but he rather regretted the fact that he was not able to wear Chinese labelled sportswear because the sector was dominated by foreign-owned sports goods. His solution was to set up his own sports goods company, Li-Ning Sports Goods Company. By 2003 the company had grown to become the largest sports goods company in China with a market share of more than 30 per cent, larger than companies such as Nike and Reebok. It now has 1000 employees across China, 10 subsidiaries and 700 licensed stores. The company has production plants and a design centre in Guangdong.

The Chinese market environment

In the 1990s, although China was still at relatively early stages of economic development, the huge market and high growth rates enabled dynamic businesses such as Li-Ning to build strong revenues at home. However, it was not always a smooth ride. In China in the late 1990s the company suffered lower sales due to the restructuring of the State Owned Enterprises (SOE). SOEs had traditionally bought equipment for their own sports teams but had to cut back during the more difficult economic times. Li-Ning made up for this reduction in revenues through international development and has started exporting products into the European market in countries such as Spain, France and Greece.

Since joining the World Trade Organisation many Chinese tariff and other trade barriers have reduced, allowing sports goods companies from the West, such as Nike and Adidas, to compete more strongly in China but Li-Ning has fought back by building its own brand and promoting its products.

At 57 Li-Ning is probably too old to be the sporting hero of the new generation of Chinese but Li-Ning sports goods could be on the way to becoming the 'cool' brand favourite of a worldwide market segment of sporting youngsters.

Source: Adapted from various sources, including: The Straits Times (Singapore), 31 January 2001, South China Morning Post, 29 January 2002, Advertising Age, 13 January 2003, and The Economist, 2 August 2003.

The task

1 Analyse and evaluate the major environmental influences that will impact on Li-Ning in his attempt to become a global player.

2 Propose and justify an effective segmentation strategy that will form the basis on which Li-Ning can build a global marketing strategy.

3 Choose one particular global segment from question 2. Draw up a market profile analysis for that segment with reference to Li-Ning. This should form the basis on which Li-Ning can enter and develop the global segment you have specified.

4 Make recommendations to Li-Ning on how he should develop the segment identified. In doing so you will need to fully apprise him of the challenges and problems he will face and how you think he should solve these.

Useful Web sites

english.li-ning.com.cn
1chinastar.com
www.china.org
www.wto.org
www.globalexchange.org
www.ita.doc.gov/tradestats
www.worldbank.com
www.foreign-trade.com
www.chinaci.net
www.chinasportswear.net
www.made-in-china.com

Getting started

For a company to operate in its own domestic market there are considerable difficulties in understanding and in forecasting the future facing the company. In international markets it is exceedingly difficult to obtain a comprehensive understanding of the relevant market environment. In tackling task 1 it is useful to categorise the elements of the environment into social and cultural, legal, economic, political and technological forces (SLEPT).

In the increasingly global marketplace companies are trying to identify methodologies for segmenting and evaluating international markets that transcend national and cultural boundaries. In task 2 you are asked to develop a segmentation strategy. It is important here to remember that simply segmenting the market on a geographical basis will be too simplistic and not form a basis on which Li-Ning can build a global niche strategy. You will need a hierarchical approach where your segmentation strategy has several steps and can incorporate the multi-dimensional aspects of a global niche segment.

In task 3 we focus on the role of international market analysis. It is important for Li-Ning to develop a systematic method for building a market information system on the international markets the company has prioritised. The 12C framework is a useful tool when developing profiles of international markets. Finally in task 3 we need to think through the implications of our research and consider the issues the analysis has highlighted that Li-Ning has to consider if he is to succeed in his ambitions. Of particular importance is to consider these issues in the light of possible resource/cultural/management constraints that may face Li-Ning.

In summary, therefore, the framework shown in Figure 1 provides a guide to the key factors that need to be considered in tackling the task identified.

The way forward

After reading part 2 of the textbook you may wish to return to plan the next stage of Li-Ning's strategy. The most important issue is deciding how quickly the firm should develop internationally and how – country by country, concentrating on a particular segment or seeking global distribution. You should define a strategy that builds upon the firm's competitive advantage, identifying a positioning strategy that meets the needs of the target segment you have chosen. Then you should identify the criteria that will determine the choice of market entry.

After reading part 3 you will be in a position to define the implementation plan and make decisions on the marketing mix elements, relationship building and supply chain management. You can identify how management and technology systems might support the international expansion. Finally, you will be able to identify the monitoring and control systems that will be used.

Integrative learning activities

A series of learning activities presented at the end of each part. Each one integrates the 4 chapters of the associated part.

PART 1

ANALYSIS

1 An introduction to international marketing

2 The international trading environment

3 Social and cultural considerations in international marketing

4 International marketing research and opportunity analysis

Introduction: Aims and objectives

Knowledge and an understanding of the markets in which companies operate are important for all business activities. In international markets, because of geographical distances and the complexities of operating in a number of disparate markets where risk and uncertainty are high, the need for knowledge and understanding becomes of paramount importance. It is this issue that is central to Part 1 of this book. The chapters within this part concentrate on helping the reader generate a greater understanding of the concepts of the international marketing process and the international environment within which companies operate. It aims to extend the range of understanding to enable the reader to deal with international marketing situations and develop the skills to analyse and evaluate non-domestic markets to enable their firms to compete effectively in world markets.

In Chapter 1 we focus on the international marketing environment. The book uses the SLEPT approach to understanding the complexities of the environmental influences on international marketing, thus enabling the reader to acquire an appreciation of the complexities of marketing on an international basis. We examine what is meant by international marketing and examine the reasons for success and failure in international marketing strategies and the characteristics of best international marketing practice.

In Chapter 2 the focus is on gaining an understanding of the international trading environment. We first examine, at a macro level, the development of international trading structures and the changes in trading patterns, as well as examining the major international bodies formed to foster world trade. The evolution of trading regions is analysed and the implications to international marketing companies assessed.

In Chapter 3 we take a fairly detailed approach to examining the social and cultural influences in international marketing. The components of culture are examined together with the impact of these components on international marketing. We then look at how cultural influences impact on buyer behaviour across the globe both in consumer markets and in business-to-business markets and discuss methods that can be used to analyse cultures both within and across countries.

In Chapter 4 the focus is on the identification and evaluation of marketing opportunities internationally. Segmentation of international markets is discussed, and how to prioritise international opportunities. The marketing research process and the role it plays in the development of international marketing strategies are also examined. The different stages in the marketing research process are discussed, with particular attention being paid to the problems in carrying out international marketing research in foreign markets and coordinating multi-country studies.

CHAPTER 1

AN INTRODUCTION TO INTERNATIONAL MARKETING

Introduction

Managers around the globe are recognising the increasing necessity for their companies and organisations to develop the skills, aptitudes and knowledge to compete effectively in international markets.

The emergence of a more open world economy, the globalisation of consumer tastes and the unabated construction of global electronic highways all increase the inter-dependency and inter-connections of nation economies across the globe. The need for managers to develop the skills to respond to these pressures affects companies of all sizes.

In this chapter, the reader will be introduced to the concepts of international marketing, enabling them to acquire an appreciation of the complexities of marketing on an international basis and of how this activity differs from operating purely in domestic markets. In the following sections we will define international marketing, examine the important trends in the global marketing environment and introduce the reader to the international marketing management process.

Learning objectives

After reading this chapter you should be able to:

- Explain and use the SLEPT factors to assess international markets

- Discuss the differences between export marketing, international and global marketing

- Understand the criteria required to evaluate a company's international marketing strategy

THE STRATEGIC IMPORTANCE OF INTERNATIONAL MARKETING

Last year's international trade in merchandise exceeded US$7 trillion and world trade in services is estimated at around US$1.5 trillion. Whilst most of us cannot visualise such huge amounts, it does serve to give some indication of the scale of international trade today.

This global marketplace consists of a population of 6 billion people which is expected to reach 10 billion by 2050 according to the latest projections prepared by the United Nations.

Global wealth is increasing and this is again reflected in higher demand. Increasing affluence and commercial dynamism has seen nations across Asia, central and Eastern Europe emerge as high growth economies. Increasing affluence and demand simply means that consumers will actively seek choice with the result that competition is emerging as companies compete to win the battle for disposable income. Countries, or at least large sections of them, are moving into a world which deals not in commodity purchase, maize or rice, into consumer goods i.e. packaged and marketed to their citizens' personal needs.

Population growth and increased affluence together have helped create a 'global youth culture'. Teenagers now account for 30 per cent of the population globally. In many countries, more than half the population is pre-adult, creating one of the world's biggest single markets, the youth market. Everywhere adolescents project worldwide cultural icons, Nike, Coke, Gap and Sony Walkman, as well as Sega, Nintendo and the Sony Playstation. When 'virtual reality' is commonplace, the one-world youth culture market will exceed all others as a general category for marketers. Parochial, local and ethnic growth products may face difficult times.

Older consumers are also increasingly non-national in their identity, not in their personal identity but from the perspective of the consumable fabric of their lives. They drive international cars, watch international programmes on television, use international hardware and software. International consumption is accelerating and boundaries of product ownership are increasingly blurred.

On the supply side, multi-national and global corporations are increasing in size and embracing more global power. The top 500 companies in the world now account for 70 per cent of world trade and 80 per cent of international investment. Total sales of multi-nationals are now in excess of world trade, which gives them a combined gross product of more than some national economies.

To deal with the size of the global economy, companies are consolidating through mergers, acquisitions and alliances to reach the scale considered necessary to compete in the global arena. At the same time, there is a trend towards global nationalisation, seeking world standards for efficiency and productivity. Toyota and General Motors have a joint venture in California called Nummi. Daimler-Benz have taken over Chrysler and VW have taken over the Bentley brand and their UK production facilities. Glaxo Wellcome formed a number of global alliances in the pharmaceutical market, creating the world's largest research-based pharmaceutical company. General Electric formed a strategic alliance with the French aircraft company Snecma. Such trends can also be seen in the service sector. In the US, Morgan Stanley and Dean Witter merged to offer global investment as well as global private banking and credit card services. There has also been an increase in the number of joint ventures and international strategic alliances to gain access to global markets. Xerox entered into a joint venture with Fuji to gain access to the Japanese market. Motorola and Fujitsu joined together to exploit opportunities in the global telecommunications market and Vodafone have joined with Omnitel to enable them to compete more effectively in Italy.

The global marketplace is simultaneously becoming inter-dependent, economically, culturally and technically through the consistent thrust in technological innovation. Information moves anywhere in the world at the speed of light and what is becoming known as the global civilisation is being facilitated by the convergence of long distance telecoms, cuts in the cost of electronic processing and the growth of Internet access.

The combination of all these forces has meant that all companies need to develop a marketing orientation which is international and have managers who are able to analyse, plan and implement strategies across the globe. It is for these reasons that international marketing has become such a critical area of study for managers and an important component of the marketing syllabus of Business faculties in universities.

So perhaps now we should turn our attention to examining exactly what we mean by international marketing.

What is international marketing?

Many readers of this textbook will have already followed a programme of study in marketing but, before explaining what we mean by international marketing, let us reflect for a few moments on our understanding of what is meant by marketing itself. The Chartered Institute of Marketing defines marketing as the 'Management process responsible for identifying, anticipating and satisfying customer requirements profitably'. Thus marketing involves:

- focusing on the needs and wants of customers
- identifying the best method of satisfying those needs and wants
- orienting the company towards the process of providing that satisfaction
- meeting organisational objectives.

In this way, it is argued, the company or organisation best prepares itself to achieve competitive advantage in the marketplace. It then needs to work to maintain this advantage by manipulating the controllable functions of marketing within the largely uncontrollable marketing environment made up of SLEPT factors, i.e. Social, Legal, Economic, Political and Technical.

How does the process of international marketing differ? Within the international marketing process the key elements of this framework still apply. The conceptual framework is not going to change to any marked degree when a company moves from a domestic to an international market; however, there are two main differences. First, there are different levels at which international marketing can be approached and, second, the uncontrollable elements of the marketing environment are more complex and multi-dimensional given the multiplicity of markets that constitute the global marketplace. This means managers have to acquire new skills and abilities to add to the tools and techniques they have developed in marketing to domestic markets.

International marketing defined

At its simplest level, international marketing involves the firm in making one or more marketing mix decisions across national boundaries. At its most complex, it involves the firm in establishing manufacturing facilities overseas and coordinating marketing strategies across the globe. At one extreme there are firms that opt for 'international marketing' simply by signing a distribution agreement with a foreign agent who then takes on the responsibility for pricing, promotion, distribution and market development. At the other extreme, there are huge global companies such as Ford with an integrated network of manufacturing plants worldwide and who operate in some 150 country markets. Thus, at its most complex, international marketing becomes a process of managing on a global scale. These different levels of marketing can be expressed in the following terms:

- **Domestic marketing**, which involves the company manipulating a series of controllable variables such as price, advertising, distribution and the product in a largely uncontrollable external environment that is made up of different economic structures, competitors, cultural values and legal infrastructure within specific political or geographic country boundaries.

- **International marketing**, which involves operating across a number of foreign country markets in which not only do the uncontrollable variables differ significantly between one market and another, but the controllable factors in the form of cost and price structures, opportunities for advertising and distributive infrastructure are also likely to differ significantly. It is these sorts of differences that lead to the complexities of international marketing.

- **Global marketing management**, which is a larger and more complex international operation. Here a company coordinates, integrates and controls a whole series of marketing programmes into a substantial global effort. Here the primary objective of the company is to achieve a degree of synergy in the overall operation so that by taking advantage of different exchange rates, tax rates, labour rates, skill levels and market opportunities, the organisation as a whole will be greater than the sum of its parts.

This type of strategy calls for managers who are capable of operating as international marketing managers in the truest sense, a task which is far broader and more complex than that of operating either in a specific foreign country or in the domestic market. In discussing this, Terpstra and Sarathy (2002) comment that 'the international marketing manager has a dual responsibility; foreign marketing (marketing within foreign countries) and global marketing (co-ordinating marketing in multiple markets in the face of global competition)'.

Thus, how international marketing is defined and interpreted depends on the level of involvement of the company in the international marketplace. International marketing could therefore be:

- **Export marketing**, in which case the firm markets its goods and/or services across national/political boundaries.

- **International marketing**, where the marketing activities of an organisation include activities, interests or operations in more than one country and where there is some kind of influence or control of marketing activities from outside the country in which the goods or services will actually be sold. Sometimes markets are typically perceived to be independent and a profit centre in their own right, in which case, the term multi-national or multi-domestic marketing is often used.

- **Global marketing**, in which the whole organisation focuses on the selection and exploitation of global marketing opportunities and marshals resources around the globe with the objective of achieving a global competitive advantage.

The first of these definitions describes relatively straightforward exporting activities, numerous examples of which exist. However, the subsequent definitions are more complex and more formal and indicate not only a revised attitude to marketing but also a very different underlying philosophy. Here the world is seen as a market segmented by social, legal, economic, political and technological (SLEPT) groupings.

In this textbook, we will incorporate the international marketing issues faced by firms, be they involved in export, international or global marketing.

For all these levels the key to successful international marketing is being able to identify and understand the complexities of each of these SLEPT dimensions of the international environment and how they impact on a firm's marketing strategies across their international markets. As in domestic marketing, the successful marketing company will be the one that is best able to manipulate the controllable tools of the marketing mix within the uncontrollable environment. It follows that the key problem faced by the international marketing manager is that of coming to terms with the details and complexities of the international environment. It is these complexities that we will examine in the following sections.

THE INTERNATIONAL MARKETING ENVIRONMENT

The key difference between domestic marketing and marketing on an international scale is the multi-dimensionality and complexity of the many foreign country markets a company may operate in. An international manager needs a knowledge and awareness of these complexities and the implications they have for international marketing management.

There are many environmental analysis models which the reader may have come across. For the purposes of this textbook, we will use the SLEPT (Social, Legal, Economic, Political and Technological) approach and examine the various aspects and trends in the international marketing environment through the social/cultural, legal, economic, political and technological dimensions, as depicted in Figure 1.1.

Social/cultural environment

The social and cultural influences on international marketing are immense. Differences in social conditions, religion and material culture all affect

---

FIGURE 1.1

The environmental influences on international marketing

consumers' perceptions and patterns of buying behaviour. It is this area that determines the extent to which consumers across the globe are either similar or different and so determines the potential for global branding and standardisation.

A failure to understand the social/cultural dimensions of a market is a prime reason for failure as McDonald's found when they moved into India following the opening up of that market (see Illustration 1.1).

Cultural factors

Cultural differences and especially language differences have a significant impact on the way a product may be used in a market, its brand name and the advertising campaign.

Coca-Cola had to withdraw their two-litre bottle from Spain when they found that Spaniards did not own fridges with sufficiently large compartments. Johnson's floor wax was doomed to failure in Japan as it made the wooden floors very slippery and Johnson's failed to take into account the custom of not wearing shoes inside the home.

Initially, Coca-Cola had enormous problems in China as Coca-Cola sounded like 'Kooke Koula' which translates into 'A thirsty mouthful of candle wax'. They managed to find a new pronunciation 'Kee Kou Keele' which means 'joyful tastes and happiness'.

ILLUSTRATION 1.1   India spices things up!

The McDonald's formula, hugely successful as it is, was always going to have to be adapted to a place where killing cows is sacrilege. But burger joints are not the only ones that need to be careful; other western firms tempted by India's growing middle class have had to be sensitive to the country's definite tastes.

McDonald's, which now has seven restaurants in India, was launched there a year ago. It has had to deal with a market that is 40 per cent vegetarian; with the aversion to either beef or pork among meat-eaters, with a hostility to frozen meat and fish, and with the general Indian fondness for spice with everything.

To satisfy such tastes, McDonald's has discovered that it needs to do more than provide the right burgers. Customers buying vegetarian burgers want to be sure that these are cooked in a separate area in the kitchen using separate utensils. Sauces like McMasala and McImli are on offer to satisfy the Indian taste for spice. McDonald's promises to introduce a spiced version of its fries soon.

Although its expansion has been faster in India than in some other Asian countries such as Indonesia, it has hardly been rapid. Yet, at least, the firm has avoided the disasters of some other big American names.

A few years back, violent protests in Bangalore in southern India over the quality of its food temporarily closed KFC which sells fried chicken.

Three years ago, Kellogg made a splash pitching breakfast cereals as a healthier alternative to the heavy Indian breakfast. Indians were unimpressed. Kellogg, facing mounting losses, is now selling to a westernised niche market instead.

Foreign companies have got three things wrong in India. They overestimated the size and disposable income of the much-touted Indian middle class. They underestimated the strength of local products in the markets they were entering and they overestimated the value of their reputation. Indian consumers seem unimpressed by the glamour of the western brands, and food companies are scaling down their plans accordingly.

Others are playing it safe. For years Wimpy has restricted itself to only a few outlets. Burger King has stayed out of the market altogether. Three years after Heinz went into India by taking over Glaxo's food business, it is still chewing over the idea of introducing Indians to the joys of tomato ketchup. An extra pinch of spice might do the trick.

Question How can foreign companies ensure they avoid cultural insensitivity when going into new markets?

Source: Adapted from *The Economist*, 22 November 1997

Other companies who have experienced problems are General Motors which experienced difficulties with its brand name 'Nova' in Spain ('no va' in Spanish means 'no go'), Pepsi Cola which had to change its campaign 'Come Alive With Pepsi' in Germany as, literally translated, it means 'Come Alive Out of the Grave' and McDonald's whose character Ronald McDonald failed in Japan because his white face was seen as a death mask.

To operate effectively in different countries requires recognition that there may be considerable differences in the different regions. Consider Northern Europe versus Latin Europe, the Northwest of the USA versus the South or Tokyo and Taiwan. At the stage of early internationalisation it is not unusual for Western firms to experience what appear to be cultural gaps with their counterparts in Latin America and Asian countries as well as in different regions of those countries. There are many examples where companies simply do not find their way into a market or where their performance is less than successful. Only a very small proportion of the failures or the major difficulties are made public. A campaign by Camay Soap which showed a husband washing his wife's back in the bath was a huge success in France but failed in Japan. Not because it caused offence, but because Japanese women viewed the prospect of a husband sharing such a time as a huge invasion of privacy.

On the other hand, there are visible signs that social and cultural differences are becoming less of a barrier. This has led to the emergence of a number of world brands such as Microsoft, Intel, Coca-Cola, McDonald's, Nike etc., all competing in global markets that transcend national and political boundaries. But many have confused globalisation with homogenisation; cultural differences between, and often within, countries can affect the success of such brands.

There are a number of **cultural paradoxes** which exist. For example, in Asia, the Middle East, Africa and Latin America there is evidence both for the westernisation of tastes and the assertion of ethnic, religious and cultural differences. These differences do not necessarily constitute unbridgeable cultural chasms in all sectors of a society. Instead there are trends toward similarities both in cultures and outlooks of consumers. There are more than 600 000 Avon ladies now in China and a growing number of them in Eastern Europe, Brazil and the Amazon.

In northern Kenya you may find a Sambhuru warrior who owns a cellular telephone. Thus, whilst there is a vast and, sometimes, turbulent mosaic of cultural differences, there is also evidence that a global village is potentially taking shape which, as Kenichi Ohmae (1994) said, 'will be a nationless state marked by the convergence of customer needs that transcends political and cultural boundaries'.

The social/cultural environment is an important area for international marketing managers and will be returned to in a number of chapters where we examine the various aspects of its strategic implications. In Chapter 3, we devote a full chapter to the examination of the social and cultural influences in international marketing. In Chapter 5, we will examine the forces driving the global village and its strategic implication to companies across the world.

Social factors

Growth and movement in populations around the world are important factors heralding social changes. Eighty per cent of the world's population live in developing countries; by 2025 this is likely to reach 85 per cent. Two out of every five people live in China and India. Figure 1.2 details the changes in the regional population around the globe. As can be seen, whilst world population is growing dramatically, the growth patterns are not consistent around the world.

Over the next half century, Africa's population will almost treble. In 1995, 700 million people lived in Africa: by 2050 there will be just over 2 billion. China's population will rise much more slowly from 1.2 billion to 1.5 billion. With a population of 1.53 billion people, India will have more inhabitants than China in 50 years' time. Europe is the only region where the population is expected to decline; any increase in population in high income countries is entirely due to migration.

There are also visible moves in the population within many countries leading to the formation of huge urban areas where consumers have a growing similarity of needs across the globe. By 2010, 50 per cent of the world's population will live in urban areas. The world is moving into gigantic conurbations. The population of Greater Tokyo is soon to be close to 30 million and Mexico City 20 million. Cities such as Lagos, Buenos Aires and Djakarta will soon outstrip cities such as Paris, London and Rome. In the year 2015, no European city will be in the top 30 and 17 of the world's mega cities of 10 million plus will be in the Third World. This has powerful implications for international marketing. These cities will be markets in themselves. Urban dwellers require similar products (packaged conveniently and easy to carry). Similarly, they demand services, telephones and transportation of all kinds and modern visual communications. It also means for the incoming company that customers are accessible. They are identifiable and firms can communicate with them efficiently via supermarkets, advertising and other marketing communication tools. Table 1.1 shows the ten mega cities in the world forecast for 2015.

Legal environment

Legal systems vary both in content and interpretation. A company is not just bound by the laws of its home country but also by those of its host country and by the growing body of international law. Firms operating in the **European Union** are facing ever-increasing directives which affect their markets across Europe. This can affect many aspects of a marketing strategy — for instance advertising — in the form of media restrictions and the acceptability of particular

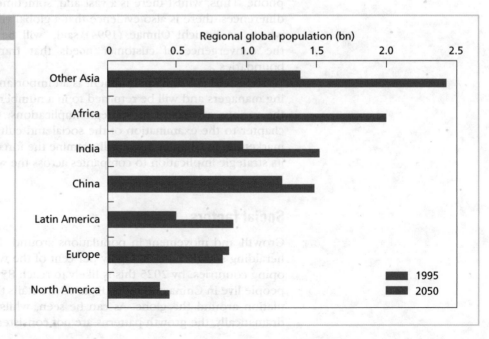

FIGURE 1.2

Regional breakdown of global population

Source: Population Division, Department of Economic and Social Affairs, United Nations Secretariat, *World Population Prospects. The 1996 Revision*, United Nations, New York

creative appeals (see Illustration 1.2). Product acceptability in a country can be affected by minor regulations on such things as packaging and by more major changes in legislation. In the USA for instance, the MG sports car was withdrawn when the increasing difficulty of complying with safety legislation changes made exporting to that market unprofitable. Kraft Foods sell a product called Lifesavers in many countries. They are very similar to the Nestlé Polo brand, who, using EU law, attempted to stop the sale of Lifesavers in the EU purely to protect their market share.

It is important, therefore, for the firm to know the legal environment in each of its markets. These laws constitute the 'rules of the game' for business activity. The legal environment in international marketing is more complicated than in domestic since it has three dimensions: (1) local domestic law; (2) international law; (3) domestic laws in the firm's home base.

TABLE 1.1	The world's ten mega cities in 2015		
City		Country	Population (millions)
Tokyo		Japan	26.4
Mumbai		India	26.1
Lagos		Nigeria	23.2
Dhaka		Bangladesh	21.1
Sao Paulo		Brazil	20.4
Karachi		Pakistan	19.2
Mexico City		Mexico	19.2
New York		USA	17.4
Jakarta		Indonesia	17.3
Calcutta		India	17.3

Source: United Nations

ILLUSTRATION 1.2   When is a Parma ham not a Parma ham?

The European Court of Justice has decided that it is illegal for the world-famous Parma ham to be sliced and packaged outside the Italian region that gives Parma ham its name. The ruling was a victory for the 200 or so producers of Parma ham who had launched their legal action against Asda, a UK food retailer. The case hinged on the court's interpretation of geographical indications – EU-protected trademarks that recognise the importance of products closely associated with a particular place, whether it be Parma ham, French champagne, Spanish sherry or Stilton cheese from Britain. The Parma producers argued that slicing the ham was an important process that had to be done locally. Asda argued they should be free to slice and pack the ham where they chose in order to cut costs and reduce the price to consumers. The court showed it was more concerned with the protection of the ham producers' rights than market efficiency.

The question is, how will the world view the decision. Some commentators use such examples to question the commitment of the European Union to freeing trade and becoming more competitive.

Question Do you think the court decision protects local market diversity across European markets or does it act as a restrictive trade practice?

Source: Adapted from *The Economist*, 21 May 2003

■ *Local domestic laws.* These are all different! The only way to find a route through the legal maze in overseas markets is to use experts on the separate legal systems and laws pertaining in each market targeted.

■ *International law.* There are a number of 'international laws' that can affect the organisation's activity. Some are international laws covering piracy and hijacking, others are more international conventions and agreements and cover items such as IMF and World Trade Organization (WTO) treaties, patents and trademarks legislation and harmonisation of legal systems within regional economic groupings e.g. the European Union.

■ *Domestic laws in the home country.* The organisation's domestic (home market) legal system is important for two reasons. First, there are often export controls which limit the free export of certain goods and services to particular marketplaces, and second, there is the duty of the organisation to act and abide by its national laws in all its activities whether domestic or international.

It will be readily understandable how domestic, international and local legal systems can have a major impact upon the organisation's ability to market into particular overseas countries. Laws will affect the marketing mix in terms of products, price, distribution and promotional activities quite dramatically. For many firms, the legal challenges they face in international markets is almost a double-edged sword. Often firms operating internationally face ethical challenges in deciding how to deal with differing cultural perceptions of legal practices as in the dilemma posed below.

In many mature markets they face quite specific and, sometimes, burdensome regulations. In Germany, for instance, environmental laws mean a firm is responsible for the retrieval and disposal of the packaging waste it creates and must produce packaging which is recyclable, whereas in many emerging markets there may be limited patent and trademark protection, still evolving judicial systems, non-tariff barriers and an instability through an ever-evolving reform programme.

Recently, McDonald's had a legal case they brought to win the right to use their brand name in South Africa dismissed, on the grounds that it was already used by

---

DILEMMA 1.1	**Ethical dilemma**

Wearwell PLC has a chain of competitively priced garment retail outlets across Europe. They make regular and frequent bulk purchases from manufacturers in South Asia who offer good quality, low-priced ready-to-wear garments. Price is a key factor in the sourcing decision as European competition is very fierce in this sector of the garment market. The company has never made visits to the factories where the garments are made or involved itself in any kind of inspection of working conditions.

An international trade union representing textile and garment workers has spent considerable resources gathering data on the textile industries in different countries. They have recently conducted a survey covering several of the countries from which Wearwell source their products. The findings of the survey suggest there is a serious problem of abusive and restrictive working practices in many textile factories. None of the factories from which the company has traditionally sourced their products have been named. Even so, the marketing director is concerned about the possible impact such surveys may have on their brand image in the European markets if their company is ever linked to such practices. However, the finance director views the cost of auditing their international suppliers as prohibitive and in any case quite impractical.

Question Is the marketing director right to be concerned? What action should the company take?

Source: Dr Keith Jones

several indigenous firms in the fast-food market. Some governments are reluctant to develop and enforce laws protecting intellectual property partly because they believe such actions favour large, rich, multi-nationals.

Anheuser Busch (USA) and Budvar (Czech Republic) have been in constant litigation over the right to use Budweiser in the European Union. Both companies have recently been legally deemed the right to use it.

Piracy in markets with limited trademark and patent protection is another challenge. Bootlegged software constitutes 87 per cent of all personal computer software in use in India, 92 per cent in Thailand and 98 per cent in China, resulting in a loss of US$8 billion for software makers a year. In the case study at the end of Chapter 1, Tokai guitars were accused of breach of copyright in Germany. They won their case in court but at huge financial cost to the company.

India has been seen by many firms to be an attractive emerging market beset with many legal difficulties, bureaucratic delay and lots of red tape. For example, shoes cannot be imported in pairs but have to be imported one at a time. This causes huge problems for shoe manufacturers who need to import shoes as production samples. The way many of them overcome the problem is by importing the left shoe via Madras and the right shoe via Mumbai. Companies such as Mercedes Benz, Coca-Cola and Kellogg have found the vast potential of India's market somewhat hard to break into. Its demanding consumers can be difficult to read and local rivals can be surprisingly tough. Political squabbles, bureaucratic delays, infrastructure headaches and unprofessional business practices create one obstacle after another. Foreign companies are often viewed with suspicion.

Economic environment

It is important that the international marketer has an understanding of economic developments and how they impinge on the marketing strategy. This understanding is important at both a world level in terms of the world trading infrastructure such as world institutions and trade agreements developed to foster international trade, at a regional level in terms of regional trade integration and at a country/market level. Firms need to be aware of the economic policies of countries and the direction in which a particular market is developing economically in order to make an assessment as to whether they can profitably satisfy market demand and compete with firms already in the market.

Amongst the 200 or so countries in the world, there are varying economic conditions, levels of economic development and **Gross National Income** (GNI) per capita. Gross National Income in the world is US$33 trillion; however, it is not shared equitably across the world. The United Nations classes 75 per cent of the world's population as poor, that is, they have a per capita income of less than US$3470, and only 11 per cent of the population as rich, meaning they have a per capita income of more than US$8000. Perhaps more startling is the UN claim that the richest 50 million people in the world share the same amount of wealth as the poorest 3000 million. Such disparities of incomes set particular challenges for companies operating in international markets in terms of seeking possible market opportunities, assessing the viability of potential markets as well as identifying sources of finance in markets where opportunities are identified but where there is not capacity to pay for goods.

Another key challenge facing companies is the question as to how they can develop an integrated strategy across a number of international markets when there are divergent levels of economic development. Such disparities often make it difficult to have a cohesive strategy, certainly in pricing. Table 1.2 gives an indication of the diversity of purchasing power across a number of selected countries. Per capita Gross National Income has been weighted to reflect what a consumer can actually buy with a dollar in the country being measured; this is what is meant by the term **purchasing power parity** (PPP). Reporting the figures this way gives a more accurate reflection of the real differences in purchasing power between countries.

The Economist 'Big Mac' Index is a useful tool which illustrates the difficulties global companies have in trying to achieve a consistent pricing strategy across the world. This index gives a guide to the comparative purchasing power across countries by examining their economies in terms of how many minutes somebody needs to work to buy a 'Big Mac' as priced in the US.

Figure 1.3 shows that the average worker in Caracas has to toil for 117 minutes to earn enough money to buy a Big Mac. At the other extreme, a worker in Tokyo needs to work for only nine minutes and a New Yorker 20 minutes. This causes problems for McDonald's in trying to pursue a standard product image across markets. Priced in US dollars, a Big Mac in Iceland would cost US$5.79, whereas in the Philippines it costs US$1.23.

In order to examine these challenges further we divided the economies into developed economies, **emerging economies** and **less developed economies**.

TABLE 1.2	Gross National Income per capita (GNIpc) across the world (weighted for purchasing power parity (ppp))

Country	GNIpc (ppp) (US$)
Luxembourg	48 560
USA	34 280
Denmark	28 490
Netherlands	27 390
Germany	25 420
United Kingdom	24 340
Singapore	21 630
Greece	17 520
Hungary	11 990
South Africa	10 910
Poland	9 370
Chile	8 840
Uruguay	8 250
Brazil	7 070
Thailand	6 230
Turkey	5 830
Philippines	4 240
China	4 070
Indonesia	2 890
India	2 820
Zimbabwe	2 220
Vietnam	2 070
Bangladesh	1 620
Nigeria	790
Tanzania	520
Sierra Leone	460

Source: World Bank: World Development Indicators

The developed economies

The developed economies of the **North American Free Trade Area (NAFTA)**, **European Union (EU)** and **Japan** account for 80 per cent of world trade. For many firms this constitutes much of what is termed the global market. Even though many companies call themselves global, most of their revenues and profits will be earned from these markets. In the US car market, for instance, 85 per cent of cars produced there are sold there. In the European Union nearly 70 per cent of the international goods traded are traded within the European Union; in NAFTA, 50 per cent of goods exported are to other members of NAFTA. This leads some commentators to argue that most competition, even in today's global marketplace, is more active at a regional level than a global level. It is from these developed economies that the global consumer with similar lifestyles, needs and desires emanates. However, emerging markets are now becoming more economically powerful and moving up the ranks such that by the year 2020 it is projected that China, South Korea and Taiwan will be amongst the top tier of national economies.

The emerging economies

In countries such as China, Mexico, Vietnam and India there is a huge and growing demand for everything from automobiles to cellular phones. Many of the countries which were seen only a few years ago as 'lesser developed countries' (LDCs) have shown considerable economic advancement. Countries such as China, Mexico, Chile, Hungary, Poland, Turkey, the Czech Republic and South Africa are all viewed as key growth markets.

In these emerging markets, there is an evolving pattern of government-directed economic reforms, lowering of restrictions on foreign investment and

---

Working time required to buy a Big Mac (in minutes)

Source: Adapted from *The Economist*

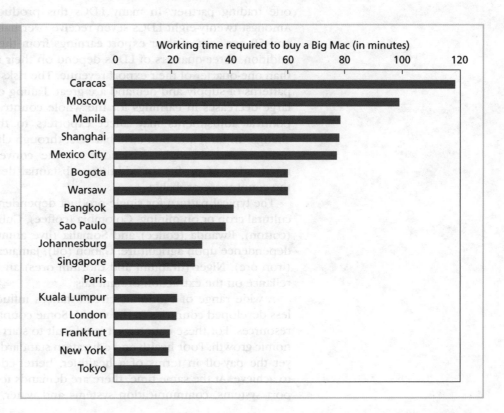

increasing privatisation of state-owned monopolies. All these herald significant opportunities for the international marketing firm.

Such markets often have what is termed as a 'dual economy'. Usually there tends to be a wealthy urban professional class alongside a poorer rural population. Income distribution tends to be much more skewed between the 'haves' and the 'have nots' than in developed countries. From negligible numbers a few years ago, China now has a middle class of 82 million which is forecast to grow to 500 million in the next century. Brazil and Indonesia have middle classes of 15 million each.

High economic growth is often accompanied by high inflation. Countries such as Russia, Brazil, Mexico and Argentina have all recently suffered from high rates of inflation and, in the developing world, it tends to be a more persistent problem than in the developed world where most countries have experienced single digit inflation for some years.

Venezuela has an inflation rate of 33.5 per cent and Turkey one of 29.5 per cent. Both countries are seen as potentially high growth markets, but with huge economic challenges.

Tied to an inflationary environment are generally high levels of external debt. Total external debt of lesser developed countries exceeds US$1 trillion. As countries have to prioritise the servicing of external debt, it invariably leaves little availability of **hard currency** to buy imported products.

Less developed countries (LDCs)

This group includes underdeveloped countries and developing countries. The main features are a low GDP per capita (see Table 1.2), a limited amount of manufacturing activity and a very poor and fragmented infrastructure. Typical infrastructure weaknesses are in transport, communications, education and healthcare. In addition, the public sector is often slow-moving and bureaucratic.

It is common to find that LDCs are heavily reliant on one product and often on one trading partner. In many LDCs this product is the main export earner. Amongst twenty-eight LDCs seven receive over half and nine receive between 25 and 50 per cent of their export earnings from their main export commodity. In addition, three-quarters of LDCs depend on their main trading partner for more than one-quarter of their export revenue. The risks posed to the LDC by changing patterns of supply and demand are great. Falling commodity prices can result in large decreases in earnings for the whole country. The resultant economic and political adjustments may affect exporters to that country through possible changes in tariff and non-tariff barriers, through changes in the level of company taxation and through restrictions on the convertibility of currency and the repatriation of profits. In addition, substantial decreases in market sizes within the country are probable.

The typical pattern for single-product dependence is the reliance on one agricultural crop or on mining. Colombia (coffee), Cuba (sugar), Ghana (cocoa), Mali (cotton), Rwanda (coffee) and Somalia (live animals) are examples of extreme dependence upon agriculture. Gabon (oil), Jamaica (base metal ores), Mauritania (iron ore), Niger (uranium and thorium ores) and Nigeria (oil) are examples of reliance on the extraction of minerals.

A wide range of economic circumstances influences the development of the less developed countries in the world. Some countries are small with few natural resources. For these countries it is difficult to start the process of substantial economic growth. Poor health and education standards need money on a large scale, yet the pay-off in terms of a healthier, better-educated population takes time to achieve. At the same time, there are demands for public expenditure on transport systems, communication systems and water control systems. Without real prospects for rapid economic development, private sources of capital are reluctant to invest in such countries. This is particularly the case for long-term infrastructure projects and, as a result, important capital spending projects rely heavily on world aid programmes.

Currency risks

Whilst we have examined economic factors within markets, we also need to bear in mind that in international marketing transactions invariably take place between countries and so the exchange rates and currency movements are an important aspect of the international economic environment. On top of all the normal vagaries of markets, customer demands, competitive actions and economic infrastructures, foreign exchange parities are likely to change on a regular if unpredictable basis. In the past year currency movements have been markedly more volatile than for several years. The euro has risen by about 25 per cent against the dollar in the past year. The dollar has lost more than 15 per cent of its value against a broader range of currencies and the Japanese yen has been appreciating strongly, causing consternation for the Japanese government at a time when they have been trying to deal with a deflationary economy. In Britain, the pound has slumped to its lowest level for six years against the euro.

As the reader can see, world currency movements, stimulated by worldwide trading and foreign exchange dealing, is an additional complication in the international environment. Companies operating in international markets that guess wrongly as to which way a currency will move can see their international business deals rendered unprofitable overnight. Businesses that need to swap currencies to pay for imported goods, or because they have received foreign currency for products they have exported, can find themselves squeezed to the point where they watch their profits disappear.

In Europe, the formation of the European Monetary Union has led to greater stability for firms operating in the market. For the first years of its life, the euro seemed only to move downwards. At its low point, it had lost more than a fifth of its value against the dollar at its launch in January 1999. However, since then it has continued to rise steadily. The formation of the European Monetary Union and the introduction of the single currency across Europe has had important implications for pricing strategies as we will discuss in Chapter 2, when we examine regional trading agreements, and in Chapter 11, when we look at pricing issues in international marketing.

Political environment

The political environment of international marketing includes any national or international political factor that can affect the organisation's operations or its decision making. Politics has come to be recognised as the major factor in many international business decisions, especially in terms of whether to invest and how to develop markets.

Politics is intrinsically linked to a government's attitude to business and the freedom within which it allows firms to operate. Unstable political regimes expose foreign businesses to a variety of risks that they would generally not face in the home market. This often means that the political arena is the most volatile area of international marketing. The tendencies of governments to change regulations can seriously affect an international strategy, providing both opportunities and threats. One only has to consider the volatility of the politics in the former Yugoslavia, Russia and in China over the past few years to appreciate the need for firms to monitor the political risk factors.

Political risk is defined as being: a risk due to a sudden or gradual change in a local political environment that is disadvantageous or counter productive to foreign firms and markets.

The types of action that governments may take which constitute potential political risks to firms fall into three main areas:

- *Operational restrictions.* These could be exchange controls, employment policies, insistence on locally shared ownership and particular product requirements.

- *Discriminatory restrictions.* These tend to be imposed on purely foreign firms and, sometimes, only firms from a particular country. The USA has imposed import quotas on Japan in protest at non-tariff barriers which they view as being imposed unfairly on US exporters. They have also imposed bans on imports from Libya and Iran in the past. They tend to be such things as special taxes and tariffs, compulsory sub-contracting, loss of financial freedom.

- *Physical actions.* These actions are direct government interventions such as confiscation without any payment of indemnity, a forced takeover by the government, expropriation, nationalisation or even damage to property or personnel through riots and war. In 2001 the Nigerian government claimed ownership of Shell's equipment and machinery without any prior warning.

The events of 11 September 2001 made many companies who operate in international markets aware of the impact political events can have on global markets. Even now, the global airline industry is still reeling from the after-shock of 11 September. Since then, the invasions of Afghanistan and Iraq have brought market development opportunities for some but market devastation for others and higher political risk in neighbouring markets for all. The instability in the Middle East and the continued threat of global terrorism have served to heighten the awareness of firms of the importance of monitoring political risk factors in the international markets in which they operate. The accession of the ten new members to the European Union from Southern, Central and Eastern Europe will also have significant implications for companies operating in the European markets. A number of the accession candidates are perceived as areas of relatively high political risk and yet potentially having huge market opportunities. An unstable political climate can expose firms to many commercial, economic and legal risks that they would not face in their domestic markets.

Lesser developed countries and emerging markets pose particularly high political risks, even when they are following reforms to solve the political problems they have. The stringency of such reforms can itself lead to civil disorder and rising opposition to governments, as has been recently seen in Indonesia, Venezuela, Brazil and Argentina.

Civil unrest is often accompanied by high illiteracy (the UN estimate that one in five people in the world is illiterate), poor health and a large proportion of the population living in poverty; 73 per cent of the population in Brazil live in poverty compared to 7 per cent in Spain.

Investment restrictions are a common way governments interfere politically in international markets by restricting levels of investment, location of facilities, choice of local partners and ownership percentage.

When Microsoft opened its Beijing office, it planned to use its Taiwan operations to supply a Mandarin language version of Windows. The government not only wanted such an operating system to be designed in China but also insisted on defining the coding standards for Chinese characters' fonts, something Microsoft had done independently everywhere else in the world. In a flurry of meetings with officials, Bill Gates argued that the marketplace not the government should set standards. But the Chinese electronics industry threatened to ban Windows and president Jiang Zemin personally admonished Gates to spend more time in China and 'learn something from 5000 years of Chinese history'. Gates sacked the original management team and promised to cooperate with Beijing.

FIGURE 1.4 — Country associated risks

Economic factors

Population and income
- Size and sectoral distribution
- Economic growth and per capita income
- Population growth and control
- Income distribution

Workforce and employment
- Size and composition
- Sectoral and geographic distribution
- Productivity
- Migration and urban unemployment

Sectoral analysis
- Agriculture and self-sufficiency
- Industrial growth and distribution
- Size and growth of the public sector
- National priorities and strategic sectors

Economic geography
- Natural resources
- Economic diversification
- Topography and infrastructure

Government and social services
- Sources and structure of government revenues
- Sectoral and geographic pattern of expenditures
- Size and growth of the budget deficit
- Rigidities in spending programmes
- Regional dependency on central revenue sources

General indicators
- Price indices
- Wage rates
- Interest rates, money supply, etc.

Foreign trade and invisibles
- Current account balance and composition
- Income and price elasticity of exports and imports
- Price stability of major imports and exports
- Evolution of the terms of trade
- Geographic composition of trade

External debt and servicing
- Outstanding foreign debt, absolute and relative levels
- Terms and maturity profile
- Debt servicing to income and exports

Foreign investment
- Size and relative importance
- Sectoral distribution
- Geographic (by origin) and regional distribution
- Court proceedings in disputes

Overall balance of payments
- Trends in the capital account
- Reserve position
- Capital flight and 'errors and omissions'

General indicators
- Exchange rates (official and unofficial)
- Changes in international borrowing terms

Political factors

Composition of population
- Ethnolinguistic, religious, tribal or class heterogeneity
- Relative shares in economic and political power
- Immigration and emigration

Culture
- Underlying cultural values and beliefs
- Religious and moral values
- Sense of alienation with foreign or modern influences

Government and institutions
- Constitutional principles and conflicts
- Resilience of national institutions
- Role and strength of the army, church, political parties, press, educational establishment, etc.

Power
- Key leaders' background and attitudes
- Main beneficiaries of the *status quo*
- Role and power of the internal security apparatus

Opposition
- Strength, sources of support, effectiveness

General indicators
- Level and frequency of strikes
- Riots and terrorist acts
- Number and treatment of political prisoners
- Extent of official corruption

Alignments
- International treaties and alignments
- Position on international issues, UN voting record

Financial support
- Financial aid, food and military assistance
- Preferential economic and trade linkages

Regional ties
- Border disputes
- External military threat or guerrilla activity
- Nearby revolution, political refugees

Attitude towards foreign capital and investment
- National investment codes
- Polls of local attitudes towards foreign investors

General indicators
- Record on human rights
- Formal exiled opposition groups
- Terrorist acts in third countries
- Diplomatic or commercial conflict with home country

Source: El-Kahal (1994)

However, the recent trends of trade agreements, privatisation and market reforms are all working to remove trade impediments.

Globally, trade agreements have been making consistent progress over the past forty years. The **World Trade Organisation** (formerly known as GATT) has led to a series of worldwide agreements which have expanded quotas, reduced tariffs and introduced a number of innovative measures to encourage trade amongst countries. Together with the formation of regional trading agreements in the European Union, North and South America and Asia, these reforms constitute a move to a more politically stable international trading environment. An understanding of these issues is critical to the international marketing manager which is why in Chapter 2 we examine in some detail the patterns of world trade, the regional trading agreements and the development of world trading institutions developed to foster international trade.

The political and economic environments are greatly intertwined and, sometimes, difficult to categorise. It is important, however, that a firm operating in international markets assesses the countries in which it operates to assess not only the economic and political risk but also to ensure they understand the peculiarities and characteristics of the country's market they wish to develop. Illustration 1.3 gives the example of Cadbury's, who caused huge offence by their misreading of political sentiments in India. In Chapter 4 we will examine in some detail the procedures, tools and techniques which can help the analysis and evaluation of opportunities. In this chapter, Figure 1.4 provides a summary of the key political and economic factors firms need to evaluate in a foreign country market in order to assess the associated levels of risk.

Technological environment

Technology is a major driving force both in international marketing and in the move towards a more global marketplace. The impact of technological advances can be seen in all aspects of the marketing process. The ability to gather data on markets, management control capabilities and the practicalities of carrying out

---

ILLUSTRATION 1.3   **Cadbury's in political faux-pas**

The Indian division of Cadbury-Schweppes suffered embarrassment around the world and incensed large swathes of Hindu society by running a newspaper advertisement comparing its Temptations chocolate to the war-torn region of Kashmir. The ad carried the tagline:

'I'm good. I'm tempting. I'm too good to share. What am I? Cadbury's Temptations or Kashmir?'. To make sure nobody missed the point, the ad's creators laid the 'too good to share' catch-line over a map of Kashmir.

The ad caused a national outcry. Arguments over Kashmir have taken India and Pakistan to the brink of nuclear war and so using them to sell chocolate was perhaps not the wisest thing to do. Indian politicians were shocked at the very mention of sharing the territory and so threatened nationwide protests. To add insult to injury the advertise-

ment was timed to appear on 15 August, India's Independence Day. Cadbury's British roots may have made the ad even harder to swallow. It was British colonial rulers who, at partition in 1947, drew the boundary line between India and Pakistan that the two nations have battled over ever since.

Though Cadbury India has apologised, it does show that, even in peripheral markets, multi-nationals can't hide their blunders for long.

Question   What are the dangers of a company making such blunders when it operates globally?

Source: Adapted from *The Economist*, 22 August 2002, and BBC News Online, 7 October 2002

the business function internationally over the past few years have been revolutionised with the advancement of electronic communications.

Satellite communications, the Internet and the World Wide Web, client–server technologies, ISDN and cable as well as e-mail, faxes and advanced telephone networks have all led to dramatic shrinkages in worldwide communications.

Shrinking communications

Shrinking communications means, increasingly, that in the international marketplace information is power. At the touch of a button we can access information on the key factors that determine our business. News is a 24 hours a day service. (BBC24 offers global transmission and communication of events throughout the world.) Manufacturers wanting to know the price of coffee beans or the relevant position of competitors in terms of their share price or in terms of new product activity have it at their immediate disposal.

As satellite technology renders land cables and telephone lines redundant, developing countries are abandoning plans to invest in land-based communication. They are bypassing terrestrial communication systems, enabling them to catch up with and, in some cases, overtake developed countries in the marketplace. In emerging economies consumers are jumping from no telephone to the latest in global communications technology. China currently has 85 million mobile telephone users, ranking second in the world. Wireless application protocol (WAP) technology allows online shopping services to be available to mobile phone users whilst they are on the move, wherever they happen to be in the world. The use of Global System for Mobile Communications (GSM) technology enables mobile phone operators to determine the location of a customer globally to send them relevant and timely advertising messages.

British Airways operates its worldwide 'exceptional request' facility, such as wheelchair assistance needed for a passenger, from a centre in Mumbai. The ease of hiring computer-literate graduates by the hundred, who are intelligent, capable, keen and inexpensive to hire, as is local property to rent, makes India an attractive location (see Illustration 1.4). The cost of transmitting data processing

---

ILLUSTRATION 1.4   Indian brands emerge from the shadows

FLEXCUBE is the world's best-selling banking-software product. For many years Indian technicians have been beavering away writing code to be sold as an American or European brand. Now India's own brands are starting to fight in the global markets in their own right.

Indian marketing professionals have been arguing for some time that IT exports would be more secure if they relied less on outsourcing and were 'products', where the Indian seller owns the intellectual property, not just the brainpower-for-hire. Mixing his metaphors wildly, Rajesh Hukku, the founder and chairman of i-flex, argues that Indian firms otherwise risk being doomed forever to providing 'the cheap labour at the bottom of the food chain'.

At a time when there has been a protectionist backlash in America and Europe against the outsourcing of IT jobs to India and fears of decline in the industry as margins and

costs are being further reduced, Indian software firms are emerging from the shadows and fighting in the global market under their own brand names.

Last year, Nasscom, the Indian industry's lobby group, estimated that India captured just 0.2 per cent of a global market of US$180 billion for software products. It expects that to increase, but recognises the obstacles. The product business depends on heavy investment in sales, marketing and branding and the ability to market globally against fierce and rich competitors.

Question How should new brands in developing countries compete against established US global brands?

Source: Adapted from *The Economist*, 8 May 2003

from London to Mumbai, a distance of some 7000 miles, is no more than sending the same information 7 miles. British Airways now plans to run its worldwide ticketing operation from Mumbai.

The Internet and the World Wide Web (WWW)

The Internet and the access gained to the World Wide Web is revolutionising international marketing practices. EasyJet estimate 90 per cent of its ticket reservations are made online. EToys, a virtual company based in the US, has no retail outlets but a higher market capitalisation than Toys'R'Us. Firms ranging from a few employees to large multi-nationals are now realising the potential of marketing online and so have developed the facility to buy and sell their products and services online to the world.

An estimated 500 million people now have access and this is expected to reach 765 million by the end of 2005. The United Nations estimate that global e-business is now worth US\$200 billion and could grow to as much as US\$10 trillion by 2005. Most of this is business-to-business (B2B), not business-to-consumer (B2C) purchases. By 2005, 80 million households across Europe will have interactive television services via digital television and the interactive shopping services it offers. This explosion of online international marketing activity and the associated emergence of the global information highway will impact on all businesses.

The Internet has meant huge opportunities for small and medium-sized enterprises (SMEs) and rapid internationalisation for many. It has enabled them to substantially reduce the costs of reaching international customers, reduce global advertising costs and made it much easier for small niche products to find a critical mass of customers. Because of the low entry costs of the Internet it has permitted firms with low capital resources to become global marketers, in some cases overnight. There are, therefore, quite significant implications for SMEs which will be examined further in Chapter 5, where we discuss in some detail the issues in international marketing pertinent to SMEs.

For all companies, the implications of being able to market goods and services online have been far reaching, The Internet has led to an explosion of information to consumers giving them the potential to source products from the cheapest supplier in the world. This has led to the increasing standardisation of prices across borders or, at least, to the narrowing of price differentials as consumers become more aware of prices in different countries and buy a whole range of products via the net. In B2C marketing this has been most dramatically seen in the purchase of such things as flights, holidays, CDs and books. The Internet, by connecting end-users and producers directly, has reduced the importance of

---

DILEMMA 1.2   The nude economy

Some businessmen suggest the new E-Business economy should be called the nude economy because the Internet makes trading so much more transparent and exposed. This could be a big opportunity for companies competing internationally, but it could also be a big dilemma. By making it easier for sellers and buyers to compare prices, companies can cut out the middleman, reduce transactions costs and reduce barriers to trading on international markets. This could make it very competitive and mean some companies are no longer able to compete in what could be a hostile and cut-throat environment.

Question What do you think companies should do to compete effectively in such an international market environment?

traditional intermediaries in international marketing (i.e. agents and distributors) as more companies have built the online capability to deal direct with their customers, particularly in B2B marketing. To survive, such intermediaries have begun offering a whole range of new services, the value-added of their offering no longer being principally in the physical distribution of goods but rather in the collection, collation, interpretation and dissemination of vast amounts of information. The critical resource possessed by this new breed of 'cybermediary' is information rather than inventory. The Internet has also become a powerful tool for supporting networks both internal and external to the firm. Many global firms have developed supplier intranets through which they source products and services from preferred suppliers who have met the criteria to gain access to their supplier intranets. It has become the efficient new medium for conducting worldwide market research and gaining feedback from customers.

Thus the Internet produces a fundamentally different environment for international marketing and requires a radically different strategic approach affecting all aspects of the marketing process. Not all forays into Internet marketing have been successful. Many early dotcom high growth companies became 'dot.bombs' when they failed to sustain their early promise. Levi Strauss stopped its Internet selling operation after finding the cost of servicing returned goods was greater than the revenue generated from new sales.

The dual technological/cultural paradox

On the one hand commentators view technological advancement and shrinking communications as the most important driving force in the building of the global village where there are global consumers who have similar needs. On the other hand, to access this global village a person invariably needs a command of the English language and access to a whole range of equipment. In many markets we yet again stumble against the paradox that whilst in some countries there is a market of well-educated and computer-literate people, in other countries the global electronic highway completely bypasses them.

Despite all that has been said in previous sections, many developing and emerging markets are characterised by poor, inadequate or deteriorating infrastructures. It is estimated that only 7 per cent of the world's population has direct access to a PC and only 4 per cent have direct access to the Internet. Essential services required for commercial activity, ranging from electric power to water supplies, from highways to air transportation and from phone lines to banking services are often in short supply or unreliable. Fifty per cent of the world has still, even today, never used a telephone.

There are also major disparities in the cost of accessing the Internet. In the USA, accessing the Internet for 20 hours per month would cost 1 per cent of a person's average income; in Mexico it would cost 15 per cent of a person's average income. However, in Bangladesh the same amount of access is equivalent to 278 per cent of the average income and in Madagascar 614 per cent, hardly making access to the Internet feasible for the average person, even if it is technically available.

The huge population shifts discussed earlier have also aggravated the technical infrastructure problems in many of the major cities in emerging markets. This often results in widespread production and distribution bottlenecks, which in turn raises costs. 'Brown outs', for instance, are not uncommon in the Philippines, even in the capital city Manila, where companies and offices regularly lose electric power and either shut down in those periods or revert to generators. Fragmented and circuitous channels of distribution are a result of lack of adequate infrastructure. This makes market entry more difficult and the efficient distribution of a product very difficult. Pepsi Cola in Eastern Europe have a large number of decentralised satellite bottling plants in an attempt to overcome the lack of a distribution infrastructure.

The reader will find that we will examine the impact of the Internet and the WWW on the relevant marketing practices and processes as we move through the chapters of the book. In Chapter 12 of this edition we devote a whole chapter to examining the implications for the international marketing strategies of companies of such trends in technology environment in some detail.

Stakeholder expectations

The complexities of the international marketing environment mean another major difference for companies competing on international markets is that the company has many more organisations and people who have a stake in how they conduct their business and so consequently many more stakeholders whose differing expectations they have to manage. The ability of a company to pursue its chosen marketing strategy is determined to a large degree by the aims and expectations of the stakeholders, who directly or indirectly provide the resources and support needed to implement the strategies and plans. It is important to clearly identify the different stakeholder groups, understand their expectations and evaluate their power because it is the stakeholders who provide the broad guidelines within which the firm operates. Figure 1.5 identifies the typical stakeholders of a multi-national enterprise. Body Shop, the environmentally conscious UK toiletries retailer, is always likely to have problems balancing the widely differing pricing and profit expectations and environmental concerns of its franchisees, customers and shareholders.

Whilst the senior management of the firm aim usually to develop and adopt strategies which do not directly oppose these stakeholder expectations, they do, of course, frequently widen or alter the firm's activities due to changes in the market and competition. Moreover, a wide range of stakeholders influence what **multi-national enterprises (MNEs)** do by giving greater attention to the

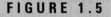

FIGURE 1.5

Some typical stakeholders of multi-national enterprises

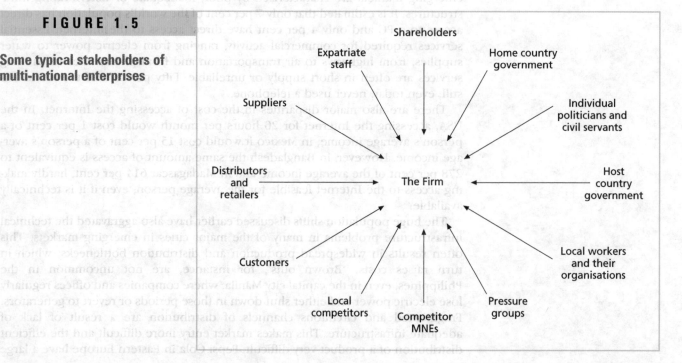

political, commercial and ethical behaviour of the organisations as well as taking more interest in the actual operation of the business and the performance and safety of the products. As a result of this, companies need to explain their strategies and plans to shareholders through more detailed annual reports, to staff through a variety of briefing methods and to pressure groups and the community in general through various public relations activities, particularly when their activities have an impact on the local environment or economy. In international marketing it is particularly important that the firm addresses the concern of its host country stakeholders, who may be physically and culturally very distant from the headquarters.

Particular attention should be paid to the different expectations of the stakeholders and their power to influence the firm's strategic direction. Given the different expectations of the firm's stakeholders it is inevitable that conflicts will occur. For example, shareholders usually want a high return on their investment and may expect the firm to find countries with low production costs, but the workers in these countries want an adequate wage on which to live. It is often the firm's ability to manage these potential conflicts that leads to success or failure in international marketing.

International pressure groups are another important stakeholder MNEs have to manage. Global communications and the ability of the World Wide Web to draw together people with shared interests have led to the growing power of globally based pressure groups. Such has been the success of a number of these, it is now the case that pressure-groups are seen by many global operators as one of the key stakeholders to be considered in international strategy decision making. The role of pressure groups in global markets tends to be to raise awareness of issues of concern. Among those that have received wide press coverage affecting international marketing strategies are:

- the Greenpeace efforts to raise awareness to threats on the environment
- the anti-globalisation lobby demonstrating against the perceived dark global forces they see manifested in the World Trade Organisation
- the anti-child labour movement.

Gap, the clothes manufacturer and retailer, responded to the revelation that companies who had a licence to produce their products were using child labour by applying the employment guidelines and dismissing the 'child'. This only exacerbated the anger of the pressure groups. Levi, another target of the anti-child labour movement, finding themselves exposed to the same bad publicity, dismissed the child but agreed to fund the child's education up to the point when they would be eligible to seek employment. This pacified the pressure group in the short term but one is left wondering what Levi would do if they subsequently discovered that there were another few thousand under-age employees across other factories they use, or if there was a sudden influx of employees that were recruited and then declared themselves as under-age in order to seek educational support.

One of the main roles of international public relations is to try to manage the expectations and aspirations of pressure groups and all the stakeholders of a company. In international marketing one of the key responsibilities is to establish good practice to respond to publicity generated by pressure groups on issues where they have been seen not to meet stakeholder expectations.

As the international business environment becomes more competitive, dynamic and complex, there is a greater need for individual managers to be aware not simply of their immediate situation, but also of the possible impact of changes taking place in surrounding areas too. Individual national markets can be both surprisingly similar and surprisingly dissimilar in nature, and it is important to understand these linkages and the implications of the changes that take place.

There is a strong argument for adopting a standardised approach to analysing environmental changes, for example by using the marketing profile analysis discussed in Chapter 4, because this allows comparisons to be made and specific issues to be addressed in a thorough and logical way in order to obtain as precise and complete a picture as possible.

DIFFERENCES BETWEEN INTERNATIONAL AND DOMESTIC MARKETING

As we have seen in the previous sections, there are many factors within the international environment which substantially increase the challenge of international marketing. These can be summarised as follows:

1 *Culture*: often diverse and multi-cultural markets

2 *Markets*: widespread and sometimes fragmented

3 *Data*: difficult to obtain and often expensive

4 *Politics*: regimes vary in stability – political risk becomes an important variable

5 *Governments*: can be a strong influence in regulating importers and foreign business ventures

6 *Economies*: varying levels of development and varying and sometimes unstable currencies

7 *Finance*: many differing finance systems and regulatory bodies

8 *Stakeholders*: commercial, home country and host country

9 *Business*: diverse rules, culturally influenced

10 *Control*: difficult to control and coordinate across markets.

Porter (1986) identified that the forces driving international marketing could be divided into currents and cross currents.

Currents are the macro forces such as the growing homogeneity of markets, the drive towards regionalisation, the rise of the emerging markets and shrinking communications.

Cross currents are the emergent trends in international marketing strategies which are driving international competition to behave in new and, sometimes, innovative ways which are changing the bases of international competitive advantage. Cross currents, therefore, are such things as strategic alliances, the growth of marketing on the Internet, R&D (research and development) cooperation, increasing involvement by governments in international trade, the growth of pirating and grey marketing.

The international competitive landscape

A major difference for managers operating on international markets is the impact all these currents and cross currents have on the competitive landscape. Wilson and Gilligan (2003) define marketing as 'getting the competitive advantage and keeping it'. The task of achieving this in a competitive environment where firms are subject to local, regional and global competition can be immensely challenging. This is especially so if indigenous local competitors are supported by the government of the country.

Across international markets, advanced countries are seeing significant competition from both emerging markets and less developed countries who are exploiting modern technology and their own low labour costs to compete in markets no longer so protected by tariff walls.

The complexity of competition is also heightened by the strategic use of international sourcing of components by multi-nationals and global firms to achieve competitive advantage.

This means, given the nature of the challenges and opportunities identified above and the speed of change within the international environment, substantially different pressures are being placed upon management than if they were purely operating in domestic markets. It follows from this that the manager of international marketing needs a detailed knowledge and understanding of how particular environmental variables impact on a firm's international marketing operations. An interesting example of this is the beauty industry, as seen in Illustration 1.5.

In the next section we will examine the characteristics of international marketing strategies that both fail and succeed before finally going on to consider what are the necessary components of a successful international marketing strategy.

INTERNATIONAL MARKETING STRATEGIES

Reasons for failure

As we have seen from the various examples given throughout the chapter, sometimes firms fail in their efforts to develop the international markets they have targeted.

ILLUSTRATION 1.5   The beautification of the ageing baby boomers

Analysts at Goldman Sachs estimate that the global beauty industry is worth about 100 billion dollars a year and is growing at up to 7 per cent a year, more than twice the rate of the developed world's GDP. This growth is being driven by richer, ageing baby-boomers and increased discretionary income in the West, and by the growing middle classes in developing countries. China, Russia and South Korea are turning into huge markets. In India, sales of anti-ageing creams are growing by 40 per cent a year. Avon is expanding rapidly in Eastern Europe and Russia as well as in South America. Brazil now has more than 900 000 Avon Ladies.

Global competition in the market is becoming increasingly intense. Unilever and Procter & Gamble, facing maturity in many of their traditional businesses, are devoting more resources to developing global beauty brands. Luxury product manufacturers such as Dior, Chanel and Yves St Laurent are moving into mainstream beauty products and

many of the global giants are growing by buying up smaller brands. Japan's Kao have gone into the hair dye market by buying John Frieda while Estée Lauder has acquired Stila, MAC and Bobbi Brown, all of which are innovative and growing make-up brands.

The traditional global beauty brands established by such companies as L'Oréal, Arden and Rubenstein are now having to fight hard in a global market where traditionally they have earned huge margins and enjoyed continuous growth for many years.

Question Outline the reasons for the changing structure of the global beauty market.

Source: Adapted from *The Economist,* 22 May 2003

Perlmutter (1995), examining the reasons why firms did not manage their international markets effectively, identified nine cross-cultural management incompetencies which led to failure across a spread of country markets. He defined these core incompetencies as 'the bundle of activities and managerial skills that are mis-matched in a great variety of countries where firms do business'.

The first three are interrelated and relate to the failure to be market driven.

1   Inability to find the right market niches.

2   Unwillingness to adapt and update products to local needs.

3   Not having unique products that are viewed as sufficiently higher added-value by customers in local markets.

4   A vacillating commitment. It takes time to learn how to function in countries such as Japan.

5   Assigning the wrong people. Picking the wrong people or the wrong top team in an affiliate.

6   Picking the wrong partners. There is a list of difficulties in building alliances. A main limitation is picking partners who do not have the right bundle of capabilities to help reach the local market.

7   Inability to manage local stakeholders. This includes an incompetence in developing a satisfactory partnership relationship with unions and governments.

8   Developing mutual distrust and lack of respect between HQ and the affiliates at different levels of management.

9   Inability to leverage ideas developed in one country to other countries worldwide.

Reasons for success

Hamel and Prahalad (1996) suggest the firms operating globally that succeed are those that perceive the changes in the international environment and are able to develop strategies which enable them to respond accordingly. The firms that will do well will base their success largely on the early identification of the changes in the boundaries of markets and industries in their analysis of their international marketing environment. Management foresight and organisational learning are therefore the basis of a sustainable competitive advantage in global markets.

The increasing **globalisation** of business, particularly because it is being driven by information technology, has led many firms to re-examine what contributes to their global competitive advantage. They have recognised the fact that it is the pool of personal knowledge, skills and competencies of the firm's staff that provides its development potential and they have redefined themselves as 'knowledge-based' organisations. Moreover, these firms have acknowledged that they must retain, nurture and apply the knowledge and skills across their business if they wish to be effective in global markets. The growth potential of international markets can only be exploited if the firm becomes a learning organisation in which the good practice learned by individual members of staff in one market can be 'leveraged' and built upon throughout its global activity.

However, firms are increasingly vulnerable to losing these valuable personal assets, because of the greater mobility of staff, prevalence of industrial espionage and the security risks and abuse associated with the Internet. Moreover, with the increase in communications it is becoming more difficult to store, access and apply the valuable knowledge that exists amongst the huge volume of relatively

ILLUSTRATION 1.6	FISHERMAN'S FRIEND

FISHERMAN'S FRIEND lozenges were initially developed for sailors and Fleetwood fishermen who were working in the severe North Atlantic fishing grounds. For a whole century the company made around 14lb of lozenges a month which were only sold in the local area. However, when Doreen Lofthouse joined the company she set about expanding the market by selling into towns throughout Lancashire and Yorkshire. Distribution then spread throughout the UK, before expanding overseas. Norway was a logical starting point and it is now the market with the highest sales per head of population. Surprisingly, the lozenge was a success in many hot countries too. Italy at one point was the largest export market before being overtaken by Germany. Although the lozenge needs no adaptation – a cough needs no translation – promotion of FISHERMAN'S FRIEND differs greatly from country to country. The traditional concept has been the centre of advertising in the UK, but overseas promotional themes are quite different. An Italian TV commercial showed a girl who breathed so deeply after eating a lozenge that the buttons pop off her blouse to reveal her cleavage; in Denmark a man breathes fire; in the Philippines butterflies flutter against pastel shades accompanied by gentle music. FISHERMAN'S FRIEND is now available in over 100 countries worldwide and in many it is seen as a strong sweet, not as medicated confectionery. Exports now account for over 95 per cent of the company's total production.

Question What are the reasons for the success of FISHERMAN'S FRIEND?

Source: Fisherman's Friend

Source: Fisherman's Friend

Source: Fisherman's Friend

worthless data that the company deals with. Consequently, effective knowledge management is now critical for success. This means having Web-enabled database systems that facilitate effective data collection, storage in data warehouses and data mining (the identification of opportunities from patterns that emerge from detailed analysis of the data held).

Successful global operators use the knowledge gained to assess their strengths and weaknesses in light of their organisational learning and ensure they have the company capability and resources to respond to their learning in order to sustain their competitive advantage. This is particularly important in international markets as, for example, customer and brand loyalty may be much stronger in certain markets than others, and products that may be at the end of their life in the domestic market may be ideal for less sophisticated markets. In the dynamic international markets, therefore, if a firm is to succeed it must develop the ability to think, analyse and develop strategic and innovative responses on an international, if not global scale, perhaps such as Mrs Lofthouse did for the FISHERMAN'S FRIEND in Illustration 1.6.

Characteristics of best practice in international marketing

It is apparent, therefore, that firms and organisations planning to compete effectively in world markets need a clear and well-focused international marketing strategy that is based on a thorough understanding of the markets which the company is targeting or operating in. International markets are dynamic entities which require constant monitoring and evaluation. As we have discussed, as markets change so must marketing techniques. Innovation is an important competitive variable, not only in terms of the product or service but throughout the marketing process. Counter-trading, financial innovations, networking and value-based marketing are all becoming increasingly important concepts in the implementation of a successful international strategy.

The challenge, then, of international marketing is to ensure that any international strategy has the discipline of thorough research and an understanding and accurate evaluation of what is required to achieve the competitive advantage. Doole (2000) identified three major components to the strategies of firms successfully competing in international markets:

- *A clear international competitive focus* achieved through a thorough knowledge of the international markets, a strong competitive positioning and a strategic perspective which was truly international.

- *An effective relationship strategy* achieved through strong customer relations, a commitment to quality products and service and a dedication to customer service throughout international markets.

- *Well-managed* organisations with a culture of learning. Firms were innovative and willing to learn, showed high levels of energy and commitment to international markets and had effective monitoring and control procedures for all their international markets.

SUMMARY

- In this chapter we have discussed the growing strategic importance of international marketing and examined the issues associated with successfully competing in international markets.

- The environments in which international companies must operate are typically characterised by uncertainty and change – factors which, taken together, increase the element of risk.

- Marketing managers need to have a properly planned approach to any international activity since, without this, the costs and likelihood of failure are likely to increase.

- We have examined the major changes in the macro global environment which have taken place as old political structures collapse, major **trading blocs** develop and the global village emerges through technological advances.

- Many nations are undergoing change and consumers generally are becoming more demanding and more discriminating.

- Faced with changes such as these, the implications for international marketing management are significant and it is to these challenges that we turn our attention in the following chapters.

- The reader has been introduced to many of the concepts that are important to the international marketing management process and will have gained an understanding of the issues to be addressed.

- In the following chapters the international trading environment and the trends and developments in trading patterns will be examined.

KEYWORDS

cross currents	international marketing
cultural paradox	international trade
currents	less developed countries
emerging economies	multi-national enterprise
European Union	North American Free Trade Area
export marketing	piracy
global marketing	purchasing power parity
global youth culture	trading blocs
globalisation	world trade
gross national income	World Trade Organisation
hard currency	

History of Tokai and birth of Tokai UK

The Tokai Company was founded in 1947 in Hamamatsu, Japan and produced all forms of musical instruments, including a large range of pianos. Tokai instruments first appeared in the UK in the early 1980s when they were imported by a company called Bluesuede Music. At that time the two biggest names in electric guitars were those produced by the American companies Fender and Gibson, who both produced high quality electric guitars but at a price that was prohibitive for the average amateur guitarist. Tokai competed against Fender, with products that replicated the Fender quality and also closely resembled their guitars but for half the price. Not surprisingly the Tokai product stood alone in the marketplace and competed with Fender by making quality instruments available to customers who couldn't afford a genuine Fender or Gibson guitar. Tokai's biggest seller at the time was the ST50 which resembled the famous Fender Stratocaster. However, Fender issued writs against Tokai which forced them to change the designs so as to not infringe Fender's copyright. Imports continued on for a further three years and Bluesuede Music did remarkably well with the product, using sales agents out on the road selling guitars to retailers. Unfortunately, in the mid-eighties one of the partners left Bluesuede owing the company and Tokai a lot of money. At that point Bluesuede had to stop the import of Tokai guitars.

At the beginning of 2002 Nick Crane, a British entrepreneur, went to Japan to see Mr Shohei Adachi, the managing director of Tokai, and agreed a deal to import the company's guitars once more into the UK. This started as a small operation and the products began to trickle into the UK. Shortly afterwards Nick Crane approached Bob Murdoch, who had 25 years' experience in the music wholesale and retail business. Bob Murdoch saw the potential of these instruments on the European market and became a partner in Tokai UK in early 2002. The company began by working from a small garage, but over the subsequent 18 months turnover increased by 200 per cent and they are now selling into Ireland, Italy and Spain. They had a huge market in Germany but, as we will see later, have now pulled out of the market. Tokai UK now operates from premises on an industrial estate at Dinnington, South Yorkshire. Nick Crane left the company to follow other interests in Spain; Bob Murdoch bought out his partner and now has overall control of Tokai UK and plans to launch Tokai across the pan-European market.

Objectives

Bob Murdoch's objectives for Tokai UK are:

- To expand the business across the European Union.
- To develop new guitar models with Tokai Japan to meet the needs of the European market.
- To expand the dealer network across Europe.
- To develop a pricing strategy across the European markets which will help them generate the revenues to improve quality but still remain a competitively priced product.

Tokai product range and policy

Tokai guitars are mainly produced in Japan. The factory employs 60 people and guitars are produced in several formats. Some guitars are also produced in Korea but are of lower quality and do not feature in the Tokai UK portfolio.

Tokai offer a wide range of electric guitars within their product portfolio, catering for every genre and playing style.

Within their range is the AST50, supplied in a single model which was the top-selling model during the early-80s venture into the UK. This is supported by the ATE55, supplied in two models plus a left-hand version. Both of these models are Fender-type guitars.

However, today the Loverock model in one of its many forms has taken over as best seller and currently outsells the AST50 by some 5 to 1. The Loverock is a Gibson Les Paul-style guitar and extremely popular amongst rock guitarists. Tokai UK supply this model in five variations plus left-hand version.

Source: Tokai Guitars

Tokai also produce bass guitars and semi-acoustic electric guitars. The semi-acoustic ES model is produced in two model variants.

An innovative guitar produced by Tokai is the Talbo aluminium-bodied guitar, which produces a quite unique sound. However, perhaps this was a little ahead of its time and has not proved to be a good seller in the European market. The Talbo is also supplied in a wooden version with a hollow maple body. The range consists of three aluminium-bodied instruments and two wooden-bodied instruments.

Tokai UK has also designed two new models of electric guitar which were unveiled at the Frankfurt Music Exhibition, the Tsunami (big wave) and the Loverock 2, a double cutaway version of the standard Loverock. Response to the new models has been very good, especially towards the Loverock 2, with the next three months' production of this model all presold. Tokai UK are also working in conjunction with Trevor Wilkinson, of Wilkinson tremolos and guitar bridges, to produce new models and to strive to improve the quality of existing models. This demonstrates the company's commitment to design, innovation and quality. The custom shop in Japan also manufactures two semi-acoustic guitars, the ALS320 and the UES320, in very small numbers, essentially to special order. These represent the ultimate in Tokai quality for the enthusiast.

Pricing

Tokai is facing a dilemma as to how to achieve a consistent pricing policy for their products across the European market. In the UK, Tokai prices for electric guitars range at RRP from £399 to £800 approx. These prices compare very favourably to competitor's products of similar quality. Gibson prices start at around the £800 mark and Fender start at £409 for the Mexican product. The exceptions are the custom shop ALS320 at £1800 and the UES320 at £2500.

This represents prices that attract buyers but still allow retailers to make reasonable profits on the instruments. Of course discounting exists, but would come off the retailers' margin. Tokai UK maintain this policy is better for dealers as it gives them a feeling of allegiance to Tokai UK, and causes the dealers to feel honour bound to react quickly to any problems customers might have, no matter how small.

Tokai UK are also unique in that they do not charge a premium for left-handed guitars; they feel that it is wrong to discriminate against a customer simply because he/she happens to be left-handed. All other companies charge a premium.

Distribution

Tokai UK distributes its instruments throughout the UK and Ireland, and also to a limited number of outlets in Spain and Italy. In Germany, Tokai was taken to court by Gibson Guitars for breach of copyright and so had to pull out of the market. However, Tokai won the court action; copyright was not seen to have been breached and Tokai were able to prove they had a strong brand identity in their own right and were not trading on the Gibson name, even if they were selling guitars of a similar style. However, the fear of legal action and the potential financial costs involved has meant Tokai has not gone back into the German market as they have decided they prefer to follow opportunities in more profitable markets that do not have such a threat of legal action.

When Tokai UK was founded in 2001 the company started with 15 active accounts that would buy from every shipment. To date, the company has 60 active accounts and a further 25 accounts buying from every third shipment.

The accounts are shops across their European markets ranging from the very large multi-outlet music mega stores, through the middle of the road large one-off music shops, to the very small owner-operator music shops. Tokai UK prefer the middle of the road shops because they feel the brand gets greater exposure and sales attention from these types of outlets. The brand can tend to get lost amongst the vast range of products stocked by the mega stores.

Because of the commitment to quality given by Tokai the dealers tend to reciprocate by paying invoices on time and handling customer problems quickly and efficiently. However, Tokai UK does want to grow and expand its network over the forthcoming years.

Promotion

Tokai UK do advertise in the specialist media aimed at guitar enthusiasts such as *Guitar* magazine etc. Their major exposure to the trade is not surprisingly via exhibitions. They exhibit at major exhibitions such as the NEC Birmingham UK, which is the major music exhibition for the trade in the UK. They will continue to exhibit at the Frankfurt exhibition and plan to launch new models there.

They also plan to exhibit at numerous other trade fairs across Europe in the forthcoming years, but plan to concentrate on the smaller, more intimate ones. They hope to take orders from these and expand their dealer network.

They produce a full-colour catalogue for dealers and customers. They have produced a Web site (*www.tokai-guitars.co.uk*) for the benefit of dealers and end customers. Also, numerous Tokai enthusiast Web sites exist, consisting of chat rooms where enthusiasts can exchange anecdotes or just chat about guitars in general and Tokai in particular, and there are Web forums for Tokai players where views can be sought or exchanged.

The future

Tokai UK's expressed aim is to expand over the next few years but keeping to the ethos of maintaining quality. The major inhibiting factor to the growth of Tokai UK is the level of production possible at the factory in Hamamatsu. There appears to be little scope to expand into Europe in a big way unless the factory expands, as demand for the product remains unfulfilled in the UK.

Questions

1 Identify the strengths and weaknesses of Tokai UK's international strategy.

2 What are the key issues they need to address if they are to succeed in the European market?

3 Suggest methods by which Tokai UK could expand into the European market.

Source: Peter Lancaster, Senior Lecturer, Sheffield Hallam University

DISCUSSION QUESTIONS

1 What are the major environmental influences which impact on international marketing? Show how they can affect international marketing strategies.

2 Using examples, examine the reasons why marketing strategies fail in international markets.

3 Identify three major global pressure groups. Examine how they have influenced the international marketing strategies of particular firms.

4 What skills and abilities are necessary requirements for an effective international marketing manager? Justify your choices.

5 Evaluate the impact and opportunities of e-business development for a service organisation. What are the potential dangers of e-business?

REFERENCES

Dicken, P. (2003) *Global Shift: Reshaping the Global Economic Map in the 21st Century*, 4th edn, Sage Publications.

Doole, I. (2000) 'How SMEs Learn to Compete Effectively on International Markets', Ph.D.

El-Kahal, S. (1994) *Introduction to International Business*, McGraw-Hill.

Haliburton, C. (1997) 'Reconciling global marketing and one to one marketing – A global individualism response', in Doole, I. and Lowe, R. (eds), *International Marketing Strategy – Contemporary Readings*, ITP.

Hamel, G. and Prahalad, C.K. (1996) *Competing for the Future*, Harvard Business School Press.

Hamill, J. (1997) 'The Internet and International Marketing', *International Marketing Review*, 14 (5).

Herbig, P. and Hale, B. (1997) 'Internet, the challenge of the 20th Century', *Electronic Networking Applications and Policy*, 7 (2): 95–100.

Hofstede, G. (2000) *Cultural consequences*, 3rd edn, Sage Publications.

Jain, S.C. (2001) *International Marketing*, 6th edn, Southwestern.

Ohmae, K. (1994) *The Borderless World: power and strategy in the interlinked economy*, HarperCollins.

Perlmutter, M.V. (1995) 'Becoming globally civilised, Managing across culture', Mastering Management Part 6, *Financial Times*, 1 December.

Porter, M.E. (1986) *Competition in Global Industries*, Harvard Business School Press.

Quelch, J.A. and Klein, L.R. (1996) 'Internet and International Marketing', *Sloane Management Review*, Spring.

Rugimbana, R. and Nwankwo, S. (2003) *Cross Cultural Marketing*, Thomson Learning.

Terpstra, V. and Sarathy, R. (2002) *International Marketing*, Dryden Press.

Wilson, R. and Gilligan, C. (2003) *Strategic Marketing Management: planning implementation and control*, 3rd edn, Butterworth-Heinemann.

THE INTERNATIONAL TRADING ENVIRONMENT

CHAPTER

2

Introduction

International marketing takes place within the framework of the international trading environment. If the reader is to have the skills necessary to develop international marketing strategies, some understanding of the parameters of the international trading environment in which they operate is needed.

In this chapter we examine the development of international trade in recent years. We will analyse the growth and changing pattern of international trade and discuss the institutions that aim to influence international trade.

We will also look at the changing regional trading blocs and the implications these have on trading structures around the globe.

Learning objectives

After reading this chapter the reader should be able to;

- Discuss the effects and implications of the factors impacting on world trade

- Explain the key trends in the major regional trading blocs around the globe

- Understand the role of the major world institutions that foster the development of multilateral free trade across the world

WORLD TRADING PATTERNS

The world economy consists of over 250 nations with a population of 6 billion and an output (GDP) totalling US$33 trillion. In the year 2003 global GDP grew by 3.0 per cent. In 2003 international trade in merchandise totalled US$7 trillion and trade in services is currently estimated to be about US$1.5 trillion. However, this may be well below the true figure.

Together, East Asia, North America and the European Union account for 80 per cent of world trade and 85 per cent of world direct investment.

Europe and the US alone account for 56 per cent of world GDP but only 11 per cent of the world population. Figure 2.1 displays the regional composition of the world economy compared to the population of the regions.

The economic weakness of Africa, Eastern Europe, Russia and the Middle East is highlighted by their congregation in the lower sections. Cumulatively, these regions accounted for only 14 per cent of world GDP. However, Central and Eastern European economies are growing at a rate of 4 per cent per annum. Their share of world exports is growing at a similar rate and so their position looks set to change in the next few years. Asia represented 33 per cent of world GDP (including Japan) and 59 per cent of the world's population.

Japan was until recently seen as an economic powerhouse. However, progress recently has been more subdued as the Japanese economy has matured. It is currently dealing with the challenges of a deflationary economy, serious structural problems and weaknesses in its financial sector. In addition, much manufacturing activity has been transferred to economies with cheaper labour costs.

In the past thirty years, the developing economies of Asia have increased their share of world exports from 6.6 per cent to 18.4 per cent. In the aftermath of the financial crisis of 1998 Asia's trade and output recovered impressively. The newly industrialised Asian economies are forecast to grow by 4.5 per cent in 2004 compared to 2.9 per cent forecast for advanced economies such as the European Union and the USA.

Despite concern over its **trade deficit** and its fears of a recession, America remains by a wide margin the world's biggest exporter (see Table 2.1). In 2003 it sold merchandise worth US$730 billion, accounting for 12 per cent of the global total. It is also the biggest exporter of services, accounting for 18 per cent of global exports of services. This puts it far in front of any other competitors. The UK, the next largest supplier of services, has only 7.45 per cent of world exports. France, Japan and Germany have approximately a 5.5 per cent share of world service exports each.

FIGURE 2.1

Regional composition of world GDP and population

Source: Market Intelligence Department, NatWest Group (1998)

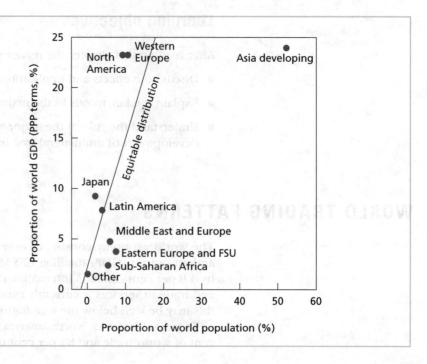

TABLE 2.1

Percentage of the total of world exports in merchandise, 2003

Country	Percentage %
United States	11.9
Germany	9.3
Japan	6.6
France	5.2
Britain	4.4
China	4.3
Canada	4.2
Italy	3.9
Netherlands	3.1
Hong Kong	3.1

Source: WTO.org

TABLE 2.2

Forecasts in per cent changes in consumer prices and real GDP/GNP 2004

Country	% inflation rate	% growth rate
Argentina	19.5	5.2
Australia	2.9	3.4
Belgium	1.5	2.3
Brazil	16.7	3.4
Canada	2.3	3.3
China	1.0	9.9
Czech Republic	−0.1	1.5
EU	1.6	2.2
France	1.4	2.4
Germany	1.1	1.9
Hong Kong	−2.1	5.0
India	4.1	2.6
Italy	2.2	2.0
Japan	−0.5	0.6
Malaysia	1.0	5.6
Mexico	5.3	2.3
Netherlands	2.2	0.4
Poland	0.3	2.1
Russia	14.7	5.2
Singapore	0.8	1.6
South Africa	12.5	3.0
South Korea	3.7	3.7
Spain	2.7	2.9
Taiwan	−0.1	3.2
Thailand	1.6	6.1
Turkey	29.5	11.4
UK	1.3	2.7
USA	1.9	3.5
Venezuela	33.5	−16.7

Source: IMF World Economic Outlook

In merchandise exports, Germany accounted for 9.3 per cent of exports and Japan 6.6 per cent. China continued to move up the rankings in 2003, to sixth place, with 4.3 per cent of world exports.

The UK's share of global merchandise exports has declined appreciably over the past thirty years. Compared with a 7.5 per cent share in the mid-1960s, the UK currently accounts for only 4.4 per cent of global visible exports. The pattern of change over the period is very similar to that of US exports, with a sizable decline in the ten years to the mid-1970s followed by relative stability since. German exports, by contrast, held their share.

The pronounced change in the geographical structure of UK exports over the past three decades largely reflects the consequences of the UK's accession to the European Union. In 1970, less than a third of UK exports went to countries that now constitute the EU. This proportion is now 55 per cent. The main 'losers' in terms of the share of UK exports were Commonwealth countries such as Australia and New Zealand whose share fell to 2.0 per cent. The US, however, has a 12 per cent share of UK exports. The advanced economies in total now account for over 80 per cent of UK exports compared with 70 per cent in 1970.

Future prospects

World trade volume in 2003 stabilised for the first time in many years, although it is forecast to regain its growth in 2004. World Gross Domestic Product (GDP) also registered zero growth for the first time in many decades. Table 2.2 examines the annual percentage change in gross domestic product (GDP) and consumer prices (inflation) forecast for 2004. China, Malaysia, Thailand and Turkey are all expected

TABLE 2.3	Forecasted balance of payments current accounts, 2004	
	Country	**US$ billion**
	Argentina	+8.9
	Australia	−17.0
	Brazil	+17.0
	China	+33.5
	Germany	−3.4
	Hong Kong	+13.8
	Japan	+120.6
	Mexico	−14.5
	Malaysia	−4.8
	Netherlands	+19.9
	Poland	−5.0
	Russia	+38.0
	Saudi Arabia	−12.8
	Singapore	+18.7
	Taiwan	+26.0
	UK	−0.3
	USA	−220.5
	EU	+78.2

Source: World Bank: World Development Indicators

to maintain growth rates in excess of 5 per cent per annum. On the other side Venezuela's economy is expected to contract by 16 per cent. In Table 2.3, China, Japan, Russia and Taiwan all exhibit strong healthy balance of payment surpluses, as does the European Union. The US, however, is still forecast to have a large trade deficit (US$200 billion) over the next five years. In Chapter 1 we discussed the difficulties of marketing to countries with high inflation rates. According to Table 2.2 firms are likely to have difficulties in such markets as Argentina, Brazil, Venezuela, South Africa and Turkey where inflation is in excess of 10 per cent. Latin America is a particular area of concern given the economic and political challenges facing such countries as Argentina, Brazil, Venezuela and Colombia.

REASONS COUNTRIES TRADE

International trade is a vital part of world economic activity but it is not a new phenomenon and whilst the growth of international trade has accelerated in the past forty years, it goes back far beyond then and has been developing throughout the ages since the time when barter was used.

The great growth period for trade was in the eighteenth and nineteenth centuries when many of today's important trading links were forged and developed.

A major source of many of the conflicts in the nineteenth century was the desire by nations to win the right to trade in foreign markets. One of the reasons why Great Britain went to war with Napoleon was to open the French markets to our newly industrialised nation. The colony of Hong Kong and the associated New Territories returned to China in 1997 were acquired by the UK in the early nineteenth century for trading purposes.

The reasons nations trade are many and varied: the two key explanations of why nations trade, however, are based on the theory of comparative advantage and the **international product life cycle**.

The theory of comparative advantage

The rationale for world trade is based largely upon Ricardo's theory of comparative advantage. At its simplest level, the theory suggests that trade between countries takes place because one country is able to produce a product at a lower price than is possible elsewhere. An illustration of this is provided by the way in which Japanese companies such as Sony and Hitachi came to dominate the European television market. Their strategy was based upon higher product quality, better design and, more importantly for our purposes here, the lower prices that were made possible by far greater economies of scale and better manufacturing technology than was currently being achieved by the European producers.

It is this notion of relative cost that underpins world trade; in other words, countries should concentrate upon producing products in which they have a comparative advantage over their foreign competitor countries.

How comparative advantage is achieved

A comparative advantage can be achieved in a variety of ways.

- **Sustained period of investment.** This may well lead to significantly lower operating costs.

■ **Lower labour cost**. A firm operating internationally may locate a manufacturing plant in one of the **newly industrialised economies** (NIEs), to take advantage of the lower labour costs there. In 1998, the average hourly wage in the USA was US$17.20, in South Korea it was US$7.40, in Taiwan US$5.82, in Brazil US$4.28 and in China 25 cents! Many developed countries complain of the disadvantage this creates for them in trying to compete in international markets.

This competitive disadvantage is further compounded by the government subsidies and support given in such countries. However, as Illustration 2.1 points out, such countries can be viewed as an opportunity rather than a threat.

■ **Proximity to raw materials**. This is another way to achieve comparative advantage as has been the case with Australia's reserves of coal and mineral ores.

■ **Subsidies to help native industries**. When the US announced increased wheat subsidies to US farmers, they outraged the Australian and Canadian wheat farmers who saw it as a direct attack on their international markets. Without comparable government support, they felt they were unable to compete with US wheat in these markets.

■ **Building expertise in certain key areas**. This is another way to achieve comparative advantage. The Japanese identified biotechnology as a key area where they have comparative strength and so have targeted it as a priority research area for the new millennium.

ILLUSTRATION 2.1   China: Opportunity or threat?

China, a country of 1.3 billion people, willing to work long hours for pitifully low pay, is now a member of the World Trade Organisation and the world's biggest net recipient of foreign direct investment. Companies across the globe are starting to realise that Chinese companies may prove a threat to their established markets just as the Japanese did a few decades ago. Chinese companies are becoming globally competitive in motorbikes, toys, shoes, fridges and microwaves as well as many other products.

But is the fear that China is a major competitive threat justified? *The Economist* argues that such doomsday pessimists who think so are incorrect.

Firstly, they argue, increased trade benefits everyone, profiting buyers and sellers alike. It depends for its benefits not on competitive advantage, but on comparative advantage, a crucial distinction. Thus China may indeed be a cheaper place to manufacture everything than, say, Japan. But that does not mean that all manufacturing will or should shift from Japan to China. The central insight of trade theory is that, in such a situation, both countries will gain from specialising in goods in which they hold a comparative advantage (China in low-end manufacturing, Japan in higher value-added goods and services, say) and then trading with each other.

Secondly, whilst China is becoming increasingly important on the world stage, its exports are still relatively small, about the same as Italy, and its trade surplus is the same as Canada's and shrinking. Which brings us to the final point: China has vast potential as an export market. China's contribution to world demand is vital. Its share of world GDP is 12 per cent. Although much foreign investment in China is aimed at exports, even more is intended to satisfy domestic demand. Far from being flattened by Chinese exports, the rest of East Asia is seeing fast-rising higher-value exports to China. Volkswagen counts China as its second biggest market for cars after Germany. Legend Group, China's biggest computer-maker, is mostly supplying rising domestic demand. As WTO membership opens China's markets to competition, its importance as a source of demand will grow.

Question Do you think Chinese companies pose a substantive competitive threat to established global brands?

Source: Adapted from 'China: Eating your Lunch', *The Economist,* 13 February 2003

Some countries use international trade to buy in a **comparative advantage**, buying in highly developed products and so speeding up their development. Porter (1990) suggests that countries can build a national advantage through four major attributes:

- *Factor conditions*: the nation's position in factors of production such as skilled labour or infrastructure necessary to compete.
- *Demand conditions*: the nature of demand in the home country.
- *Related and supporting industries*: the presence or absence of supplier industries and related industries that are internationally competitive.
- *Firm strategy, structure and rivalry*: the conditions in the nation governing how companies are created, organised and managed and the nature of domestic rivalry.

The international product life cycle

The theory of comparative advantage is often used as the classic explanation of world trade. Other observers, however, believe that world trade and investment patterns are based upon the product life cycle concept. Writing from an American perspective, Vernon and Wells (1968) suggested that on an international level, products move through four distinct phases:

1 US firms manufacture for the home market and begin exporting.

2 Foreign production starts.

3 Foreign products become increasingly competitive in world markets.

4 Imports to the USA begin providing significant competition.

This cycle begins with the product being developed and manufactured in the USA for high-income markets, subsequently being introduced into other markets in the form of exports. The second phase begins to emerge as the technology is developed further and becomes more easily transferable. Companies in other countries then begin manufacturing and, because of lower transportation and labour costs, are able to undercut the American manufacturers in certain markets. The third phase is characterised by foreign companies competing against US exports which, in turn, leads to a further decline in the market for US exports. Typically, it is at this stage that US companies either begin to withdraw from selected markets or, in an attempt to compete more effectively, begin investing in manufacturing capacity overseas to regain sales.

The fourth and final stage begins when foreign companies, having established a strong presence in their home and export markets, start the process of exporting to the US and begin competing against the products produced domestically.

It is these four stages, Vernon suggests, that illustrate graphically how American firms eventually find themselves being squeezed out of their domestic markets having enjoyed a world monopoly just a few years earlier.

Although the product life cycle provides an interesting insight into the evolution of multi-national operations, it needs to be recognised that it provides only a partial explanation of world trade since products do not inevitably follow this pattern. First, competition today is international rather than domestic for all goods and services. Consequently, there is a reduced time lag between product research, development and production, leading to the simultaneous appearance of a standardised product in major world markets. Second, it is not production in the highly labour-intensive industries that is moving to the low labour cost countries but the capital-intensive industries such as electronics, creating the anomalous situation of basing production for high-value, high-technology goods in the countries least able to afford them. Nor does the model go very far in explaining the rapid development of companies networking production and marketing facilities across many countries. Thus global business integration and sharing of R&D, technological and business resources is seen as a more relevant explanation of today's world trade.

It is estimated that somewhere in the region of 50 per cent of international trade is now by global or multi-domestic corporations trading with each other. More and more industrial products sold throughout the world are assembled in one country from components manufactured in others.

BARRIERS TO WORLD TRADE

Marketing barriers

Whilst countries have many reasons for wishing to trade with each other, it is also true to say that all too frequently an importing nation will take steps to inhibit the inward flow of goods and services.

One of the reasons international trade is different from domestic trade is that it is carried on between different political units, each one a sovereign nation exercising control over its own trade. Although all nations control their foreign trade, they vary in terms of the degree of control. Each nation or trading bloc invariably establishes trade laws that favour their indigenous companies and discriminate against foreign ones.

Thus, at the same time as trade has been developing worldwide, so has the body of regulations and barriers to trade. Onkvisit and Shaw identify 850 ways of reducing imports and claim nations have been known to use all of them. Their research shows that large proportions of many manufactured goods are *overtly protected*, the main protagonists being the USA, Italy, France and Germany.

However, the major barriers to trade are becoming increasingly covert, i.e. non-tariff barriers which are often closely associated with the cultural heritage of a country and very difficult to overcome. The complex distribution patterns in Japan are one such example. Thus, whilst Japan is seen not to have many overt barriers, many businesses experience great difficulties when trying to enter the Japanese market.

Trade distortion practices can be grouped into two basic categories: **tariff** and **non-tariff barriers** as illustrated in Figure 2.2.

Tariff barriers

Tariffs are direct taxes and charges imposed on imports. They are generally simple, straightforward and easy for the country to administer. Whilst they are a barrier to trade, they are a visible and known quantity and so can be accounted for by companies when developing their marketing strategies.

Tariffs are used by poorer nations as the easiest means of collecting revenue. The Bahamas for example has a minimum import tax of 30 per cent on all goods, and some products are taxed even higher. Tariffs are also imposed to protect the home producer, as in the US and Australia. Both of these countries have high tariff walls for certain industries they wish to protect – for example, cars and agricultural products. The trend towards the lowering of tariff barriers across the globe in recent years (the average tariff is now 5 per cent whereas in 1945 it was 45 per cent), together with the opening up of new markets to foreign investment, notably Asia and Eastern Europe, has greatly complicated the decision for many companies as to where to place manufacturing facilities.

These trends have made global production much more possible, but it has also reduced the need for many overseas plants. Markets that previously demanded local production facilities because tariff levels made importing prohibitive can now be supplied from non-domestic sources.

A good example of these dynamics can be found in the Australian automotive sector. Over the past decade, the tariff on imported cars has fallen from 57.5 per cent to 22.5 per cent, whilst the number of imported cars has risen from less than 15 per cent of the total market to about half. One large car maker, Nissan, has abandoned Australian manufacturing as a result and other car makers, such as Toyota, have threatened to follow suit unless the pace of tariff reduction slows down.

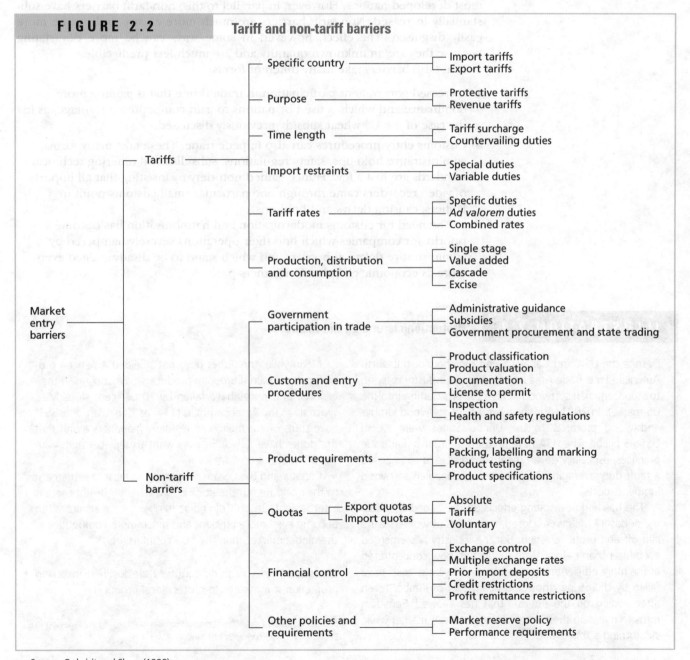

FIGURE 2.2   **Tariff and non-tariff barriers**

Source: Onkvisit and Shaw (1998)

Tariffs can take many forms, as can be seen in Figure 2.2. The most common forms, however, are:

- *Specific*: charges are imposed on particular products either by weight or volume and usually stated in the local currency.
- *Ad valorem*: a straight percentage of the import price.
- *Discriminatory*: in this case the tariff is charged against goods coming from a particular country either where there is a trade imbalance or for political purposes.

Non-tariff barriers

In the past forty years, the world has seen a gradual reduction in tariff barriers in most developed nations. However, in parallel to this, non-tariff barriers have substantially increased. Non-tariff barriers are much more elusive and can be more easily disguised. The effect, however, in some ways can be more devastating because they are an unknown quantity and are much less predictable.

Non-tariff barriers take many different forms:

- Increased government participation in trade is one that is gaining more dominance and which is used by nations to gain competitive advantage, as in the case of the US wheat subsidy previously discussed.
- Customs entry procedures can also impede trade. These take many forms; administrative hold-ups, safety regulations, subsidies and differing technical standards are just a few. France gained notoriety by insisting that all imports of video recorders came through one particular small customs point in Poitiers, causing delays and hold-ups.

The need for customs modernisation and harmonisation has become a priority for companies which find their operations severely hampered by administrative delays at borders and which stand to be disadvantaged even more as economic globalisation gathers pace.

ILLUSTRATION 2.2   **Protectionists end up the losers**

Despite the USA and Canada being members of the North American Free Trade Area, the US lumber industry is trying to stop Canadian softwood lumber exports getting into the US market. In 2001, Canadian exports of softwood lumber and wood products to the United States were worth US$6.5 billion. The USA have accused them of unfair trade practices, especially government subsidies, and so imposed a tariff duty averaging 27 per cent on Canadian softwood lumber exports.

This has had devastating effects on the Canadian industry, or has it? Mills were closed, thousands of workers were laid off and profits crashed. But the industry has emerged even fitter than before. With production now concentrated at the more efficient mills, the industry's average costs have fallen by US$65 per thousand board feet of lumber (even after adding on the duties). That has allowed Canadian firms to maintain their share of the American market while still turning a thin profit.

Meanwhile, the duties have not shielded American producers from pain. European producers have increased their exports, and prices have fallen by 10 per cent since May. Twice as many American mills (114) as Canadian ones (51) have shut, or cut their output. Many managers admit that the duties have failed. So they want to replace them with export quotas.

Canada and the US are now trying to reach a settlement to their dispute but the irony is that whether or not there is a settlement, British Columbia's lumber producers are set to become even more efficient and much more competitive in the global market than their US counterparts.

Question Do you think countries are justified in taking protectionist measures to protect local producers?

Source: Adapted from 'The softwood lumber dispute: A simple lesson in Economics', *The Economist*, 30 January 2003

Clearly the extent of customs delays and red tape varies enormously from country to country but everywhere there is a need for governments to take account of business needs for simple, transparent, coordinated and harmonised customs procedures.

■ Quantitative restrictions such as quotas are another barrier. These are limits on the amount of goods that may enter a country. An import quota can be more restrictive than a tariff as there is less flexibility in responding to it. The Japanese car industry faced quotas both in Europe and the US and so developed manufacturing capacity in these markets as a means of overcoming the barriers. The US also imposes quotas on textile imports from China. However, China, according to the US, has been transshipping textiles through other ports such as Hong Kong in order to circumvent the quota. Even a decade after the formation of NAFTA, the US lumber industry is lobbying against the import of Canadian softwood, as can be seen in Illustration 2.2.

■ Financial controls were last seen in the UK in the mid-1970s but are used today in Mexico and Eastern Europe where high inflation and lack of hard currency require stringent monetary control. This is probably the most complete tool for the regulation of foreign trade as it gives the government a monopoly of all dealings in foreign exchange. A domestic company earning foreign exchange from exporting must sell it to the national bank and, if goods from abroad need to be bought, a company has to apply for foreign exchange. Thus foreign currency is scarce. The **International Monetary Fund** has placed stringent controls on several countries, in particular Indonesia, Brazil and Argentina. The latter countries especially have huge external debts which are viewed as unsustainable.

Countries practising exchange controls tend to favour the import of capital goods rather than consumer goods. The other major implication to companies operating in foreign markets is the restrictions on repatriating profits in foreign currency, requiring either counter-trade dealings or the use of distorted transfer prices to get profits home (see Chapter 11 on pricing issues).

Non-tariff barriers become much more prevalent in times of recession. In the US and Europe we have witnessed the mobilisation of quite strong political lobby groups, as indigenous industries, which have come under threat, lobby their governments to take measures to protect them from international competition.

The last major era of protectionism was in the 1930s. During that decade, under the impact of the most disastrous trade depression in recorded history, most countries of the world adopted high tariffs and abandoned their policies of free trade. In 1944 there was a reaction against the high tariff policy of the 1930s and significant efforts were made to move the world back to free trade. In the next section we will look at the world institutions that have been developed since that time to foster international trade and provide a trade climate in which such barriers can be reduced.

THE DEVELOPMENT OF WORLD INSTITUTIONS TO FOSTER INTERNATIONAL TRADE

In the 1930s international trade was at a low ebb, protectionism was rife and economies were strangling themselves. Several initiatives were born, primarily out of the 1944 Bretton Woods conference, to create an infrastructure that fostered trading relations. These initiatives fell into three areas:

■ Need for international capital: IBRD

■ International liquidity: IMF
■ Liberalisation of international trade and tariffs: GATT/WTO.

International Bank for Reconstruction and Development (IBRD)

The **World Bank**, officially called the International Bank for Reconstruction and Development, was founded together with the International Monetary Fund (IMF) in 1944. The World Bank began operating in June 1946 and membership of the Bank is open to all members of the IMF. Currently, there are 130 member countries. The Bank is owned and controlled by its member governments. Each member country subscribes to shares for an amount relative to its economic strength. The largest shareholder in the World Bank at the moment is the United States.

The primary purpose of the Bank is to provide financial and technical help for the development of poorer countries. Currently it lends about £10 billion a year to help raise the standard of living in poorer countries.

The scope of the Bank's operations has increased phenomenally during the past two decades. For example, in the year 2000 it provided more than five times as much financial help to developing countries than in any year of the 1960s. The Bank provides support for a wide variety of projects related to agriculture, education, industry, electricity, rural development, tourism, transportation, population planning, urban development, water supply and telecommunications. The Bank lends money only for productive purposes and gives serious consideration to the prospects of repayment before granting the loan.

Whilst the countries who are members subscribe to the share capital of the World Bank, it relies mainly on private investors for its financial resources through borrowing in various capital markets. In this way, private investors become involved in the development efforts of developing countries. Since the IBRD obtains most of its funds on commercial terms, it charges its borrowers a commercial rate of interest. Loans are usually repayable over a twenty-year period.

This has led to what has been euphemistically termed the 'debt crisis'. Many of the poor developing countries who have been the recipients of large capital loans

TABLE 2.4	The heavy burden of debt	
	Debt US$Billion	% GDP
Argentina	168.0	61
Brazil	175.0	31
Mauritania	2.5	241
Mexico	140.0	25
Nicaragua	6.0	262
Poland	40.0	25
Russia	120.0	48
Sierra Leone	1.2	171
Syria	22.4	136
Thailand	70.0	58
Turkey	98.0	49

Source: WTO World Development Indicators 2003

are now finding it impossible to meet the burden of debt facing them. In 2003 it was estimated that developing countries owed US$1.2 trillion to the world's richest nations. Table 2.4 illustrates the heavy burden of debt that some countries may face. In some cases, such as Sierra Leone, Syria and Nicaragua, countries have debt burdens well in excess of their Gross National Income (GNI). There is now international agreement that international reforms are needed in order to achieve more sustainable debt platforms and many campaigns are fighting for the debts of many countries to be written off completely.

International Development Association

In the 1950s it became obvious that many of the poorer countries needed loans on much easier terms than the World Bank could provide. The International Development Association was established in 1960 to help meet this need. It was made an affiliate of the World Bank and was to be administered in accordance with the Bank's established methods.

Almost all of the **International Development Association**'s loans are granted for a period of fifteen years without interest, except for a small charge to cover administrative overheads. Repayment of loans does not start until after a ten-year period of grace. Both the IDA and the IBRD lay down quite stringent requirements that have to be met before any loans are granted. In many cases this has meant that in order to be granted the investment the countries have had to make quite hard political decisions in order to achieve the balanced budget required. In some cases this has led to severe hardship and social disorder for which the institutions have been severely criticised.

International Monetary Fund (IMF)

The objective of the IMF was to regain the stability in international exchange rates that had existed under the gold standard. Although the system of pegged rates failed to keep up with the growth in international trade, the functions of the IMF have continued to develop.

The main function is to provide short-term international liquidity to countries with **balance of payments** deficit problems enabling them to continue to trade internationally. The IMF, with its 130 members, provides a forum for international monetary cooperation enabling the making of reciprocal agreements amongst countries and the monitoring of the balance of payments positions of countries. Thus it serves to lessen the risk of nations taking arbitrary actions against each other as happened in the 1930s and also can sound a warning bell for nations with potential liquidity problems.

The IMF's seal of approval is, for emerging markets, essential to attract foreign investment and finance. It is also a precondition of financial assistance from the Fund. Brazil and Turkey have been recent recipients of IMF funding. Turkey got help, in spite of the government's persistent failure to stick to its policy obligations. Recently, Brazil received the Fund's largest-ever loan. This was seen as a big risk for the IMF. Several prominent economists argued that Brazil's huge foreign-debt burdens were unsustainable and so the loan would only add to their burden.

The IMF also intervened in Argentina in 2001 to the tune of US$8 billion. The economic crisis at the end of 2001 saw the abandonment of the one-for-one currency peg with the American dollar and the government defaulting on a US$800 million debt owed to the World Bank; this was the biggest debt default in IMF history and greatly soured relations between the IMF and Argentina. Although relations have now improved, many Argentines remain resentful at what they regard as harsh treatment of their country by the IMF conditions set down for the loans being made. Argentina's external government debt stands at US$100 billion; they have recently been granted a further US$6.6 billion loan by the IMF to cover repayments due to the International Monetary Fund itself during 2003.

The World Trade Organisation

The predecessor of the World Trade Organisation was the General Agreement on Tarriffs and Trade (GATT). Established in January 1948, it was a treaty not an organisation, with the signatories being contracting parties. Prior to the Doha Round which commenced in 2001 there had been a series of eight trade liberalisation 'rounds'. These entailed tens of thousands of tariff concessions on industrial goods and covered trade flows worth hundreds of billions of dollars. Twenty-three countries participated in the 1948 opening round when 45 000 tariff concessions were agreed covering US$10 billion worth of trade. Under the first eight GATT rounds, the average tariff on manufactured products in the industrial world fell from around 45 per cent in 1947 to under 5 per cent. This has been an important engine of world economic growth which, in turn, has stimulated further increases in world trade. Signatories to these treaties account for some 90 per cent of world trade.

The last round of negotiations to be completed was the Uruguay Round with 107 participants. It was widely seen as the most complex and ambitious round ever attempted. This was due to the sheer volume of its coverage – fifteen sectors and US$1 trillion worth of trade. An important part of the treaty was the formation of the World Trade Organisation, which commenced in 1995 and replaced GATT. The WTO currently has 144 members and another 29 countries who have observer status. The newest member is China.

The WTO preaches a gospel of multilateral trade and most-favoured-nation status which obliges each signatory to the treaties to grant the same treatment to all other members on a non-discriminatory basis. It has evolved regulations which it has tried to enforce through its adjudicatory disputes panels and complaints procedures. The WTO has been the final arbitrator in a number of trade disputes, most notably between the USA and China in disputes over copyright, piracy and the use of brand names and between the USA and the European Union. The USA considers the EU's refusal to approve genetically modified (GM) foods illegal under the WTO trade rules and in 2003 launched a formal complaint against them. Barring US producers from exporting GM crops to the EU is estimated to cost US producers several hundred million dollars a year. Interestingly, however, the WTO has recently allowed the EU to impose up to US$4 billion of tariffs against America as recompense for a US foreign tax sales break which the WTO has deemed an illegal subsidy.

The main aim of the WTO is to promote a free market international trade system. It promotes trade by:

■ working to reduce tariffs

■ prohibiting import/export bans and quotas

■ eliminating discrimination against foreign products and services

■ eliminating other impediments to trade commonly known as non-tariff barriers.

The latest round of negotiations, called **The Doha Round**, commenced in 2001 and will take several years to complete. In this round members of the WTO are attempting to liberalise trading rules in a number of areas, including agricultural subsidies, textiles and clothing, services, technical barriers to trade, trade-related investments and rules of origin.

Over three-quarters of the WTO members are developing countries. The Doha Round has been dubbed the Development Round as it is specifically aiming to ease trading restrictions for these countries. It is estimated that developing countries face trade barriers four times those applied by rich countries to each other. These barriers reduce export earnings by US$100 billion per annum. Two of the main problem areas for negotiators are the international trading of textiles and agriculture, which accounts for 70 per cent of developing countries' exports. Average tariffs for textiles are 15–20 per cent compared to an average of 3 per cent for industrialised goods. In the European Union and the USA agricultural subsidies amount to US$1 billion per day, six times the annual amount spent on aid by these two regions.

THE DEVELOPMENT OF WORLD TRADING GROUPS

It is believed by some that during the fifty years of global economic expansion under the auspices of GATT, despite the long-term commitments to multilateral trade, there has been an unstoppable momentum of the creation of giant trading blocs.

The formation of the European Monetary Union in 1999 was, perhaps, the most significant of these. When the European single market was formed in 1993, the United States effectively became the second largest market in the world. Who will dominate the international markets of the twenty-first century depends upon the outcome of the competitive battle now commencing. The fear that the world economy may divide into three enormous trading blocs dominated by the world's major trading regions, the EU, NAFTA and China/Japan, rather than a world of multilateral free trade is a recurrent fear. Some commentators argue that national economies are becoming vulnerable to the needs of the trading blocs within which trade is free, currencies are convertible, access to banking is open and contracts are enforceable by law. Whilst this scenario may be a long way from the present position, we are already seeing the formation of trading blocs such as the North American Free Trade Association (NAFTA), Association of South East Asian Nations (ASEAN) and the formation of the European Monetary Union.

In this section we will examine in detail the regional trading blocs that are emerging but first let us examine different forms of trade agreements.

Forms of market agreement

There are nine levels of market association ranging from limited trade cooperation to full-blown political union (see Table 2.5). At the lower level of association, agreements can be purely for economic cooperation in some form, perhaps a decision to consult on or coordinate trade policies. At the next level of cooperation, there will be the development of trade agreements between countries on either a bilateral or multilateral basis. Often these are for a particular sector – for example the multi-fibre agreement on textiles. Sometimes such agreements, especially trade preference ones, will act as a forerunner to closer ties. As far as formal trade groupings are concerned, there are five major forms: free trade areas, customs unions, common markets, economic unions and political unions.

Free trade area

The free trade area type of agreement requires different countries to remove all tariffs amongst the agreement's members. Let us assume that there are three

TABLE 2.5 Main types of trade associations

Type	Description	Degree of policy harmonisation amongst members	Common external tariff	Free movement of capital and people	Example
Economic cooperation	Broad agreement for consultations on and possible coordination of economic trade policies	None/very low	No	No	Canada–EC framework agreement, APEC
Bilateral or multilateral trade treaty	Trade regulation and often, but not necessarily, liberalisation in one or more specified sector(s)	Low	No	No	The Peru, Chile accord
Sectoral free trade agreement	Removal of internal tariffs in a specified sector may include non-tariff barrier reduction	Medium (within specified sector(s))	No	No	The multi-fibre agreement
Trade preference agreement	Preferred trade terms (often including tariff reduction) in all or most sectors, possibly leading to free trade area	Low/medium	No	No	South African Development Cone (SADC)
Free trade area (or agreement)	Removal of internal tariffs and some reduction of non-tariff barriers in all or most sectors	Medium	No	No	ASEAN, NAFTA, Mercosur
Customs union	Free trade area but with a common external tariff, harmonisation of trade policy toward third countries	Medium/high	Yes	Possibly	Economic Community of West African States, ANCOM, CACM
Common market	Customs union, but with provisions for the free movement of capital and people, removal of all trade barriers, elaborate supranational institutions, significant harmonisation of internal market structure and external policies	Medium	Yes	Yes	European single market
Economic union	Common market, but with integration of monetary policies, possibly common currency, significant weakening of national powers of member states	Very high	Yes	Yes	European Monetary Union
Political	Full or partial federalism, including sharing of powers between supranational institutions and national governments	Highest	Yes	Yes	Would resemble federal states (e.g. US, Canada, Germany)

Source: unknown

nations – A, B and C – that agree to a free trade area agreement and abolish all tariffs amongst themselves to permit free trade. Beyond the free trade area A, B and C may impose tariffs as they choose. The EEA (European Economic Area) formed between the EU and EFTA and the LAFTA (Latin American Free Trade Area) illustrate the free trade area type of agreement, as does NAFTA, the agreement between the USA, Canada and Mexico, and the ASEAN agreement.

Customs union

In addition to requiring abolition of internal tariffs amongst the members, a customs union further requires the members to establish common external tariffs. To continue with the example (countries A, B and C), under a customs union agreement B would not be permitted to have a special relationship with country X – A, B and C would have a common tariff policy towards X. Prior to 1993, the EC was, in reality, a customs union. The objective of Mercosur is to form a customs union. Their cooperative effort started as a free trade area and now they intend to develop into a customs union.

Common market

In a common market type of agreement, not only do members abolish internal tariffs amongst themselves and levy common external tariffs, they also permit free flow of all factors of production amongst themselves. Under a common market agreement, countries A, B and C would not only remove all tariffs and quotas amongst themselves and impose common tariffs against other countries such as country X, but would also allow capital and labour to move freely within their boundaries as if they were one country. This means that, for example, a resident of country A is free to accept a position in Country C without a work permit.

The European Union prior to 1999 was essentially a common market with full freedom of movement of all factors of production. The Andean nations in South America have formed ANCOM and the Central American nations have formed CACM. However, these are more association agreements than common markets.

Economic union

Under an economic union agreement, common market characteristics are combined with the harmonisation of economic policy. Member countries are expected to pursue common fiscal and monetary policies. Ordinarily this means a synchronisation of money supply, interest rates, regulation of capital market and taxes. In effect, an economic union calls for a supranational authority to design an economic policy for an entire group of nations. This was the objective of the European Monetary Union.

Political union

This is the ultimate market agreement amongst nations. It includes the characteristics of economic union and requires, additionally, political harmony amongst the members. Essentially, it means nations merging to form a new political entity. Thus Yugoslavia, which was created after the First World War, was a political union, as was the Soviet Union – both of which have now disintegrated.

Figure 2.3 shows the major trading regions which have significantly developed in the past decade together with their member countries. In the following sections we will examine these major trading groups and the developments they have undergone.

THE EUROPEAN UNION

Since 1987 and the signing of the Single European Act, Europe has undergone momentous changes, the key amongst these being:

- the **Single European Market** (SEM)
- formation of the European Monetary Union (EMU)
- the expansion of the European Union (EU) to include members of the European Economic Area (EEA) and the accession of new members from Central, Eastern and Southern Europe.

The Single European Market

The formation of the SEM meant that Europe became the largest trading bloc in the world with a population of 380 million people making it a powerful competitive force in the global markets. This, of course, was the key objective of the moves towards a unified market. In the early 1980s it was recognised that if European companies were to compete successfully in the increasingly interdependent and global economy, a free and unbridled large internal market was necessary. This would enable companies to develop the critical mass needed to compete globally. The highly fragmented and restricted European market was seen as a major barrier to the ability to compete in global markets.

The SEM was formed as a result of the signing of the Single European Act in 1987 which created, within Europe, 'an area without internal priorities in which the free movement of goods, personal services and capital is ensured in accordance with the provision of the Treaty of Rome'.

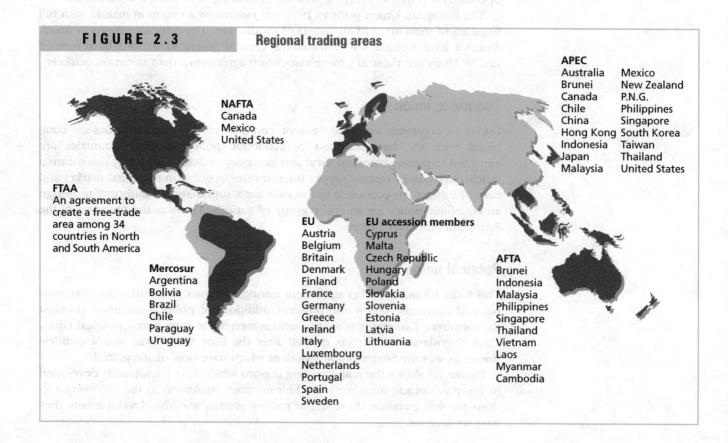

FIGURE 2.3 **Regional trading areas**

APEC
Australia	Mexico
Brunei	New Zealand
Canada	P.N.G.
Chile	Philippines
China	Singapore
Hong Kong	South Korea
Indonesia	Taiwan
Japan	Thailand
Malaysia	United States

NAFTA
Canada
Mexico
United States

FTAA
An agreement to create a free-trade area among 34 countries in North and South America

Mercosur
Argentina
Bolivia
Brazil
Chile
Paraguay
Uruguay

EU
Austria
Belgium
Britain
Denmark
Finland
France
Germany
Greece
Ireland
Italy
Luxembourg
Netherlands
Portugal
Spain
Sweden

EU accession members
Cyprus
Malta
Czech Republic
Hungary
Poland
Slovakia
Slovenia
Estonia
Latvia
Lithuania

AFTA
Brunei
Indonesia
Malaysia
Philippines
Singapore
Thailand
Vietnam
Laos
Myanmar
Cambodia

The key changes were:

- **Removal of tariff barriers**: a single customs-check at all intra-EU borders enabling goods and services to move freely across Europe.

- **Removal of technical barriers**: a major impediment to trade was the differing complex standards required in each country. Harmonisation of these standards has paved the way for product standardisation throughout Europe.

- **Public procurement**: public procurement amounts to 15 per cent of EU GNP, only 2 per cent of which went to foreign suppliers. By opening up the market to all European suppliers and by ensuring its enforcement, it is estimated that €17.5 billion are saved per annum.

- **Free movement of labour and workers' rights**: nationals of member states now have the right to work in other member states.

- **Opening up of professions**: through mutual recognition of qualifications, professionals in certain categories have their qualifications recognised by other member states.

- **Financial services**: the opening-up of banking, insurance and investment services through the introduction of a single banking licence and the harmonisation of banking conditions.

- **Transport, haulage and coastal cabotage**: road haulage permits and quotas have been abolished. A more competitive air transport industry is also being pursued, as is unlimited cabotage for transport through the SEM. Thus, trucks are now allowed to pick up goods in any EU country and drop them off where required without the bureaucracy of permits and border documentation.

- **Company law**: several European developments in the area of company law are taking place in the fields of takeover bids, health and safety, cross-border merger, etc. The road to greater control from Brussels is now becoming especially apparent in this area.

- **Fiscal barriers**: there are many EU variations of fiscal policies, e.g. VAT. The UK has a standard rate of 17.5 per cent whereas France has six rates varying from 2.1 to 33.33 per cent. Moves are being made to reduce these disparities.

- **The environment**: the European Environment Agency was established to try to provide an integrated and Europe-wide policy for environmental protection.

Most analysts agree that the SEM has greatly enhanced market opportunities for European companies. Since its formation it is estimated to have created about 2.5 million jobs and generated prosperity equivalent to €877 billion. As a result of its formation, there is a potential home market of 380 million consumers for companies within its walls. Intra-regional trading amongst EU members accounts for 70 per cent of all intra-trade. With such inter-dependency, it is little wonder that so much effort has been put into completing the unified market. However, a decade or so on from the formation of the SEM, whilst most goods are now crossing Europe's national borders with little or no hindrance, the liberalisation of trade in services has not made the same progress. Europe's service providers are hindered by all sorts of petty bureaucratic rules, often justified on health, safety or consumer-protection grounds, which discourage them from entering new European markets. In some cases, the European Commission has itself hampered the development of the single market by granting certain industries exemptions from the normal rules of fair competition. But these exemptions are starting to be undone. One of the most famous cases is that of new cars. British motorists have long been outraged that the prices in their local showrooms are so much higher than on the continent. Their attempts to buy cars more cheaply across the Channel have often been frustrated because of restrictions that the car makers were allowed to impose on dealers. However, from 2005, car makers will no longer be able to threaten to stop supplying, for example, a Belgian car dealer who advertises directly to British motorists and sets up a delivery service in Britain.

European Monetary Union (EMU)

The idea behind a single European currency has been around since the early 1960s. As trade between member countries increased, various attempts were made to stabilise exchange rates. Previous systems such as the **Exchange Rate Mechanism** (ERM) attempted to create monetary stability through a system of fixed and floating exchange rates. This proved, however, to be incapable of coping with capital flows, which resulted in problems for sterling and the lira in September 1992, with the remaining currencies also facing problems the following year. Pressure for further integration in the Community resulted in the move to monetary union and a single European currency, following, as a logical conclusion, to the Single Market. **European Monetary Union** (EMU) commenced in 1999 in the sense that the European Central Bank took control of interest rates. Businesses, however, did not have to trade or pay wages in euros until 2002.

EMU started with eleven founder members. Whilst Britain has not joined EMU, if UK firms trade in the European Union both the manufacturing and service sectors will be affected by the single currency. Companies in both sectors have had to convert their customer invoices and accounts, credit notes and prices into euros. Companies that use computer systems for their customer and/or supplier accounts have adapted them to deal with euros. The estimated conversion cost in computers, tills, packaging and billing was estimated to be over US$1 billion. On the other hand, companies with customer and supplier bases largely outside the EU face little or no impact on their businesses.

Strategic implications

The strategic aspects of EMU are notoriously difficult to judge. EMU is not just a monetary event but one that has had a serious impact on the real economy. Prices and wages have become transparent; consumers now shop around for the best deals; middlemen try to exploit any prevailing regional price differences and margins everywhere are now coming under pressure.

The competitive environment is viewed by many as being tougher under EMU. The change has affected companies both inside and outside the EMU zone, it is just that companies operating inside the eurozone have had to adjust more quickly than companies operating outside the zone.

In some cases, it has taken outsiders longer to sense the changes EMU has brought. By the time the UK eventually joins EMU, UK companies might find that their competitors are significantly ahead, in their logistical as well as strategic preparations.

Some large European companies, BMW, Daimler-Benz and Siemens for example, use the euro as their in-house currency. Hewlett Packard have abolished national prices for office supplies. Schering recently introduced a new drug for multiple sclerosis at a single pan-European price. Marks and Spencer quote all prices in euros as well as the local currency.

The question is, which industries do commentators expect to be winners in the new competitive landscape and which have lost from the introduction of the euro? Amongst significant losers have been the banks, which have lost their business of buying and selling European currencies. The biggest difference, however, has not been between industries but between efficient, flexible companies and those that have stuck to their old national ways.

Companies that have concentrated on their national markets have been particularly vulnerable to takeover or extinction at the hands of their more far-sighted European competitors. Those businesses already used to competing internationally have had a strong advantage. As sources of supply widen, specialisations based on national talents have developed further. French and German companies, for example, run call-centres from Dublin, where multilingual Irish operators (or continental expatriates) provide advice or take orders over the telephone more cheaply and flexibly than would be possible in the companies' home countries. Another effect of the single currency has been to open the European market for those small and medium-sized companies who have previously

---

ILLUSTRATION 2.3   Skoda has the last laugh

The Czech word skoda means pity or shame. Thus, on spying a passing Skoda car, Czechs used to say there goes a shame, and nobody would much argue. However, Skoda Autos (of the Czech Republic), once a butt of jokes, has now completely overhauled its image and its profitability with the help of its German partner Volkswagen who have the controlling share in Skoda. The company employs some 4 per cent of the Czech workforce, or 150 000 people, directly or indirectly. An impressive 14 per cent of Czech exports are attributable to Skoda and its suppliers. These other firms now account for US$3 billion in combined revenues.

The production line near Prague now makes one of a growing number of world-class mass-market manufactured products developed in Eastern Europe and being marketed across the pan-European market. Productivity is higher than Western levels and labour costs are much lower than at other VW plants in Europe. Analysts reckon that Skoda is the most successful former Communist company anywhere. Production has tripled since 1991. In 1997, Skoda overtook Fiat's Polish affiliate as Central Europe's largest car manufacturer. Despite a three-year recession in the Czech Republic,

Skoda has doubled its sales since 1995 to US$3.2 billion, and last year it made a respectable profit of US$75m. Last year VW bought the remaining 30 per cent stake owned by the Czech government for a further US$320m.

The growth has been driven by exports. In 1991, around 30 per cent of Skodas were sold abroad; now around 80 per cent are exported. Skoda has plants in Poland and Bosnia, and one on the way in India. Its controlled expansion into Western Europe has continued apace, especially into Germany, the firm's biggest Western market.

Volkswagen's presence in Central Europe has had three advantages. First, it increased Volkswagen's leadership in Europe through the conquest of local Central European markets. Second, it increased competitiveness through local manufacturing and purchases. Third, it has allowed them the possibility of using Skoda to penetrate other emerging markets in Europe, Russia and Asia.

Question Fully evaluate the reasons for Skoda's success.

Source: adapted from *The Economist*, 2001

Source: Tim Gutt

Skoda's new Skoda Superb from Skoda.

Source: Tim Gutt

concentrated on their domestic customers. It has been estimated that currency fluctuations and the costs of dealing with them previously deterred a third of small and medium-sized German companies from venturing abroad. Many that did export concentrated exclusively on countries where currencies were informally linked to the D-Mark, such as Austria and the Netherlands.

Widening European membership

Enlargement of the European Union has happened at several stages of its development over the past fifty years, and there have been four previous enlargements. In 1993 the European Council adopted the 'Copenhagen Criteria' for admission to the EU. These require that member countries attain the following:

- Stable institutions guaranteeing democracy and the rule of law.
- A functioning market economy, as well as the capacity to cope with the competitive pressure and market forces within the EU.
- The ability to fulfil membership obligations, including adherence to the aims of political, economic and monetary union.

Thirteen countries from Southern, Central and Eastern Europe have applied to gain access to the EU, ten of which are expected to join in 2004. They are Cyprus, Malta, Czech Republic, Hungary, Poland, Slovakia, Slovenia, Estonia, Latvia and Lithuania. If all thirteen join (including the other three candidates, Bulgaria, Turkey and Romania), together they will increase the EU's population by 45 per cent but only raise its GDP by 17 per cent.

The annual growth rate amongst the accession countries in Central and Eastern Europe has been between 2 and 6 per cent compared to 1–2 per cent in the existing EU members. It is reasonable to expect such a differential to

---

ILLUSTRATION 2.4   **ABB's Central European strategy**

ABB's strategy in Central and Eastern Europe had two motivators: high local demand in energy-related businesses and low-cost manufacturing which enhances the group's global competitiveness.

ABB felt the optimum strategy for the division of labour was to manufacture high-tech products in the West and standard products in emerging countries.

In Central Europe ABB's presence has been massive and precocious. In 2002 the company employed 24 000 people in the region; worldwide it has 215 000 staff. The company's focus was on Poland, Hungary and the Czech Republic.

ABB's largest Central European subsidiary exports gas turbines, low-pressure turbine rotors and generators worldwide. Polish plants within the ABB group tend to export more than 20 per cent of their production.

This implies that local production meets the group's worldwide quality standards and that the group integrates all its activities into a unified manufacturing network. Since the cost of a turbine manufactured in Poland may be 40 per cent lower than competing products from Western Europe, ABB's competitive advantage at a global level is increased.

However, this rosy picture has now turned sour. ABB, once seen as Europe's answer to GE, is seen as a stricken engineering group struggling for months with a severe financial and operational crisis. The current chairman was confident that ABB would meet its targets for improving earnings and reducing its US$5.2 billion of debt. However, this confidence now looks misplaced. The price of its shares has collapsed and its future looks uncertain. Bad investments, severe liabilities due to asbestos claims against it and a faltering strategy have all been factors contributing to the downfall.

Question What do you think are the reasons for ABB's change of fortune?

Source: Adapted from *FT Exporter* and *The Economist*

continue in the medium term and, as such, Central Europe may be considered a younger and faster-growing version of Western Europe.

Depending on the country and industry, growth potential in Central Europe is extremely high. The consumer goods market, for example, which was almost virgin territory in 1989, has undergone tremendous growth. Sony's sales in the region have risen 30 per cent annually in recent years whilst Skoda's sales have risen by 21 per cent annually since 1996 (see Illustration 2.3).

The second major attraction for business is cost. The average labour cost in the Czech Republic was only US$4 per hour compared with US$30 in Germany. Relative to other emerging regions, Central Europe has a high level of education, a skilled labour force, a number of good and even excellent engineers and a strong technological and scientific tradition. It was for such reasons that ABB invested so heavily in Central Europe. However, it was not the recipe for success (see illustration 2.4).

THE FREE TRADE AREA OF THE AMERICAS (FTAA)

In 1994, the US, Canada and Mexico created the world's richest market – the North American Free Trade Area (NAFTA). NAFTA created a single market of 360 million people producing over US$6 trillion in annual output. Their combined intra-trade amounted to over US$300 billion and they estimate that NAFTA has added US$30 billion per annum to their combined GDP.

The main provisions of the NAFTA agreement aimed to:

- Eliminate tariffs on manufactured goods.

- Eliminate tariffs on 57 per cent of the agricultural produce from Mexico.

- Harmonise and streamline customs procedures and bureaucracy.

ILLUSTRATION 2.5	When is a catfish not a catfish?

The mighty USA is feeling threatened because of imports of catfish coming into the country from Vietnam. Since formalising a trade deal two years ago, Americans have bought 17m lb (7.7m kilos) of Vietnamese catfish a year, the price of catfish has almost halved and they fear this could put US producers with higher costs out of business. However, instead of submitting to the free-market principles, America's lobbyists and lawmakers are seeking to crush the Vietnamese producers by passing a law restricting the use of the word catfish to American varieties.

When the new law failed to dent sales of the import formerly known as catfish, American farmers decided to launch an anti-dumping suit. Their petition contends that companies in Vietnam, where the average income per person is about a fiftieth of America's, are subsidising rich Americans' taste for catfish. The Vietnamese government meddles in its economy so much, they claim, that it is impossible to make a true assessment of the local producers' costs. So they asked the Department of Commerce to work out how much it would cost to raise hypothetical catfish in India, fillet and freeze them in imaginary factories, and ship them in phantom boats to America. If these turned out to cost more than the fleshier Vietnamese sort, it would be proof, the Americans say, that Vietnamese producers are unfairly subsidised and should pay a tariff of up to 190 per cent.

The Vietnamese government is indignant. It points out that its booming catfish industry benefits America, by cutting costs for consumers and boosting demand for American exports such as grain for catfish feed. It is threatening to launch a suit of its own, against subsidised imports of American soya beans.

Question How would you recommend the Vietnamese producers protect themselves against the US action?

Source: Adapted from *The Economist* 2003

- Liberalise telecommunications, transport, textiles, banking and finance.

- Establish a NAFTA trade commission to settle trade disputes.

The attractive feature of NAFTA is that by virtue of the fact that Mexico is at a different stage of economic development from the US and Canada, the gains through specialisation have been relatively large, allowing the US to specialise in more complex products that are intensive in their use of knowledge, technology and capital equipment.

The available evidence suggests that this is precisely what has happened. US exports to Mexico of electronic goods and transport equipment have increased substantially. Meanwhile, most of the anecdotal evidence about US workers harmed by NAFTA comes from light manufacturing industries and agriculture.

However, it must be said that the scale of change induced by NAFTA is probably quite small relative to other factors impinging on the US economy over the last decade, such as technological change and reductions in defence spending.

For many, the creation of NAFTA was a US response to the formation of the single market in Europe. However, for others it has signalled the era of US protectionism (see Illustration 2.5) and the drive by the US to create a free trade area across the Americas. The objective is to create a free trade area consisting of thirty-four democracies by the year 2005.

This involves negotiations with the Central American Common Market, the Andean Community and Mercosur. However, since the political and economic crises in various Southern American nations, negotiations have been slowed down somewhat, with some countries, e.g. Brazil, now very sceptical as to its likely success.

Mercosur

Mercosur is the customs union linking Brazil, Paraguay, Uruguay, Argentina, Bolivia and Chile. This South American Southern cone is the fourth largest integrated market in the world and consists of 300 million people with a combined GNP of over US$1 trillion.

The creation of Mercosur was seen as an integral part of the formula to conquer inflation, expand the size of its markets and attract substantial foreign direct investment, and this was very successful for several years.

However, Uruguay, Brazil and Argentina have now gone through a period of turbulence and face huge political and economic challenges, which have hindered the progress of the formation of the trading bloc.

Argentina's prices rose by 48 per cent in 2003, its exchange rate decreased by 70 per cent and GDP is 20 per cent less than it was in 1998. If one adds to this the huge debt defaults and the high levels of poverty and corruption, it is little wonder that foreign investors have been deterred. The picture is not the same in all of South America. Chile is performing strongly, has sound policies and is well integrated into the global economy. Columbia and Ecuador are viewed by the IMF to be following a sound reform programme and both have growing economies.

As trade barriers have fallen, especially in intra-regional trade, many multinationals have tried to bring the Mercosur countries into their worldwide strategy. For example, Unilever as part of its drive to dominate the global ice-cream industry bought Kibon, Brazil's largest ice-cream maker. However, besides the challenges described above, these companies have found there are three strategic issues they have faced when trying to build a presence in the Mercosur markets:

- *Infrastructural weaknesses*: although the region has achieved remarkable growth in internal trade in the past few years, its infrastructure has to be substantially improved to facilitate a more competitive flow of materials, machinery and goods. This will allow corporations to develop fully integrated regional strategies. As things stand, the inefficient infrastructure hampers companies' efforts to achieve the economies of scale needed for regional competitiveness.

- *The need to develop industrial 'clusters'*: a nation's successful industries are usually linked through clusters of vertical and horizontal relationships. The vehicle assembly industry based in Sao Paulo, which has been successful for decades, illustrates how clustering of related businesses (glass, rubber, pistons and steel) is a driving force behind an industry's competitiveness. Such clusters should increase the opportunities for small and medium-sized companies – not just the big corporations – to profit from the process of regional economic integration.

- *The business mindset*: a major obstacle to development is the business culture amongst traditional entrepreneurs. A mindset based on paternalism, centralisation of authority and casual opportunism can pose problems for carrying out business in such countries.

The development of the Latin American markets is essential if the economies of the region are to compete effectively in a much larger area – as will happen if the FTAA (Free Trade Area of the Americas) becomes a reality. Mercosur, the Andean Pact and other trade agreements in the region are regional training fields for the new structures to come.

Companies in the area are becoming familiar with the complexities of the new business landscape and trying to increase their cross-border capabilities. Whether they will flourish in the larger, more integrated, global economy that will be the competitive playing ground if the USA succeeds in its aspirations for the FTAA is yet to be seen.

THE ASIAN PACIFIC TRADING REGION

Asia Pacific Economic Cooperation (APEC)

The US is also a member of APEC (Asia Pacific Economic Cooperation). APEC is essentially a forum amongst twenty-three Asia Pacific nations to discuss means and ways to build economic and trade cooperation. Some members of the group would like an Asia-Pacific trading bloc to emerge as they fear being excluded from traditional US markets. This would mean that Japan and the US would be in one regional bloc. Combining FTAA, East Asian and Australasian countries into one Asia-Pacific bloc would mean that nearly 70 per cent of their trade would be intra-regional. However, there is marked resistance amongst Asian members of APEC for an enhanced role of the group although the US is giving a high priority to the APEC grouping and intends to forge closer trade and investment ties across the Pacific. A new round of trade talks commenced in 2001 to energise the process to achieve this objective.

The Asia Pacific region has had the fastest growth in the world for thirty years and, despite a downturn in 1998, East Asia is the principal export market for US products. Transpacific trade is 50 per cent greater than its transatlantic trade and more than 40 per cent of US trade is now in the Asian region. To foster this growth, the United States supports a more active APEC that will take on a role as a forum for consultations on trade policy and expansion of trade and investment, with a goal of lowering trade barriers in the region and supporting a multilateral system of free trade.

The Asian Free Trade Area (AFTA)

The members of the **Association of South East Asian Nations** (ASEAN) – Thailand, Indonesia, Singapore, Brunei, Malaysia and the Philippines, together with Vietnam, Myanmar, Cambodia and Laos, have agreed to form an **Asian Free Trade Area** (AFTA) by the year 2005.

This will create a largely tariff-free market of 500 million people. The scheme aims to reduce tariffs on internal trade to a common preferential tariff of 0–5 per cent. Total trade of the AFTA members is US$720 billion and they have a combined GNI of US$737 billion.

However, some observers are sceptical about the development. Geographical distances and cultural disparities have meant that previous attempts at closer economic integration have failed. These nations are keenly competitive and previously have not kept to agreements to lower trading restrictions. Nevertheless, the Asian economies are pulling closer together than ever before and this trend is likely to accelerate the potential formation of an Asian Economic Region by 2020. But where European (EU) and North American (NAFTA) integration has been based on treaties, in Asia it is based on market forces, the chief force being the region's fast rate of growth. By the year 2010, Asia should account for about a third of world production. Increasingly growth is also coming from intra-Asian trade which recent estimates have put as high as 40 per cent.

Barriers to developing a cohesive trading region

Whilst an Asian Pacific trading bloc may never have the cohesion of either Europe or America, as the fastest-growing economic region in the world any move towards integration will be watched closely by international competitors. Investment there is dominated by Japanese companies which are providing 75 per cent of all foreign investment in China, Hong Kong and the ASEAN countries.

Thus, even if AFTA does not become a viable trading area, there are regional pressures beginning to emerge. Of key importance in this region is the reaction of Japan to the North American and European trading blocs. Ironically, the US is opposing any move towards an Asian Free Trade Area, emphasising the role of APEC which includes Japan, Australia, New Zealand and China.

There are particular barriers to developing a liberalised Asia Pacific trading bloc. Firstly, there is a huge diversity amongst the nation states, not just culturally but historical and religious as well as economic. Japan currently has a GDP per capita of US$23 400, Myanmar US$1 200. Politically, the countries embrace very different systems. Democratic structures in many of these markets, e.g. Indonesia, are either non-existent or too weak to ensure the economic fairness necessary to sustain the progress to regulation of markets and trust in the rule of law which is crucial to any commercial relationship.

Furthermore, the geographical area is huge and there are no natural groupings of nation states. There is also uncertainty as to the future intentions of Japan in the region but perhaps, more significantly, huge uncertainty as to the role China will play in this region over the next decade.

THE CHINESE ECONOMIC AREA

The centre of gravity and dynamism of the Asia Pacific economy in the decade ahead is most likely to be the Chinese economic area. This consists of China, Hong Kong and Taiwan. This is a prediction that could conceivably fall flat due to political circumstances. The implosion of China, driven by the huge income discrepancies that are emerging within social groups and between regions on the one hand and the increasingly apparent illegitimacy of the Communist Party on the other, is not a totally implausible scenario.

However, the past decade has seen a phenomenal rate of growth in China itself. China's GDP is estimated to be around US$1,200 billion and has a current growth rate of 9.9 per cent. Moreover, according to a study by China's Academy of Social Science (CASS), by 2030 it will have become the world's largest economy, surpassing even the US. Some Western studies have even estimated that China's economy will have achieved top spot a decade earlier than this.

The World Bank report China 2020 estimates that China will achieve an annual growth rate of 6.5 per cent for the next 20 years – making it the world's second largest exporter after the US. This in itself has meant that Western firms, when selling export goods on world markets, are themselves facing new marketing challenges. In 2001 China became a member of the World Trade Organisation and is now becoming increasingly integrated into the global economy and more open to Western companies. As part of the agreement to its accession to the WTO it is eliminating over 70 non-tariff barriers and reducing the average tariff on goods from 17 per cent to 10 per cent. In the past year there have been some major contracts won by Western companies in the Chinese market. Motorola has a US$400 million contract to build a high-speed communications network and Lucent Technologies have been contracted to supply US$427 million of network equipment. However, it is the potential market for automotives in China, set to grow at a rate of 15 per cent per annum which is attracting most international interest. Volkswagen is reported to be investing €3 billion in the coming years, which is more than the whole of its investment over the past fifteen years.

Overall levels of direct investment in China remain strong. In 2002 it attracted a record US$52.7 billion foreign direct investment, surpassing the US to become the world's premier destination for investment flows as companies become increasingly attracted by cheap labour, robust economic growth and market deregulation. The UK is pledged to invest US$11.93 billion in the next three years. However, all this investment has helped China to achieve rapid economic development but it has been spread unevenly across the country. For example, the southern coastal regions of China, typified by Guangzhou Province, have grown out of all recognition compared with the rest of the country.

DILEMMA 2.1   The dilemma of the long supply chain

Whitline sell a range of premium kitchen accessories. Their principal international markets are the US, Australia and Northern Europe. They have become aware that a number of their competitors, particularly in the US, have become enthusiastic participants and members of the Ethical Trading Initiative (ETI). Whitline's own company research has shown indications that a growing number of consumers across their priority international markets are concerned about the ethical origins of the goods they purchase.

However, to become a member of the ETI would require a comprehensive and costly series of verification visits to suppliers with repeat visits at regular intervals. Over 60 per cent of the products sold by Whitline are sourced in China and East Asia. Often their products are bought through intermediaries and so they have little contact with the original manufacturers. The process then of verifying the ethical practices of the original supplier could involve the company in considerable costs and effort.

Question How important do you think such ethical issues are in building a brand image across international markets? What action do you think Whitline should take?

Source: Dr Keith Jones

Figures supplied by the Chinese authorities underline this regional disparity; the eastern seaboard produces 53 per cent of China's GDP, the middle provinces 31 per cent and the western provinces 16 per cent.

Companies that have succeeded in China include Siemens, Johnson, Motorola and Volkswagen. It should come as no surprise that companies, however, have faced severe difficulties in establishing themselves in China and some car manufacturers especially have suffered huge losses. The main problems they have faced centre around the following areas: Chinese bureaucrats pushing for over-capacity, inconsistent regulations, red tape leading to significant increases in costs, insufficient protection of intellectual property, illegal business practices, debt collection and government taxation policies (see Dilemma 2.1).

SUMMARY

- In this chapter we have discussed the major developments in international trade over the past forty years. In that time multilateral trade has flourished and a number of institutions have been developed to foster international trade.

- The World Bank, the IMF and the WTO all play important roles in ensuring a multilateral and fair international trading environment. It is important for the reader to have an understanding of how they may impact on the international marketing strategy of a company.

- The major trading regions around the globe are at different stages and their continuing development has been discussed.

- In recent years there have been substantive changes in the global competitive structures as emerging markets strengthen their economic foundations and regional trading areas become more cohesive.

- Europe now has monetary union. Free trade areas are emerging in Asia, the Pacific and the Americas. This is moving world trade to a more regionally focused trading pattern.

- China is developing the potential to dwarf most countries as it continues its rapid development and speedy economic growth.

KEYWORDS

Asian Free Trade Area
Association of South East Asian
    Nations
balance of payments
comparative advantage
Copenhagen criteria
European Monetary Union
Exchange Rate Mechanism
Free Trade Area of the Americas
International Development
    Association

International Monetary Fund
international product life cycle
Mercosur
newly industrialised economies
non-tariff barriers
Single European Market
tariff barriers
the Doha Round
trade deficit
United Nations
World Bank

CASE STUDY   B F Rail

B F Rail employs 20 people and has a turnover of approximately £3.0 million. The company manufactures hot and cold pressed track components for rail systems. Traditionally these components served the UK mining market. The major customer of the firm, prior to 1990, was British Coal whose large number of mines, in 1985, accounted for 95 per cent of the firm's turnover.

In the period 1985 to 1990, British Coal underwent a major mine closure programme. Thirty-eight of the mines to which B F Rail supplied rail components closed in this period. This constituted lost sales of £900 000 per annum.

Mr Baker, the Managing Director, carried out an analysis of the company's operations and concluded that the competition in the UK was now so fierce, that if the company did not diversify and widen the customer base, it would not survive.

The Managing Director also recognised two important factors crucial to the future development of the firm. Firstly, that whilst they had traditionally supplied rail components to the mining sector, their products were equally suitable for any tunnels requiring light railways. All tunnels in their construction phase were viewed as requiring light railways. Secondly, as a small company in a specialist niche market, B F Rail recognised that, in order to diversify its customer base, it had to develop internationally.

B F Rail identified two target markets in which they could effectively compete internationally: industrial suppliers of railways and the tunnel construction industry. As a small company, the Managing Director viewed the major barriers faced to be the lack of resources and the lack of experience competing internationally. To overcome these hurdles B F Rail built an international strategy based on the principle of building a network of partners in the key sectors identified. An example of the partnerships established was the one developed with a supplier of steel for railway tracks to supply the complementary components required by their customers. A number of partnerships were also formed with major construction contractors that helped B F Rail exploit the opportunities identified in the tunnel construction market.

The USA was a key market for B F Rail. Their partner in the USA was McNallys, a tunnel construction contractor, and it was through them that B F Rail at this time built a presence in the Canadian market. From very small beginnings, the Canadian market grew to £165 000 per annum. B F Rail has two agents representing them there and has plans to further develop the market.

B F Rail obtained the first international contract in 1990 in Germany. In the period 1990 to 2003 it built a sound international business in the USA, Canada and Spain and to a lesser extent in Ireland. In the late nineties, despite the relatively hostile climate of the increasing strength of sterling, B F Rail continued to build its international business and exports now account for 60 per cent of its turnover.

B F Rail's largest market in Europe had been Germany. The business had been based in construction projects to upgrade the infrastructure of East Germany, particularly in the building of tunnels for fresh water and sewage. However, the decline of the political will to invest further meant that German federal and European Union funding for many projects was no longer so easy to obtain. However, by networking the German contractors with whom they had been working, B F Rail secured new business in Eastern Europe by acting as a subcontractor to the German company.

The accession of the new Central and Eastern European members to the European Union is viewed as a potential opportunity for B F Rail as countries endeavour to improve their infrastructure to meet European standards. Opportunities have been identified in countries such as Poland, Slovenia and Bulgaria. However, whilst there are market opportunities, these countries face huge economic challenges, have limited capital resources and face huge debt repayments to the World Bank.

In Spain, B F Rail recently suffered at the hands of what turned out to be an unscrupulous distributor who left B F Rail with unpaid debts, which proved hard to recover. However, given their understanding of the number of European-funded construction projects under way, B F Rail viewed it as a market where they needed to have a presence. By maximising on an opportunity presented through a major UK customer with operations in Spain, B F Rail identified a new potential distributor in Spain. They developed a joint marketing approach to bid for tenders resulting from EU-funded projects, which has started to achieve its first tangible outcomes.

In Europe, B F Rail has had some success in being involved in projects that had received EU funding. Recently, however, Mr Baker realised that in order to develop further he needed to develop a more global profile and so is now trying to develop the market for the supply of track components for light industrial railways in new markets which are much further afield. This meant trying to develop lesser developed and emerging markets where infrastructure developments were taking place.

The major opportunities for development in the industrial railway sector were seen to be the infrastructure developments in many African countries being funded through aid projects or through loans from the World Bank. B F Rail's first contract in Africa was a World Bank funded project in

Angola. However, they were not able to bid for this contract on their own. Their route to Angola was through a German contact with whom they tendered for the contract as one of a number of partners. The participation in the World Bank project signalled a step change in B F Rail's international profile.

They have now recently won a similar contract in Nigeria. Interestingly, the contract for the Nigerian railways came through a South African connection made several years ago, which, at that time, failed to lead to any business development in South Africa. The relationship has been carefully nurtured by Mr Baker and led to the two companies putting in a joint tender for the Nigerian contract.

Questions

1 Evaluate the opportunities and threats to B F Rail of its approach to targeting infrastructure development projects being funded by the World Bank and other international institutions.

2 What are the key issues facing the further international development of B F Rail?

3 What recommendations would you make to Mr Baker to enable him to achieve his objective of developing a global profile?

Source: Isobel Doole, Sheffield Hallam University

DISCUSSION QUESTIONS

1 Identify barriers to the free movement of goods and services. Explain how barriers influence the development of international trade.

2 What do you consider to be the macro forces impacting on the development of world trade? Show by examples how they are changing the nature of international business.

3 Discuss the impact of China's membership of the WTO for firms trying to compete in the Chinese Economic Area.

4 Evaluate the importance of full monetary union within the European Union to a company marketing to the European market.

5 Recent mega mergers in the pharmaceutical and media industry are becoming increasingly evident. What is the rationale behind such mergers and how will it lead to global competitive advantage?

REFERENCES

Onkvisit, S. and Shaw, J.J. (1988) 'Marketing Barriers in International Trade', *Business Horizons*, June.

Porter, M.C. (1990) *The Competitive Advantage of Nations*, Macmillan.

Vernon, R. and Wells, L.T. (1968) 'International Trade and International Investment in the Product Life Cycle', *Quarterly Journal of Economics*, May.

USEFUL WEB SITES

http://www.economist.co
http://news.ft.com/home/uk/
http://www.imf.org
http://www.pwcglobal.com
http://www.oecd.org
http://www.un.org
http://www.worldbank.org/

SOCIAL AND CULTURAL CONSIDERATIONS IN INTERNATIONAL MARKETING

Introduction

Markets in countries around the world are subject to many influences as we saw in Chapter 1. Whilst it is possible to identify those influences common to many country markets, the real difficulty lies in understanding the specific nature and importance of these influences.

The development of successful international marketing strategies is based on a sound understanding of the similarities and differences that exist in the countries around the world. The sheer complexity of the market considerations that impinge on the analysis, strategic development and implementation of international marketing planning is a major challenge.

In this chapter we will examine the social and cultural issues in international marketing and the implications they have for strategy development.

Learning objectives

After reading this chapter you should be able to:

■ Discuss and evaluate social and cultural factors impacting on an international marketing strategy

■ Understand the cross-cultural complexities of buying behaviour in different international markets

■ Assess the impact of social and cultural factors on the international marketing process

■ Carry out a cross-cultural analysis of specified international markets

SOCIAL AND CULTURAL FACTORS

Social and cultural factors influence all aspects of consumer and buyer behaviour. The differences between these factors in different parts of the world can be a central consideration in developing and implementing international marketing strategies. Social and cultural forces are often linked together. Whilst meaningful distinctions between social and cultural factors can be made, in many ways the two interact and the distinction between the various factors is not clear-cut. Differences in language can alter the intended meaning of a promotional campaign and differences in the way a culture organises itself socially may affect the way a product is positioned in the market and the benefits a consumer may seek from that product. A sewing machine in one culture may be seen as a useful hobby, but in another culture a sewing machine may be necessary to the survival of a family.

Kotler (2003) included such things as reference groups, family, roles and status within social factors. Whilst this is a useful distinction from the broader forces of culture, social class and social factors are clearly influenced by cultural factors. Take the example of the family which is an important medium of transmitting cultural values. Children learn about their society and imbibe its culture through many means but the family influence is strong, particularly during the early formative years of a child's life. Furthermore, the way in which family life is arranged varies considerably from one culture to another. In some cultures the family is a large extended group encompassing several generations and including aunts and uncles, whilst in other cultures the family is limited more precisely to the immediate family of procreation and even then the unit might not be permanent and the father and mother of their children might not remain together for the entirety of the child-rearing process. Thus social and cultural influences intertwine and have a great impact on the personal and psychological processes in the consumer and buyer behaviour processes and, as such, play an integral part in the understanding of the consumer in international markets. Toys R Us found quite distinct differences in the type of toys demanded in their various international markets. Whereas the US children had preferred TV and movie endorsed products, Japanese children demanded electronic toys, South East Asian children wanted educational toys, and the more conservative cultures of the European markets expected a choice of traditional toys.

It is not feasible to examine all the social or cultural influences on consumer and buyer behaviour in one chapter, neither is it possible to describe all the differences between cultures across the world. In the first section we will highlight the more important socio-cultural influences which are relevant to buyer behaviour in international markets. In the following section we will focus on developing an understanding of the components of culture and its impact on consumer behaviour and the implications for international marketing strategies. We will then discuss the methodologies which can be used to carry out cross-cultural analyses to enable comparisons to be made across cultures, and finally we will examine business-to-business marketing and the impact of culture in these types of markets.

WHAT IS CULTURE?

Perhaps the most widely accepted definition of culture is that of Ralph Linton (1945): 'A culture is the configuration of learned behaviour and results of behaviour whose component elements are shared and transmitted by members of a particular society'. Or perhaps, more appropriately: 'The way we do things around here'. In relation to international marketing, culture can be defined as: 'The sum total of learned beliefs, values and customs that serve to direct consumer behaviour in a particular country market'.

Thus culture is made up of three essential components:

Beliefs: A large number of mental and verbal processes which reflect our knowledge and assessment of products and services.

Values: The indicators consumers use to serve as guides for what is appropriate behaviour. They tend to be relatively enduring and stable over time and widely accepted by members of a particular market.

Customs: Overt modes of behaviour that constitute culturally approved or acceptable ways of behaving in specific situations. Customs are evident at major events in one's life e.g. birth, marriage, death and at key events in the year e.g. Christmas, Easter, Ramadan, etc.

Such components as values, beliefs and customs are often ingrained in a society and many of us only fully realise what is special about our own culture, its beliefs, values and customs when we come into contact with other cultures. This is what happens to firms when they expand internationally and build up a market presence in foreign markets. Often the problems they face are a result of their mistaken assumption that foreign markets will be similar to their home market and so they can operate in a similar manner. Frequently in international markets the toughest competition a firm may face is not another supplier but the competition of different customs or beliefs as a result of cultural differences. This means that for a company to succeed in that market they often have to change ingrained attitudes as to the way they do business. The beliefs and values of a culture satisfy a need within that society for order, direction and guidance. Thus culture sets the standards shared by significant portions of that society which in turn sets the rules for operating in that market.

Hofstede (2001) identifies a number of layers within a national culture.

Layers of culture

- A national level according to one's country which determines our basic cultural assumptions.
- A regional/ethnic/religious/linguistic affiliation level determining basic cultural beliefs.
- A gender level according to whether a person was born as a girl or as a boy.
- A generation level which separates grandparents, parents and children.
- A social class level associated with educational opportunities, a person's occupation or profession.

All of these determine attitudes and values and everyday behavioural standards in individuals and organisations.

Given such complexities, often market analysts have used the 'country' as a surrogate for 'culture'. Moreover, culture is not something granted only to citizens of a country or something we are born with, it is something we learn as we grow in our environment. Similar environments provide similar experiences and opportunities and hence tend to shape similar behaviours.

Terpstra and Sarathy (2000) identify eight components of culture which form a convenient framework for examining a culture from a marketing perspective (see Figure 3.1).

The components of culture

Education

The level of formal primary and secondary education in a foreign market will have a direct impact upon the 'sophistication' of the target customers. A simple example will be the degree of literacy. The labelling of products, especially those with possibly hazardous side-effects, needs to be taken seriously for a market that has a very low literacy rate. ICI markets pesticides throughout the world. In developed countries its main form of communication is advertising and printed matter. In developing countries they rely heavily on training and verbally based educational programmes to get their message across.

Social organisation

This relates to the way in which a society organises itself. How the culture considers kinship, social institutions, interest groups and status systems. The role of women and caste systems are easily identifiable examples. If the firm has a history of successfully marketing to 'the housewife/homemaker', life becomes more difficult where women have no social status at all. House ownership is another. In Switzerland the majority of people rent rather than own their houses. They expect to rent property with domestic appliances already installed, which means the banks are the largest purchasers of washing machines, not individual families.

Technology and material culture

This aspect relates not to 'materialism' but to the local market's ability to handle and deal with modern technology. Some cultures find leaving freezers plugged in overnight, or servicing cars and trucks that have not yet broken down, difficult concepts to understand. In instances such as these the organisation is often faced with the choice of either educating the population (expensive and time consuming) or de-engineering the product or service (difficult if you have invested heavily in product development).

Law and politics

The legal and political environments in a foreign market are often seen as consequences of the cultural traditions of that market. Legal and political systems are often a simple codification of the norms of behaviour deemed acceptable by the local culture. This aspect was dealt with in some detail in Chapter 1. **Cultural sensitivity** to political issues in international markets is of utmost importance. Thus an advertisement for the Orange mobile phone network in Ireland with the strap-line 'The future's bright, the future's orange', clearly did not have any awareness of political sensitivities in the northern part of the country.

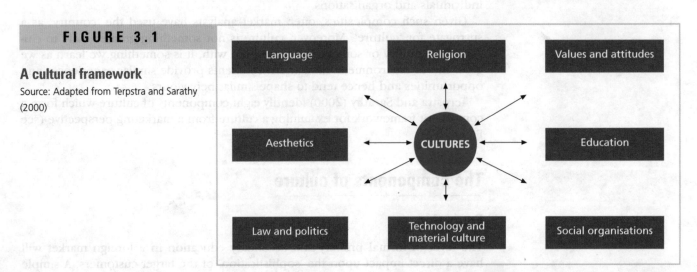

FIGURE 3.1

A cultural framework

Source: Adapted from Terpstra and Sarathy (2000)

Aesthetics

This area covers the local culture's perception of things such as beauty, good taste and design and dictates what is acceptable or 'appealing' to the local eye. A firm needs to ensure that use of colour, music, architecture or brand names in their product and communications strategies is sympathetic and acceptable to the local culture. For the unwary, there are many, many traps in this area. Colour means completely different things in different cultures and brand names often do not travel well! (See Illustration 3.1.)

Values and attitudes

The values consumers from different countries place on things such as time, achievement, work, wealth and risk taking will seriously affect not only the products offered but also the packaging and communication activities. The methods used by a firm to motivate its personnel are also strongly influenced by the local culture and practice. Encouraging local sales forces to sell more by offering cars and more money, for example, may not work in all cultures. Values are important to marketers as they can be translated into consumption vehicles as illustrated in Table 3.1.

Religion

Religion is a major cultural variable and has significant if not always apparent effects on marketing strategy. For example, the identification of sacred objects and philosophical systems, beliefs and norms as well as taboos, holidays and rituals is critical for an understanding of a foreign market. Religion, for example,

---

ILLUSTRATION 3.1   Cadbury's: Lady Purple or Aunty Violet?

Not unlike ourselves, colours may or may not be aesthetically pleasing . . . but they all have a personality. When we look at a colour a whole spectrum of thoughts, feelings and emotions are evoked in our minds. Some of these associations are instinctive in us all, others we learn from the environment in which we live. From the passionate excitement of red to the playful happiness of yellow, colours are constantly eliciting subconscious responses in us all.

For international marketers this notion is particularly pertinent. In our efforts to cue the customer into positioning our brand in a certain way, the colours used in the design, packaging and advertising of a product can send very powerful messages about the personality of our brand. However, as the meaning of colour is often derived from the cultural environment, the messages and thus the personality may fluctuate greatly across countries and cultures.

In a recent study, the Cadbury's brand was perceived very differently by UK and Taiwanese participants. Whilst in the UK Cadbury's was seen to be luxurious, stylish, expensive, classy and silkily feminine, the Taiwanese held the image of an old, warm, friendly, but essentially poor brand, low in quality and lacking in class.

In the same study, participants from the two countries were asked to discuss their perceptions of the colour purple – a colour that Cadbury's is currently attempting to register as a trademark.

Once again, the British made associations with luxury, style, sophistication, youth and femininity. The Taiwanese, on the other hand, talked of a warm, old, quiet colour, serious, a little sad but dignified. In both cultures, all the feelings, emotions and characteristics associated with the colour purple had been transferred to give very different meaning to the Cadbury's brand.

When taking colour abroad, therefore, marketers may do well to heed some of mother's most motherly advice . . . 'Looks aren't everything. It's the personality that counts!'

Question How can marketers ensure they understand such cultural sensitivities when entering new markets?

Source: Anthony Grimes, University of Hull

will affect the food that people eat and when they eat it as well as their attitudes to a whole range of products from deodorants to alcoholic drink.

In some countries religion is the most dominant cultural force. For instance, in Islamic markets, such as Saudi Arabia, no violation of religion by advertising and other promotional practices, no matter how insignificant, will go unnoticed or unpunished either by the government or the consumer. This can cause problems for advertisers. Shaving advertisements cannot be shown if the male actor shows too much of his chest. Likewise, in certain Gulf states, an advertisement where someone uses their left hand to handle food could upset local sensibilities. Major violations of religion are sometimes punished in more liberal and so called secular markets within the Islamic world. Rules surrounding religious laws require heightened insight and empathy by international companies. Comparative ads are banned as, according to the laws of Islam, pegging one product against another diminishes the sense of unity and social community. Companies need to understand the difference between two key terms, Haraam and Makruh.

Haraam are subjects or things that are absolutely unlawful and strongly prohibited in Islam, such as alcohol and cheating. These taboo subjects are totally banned in advertising and other promotional activities in Saudi Arabia, Kuwait and Iran (see Table 3.2).

TABLE 3.1	Cultural values and their relevance to consumer behaviour	
Value	*General features*	*Relevance to consumer behaviour*
Achievement and success	Hard work is good; success flows from hard work	Acts as a justification for acquisition of goods ('You deserve it')
Efficiency and practicality	Admiration of things that solve problems (e.g. save time and effort)	Stimulates purchase of products that function well and save time
Progress	People can improve themselves; tomorrow should be better than today	Stimulates desire for new products that fulfil unsatisfied needs; ready acceptance of products that claim to be 'new' or 'improved'
Material comfort	'The good life'	Fosters acceptance of convenience and luxury products that make life more comfortable and enjoyable
Individualism	Being oneself (e.g. self-reliance, self-interest, self-esteem)	Stimulates acceptance of customised or unique products that enable a person to 'express his or her own personality'
External conformity	Uniformity of observable behaviour, desire for acceptance	Stimulates interest in products that are used or owned by others in the same peer group
Youthfulness	A state of mind that stresses being young at heart and a youthful appearance	Stimulates acceptance of products that provide the illusion of maintaining or fostering youthfulness

Source: Schiffman, L.G. and Kanuk, L.L. (2000) *Consumer Behaviour*, Prentice Hall

Makruh are the subjects which are seen as distasteful. They are discouraged in Islam but are not banned. Smoking is not forbidden in Islam but it is highly discouraged.

Language

Language can be divided into two major elements: the spoken language of vocal sounds in patterns that have meaning and **silent language** which is the communication through body language, silences and social distance. This is less obvious but is a powerful communication tool. Language to many commentators interlinks all the components of culture and is the key to understanding and gaining empathy with a different culture. In the following section we will examine the different components of language.

Language and culture

Spoken language

Spoken language is an important means of communication. In various forms, for example plays and poetry, the written word is regarded as part of the culture of a group of people. In the spoken form the actual words spoken and the ways in which the words are pronounced provide clues to the receiver about the type of person who is speaking.

Chinese is spoken as the mother tongue (or first language) by three times more people than the next largest language, English. However, Chinese is overtaken by English when official language population numbers are taken into account. However, the official language is not always spoken by the whole population of a country. For example, French is an official language in Canada but many Canadians have little or no fluency in French.

English is often but by no means always the common language between business people of different nationalities. Speaking or writing in another language can be a risky activity (see Illustration 3.2).

TABLE 3.2	**Major 'Haraam' subjects in Islam**	
Abusive language	Cruelty towards living beings	Interference in performing religious duties
Adultery	Drugs (intoxicants)	Murder
Alcohol	False promises	Necromancy
Arrogance	Gambling	Pork
Backbiting	Game of chance	Prostitution
Bribery	Hoarding	Sodomy (homosexuality)
Cheating	Idol worship[2]	Usury (interest)
Comparative ads	Immodest exposure [1]	

[1] Women must cover whole body except hands and face. Men must at least be covered from navel to knees
[2] Worshipping anything and anybody other than the one and only Allah as the supreme power and creator

Source: Doole and Yaqub (1997)

In advertising, particular attention needs to be paid when translating from one language to another. The creative use of copy to gain attention and to influence comprehension of the target audience can result in a clever use of words. However, inadequate translation often results in clumsy errors. In Germany a General Motors advertisement mentioned a 'body by Fischer' which became 'corpse by Fischer'. This is clearly a straightforward translation error, directly resulting from the mistranslating of the word 'body'. The Hertz company strapline, 'Let Hertz put you in the driving seat', became 'Let Hertz make you a chauffeur'. Instead of communicating liberation and action as intended, this translation provided quite a different meaning, implying a change of occupation and status. In India an advertisement for the milky drink Horlicks was translated into Tamil as 'twenty men asleep under the tree'.

Language in Web marketing

The choice of language to use for a company Web site is now raising its head as a question for discussion amongst international marketing executives. Surprisingly, whilst English is a widely spoken language throughout the world, it is only the first language of 6 per cent of the world's population, yet 96 per cent of all e-business sites are written in English.

Managers have previously assumed that English is the international language of the Web. Whilst this was so in the early days, according to Forrester Research, Web contact time is doubled on sites localised for language and culture. Japanese businessmen, for example, are three times more likely to conduct an online transaction when addressed in Japanese. It is estimated by the US consultancy Global Reach that for every US$2 million a US site generates from domestic sales, another US$1 million is lost when non-Americans do not easily understand the Web site.

Commentators now believe that soon we will see Web sites in many other languages than English, predominantly Chinese. The proactive international marketers are therefore investigating methods by which they can offer multilingual web sites, localised to the language and cultural sensitivities of the market, as can be seen in Illustration 3.3.

ILLUSTRATION 3.2   Written language: but what does it mean?

In France the Toyota MR2, pronounced emm-er-deux, is written phonetically as merde.

The car maker AMC were confident Matador meant bullfighter. However, when they launched the Matador in South America they, to their cost, found it actually meant 'killer'.

Japanese hotel notice to hotel guests: 'You are invited to take advantage of the chambermaid'.

Acapulco hotel notice regarding drinking water: 'The manager has personally passed all the water served here'.

Visitors to a zoo in Budapest were asked: 'Not to feed the animals. If you have any suitable food, give it to the guard on duty'.

A Bangkok dry cleaner to potential customers: 'Drop your trousers here for best results'.

A Roman laundry innocently suggested: 'Ladies leave your clothes here and spend the afternoon having a good time'.

A Hong Kong dentist claims to extract teeth: 'By the latest Methodists'.

A Copenhagen airline office promises to: 'Take your bags and send them in all directions'.

Question What unusual translations have you come across when perusing international advertisements?

Source: Adapted from BBC News Online and *The Sunday Times*

Silent language

Silent language is a powerful means of communication. The importance of **non-verbal communication** is greater in some countries. In these cultures people are more sensitive to a variety of different message systems. Table 3.3 describes some of the main silent languages in overseas business.

Silent languages are particularly important in sales negotiations and other forms of business meetings. They will, in addition, influence internal communications in companies employing people from different countries and cultures.

Difficulties can arise even between cultures which are geographically close to each other but have different perceptions of language. The word *konzept* in German means a detailed plan whereas the word *concept* in French means an opportunity to discuss. Executives could meet with hugely varying expectations if a conceptual discussion was on the agenda.

ILLUSTRATION 3.3   **Localising Web sites**

Companies competing on international markets are now beginning to realise that if they are going to maximise the value from their company Web sites they need the capability to localise the content to suit the language and cultural sensitivities of the markets they are targeting. Consultants called *localisation outsourcers* have been springing up in the USA and the UK to help companies do just this. Most use a combination of human translators and machine translation technologies to translate and edit text in a culturally sensitive way.

Localisation specialists claim they can help clients protect their brands by providing control over Web-based marketing strategies on a global basis. The concept: Centralise the message, translate it, and colloquialise it. Outsourcers also examine design concerns, such as the cultural implications of colour. In many parts of Asia, for example, white is the kiss of death.

Further, localisation experts can point out legal and regulatory snares. In France, for instance, consumers enjoy a one-week grace period after they receive an online purchase. In Germany, comparative advertising is banned on the Web. In China, clients may become unnerved when they find out that encrypted Web sites are regulated by the Chinese government.

Question What are the dangers of standardising Web pages across the globe?

Source: Adapted from BBC News Online, April 2003

TABLE 3.3   **The main silent languages in overseas business**

Silent language	Implications for marketing and business
Time	Appointment scheduling. The importance of being 'on time'. The importance of deadlines.
Space	Sizes of offices. Conversational distance between people.
Things	The relevance of material possessions. The interest in the latest technology.
Friendship	The significance of trusted friends as a social insurance in times of stress and emergency.
Agreements	Rules of negotiations based on laws, moral practices or informal customs.

Source: Hall and Hall (1987)

Cultural learning

The process of **enculturation**, i.e. learning about their own culture by members of a society, can be through three types of mechanism: formally, through the family and the social institutions to which people belong, technically, through the educational processes, be it through schools or religious institutions, and informally, through peer groups, advertising and various other marketing-related vehicles.

This enculturation process influences consumer behaviour by providing the learning we use to shape the toolkit of labels, skills and styles from which people construct strategies of action, e.g. persistent ways of going through the buying process.

The process of *acculturation* is the process international companies need to go through in order to obtain an understanding of another culture's beliefs, values and attitudes in order to gain an empathy with that market. As we have seen, culture is pervasive and complex and it is not always easy for someone outside a given culture to gain an empathy with that market.

Having examined the main components of culture and the various important dimensions we will now look at how culture impacts on consumer behaviour.

CULTURE AND CONSUMER BEHAVIOUR

There are several important ways in which the various components of culture influence a consumer's perception, **attitude** and understanding of a given product or communication and so affect the way a consumer behaves in the buying process. Jeannet and Hennessey (2002) identify three major processes through which culture influences consumer behaviour as depicted in Figure 3.2.

Culture is seen as being embedded in elements of society such as religion, language, history and education (cultural forces). These elements send direct and indirect messages to consumers regarding the selection of goods and services (cultural message). The culture we live in determines the answers to such questions as: Do we drink coffee or juice at breakfast? Do we shop daily or on a weekly basis? and so affects the consumer decision process.

The body of theory on which our understanding of **consumer behaviour** is based predominantly hails from the USA. Usunier (2000) argues that the means by which international marketing managers understand consumer behaviour is flawed as sometimes the theoretical principles on which we base our understanding do not necessarily hold true across different cultures. He specifically

---

FIGURE 3.2

Cultural influences on buyer behaviour

Source: Adapted from Jeannet and Hennessey (2002)

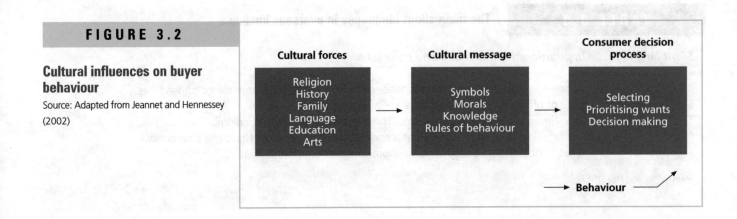

highlights four important assumptions which international marketers should question:

1 That Maslow's Hierarchy of Needs is consistent across cultures.
2 That the buying process in all countries is an individualistic activity.
3 That social institutions and local conventions are similar across cultures.
4 That the consumer buying process is consistent across cultures.

That Maslow's Hierarchy of Needs is consistent across cultures

Culture influences the hierarchy of needs (Maslow 1970) on two levels. First, the axiom that one need must be satisfied before the next appears is not true for every culture, and second, similar kinds of needs may be satisfied by different products and consumption types.

For example, in some less developed countries, a consumer may go without food in order to buy a refrigerator and, therefore, satisfy the dominant need of social status before physical satisfaction. A study identified that self-esteem needs were most important to Chinese consumers, with the least important being physiological needs. Physiological needs include food, water, shelter, etc. whereas self-esteem needs include prestige and success.

In building a presence therefore in the Chinese market, companies would need to target consumers with high self-esteem needs by linking a product such as credit cards to success in business or beer to success in sporting activities.

Likewise, similar kinds of needs may be satisfied in very different ways. For example, to a Hindu the need for self-realisation does not necessarily imply material consumption, as in Western cultures, but in fact abandoning all worldly possessions.

That the buying process in all countries is an individualistic activity

Many Western buying behaviour models are primarily based on individual purchases with reference to family decision making in the context of husband and wife decisions. They assume buying decisions are focused on an individual's decision-making process. In Asia a family may be a complex structure and so an individual would need to take into account all members of the family in making major purchase decisions. Thus the decision making is of a much more collectivist nature.

That social institutions and local conventions are similar across cultures

Institutions such as the state, the religious institutions, trade unions and the education system also influence consumer behaviour.

The UK company ROMPA, which serves the market for people with learning disabilities, found enormous cultural differences across their European market due to the varying influences the national institutions had on how charities and social institutions should be organised. In Germany the market was highly organised and strongly supported financially by the state. In Spain the state lottery was the prime benefactor through major national charities, whereas in Italy the church was the major benefactor, with very little involvement by the state.

That the consumer buying process is consistent across cultures

There are many inconsistencies in the buying processes across cultures around the globe. Three aspects which are particularly pertinent to our discussion are the differences in: the level of consumer involvement, the perception of risk in a purchase and the cognitive processes of consumers.

Consumer involvement

The Chinese are seen as having a low level of involvement when purchases are for private consumption but a high level of involvement when they are buying products for their social or symbolic value. Since the Chinese greatly value social harmony and smoothness of relationships within the extended family, the social significance of products is highly important, be it to express status, gratitude, approval or even disapproval. Heineken very successfully tapped into this need for social acceptance in their innovative campaign in Hong Kong (see Illustration 3.4).

Perceived risk

The level of risk consumers associate with a purchase varies enormously across cultures and as such it is an important variable in consumer behaviour. It will

---

ILLUSTRATION 3.4 **Heineken beats Carlsberg through the backdoor**

Between 1993 and 1998 Heineken increased its market share in Hong Kong from 5 per cent to 25 per cent.

The Heineken brewer did not achieve these remarkable share gains directly. It was the local distributor that truly understood the cultural drivers of the Hong Kong beer market. The local distributor knew the market and understood that Heineken had an enormous task against the entrenched brands with huge market shares, large advertising budgets and very effective campaigns. To spend millions of advertising dollars to achieve anything against the two major and entrenched brands, San Miguel and Carlsberg which together had over 70 per cent market share, was considered unrealistic. The distributor basically tapped a key Asian value – make people believe the beer is popular!

The Heineken beer distributor in Hong Kong achieved this by pushing the product first in aspirational, on-premise outlets to develop an up-market niche. They then followed a programme of asking on-premise staff to leave the bottles on the table by not pouring full beers into glasses and not collecting the empties. Suddenly, little green bottles were seen everywhere, being drunk by white collar, up-market types in expensive, trendy outlets. This evolved until suddenly more and more people were drinking the beer and it eventually took on its own momentum.

This general approach was viewed as the only way to beat the entrenched brand loyalty. The biggest key to marketing in Asia is not necessarily actual market share but *perceived popularity*. If a firm can convince Asians that many of their colleagues are buying the brand by building high visibility then success is much more likely.

Question Fully evaluate the reasons for the success of the Heineken strategy.

Source: Adapted from Robinson, D.Q. (1999) *Journal of Market Research Society*, 38 (1)

determine whether a consumer will go for the comfortable purchase or is willing to try new products and services. Risk incorporates three components: physical risk, financial risk and social risk.

Whereas in some countries, *physical risk* may be important (e.g. the fear of BSE in the UK beef market), others may be more sensitive to *social risk* and the loss of social status if a wrong buying decision is made (i.e. the Chinese fear of losing face). *Financial risk* closely relates to the level of economic development in a country. It is likely to be less in the more affluent economies where if a wrong purchase decision is made the financial hardship suffered may not be so profound.

The level of brand loyalty found in a market is also closely related to the **perception of risk**. There are huge variations in attitudes to brand loyalty across different cultures. In the US the standard buyer behaviour is that of *disloyalty*. A consumer will shift from one brand to another because it is standard behaviour to test several competitive products and so foster price competition. Thus in the US it is relatively easy for a new entrant to persuade Americans to try their product, but it is much harder to get them to keep buying it.

In other cultures, consumers are more fundamentally loyal, less brand conscious and not so used to cross-product comparisons. In Australia and South East Asia it is viewed that buyers have a greater need for brand security, are less confident with regard to trying unknown products and so are less willing to take risks.

Cognitive style

Western consumer behaviour models assume a logical buying process with rational steps, including the formation of awareness, the searching for information, reviewing the information, evaluating alternatives and finally making a choice. Sometimes by attacking traditional cognitive styles advertisers have had surprising success, as in the case of Skoda.

Many authors argue that internationally there are many different models of the buying process. Asian consumers tend to have a quite different cognitive style to Western consumers. The Chinese as well as the Japanese have a more synthetic, concrete and contextual orientation in their thought patterns, as opposed to the Americans who tend to have a more analytical and abstract decision-making process. Thus culture not only impacts on how we behave as consumers but on the whole decision-making process. Advertisers and marketing managers need, as in the case of Skoda in Dilemma 3.1, to examine how they can exploit such nuances in building their global brands.

DILEMMA 3.1   Skoda

Skoda, a subsidiary of Volkswagen, adopted a pan-European approach to building its brand profile in Europe. All advertising therefore was developed centrally and concentrated on building the product profile. The new Skoda marketing manager questioned this approach, arguing that there was a failure in previous pan-European advertising campaigns to recognise that the brand meant something quite different in most Western European countries and, consequently, the campaigns were not connecting with the target audience. In the UK, for instance, Skoda had to put up with a fair amount of ridicule. Even having their cars endorsed by independent critics and being named Car of the Year did nothing to change the strong negative public perception of the brand. However, the European advertising budget for Skoda was very small compared to its main rivals and so economies of scale were a consideration.

Question How would you solve the dilemma?

ANALYSING CULTURES AND THE IMPLICATIONS FOR CONSUMER BEHAVIOUR

As we have seen in previous sections, there are many social and cultural influences which determine our values, beliefs and customs which combine to form a **cultural identity** which in turn influences the process of decision making when buying products. All these aspects need to be examined to understand the consumer in any international market. The framework depicted in Figure 3.3 summarises many of the issues we have been discussing and may prove useful to the reader as a framework for assessing the impact of social and cultural influences in a particular market.

Blackwell *et al*. (2001) 'suggest' the following steps should be undertaken when analysing consumer behaviour in international markets. They propose if a company is to fully empathise with a culture they must pose a series of questions about buyer behaviour, culture and the suitability of various marketing communications approaches for that culture. These steps consist of:

■ **Determine relevant motivations in the culture**: What needs are fulfilled with this product in the minds of members of the culture? How are these needs presently fulfilled? Do members of this culture readily recognise these needs?

■ **Determine characteristic behaviour patterns**: What patterns are characteristic of purchasing behaviour? What forms of division of labour exist within the family structure? How frequently are products of this type purchased? Do any of these characteristic behaviours conflict with behaviour expected for this product? How strongly ingrained are the behaviour patterns that conflict with those needed for distribution of this product?

FIGURE 3.3

Model of consumer behaviour in international markets

Source: Adapted from Liv Kirby from Hawkins *et al.* (1992)

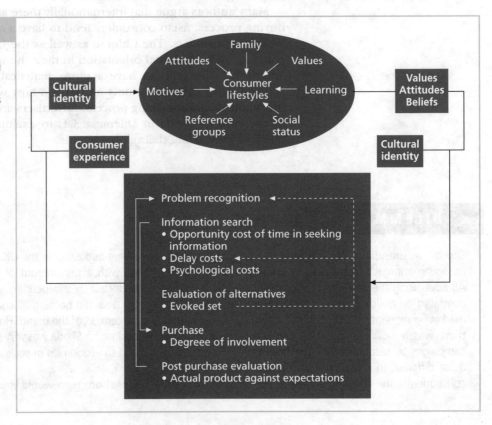

- **Determine what broad cultural values are relevant to this product**: Are there strong values about work, morality, religion, family relations and so on that relate to this product? Does this product denote attributes that are in conflict with these cultural values? Can conflicts with values be avoided by changing the product? Are there positive values in this culture with which the product might be identified?

- **Determine characteristic forms of decision making**: Do members of the culture display a studied approach to decisions concerning innovations or an impulsive approach? What is the form of the decision process? Upon which information sources do members of the culture rely? Do members of the culture tend to be rigid or flexible in the acceptance of new ideas? What criteria do they use in evaluating alternatives?

- **Evaluate promotion methods appropriate to the culture**: What role does advertising occupy in the culture? What themes, words or illustrations are taboo? What language problems exist in present markets that cannot be translated into this culture? What types of sales staff are accepted by members of the culture? Are such sales staff available?

- **Determine appropriate institutions for this product in the minds of consumers**: What types of retailers and intermediary institutions are available? What services do these institutions offer that are expected by the consumer? What alternatives are available for obtaining services needed for the product but not offered by existing institutions? How are various types of retailers regarded by consumers? Will changes in the distribution structure be readily accepted?

Self-reference criterion

As we have discussed, it is of crucial importance when examining foreign markets that the culture of the country is seen in the context of that country. It is better to regard the culture as different from, rather than better or worse than, the home culture. In this way, differences and similarities can be explored and the reasons for differences can be sought and explained. The differences approach avoids the evaluative and often superior approach based on one's own self-reference criterion.

'Self-reference criterion' (SRC) characterises our unconscious reference to our own cultural values when examining other cultures. Usunier (2000) suggests a four-step approach to eliminate SRC.

1 Define the problem or goal in terms of home country cultural traits, habits and norms.

2 Define the problems or goals in terms of the foreign culture, traits, habits and norms.

3 Isolate the SRC influence in the problem and examine it carefully to see how it complicates the problem.

4 Redefine the problem without the SRC influence and solve for the foreign market situation.

The process of enculturation to gain empathy with a foreign country market is not an easy one and requires:

- *Cultural empathy*: the ability to place yourself in the position of the buyer from another culture. In this way a strong attempt is made to understand the thinking approaches, the decision-making process and the interactions between this and the cultural and other forces influencing the buyer.

■ *Neutrality*: the ability to identify the differences that exist without making value judgements about 'better' or 'worse' cultures. Inevitably, self-reference will exist. If the focus is placed on differences rather than superiority, the chances of achieving accurate cross-cultural analysis are increased.

To ensure they achieve this, companies follow a number of policies. They may recruit foreign staff at their head office, collaborate with local firms when entering a new market or they may put managers through acculturation programmes. Guinness understood the importance of avoiding SRC in developing their knowledge base of the new international markets in which they were operating. It is for this reason they ensured they had a management team in each market which was truly multi-national as well as including managers with a local knowledge. Perhaps this is where the US company buying a German company went wrong (see Dilemma 3.2).

CROSS-CULTURAL ANALYSIS

So far our discussions have been primarily concerned with understanding what is meant by culture, examining its components and surveying its influence on consumer behaviour and how that differs across cultures.

However, strategists and students of international marketing need to move beyond this and endeavour to develop ways to compare and contrast consumers, market segments and buyers across cultures.

International marketers need appropriate frameworks or conceptual schemata to enable comparisons to be made and contrasts and similarities to be drawn.

For the most part, **cross-cultural** classification approaches tend to be either mere lists or incredibly theoretical complex structures. There is a recognised lack of a universal, broadly generalisable framework within which to visualise national cultures. Consequently, the work of Hofstede (2001) and Hall and Hall (1986) is seen as holding the maximum potential for providing methods for cross-cultural analysis. In the following sections we will look at the work of each of these writers and examine how the concepts they propose can be used by firms in attempting to analyse consumer behaviour across cultures. We will then highlight

---

DILEMMA 3.2	Mittelstand vs US executives

A US company recently bought into a 180-year-old family-owned Mittelstand in Germany. The US company thought the purchase would give them a good base for the European market. They were particularly interested in Germany as it was viewed by them as the largest and most technically sophisticated market in Europe. As a financially driven company the new US owner needed to ensure a high rate of return on its investment and so needed to examine costings in the company closely and introduce efficient US working practices to cut costs. The company canteen was closed in the belief that rather than eat a full hot meal, workers could eat sandwiches whilst working. Morning cheerleader sessions were introduced to motivate staff. Managers were addressed by their first names to build

relationships. Unfortunately such practices led to a breakdown of the deal. The German managers were grossly insulted by the informal form of address. The workers took industrial action against the loss of hot midday meals and the staff refused to join cheerleader sessions. To add to the new owner's problems they found it very difficult to extract accurate financial information because the financial side of the business had traditionally been handled by tax advisers outside the company, not by managers within it.

Question How could the new owner have avoided the breakdown of the deal? Do you think they should persevere and rectify the situation or withdraw?

some of the frameworks which have been developed by later authors building on their work.

Hall's high/low context approach

Hall and Hall's (1987) main thesis was that one culture will be different from another if it understands and communicates in different ways. They therefore saw languages as the most important component of culture.

The language differences between some cultures will be large and therefore there will be marked differences in their cultures. Language and value differences between the German and Japanese cultures, for instance, are considerable. There are also differences between the Spanish and Italian cultures but they are much less; both have languages based on Latin, they use the same written form of communication and have similar although not identical values and norms.

In different cultures the use of communication techniques varies. In some languages communication is based on the words that are said or written (spoken language). In others, the more ambiguous elements such as surroundings or social status of the message-giver are important variables in the transmission of understanding (silent language). Hall used these findings to classify cultures into what he referred to as 'low context cultures' and 'high context cultures'.

- **Low context cultures** rely on spoken and written language for meaning. Senders of messages encode their messages expecting that the receivers will accurately decode the words used to gain a good understanding of the intended message.

- **High context cultures** use and interpret more of the elements surrounding the message to develop their understanding of the message. In high context cultures the social importance, knowledge of the person and the social setting add extra information and will be perceived by the message receivers. Figure 3.4 shows the contextual differences in the cultures around the world.

With the Swiss, in particular, having a high explicit content in their communications, at one extreme are the low context cultures of Northern Europe. At the other extreme are the high context cultures. The Japanese have subtle and complex ways of communicating with people according to their age, sex and the relative and actual social positions of the people conversing.

The greater the contextual difference between those trying to communicate, the greater the difficulty firms will have in achieving accurate communications.

Hofstede's cultural dimensions

Hofstede (2001) was primarily interested in uncovering differences in work-related values across countries. He originally identified four dimensions of culture: **individualism**, power distance, uncertainty avoidance and masculinity. These dimensions, it was argued, largely account for cross-cultural differences in people's belief systems and behaviour patterns around the globe.

Individualism

Individualism (IDV) describes the relationship between an individual and his or her fellow individuals in society. It manifests itself in the way people live together such as in nuclear families, extended families or tribes and has a great variety of value implications. At one end of the spectrum are societies with very loose ties between individuals. Such societies allow a large degree of freedom and everybody is expected to look after his or her own self-interest and possibly that of the immediate family. Societies of this type exemplify high individualism (high IDV) and display loose integration. At the other end are societies with very strong ties between individuals. Everybody is expected to look after the interests of their in-group and to hold only those opinions and beliefs sanctioned by the in-group which, in turn, protects the individual. These 'collective' (low IDV) societies show tight integration. Hofstede identified highly individualistic countries as the USA, Great Britain and the Netherlands. Collectivist countries were Colombia, Pakistan and Taiwan. The mid-range contains countries such as Japan, India, Austria and Spain.

Power distance

Power distance (PDI) involves the way societies deal with human inequality. People possess unequal physical and intellectual capacities which some societies allow to grow into inequalities in power and wealth. However, some other societies de-emphasise such inequalities. All societies are unequal but some are more unequal than others (Hofstede 1994). The Philippines, India and France score relatively high in power distance. Austria, Israel, Denmark and Sweden show relatively low PDI scores, while the United States ranks slightly below midpoint.

Combining power distance and individualism reveals some interesting relationships (see Figure 3.5). Collectivist countries seem to show large power distance but individualist countries do not necessarily display small power distance. For example, the Latin European countries combine large power distance with high individualism. Other wealthy Western countries combine smaller power distance with high individualism. It is interesting to observe that in Hofstede's sample, almost all developing countries tend to rate high on both collectivism (low individualism) and power distance. Of the countries Hofstede

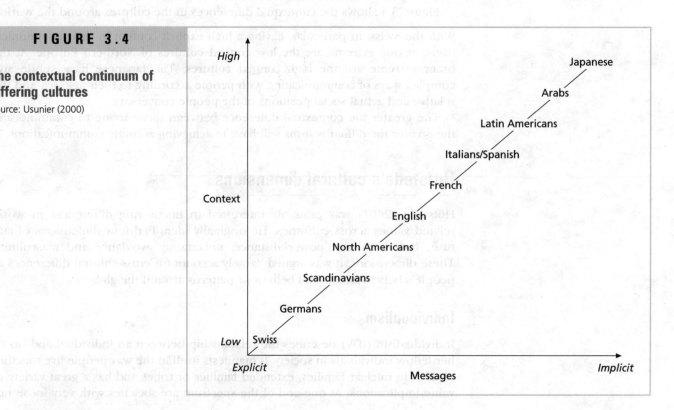

FIGURE 3.4

The contextual continuum of differing cultures

Source: Usunier (2000)

studied, only Costa Rica combined small power distance with high collectivism (low individualism).

Uncertainty avoidance

Uncertainty Avoidance (UA) reflects how a society deals with uncertainty about the future, a fundamental fact of human existence. At one extreme, weak UA cultures socialise members to accept and handle uncertainty. People in such cultures tend to accept each day as it comes, take risks rather easily, do not work too hard and tolerate opinions and behaviour different from their own. Denmark, Sweden and Hong Kong all rated low in UA. The other extreme – strong UA societies – fosters the need to try to beat the future, resulting in greater nervousness, aggressiveness and emotional stress. Belgium, Japan and France ranked relatively high in uncertainty avoidance while the United States scored somewhat below midpoint.

Masculinity

Masculinity (MAS) deals with the degree to which societies subscribe to the typical stereotypes associated with males and females. Masculine values stress making money and the pursuit of visible achievements. Such societies admire individual brilliance and idolise the successful achiever, the superman. These traditional masculine social values permeate the thinking of the entire society, women as well as men. Hofstede's research indicated that within his sample, Japan, Austria, Venezuela and Italy ranked highest in masculinity.

In more feminine societies, both men and women exhibit values associated with traditionally feminine roles such as endurance and an emphasis on people rather than money. Societal sympathy lies with the underdog, the anti-hero rather than the individually brilliant. Sweden, Norway, the Netherlands and Denmark rank as some of the most feminine societies studied by Hofstede. The United

---

FIGURE 3.5

Power distance/individualism dimensions across cultures

Source: Hofstede (2001)

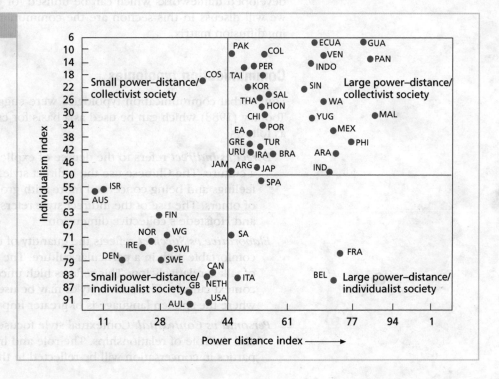

States scored fairly high on the masculinity dimension, placing it near the top one-third.

An assertive salesperson would be better accepted therefore in a highly masculine culture such as Austria than in Denmark's more feminine culture. The level of masculinity also explains part of the perception that business people have of each other. In feminine countries where relationships are more highly valued the supplier–client relationship is seen much more as a partnership than in more masculine cultures. Thus the affective aspects of the business relationship are seen as of vital importance, particularly in negotiations as we will see in the section on cross-cultural negotiating later in this chapter.

Confucian dynamism

Later work by Hofstede revealed a fifth dimension, 'Confucian dynamism'. Confucian dynamism assesses cultures to the degree they are universalistic or particularistic. Universalistic cultures believe that what is true and good can be determined and defined and can be applied everywhere. Particularistic cultures evolve where 'unique circumstances and *relationships* are more important considerations in determining what is right and good rather than abstract rules'. Confucian philosophy traditionally pervades Chinese culture. Its major characteristics include a strong bias towards obedience, the importance of rank and hierarchies and the need for smooth social relations. Within Confucian ethics, four relations were basic, between: ruler and those ruled, father and son, husband and wife, and friend and friend. Everyone is expected to know where they stand in the hierarchy of human relations and one's place carries with it fixed standards of how one behaves towards others.

Culture/communication typologies

Following on from the research by Hall and Hofstede a number of writers have developed frameworks which can be utilised for cross-cultural analysis. The two we will discuss in this section are the communication typologies and the learning/diffusion matrix.

Communication typologies

Four verbal communication typologies were suggested by Gudykunst and Ting-Toomey (1988) which can be used as a basis for cross-cultural analysis. These are as follows:

Direct vs Indirect refers to the degree of explicitness of the verbal message of a culture. The Chinese use the indirect style, often hiding their real feelings and being concerned more with group harmony and the feelings of others. The use of the indirect style refers to Hall's high context culture and Hofstede's collective dimension.

Elaborative vs Succinct reflects the quantity of talk that people feel comfortable with in a particular culture. The succinct style is where quantity of talk is relatively low. This reflects high uncertainty avoidance and a high context culture. Elaborative styles may be used more in low context cultures where the spoken language is of greater importance, as in the US.

Personal vs Contextual. Contextual style focuses on the role of the speaker and the role of relationships. The role and hierarchical relationship of the parties in conversation will be reflected in the form of address and words that are used. This type of communication reflects high power distance, collectivism and high context cultures such as Japan.

Instrumental vs Affective defines the orientation of the speaker. In the affective verbal style the speaker is process orientated. There is concern that neither the speaker nor the receiver will be put in an uncomfortable position. The speaker also listens to and closely observes the receiver in order to interpret how the message is being taken. This is a reflection of a high context, collective culture such as South East Asia.

Cross-cultural/diffusion and learning matrix

The speed of learning and the degree of involvement are essential ingredients of the individual consumer behaviour process. In cross-cultural comparisons, it is possible to analyse the consumer behaviour from this micro perspective.

Wills *et al.* (1991) use the dimensions of diffusion/learning to suggest a cross-cultural analysis model examining the relationships between the context of a culture and the rate of diffusion of new products which varies considerably across cultures. The rate of learning will impact on the rate of diffusion of any new product. By comparing the diffusion rate to whether a culture is high or low context (see Figure 3.6), a firm can gain a much better understanding of the type of strategies to employ to increase the pace of learning and so the rate of diffusion.

SOCIAL AND CULTURAL INFLUENCES IN BUSINESS-TO-BUSINESS MARKETING

Much of the discussion relating to the influences of social cultural factors on international marketing assumes a market for predominantly fast-moving consumer goods where decisions are made on either a family or individual basis. Yet a considerable proportion of exports relates to industrial goods and services where companies are primarily concerned with company-to-company or business-to-business marketing and dealing, therefore with primarily organisational or even government buyers. The question we need now to address is how relevant are the social/cultural factors we have been discussing to these types of markets.

In business-to-business marketing there are essentially two types of buyers, organisations and governments. In this section we will highlight some of the social/cultural influences on these types of buyers which are particularly relevant

FIGURE 3.6		
Interrelationship between context and diffusion Source: Wills *et al.* (1991)	High context/Fast diffusion South East Asia Japan	High context/Slow diffusion India Asia
	Low context/Fast diffusion Scandinavia USA Canada	Low context/Slow diffusion UK Eastern Europe

to international marketing. Following this we will discuss the impact of culture on cross-cultural negotiating styles and the practice of gift giving in international business relationships.

Organisational buyers

Business buying decisions are influenced by decisions about technology, the objectives and tasks of the company, the organisational structure of the buying company and the motivations of people in the company. The technology decision is an interesting area. Some companies rely on their own internal capability to produce solutions to problems they need to solve in the areas of the technology and how to manufacture the product. However, Japanese companies have encouraged their suppliers to help them by providing technological improvements. This approach is now influencing business practices across the world. The US adversarial approach of developing a precise buying specification and then challenging supplying firms to win the contract by providing the best deal is now less common.

Culture at the organisational level can play a significant part in the way in which the various roles are enacted. When it comes to international encounters, humour for instance can be a double-edged sword. The dangers of a joke backfiring are increased when the parties concerned do not share a common culture. Different cultures have different beliefs and assumptions which determine when humour is considered appropriate, what can be joked about and even who can be joked with. Attitudes to uncertainty, status and the sanctity of business influence the extent to which humour is allowed to intrude on proceedings (see Illustration 3.5).

ILLUSTRATION 3.5 **The use of humour in international meetings**

In cultures where the desire to avoid uncertainty is high, as in Germany, humour with its inherent ambiguity is likely to be restrained. Levity will be welcomed to the extent it contributes to the *Arbeitsklima* (working environment) and supports the highly task-oriented German company.

Status is another important consideration. In some countries people may loosen up as they get promoted but in more hierarchical cultures, such as France, the reverse is more likely to be the case. Seniority is largely determined by intellectual achievement and academic credentials. Consequently, French *cadres* (executives) are keen to avoid being branded lightweight. So whilst clever and sophisticated humour is acceptable, the risk of appearing foolish, with the accompanying loss of credibility and intellectual standing, tends to inhibit other forms of humour. Self-mocking humour may be completely misunderstood.

In many Western business cultures teasing is routinely used as a means of social control.

Typically it serves to chastise a late-comer to a meeting or to mark mild displeasure whilst avoiding confrontation.

But in certain Asian cultures, making fun of someone may leave managers feeling uncomfortable. In Japan managers use after-hours drinking as a functional equivalent to criticising with humour.

American managers invariably use jokes to warm up speeches and presentation but, once the real business starts, attempts at humour may be met with a frosty silence. Americans have invested heavily in a set of political and economic values embedded in individual liberty and economic opportunity. It follows that business is taken more seriously than in other Anglo-Saxon cultures such as Britain.

International managers have to proceed with caution but humour remains a vital means of bridging cultural differences.

Question What other useful techniques can you think of to help bridge cultural differences?

Source: Adapted from Barsoux, J.L. (1997) *Financial Times*, 17 February

There are a number of different corporate cultural characteristics in European countries which influence buyer behaviour. The French have a hierarchical system of management with a strong tendency to centralism. Consequently it is often difficult for sales people to reach the top manager as they may well be buffered behind half a dozen assistants. Spanish and Italian decision making tends to be highly autocratic based on the model of the family; decision making is shared, with systems that tend to be informal. The German position is influenced by earned respect for formal qualifications and technical competence. Leadership depends upon respect rather than subservience.

Government buyer behaviour

In many countries the government is the biggest buyer, far larger than any individual consumer or business buyer. Governments buy a wide range of goods and services: roads, education, military, health and welfare. The way in which governments buy is influenced by the extent to which public accountability in the expenditure of public money is thought important.

It has been estimated that 20 per cent of the gross domestic product of the European Union is controlled through the value of purchases and contracts awarded by the public sector. In the US approximately 30 per cent of the gross national product is accounted for by the purchases of US governmental units. For some companies their international business comprises of government buyers in different countries. It is important, therefore, to understand the government buying processes.

Usual forms of buying procedure are the open tender and selective tender. In open bid contracts, tenders are invited against a tight specification, contracts are usually awarded to the lowest price bid. Selective tender contracts are offered to companies who have already demonstrated their ability in the area appropriate to the tender. Only those companies on the selective tender list will be invited to tender. As with open tender, the lowest price is often used to adjudicate the bids.

In the European Union specific rules have been drawn up in an attempt to remove the barriers between potential suppliers of government contracts from different countries of the EU. Suppliers from all EU member states should have an equal opportunity to bid for public authority contracts and public works contracts must be advertised throughout the EU.

The business-to-business buying process

Various models of the buying process have been developed by different writers. Robinson *et al.* (1979) divide classes of buying into straight re-buy, modified re-buy and new task.

A straight re-buy represents the bulk of the business buying. The buy signal is often triggered through information systems when stock levels reach a predetermined replenishment point. The modified re-buy indicates a certain level of information search and re-evaluation of products/services and supplies before the purchase is made. The new task represents an area of considerable uncertainty in which the company needs to make decisions about what it wants, about performance standards and about supplier capabilities. The new task, particularly if the purchase is of major importance to the company, will involve senior management and might take a long time to complete.

The way in which a company manages each of the buy classes will be influenced by cultural factors. Companies with a strong ethnocentric orientation may limit their search for suppliers to suppliers from their own country. For more internationally oriented companies, the country of origin effect will distort information collection and appraisal. The influence of established relationships in cultures in which personal contacts and relationships are important will act as a barrier to companies which operate in a more formal way.

Relationship marketing is very important in business-to-business marketing where companies may gain competitive advantage not necessarily through the product but through the added value they have built through their relationship. This is especially important in markets such as China. The Chinese rely heavily on personal relationships in business dealings. It is important for foreign companies to understand the dynamics of these relationships (known as *guanxi*). There is a saying in Chinese, 'If you do not have a relationship you do not exist!'

Personal selling and negotiation between the buyer and seller as they go through the interaction process in order to build a business relationship which is mutually beneficial is an important part of international marketing. It is in this process of negotiation and relationship building where cultural factors have their greatest impact.

The role of culture in negotiation styles

Culture can be a major determinant in the success or failure of business negotiations. In Saudi Arabia business may look informal and slow paced but in negotiations a businessman would be grossly insulted if they were expected to negotiate with a representative rather than the top person.

If cases of intra-cultural bargaining are examined some surprising factors come to light. In one carried out by Druckman, examining the bargaining behaviour of three cultures – India, Argentina and the United States, he identified that Indian negotiators bargained longer, were more competitive and maximised their gains relative to US and Argentinian negotiators.

However, some commentators suggest that whilst a lack of understanding of the cultural differences in negotiation styles may be a major cause of negotiation failure, awareness of cultural differences may not be a major factor in negotiation success, unless that awareness is accompanied by a deeper understanding of how culture impacts on the whole negotiation process.

The first stage, *non-task sounding*, describes the process of establishing rapport between members of the negotiation teams. Japanese negotiators would spend considerable time and money entertaining foreign negotiating teams in order to establish a rapport, whereas US executives saw the delays as frustrating and the money spent wasteful. GEC Alsthon sales executives found Karaoke sessions very useful when negotiating with the North Koreans for a contract for high-speed trains between Seoul and Pusan. The firm underststood from the outset that the first stage of negotiations needed to include a broad range of activities, such as singing, to help establish a rapport on which the relationship could be built.

The *task-related exchange of information stage* describes the exchange of information that defines the participants' needs and expectations. Well over 90 per cent of all large Japanese companies and most of the smaller ones used a decision-making process called *ringi*. The system is based on the principle that

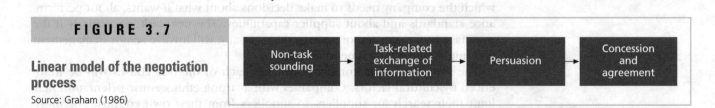

FIGURE 3.7

Linear model of the negotiation process
Source: Graham (1986)

decisions are made only when a consensus is reached by the negotiating team. Proposals are circulated amongst the negotiating team and the affected individuals in the main office staff, for each to affix their own personal seal of approval. Without the group's approval, which takes a long time to acquire, no proposal will be accepted. What may appear to US negotiators as stalling tactics is often simply the different process by which the Japanese reach a decision.

The *persuasion stage* for US executives is the one that consumes time, whereas for Japanese negotiators who have previously taken the time to understand each other's expectations, it is seen as unnecessary. Japanese negotiators as a result may remain silent. This is not because they do not agree with the proposal but because they are either waiting for more information or that for them, agreement has been reached and therefore negotiations are complete.

This often leads to misunderstanding at the *concession and agreement stage*. An extension of the Japanese preference for establishing strong personal relationships is their dislike for the formal Western-style contract. A loosely worded statement expressing mutual cooperation and trust developed between negotiating parties is much preferred. The advantage of these agreements is that they allow a great deal of flexibility in the solution of unforeseen problems, whereas Western negotiators may feel the need to bargain to the end and do not see their job as complete until they have actually obtained a signature. Table 3.4 gives an interesting summary of differences in buyer–seller negotiating styles in selected countries.

Usunier (2000) suggests a number of ways to minimise cultural impact in negotiations in order to build effective transcultural relationships.

- **Adaptation**. In international business meetings, people who do not appear to feel the need to adapt may be considered indolent: 'Those who adapt are aware of differences, whereas those to whom others adapt remain unaware'.

- **Interpreters**. Be aware that interpreters influence meaning. They may translate better from one language into another than in the opposite direction. The loyalty of interpreters needs to be considered. Are they more in favour of one party than the other? Should you use your own interpreter? Should you use several interpreters to reduce stress errors and bias?

- **Cultural blocks**. Not everything will translate – it is not possible to translate meaning exactly for all elements in an interpretation. Culture-specific elements will block some attempts at translation.

- **The stereotype**. Avoid negative stereotyping which is likely to increase negotiation conflicts and difficulties.

- **Inter-cultural preparation**. Good prior preparation in inter-cultural understanding is a necessary investment to improve international business effectiveness.

Ethical issues in cross-cultural marketing

Cultural sensitivity is often at the heart of the ethical dilemmas that managers face when operating in international markets. There are few, if any, moral absolutes and few actions for which no one can provide reasonable justification. Almost every action can be justified on the basis that it is acceptable in one particular culture. In thinking about ethics managers need to be aware that simply defining what is ethical by the standards, values and actions from their own culture may be insufficient in satisfying all the stakeholders of a multi-national enterprise. What is often seen as an acceptable business practice in one culture can be seen as ethically questionable in another. The SRC effect discussed earlier is particularly relevant to the discussion of how cultural sensitivities impact on what is an ethical business practice. Managers from different cultures will always be able to challenge, for instance, the US, Indian or Japanese perspective of what is ethical.

The **ethical challenges** facing international marketing managers are many. In recent years such issues as environmental abuse, the use of child labour, poor working conditions and the low levels of pay in Third World factories have received particular attention. Western consumers in choosing brands look for

TABLE 3.4	Differences in buyer–seller relationships styles			
International market	**Climate**	**Importance of relationships**	**Process**	**Decision making**
United States	Sometimes viewed as an aggressive or confrontational climate	Of less importance. Focus is on achieving desired results	Ordered process where each point is discussed in sequence	Can be either an individual or group decision process
Canada	Positive, polite climate. Hard sell will not work here	Of less importance. Focus is on achieving desired results	Ordered process where each point is discussed in sequence	Can be either an individual or group decision process
Latin America	Positive and hospitable climate	Personal, one-on-one relationships very important	Relationship building through socialisation will precede negotiations	Decisions are usually made by a high-level individual
United Kingdom	Traditional, polite climate. Hard sell will not work here	Of less importance. Focus is on achieving desired results	Ordered process where each point is discussed in sequence	Can be either an individual or group decision process
Germany/ Austria	Rigid, sober climate	Low. Germans remain aloof until negotiations conclude	Systematic process with emphasis on contractual detail	Even the most routine decisions are made by top-level officials
France/ Belgium	Formal, bureaucratic climate. Hard sell will not work here	Formal, arm's-length relationships with attention to etiquette	French teams use argument to generate discussion	Usually a group process headed by a senior negotiator
Japan	Formal polite climate with many idiosyncratic nuances	Great importance. Long-term relationships are what matter most	First all general items are agreed on, then details are discussed	A total group process with all levels involved in the final decision
China	Bureaucratic climate with an abundance of 'red tape'	Very important. Traditional, cultural courtesies are expected	Discussions are long and repetitive. Agreements must be in writing	Usually a group process headed by a senior negotiator
Russia	Bureaucratic climate with an abundance of 'red tape'	Low. Russians will remain reserved until negotiations conclude	Cumbersome process due to bureaucratic constraints	Usually a group process headed by a senior negotiator

Source: Lewin and Johnston (1997)

reassurance that the product has been produced in what they see as a socially responsible manner (see Illustration 3.6). Many sportswear brands such as Nike, Levi and Gap have suffered adverse publicity when it has been made known that child labour has been used to produce their products. Anita Roddick built the Body Shop empire on the basis of ensuring her ingredients came from authentic sources of supply which did not lead to the destruction of the environment and that the indigenous producers received a fair price for the products they sold. She has recently launched an *ethical fashion chain*. Her key selling points for the new range of clothes are that they are free from child slavery and that the people that make them are able to earn a proper living wage and enjoy good working conditions.

Consumers globally are becoming better informed through better education and faster and more effective communications. Increasingly, therefore, they are able to question the actions of multi-national enterprises, as we saw in the discussion of the role of pressure groups in Chapter 1. For their part, whilst the largest multi-nationals are extending their influence within the global markets, they are becoming more vulnerable to criticism. Over the past few years, quality and service have improved considerably but now firms are increasingly expected to ensure that their behaviour is ethical and in the interests of the global community which makes up their market.

However, international marketing executives when operating across cultures will find themselves facing moral and ethical dilemmas on a daily basis on a wide range of issues. Some of the ones currently receiving particular attention are bribery and corruption, counterfeiting and piracy.

ILLUSTRATION 3.6	How the ethical consumer makes decisions

Ethical consumerism is of course nothing new; the campaign against Nestlé's sale of baby milk into Africa and boycotts of South African products during the days of apartheid have attracted widespread support.

Ethical consumers have helped to raise awareness of Third World debt and, as a result, prompted government action. And clearly, they tap into a latent anti-Americanism; people love eating McDonald's, but are happy to protest against them for a variety of reasons; protection of the rainforest, anti-globalisation, to name but two.

Most consumers are moderate but the issues these campaigners raise are steadily changing their expectations of corporate social responsibility and this, in turn, is influencing their purchase behaviour.

For example, concerns about animal welfare have fuelled demand for Freedom Food, organic meat and dolphin-friendly tuna, while growing environmental awareness has prompted a massive growth in organic/quasi-organic and bio-dynamic products. Greater social awareness has led to the development of Fair Trade products and anti-child-labour campaigns.

However, some moderate ethical consumers are highly selective about what they will boycott: many vegetarians eat non-vegetarian cheese or wear leather shoes; people who openly claim to be concerned with the environment use their cars instead of public transport; fashion conscious youngsters buy Nike trainers if that's what the fashion pack dictates; and people resist paying a couple of pence extra for Fair Trade coffee even though they claim to be concerned about Third World labour exploitation.

The question is, should multi-nationals take note of such moderate ethically aware people? These consumers may not protest at WTO summits but are they becoming aware of what the global pressure groups are demanding? and will they change their purchasing behaviour in the future?

International marketers need to be able to anticipate consumer demands across a range of cultural markets. So even if awareness of ethical issues has not changed actual buying behaviour, how should international marketing managers respond to such challenges?

Question How far do you think ethically aware consumers translate their beliefs into purchasing behaviour across the globe?

Source: Adapted from Seligman, P. *Financial Times Information*, 11 July 2002

Bribery and corruption

An integral part of conducting business internationally is the practice of gift giving. However, in many Western countries such practice is seen as bribery/ corruption and is tightly regulated and controlled. Business gift giving (or bribery depending on your view), if improperly executed, could stop sensitive negotiations and ruin new and potential business relationships. German and Swiss executives tend to feel uncomfortable accepting gifts, which they view as bribes, as they will not want to be seen as being under obligation to the other party. However, business gift giving in many cultures is an important part of persuasion. In cultures where a business gift is expected but not given, it is an insult to the host. In China it would be virtually impossible to gain any local government approval without offering financial inducements.

Cultures that view bribery as an acceptable business practice tend to fall into Hall's high context category. In such a culture the communication style is more implicit, non-verbal and is more reliant on hidden cues in the context of personal relationships. In Japan, for example, a highly developed and affluent society, gift-giving practices are widespread in the business culture. Refusing to participate in gift giving in such cultures can cause hard feelings and misunderstandings between business clients. In high context cultures, financial inducements are often seen as important steps in bringing a person into the inner circle of a business relationship or to strengthen the relationship between a buyer and a seller.

By contrast, people in low context cultures rely on explicit contracts, communication is more formal and explicit and negotiations based on a more legalistic orientation. Laws applying to bribery tend to be very well laid out. In some cultures, all business gifts will be viewed as illegal bribes; on the other hand, other cultures view gifts, pay-offs and even bribes merely as a cost of business. Bribery and corruption are part of the commercial traditions of many parts of Asia, Africa and the Middle East. Transparency International, a global counter-corruption watchdog, ranks Indonesia as the most corrupt country followed closely by Vietnam. They estimate in Vietnam that 20 per cent of infrastructure spending finds its way into the pockets of corrupt officials.

Piracy

Piracy has been a particular problem to the global music and software industry. The advent of digital technology and the ability to download from the Internet has made the copying of such things as CDs much easier. Ninety-eight per cent of software in China is estimated to be pirated software. The music industry too has financially suffered from such practices. It is estimated that 27 per cent of Americans and 13 per cent of Europeans download music, which the music industry sees as a major cause for the decline in sales worldwide.

However, whether piracy is the cause is questioned by some commentators. They argue that, whilst some consumers are buying fewer CDs it has actually led to others to buy more. The decline in sales, it is suggested, is more likely to be due to fiercer competition and the market maturing than just a result of piracy.

Even on piracy different cultures have varying perspectives. The US courts take a very stringent view and prosecute offenders that are caught. In China and India views on intellectual property rights are much more difficult to define. The International Intellectual Property Alliance claims that 90 per cent of musical recordings sold in China are pirated. Whilst officially regulations are being put in place to ban such practice, in fact very little has been done to control it. Even amongst professionals there are differing views. Robbie Williams, a UK superstar, recently publicly stated that he thought there was nothing wrong with piracy and that there was very little anyone could do about it.

Counterfeiting

A counterfeit is something that is forged, copied or imitated without the perpetrator having the right to do it, and with the purpose of deceiving or defrauding (whereas piracy does not attempt to defraud but openly sells as a pirated copy). In China at least US$16 billion-worth of goods sold each year inside the country are counterfeit. Procter & Gamble estimates that 10–15 per cent of its revenues in China are lost each year to counterfeit products. The Ukraine now exports counterfeit optical discs; Russia markets counterfeit software; while Paraguay markets imitation cigarettes. Counterfeit pharmaceuticals are routinely marketed to countries unable to afford the expensive products of the authentic drug companies; often these are sub-standard, or have fake labels. It is estimated by the World Health Organisation that between 5 and 7 per cent of drugs sold are counterfeits, with potentially fatal consequences.

American industries lose US$200–250 billion a year to counterfeiting. The fact that many global manufacturers have moved their production to Third World countries is seen by some to have opened the floodgates to counterfeiting. The global brands have been able to take advantage of low labour costs but gave insufficient attention to securing intellectual property rights in such countries. In today's markets, where so much of the added value of a product is in its brand identity, counterfeiters have been able to exploit consumers' expectations of quality and service with counterfeit products. The Internet has also helped build the market for counterfeit products; it is estimated that approximately US$25 billion-worth of counterfeit goods are traded each year over the Internet.

Much of the problem stems from cultural attitudes to the rights of anyone to own intellectual property. The Chinese have argued that if all ideas were copyrighted they should be able to patent the compass, ice-cream, noodles and many other products they have given to the world. This has led to inadequate laws on intellectual property rights (IPR) in many countries. By 2006, all members of the World Trade Organisation, however, should have started the process of implementing TRIPS, an international treaty on IPR that lays down basic rules for protection and enforcement. Some countries, notably China, since joining the WTO have introduced laws so companies can protect their intellectual property assets. How those rights are enforced in practice, however, remains to be seen. In Europe, the European Commission has proposed new rules to harmonise member states' legislation on IPR enforcement. This is particularly important as the EU prepares to embrace new members, such as Poland, where counterfeiting is a serious problem.

Although nations and organisations often provide ethical guidelines on bribery, counterfeiting etc., ultimately international managers have to make decisions based on their own personal views of what is and is not ethical. Managers need to form a view when operating across different cultures as to what constitutes ethical decision making within an organisation. In taking such a view, managers need to reflect on how their views on what constitutes ethical behaviour reflect changing societal views of acceptable behaviour, how decisions will be viewed by stakeholders and the perceived and real impact upon the organisation of making those decisions. Central to their concerns is the importance the company places on the need for an ethically responsible approach to their operations in the global markets. However, interwoven within this are the commercial concerns of the business.

Companies are increasingly of the view that organisational behaviour considered to be unethical can decrease a firm's wealth, whilst behaviour considered by stakeholders to be ethical can enhance a company's competitive advantage on global markets. Attempting to take an ethically responsible decision, though, could mean the loss of perhaps an efficient and cheap source of supply or in some cases the loss of a potential deal. Therefore, any decision would need very careful consideration.

The consequence of an ethically responsible approach would involve increased resources and attention being applied to a number of areas, such as:

- The increased need for accurate and timely information.
- Increased attention to press, public reaction and global pressure groups.
- Closer relationships with stakeholders and members of the supply chain to ensure all interests are taken into consideration.
- Being prepared, when serious risks are identified, to take positive and constructive action.

SUMMARY

- The influence of social and cultural factors in international marketing is complex and often extremely difficult for a firm operating in a foreign market to analyse and understand.

- If the firm is operating across a number of markets and looking for consistent methods of analysing their markets, the cultural differences pose particular challenges.

- This chapter has focused on developing an understanding of the components of culture and how these components impact on consumer beliefs, values, attitudes and purchasing behaviour.

- Culture also affects the way that business is carried out in different markets.

- Culture has a significant impact, therefore, on the international marketing strategies of firms, both in consumer and business-to-business markets.

- The reader should have acquired an awareness of the possible methods that can be used to categorise differences across cultures to enable a cross-cultural analysis to be carried out.

KEYWORDS

attitudes	individualism
beliefs	low context cultures
consumer behaviour	non-verbal communications
cross-cultural	perceived risk
cultural identity	piracy
cultural sensitivity	self-reference criterion
customs	silent language
enculturation	social and cultural factors
ethical challenges	spoken language
high context cultures	

The Beckham brand: Real Madrid vs Manchester United in the Far East

On 14 July 2003 *Newsweek International* observed that one man 'has become the hottest marketing machine in the sports world since Michael Jordan'.

Like the world-famous basketball star, his global appeal goes far beyond football, spanning the glamorous touch-points between sport, fashion and entertainment. He is a one-man brand – a sportsman, a model, a teenage fantasy, a gay icon and the face of Marks & Spencer's schoolwear. He is David Beckham.

Last year, he and his celebrity wife, Victoria, earned £15.5 million (£0.3 million more than the Queen) and his ability to generate revenue for his club, Manchester United, is no less impressive. Global consultancy Interbrand currently value the Beckham brand at around £50 million.

On 13 June 2003, Florentino Perez, the president of Real Madrid, announced that he had agreed a £25 million deal to transfer Beckham to the world-famous Spanish club. On the same day, the player and his wife were appearing in Tokyo, at the height of their 'promotional tour' of the Far East. Within hours the streets were flooded with Real Madrid shirts bearing Beckham's name.

The deal followed years of market research in the Far East, an enormous and rapidly growing market. These studies indicated that Beckham was the only individual player, not currently on their books, who had the power to significantly affect consumer preferences and behaviour in this part of the world.

Evidence of this was provided by scenes of Beckham-mania during the 2002 World Cup in Japan. Whilst the Beckham haircut spread like nits across the heads of young boys, the screaming Beckhamettes reached fever pitch on his departure, when the tears flowed and worlds collapsed.

Perez made no secret of the fact that the decision to buy Beckham was based as much on his international marketing power as on his footballing talent. After many years of operating with a business model that flew in the face of all corporate and financial wisdom, football clubs are responding to the near extinction of many of their own with a new emphasis on business strategy.

None more so than Real Madrid, a club with global reach that, despite having a larger fan base, still ranks second to Manchester United in financial terms. The main reason for United's dominance is its enormous following in the Far East, where it is estimated the club has nearly 17 million supporters. By contrast, Real Madrid has a relatively weak position in these markets – Perez hopes that the signing of David Beckham will change all that.

His rationale is simple: the appeal to Asian fans is pre-dominantly that of the player, not the club. In which case,

Real Madrid can buy the loyalty of fans simply by buying the player they follow.

His view is supported by leading agency FutureBrand, who estimate that one-third of the 17 million Manchester United fans in Asia support Beckham, rather than the club. According to FutureBrand consultant Samantha McCollum, 'Many fans in Asia watch a team because of the individual star players. When those players are transferred, quite often they will swap allegiances to a club and will follow the player. It's certainly very different to how things are in the UK, where you are committed to a club.'

Given this, Real Madrid can expect to attract around 5 million more fans in the Asian market. According to sports marketing firm Apex, the £25 million they paid for Beckham will be recouped in additional shirt sales alone within the four years of his contract. Michael Sterling, a sports analyst at Field Fisher Waterhouse in London, believes that Beckham will generate between £6 million and £10 million per year for his new club, largely because of the nature of the Asian markets.

So why on earth would the executives at Manchester United be prepared to sell such a powerful asset? Well, the reasons are both diverse and complex, but one contributory factor is seen to be their different approach to marketing strategy. Their view is that the club is bigger than the player, and their marketing activities reflect this. In official pictures, for example, they insist that at least three players are featured.

Furthermore, merchandising – an essential element in leveraging the Beckham brand – accounts for just 7 per cent of United's revenue, with ticket sales and media rights making up the majority of their income. The under-lying assumption is that Manchester United fans will keep watching, Beckham or no Beckham!

A marked contrast from the Real Madrid strategy, of which the timely announcement in Tokyo was only the beginning. Having secured the brand, leveraging its value has now become the critical concern, and in recent weeks two questions have been rapidly addressed.

The first, where would Beckham play his first eagerly awaited game for the club, was straightforward. It would not be in the club's famous Bernabeu stadium, nor anywhere in Spain, but on 2 August, in China. From here the team would embark on a tour of the Far East that would quickly take in Japan.

The second, however, proved a little more tricky - what number shirt would Beckham be wearing?

The player had long been associated with the number 7 – a number that has assumed great significance amongst European football fans, having previously been worn by the likes of Kevin Keegan and Kenny Dalglish. At Real Madrid, however, that number had been cultivated as a key brand asset of Raul, himself an international star for a number of years.

The club decided that the number associated with the Beckham brand would, and could, be changed in the key target markets of the Far East, and so they set to work. The obvious choice was the number 4 shirt, worn by Hierro, the retiring Real and Spain captain. The number 4, however, is considered to be unlucky in many parts of the Far East and so this was rejected.

The delay merely fuelled the fervour that had surrounded the announcement of his transfer. The icon continued his tour, the crowds clamoured and wept as a giant chocolate replica of the great man was unveiled. And the brand value crept ever higher.

Finally, it was revealed. The new Madrid–Beckham brand would be encapsulated in the number 23. Why? Maybe we'll never know, but it's not difficult to imagine the rush of adoration in the hearts of Asian sports fans, as they recall the number 23 rising powerfully and majestically, reaching

for the skies, blazing bright beneath the shoulders of one . . . Michael Jordan.

Questions

1 What assumptions about consumer behaviour in the Far East underpinned the marketing decisions of both Real Madrid and Manchester United?

2 From a cross-cultural perspective, do you think the values and motivations of football consumers in the Far East differ from those of their European counterparts?

3 From a cultural perspective, why might an individual promotional tour of Japan be more successful than one of Spain?

4 What other cultural and behavioural considerations might you take into consideration when designing a strategy for the Beckhams in the Far East? What implications might these have for Real Madrid's international marketing strategy?

Source: Anthony Grimes, University of Hull

DISCUSSION QUESTIONS

1 Discuss the view that culture lies at the heart of all problems connected with international marketing.

2 What is culture? Is it important for international marketers to take account of it or is globalisation going to make it a thing of the past?

3 Given the cultural sensitivities to ethical dilemmas, can there ever be a global harmonisation of ethical business practices in international marketing?

4 How do social and cultural influences impact on international business negotiations? Using examples, advise a company preparing for cross-cultural negotiations.

5 It has been suggested that firms from developed countries should market to developing countries by establishing partnerships in a neighbouring developing country. Explain the reasons behind such a proposition and the implications for a firm developing a globalisation strategy.

REFERENCES

Blackwell, R.D., Minniard, P.W. and Engel, J.L. (2001) *Consumer Behaviour*, 5th edn, The Dryden Press.

Doole, I. and Yaqub, A.C. (1997) Integrated Communications: the challenge of Saudi Arabia, *Academy of Marketing Conference proceedings*, July.

Druckman, D. (1977) *Negotiations, social-psychological perspectives*, Sage.

Graham, J.L. (1986) 'Across the negotiating table from the Japanese', *International Marketing Review*, Autumn.

Graham, J.L., Hodgson, J.D. and Sano, Y. (2000) *Doing business with the new Japan*, Rowman and Littlefield Publishers.

Gudykunst, W.B. and Mody, B. (2002) *Handbook of international and intercultural communication*. 2nd edn, Sage Publications.

Gudykunst, W.B. and Ting-Toomey, S. (1988) *Culture and Interpersonal Communication*, Sage Publications.

Hall, E.T. and Hall, M.R. (1986) *Hidden Differences: doing business with the Japanese*, Anchor Press.

Hawkins, D.I., Best, R.J. and Coney, K.A. (1992) *Consumer Behaviour: Implications for Marketing Strategy*, 5th edn, Irwin.

Hawrysh, B.M. and Zaichkowsky, J.L. (1990) 'Cultural approaches to negotiations: Understanding the Japanese', *International Marketing Review*, 7 (2).

Hofstede, G. (2001) *Culture's consequences: international differences in work-related values*, 2nd edn, Sage.

Hofstede, G. (1994) 'The business of international business is culture', *International Business Review*, 3 (1).

Jeannet, J.-P. and Hennessey, H.O. (2002), *Global Marketing Strategies,* 5th edn, Houghton Miffin.

Kale, S.H. (1991) 'Culture specific marketing communications: an analytical approach', *International Marketing Review*, 8 (1).

Kotler, P. (2003) *Marketing Management*, 11th edn, Prentice Education Intn.

Lee, J.R. and Olson, W.C. (1994), *Theory and Practice of International relations*, 2nd edn, Prentice Hall.

Lewin, J.E. and Johnston, W.L. (1997) 'Managing the International Salesforce', *Journal of Business and Industrial Marketing*, 12 (3/4).

Linton, R. (1945) *The Cultural Background of Personality*, Appleton Century.

Maslow A.H. (1970) *Motivation and Personality*, 2nd edn, Harper and Row.

Robinson, P.J., Faris, C.W. and Wind, Y. (1979) *Industrial Buying and Creative Marketing*, Allyn and Bacon.

Schiffman, L.G. and Kanuk, U. (2000) *Consumer Behaviour*, 7th edn, Prentice Hall.

Terpstra, V. and Sarathy, R. (2000) *International Marketing*, 8th edn, Dryden Press.

Toyne, B. and Walters, P.G.P. (1993) *Global Marketing Management: A Strategic Perspective*, Allyn and Bacon.

Welford, R. and Prescott, K. (1994) *European Business, An Issue Based Approach*, Pitman.

Wills, J.I., Samli, A.C. and Jacobs, L. (1991) 'Developing global products and marketing strategies; a construct and a research agenda', *Journal of the Academy of Marketing Science*, 19 (Winter), 1–10.

Usunier, J.C. (2000) *Marketing Across Cultures*, 2nd edn, Prentice Hall.

INTERNATIONAL MARKETING RESEARCH AND OPPORTUNITY ANALYSIS

Introduction

Discussions in previous chapters have illustrated the highly risky and complex environment in which the international marketing manager operates. If a company is to survive in the international marketplace, it is important that it searches for methods to reduce, as far as possible, the risk of making a wrong decision.

This is why **marketing research** is so fundamentally important to the international marketing process, for whilst it cannot help a manager reduce risk to the point of zero, it can ensure that the starting point for decision making is knowledge, rather than guesswork. Lack of knowledge of foreign markets is one of the first major barriers an international marketing manager has to overcome. An effective marketing research strategy is the first step in overcoming that barrier.

The purpose of this chapter is to examine the place of marketing research in international strategy and the contribution it makes to the decision-making process. We shall, therefore, be examining such concepts as the role of marketing research and opportunity analysis in international markets and the building of an international marketing information system. We shall also examine some of the aspects of primary marketing research in international markets and discuss the practicalities and problems in implementing multi-country studies.

Learning objectives

On completion of this chapter the reader should be able to:

- Appreciate the key roles of marketing research in international marketing
- Understand the concepts and techniques to identify and evaluate opportunities internationally
- Build a market profile analysis of a foreign country market
- Discuss the difficulties and issues that arise in developing multi-country primary research studies

THE ROLE OF MARKETING RESEARCH AND OPPORTUNITY ANALYSIS

Marketing research can be defined as the systematic gathering, recording, analysis and interpretation of data on problems relating to the marketing of goods and services.

The role of research is primarily to act as an aid to the decision-maker. It is a tool that can help to reduce the risk in decision making caused by the environmental uncertainties and lack of knowledge in international markets. It ensures that the manager bases a decision on the solid foundation of knowledge and focuses strategic thinking on the needs of the marketplace, rather than the product. Such a role is, of course, necessary in all types of marketing.

In international marketing, because of the increased uncertainties and complexities in world markets, the capacity to ensure a systematic planned process in the research and the use of secondary information, prior to field research, is of paramount importance if quality information is to be obtained. The **research process** (Malhotra *et al*. 1997) consists of six key stages. These steps are the logical process for any research study to go through in its implementation and will be relevant for all research studies:

1 *Defining the problem*. It is important to decide what information is needed and set the objectives of the research ensuring it is both commercially worthwhile and that the objective is feasible and achievable.

2 *Developing the approach to be taken*. The planning phase will concern itself with timescales, resources to carry out the work and the expertise required to meet the objectives. Also the decision as to whether a qualitative or quantitative approach is to be taken.

3 *Designing the research*. In designing the research strategy consideration will be given to the different action steps that need to be taken. Ensuring full use of secondary data sources will be important, as will the use of a pilot study to ensure the development of an effective and meaningful questionnaire.

4 *Carrying out the field work*. Decisions as to how the questionnaires will be administered (telephone, mail, personal interviews or focus groups) will be made as well as decisions as to who will do the work and what resources are required.

5 *Analysing the data*. The data analysis stage will need to take full account of the objectives of the research and the client's needs. Many researchers will argue that the methodology to be used should be decided in the first stages of the research planning as it will impact on the questionnaire design and how the interviews are administered.

6 *Preparing the report and presentation*. The report and presentation are the researcher's outputs and vital in establishing the credibility of the research methods used and the validity of the findings of the research.

THE ROLE OF INTERNATIONAL MARKETING RESEARCH

The ability for research to deliver fast and yet sensitively analysed results across a range of different countries in today's global markets is crucial for competitive success. In the past decade, we have seen the development of improved techniques, data availability and new research supplier networks in many developing countries. There has been an increase in the usage of continent-wide or even worldwide surveys which transcend national boundaries, the development of global niche marketing with differing research requirements, and a rapid increase in the rate and spread of product innovation with which research must keep pace. The old days of slow-moving local or national test marketing results are long gone.

There has also been an information explosion. The availability of online databases, CD ROMS and the World Wide Web has transformed the nature of international marketing research and the role it plays in the marketing process. The international market research industry has had to develop the ability to meet these challenges.

Research into international market issues can incorporate three major roles:

- **cross-cultural research**, the conducting of a research project across nation or culture groups;

- **foreign research**, research conducted in a country other than the country of the commissioning company;

- **multi-country research**, research conducted in all or important countries where a company is represented (Terpstra and Sarathy, 2000).

This does not, however, in any way convey the enormity of the task involved in developing an international market intelligence system which would be sufficient to provide the information necessary to make sound international marketing decisions. Such an information system would not only have to identify and analyse potential markets, but would also have to have the capacity to generate an understanding of the many environmental variables discussed in the previous three chapters. Many levels of environmental factors will affect international marketing decisions, from macro-level economic factors to political-legal factors, as well as the micro market structures and cultural factors affecting the consumer. What Johannson said way back in 1972 still holds true today:

> In international activities, uncertainty is generally greater and the difficulties in getting information are also greater. It is the lack of market knowledge which is the greatest obstacle to the first foreign venture and it is access to such knowledge which makes it possible for the internationally experienced company to extend their activities to new markets.

As such, the role of the international market researcher is to provide an assessment of market demand globally, an evaluation of potential markets and of the risks and costs involved in market entries, as well as detailed information on which to base effective marketing strategies.

To achieve this the researcher has primarily three functions to carry out:

1 Scanning international markets to identify and analyse the opportunities.

2 Building marketing information systems to monitor environmental trends.

3 Carrying out primary marketing research studies for input into the development of marketing strategies and to test the feasibility of the possible marketing mix options, both in foreign country markets and across a range of international markets.

In the next three sections we will examine each of these in some detail.

OPPORTUNITY IDENTIFICATION AND ANALYSIS

Scanning international markets

There are approximately 200 countries in the world. Even a large multi-national corporation would find it difficult to resource market development in all these countries. Thus the first task for the researcher is to scan markets to identify which countries have the potential for growth. International markets are scanned primarily at this stage to identify countries that warrant further research and analysis, thus the researcher will look for countries that meet three qualifying criteria:

1 **Accessibility**. If a company is barred from entering the market, it would be an ineffective use of resources to take research further. The scanning unit would assess such things as tariffs, non-tariff barriers, government regulation and import regulations to assess the accessibility of the market. Japan is seen as a highly profitable potential market but is viewed by some as inaccessible due to the perception of the difficulties involved in overcoming trade barriers.

2 **Profitability**. At this level the researcher would assess factors that at a macro level could render the market unprofitable – for example, the availability of currency, the existence of exchange regulations, government subsidies to local competition, price controls and substitute products. Eastern European markets, including Russia, are fully accessible, but many companies question the ability of trade partners in some countries to pay. The extra risk of non-payment reduces the profit return calculations of those markets.

3 **Market size**. An assessment is made of the potential market size to evaluate whether future investment is likely to bear fruit.

The specific indicators a company will look for tend to be very product/market specific. Thus a hand tool manufacturer in the north of England specialising in tools for woodworking craftsmen looked for evidence of a hobby market (accessibility), high levels of disposable income (profitability) and large numbers of educated, middle-aged men with leisure time (market size).

At the scanning stage the researcher is attempting to identify countries where marketing opportunities exist. Having identified those opportunities, the researcher will need to make an assessment of their viability for further investigation. In principle, there are three types of market opportunities:

1 **Existing markets**. Here customers' needs are already serviced by existing suppliers; therefore, market entry would be difficult unless the company has a superior product or a totally new concept to offer the market.

2 **Latent markets**. In this type of market there are recognised potential customers but no company has yet offered a product to fulfil the latent need. As there is no direct competition, market entry would be easier than in existing markets as long as the company could convey the benefits of its product to the market. Coca-Cola and Pepsi Cola dominate the global market. Qibla Cola, however, has tapped into a latent market by targeting consumers who do not want to buy a US brand. They have launched their cola not on its product benefits but as an alternative for consumers around the globe who oppose US policies in the Middle East.

3 **Incipient markets**. Incipient markets are ones that do not exist at present but conditions and trends can be identified that indicate the future emergence of needs that, under present circumstances, would be unfulfilled. It may be, of course, that existing companies in the market are positioning themselves to take advantage of emerging markets but at present there is no direct competition.

The nature of competition can be analysed in a broadly similar way, with three distinct product types: competitive products, improved products and breakthrough products. A competitive product is one that has no significant advantages over those already on offer. An improved product is one that, whilst not unique, represents an improvement upon those currently available. A breakthrough product, by way of contrast, represents an innovation and, as such, is likely to have a significant competitive advantage.

The level and nature of competition that a firm will encounter can therefore be analysed by relating the three types of demand to the three types of product. This is illustrated in Figure 4.1 and can be used as a basis for determining, first, whether market entry is likely to succeed, and second, whether the company possesses any degree of competitive advantage. This, in turn, provides an insight into the nature of the marketing task needed. In saying this, however, it needs to be emphasised that this sort of analysis provides an initial framework for analysis and nothing more. What is then needed is a far more detailed assessment of the degree of competitive advantage that the company possesses.

Obviously the greatest opportunities, together with the greatest risk and potential for profit, are in the identification of incipient markets. The problem is, because markets do not yet exist, neither does market data. Researchers, therefore, use analytical techniques to make sure they identify and recognise conditions in incipient markets, thus enabling their companies to develop strategies by which to be first into the market.

In the research techniques used, the basic principle is to compare, contrast or correlate various factors in the market under study with some external variant to identify similarities within the market or with other markets, thus assessing whether the right conditions exist for a market to emerge.

Some of the key techniques used are the following.

FIGURE 4.1   Product/market combinations and the scope for competitive advantage on market entry

Type of product	Type of market			
	Existing	**Latent**	**Incipient**	
Competitive			Existing brands are positioned to take advantage of possible developing needs; no direct competition, but consumers need to be found and then persuaded of the product's value to them. Risk and cost of failure may be high	Low
Improved	Superior product offers competitive advantage and eases market entry	Increasingly advanced profile offers greater benefits to the market; no direct competition		Cost and risk of launching the product
Breakthrough	Breakthrough product offers self-evident superiority and the competitive advantage is high	Breakthrough product offers siginificant advantages but markets need to be identified and developed. Little likelihood of competitors in the short and medium term, but consumer resistance may be high		High
	Low	Cost and risk of opening up the market		High

Source: Gilligan and Hird (1985)

Demand pattern analysis

In this technique, it is assumed that countries at different levels of economic development have differing patterns of demand and consumption. By comparing the pattern of demand in the country under study with the pattern of demand in an established market when the product was first introduced, a broad estimate of an incipient market can be achieved. An example of how Kodak use econometric indicators is given in Illustration 4.1.

Multiple factor indices

This assumes that the demand for a product correlates to demand for other products. By measuring demand for the correlated product, estimates of potential demand can be made. For example, a manufacturer of frozen foods may make an assessment by measuring the number of houses with freezers.

Analogy estimation

Analogy estimation is used where there is a lack of market data in a particular country. Analogies are made with existing markets – perhaps the US – comparing and contrasting certain ratios to test for market potential. This technique arouses mixed levels of enthusiasm, since experiences with it have been variable. In addition, it is an expensive technique to implement and doubts have been expressed about the accuracy of its forecasts. Those who have used it typically adopt one of two approaches:

- A cross-section approach, where the product-market size for one country is related to some appropriate gross economic indicator in order to establish a ratio. This ratio is then applied to the specific country under analysis to estimate the potential for the product-market in that country.

- A time-series approach based on the belief that product usage moves through a cycle. Thus one assumes that the country under analysis will follow the same pattern of consumption as a more advanced economy, albeit with a predetermined time-lag.

DILEMMA 4.1	Dutch flowers to the US

The dominant markets for cut flowers are Western Europe, the US and Japan. Western Europe is by far the largest market, currently three times the size of the US. Research carried out by the Dutch Flower Council, however, indicates rapid growth in the market in the US. In Europe the Dutch growers face intense competition from North and West Africa and, more recently, from South and East Africa and Israel. The main suppliers to the US market are Mexico, Central and Southern America and, increasingly, the Caribbean basin.

Question The dilemma for the Dutch growers is should they use their limited resources to continue to build their presence in Western Europe or should they try to develop a presence in the US market and, if so, how should they go about it?

Source: Professor Steve Carter

Regression analysis

This technique is typically used to complement an analogy approach. Regression analysis is particularly useful in enhancing the likely accuracy and eventual confidence that can be placed on cross-sectional studies.

Macrosurvey technique

This method is essentially anthropological in approach and can help companies to establish themselves early in emerging countries with obvious long-term marketing benefits. The technique is based on the notion that as a community grows and develops, more specialised institutions come into being. Thus, one can construct a scale of successively more differentiated institutions against which any particular country can be evaluated to assess its level of development and hence its market potential.

These techniques highlight the importance of **comparative research** and regular market screening if incipient demand is to be identified at an early stage. However, the value of several of the techniques does rest upon the assumption that all countries and their consumption patterns will develop along broadly common lines. If firms are to make effective use of many of these techniques, the

---

ILLUSTRATION 4.1   **Kodak's use of consumer research to assess global market potential**

In a global organisation, there is more of a focus on econometric research and multi-country benchmarking.

At the corporate level, Kodak wants to pinpoint where to invest finite resources for longer-term pay-offs whether it be in manufacturing or setting up a marketing company or expending large amounts of advertising dollars. Research also provides a common planning framework for the company's different units.

In the global arena, econometric aspects – the economic development mechanisms that produce income for the purchase of both consumer goods and industrial goods – become highly significant. Also important is multi-country benchmarking due to the lack of readily available information and the fact that most products still go through highly specialised channels.

Kodak has been working with the World Bank to develop a framework for improved understanding of the economic engine that drives a country's development.

The analysis began with thirteen primary measures of a country's state of development – industrial infrastructure, disposable income, etc. Multivariate clustering techniques were then applied to these measures to try to give some finite meaning to the notions of developed, developing and undeveloped economies.

It was found that economic parameters were highly interrelated. There is a very long period of time during which money is poured into a country just to develop the support infrastructure – business, roads, education etc. Only in the relatively later stage does the consumer economy seem to develop more fully.

Attitudinal research gives Kodak an understanding of perceptions, preferences and brand images specific to potential target markets. In trying to develop a strategy around cameras, for example, Kodak conducted a trade-off exercise involving several broad camera attributes: picture quality, film loading, skill required, size and weight, durability, appearance and range.

The study was conducted in eight countries and resulted in perception maps of basic camera types that were virtually identical across all the countries, with picture quality and weight ranked as the most important camera characteristics.

This information gave Kodak the ability to put together a fairly good global strategic framework for their global markets. It also allows them to think carefully about alternatives and improve their understanding and appreciation of risk. It is research such as this that has contributed many millions of dollars to the organisation over the past decade.

Question Examine how such information can be used as a basis for developing an international marketing strategy.

Source: Adapted from *The Economist*, March 1998 and *Interfaces*, Sept/Oct 2001

assumption of common economic development patterns must stand. Increasingly, however, evidence is emerging to suggest that global commonality does not exist to this degree and there are strong arguments for companies grouping country markets for the purposes of this sort of comparative analysis.

Risk evaluation

As previously stated, incipient markets offer the greatest opportunity for profit potential, but with profit comes risk.

The risk factor in opportunity analysis cannot be over-estimated. Sometimes political risk itself can be the most important determining factor to the success or failure of an international marketing campaign. In the markets where opportunities have been identified, researchers need to make an assessment first as to the type of risk apparent in that market (political, commercial, industrial or financial), and second as to the degree of that risk. Matrices such as the one identified in Figure 4.2 can be useful in carrying out such assessments.

Over recent years marketers have developed various indices to help assess the risk factor in the evaluation of potential market opportunities. Two such indices are the Business Environment Risk Index (BERI) and the Goodnow and Hansz temperature gradient.

BERI

BERI provides country risk forecasts for fifty countries throughout the world and is updated three times a year. This index assesses fifteen environment factors, including political stability, balance of payments volatility, inflation, labour productivity, local management skills, bureaucratic delays, etc. Each factor is rated on a scale of 0–4 ranging from unacceptable conditions (0) to superior conditions (4). The key factors are individually weighted to take account of their importance. For example, political stability is weighted by a factor of 2.5. The final score is out of 100 and scores of over 80 would indicate a favourable environment for investors and an advanced economy. Scores of less than 40 would indicate very high risk for companies committing capital.

FIGURE 4.2

The four-risk matrix

Country						
Risk level	A	B	C	D	E	F
Risk type	Low	Moderate	Some	Risky	Very risky	Dangerous
Political						
Commercial						
Industrial						
Financial						

The Goodnow and Hansz temperature gradient

This classification system rates a country's environmental factors ture gradient whereby environmental factors are defined as being hot to moderate to cold. This system examines such factors as po economic development and performance, cultural unity, legal barriers and geo-cultural barriers. Relative positive values on the gradient give degrees of hotness. Relative negative values indicate degrees of coldness. Thus, an advanced economy such as the USA would achieve a relatively hot score whereas a less developed economy such as India would be given a relatively cold score.

The main value of subscribing to such indices is to give companies an appreciation of the risk involved in opportunities identified. There are various publications such as *The Economist* which also publish country risk ratings, so information on risk evaluation is readily available to the researcher.

Major global corporations such as IBM, Honeywell and ICI have specialist political risk analysts, monitoring environmental trends to alert senior managers to changes and developments which may affect their markets.

INTERNATIONAL MARKETING SEGMENTATION

At the scanning stage, the manager researching international markets is identifying and then analysing opportunities to evaluate which markets to prioritise for further research and development. Some system then needs to be designed to evaluate those opportunities and try to reduce the plethora of countries to a more manageable number. To do this, managers need to divide markets into groups so they can decide which markets to give priority or even to target.

Market segmentation is the strategy by which a firm partitions a market into sub-markets or segments likely to manifest similar responses to marketing inputs. The aim is to identify the markets on which a company can concentrate its resources and efforts so that they can achieve maximum penetration of that market, rather than going for perhaps a market-spreading strategy where they aim to achieve a presence, however small, in as many markets as possible.

The **Pareto law** usually applies to international marketing strategies with its full vigour. The most broad-based and well-established international firms find that 20 per cent of the countries they serve generate at least 80 per cent of the results. Obviously these countries must receive greater managerial attention and allocation of resources. The two main bases for segmenting international markets are by geographical criteria (i.e. countries) and transnational criteria (i.e. individual decision-makers).

DILEMMA 4.2   Optcan assess Saudi Arabia

A Canadian company, Optcan, is in the business of FSOs (Free Space Optics), an emerging technology that transports data via laser technology. They are considering entering the Saudi Arabian market and so wish to carry out a feasibility study to help them decide whether they should set up a presence in the market. However, there is no actual market data as there is no company, as yet, operating directly in the market.

Question How should Optcan evaluate whether Saudi Arabia is potentially viable and how should they assess the level of potential risks involved?

Geographical criteria

The traditional practice is to use a country-based classification system as a basis for classifying international markets. The business portfolio matrix (Figure 4.3) is indicative of the approach taken by many companies. In this, markets are classified in three categories.

Primary opportunity

These markets indicate the best opportunities for long-term strategic development. Companies may want to establish a permanent presence and so embark on a thorough research programme.

Secondary opportunity

These are the markets where opportunities are identified but political or economic risk is perceived as being too high to make long-term irrevocable commitments. These markets would be handled in a more pragmatic way due to potential risks identified. A comprehensive marketing information system would be needed.

Tertiary opportunity

These are the catch-what-you-can markets. These markets will be perceived as high risk and so the allocation of resources will be minimal. Objectives in such countries would be short term and opportunistic, companies would give no real commitment. No significant research would be carried out.

Figure 4.3 illustrates the business portfolio matrix. The horizontal axis evaluates the attractiveness of each country on objective and measurable criteria (e.g. size, stability and wealth). The vertical axis evaluates the firm's compatibility with each country on a more subjective and judgemental basis. Primary markets would score high on both axes.

This is a particularly useful device for companies operating in a portfolio of markets to prioritise market opportunity. Ford Tractor carried out such an analysis of key markets. In assessing market attractiveness they explored four basic elements: market size, market growth rate, government regulations and economic and political stability. Competitive strength and compatibility were defined in the international context and such factors as market share, market representation, contribution margin and market support were examined. Using this analysis they identified Kenya, Pakistan and Venezuela as primary markets.

Equally, a company may use the BERI index, Hofstede's cultural dimensions or the Goodnow and Hansz country temperature gradient as a basis for classifying countries. Whatever measurement base is used, once the primary markets have been identified, companies usually then use standard methods to segment the markets within countries using such variables as demographic/economic factors, lifestyles, consumer motivations, geography, buyer behaviour, psychographics, etc.

Thus the primary segmentation base is geographic (by country) and the secondary bases are within countries. The problem here is that depending on the information base, it may be difficult to fully formulate secondary segmentation bases. Furthermore, such an approach can run the risk of leading to a **differentiated marketing** approach which may leave the company with a very fragmented international strategy.

A major drawback with the country-based approach is the difficulty in applying the segmentation strategy consistently across markets. If a company is to try to achieve a consistent and controlled marketing strategy across all its international markets, it needs a transnational approach to its segmentation strategy.

Transnational segmentation

To achieve a transnational approach, the country as a unit of analysis is too large to be of operational use. An alternative approach is to examine the individual decision-maker (Walters 1997). Key bases for segmentation would include, therefore, such variables as demographic, psychographic and behavioural criteria.

Demographic variables have obvious potential as cross-national segmentation criteria. The most commonly used variables include sex, age, income level, social class and educational achievement. Frequently, use is made of a battery of demographic variables when delineating transnational market segments.

Psychographic segmentation involves using 'lifestyle' factors in the segmentation process. Appropriate criteria are usually of an inferred nature and concern consumer interests and perceptions of 'way of living' in regard to work and leisure habits. Critical dimensions of lifestyle thus include activities, interests and opinions. Objective criteria, normally of a demographic nature, may also be helpful when defining lifestyle segments. *Research International*, when researching the transnational segments of young adults globally, divided them into four broad categories. 'Enthusiastic materialists' are optimistic and aspirational and to be found in developing countries and emerging markets like India and Latin

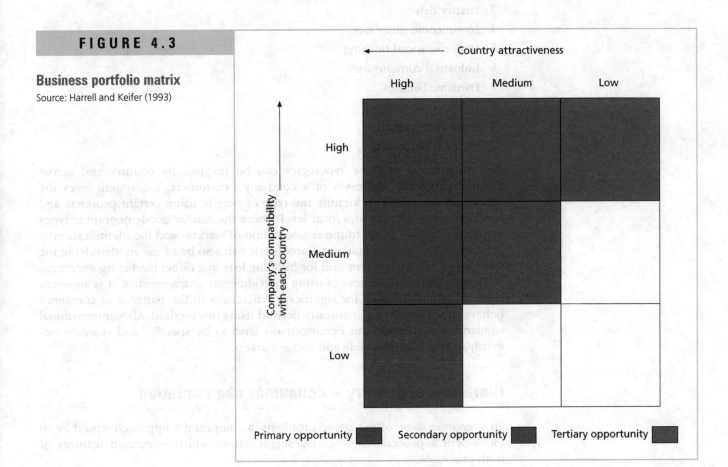

FIGURE 4.3

Business portfolio matrix
Source: Harrell and Keifer (1993)

America. 'Swimmers against the tide' on the other hand demonstrate a degree of underlying pessimism and tend to live for the moment and are likely to be found in southern Europe. In northern Europe, the US and Australasia are the 'new realists', looking for a balance between work and leisure with some underlying pessimism in outlook and, finally, the 'complacent materialists' are defined as passively optimistic and located in Japan.

Behavioural variables also have a lot of potential as a basis for global market segmentation. In particular, attention to patterns of consumption and loyalty in respect of product category and brand can be useful, along with a focus on the context for usage. Variables such as the benefit sought or the buying motivations may be used. Behaviourally defined segments may be identified in terms of a specific aspect of behaviour which is not broad enough to be defined as a 'lifestyle'. Goodyear have effectively used behavioural characteristics to develop a global segmentation strategy (see Illustration 4.2).

EuroMosaic

One of the trends enabling segmentation, using individualistic characteristics, to become a feasible strategy for many companies is the development of geodemographic databases. One such database is the CCN EuroMosaic. This is claimed to be the first pan-European segmentation system allowing the classification of 380 million consumers across the European Union on the basis of the types of neighbourhood in which they live. Ten EuroMosaic types have been identified:

1 Elite suburbs
2 Average areas
3 Luxury flats
4 Low-income inner city
5 High-rise social housing
6 Industrial communities
7 Dynamic families
8 Low-income families
9 Rural agricultural
10 Vacation retirement

The distribution of these typologies can be mapped by country and across Europe. Given the addresses of a company's customers, the system gives the researcher the ability to identify the type of people using certain products and services and to identify at a local level where the similar geodemographic types are, thus acting as an aid to the segmentation of markets and the identification of primary and secondary markets. EuroMosaic will also be of use in identifying the sample in a research survey and for building lists in a direct marketing exercise.

Despite the attractiveness of using individualistic characteristics, it is apparent there is strong potential for significant differences in the patterns of consumer behaviour within global segments derived using this method. Also, international similarities in lifestyle and behaviour do tend to be specific, and relevant primarily to specialist products and niche markets.

Hierarchical country – consumer segmentation

To overcome some of the above problems, a compromise approach would be to implement a procedure for global segmentation which integrated features of both processes.

ILLUSTRATION 4.2   Goodyear global segmentation research

Goodyear Tyre and Rubber Company investigated the feasibility of developing a segmentation strategy that could be applied globally to their world markets. The requirement was that the strategy would provide a practical base for an international marketing strategy and prove to be consistent and durable.

This is an important part of their objective to gain 1 per cent market share globally and a further 2 per cent of the US market by 2005.

After considerable research they identified three decision orientations which could constitute primary attitude segments when buying tyres: brand, outlet and price.

From consumer research they then developed six consumer segments:

1 The *Prestige Buyer* makes the brand decision first and the outlet decision second. This segment is male-dominated, very 'upscale', brand and retailer loyal, does very little information gathering prior to making a purchase and is predisposed to major brands.

2 The *Comfortable Conservative* looks for the outlet first and the brand second. This segment has the same characteristics of the first group but includes more women who are dependent on the retailer for expert advice. These shoppers tend to develop a lasting relationship with a retailer.

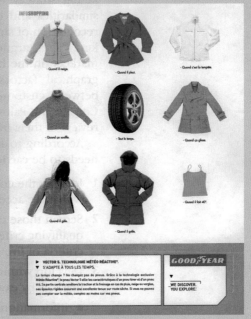

Source: Goodyear

3 The *Value Shopper* considers brand first and price second. This segment is seen as Mr Average. Its members are predisposed to major brands, have a very low retailer loyalty and search for information extensively to educate themselves prior to making the purchase.

4 The *Pretender* wants a major brand but the price ultimately determines the choice. The first decision is price, the second is brand. This group has two sub-segments – the aspiring young and emulating old – but all these shoppers exhibit very little loyalty to retailers or brands and do a lot of information searching.

5 The *Trusting Patron* chooses the outlet first and the price second. This group is somewhat 'downscale', heavily female and extremely retailer loyal. The brand is totally unimportant and little searching for information is undertaken.

6 The *Bargain Hunter* shops for price first, outlet second but price is really the only consideration. This group primarily consists of young, 'downscale' people who have low retailer and brand loyalty and who delay the tyre purchase as long as possible.

Question Do you think these segments are valid across all global markets?

Source: Adapted from *Marketing News* (1996) and *Rubber and Plastic News* (2003)

Source: Goodyear

Kale and Sudarshan have outlined a process to formulate strategically equivalent segments (SES) that transcend national boundaries. On this basis the marketing strategy would follow the premise that world markets consist of both similarities and differences and that the most effective strategies reflect a full recognition of similarities and differences across markets rather than within markets. They argue that companies competing internationally should segment markets on the basis of consumers, not countries. Segmentation by purely geographical factors leads to national stereotyping. It ignores the differences between customers within a nation and ignores similarities across boundaries. Colgate and Palmolive reached such a conclusion when carrying out an analytical review of their own segmentation strategies and use the hierarchical approach.

According to Kale and Sudharshan, to achieve SES, the segmentation process needs to be carried out in stages:

1 Identify the countries that have the infrastructure to support the product and which are accessible to the company.

2 Screen those countries to arrive at a shorter list of countries that meet certain qualifying criteria, e.g. a frozen dessert manufacturer may set a qualifying criteria of five million refrigerators per market.

3 Develop within these countries micro-segments, e.g. segment those potential markets by examining such factors as:

- information search behaviour
- product characteristics required.

The outcome of this process would be a series of micro-segments within qualified countries.

4 Having disaggregated, the aggregation process then commences by looking for similarities across segments. Factor analysis of the behavioural patterns of these segments would enable managers to understand the characteristics of the demand of each segment as regards marketing mix issues. Each micro-segment would therefore be rated on several strategic factors in terms of potential response.

5 Cluster analysis is then used to identify meaningful cross-national segments, each of which, it is thought, would evoke a similar response to any marketing mix strategy.

It is argued that this approach would enable marketers to design strategies at a cross-national segment level and so take a more consumer-orientated approach to international marketing. In prioritising markets, companies would use consumers as their primary base. Some writers argue that companies still need a secondary segmentation stage to identify the key countries where these transnational segments can be found.

THE INTERNATIONAL MARKETING INFORMATION SYSTEM

Building the information base

Having completed the scanning stage, the researcher will have reduced the number of potential countries to a feasible number requiring further research. The company needs a systematic method for evaluating the markets identified. This is primarily the role of the **marketing information system** (MIS).

In building any MIS, the objective of the company is to develop a cost-effective communication channel between the environment in which the company operates and the decision-makers. As is discussed in Chapter 5, one of the great difficulties in international marketing planning is the long communication lines between headquarters and subsidiaries. This often causes inadequate dataflow which results in misunderstandings and wrong decisions being made.

An effective MIS can contribute to solving these problems and provide a solid base for strategic decisions to be made. Using the 12C environmental analysis model in Table 4.1 we can identify some of the major inputs that an international marketing information system should contain.

The information input into the MIS is used to draw up a **market profile analysis** as shown in Figure 4.4.

The objective of a market profile analysis is to enable the company to use the environmental information built up in the system to identify opportunities and problems in the potential marketing strategies. For example, the fact that television advertising is prohibited in a country will have major implications for a promotional strategy.

It is this type of detailed assessment that helps companies determine the degree of competitive advantage they may possess and to determine the most appropriate method of market entry. Using consistent frameworks also enables the researcher to make cross-country comparisons much more easily.

TABLE 4.1	The 12C framework for analysing international markets

Country
- general country information
- basic SLEPT data
- impact of environmental dimensions

Concentration
- structure of the market segments
- geographical spread

Culture/consumer behaviour
- characteristics of the country
- diversity of cultural groupings
- nature of decision-making
- major influences of purchasing behaviour

Choices
- analysis of supply
- international and external competition
- characteristics of competitors
- import analysis
- competitive strengths and weaknesses

Consumption
- demand and end use analysis of economic sectors that use the product
- market share by demand sector
- growth patterns of sectors
- evaluation of the threat of substitute products

Contractual obligations
- business practices
- insurance
- legal obligations

Commitment
- access to market
- trade incentives and barriers
- custom tariffs

Channels
- purchasing behaviour
- capabilities of intermediaries
- coverage of distribution costs
- physical distribution
- infrastructure
- size and grade of products purchased

Communication
- promotion
- media infrastructure and availability
- which marketing approaches are effective
- cost of promotion
- common selling practices
- media information

Capacity to pay
- pricing
- extrapolation of pricing to examine trends
- culture of pricing
- conditions of payment
- insurance terms

Currency
- stability
- restrictions
- exchange controls

Caveats
- factors to beware of

Sources of information

In building an MIS, companies would utilise a variety of information services and sources. The starting point for most international researchers in the UK is Trade Partners UK. This government department provides a variety of information services. The majority of Western nations have similar government-sponsored organisations helping exporters to develop information on international markets.

Some reports have been critical of the deficiencies in the provision of market intelligence by government departments and of firms' abilities to use this information, the main criticisms being:

- information is non-specific to particular industries
- firms experience problems with the bureaucratic nature of some government services
- data is often in a form which is unsuitable for the company's needs, or too general to be of use
- services have been available only in the capital city
- inadequate publicity about the information and services available.

Other institutions that offer advice and information to companies researching international markets include:

- business libraries
- university libraries
- international chambers of commerce
- International Market Intelligence Centre (Trade Partners UK)
- business links
- embassies
- banks
- trade associations
- export councils
- overseas distributors
- overseas sales subsidiaries
- foreign brokerage houses

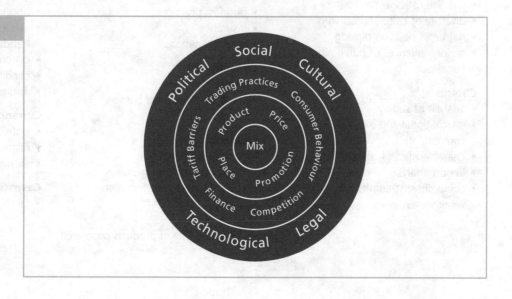

FIGURE 4.4

Market profile analysis

■ foreign trade organisations such as JETRO (Japanese Export Trade and Research Organisation).

Online databases

One of the main developments in international secondary information over the past five years has been the emergence of a plethora of Internet sites, online and CD ROM databases as well as company customer response management (CRM) databases. Nokia's analysis of its own CRM database allowed it to identify that their customers viewed phones as fashion accessories. This enabled Nokia to reposition themselves and steal global market share from Ericsson.

Online databases are systems which hold computerised information which can be accessed through the Internet, allowing a wide range of information to be available from an online database to a manager in a matter of seconds. Information can be transmitted from anywhere in the world instantaneously, bringing obvious benefits.

There are numerous advantages of using online databases. The databases are regularly updated – two or three times per day – and are therefore much more current than traditional printed sources. Retrieving information online is much more cost effective than manual searching and is considerably faster. Many online databases can be accessed 24 hours a day, seven days a week. You also retrieve and consequently pay for only the information you want.

Table 4.2 gives examples of some of the online databases that managers researching international markets may find useful.

TABLE 4.2	Online databases
Company Information	
Duns European Marketing Database:	1.8 million companies in 16 countries
European Kompass:	320,000 companies
Datastream:	Financial data on companies worldwide
Extel:	Worldwide company information
McCarthys:	Articles on companies/industries
Predicast:	Worldwide business and industry information
Trade Data	
Textline:	Reuters
Comtrade:	UN Foreign trade database
Tradstrat:	Import/export on 22 countries
Croners:	Wide range of data on EC/USA/JAPAN
Eurostar – context:	EU statistical data
IMF/World Bank/UN:	World trade statistics
Market Information	
Business International:	Market forecasts worldwide
Euro Monitor:	Covers market reports on 100 consumer markets in Europe and USA
Profound/MAID:	Full text market research reports
Informat:	Abstracts from 500 newspapers and trade journals
PTS Prompt:	Abstracts/articles from 1500 trade journals
Mintel:	Market reports

Organisations in developing countries are increasingly using online computerised databases for their market research work as more of these countries become equipped with telecommunication facilities. The type and volume of trade information available through online databases has expanded dramatically over recent years, with new databases of interest to business and trade organisations continuously being introduced to the market.

The use of the Internet for marketing intelligence, therefore, is one of the most important ways in which connectivity can improve a firm's ability to develop international markets. Buying or commissioning market research reports can be a prohibitively expensive business. For a fraction of the cost and in many cases free of charge, much of the same information can be gathered from the **World Wide Web** (WWW). The volume of relevant international marketing information available on the Web is too extensive to describe in detail in this chapter but includes numerous online newspapers and journals, an extensive list of individual country and industry market research reports, trade lists of suppliers, agents, distributors and government contacts in a large number of countries, details on host country legislation covering imports, agency agreements, joint ventures, etc.

Some of the best sites for undertaking general country screening and international marketing research include:

- Brand data: www.brandchannel.com; www.gbrands.com; www.globalstrategies.com
- Business Week: www.businessweek.com
- CIA: www.ciafactbook.com
- Economist: www.economist.com
- European Union: www.europa.eu.int
- International Business Resources: www.ciber.bus
- Trade Partners UK: www.tradepartners.gov.uk
- UK chambers of Commerce: www.britishchambers.org.uk
- UK government: www.gov/foreign-trade

DILEMMA 4.3   How to research the Canadian Market

The account manager of a small food manufacturer in Groningen, the Netherlands, was keen to expand the business in Canada. The company has 50 employees and manufactures a traditional Dutch ready-meal dish. The account manager was convinced from her knowledge of the marketplace that there were huge opportunities in Canada. Canada and the Netherlands had a strong relationship with a larger number of Dutch expatriates residing in Canada; English and French were the key 'second languages' for the account manager and her fellow employees. She had also read in a European Food Association newsletter that a UK manufacturer of a UK traditional dish, 'bangers and mash', had entered the Canadian market and used it as a springboard into the US. As a small company the board of directors were reluctant to invest in overseas markets without the possibility of substantial return; the home market had

declined and resources to invest were precious. Having persuaded the board to consider exporting, another member of the board felt that testing a market with closer proximity to the Netherlands such as Germany would be cheaper and easier.

The account manager had four weeks to provide a business case for Canada.

Question Without visiting the marketplace and no budget to purchase market information, how could the account manager identify sufficient evidence in such a short period of time to substantiate her proposal to invest in Canada?

Source: Alexandra Anderson

- US Government: www.Stat-usa.gov; www.dataweb.usitc.gov; www.exportusa.gov
- United Nations: www.un.org
- World Bank: www.worldbank.com
- World Fact Book: www.bartleby.com
- World Trade Organisation: www.wto.org

These are just a few examples of the large number of Web sites which provide access to sources of international trade and marketing data as well as other useful services.

Problems in using secondary data

In carrying out marketing research internationally, problems arise by virtue of the very nature of the number and complexities of the markets being investigated. Whilst the use of **secondary data** is essential in international marketing research, the reader needs to be aware of its limitations and some of the problems that occur in using secondary data.

Perhaps the most frequently discussed issue is the availability and accessibility of quality secondary information in international markets. The collection of secondary data concerning the economy and the business infrastructure in some countries is still new and, even if the data is available, it may have to be viewed with scepticism. One of the reasons for the distortion of data in some countries is the political considerations of governments.

The International Labour Organisation found the actual unemployment rate in Russia was 10 per cent rather than the officially reported 2 per cent. The Indian government estimates that India's middle class numbers 250 million but, according to a recent survey of consumer patterns conducted by the National Council of Applied Economic Research in Delhi, the Indian middle-class probably totals 100 million at best and there is much stratification amongst them.

However, this problem might be solved by obtaining authentic data from international organisations such as the OECD, EU, World Bank, etc. The inconsistencies which can be found in the classification of various types of data in various countries are also a problem when carrying out any comparative analysis across markets.

Terpstra and Sarathy (2000) say that the most important problem associated with the secondary data, especially in developing countries, is its scarcity. Another problem which can be quite misleading is the timeliness of the collected secondary data. The data might have been collected five or even ten years earlier and never updated and therefore outdated information is often used.

Many countries attempt to attract foreign investment by overstating certain factors that make the economic picture look better. On the other hand, some countries understate certain factors, making the economic situation appear worse in order to attract foreign aid (see Illustration 4.3).

The Asia-Pacific market is an important market and so obtaining reliable information in this region is of crucial importance for many companies. In a recent survey by INSEAD of one thousand managers of European companies operating in the Asia-Pacific region, it was found that only in Japan and Singapore were companies able to easily access data that was viewed as being of a reliable quality. In China, Taiwan and Vietnam, data was not trusted by researchers. Even though Japanese data was relatively accessible, there were still difficulties due to the fact that the information was over-abundant and so it was difficult to select and interpret the relevant data or to give it any practical application.

None of the limitations discussed above should devalue the importance of secondary data in international marketing research. For many smaller companies lacking the resources to carry out primary research in markets which are geographically distant, it may be the only information where there is relative ease of access.

PRIMARY RESEARCH IN INTERNATIONAL MARKETS

We have discussed scanning international markets to identify potential market opportunities and the building of market information systems from which the market profile analysis is formulated. So far we have only discussed obtaining information from secondary sources. It is unlikely that a researcher will be able to obtain the information for input into a marketing information system from secondary sources alone. After exhausting these sources the researcher will need to embark on the collecting of primary data to obtain the information required.

In the following sections we will discuss the issues facing the researcher which should be considered when endeavouring to carry out primary research studies. To do this we use the seven-step framework (Malhotra *et al*. 1997) as depicted in Figure 4.5.

Problem definition and establishing objectives

The precise definition of the marketing research problem is more difficult and more important in international marketing research than in domestic marketing research. Unfamiliarity with the cultures and environmental factors of the coun-

---

ILLUSTRATION 4.3   **Statistics in Siberia**

Amidst a growing concern for the environment and the introduction of both domestic and international legislation and guidelines for the permissible levels of pollutants and emissions, the emerging Eastern European states in the 1990s were desperately trying to find new markets for their surplus production to generate the wealth required to rebuild economies. No more so than in Western Siberia, where the old Soviet practice of grouping together key industries into geographic zones created a large number of mono-industry towns, primarily dependent upon coal mining and chemical production.

Conscious of the need to remove any possible barriers to international trade and in response to Western pressure, chemical plants were tasked with reducing pollutant emissions. Acceptable levels were agreed and companies were instructed to regularly monitor and report emission levels. Fines were imposed for any transgression.

The local administration (government) had responsibility for monitoring, control and checking, and so recorded and reported the local companies' compliance with the agreements made. This information was made publicly available.

Official data on emissions in 2001 revealed that rates were improving, but still 10 per cent above agreed levels. However, the official figures ignored a number of important points. First, few companies had monitoring equipment that worked, and so estimated their emission levels. Secondly, the administration had no monitoring equipment at all and so accepted the returns without question. Finally, no fines were ever imposed. The economy was in such a poor state, it was thought no one could afford to pay them anyway.

Thus whilst official data painted a picture of progress, the real picture was far different.

Question   Fully evaluate the problem of using secondary data such as this in international markets.

Source: Andy Cropper

tries where the research is being conducted can greatly increase the difficulty of attaining accurate findings.

On a practical level, the differences in climate and infrastructure create problems. A survey on floor-cleaning products across Europe would have to take account of the fact that Scandinavians have wooden floors, there are lots of tiled and stone floors in the Mediterranean and in the UK many houses have carpets.

Many international marketing efforts fail not because research was not conducted but because the issue of comparability was not adequately addressed in defining the marketing research problem. This is why, as we saw in Chapter 3, it is so important to isolate the impact of self-reference criteria (SRC) and the unconscious reference to our own cultural values when defining the problem we are attempting to research in international markets.

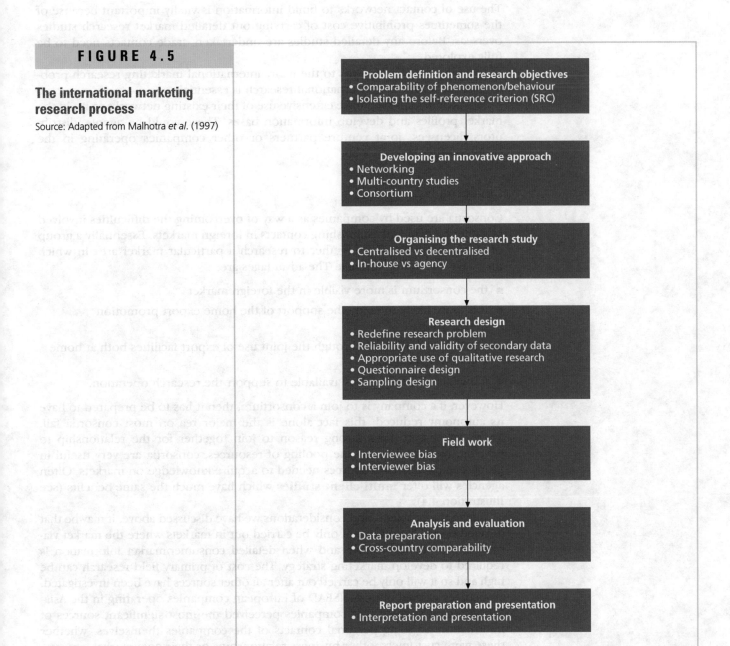

FIGURE 4.5

The international marketing research process

Source: Adapted from Malhotra *et al.* (1997)

Problem definition and research objectives
- Comparability of phenomenon/behaviour
- Isolating the self-reference criterion (SRC)

Developing an innovative approach
- Networking
- Multi-country studies
- Consortium

Organising the research study
- Centralised vs decentralised
- In-house vs agency

Research design
- Redefine research problem
- Reliability and validity of secondary data
- Appropriate use of qualitative research
- Questionnaire design
- Sampling design

Field work
- Interviewee bias
- Interviewer bias

Analysis and evaluation
- Data preparation
- Cross-country comparability

Report preparation and presentation
- Interpretation and presentation

Developing an innovative approach

It is important in international marketing research to maintain flexibility in the approach you may have in the initial stages of the research. In the first stage of primary research, companies often use informal means to gather preliminary information and extensive use is made of the network of contacts available to the company both at home and abroad. It is unlikely that a full understanding of the foreign market will be obtained without visiting that market to gain information first hand. The first steps in doing this would be by networking and obtaining information through relatively informal means such as networking consortia or multi-country studies.

Networking

The use of contact networks to build information is vitally important because of the sometimes prohibitive cost of carrying out detailed market research studies overseas. Before any detailed studies are undertaken, trade contacts need to be fully explored.

In order to find solutions to the many international marketing research problems, improvisation in international research is essential.

Most companies will make extensive use of their existing networks to build the market profiles and develop information bases. These could be agents, distributors, licensees, joint venture partners or other companies operating in the country under investigation.

Consortia

Consortia are used by companies as a way of overcoming the difficulties involved in gathering data and establishing contacts in foreign markets. Essentially a group of companies will come together to research a particular market area in which they have a common interest. The advantages are:

- the consortium is more visible in the foreign market
- it is more likely to enjoy the support of the home export promotion organisation
- it achieves economies through the joint use of export facilities both at home and in foreign markets
- it increases the resources available to support the research operation.

However, if a company is to join a consortium, then it has to be prepared to have its autonomy reduced; this fact alone is the major reason most consortia fail. There also has to be a strong reason to join together for the relationship to develop. Nevertheless, by the pooling of resources, consortia are very useful in giving companies the resources needed to acquire knowledge on markets. Often agencies will offer **multi-client studies** which have much the same benefits (see Illustration 4.4)

Due to the problems and considerations we have discussed above, it may be that detailed research studies will only be carried out in markets where the market viability is seen to be positive and when detailed consumer/market information is required to develop marketing strategy. The cost of primary field research can be high and so it will only be carried out after all other sources have been investigated.

A survey carried out by INSEAD of European companies operating in the Asia-Pacific region showed that companies perceived the most significant sources of information as being personal contacts of the companies themselves, whether these were customers, other business relationships or their own market surveys.

A second tier of usefulness was then identified as consisting of other direct sources such as government contacts and contacts with competitors or trade associations. Finally, there was a third tier comprising publicly available information such as newspapers and magazines. This information may be widely read but relatively little weight seems to be given to its strategic value. The importance of directly collected information seems to confirm the view that business in Asia depends more heavily on the creation of a network of relationships than on analysis of hard data collected through published surveys or other published information.

The collection of primary data

The cost and effort of collecting primary data in new markets is far higher than that of collecting such data in the domestic market. This is particularly the case in developing countries where no marketing research infrastructure or experience is available. Primary research in these circumstances would entail substantial investment costs in developing basic information relating, for example, to sampling frames or trained qualified interviewers. This, of course, reinforces the importance of secondary data for research purposes and the need for a systematic planning process when embarking on a primary research project.

Organising the research study

There are two major organisational questions which the international marketing manager will need to address:

- Should the research be carried out by foreign local subsidiaries or should all marketing research be centralised at headquarters?
- Should the fieldwork be carried out in-house or by an agency?

ILLUSTRATION 4.4   Use of multi-client studies

Multi-client studies have the advantage of enabling the client to participate in large surveys with quite focused questions at a much smaller expense than would be the case otherwise. A significant growth in this type of field research has been seen in the past few years, particularly since the opening up of the Eastern bloc where the practical difficulties in carrying out research are enormous. These studies have specific target audiences in specified countries and offer fast analysis. An example of one is as follows:

The East European Omnibus

Guaranteed:	to run each and every month in the Czech Republic, Slovenia and Hungary 1000 face-to-face interviews per country in respondents' homes.
Genuinely comparable:	no subcontracting, using only qualified field force means absolutely identical methods, procedures and quality controls every time in every country.
High quality:	all interviewer training, supervision, back-checking and other procedures are to the same high standards. True random pre-selected sample.
Fast:	results two weeks after field work.

Other services include: expertly organised focus groups in any part of the region, local telephone centre, hall tests and business research.

Question Identify a number of examples where multi-client studies would be effective in international marketing research.

Centralisation vs decentralisation

If a centralised approach is adopted, then decisions have to be made regarding the specific responsibilities of the operating unit and what managerial arrangements should exist between the unit and headquarters staff. Further to this, decisions have to be taken as to what relationship is to exist between the local research staff who are ultimately responsible to headquarters and the local line management.

If a decentralised approach is chosen, then arrangements have to be made for research findings to be transferred from one operating unit to another. There is also then the question as to who has the overall responsibility for administering and overseeing the market research budget to ensure that resources are not wasted by a possible duplication of research effort.

Such issues are complex and are also related to overall organisational issues which are examined in some depth in Chapter 5. In this chapter we will concentrate our discussion on the decision as to whether the company should carry out international research itself, or should involve independent research agencies.

In-house or agency

Whether the company chooses to do all the research in-house or to use an agency will largely be determined by factors such as company resources, market expertise and product complexity.

If a company operates in a specialist industrial market with highly technological and complex products and has significant experience in the market, it may have no choice but to carry out research itself as it may be difficult to find an agency with the necessary competence.

However, if the company is operating in the consumer field then a different scenario applies. Consumer research may require an established field force and the size of the markets may mean that a research company with field work resources is needed. A priority could well be to obtain an independent objective assessment of a foreign country; this could require specialist interviewing skills which a company alone might not be able to resource and thus would require the services of an agency. If the company is carrying out a **multi-country study** and needs a consistent research approach across all markets, then an international agency with resources across markets may be much more able to handle the research programme. Often, however, research in foreign markets may require a local firm that can do the field work, gather data and provide some analysis and interpretation. The selection and use of a foreign firm may be extremely important to the success of the whole project.

In choosing an agency, a company has six basic options:

- a local agency in the market under investigation
- a domestic agency with overseas offices
- a domestic agency with overseas associate companies
- a domestic agency which subcontracts field work to an agency in the market under investigation
- a domestic agency with competent foreign staff
- a global agency with offices around the world.

Which solution is best for the researcher will depend on a number of factors: the ease of briefing the agency, supervising and coordinating the project, the probability of language problems arising, the requirements of specialist market knowledge, the standard of competence required and the budget available.

Thus no single option is universally the best to select. It is primarily dependent on the budget available, the requirements of the research, the expertise within the company and, of course, the market under investigation. In a research study in Saudi Arabia the UK agency wished to maintain control and coordination of the project. However, Western interviewers would have had little success in eliciting meaningful information from Saudi businessmen. Therefore it was decided to employ a Cypriot field work agency to translate the questionnaire into Arabic and carry out the required field work. This led to communication and certain control problems but was the only realistic methodology to obtain the required information.

It may often be that in a multi-country study a combination of agencies are used. A typical multi-country study will go through the following steps:

1 The project is discussed at length with the client.
2 The field work agencies in each country are selected.
3 The questionnaire is designed centrally.
4 The questionnaire is translated locally and the translation is checked centrally.
5 The questionnaire is piloted locally.
6 The questionnaire is finalised centrally.
7 The inteviewers are briefed locally by an executive of the central company.
8 The field work is carried out locally.
9 The coding and editing plan is provided for the local agencies.
10 The edited and coded questionnaires are returned to head office.
11 A coding and editing check is carried out centrally.
12 Computing and analysis are carried out centrally.

Research design

In formulating a research design, considerable effort is needed to ensure that the methods used will ensure comparability of data. In order to handle problems such as cultural bias in research design and interpretation of data, etc., perspectives of researchers from different countries and cultures could be incorporated in the process so that the bias is minimal. However, this method will only work if there are no major problems of communication between researchers from different environments. If this is not the case, there is a possibility that some other kind of unknown bias might be introduced into the research process which could be even more harmful. Therefore a study of the cultural and social values and the method of conducting research in the host country could play an important role in facilitating the process of international marketing research.

One of the first factors to consider in developing a research design is the reliability and validity of the secondary data used. As we have previously discussed, the accuracy of secondary data varies enormously across countries. This means that the database being used to develop primary research may be inaccurate or highly biased or lack the capability to make multi-country comparisons.

Further to this, the research design needs to incorporate methods which will be feasible in the foreign country markets as well as allowing the international researcher to obtain meaningful and relevant findings.

For example, in India, illiteracy affects 64 per cent of the population outside the main areas, there are hundreds of languages and there can be very real fears that the interviewer is a government inspector in disguise. With such a scenario, a researcher would have problems throughout the research process in establishing the basic sample, designing the questionnaire and applying analytical techniques. However, India also has an affluent and educated middle class that in absolute terms is larger in size than the total population of any Western European country.

Social and cultural factors are one of the most important issues which affect the process of international marketing research. Thus in collecting primary data, the researcher needs to consider the issues facing them in evaluating the possible methods under consideration.

In this context, qualitative research, survey methods, questionnaire design and sampling considerations are particularly important.

Qualitative research

Because the researcher is often unfamiliar with the foreign market to be examined, qualitative research is crucial in international marketing research. In the initial stages, **qualitative research** can provide insights into the problem and help in developing an approach by generating relevant research questions and hypotheses, models and characteristics which influence the research design. Thus, qualitative research may reveal the differences between foreign and domestic markets. It may also help to reduce the psychological distance between the researcher and the respondent. In some cases, the researcher must rely on qualitative research since secondary data may not be available. Some problems associated with qualitative techniques in developing countries are such things as accessibility (different concept of time), sampling (extended demographic factors such as religion and tribal membership), shorter span of attention and less familiarity with abstract thinking.

Focus groups can be used in many settings, particularly in industrialised countries. In some cultures, though, such as in the Middle or Far East, people are hesitant to discuss their feelings in a group setting. In these cases, in-depth interviews can be used.

The use of projective techniques is sometimes appropriate. Association techniques (word association), completion techniques (sentence completion, story completion) and expressive techniques (role playing, third-person technique) involve the use of verbal cues and so are all good cross-cultural research techniques. An interesting example of qualitative research in international markets is given in Illustration 4.5.

Survey methods

There are several issues to consider in evaluating the various interviewing methods available.

Telephone interviewing: in the US, Canada and Europe, the telephone has achieved almost total penetration of households. In most developing nations, however, only a few households have telephones (e.g. many African countries, India, Brazil). Even in countries like Saudi Arabia, where telephone ownership is extensive, telephone directories tend to be incomplete and out of date.

Therefore, telephone interviews are most useful when employed with relatively upscale consumers who are accustomed to business transactions by phone or consumers who can be reached by phone and can express themselves easily. With the decline of costs for international telephone calls, multi-country studies are now often conducted from a single location.

Mail interviewing: because of low cost, mail interviews continue to be used in most developed countries where literacy is high and the postal system is well developed. In Africa, Asia and South America, however, the use of mail surveys and mail panels is low because of illiteracy and the large proportion of population living in rural areas. Mail surveys are, typically, more effective in industrial international marketing research.

No questionnaire administration method is superior in all situations. Table 4.3 presents a comparative evaluation of the major modes of collecting primary data in the context of international marketing research.

Questionnaire design

The questionnaire or research instrument should be adapted to the specific cultural environment and should not be biased in terms of any one culture. This requires careful attention to each step of the questionnaire design process. It is

---

ILLUSTRATION 4.5   The use of qualitative research to overhaul global brand image

Unilever, using a range of qualitative research techniques, such as focus groups, psychological testing and in-depth interviewing, have spent several years investigating the attitude to dirt of their consumers in a number of different cultures.

As a result of their research they have recently re-launched their leading soap powder on the premise that 'dirt is good' – completely contrary to the line soap powders advertisements usually take – that 'dirt is bad'. The advertisements promote the image of children playing on the beach in the sand and ask consumers to think differently about how children get their clothes dirty. They suggest playing isn't about creating dirty clothes but about kids being creative and so the clothes that need washing as a

result of their playing should be a cause of celebration for their mums, not despair.

The Unilever brand in most countries is known as Omo. In the US it is called Wisk, in France, Skip and in the UK, Persil. Unilever plan to launch the campaign across its global markets, starting in Europe, in a bid to reposition the concept of their brand in the eyes of their consumers. If they succeed they may well throw down the gauntlet to their arch rivals Procter and Gamble.

Question Identify the main benefits of using qualitative research when deciding to enter a new international market.

Source: Adapted from *Marketing*, May 2003

TABLE 4.3   A comparative evaluation of survey methods for use in international marketing research

Criteria	Telephone	Personal	Mail
High sample control	+	+	–
Difficulty in locating respondents at home	+	–	+
Inaccessibility of homes	+	–	+
Unavailability of a large pool of trained interviewers	+	–	+
Large population in rural areas	–	+	–
Unavailability of current telephone directory	–	+	–
Unavailability of mailing lists	–	+	–
Low penetration of telephones	–	+	+
Lack of an efficient postal system	+	+	–
Low level of literacy	–	+	–
Face-to-face communication culture	–	+	–

Note: + denotes an advantage: – denotes a disadvantage
Source: Malhotra *et al.* (1997)

important to take into account any differences in underlying consumer behaviour, decision-making processes, psychographics, lifestyles and demographic variables.

The use of unstructured or open-ended questions may be desirable if the researcher lacks knowledge of the possible responses in other cultures. Unstructured questions also reduce cultural bias because they do not impose any response alternatives. However, unstructured questions are more affected by differences in educational levels than structured questions. They should be used with caution in countries with high illiteracy rates.

The questions may have to be translated for administration in different cultures. A set of guidelines has been proposed by Brislin (2001) for writing questionnaires in English so that they can be easily translated. These include:

- use short and simple sentences
- repeat nouns rather than using pronouns
- avoid metaphors
- avoid adverbs and prepositions related to place and time
- avoid possessive forms
- use specific rather than general terms
- avoid vague words
- avoid sentences with two different verbs if the verbs suggest different actions.

The problems of language and translation were discussed in Chapter 3 and equally apply in marketing research. A translation of a questionnaire might be grammatically correct but this does not necessarily mean that it is conveying the appropriate message. For example: value for money is not a common phrase in Spain; the equivalent phrase is 'price for product'. In the Middle East 'payment' is a transactional word; it refers to repaying a debt and so would be inappropriate in the context of purchasing a product.

Another problem is that countries sometimes have more than one official language: a decision has then to be made as to what the most appropriate language is. In Malaysia and Singapore, for instance, consumer surveys regularly employ three languages (English, Malay and Chinese). An interviewer may need a command of several languages or dialects to undertake field work. In Pakistan, the official language is Urdu, but most of the official work in government departments is done in English. However, most local nationals who understand English also usually understand Urdu. There is also a particular segment of social class in the country which prefers English to Urdu in their daily routines. Thus should the researcher use English or Urdu?

The literal translation of a questionnaire can pose problems. A different language is not just a matter of different spellings but of different linguistic concepts. This is why translation agencies recommend back translation into the original language This identifies and corrects many of the problems faced in simple translation. The technique of 'decentring' in translation, where the material is translated and retranslated each time by a different translator, also minimises mistakes being made.

Sample frame

The problems of obtaining valid sampling frames tend to be more complicated in researching international markets. It might be difficult or even impossible to obtain a reliable sampling frame. Due to problems associated with the validity and reliability of secondary data in some countries, experience and judgement need to play an important part in constructing the sample where there is the lack of a reliable database. It may mean that accepted techniques of marketing research in developed countries cannot always be directly transferred even to other developed countries where data might have to be collected through less formalised methods. This applies especially in countries lacking a marketing infrastructure where, unless sufficient care is taken in selecting the sampling frame, the sample chosen will invariably be distorted.

Field work

Interviewee bias

The major problems in field work are errors caused through bias in the interviewing stage of the process which can mean that reliable multi-country studies where results can be compared and contrasted across different countries are sometimes difficult to achieve.

Different cultures will produce a varied response to interviews or questionnaires. For example, purchase intentions for new products frequently peak in Italy because Italians have a propensity to over-claim their likelihood to buy, whereas German results are much closer to reality. If Germans say they will buy a product they probably will.

Another problem is that in some countries it is not possible for the female members of a household to respond personally to a survey. In such countries, mail questionnaires for researching the female market might obtain a much better rate of response.

In some countries the rate of response of a particular segment of society might be quite low due to tax evasion problems, respondents being unwilling to provide any information which gives an idea of their economic status (Terpstra and Sarathy 2000). Even within the same country, different social classes of customers could have differing responses to marketing research techniques. In some cultures the respondent may cause bias by attempting to please the interviewer and give the answers they think they want to hear. This happened to BSN in Japan. The French conglomerate carried out a study in Japan to find out people's attitudes to yogurt. The results indicated that the Japanese were becoming much more Westernised in their food and eating habits and that there was a potential market for yogurts. BSN launched their products, set up distribution and invested heavily in promotion. However, the sales were disappointing. Follow-up research showed that the questions used in the original research were too simplistic to elicit accurate responses. The Japanese were far too polite to reply NO to a question. Therefore the responses to yes/no questions were highly misleading. Likewise, they did not wish to offend Westerners by criticising the usage of a spoon as an eating implement.

Interviewer bias

Interviewer biases are often due to communication problems between the interviewer and respondents. Several biases have been identified in multi-cultural research, including rudeness bias, 'I can answer any question' bias, courtesy bias, sucker bias, hidden premises bias, reticence–loquaciousness bias, social desirability, status difference bias, racial difference bias and individual group opinion bias (Malhotra *et al.*, 1997).

Extensive training and close supervision of the interviewers and other field staff may be required to minimise these biases.

The selection, training, supervision and evaluation of field workers are critical in multi-country research. Local field work agencies are unavailable in many countries. It may be necessary therefore to recruit and train local field workers or import trained foreign workers. The use of local field workers is desirable as they are familiar with the local language and culture. They can thus create an appropriate climate for the interview and be sensitive to the concerns of the respondents.

Data analysis

A number of issues need to be considered at the data analysis stage. First, in preparing data for analysis in multi-country or cross-cultural studies, how do you deal with 'outliers'? These are countries where the data is quite obviously different from the bulk of the data. It may not be a problem at all but, likewise, it could be due to some cultural bias, a problem in the sampling or a problem of translation in the questionnaire.

Second, the issue of how to ensure comparability of data across cultures. Some researchers prefer to standardise data to ensure comparability. In contrast, others prefer statistics based on unstandardised data on the basis that this allows a truer comparative analysis.

Report preparation and presentation

In any research study there is the chance of cultural bias in the research findings. International research often involves researchers from one cultural environment conducting research in another cultural environment or communicating with researchers from another cultural environment. In international research situations, effective communication between the respondents and the researcher is essential to avoid problems of misinterpretation of the data. The phenomenon of cultural self-reference criteria is cited as a possible cause of the misinterpretation of data and can lead to a quite systematic bias in the findings. The reader is referred to the discussion in Chapter 3 and the discussion on the steps that can be taken to remedy self-reference criteria.

Some agencies follow the practice of always ensuring foreign market studies are written in the local language and include interpretation as well as analysis. The nuance can then be discussed with the translator.

Face-to-face debriefings with agencies and researchers are also a good way to synthesise the results from multi-country surveys and form coherent conclusions through open discussions with representatives who have participated in the research across a range of countries.

Continuous research

In this chapter, in order to discuss the relevant issues in a logical manner, we have used the six-step research design framework. It is perhaps important to stress, however, that international market research, whilst expensive, is by no means a 'one-off' activity. In today's dynamic environment where changes occur almost on a daily basis in some rapidly growing markets (e.g. China), it is important that research be on a continuous basis to ensure a company keeps ahead of its competition.

SUMMARY

- In this chapter we have examined the three main roles of the international marketing researcher, scanning international markets, building up market profiles and carrying out primary research across global markets.

- The issues that are raised in identifying and analysing opportunities across the globe have been discussed.

- Segmentation provides the basis for exploiting opportunities. Several models used in the segmentation process of international markets have been presented.

- In examining the international marketing research process the six-step research design framework has been used and at each stage the relevant issues for the international marketer highlighted.

- Within this chapter, we have illustrated the strategic importance of opportunity analysis and the contribution that the information system and market research can make to the decision-making process.

- International research is, in many cases, a complex, expensive and time-consuming task and evidence suggests that for these reasons many international firms fail to research markets to the extent that is really necessary.

- The consequences of this are significant in terms of both missed opportunities and the failure to meet existing and developing market demand.

KEYWORDS

comparative research
cross-cultural research
differentiated marketing
existing markets
global segments
incipient markets
latent markets
marketing information system
marketing research
market profile analysis
market segmentation

multi-client studies
multi-country studies
online databases
Pareto law
primary data
qualitative research
research process
secondary data
transnational segmentation
World Wide Web

CASE STUDY   The Day Chocolate Company

In 1998 Kuapa Kokoo, a cooperative of small-scale cocoa farmers in Ghana, voted at their AGM to set up The Day Chocolate Company. The NGO Twin Trading, along with The Body Shop, were also involved in creating the new company and, together with Kuapa Kokoo, share its ownership, with Kuapa owning 33 per cent of the shares. In a unique step, The Department for International Development guaranteed a bank loan.

The Day Chocolate Company buys all its cocoa at Fairtrade prices which means the farmers receive a guaranteed minimum price of US$1600 per tonne of cocoa, plus a social premium of US$150 per tonne which they invest in farm and community development projects. Day Chocolate's products, under the two brand names Divine and Dubble, can therefore carry the Fairtrade Mark licensed by the international Fairtrade Labelling Organisation's (FLO) representative body in the UK, the Fairtrade Foundation.

The Day Chocolate Company started out with the mission to bring Fairtrade chocolate to the mainstream UK market. Their milk chocolate recipe was developed with UK tastes in mind, and both Divine and Dubble were created to a quality standard and, with the innovative marketing support, designed to compete with major brands. Prices also matched those of equivalent products already available on the market.

Armed with a delicious product and a compelling story, and the clout of supporting charities Comic Relief and Christian Aid, Day Chocolate has succeeded in getting both Divine and Dubble listed in all the top UK supermarkets, as well as many independents. They also supply chocolate for own label products in the Co-op and Starbucks in the UK. The company now also has the USA and other countries in their sights.

Source: The Day Chocolate Company

Target market and ethical consumer

The past five years have seen an increasing number of people start to question the provenance of the foods they buy, and the integrity of the companies who make them. These 'Concerned Consumers' make an ideal target for Fairtrade. Consumer numbers aware of and open to the concept of Fairtrade products have grown steadily over the ten years since they were first introduced in the UK. A third of all UK consumers now recognise the Fairtrade Mark, and the fact that Day Chocolate's turnover has doubled in the past year is testament to the fact that consumers are turning their concerns into action.

The Worldwatch Institute (www.oneworld.org) suggests that consumers are becoming much more informed through information on product labels – examining lists of ingredients and sources as well as endorsements by environmentally aware organisations. Various Web sites to inform consumers of where there are ethical choices to be made are also springing up, encouraging more and more consumers to choose the 'ethical' alternative. Retailers in turn are becoming more ethically aware. The Co-op is leading the way in championing Fairtrade products, and other companies such as Starbucks are looking to where they can improve their ethical credentials, particularly in their supply chain.

The Day Chocolate Company now has two successful brands, established due to their product excellence and the resonance of the Fairtrade message with today's consumer. How do they now keep those brands growing alongside the market leaders, bearing in mind their restricted resources? How do they communicate brands' success, while addressing the potential conflict in the consumer's mind between commercial success and worthy values? How do they take the message to new countries and new cultures with very different consumer behaviour and attitudes?

Questions

1 Advise The Day Chocolate Company as to how they should collect the necessary information on which they can build a global marketing plan.

2 On what basis should Divine segment the global markets if their segmentation strategy is to form a basis for a global marketing plan?

3 What suggestions would you make to The Day Chocolate Company to help them develop internationally?

Jeanette Baker, Sheffield Hallam University
Source: Adapted from www.divinechocolate.com

DISCUSSION QUESTIONS

1 What are the dangers of translating questionnaires that have been designed and used in one country for use in multi-country studies? How would you avoid these dangers?

2 Many companies are looking to emerging markets in their internationalisation programmes. What are the problems in researching these markets? How, if at all, may they be overcome?

3 Identify the principal methods that companies might use in assessing and reviewing opportunities across international markets. Suggest the alternative means by which firms can prioritise and segment international markets.

4 As firms become more global so does their requirement to gather global information. Outline the key categories of a global information system and explain their relevance.

5 Citing specific examples, show how researching the Web can help international marketers. What are the problems and limitations of using Web-based sources.

REFERENCES

Brislin, R.W. (2001) *Understanding Cultures Influence on Behaviour*, 2nd edn, Harcourt.

Czinkota, M.R. and Ronkainen, I.A. (2002) *International Marketing*, Harcourt.

Douglas, C. (1999) *International Marketing Research*, 2nd edn, Prentice Hall.

Gilligan, C. and Hird, M. (1985) *International Marketing*, Routledge.

Gorton, K. and Doole, I. (1989) *Low Cost Marketing Research*, John Wiley.

Hamill, J. and Stevenson, J. (2002) 'Internet Forum', *International Marketing Review*, 19 (5): 545.

Hammersveld, M.V. (1989) 'Marketing Research, Local, Multi-Domestic or International?', *Marketing and Research Today*, 17.

Harrell, G.D. and Keifer, R.D. (1993) 'Multinational Market Portfolio in Global Strategy Development', *International Marketing Review*, 10 (1).

Johannson, J. (1972) *Exportstrategiska problem*, Stockholm Press.

Kale, S.H. and Sudharshan, D.A. (1987) 'A Strategic Approach to International Segmentation', *International Marketing Review*, Summer.

Malhotra, N.K., Agrawal, J. and Peterson, M. (1997) 'Methodological Issues in Cross Cultural Marketing Research', *International Marketing Review*, 13 (6): 7–43.

Paliwoda, S. and Thomas, M.J. (1998) *International Marketing*, 3rd edn, Butterworth Heinemann.

Terpstra, V. and Sarathy, R. (2000) *International Marketing*, 8th edn, Dryden Press.

Walters, P.G.P. (1997) 'Global Market Segmentation: Methodologies and Challenges', *Journal of Marketing Management*, 13: 165–77.

INTEGRATIVE LEARNING ACTIVITIES

An introduction

Successful international marketing is about taking a planned approach to analysis, strategy development and implementation. The chapters of this book focus upon providing the underpinning knowledge to support the process of planning an international marketing strategy. The purpose of the three integrated learning activities at the end of each of the three parts of the book is to integrate the four chapters that make up each of the parts. More importantly, however, is that as a whole, the three activities provide a framework for planning an international marketing strategy and give the opportunity for readers to consider the practical issues involved in developing, planning and implementing an outline international marketing strategy.

Learning objectives

On completing the three integrated learning activities the reader should be able to:

■ Critically analyse the international marketing environment of a given company situation

■ Apply relevant concepts and models to each of the development stages of an international marketing strategy

■ Make clear links between analysis and the chosen response. The issues identified in the analysis should lead directly to the development and implementation of a strategy

■ Develop a realistic and cohesive international marketing strategy

The aims of the integrated learning activities (ILAs) therefore are much wider in scope than the short case studies found at the end of each chapter. The objective is to provide a vehicle through which the reader is able to develop practical skills in research, analysis, evaluation and strategy development. In completing these

activities you will need to synthesise the various strands and themes explored throughout the book and apply them to a practical situation. To complete each of the activities the reader must move well beyond the boundaries of the textbook, researching new material and exploring the interplay of the concepts discussed in the text and possible solutions to the practical problems identified in each activity.

Each ILA depicts very different scenarios.

Part One: Li-Ning is a Chinese entrepreneur taking the first major steps in highly competitive, international markets that are dominated by famous brands, such as Nike and Adidas. How does the small Chinese business identify a global niche through which it could compete against the global players?

Part Two: The beauty industry is a highly competitive, high growth global market incorporating a number of different global players including very strong firms, smaller niche players and some large firms that are under-performing. All the firms face competitive challenges in maintaining their global positions as well as huge potential changes in the global marketing environment. The question is, how should they react to the competitive challenges in developing their future strategic direction?

Part Three: ISS is a Danish-based people management business that is susceptible to differences in expectations between cultures but is, nevertheless, growing very rapidly based on corporate standards and values that are different from the norm in the industry. However, as a service firm, how do they implement their international marketing plan? and how does a service firm establish a consistent image across a number of different international markets?

In each of the activities a series of questions is posed, together with suggestions on how to get started, a framework depicting the key factors to consider in completing the task and suggested Web sites you may find useful.

Additional observations are also made that will assist you in addressing the key issues and how you could develop the activity further.

In all the activities we have provided only outline information on the scenarios. A key skill in international marketing is finding information about international markets, analysing it, deciding what is most important and preparing a structured, logical rationale for the decisions that must ultimately be made. In each activity, therefore, you will need to seek information outside of the case to complete the task. Much of the information you can use is available online. You should not have to approach staff in the organisations depicted for further information to complete the task.

The firm is also ...
tudes to sport ...
from the C...
pared to ...
that ...

INTEGRATIVE LEARNING ACTIVITY

International marketing planning: analysis

Introduction

In this activity we explore the issues facing a Chinese entrepreneur in his efforts to develop a global marketing strategy which will help his company explore the international marketing opportunities identified.

As a medium-sized enterprise he faces issues as to how he should internationalise and how quickly, but perhaps most importantly at this stage he needs to develop a thorough understanding of the complexities of the international marketing environment in which he is competing and decide how to segment the global market, which segment he should target and develop a positioning strategy to achieve competitive leverage. Increasing global competition in this market necessitates greater innovation not just in products and services, but in all aspects of the operation of the firm. To understand such issues we need to build the skills to research, analyse and evaluate how such factors impact international strategy development. It is such skills it is hoped the reader will develop in this activity.

Learning objectives

On completing this activity the reader should be able to:

- Identify and analyse international market opportunities
- Use appropriate conceptual frameworks to develop a trans-national segmentation methodology on which to base a global marketing strategy
- Identify sources of information, methods of information collection and methods of information analysis suitable for international marketing operations
- Understand the complexities of researching international markets and be able to identify possible solutions

Robin Lowe, Sheffield Hallam University

The scenario: Li-Ning

China's best known gymnast, Li-Ning, won three gold medals at the 1984 Olympics but he rather regretted the fact that he was not able to wear Chinese labelled sportswear because the sector was dominated by foreign-owned sports goods. His solution was to set up his own sports goods company, Li-Ning Sports Goods Company. By 2003 the company had grown to become the largest sports goods company in China with a market share of more than 30 per cent, larger than companies such as Nike and Reebok. It now has 1000 employees across China, 10 subsidiaries and 700 licensed stores. The company has production plants and a design centre in Guangdong.

The Chinese market environment

In the 1990s, although China was still at relatively early stages of economic development, the huge market and high growth rates enabled dynamic businesses such as Li-Ning to build strong revenues at home. However, it was not always a smooth ride. In China in the late 1990s the company suffered lower sales due to the restructuring of the State Owned Enterprises (SOE). SOEs had traditionally bought equipment for their own sports teams but had to cut back during the more difficult economic times. Li-Ning made up for this reduction in revenues through international development and has started exporting products into the European market in countries such as Spain, France and Greece.

Since joining the World Trade Organisation many Chinese tariff and other trade barriers have reduced, allowing sports goods companies from the West, such as Nike and Adidas, to compete more strongly in China but Li-Ning has fought back by building its own brand and promoting its products.

...very aware of Chinese customer attitudes. ...Only 15 per cent of people aged 15–35 ...hinese mainland play sport regularly com... 50 per cent in the US. Most Chinese believe ...success in life comes from academic achievement ...nd making money, and they do not care so much about their health. Li-Ning must increase the market size to grow further and to do that it has to change attitudes, and this is part of its advertising campaign, referred to below.

International marketing environment

In developed countries sports goods markets are dominated by competitors with innovative and stylish products, strong brands, and sophisticated marketing and advertising campaigns. Global customers are aware of product endorsement by sports stars, sponsorship deals and advertising programmes on a global basis. Sports goods brands are increasingly becoming fashion brands. Li-Ning has to understand the similarity in the global markets and needs of the global customer segments, but also the subtle differences in purchasing behaviour, product usage and local market structure.

Company expertise and marketing capability

Having taken its first tentative steps in international markets Li-Ning is now starting to build a more sophisticated product offering for its home market. This will provide a better launch pad for a global assault. For example, Li-Ning is improving product design by using European and South Korean designers and launching more innovative products.

Part of Li-Ning's competitive advantage has traditionally been maintaining prices that are low by international standards. By Chinese standards, however, the prices of Li-Ning sports equipment are quite high – sports shoes cost 198–388 yuan and T-shirts 90–200 yuan. However, the firm believes that through brand building activity it will be possible to double the prices of their most expensive products over the next few years. This in turn will help Li-Ning to generate the revenue at home to enable them to compete more effectively in export markets. The question, of course, is whether the market will accept higher prices.

To support its brand building both at home and abroad the firm has begun to promote its products more heavily. In 2003 Li-Ning launched an advertising campaign on Chinese television with an expenditure eight times its previous level, using the mottos 'Goodbye' (to the hard lives of the past) and 'Anything is possible' (the future is filled with unlimited oppor-

tunities), echoing Nike's 'Just do it' campaign. It also began sponsorship deals for teams in France and Russia, even though the firm did not do any international advertising.

The firm is building capability throughout the business. For example, with his business partner, Singapore Internet entrepreneur Danny Toe, Li-Ning has set up two businesses supported by Internet Web sites, Etosports, a sports portal, and Etochannel, a technology platform for sports e-business. These businesses support the sportswear business and will be essential for international development.

Future growth prospects

At the age of 37, Li-Ning is the chief strategist for the business but is modest about the firm's impressive success. Li-Ning is one of a small number of Chinese businesses that could become a global player. To succeed, the firm must build a strong and secure home market as the basis for international expansion. Therefore, it must constantly monitor the Chinese market environment. Sport is increasingly becoming a global business as the case at the end of Chapter 3 shows. Consequently, Li-Ning will have to compete with Nike, Reebok and Adidas in the international market, not only to generate growth, but also to avoid becoming vulnerable in the Chinese market. Li-Ning needs to monitor the international market environment for sports goods, specifically identify a global customer segment that it can serve and understand the purchasing behaviour of those customers.

The 2008 Beijing Olympics offer Li-Ning an exceptional, well-timed opportunity. Given the global television audience for the Olympic Games this offers the firm a unique opportunity to gain visibility amongst a worldwide audience. The Beijing Olympics Preparatory Committee (BOPC) has already begun work and Li-Ning is one of 33 companies that have signed agreements to use the 5 rings logo. The Olympics may well help raise interest in sport in China, too, and expand Li-Ning's local market.

Interestingly, the Olympics may have another beneficial effect by tackling another environmental factor over which Li-Ning has little control. The International Olympic Committee relies on sponsorship for most of its income and Beijing hopes to pay for most, if not all, of the cost of the stadia from sponsorship. But China is the capital of counterfeiting, which could reduce the income from sponsorship and upset the relationship between China and the IOC. It is likely, therefore, that at least in this area the Chinese authorities will tackle counterfeiters more aggressively than ever before. This will assist Li-Ning just as much as Nike and Adidas.

At 37 Li-Ning is probably too old to be the sporting hero of the new generation of Chinese but Li-Ning sports goods could be on the way to becoming the 'cool' brand favourite of a worldwide market segment of sporting youngsters.

Sources: Adapted from various sources, including: *The Straits Times* (Singapore), 31 January 2001, *South China Morning Post*, 29 January 2002, *Advertising Age*, 13 January 2003, and *The Economist*, 2 August 2003.

The task

1 Analyse and evaluate the major environmental influences that will impact on Li-Ning in his attempt to become a global player.

2 Propose and justify an effective segmentation strategy that will form the basis on which Li-Ning can build a global marketing strategy.

3 Choose one particular global segment from question 2. Draw up a market profile analysis for that segment with reference to Li-Ning. This should form the basis on which Li-Ning can enter and develop the global segment you have specified.

4 Make recommendations to Li-Ning on how he should develop the segment identified. In doing so you will need to fully apprise him of the challenges and problems he will face and how you think he should solve these.

Useful Web sites

www.english.li-ning.com.cn
www.1chinastar.com
www.china.org.
www.wto.org
www.globalexchange.org
www.ita.doc.gov/tradestats
www.worldbank.com
www.foreign-trade.com
www.chinaci.net
www.chinasportswear.net
www.made-in-china.com

Getting started

For a company to operate in its own domestic market there are considerable difficulties in understanding and in forecasting the future facing the company. In international markets it is exceedingly difficult to obtain a comprehensive understanding of the relevant market environment. In tackling task 1 it is useful to categorise the elements of the environment into social and cultural, legal, economic, political and technological forces (SLEPT).

In the increasingly global marketplace companies are trying to identify methodologies for segmenting and evaluating international markets that transcend national and cultural boundaries. In task 2 you are asked to develop a segmentation strategy. It is important here to remember that simply segmenting the market on a geographical basis will be too simplistic and not form a basis on which Li-Ning can build a global niche strategy. You will need a hierarchical approach where your segmentation strategy has several steps and can incorporate the multi-dimensional aspects of a global niche segment.

In task 3 we focus on the role of international market analysis. It is important for Li-Ning to develop a systematic method for building a market information system on the international markets the company has prioritised. The 12C framework is a useful tool when developing profiles of international markets. Finally, in task 4 we need to think through the implications of our research and consider the issues the analysis has highlighted that Li-Ning has to consider if he is to succeed in his ambitions. Of particular importance is to consider these issues in the light of possible resources/cultural/management constraints that may face Li-Ning.

In summary, therefore, the framework shown in Figure I provides a guide to the key factors that need to be considered in tackling the task identified.

The way forward

After reading part 2 of the textbook you may wish to return to plan the next stage of Li-Ning's strategy. The most important issue is deciding how quickly the firm should develop internationally and how – country by country, concentrating on a particular segment or seeking global distribution. You should define a strategy that builds upon the firm's competitive advantage, identifying a positioning strategy that meets the needs of the target segment you have chosen. Then you should identify the criteria that will determine the choice of market entry.

After reading part 3 you will be in a position to define the implementation plan and make decisions on the marketing mix elements, relationship building and supply chain management. You can identify how management and technology systems might support the international expansion. Finally, you will be able to identify the monitoring and control systems that will be used.

FIGURE I

Li-Ning: Key factors to consider

The element of the plan	Some concepts, models and issues to be addressed
Environment	• The global SLEPT factors, including political and economic issues and socio/cultural factors affecting the opportunities for the firm • The changing global trends in competition and customer expectations that impact on Li-Ning's business • The international challenges to be met
Home and possible international markets	• The level of market development and competitive structures • Prioritisation of markets using country attractiveness and latent-incipient assessment of markets • Commercial, home, host country stakeholder expectations and ethical issues
Company capability	• SWOT, competitive advantage • Products: international product life cycle, knowledge and capability
Segmentation	• Basis of segmentation/criteria for global segmentation/global niche possibilities • Hierarchy of segmentation
Market information	• Market profile analysis and the information systems, data collection and management to support it • Market and environmental risk and potential commercial opportunity using the 12C framework
Strategic options	• Potential strategic alternatives for Li-Ning • The challenges faced and potential responses to the issues identified in the analysis. • The resource constraints of Li-Ning

STRATEGY DEVELOPMENT

5 International niche marketing strategies for small and medium-sized enterprises (SMEs)

6 Global strategies

7 Market entry strategies

8 International product and service management

Introduction

Having identified and analysed the opportunities that exist within international markets in the first section of the book, we now turn our attention to the ways in which firms can use international marketing to develop their international business in order to exploit these opportunities profitably. The focus in Part 2 is on developing an international marketing strategy that is appropriate for the firm, given the environment and market context in which it is working, the firm's capability, and the ambition of its management. Throughout the section are a number of themes, including the need for the management of the firm to plan their international marketing and take decisive action to deal with the challenges that are posed.

The first chapter in Part 2, Chapter 5, concentrates on the international marketing strategies of small and medium-sized enterprises and deals with firms taking their first steps in international markets or marketing to international customers from their home base through to those dynamic small firms that have the ambition and capability to grow fast to become the major global players of the future.

When we think of globalisation it is the very largest firms in the world that come to mind. Chapter 6 is concerned with the global strategies of the firms that operate within a global context and build brands that are instantly recognisable. Their global strategies aim to appeal to worldwide customers and ensure that as many customers as possible choose the products and services.

For any firm moving into a new international market the key step is to decide which market entry method should be chosen in order to achieve the best outcome from the investment that is made. In Chapter 7 we discuss the factors that firms must consider in selecting an appropriate market entry method.

In Chapter 8 we consider the product and service management strategy and focus upon the need to have a portfolio of products and services that meet the current and future needs of global customers.

INTERNATIONAL NICHE MARKETING STRATEGIES FOR SMALL AND MEDIUM-SIZED ENTERPRISES (SMEs)

Introduction

Small and medium sized enterprises (SMEs) have always been significant creators of wealth and employment in domestic economies, but are a less powerful force outside their home territory usually because of their limited resources. Indeed, many SMEs, despite what may be obvious business capability, never move into international markets at all. However, for reasons which will be explored in this chapter SMEs have growth potential, both in fast-growing business sectors that involve applying new technology and in market niches, where innovation in mature industry sectors can lead to new opportunities.

In this chapter we discuss the factors which influence the patterns of international development of small and medium-sized firms, including the strategic options available to them, and the particular problems they face in implementing their strategy.

The traditional model of SME internationalisation is exporting, in which goods are manufactured in one country and transferred to buyers in other countries, but many SMEs are involved in a broader range of international marketing activity and it is for this reason we prefer the term niche marketing. For example, small service providers generate revenue from customers in foreign markets either by providing services from the home country which customers can access wherever they are situated (for example, information and advice supplied via the Internet) or by providing services in the firm's home country, and requiring the customers to visit (for example, tourism, training and education residential courses). To be successful, however, all these approaches require an understanding of the various dimensions of international marketing.

Learning objectives

After reading this chapter you should be able to:

- Appreciate the nature and the types of international marketing undertaken in the SME sector
- Compare the different strategic approaches to international marketing adopted by SMEs
- Understand the factors affecting SME international strategic management

- Identify the characteristics of the different stages of international development of SMEs
- Be able to evaluate the factors for success and failure in SME international marketing

THE SME SECTOR AND ITS ROLE WITHIN THE GLOBAL ECONOMY

A number of definitions of the small and medium-sized firm sector exist but the most commonly used terms relate to the number of employees in the company. The European Union, for example, has recently changed its definition of SMEs from those firms employing less than 500 staff to those employing less than 250. This characterisation, however, effectively includes 99 per cent of all firms in Europe and accounts for roughly 50 per cent of employment and, because it includes sole operators as well as quite sophisticated businesses, is not particularly useful for segmenting the smaller firms sector.

In this chapter, therefore, the review of smaller firm strategies is not restricted to firms with a specific number of employees but also includes issues which apply to businesses in general which think and act like small and medium-sized enterprises. The reason for adopting this stance is that a garment-making firm with 250 employees has a very restricted capacity to internationalise, whereas a 250 employee financial services or computer software company could be a significant international player. Many quite large businesses take business decisions within the family group in much the same way that small firms take decisions. Moreover, many of the fastest-growing international firms very rapidly grow through the 250 employee ceiling without making significant changes to their international strategic approach. The discussion instead relates to issues affecting firms which could not in any way be described as large MNEs with real global power.

Of the huge number of SMEs only a small percentage, perhaps less than 5 per cent, grow significantly but many of them are likely to be exporters. Indeed, Austrade, the Australian government trade department suggests that successful exporting activity is a major predictor of growth in Australian SMEs. In Pakistan (see Dilemma 5.2) SMEs contribute 40 per cent towards GDP and 50 per cent towards export earnings. However in a study of the 100 fastest-growing firms in the UK, Oldfield (1997) reports that more than half do not export at all, less than 15 per cent achieve half their sales from exports and six of the top ten do not export at all.

The SME sector is becoming more important as a creator of wealth and employment because large firms down-sized during the 1990s by reducing their workforce, rationalised their operations and have concentrated on increasingly out-sourcing their non-core components, often to smaller firms. Employment in the public sector has been decreasing during this same period due to the extensive privatisation of public sector owned utilities and agencies, such as gas, electricity, water and telephones, and the increased volume of public sector services, such as cleaning and catering which have been contracted out to private organisations. In many countries this has left the small and medium-sized firms sector as the only significant growing source of wealth and employment. However, SMEs that market their products and services in the domestic economy often grow at the expense of other domestic SMEs because of the relatively limited home market, whereas export markets offer seemingly unlimited scope for SMEs to grow.

As we have seen in the previous chapters the international marketing environment is potentially very hostile. It is a small wonder, therefore, that many companies ignore the export potential of the products and services and concentrate instead on their domestic markets. But although many firms view international markets with trepidation, others still make their decision to go international.

THE NATURE OF INTERNATIONAL MARKETING IN SMEs

In exploiting these opportunities to generate revenue from international markets SMEs have a number of alternative strategies which provide a useful method of categorisation of SME internationalisation.

- **Exporting** is primarily concerned with selling domestically developed and produced goods and services abroad.
- **International niche marketing** is concerned with marketing a differentiated product or service overseas, usually to a single customer segment, using the full range of market entry and marketing mix options available.
- **Domestically delivered or developed niche services** can be marketed or delivered internationally to potential visitors.
- **Direct marketing including electronic commerce** allows firms to market products and services globally from a domestic location.
- **Participation in the international supply chain** of an MNE can lead to SMEs piggybacking on the MNE's international development. This may involve either domestic production or establishing a facility close to where the MNE's new locations are established in other countries.

Exporting

For many firms exporting is the first significant stage in the internationalisation process as it provides the advantage of considerably expanded market potential with relatively little commitment and limited associated risk. Czinkota (1994) suggests that exporting is essentially marketing expansion and is akin to looking for new customers in the next town, next state or on another coast. Exporting, when defined as the marketing of goods and/or services across national and political boundaries, is not solely the preserve of small and medium-sized businesses, nor for many firms is it a temporary stage in the process of internationalisation. Many firms, both large and small, do not progress beyond the stage of relatively limited involvement in international markets.

Motivation

A number of writers have studied the major **motivations** for beginning exporting but Katsikeas (1996) notes that the vast majority of this research surveyed firms in the US. Given that considerable differences exist between countries Katsikeas suggests that generalisations can be misleading. Moreover, the firm's motivation in its ongoing marketing activities may differ from its initial international involvement.

The research draws the important distinction between whether the motivations to export are principally reactive stimuli or proactive stimuli. Two examples of reactive strategies are as follows: if a product has reached maturity or is in decline in the home market, the company may find new foreign markets where the product has not reached the same stage and which therefore offer potential for further growth. Companies may seek new markets abroad to utilise their production facilities to their full capacity. In these circumstances companies may well embark on marginal pricing and sell at lower prices on the export markets, seeking only a contribution to their overall cost for their home base market.

Katsikeas identifies the following reactive stimuli:

- adverse domestic market conditions
- an opportunity to reduce inventories
- the availability of production capacity
- favourable currency movements
- the opportunity to increase the number of country markets and reduce the market-related risk
- unsolicited orders from overseas customers.

Proactive stimuli for exporting include market diversification. If a company sees only limited growth opportunities in the home market for a proven product it may well see market diversification as a means of expansion. This could mean new market segments within a domestic market but it may well mean geographic expansion in foreign markets. Thus companies try to spread risks and reduce their dependence on any one market. Equally the firm may identify market gaps. The proactive company with a well-managed marketing information system may identify foreign market opportunities through its research system. This could, of course, be by undertaking formal structured research or by identifying opportunities through a network of contacts scanning international markets for potential opportunities.

Katsikeas identifies the following proactive stimuli:

- attractive profit and growth opportunities
- the ability to easily modify products for export markets
- public policy programmes for export promotion
- foreign country regulations
- the possession of unique products
- economies resulting from additional orders.

And certain managerial elements including:

- the presence of an export-minded manager
- the opportunity to better utilise management talent and skills
- management beliefs about the value of exporting.

In researching a group of Cypriot exporters, Katsikeas found that both proactive stimuli, including having an export-minded manager, attractive growth and profit opportunities and reactive stimuli, including receiving unsolicited orders, were particularly important.

Illustration 5.1 is a good example of how the disappearance of an apparently secure and reliable market forced Sure Mining (SMP) to develop its export activity rapidly and in so doing reinvent the firm.

Barriers to internationalisation

Many companies with export potential never become involved in international marketing, and a series of export studies have found that it is often a great deal easier to encourage existing exporters to increase their involvement in international markets than to encourage those who are not exporting to begin the process. The reasons given by companies for not exporting are numerous. The biggest **barrier to entry** into export markets is seen to be a fear by these companies that their products are not marketable overseas, and they consequently become preoccupied with the domestic market.

Barker and Kaynack (1992) listed the most important areas which non-exporters identified as barriers to exporting:

- too much red tape
- trade barriers
- transportation difficulties
- lack of trained personnel
- lack of export incentives
- lack of coordinated assistance
- unfavourable conditions overseas
- slow payment by buyers
- lack of competitive products
- payment defaults
- language barriers.

Experienced exporters tend not to highlight issues such as the bureaucracy associated with international markets and trade barriers, which suggests that they have overcome the problems through managerial proactivity, for example, by training staff and seeking expert assistance, so that these potential problem areas can be dealt with.

ILLUSTRATION 5.1   SMP

SMP are manufacturers of hot and cold pressed track components for rail systems. In the 1980s, British Coal was SMP's principal customer accounting for 95 per cent of its turnover. By 1990 the Coal Mine closure programme in the UK had commenced and the company was rapidly losing its traditional customer base. At that time there was a vivid recognition of the fact that if they did not diversify and widen their customer base they would not survive.

SMP saw themselves as principally serving the mining market. In 1990 they reformulated their company structure and developed a marketing strategy to take the company forward. There were two principal components to this strategy: first a redefinition of their market from mining to 'anywhere there is a tunnel'; second a decision was made to develop the export markets.

From a zero base in 1990, exports in 2000 accounted for 50 per cent of their turnover, with plans in place to increase this to 60 per cent by 2005.

The strategy put in place has proved successful for three major reasons. First, the top management have a very clear vision as to the type of company they wish to build. The Managing Director demonstrates a great deal of tenacity and resilience in driving his company forward internationally

and puts enormous energy into ensuring its success. This has often meant fighting internal battles as well as external.

Second, Sure Mining identified quite clearly two target markets where they could effectively compete; industrial suppliers of railways and the construction industry. Being a small company and without experience they then built a series of strategic alliances involving piggyback operations and other types of partnerships to help them exploit the market opportunities identified.

Third, they made an explicit commitment to a quality policy throughout the company. *'Quality processes are very important to us, it is important to show our international customers we have professional procedures in place. It is no good us acting like market traders, engineers don't want that'.*

Following this strategy has enabled the company not only to survive the collapse of their traditional home market but to develop a healthy and diverse customer base in at least a dozen countries which gives a strong foundation for future growth.

Question What are the main reasons for SMP's success in moving from a domestic firm to a successful exporter?

Niche marketing

Having identified the motivations and barriers to exporting it is tempting to conclude that many exporters are characterised by being product oriented – selling abroad the products and services that are successful in the domestic market. Moreover, exporters often seem to throw away their successful domestic marketing strategies in international markets, preferring instead to effectively delegate their marketing to agents and distributors. In doing this they seem to overlook the alternative market entry and marketing mix strategies that are available to them and instead opt for a strategy of least involvement. In many cases this approach may meet the exporting firm's immediate objectives, especially if, for example, they are simply seeking to off-load excess production capacity, but it does not provide them with a sound basis for substantially increasing their international market presence.

By contrast, **international niche marketing** occurs where firms become a strong force in a narrow specialised market of one or two segments across a number of country markets. Illustration 5.2 of Beatson Clark shows how a traditional manufacturing exporter has redefined its business to become a niche marketer.

Brown and McDonald (1994) explain that the segments must be too small or specialised to attract large competitors and true niche marketing does not include small brands or companies that are minor players in a mass market offering undifferentiated products. For the international niche to be successful the product or service must be distinctive (highly differentiated) and be recognised by consumers and other participants in the international supply chain and have clear positioning.

To sustain and develop the niche the firm must:

- have good information about the segment needs;
- have a clear understanding of the important segmentation criteria;
- understand the value of the product niche to the targeted segment(s);
- provide high levels of service;
- carry out small scale innovations;
- seek cost efficiency in the supply chain;
- maintain a separate focus, perhaps, by being content to remain relatively small;
- concentrate on profit rather than market share; and
- evaluate and apply appropriate market entry and marketing mix strategies to build market share in each country in which they wish to become involved.

Illustration 5.3 gives an example of a firm which has identified market opportunities but it emphasises that small firms must be very clear about the success criteria in an export niche market and the limits of their ambition.

There are, therefore, significant differences between the traditional view of exporting and international niche marketing and these are summarised in Figure 5.1.

Niche marketing of domestically delivered services

In the past this category of international marketing has largely been dominated by the travel industry with domestic firms such as hotels, tour operators and leisure attractions generating foreign earnings for the country by attracting visitors. International place marketing of cities, regions and countries, such as

Prague, the wildlife reserves of Botswana and Vietnam is increasingly important for economic success in certain areas. Those responsible for international marketing activity often are part of a very small department within a much larger

---

ILLUSTRATION 5.2 Beatson Clark: Defining a niche in a commodity market

Beatson Clark are manufacturers of glass containers for the pharmaceutical, food and drinks industry. They export to over 100 countries worldwide. The global glass container market is highly competitive and virtually all countries have their large indigenous producers who sell the containers as commodity products. This makes it difficult to compete considering the high costs involved in physically distributing large glass containers to overseas markets.

Beatson Clark have developed a very effective niche market strategy by focusing on low volume small items which are not of great interest to the large producers. Their competitive advantage has been developed internationally by building a highly effective customer service operation servicing customers throughout the world.

The company offer a design service for the small items which is too much hassle for their major competitors. In each market the company builds up close relationships with a number of trusted distributors who operate in the packaging market and have a good customer base. The company keeps in regular contact with all their international partners sometimes contacting to them 10–15 times a day.

They have then built an effective customer service operation to service all customers wherever they are. This is based on three fundamental principles. First, there is an explicit commitment to quality which is shared throughout the company. All prospective customers throughout the world are sent a signed letter from the MD setting out the commitment to quality procedures and there is an explicit process for translating the company's quality policy into departmental goals.

Second, the company has a team who are dedicated to the effective movement of goods throughout the world and take full responsibility for ensuring safe delivery of all orders to their international destinations, which is no easy task in the glass business!

Third, the company place great emphasis on establishing effective monitoring procedures to measure their performance in customer service as well as their financial performance by customer, order, country etc. to ensure at all times they have full control in their international operations.

This has meant the company has been able to build an international strategy which operates on good margins, is relatively low risk and has achieved a steady rate of growth whilst enabling the company to achieve an element of control in the marketplace.

Question How did the firm reduce its vulnerability to international competition in a commodity market?

ILLUSTRATION 5.3 Encouraging SMEs to export in the Philippines

For government trade and industry secretaries, encouraging SMEs to develop and grow and, in particular, export is an important part of the job and they will use many methods to get the message across.

Hosted by DTI secretary Mar Roxas, 'One on One Tayo Kay Mar Roxas' is a radio show, which uses inspiring stories to encourage Filipino business people to turn the crises that affect many of them into international opportunities. The show, however, also highlights some interesting routes to starting a business.

Jovel Ciriano left his job of 5 years with IBM Philippines after his London-based mother kept asking him to send Filipino delicacies to give away to friends. The requests inspired him in 2000 to set up Pinoydelikasi.com, an e-store that sells *danggit*, dried squid and *turrones de casuy* online to countries like Asia, Europe and the US.

Gil Nemono at 29 left a very well-paid job to concentrate on selling fruit juices to the canteen of his MBA classmate in a bank. Starting with just one blender and capital of P5000 (Philippino Peso), he started selling to offices and canteens. Very soon the juice business Nutrilicious was selling P50 million. Whilst concentrating on juice dispensers in canteens, retail outlets and fast food chains (such as Pizza Hut, Max's and Tropical Hut) Nutrilicious are now exporting purees and juices to the US, Canada, South Korea, Japan and Guam.

Question Where do international market opportunities come from for a very small firm?

Source: Adapted from radio show for Pinoy entrepreneurs, *Philippine Daily Enquirer*, 3 March 2003

authority. However, with increased international travel and improved access to worldwide communications a much wider range of services to visiting customers is being offered. Examples include the provision of education, specialised training, medical treatment, sports, cultural and leisure events and specialist retailing, for example, of luxury goods.

Clearly these activities lead to wealth and jobs being generated in the local economy in much the same way as exporting and niche marketing. The international marketing strategy processes and programmes are similar, too, in that the products and services must meet the requirements of international customer segments. Consequently issues of standardisation and adaptation of the marketing mix elements are equally important. The additional challenge is that the benefits obtained from the service provided must be unique and superior, and thus outweigh the benefits to the consumer of locally available services as well as the cost of travel that the customers will incur in the course of their purchase.

In addition to the services designed to be offered to individuals in both consumer or business-to-business markets a whole range of additional services which fall into this category of being domestically delivered are concerned with developing solutions for opportunities or problems identified abroad. These might include technology developments, such as research into new drugs, trial and testing facilities, software development and product and packaging design services. One example of this is NXT which has developed flat panel loudspeakers, ideal for public address systems and home audio use. Rather than make the final product it is licensing its portfolio of technology comprising 100 patents and patent applications to manufacturers, such as NEC, Samsung, Fujitsu and Harman International. Given that 2–3 billion speakers are sold in the world each year a royalty of US$1 per speaker on 1 per cent of the market would generate considerable revenue for NXT.

Importing and reciprocal trading

Importing is clearly the opposite process to international marketing and as such might be seen by governments as 'exporting' jobs and potential wealth. However, the purpose of raising this issue here is to highlight the nature of international trade as it is today. Rarely do supply chains for products and services involve solely domestic production and delivery. More usually 'exporting' and

---

FIGURE 5.1

The difference between exporting and international niche marketing

	Exporting	International marketing
Marketing strategy	Selling production capacity	Meeting customer needs
Financial objective	To amortise overheads	To add value
Segmentation	Usually by country and consumer characteristics	By identifying common international customer benefit
Pricing	Cost based	Market or customer based
Management focus	Efficiency in operations	Meeting market requirements
Distribution	Using existing agents or distributors	Managing the supply chain
Market information	Relying on agent or distributor feedback	Analysing the market situation and customer needs
Customer relationship	Working through intermediaries	Building multiple level relationships

'importing' become inextricably linked and so the challenge becomes one of adding value to imported components and services, no matter from where they are sourced, so that they can then be re-exported in order to effectively and profitably meet the international customers' needs.

Importing activity can also considerably enhance the company's potential to network, leading ultimately, perhaps, to **reciprocal trading** in which, as a result, the supplier might take other products or services in return from the customer.

Direct marketing and electronic commerce

A rapidly growing area of international trading is direct marketing and, in particular, **electronic commerce**. Direct marketing offers the benefits of cutting out other distribution channel members, such as importers, agents, distributors, wholesalers and retailers by using a variety of communications media, including post, telephone, television and networked computers. All these allow borders to be crossed relatively easily and at modest cost without the SME having to face many of the barriers already highlighted in this chapter.

Direct marketing also has a number of disadvantages. Despite the range of media available, communicating can still be problematic and there is always the danger of cultural insensitivity in the communications. If customers speak different languages then it may be necessary for online retailers to have multi-lingual Web sites. This can add cost in setting up and servicing the Web site. The continued growth of the retailer of online ethnic foods, discussed in Illustration 5.3, may depend on selling to international customers who do not speak the home country language. Because of the need to manage large numbers of customers it is necessary to use databases which must be up to date, accurate and be capable of dealing with foreign languages. Even an incorrectly spelt name can be insulting to the recipient.

It is electronic commerce that is expected to grow fastest over the next few years. The Internet provides smaller firms with a shop window to the world without a member of staff needing to leave the office. It can provide the means of obtaining payment, organising and tracking shipment and delivery. For some products and services it can provide the means by which market information can be accumulated and new ideas can be collected, developed and modified by customers and other stakeholders.

Electronic commerce has also led firms to redefine their business and it can also be a business in its own right. For example, many electronic commerce services take the form of information transfer and this forms the basis of the product or service itself, for example specialist advice on personal finance, travel and hobbies.

As well as being a route to market in its own right in the form of direct commerce, the Internet as an interactive marketing information provider will have an increasingly important role in each of the above international niche marketing activities.

Hamill (1997) suggests that e-mail has a number of advantages over more traditional forms of communication, such as telephone, postal and fax, most commonly used by companies. It is more cost-effective over long distances and does not rely on real time presence, which is a particular advantage when different time zones are involved. It is a very reliable and flexible method since graphics, drawings, etc. can be transferred as well as text. Individuals may become more rather than less communicative using e-mail which is best seen as supporting rather than replacing personal, face-to-face relationships. As an increasing number of competitors start to form relationships with international suppliers, partners, agents, etc., using electronic communications, SMEs who are not connected face being shut out of the network.

Internet offers the benefits to SMEs of real time communications across distances, and the levelling of the corporate playing field leading to more rapid internationalisation as well as achieving competitive advantage by:

- creating new opportunities;

- erecting barriers to entry;

- making cost savings from online communications;

- providing online support for inter-firm collaboration, especially in research and development, as an information search and retrieval tool;

- the establishment of company Web sites for marketing and sales promotion; and

- the transmission of any type of data including manuscripts, financial information and CAD/CAM (computer aided design, computer aided manufacture) files.

Quelch and Klein (1996) argue that the Internet revolutionises the dynamics of international commerce and in particular leads to the more rapid internationalisation of SMEs. The World Wide Web reduces the competitive advantages of companies in many industries making it easier for small companies to compete on a worldwide basis. The global advertising costs as a barrier to entry will be significantly reduced as the Web makes it possible to reach a global audience more cheaply. Small companies offering specialised niche products can find the critical mass of customers necessary to succeed through the worldwide reach of the Internet. Overall the authors argue that low cost Internet communications permit firms with limited capital to become global marketers at an early stage in their development. In a survey of Web site and non-Web site owners, Bennett (1997) noted that the Web site owners tended on average to:

- be less experienced at exporting (a quarter had been exporting for less than three years; double the figure for firms without Web sites);

- use fewer foreign agents or other representatives (only 32 per cent of site owners employed foreign representatives compared with 58 per cent for those without Web sites; and

- employ significantly higher proportions of IT-literate staff.

There are some disadvantages, especially the relative ease with which it is possible to become flooded with electronic messages and orders. Whilst this may be manageable for certain products and services where production volumes can be easily increased or decreased, sales feasts and famines can cause havoc where production capacity is less flexible.

As electronic commerce becomes more sophisticated, advanced search engines are being designed to find the 'best deal' rather than identify every single offer. The implications of this are that instead of marketing being essentially passive in electronic commerce, the marketing input required in designing Web sites needs to become increasingly sophisticated in promoting the products, providing interactive product design development and safe payment arrangements. Technical and customer service support and initial customer segmentation and targeting are becoming increasingly important to the delivery of an effective, focused business. Thus, whilst many SMEs see the Internet as a low cost distribution channel, in the future greater competition and more sophisticated versions of electronic commerce may well make it more difficult for SMEs to compete. SMEs frequently face the dilemma of how to cope with powerful competitors.

THE NATURE OF INTERNATIONAL DEVELOPMENT

The internationalisation process differs enormously depending on whether the company first serves the domestic market and later develops into foreign markets (*adaptive exporter*), or is expressly established from its inception to enter foreign markets (**born global**). Adaptive and born global exporters differ in a variety of ways, including their respective market assessment processes, reasons for export involvement, managerial attitudes, and the propensity to take risks. Successful born globals are seen to surmount their distinctive challenges with flexible managerial attitudes and practices. This managerial attitude and behaviour of innate exporters is seen by writers as being more conducive to eventual success than those of adaptive exporters. On the other hand, adaptive exporters that are willing to adapt to change have generally proved to be highly successful in international markets and usually develop enormously in management and company expertise.

Many exporting firms, however, especially in high-technology or industrial markets, may internationalise through their **network** of relationships. Companies in any market establish and develop relationships through interactions in which the parties build mutual trust and knowledge. In the internationalisation process these relationships can be the critical factor as the company becomes involved in relationships that are connected by networks in which active international markets develop as a consequence of the interaction between firms. The firm is engaged in a network of business relationships comprising a number of different firms – customers, customers' customers, competitors, supplementary suppliers, suppliers, distributors, agents and consultants as well as regulatory and other public agencies. In any specific country, different networks can be distinguished. Any or all of these relationships may become the conduit for the internationalisation of a company. In these cases the internationalisation process of a company is more aptly visualised as a series of multilateral cycles rather than a linear process (see Figure 5.2).

Thus the internationalisation process manifests itself by the development of business relationships in other countries:

FIGURE 5.2

The multilateral aspects of the internationalisation process

Source: Johannson and Vahine (1992)

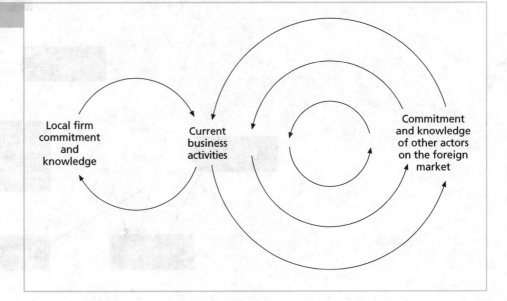

- through the establishment of relationships in country networks that are new to the firm, i.e. international extension;
- through the development of relationships in those networks, i.e. penetration;
- through connecting networks in different countries, i.e. international integration.

Networks are especially important in turbulent, high-technology industries. A study of the internationalisation process of small high-tech firms indicates that some of these companies follow the traditional internationalisation patterns, whilst others behave differently. They go directly to more distant markets and more rapidly set up their own subsidiaries. One reason seems to be that the entrepreneurs behind those companies have networks of colleagues dealing with the new technology. Internationalisation, in these cases, is an exploitation of the advantage this network constitutes.

Geographic development of SMEs

For SMEs, country market selection and development of market share within each country are particularly important for growth. Given their limited resources and narrow margin for failure it is vital that their method of country market development is effective. The various patterns of SME international development are shown in Figure 5.3.

FIGURE 5.3

Geographic development of SMEs

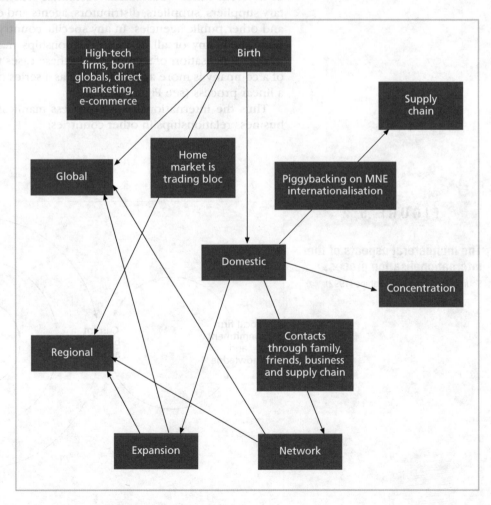

The conventional approach is for new companies to test the viability of their products in the domestic market before spreading internationally but we have already indicated that a number of firms become international players almost immediately after they have been formed either because they are born global or they operate within a common regional market. Figure 5.4 represents the internationalisation strategies in terms of the key dimensions of the number of country markets and market share.

The different patterns of international spreading are now discussed.

Market expansion and concentration

The conventional view of country selection is that from a sound domestic base SMEs develop either by choosing between expanding into many markets, gaining a superficial presence and accepting a low overall market share, or concentrating their marketing activities in a small number of markets in which a significant market share can be built. The research in this area is inconclusive about the precise reasons why firms adopt one strategy or another.

Katsikeas and Leonidou (1996) found that **market concentrators** tend, in general, to be smaller firms, because of their greater interest in export profitability and lesser concern with export sales objectives. Typically they make regular visits overseas and this appears to play a key role in their strategy for penetrating the market. Concentrators experience more problems associated with product adaptation to the needs of their customers but pricing and their marketing organisation needs present less of a problem.

Market expanders tend to be larger firms who are more concerned with export sales objectives, do more export marketing research, and have greater overall market share expectations. They place less emphasis on profitability, personal visits are less important and they perceive fewer product adaptation-related problems. E-commerce businesses are typical market expanders.

Where the domestic market is redefined

The lowering or removal of barriers between countries and the move, for example, in the EU to the harmonisation of standards, the removal of tariff barriers,

FIGURE 5.4	
Growth for niche marketers	

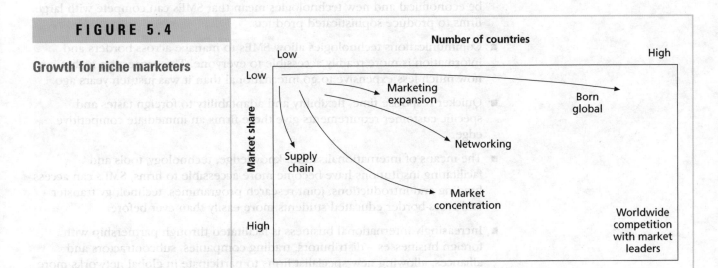

reduction of non-tariff barriers and the introduction of a common currency within a regional trading bloc mean that SMEs are more likely to be active in more than one country market because the regional market is considered to be a domestic market. This is particularly the case, for example, in mainland Europe where there are no additional costs in travelling to a neighbouring country and a common language may be used.

Where the SME is born global

SMEs market their products and services from birth in either selected overseas countries or globally because the customer segment or competition is global (especially in high technology) or because the distribution method is global, for example, direct marketing and telecommunications based international market-ing (e.g. Internet).

Knight and Cavusgil (1996) believe that in born global firms the management views the world as its marketplace from the outset and, unlike traditional com-panies, does not see foreign markets as simple adjuncts to the domestic market. They begin international trade within two years of establishing the firm and of course e-commerce is an important element of the born global operation. The majority of born globals are formed by active entrepreneurs and tend to emerge as a result of a significant breakthrough in some process or technology. They may apply cutting-edge technology to developing a unique product idea or to a new way of doing business. The products and services that born globals sell directly involve substantial value added and the majority of such products may be intended for industrial use.

According to Knight and Cavusgil several trends have given rise to the emer-gence of born global firms:

- The increasing role of niche markets especially in the developed world.

- The growing demand from consumers for specialised or customised products.

- To compete with globalising markets and worldwide competition smaller firms must specialise.

- Recent advances in process technology mean low-scale batch production can be economical and new technologies mean that SMEs can compete with large firms to produce sophisticated products.

- Communications technologies allow SMEs to manage across borders and information is more readily accessible to everyone. The suggestion is that it is now much less expensive to go international than it was just ten years ago.

- Quicker response time, flexibility and adaptability to foreign tastes and specific customer requirements give these firms an immediate competitive edge.

- The means of internationalisation, knowledge, technology, tools and facilitating institutions have become more accessible to firms. SMEs can access funding and introductions, joint research programmes, technology transfer and cross-border educated students more easily than ever before.

- Increasingly international business is facilitated through partnership with foreign businesses – distributors, trading companies, subcontractors and alliances, allowing new specialist firms to participate in global networks more easily than before.

Where the SME international development is the result of networking

Many SMEs adopt what appears to be a rather unsystematic approach to country market selection. Their patterns of development tend to be the result of a network approach where the selection of the market is not merely made on the relative attractiveness of the markets and their match with the company capability, but rather on the reduction of the risk of entering unknown markets by working with individuals or companies they know.

International development through using existing networks of contacts is more typical of Asian firms.

Nueno (2000) explains that the Chinese can be very effective entrepreneurs. Whilst 1 per cent of the population of the Philippines is ethnic Chinese they control 40 per cent of the economy, half the economies of Indonesia and Thailand are controlled by 4 per cent and 10 per cent ethnic Chinese respectively and in Malaysia two-thirds of the economy is controlled by ethnic Chinese.

In interviews with 150 Chinese entrepreneurs Kao (1993) found that Chinese-style management encompassed different political and economic systems bound together by a shared tradition but not geography. They operate effectively within a Chinese commonwealth in a network of family and clan and, because the Chinese are spread throughout the world, they can lay the foundations for stronger links amongst businesses across borders as a network of entrepreneurial relationships. A new Chinese management model is emerging which is grounded both in Chinese values, but also Western practices that encourage flexibility, innovation and the inclusion of outsiders. This shift in values has meant not only a transformation in how Chinese business people view themselves and their work but also the expansion of the emerging network. The enterprise still provides the Chinese with a means of achieving security in a disordered world and Kao suggests that the commonwealth depends on most of its entrepreneurs continuing to opt for a small business management model.

Through a global network many small units can come up with a variety of solutions at an acceptable level of risk. Whilst the Chinese are consciously moving towards a new management model that encourages growth and openness to outsiders most Chinese companies have incentives to remain small, family organisations. Such a trend is based partly on Chinese culture and partly on what now appears to be a model that is successful in the world at large. The Confucian tradition of hard work, thrift and respect for one's social network provides continuity, and the small network-based enterprise is suited to today's fast changing markets. The central strategic question for all current multi-nationals, be they Chinese, Japanese, or Western, is how to build a powerful international position through the integration of many small entrepreneurially managed units. The evolution of a worldwide web of relatively small Chinese businesses bound by undeniably strong cultural links offers an interesting working model for the future.

Supply chain internationalisation

The pattern of internationalisation of firms that are part of the supply chain of an MNE is usually determined by the international strategy adopted by the MNE. The downsizing that occurred in many large Western firms as a cost-cutting response to the recession in the late 1980s and the early 1990s led firms to think about what was their core competence and answer the question 'what business are we in?' The response to this question led a number of MNEs to identify those components and services that were part of the overall product offer but which they regarded as being peripheral to their business. As a result of this many MNEs decided to outsource more of their supplies, either from MNE specialist component makers and service providers, such as LucasVarity in the car industry, or from SMEs which have either exploited these new opportunities to grow, been the result of management buy-out of a peripheral part of the MNEs' business, or been specially set up to provide the product or service.

The reasons for MNEs to **outsource** can be summarised as follows:

- It reduces the capital requirements of the business (the supplier rather than the MNE invests in new processes and facilities).
- It overcomes the difficulty of developing quickly and maintaining in-house knowledge in many different specialist knowledge areas.
- It improves flexibility, as some firms are better equipped and can carry out small production runs, special designs and development tasks more quickly.
- The MNE can take risks in more peripheral activities where their expertise is weak, stopping the firm falling behind in the effectiveness of its non-core operations.
- The economies of scale of suppliers may make components much cheaper through outsourcing rather than from in-house supplies.
- The expertise of business support service providers, for example in transport and delivery systems, cannot be matched.
- Downsizing without outsourcing can lead to management resources becoming too stretched and unfocused.

The disadvantages of outsourcing are:

- Loss of know-how – in the 1980s a number of US businesses in many business sectors outsourced to Asian firms who subsequently opened up as competitors.
- The costs of managing the outsourced supplies – managing outsourced components and services does require time and technical expertise and, particularly in the case of IT, there have been some difficulties of integrating the service with the firm's primary strategic objectives.

Both large and smaller firms have been the beneficiaries of this increased outsourcing but for smaller firms there are particular challenges. These include:

- The need to become closely linked with one or two major customers, upon which the SME is almost entirely dependent for survival and success.
- Internationalisation is driven by the demands of the MNE. Failure to follow their product or market development demands may result in the loss of all the business as they seek alternative suppliers.
- They are under continual pressure to make operational efficiencies and design improvements in order to offer even better value for money.
- Concentration on developing the relationship with the MNE may lead to the firm becoming relatively weaker in external marketing, putting the firm at a disadvantage if it needs to find new customers when difficulties occur.

The advantages for SMEs are:

- The opportunities to learn from working with the MNE. This is likely to improve the smaller firms' strategic and operational management systems, communications and purchasing efficiency.
- They get greater business security through reliable and predictable ordering whilst the customer is successful.

- The opportunity to focus on production and technical issues rather than being diverted by the need to analyse changes to the market, customer and competition to the same degree.

Developing relationships

The key to success in working within the supply chain of an MNE is developing an effective relationship which can build upon the advantages and minimise the disadvantages of cooperative working between firms which may have some business objectives in common, but also may have a number of differences. As more SMEs become involved in international supply chains the ways in which relationships between smaller suppliers and the MNE differ between Western and Eastern styles of management become particularly significant and are explained in Illustration 5.4.

The Western way of arranging sourcing is a much more competition-based approach and has the advantage of a much sharper focus on cost reduction and profit and individual creativity whilst the Eastern way of arranging sourcing is a much more cooperative-based approach and includes ensuring that more than one strong supplier is available, expertise is shared and built upon, and the competitive focus is always on the much larger market opportunity.

Over the past few years the number of cooperative arrangements between Western and Eastern styles within one supply chain has increased and, as a result, arrangements which could be described as a combination of the two have been developed in which longer-term contracts have been agreed in order to maximise

---

| ILLUSTRATION 5.4 | Outsourcing the Western and Asian ways |

The Western way

The typical way that sourcing works in the West is that the purchasing MNE might come up with an outline design and ask for two suppliers to bid for the business. Each supplier will seek to gain competitive advantage in the negotiations by offering to deliver greater value to their customer, by identifying their requirements and preferences before working out how they might make it most efficiently. To do this they need to have a product design, production process, source of components and materials and a price. The purchasing decision will be based on the best deal for the company but this could either make or break the suppliers. Typically a short-term contract would be drawn up, during which period the chosen supplier is in fear of losing the contract and the losing supplier works hard to prove that the purchaser made the wrong choice.

The better supplier might eventually win over the longer term by gaining a larger share of the overall market, but the process of competition should ensure that customers are better served at a lower price.

The Asian way

The Asian purchasing MNE will again develop a preliminary design for its product but will invite potential suppliers not to make detailed bids but instead to make contributions that will help their alliance compete in world or regional markets. The Asian company considers the bidding to be part of a process of developing a supply chain alliance to which it will be supportive and loyal.

The winning supplier will be chosen but a condition of the contract may be that it will help the other supplier to become better. The objective behind the purchaser's approach is to improve the performance of the supply chain as a whole by getting all the participants working together with a common objective of gaining share from those companies that are prepared to work to the purchaser's agenda.

The suppliers clearly have little choice in whether they work this way or not, but the benefits they gain are in being part of a more successful supply chain and winning more business as part of this cooperative team. Whilst the weaker supplier would appear to have everything to gain from the stronger supplier, in practice the weaker player can often teach the stronger one some useful lessons.

Question As the CEO of a major manufacturer, how would you manage your SME members of the supply chain?

the cooperation between the MNE and supplier but without the insistence on sharing information with the losing contractor.

INTERNATIONAL STRATEGIC MARKETING MANAGEMENT IN SMEs

Having considered the various categories of SME internationalisation and the nature of SME international development we now turn to the factors which influence the international marketing management of SMEs. The **McKinsey 7S** framework, shown in Figure 5.5 is useful for discussing the elements.

The McKinsey 7S framework

The first three elements – strategy, structure and systems – are considered to be the hardware of successful management and as such can be implemented across international markets without the need for significant adaptation. The other four – management style, staff, skills and shared values – are the software, and are affected by cultural differences. Often it is the management of these aspects of the business that highlights good management in the best firms and relatively unimpressive management in poorer performing firms. It is quite obvious too that it is these elements of the framework which can vary considerably from country to country and provide the most significant challenges for SMEs developing from their home base into an organisation with involvement in a number of different countries.

The characteristics of these four software elements are:

Style: In organisations such as McDonald's, it is the consistency across the world of the management and their operational style that is one of the distinguishing features of the companies. For SMEs the management and operational style often reflects the personality, standards and values of the owner, and is often maintained as the firm matures, as is the case with Richard Branson of Virgin and Bill Gates of Microsoft.

Skills: The sorts of skills that are needed to carry out the strategy vary considerably between countries and also over time as the firm grows rapidly and new strategies and systems are introduced. Because the levels

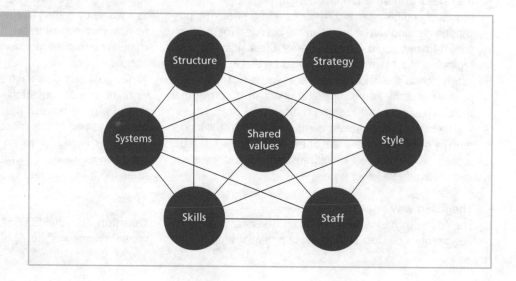

and quality of education of staff may vary considerably too, an effective human resource development strategy can be important to identify and build the necessary skills.

Staff: The people that are recruited around the world need to be capable, well trained, and given the jobs that will best allow them to make use of their talents. Recognition of the contributions of the staff, the criteria for advancement, acceptance of appraisal and disciplinary processes vary considerably between countries.

Shared values: Despite the fact that staff come from different cultural backgrounds there is a need for employees to understand what the organisation stands for, where it is going and to share the same organisational values.

The first part of this next section on international strategic management focuses broadly upon the 'hardware' and the second part on the 'software' of the McKinsey 7S framework.

The generic marketing strategies for SME internationalisation

Whilst there are an infinite number of individual implementation strategies that an SME might adopt the generic marketing strategies provide a useful starting point.

Segmentation, targeting and positioning

The principal approach to marketing strategy development follows three stages (normally referred to as segmentation, targeting and positioning (STP marketing)):

1 Identification of the various segments that exist within the sector, using the various segmentation methods which we have discussed earlier in Chapter 4. It is important for the SME to define cross-border segments with clearly identifiable requirements that it is able to serve.

2 The firm must then target the segments which appear to be most attractive in terms of their size, growth potential, the ease with which they can be reached and their likely purchasing power.

3 In seeking to defend and develop its business the firm needs to position its products or services in a way that will distinguish them from those of its local and international competitors and build up barriers which will prevent those competitors taking its business.

Competitive strategies

In order to create the competitive advantage necessary to achieve growth Porter (1990) suggests that firms should adopt one of the following three generic competitive strategies. However, each poses particular challenges for SMEs in international markets:

1 *Cost leadership* requires the firm to establish a lower cost base than its local or international competitors. This strategy has been typically adopted by companies that are located in countries with lower labour costs and who develop business usually as a component or service provider. Because of their

limited financial resources, however, SMEs that adopt a low cost strategy spend little on marketing activity and are vulnerable to either local firms or larger multi-nationals temporarily cutting prices to force the firm out of the market. Alternatively changes in currency exchange rates or other instability in the economic climate can result in newer, lower priced competitors emerging.

2 *Focus*, in which the firm concentrates on one or more narrow segments and thus builds up a specialist knowledge of each segment. Such segments in the international marketplace are transnational in nature and companies work to dominate one particular segment across a number of country markets. Typically this strategy necessitates the SME providing high levels of customer and technical service support which can be resource intensive. Moreover, unless the SME has created a highly specialised niche, it may be difficult to defend against local and international competition.

3 *Differentiation* is achieved through emphasising particular benefits in the product, service, or marketing mix, which customers think are important and a significant improvement over competitive offers. Differentiation typically requires systematic, incremental innovation to continually add customer value. Whilst SMEs are capable of the flexibility, adaptability and responsiveness to customer needs necessary with this strategy, the cost of maintaining high levels of differentiation over competitors in a number of international markets can be demanding of management time and financial resources.

Many SMEs base their international strategy on the generic strategy which has given them competitive advantage in domestic markets and then attempt to apply this same successful strategy in international markets. Of fundamental importance to the development of an effective international strategy for some SMEs is having a very strong position in the home country. US firms have benefited from having a huge domestic market. Chinese firms will also have the opportunity to become strong through exploiting the huge home market before venturing into international markets. By contrast, SMEs from emerging markets and from countries with smaller domestic markets often have to export merely to find enough customers to enable them to survive.

Growth strategies

SMEs also face a further strategic option. SMEs typically have limited resources and so need to make difficult decisions about how to use their limited resources to grow the business. Ansoff identified four growth strategies: product penetration, market development, product development and diversification, and these are shown in Figure 5.6. Following a product penetration strategy is appropriate

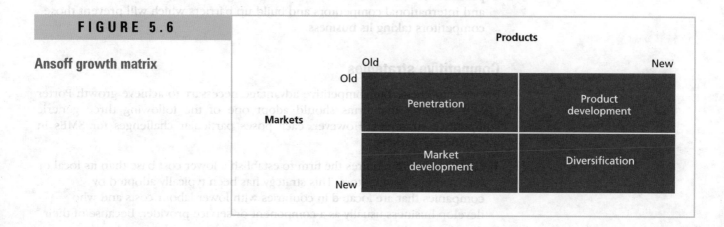

FIGURE 5.6	
Ansoff growth matrix	

if a company has an existing portfolio of products and a presence in its target markets, which offer considerable potential expansion of sales. The resources available to the company under these circumstances can be best used in concentrating on doing more of what is already being done well.

Diversification, on the other hand, is a strategy used in international markets in situations where demand for the company's existing products is falling rapidly (for example, in recent years in the defence industry), where resources are available but would not generate an acceptable return if used on existing activities or in the case of firms run by entrepreneurs, the owner often becomes rather bored with the firm's current activities and seeks out new challenges, by developing a new product for a new market.

For most companies the most obvious strategic development opportunities are in increasing geographical coverage (market development) which is discussed in Chapter 7 and product development which is discussed in Chapter 8. However, these options compete for resources and firms have to choose which approach will generate a greater return on investment.

The factors which affect the choice of an SME's international marketing strategy

Figure 5.7 indicates a number of the factors which influence the choice and development of an SME's international strategy. Particular issues include environ-

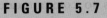

FIGURE 5.7

Factors affecting SME internationalisation

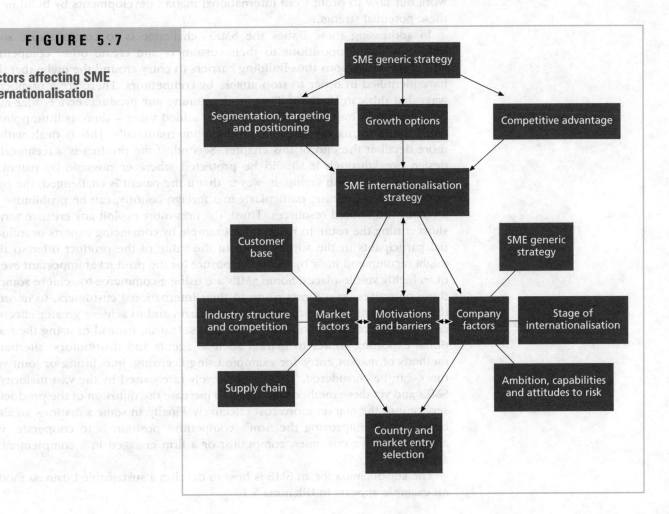

mental trends, the market and industry structure, the customer requirements from different countries, the nature and intensity of local and international competition, and the degree to which the SME can defend its niche. In SMEs, however, specific company factors are particularly important in the decision. These include the resources available, the products and services that have been developed and the firm's attitudes to international development and management of risk. These will result in the firm adopting a specific approach to individual country selection as the strategy develops.

Market factors

The most significant factor inherent in SMEs is their relatively small size and lack of power in most international markets in which they wish to be active. This puts them at a disadvantage to local competitors and MNEs as they often lack the management resources to spend researching new markets; the contacts necessary to quickly develop effective distribution of their products; sufficient financial resources to enable them to compete with the promotional spend of their competitors; and thus be strong enough to withstand a 'price war'.

The firm's smaller size means that they can offer customers the benefits of a more personal service from the firm's owners or senior managers, faster decision making and, usually, a greater willingness to listen but, of course, the SME must work out how to profit from international market developments by building on these potential strengths.

In addressing these issues the SMEs' challenge is to communicate some unique selling propositions to their customers and create other competitive advantage dimensions thus building barriers to entry around the niche that they have identified in order to stop attacks by competitors. There are a number of ways that this can be done. First, underpinning any product/service offer must be a significant improvement in customer added value – there is little point in SMEs trying to market 'me-too' products internationally. This is dealt with in more detail at the end of this chapter. Second, if the product is a technical or design breakthrough it should be protected wherever possible by patent or copyright. It is worth saying, however, that if the patent is challenged, the costs of fighting a court case, particularly in a foreign country, can be prohibitive for an SME with limited resources. Third, the firm must exploit any creative way of short cutting the route to market, for example by convincing experts or influential participants in the supply chain of the value of the product offer so they might recommend it, or by gaining exposure for the product at important events or in highly visible places. Some SMEs are using e-commerce to achieve some of these objectives: as a direct route to their international customers, to improve their efficiency in an international supply chain and to achieve greater effectiveness through collaboration with other SMEs. Fourth, instead of using the traditional exporting routes to market such as agents and distributors, alternative methods of market entry, for example using licensing, franchising or joint ventures, can be considered. They are relatively rarely used by the vast majority of SMEs and yet these methods are likely to increase the diffusion of the product or service into the market more cost effectively. Finally, in some situations an alternative way of improving the firm's competitive position is to cooperate with another firm – a customer, competitor or a firm engaged in a complementary activity.

The key dilemma for an SME is how to develop a sustainable business model. An example appears in Dilemma 5.1.

Company factors

Given the statistics it is obvious that only a minute proportion of the world's SMEs can be characterised as fast growth organisations likely to become the multi-national enterprises of the future. Therefore, it is important to realise at the outset that the majority of SMEs are developing strategies which will deliver modest growth principally in order to maintain the company's security and viability. The objective of many businesses, such as the corner shop, the market trader, and the car mechanic is to look for sufficient business to provide enough income to survive and they look no further than their domestic market.

Using research in the UK, Storey (1994) estimates that 4 per cent of SMEs contribute 50 per cent of the new jobs created and it is these few firms that are both innovative, in developing new business ideas and marketing methods, and entrepreneurial, in exploiting them commercially; they are the fast growth, international niche marketers.

The very nature of SMEs means that their smaller size and their entrepreneurial approach usually offer the advantages of flexibility and adaptability to new demands placed on them, speed of response to new opportunities and, usually, very focused management. They suffer from certain disadvantages, too, for example lack of adequate planning skills, being unwilling or unable to devote sufficient time and finances to the research and development of new business opportunities, resulting sometimes in wasted effort and some expensive failures.

Against this background must be set the obvious risk to SMEs of trading in other countries about which they have insufficient knowledge of the culture, market structure and business practices. The response of SMEs to international marketing is affected by their perceptions of this risk. At one extreme the SME will be deterred from becoming involved at all. At the other extreme the risk-taking SME will experiment with international marketing, perhaps with very little preparation, believing that the firm will be able to respond quickly enough to deal with any difficulties that emerge. More cautious SMEs will attempt to assess and manage the risks involved by evaluating the market opportunity and planning their use of management operations and financial resources to enable a cost-effective internationalisation approach to be developed.

Underlying the diversity in the range of a firm's attitudes to risk are the owners' ambition for the firm and how this fits with the firm's capabilities. To be successful the firm needs a vision of its international future which can be delivered using capabilities and resources that already exist but also include those that can

---

DILEMMA 5.1   **Building a sustainable international business model**

One of the characteristics of fast growth companies is their willingness to innovate, take risks and, where necessary, reinvent the company. South Korean company Trigem, a personal computer maker, is a typical example.

Trigem launched its eMachines onto the US market at less than US$600 per machine and took 14 per cent of the US market in August 1999. It was able to sell at this price through persuading component suppliers to cut prices in return for bulk orders and faster growth. In spring 1999 it launched an Apple iMac look-alike and was promptly sued by Apple in the US and Japan for trademark infringement.

This followed a Compaq lawsuit claiming infringement of thirteen patents, nine belonging to Intel, and coincided with an investment bank report which said that eMachines 'has not even remotely created a business model that is sustainable'.

Trigem demonstrates the importance of analysing likely competitor response to foreign market entry and building the firm's resources so that it can fight back. The dilemma is whether to completely analyse the possible response or simply try to deal with problems when they arise.

be acquired over a realistic timescale. It is often the case that successful SMEs are those that are able to clearly recognise the threats and opportunities in each marketplace, correct their weaknesses and build upon their strengths. SMEs that are unsuccessful in internationalising are those that do not understand how their market is changing, what new resources and skills are needed or are unwilling or unable to acquire them.

Systems and support networks

Typically SMEs tend not to have sophisticated systems and support networks for managing their international operations as is the case for large firms. Of course, advances in technology and the lower cost of IT systems, discussed in Chapter 12, are enabling SMEs to develop more advanced systems than they have had in the past. However, SMEs tend to rely on more informal, 'soft' systems and support networks that are based on personal contacts with family, friends, other business managers and officials for support, advice, information and knowledge.

Government support

Government support is also influential in accelerating the international development of SMEs. On a number of occasions in this chapter we have mentioned the benefits of SME international marketing in terms of the contribution it makes to the jobs and wealth creation of a country. Recognising this, most national governments offer support to SMEs for their development in general and the encouragement of exporting in particular.

Governments often provide support in the form of resources and advice but at significantly different levels, ranging from help with documentation, comprehensive country market information, export credit guarantees, trade missions and, in some cases, target country representative offices. However, Crick and Czinkota (1995) emphasise the need for policy makers to be more concerned with determining what assistance might be useful in helping firms to become more marketing oriented by being focused on satisfying customer needs by improving quality, service and specifications to meet international standards, and becoming more effective in conducting business overseas. Whilst help with language training is usually available, it is cultural training in both the social and business culture that is often more important. Other public and private sector organisations, such as Chambers of Commerce, local authorities, local business support agencies, banks and accountants also provide SMEs with a range of services to support their international marketing activity.

The dilemma illustrated in Dilemma 5.2 is concerned with how to get the best value from public money provided by governments to small firms.

Organisation structure

As an SME increases its involvement in international markets, so it needs to set up an **organisation structure** that will enable the leadership and management to effectively support, direct and control its often widespread and growing organisation. Terpstra and Sarathy (1999) have identified some of the variables which might influence the decision:

- size of the business;
- number of markets in which it operates;

- level and nature of involvement in the markets;
- company objectives;
- company international experience;
- nature of the products;
- width and diversity of the product range; and
- nature of the marketing task.

For a firm starting out in export markets, the decision is relatively simple. Either the international business is integrated within the domestic business or separated as a specialist activity. Setting up a separate activity, such as concentrating the international marketing skills and expertise in one department, avoids a situation where the international business is 'low priority', and allows the department greater independence to look specifically at international marketing opportunities.

There are, however, some disadvantages too, as it may be seen as less important by senior managers and could, as a result, create possible conflicts between domestic and international market demands. There is also the possibility of creating duplication and ineffective use of company resources. As the company develops further, it is faced with deciding how its international operations should be organised, for example by area, by product and by function. Figures 5.8 and 5.9 show typical organisational structures for organising along area and product lines. Organisation by function is only really appropriate for smaller companies with relatively simple product ranges.

| DILEMMA 5.2 | Government support for SMEs |

Most government trade and industry departments seek to encourage the creation and development of SMEs but, of course, they have a responsibility to use public money in a responsible way that achieves the best effect on the economy for the relatively small amounts of money allocated by the government. They must also avoid supporting one firm that might grow by taking business away from its neighbour. Helping SMEs to export is often seen as one of the most important activities because exporting generates foreign currency and creates wealth and jobs at home. Furthermore, competing in international markets forces small firms to raise their standards and quality.

SMEs in Pakistan provide employment to over 75 per cent of the labour force and contribute 40 per cent towards GDP and more than 50 per cent towards export earnings. The Small Business Finance Corporation in Pakistan (SBFC) has the mission 'to be a premiere financial institution providing medium & long-term, assistance (financial & technical) for the development of SMEs in Pakistan. Thus contributing to the growth of local entrepreneurs, developing export markets and providing employment opportunities'.

The exports of Pakistani fish to European countries declined after restrictions by the EU were enforced because of un-hygienic preservation and handling methods. In order to raise standards in the industry and recover the export sales the Karachi Fisheries Harbor Authority strictly enforced regulations to modify the fish holds of the traditional trawlers and the SBFC has provided small loans to poor fishermen to make suitable modifications to their boats.

Dates are grown in over 40 countries of the world and Pakistan now ranks as the fifth largest exporter with foreign earnings of US$25–30 million annually. However, there is scope for exporting more than the approx. 65 000 tons (11 per cent of total annual production). More important, however, is the opportunity to add value through packaging and processing the dates into preservatives, paste, syrup, and chocolate products. Again SBFC offers loans to SMEs to improve the quality of the dates, allow packaging to international standards and provide more hygenic and efficient processing.

Question Should the government try to support all businesses or target those with existing export business? Why, and what activities should be supported?

Source: www.pakistaneconomist.com/database1/Industry/Ind182.htm

As the firm grows it may decide to establish control in different ways, for example it may wish to control branding and corporate identity issues centrally through the use of international product managers, but at the same time it might wish to control the profitability of the business by having a chief executive in each individual country. In this way, the firm operates as a matrix structure within which individual managers might be responsible to different senior managers for different activities.

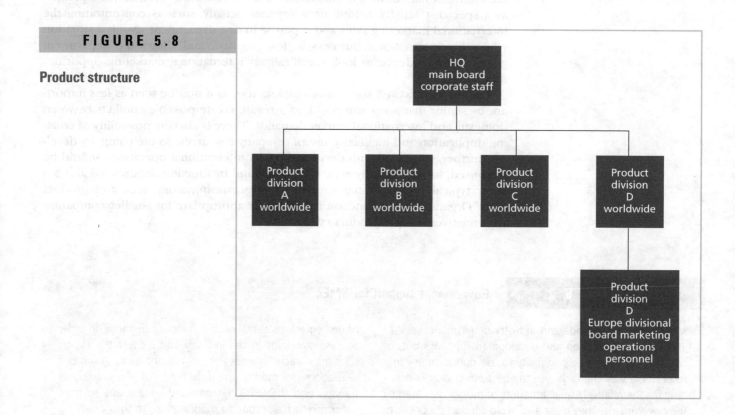

FIGURE 5.8

Product structure

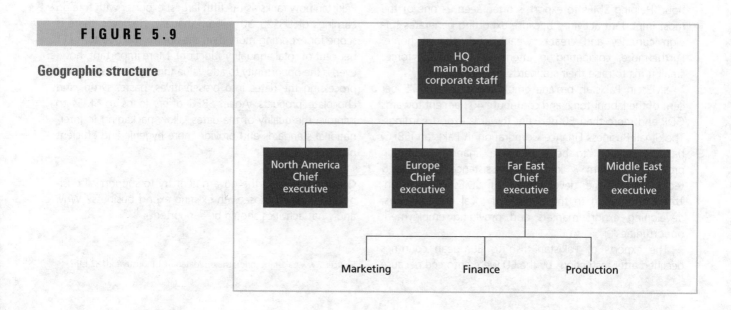

FIGURE 5.9

Geographic structure

Skills, capability and the stages of internationalisation

Having discussed the alternative categories of international marketing and the strategies which SMEs adopt we now turn to the process of SME internationalisation and the factors which lead to success and failure. In looking at a cross-section of firms involved in international trade it is possible to find some firms that are taking the major step from being a solely domestic company to generating their first revenue from foreign country sales, others that are moving from the early stages of internationalisation to a point where international marketing is totally integrated as part of the firm's activities, and a limited number of firms which are still small but have become confident world-class marketing companies.

The first step

Firms typically approach involvement in international marketing rather cautiously, as the first step towards what may appear to them to be a rather unpredictable future. For small and medium-sized firms in particular, exporting remains the most promising alternative to a full-blooded international marketing effort, since it appears to offer a degree of control over risk, cost and resource commitment. Branch and Lee (1978) treat the initiation of exporting as a diffusion of the information process and suggest that exporting is often undertaken as an innovation rather than as a managerial response to a problem. Indeed, exporting, especially by the smaller firms, is often initiated as a response to an unsolicited overseas order.

The further internationalisation of the firm is the process in which the enterprise gradually increases its international involvement. This process evolves in an interplay between the development of knowledge about foreign markets and operations on one hand and an increasing commitment of resources to foreign markets on the other. Market knowledge and market commitment are assumed to affect decisions regarding the commitment of resources to foreign markets and the way current activities are performed. Market knowledge and market commitment are, in turn, affected by current activities and operational decisions.

Thus firms start internationalisation by going to those markets that they can most easily understand. There they will see opportunities, perceive low market uncertainty and gain experience. Then as they go through the internationalisation process they will enter new more challenging markets where there is greater psychic distance. Psychic distance is defined in terms of factors such as differences in language, culture, political systems, etc., which disturb the flow of information between the firm and the market. This means that as the companies' market knowledge grows so does their commitment which in turn affects the type of strategy they decide to try.

More advanced stages of internationalisation

As companies increase their international involvement so improvements occur in the organisation, management and attitudes of those companies. Longer-term resources are committed and international business becomes part of the strategy rather than a tactical opportunity. Greater involvement in export marketing leads to better training and development, higher research and development expenditures, improvements in quality control, lower perceptions of risk, and reduced costs of doing business, all of which leads to increased performance.

Figure 5.10 provides a stage approach to conceptualising the internationalisation process based on a composite of various writers' ideas.

Lowe and Doole (1997) suggest that the internationalisation process of companies is not a gradual incremental process but a series of step changes. Firms can be characterised as being at one of the stages shown in Figure 5.3. There may be a number of factors which might initiate a step change, for example, an unexpected product or market success, the recruitment of a new chief executive, serious failure leading to a reassessment of the business and markets, the changing expectations of stakeholders, owners impatient for a more substantial return on their investment or business or family connections keen to share in the SME's success.

Expanding on these characteristics, it is possible to develop a picture of the firms at each stage.

The passive exporter

The passive exporter tends to lack any international focus, and perceives export markets as having a high hassle factor. Many passive exporters are relatively new to the export business, often reacting to unsolicited orders, and tend to see their market as essentially home based.

Such firms do not carry out research or invest in export promotion campaigns and have little direct contact with foreign companies. Firms at this stage perceive little real need to export and have no plans to do so in the future.

The reactive exporter

The reactive exporter sees export markets as secondary to the domestic markets but will put effort into dealing with key export accounts. Although they do not invest heavily in attracting export orders, once they have done business with a foreign customer they will follow up for repeat orders.

Such firms may have started to promote their export capacity and be starting to visit overseas clients. However, they have only a basic knowledge of their markets and are still undecided about their future role as an exporter.

The experimental exporter

The experimental exporter is beginning to develop a commitment to exporting and starting to structure the organisation around international activities. They are

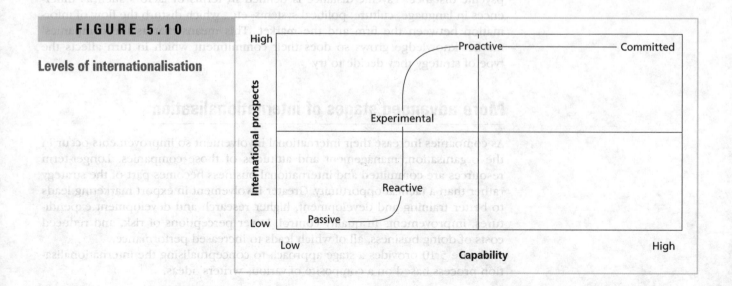

FIGURE 5.10

Levels of internationalisation

in regular contact with key accounts and are beginning to develop alliances with export partners to build better products and services and to use their information on their won markets.

Although they would prefer not to, such firms are prepared to make product adaptations to suit overseas customer needs and may have appointed dedicated export staff to look after this part of the business.

The proactive exporter

The proactive exporter is focused on key export markets, and devotes substantial amounts of time and resources to entering and developing new markets. Regular market assessment, in the form of desk research and using partners' information is carried out, and promotional materials are produced in a number of foreign languages.

Senior management regularly visit key accounts to maintain healthy relationships with clients and exporting may account for up to 50 per cent of turnover. Exporting opportunities are welcomed and seen as crucial to the business.

The well-established exporter

The committed exporter knows that exporting is integral to the business and sees the domestic market as just another market. The majority of the turnover is generated through exports and significant amounts of time are spent on this activity, with senior and middle managers frequently visiting customers.

Investment in training is substantial as skills are needed in-house and thinking on export markets is both short-term tactical and longer-term strategic with regular reviews of the overall mission and plan of action. Networks abroad provide excellent information and quality assured partners deliver on time, every time.

The firm's movement from one stage to the next, for example from reactive to experimental, experimental to proactive and proactive to world class, therefore, is not gradual. Each of these step changes requires a coordinated strategy to improve the performance of the firm. Doole (2000) has proposed ten benchmarks of international marketing practice (Figure 5.11) which indicate the most critical areas of the firms' management skills. Closer examination of the nature of these benchmarks reinforces the idea that successful international marketing is a

---

Characteristics of successful international business-to-business marketers

Source: Doole (2000)

Successful international business-to-business marketers:

1 Have a clear competitive focus in international marketplaces and a specific directional policy as to where the top management intend taking the firm.
2 Have high levels of repeat business and operate tight financial controls in export markets.
3 Have the tenacity and the resilience to face challenges and drive through change.
4 Have a perception that risk indicates a problem to be solved, not an insurmountable barrier.
5 View themselves as international niche marketers, not necessarily as good exporters.
6 Fully invest in ensuring they have thorough knowledge of the international markets in which they operate.
7 Are able to exploit distinctive product advantages in international markets.
8 Are strongly committed to supplying quality products and services to all their customers wherever they are in the world.
9 Build close relationships throughout the supply chain and invest in maintaining regular communications with their overseas partners.
10 Have a well defined communications strategy and invest in good quality promotional materials.

predictor of fast growth. Doole's research identified three key areas that SME international marketers needed to focus on to ensure success:

1 developing the characteristics of a learning organisation;
2 developing effective relationships; and
3 having a clear international competitive focus.

Learning organisation

A culture of innovation and learning throughout the firm is a common feature of successful firms that compete internationally. There is clear commitment from the top with senior management demonstrating detailed knowledge of key indicators and time and resources are invested in learning at all levels.

Investment in skills development enables the firms to be flexible in overcoming barriers and to be persistent in the face of difficulties. High levels of emotional energy are invested in the firm and staff are innovative and willing to learn. A shared vision and a sharing of experiences amongst internal partners are also key elements of the successful organisations' commitment to learning. Tight financial measurement and performance are seen as crucial.

Effective relationships

Firms who successfully compete in international markets build close relationships, not only with customers, but with others throughout the supply chain. Effective relationships are crucial and sometimes the focus of successful organisations' competitive advantage may not be the product itself but the added value given to the product and the ability to exploit opportunities by the close, meaningful and regular communication with customers, increasingly through e-commerce.

A commitment to quality procedures, a quality mission and the use of quality assured intermediaries are seen as vital. Service reliability is key to the relationships and underpins a firm's contribution to the supply chain.

Clear competitive focus

Firms establish a clear and truly international focus, demonstrating a strong competitive position in a clearly identified market. Many successful firms adopt niche marketing strategies based on a clear mission statement and a planned development strategy.

Other features usually include clearly differentiated products, strong brand positioning and high levels of flexibility in adapting products to suit particular markets.

A thorough knowledge of markets is built up through innovative and informal means of collecting information and through focused research capability, concentrating resources where they are of most use. Most successful companies have primary markets which account for at least 30 per cent of their export turnover.

MANAGEMENT STYLE AND INTERNATIONAL FAST GROWTH

Earlier in this chapter it was suggested that the vast majority of SMEs grow modestly in a risk averse series of incremental steps with a conservative management style. However, there are a small number of firms which achieve hypergrowth through commercially exploiting a revolutionary idea, business method or marketing strategy which simply leaves all the competitors behind. It is important to make the point that whilst some of these firms succeed as a result of a new technical or scientific invention, more important is the entrepreneurial flair needed to exploit the idea commercially. Some of the greatest successes are, therefore, associated with individual entrepreneurs who have the vision, determination, ability and ambition to succeed. Examples include Bill Gates, Azim Premji (see Illustration 5.5), Li Ning (see Integrative Learning Activity Part One, page 135) and Richard Branson.

In the West many of the great family business dynasties have declined in importance as these new entrepreneurs have built their business empires but Hiscock (1997) suggests that success in Asia still runs on power, prestige, influence, favours given and received, family fortune and connections. Without these even the simplest deal can come unstuck for no obvious reasons. He suggests that for example, the Chinese, Japanese, Koreans and Indians have their own special connections and their business styles come down to trust and credibility – who vouches for whom.

He identifies the six big economic groups in Asia that are growing fast as a result of networking as:

- Japanese *keiretsu* company connections;

- Koreans with *chaerbol* conglomerates;

- mainland Chinese with party and military links;

- ethnic or overseas Chinese with their stored wealth, extended family, dialect and guild connections;

- the emerging *pribumi* and *bumiputera* (indigenous) business leaders of Indonesia and Malaysia with their political connections;

- the Indians with their family dynasties.

| ILLUSTRATION 5.5 | Azim Premji – from cooking oil to IT billionaire |

In 1966 Azim Premji was 21 and studying at Stanford University when his father died suddenly. He rushed back to India and attended the first annual general meeting of the company. A vociferous and articulate shareholder told him to sell his shareholding and give it to more mature management as there was no way a person of his age and experience could lead the company. In *The Times* in 2003 it was claimed that Premji was the 41st richest person in the world with US$5.8 billion. In 2003, his company Wipro was the fourth most valuable company in India.

When Premji took over, the firm's main product was edible oils but in the 1970s the company moved into computer and printer hardware. In the 80s it moved into software. Wipro's software is used in many mobile phones, such as Nokia and NEC. Wipro also spotted the opportunity to help Indian firms with complex IT problems before multinationals, such as IBM and EDS, became established in India.

Wipro's growth in the 1990s and through into the new millennium was based on a further activity – offering outsourcing possibilities to large international firms. At the end of the 80s firms were looking to low cost manufacturing centres. Now IT is enabling firms to outsource services.

The firm manages a range of services, including call centres, financial administration, accounting, credit card renewal and marketing for clients as diverse as Thames Water, Deutsche Bank and the Scottish Parliament. Premji claims that businesses go to India because of cost but stay because of quality. The company employs 4000 graduates in its outsourcing division and there seems to be an unending source of highly qualified staff to cope with future expansion.

Question What lessons can be learned from Azim Premji's outstanding success?

Source: Adapted from Hopkins, N., The Indian Billionaire on the end of the line, *The Times*, 14 Feb 2003 and Defining moments: Azim Premji, BBC News Online, 14 July 2003

Hiscock suggests that it is networking on a grand scale that provides the basis of the international operations as there are an estimated 57 million Chinese and 18 million Indians that are living abroad. A Singaporean Chinese trader may have family connections in Taiwan, Hong Kong, Guandong Fujian or Vietnam, that can provide legal, banking and the support services when moving across borders.

The secret of high growth

For many firms high growth in revenue and profits is the ultimate goal, but this challenge is set against a global background of ever-greater competition and the increasing expectations of customers. The recession at the turn of the past two decades added to the pressure by forcing firms to restructure and downsize. This business environment seems to be hostile and yet some firms still manage to grow at a spectacular rate. It is by studying these firms, small or large, that the criteria for SME growth can be identified.

Kim and Henderson (1997) studied thirty companies around the world in order to find out what factors contributed to high growth. They failed to find links between high growth firms and what might have been thought to be obvious factors, such as having young, radical managers, being a new entrepreneurial start-up firm, having large financial investment in high technology or having a favourable competitive environment. Instead they found a fundamental difference between high- and low-growth firms in their strategic approach.

Slower growth firms typically focus upon the competition by benchmarking and seeking to meet the customers' (slightly) increased expectations. Their goal is to outperform their rivals usually by offering a little more value for a little less cost. The competitive response from the rivals is to do the same and, inevitably, this leads to a cycle of small-scale leapfrogging.

In 1983 Compaq launched its technologically excellent, IBM compatible PCs at 15 per cent lower cost than IBM and quickly gained a high market share. Within three years Compaq became the fastest company to become a Fortune 500 company.

The response from IBM was to begin a race between the two to add ever more technically sophisticated features. Neither recognised the next breakthrough – the need for lower price, user friendly and easily accessible computers which was provided by other competitors such as Dell. It ended with both facing financial crises during the 1990s.

Becoming embroiled within this competitive scenario initiates a pattern of strategic behaviour which is, in fact, opposite of that which is associated with growth. Firms become reactive, drawing in resources to respond to the short-term competitive actions and have no time or resources to think about the sorts of products and services that are needed for the future on a worldwide basis. Without this creativity the firms fall back on imitating competitors, believing the competitors' actions to be right for the market rather than really exploiting the changes taking place in their customers' needs and wants.

By contrast, high growth firms leave the competition to fight amongst themselves and, instead, seek to offer customers a quantum leap in value. The question that they need to pose is not what is needed to beat the competition but rather what is needed to win over the mass of customers. The implications of this are that it is necessary to challenge the conventional wisdom and assumptions of the industry about the basis on which firms compete and what customers value. An additional bonus from challenging the way the industry does things is that if the firm thinks on an international scale it can also lead to large cost savings as unnecessary operations are cut out. If the benefits really lead to a step change in value they will be perceived as such by customers all round the world.

In 1991, against a background of intense me-too competition, Callaway Golf the US golf club manufacturer launched its 'Big Bertha', a club with a larger head, which made playing golf more rewarding and more fun for the player. The result was a rapid increase in revenue for the company. In starting to change the way the firm thinks about its competitive strategy, it should address the following questions:

- What factors that your industry takes for granted should be eliminated?
- What factors that your industry competes on should be reduced well below the standard?
- What factors that your industry competes on should be raised well above the standard?
- What factors should be created that your industry has never offered?

By finding answers to these questions the firm can create new markets and new expectations for customers in existing markets. The Sony Walkman, low cost airlines (South West Airlines, easyJet and Ryanair) telephone and Internet banking, mobile phones (Nokia) and the illustration of Gillette (page 187) show how providing a quantum leap in value can reward the innovators. Typically it is smaller firms that are not weighed down by the industry traditions and standards that challenge conventional wisdom. If the ideas are sufficiently innovative and appealing they will create new international niche opportunities.

A number of niche brands, such as Virgin, Luxottica and Fisherman's Friend, have developed with a strong and loyal local, regional or global customer segment. Each of these successes was built on the firms recognising some often quite unexpected customer wants and needs, wherever in the world they appear, and then ensuring that they receive high-quality product offerings that are distinctive and, if possible, unique, supported by high levels of customer service. Eyretel

---

ILLUSTRATION 5.6   **Fast growth from global adaptation**

In 1990 Roger Keenan left his job as an engineer, set up office in his garage and began to search for financial backing. He wanted to develop and market his own digital recorder. He was 26, had no financial or management background and was aiming to launch a technology company, Eyretel, in the middle of the recession. He could not have picked a worse time to start.

In 1992 he had a breakthrough. With £70 000 from a backer under a government loan guarantee scheme and £155 000 from business angels (private investors) he was able to develop a digital voice recorder that could be used to record telephone calls in financial trading rooms and for emergency services. Eyretel's first big order came from an emergency service base in Virginia, US and from this beginning sales increased in the UK, US and Asia.

'To be a leading technology company, you must be big in America', Keenan says, 'We are targeting a conservative market by selling to blue-chip companies and government departments'. In fact Eyretel passed over the European markets in favour of the US in the early days but now want to find suitable managers to develop markets in France, Germany, Asia and South Africa.

With a workforce of 180 staff Eyretel's sales rose from £387 000 in 1993 to more than £12 million in 1997 and 80 per cent of its products are exported. It achieved a growth rate of 215 per cent year on year over this period and is claimed to be the UK'S fastest-growing firm.

The key to success has been the ability to adapt the product quite substantially to different market conditions and to meet different customer needs but it is designed for a global market. It is sold as a solution to a business problem, not as technology that customers ought to have.

By 2003 350 people were employed supporting 1200 customers in 10 countries.

Question   What are the challenges for a 'born global' firm?

were quick to see a new opportunity in what they considered to be a global market. They were prepared to take their first order from the international market as Illustration 5.6 explains and to develop from there.

Shared values

The core advantages of SMEs and main factors for success are their innovative capability, responsiveness, adaptability and flexibility which enable them to avoid direct competition from larger competitors. These values, which must come from senior management, must be shared and encouraged throughout the organisation. They must also be underpinned by good strategic planning and management.

Because of the small scale of operations of SMEs, staff around the world often relate quite closely to and communicate quite regularly with the owner or senior manager of the SME and so it is often the personal values of the owner and his or her view of how the products and services should be marketed that become the shared values of the organisation.

The reasons for failure

Many SMEs, however, fail to reach their full potential because they do not effectively manage their international marketing and operational activities which might affect their international success. They also stop being entrepreneurial and innovative. A number of these and other areas of weakness can seriously impede their progress in international markets or, in some cases, lead to bankruptcy. These factors include:

- failure to effectively scan the international environment
- overdependence on one product
- the ease with which larger, more powerful competitors or a number of smaller local competitors can copy the idea
- failure to respond to worldwide changes in customer needs
- failure to plan financial resources and not planning for fluctuation in currency values
- failure to manage and resource both market and operations expansion
- the prohibitive cost of enforcing patents and trademarks in foreign courts which may favour local firms.

One of the consequences of niche marketing is that success in one international market segment may lead to complacency and overdependence on that market or the erroneous belief that the firm has built up barriers to entry which will prevent the entry of potential competitors. Often, against powerful global competitors the barriers can be an illusion. The product may be superseded by an even better idea from a competitor or, alternatively, larger competitors can often gain business with an inferior product simply because of their greater promotional power or their control over the distribution channels.

Because of the often *ad hoc*, unplanned way that SMEs develop internationally they often underestimate the level of resourcing that is needed in both time and money, the difficulties and delays that may arise and consequently the length of time it takes to reach profitability in new foreign markets. The investment that is needed is often greater than the firms expect and they often fail to negotiate a suitable arrangement with their bank or other funders before difficulties emerge.

The main danger associated with international niche marketing is that the income stream is often dependent upon one single product or service idea or a very limited product portfolio. Given the capacity of competitors to copy product ideas the firm must be absolutely sure that it has built some unique competitive advantage such as a strong brand, unique technology or reliable business contacts to sustain it against the competition.

Small manufacturing firms may face particular difficulties in internationalising further, because they may need to make substantial investments in equipment and facilities if they need to significantly expand their manufacturing capacity to cope with the demand from newly created markets. For some firms it may be possible to increase capacity gradually, for example by running equipment on overtime or contracting out certain parts of the assembly process, but for others it may be necessary to make large step changes in the facility, for example buying an expensive new piece of machinery or equipping a new factory, just at the time when the firm is incurring the additional costs of entry to a new country. In this situation many firms make the decision not to go ahead with their international expansion and simply continue in their present markets. More creative SMEs find alternative ways to strengthen their international position, perhaps by finding a different way of expanding, for example by forming a joint venture or alliance with another firm, contracting out production to a firm with spare capacity or licensing the product or process or agreeing to be taken over.

THE FUTURE OF SME INTERNATIONALISATION

There are, therefore, many pitfalls for an SME that is active in international markets. For some SMEs the greatest risk is internationalising at all, particularly if they have no definable source of competitive advantage and little understanding of international marketing but, with increasing globalisation, firms such as these are no longer able to hide their inefficiency or lack of creativity in the domestic market as they will come under attack from international competitors.

Almost as risky is operating as a traditional exporter – selling excess capacity into markets about which the SME has little or no information and its managers have little cultural empathy. However, for SMEs that are innovative and ambitious, new technology and new ways of doing business offer opportunities for success on a scale never before envisaged, provided they are willing to learn, have a clear competitive focus and a strong network of connections.

SUMMARY

- SMEs have always been involved in international marketing but now have greater opportunities to develop internationally and create wealth and employment.

- New technology allows smaller firms to access information and communicate internationally in a way that was not possible before. It allows SMEs to utilise their inherent strengths of flexibility, adaptability, innovative capability and speed of response.

- Successful SME international marketers are those that build relationships with individuals and organisations that can help them understand the nature and value of the competitive advantage that they possess, and learn from their own experiences and those of others.

- The principles of international marketing can be applied to all categories of SME international activity, ranging from exporting manufactured goods, through e-commerce to marketing domestic attractions to tourists.

- SMEs use different ways of internationalising and selecting countries for market entry from incremental selection of countries, based on market potential or a network of contacts, through to high technology businesses that are 'born global'.

- The chosen SME internationalisation strategies are underpinned by generic marketing strategies but are often also affected by the management's perception of the barriers in the environment, the support that is provided in the domestic country and the specific market factors that affect their business sector.

- The stage of international development of the SME also reflects the company capability, the confidence and attitude of the senior management to internationalisation.

- There are a number of factors that lead to success and failure for SME international development, but the most significant factor is the ability of SMEs to offer customers a quantum leap in value.

KEYWORDS

7S framework	internationalisation barriers
born global	market concentrators
domestically delivered or developed niche services	market expanders
	networking
electronic commerce	organisation structure
export motivation	outsource
generic strategies	reciprocal trading
government support	small and medium-sized enterprise
international fast growth	stages of internationalisation
international niche marketing	supply chain internationalisation

CASE STUDY INDECO (pvt) Ltd

'Economic Structural Adjustment Programmes' (ESAPs) have been a feature of many Less Developed Countries (LDCs). Mainly World Bank sponsored, ESAP was introduced for a number of reasons: severe balance of payment difficulties, inability to service external debt, inappropriate domestic policies (e.g. subsidies), closed markets, state controlled prices and uncontrolled and increased government spending. Added to this many LDCs have experienced poor public sector management, idle and decaying industrial capacity and inadequate resources of foreign exchange for materials and spare parts, leading to poor quality goods and services and over-valued currencies.

Africa has been the recipient of adjustment monies for many years (US$20 billion plus). Zambia is one such recipient country. It has experienced both the positive and negative aspects of the implementation of ESAP. On the positive side the economy has 'opened up', resulting in a flood of foreign imports (due partly to domestic producers' lack of quality) and foreign direct investment due to free exchange rate regimes. Certainly more traders have entered the marketing system due to lower taxation cuts. However, Zambia has suffered many negatives from the ESAP process. Devaluation (500 per cent) has made imports expensive and imports have affected domestic production resulting in unemployment. Domestic prices have risen rapidly due to inflation and the National Debt has risen dramatically. Socially, the populace has become divided, with the rich getting richer and the poor poorer. Meanwhile, government has divested itself of many state-owned industries, these having been sold to overseas investors, making many Zambians feel that the government has 'sold off the family silver' to outsiders. Petty and serious crime have increased.

Within this scenario INDECO (the Indian Engineering Company) based in Bangalore, India, has been exporting standard products (nuts, screws, bolts, washers, clips etc.)

to Zambia for the last 10 years through a local agent. Turnover has steadily increased to its current level of US$2 million (2001), but in latter years its margins have been eroded due to the devaluation of the Zambian Kwacha and the inability of local industry (textiles, light engineering, brewing and agribusiness) to source foreign currency to pay for imports. The major Zambian industry, copper mining, is, however, relatively wealthy. Some years ago, INDECO ventured into Zambia directly by entering into an agreement for a local company to manufacture its products under licence. However, after three attempts to get it right it had abandoned the project, due to the local company's inability to manufacture to required quality standards. The local company just could not afford to import the specialist machinery. Such was the importance of the Zambian sales to INDECO, and the potential wealth due to so many South African companies now investing in Zambia (albeit a lot of it in trading), that it was worth INDECO considering venturing into Zambia directly again. The Board of INDECO met to consider the prospect.

Questions

1 As a Marketing Analyst in INDECO, advising the Main Board, write a report describing the Marketing Information required for, and its impact on, the decision to enter the Zambian market or not in Year 2002.

2 Assume the decision has been taken for INDECO to enter the Zambian market again. As the Marketing Analyst, write an International Strategic Marketing Plan for the Board, covering the years 2002–2004, based around one direct market entry method identified from your analysis of the data in Question 1.

Source: Robin Lowe, CIM/Sheffield Hallam University

DISCUSSION QUESTIONS

1 How can the smaller business compensate for its lack of resources and expertise in international marketing when trying to enter new markets?

2 Why is international niche marketing likely to be a superior approach to export selling?

3 What would you consider to be the international marketing factors that would ensure success for a long-established 200-employee manufacturer of specialist engineering components for the oil industry?

4 Why are some firms 'Born Global'? What specific risks do they face in international markets?

5 Small international marketing firms do not have the resources to systematically carry out market research. What advice would you give to a firm that wishes to enter a new emerging market?

REFERENCES

Barker, S. and Kaynak, E. (1992) 'An empirical investigation of the differences between initiating and continuing exporters', *European Journal of Marketing*, 26 (3).

Bennett, R. (1997) 'Export marketing and the Internet Experiences of Web site use and the perceptions of export barriers among UK businesses', *International Marketing Review*, 14 (5).

Branch, J. and Lee, W. (1978) 'The adoption of exports as an innovative strategy', *Journal of International Business*, 3 (2).

Brown, L. and McDonald, M.H.B. (1994) *Competitive marketing strategy for Europe*, Macmillan.

Crick, D. and Czinkota, M.R. (1995) *International Marketing Review*, 12 (3): 61–72.

Czinkota, M.R. (1994) 'A national export assistance policy for new and growing businesses', *Journal of International Marketing*, 2 (1).

Doole I. (2000) 'How SMEs learn to compete effectively on international markets', Ph.D thesis.

Hamill, J. (1997) The Internet and international marketing, *International Marketing Review*, 14, 5.

Hiscock, G. (1997) 'Meet Asia's new super rich', *Sunday Times*, 8 June.

Johannson, J. and Vahine J.E. (1992) 'The mechanism of internationalisation', *International Marketing Review*, 74.

Kao, J. (1993) 'The worldwide web of Chinese Business', *Harvard Business Review*, March–April.

Katsikeas, C.S. (1996) 'Ongoing export motivation: differences between regular and sporadic exporters', *International Marketing Review*, 13 (2).

Katsikeas, C.S. and Leonidou L.C. (1996) 'Export marketing expansion strategy: differences between market concentration and market spreading', *Journal of Marketing Management*, 12.

Kim, W.C. and Henderson, B.D. (1997) 'Value Innovation: The Strategic Logic of High Growth', *Harvard Business Review*, February.

Knight, G.A. and Cavusgil, S.T. (1996) 'The born global firm: a challenge to traditional internationalisation theory', *Advances in International Marketing*, 8.

Lowe, R. and Doole, I. (1997) 'The characteristics of exporting firms at different stages of internationalisation', *International Marketing Strategy Contemporary Readings*, International Thomson Business Press.

Nueno, P. (2000) 'The dragon breathes enterprising fire', in Bailey S. and Muzyka F. (2000) *Mastering Entrepreneurship*, FT Prentice Hall.

Oldfield, C. (1997) 'Toys and Fish vie with computers', *Sunday Times*, 7 December.

Porter, M.E. (1990) *Competitive advantage of nations*, Free Press.

Quelch, J.A. and Klein, L.R. (1996) 'The Internet and international marketing', *Sloan Management Review*, Spring.

Storey, D.J. (1994) *Understanding the small business sector*, Routledge.

Terpstra, V. and Sarathy R. (1999) *International Marketing*, 8th edn, Dryden.

GLOBAL STRATEGIES

Introduction

Having discussed the nature of international development in smaller firms we now consider the global marketing strategies of the largest firms that enable them to compete on a worldwide basis. **Globalisation** for the largest firms should be the route to maximising performance by introducing, where possible, standardised marketing programmes and processes, but at the same time, adapting certain operational activities to local needs in order to maximise short-term revenue generation. The problem that such firms face is exactly which aspects of their international activity to standardise and which to adapt because the decisions are often context specific and are affected by the particular factors which drive change within their particular industry. This leads to firms adopting a variety of global strategies, from those that are very similar from country to country to those that are substantially different in each country in which the firm operates.

In this chapter we start by considering the dimensions of the concept of globalisation before considering the alternative strategic approaches and the factors that drive strategic choice. This discussion is then followed by an examination of the strategy implementation issues that MNEs might face in managing their global business and building their global presence, with particular emphasis being placed upon global branding.

Learning objectives

After reading this chapter you should be able to:

- Appreciate the various aspects of globalisation and be able to compare and contrast the alternative global strategies
- Evaluate the factors that determine a firm's choice of global strategy
- Identify the challenges that firms face in developing a global presence
- Appreciate the role of branding in globalisation
- Understand the factors affecting global marketing management

ALTERNATIVE VIEWS OF GLOBALISATION

Over the past decade the term globalisation seems to have led to a polarisation of views. For some, globalisation is associated with opportunity, the removal of barriers and greater understanding of different cultures. Others see globalisation and MNE activity as one and the same thing, with global companies dominating international business, exploiting the resources and influencing the economy of every country and moving their factories from country to country according to which offers the lowest wage rates, with no thought either for those who lose their jobs or the well-being of those who are paid extremely low wages. In practice few companies, even those with the most familiar brand names, are truly global, as Table 6.1 shows. Taking an average of the measures of transnationality provides a picture of what are perhaps the best examples (Table 6.2). This list is significantly different from Table 6.1. The reason for this is that firms from the US have had a huge domestic market in which to grow before embarking upon international, then global activity. Chinese firms now also have a similar opportunity to grow first in a huge domestic market. By contrast, firms from smaller countries have always had to internationalise simply to grow. Table 6.3 shows the top transnational firms from developing countries.

There is no doubt, however, that the world's largest firms are seeking a worldwide presence. Driving this acceleration of global MNE activity appears to be increased competition which Sjobolom (1998) suggests is being brought about by four forces: changes in consumer expectations; technological change; deregulation; and regional forces. An example of how this has affected the telecommunications sector is shown in Illustration 6.1.

In seeking to compete successfully in increasingly globalised markets multinational enterprises realise that a precondition of long-term growth is a worldwide presence. Over the past two decades a number of writers such as Levitt and Kotler

TABLE 6.1		The top 15 transnational companies by foreign assets 2000					
2000	1999	Company	Country	Industry	Foreign assets %	Foreign sales %	Foreign employment %
1	–	Vodafone Group	UK	Telecoms	100	63	8
2	1	General Electric	US	Electronic	36	38	46
3	2	Exxon Mobil Corporation	US	Energy	68	69	65
4	47	Vivendi Universal	France	Diversified	65	49	64
5	4	General Motors	US	Automotive	25	26	43
6	3	Royal Dutch/Shell Group	UK/Netherlands	Energy	61	54	57
7	10	BP	UK	Energy	76	72	82
8	6	Toyota Motor Corporation	Japan	Automotive	36	49	Not given
9	30	Telefonica	Spain	Telecoms	64	50	48
10	50	Fiat Spa	Italy	Automotive	55	67	50
11	9	IBM	US	Electronics	49	58	54
12	12	Volkswagen Group	Germany	Automotive	57	73	49
13	–	ChevronTexaco	US	Energy	55	56	32
14	48	Hutchinson Whampoa	Hong Kong, China	Diversified	74	39	54
15	19	Suez	France	Utilities	91	75	68

Source: UNCTAD

have debated whether or not this will result in globally standardised products and services.

TABLE 6.2 — Top 15 companies: Index of transnationality* 2000

2000	1999	Company	Home economy	Industry	Index*
1	34	Rio Tinto	UK Australia	Mining	98.2
2	1	Thomson Corporation	Canada	Media	95.3
3	3	ABB	Switzerland	Machinery	94.9
4	2	Nestlé	Switzerland	Food	94.7
5	7	British American Tobacco	UK	Tobacco	94.4
6	4	Electrolux	Sweden	Electrical	93.2
7	–	Interbrew	Belgium	Food	90.2
8	–	Anglo American	UK	Mining	88.4
9	20	Astrazeneca	UK	Pharmaceuticals	86.9
10	35	Philips Electrical	Netherlands	Electrical	85.7
11	14	News corporation	Australia	Media	84.9
12	10	AkzoNobel	Netherlands	Pharmaceuticals	84.9
13	12	Cadbury Schweppes	UK	Food	84.1
14	52	Royal Ahold	Netherlands	Retail	82.5
15	–	Vodafone group	UK	Telecoms	81.4
27	26	Coca-Cola**	US	Beverages	72.7
39	24	McDonald's	US	Retail	61.8
57	49	IBM	US	IT	55.5
85	76	Ford Motor Company	US	Automotive	30.1

*The average of foreign to total assets, foreign to total sales, and foreign to total employment
**It is worth the positions of Coca-Cola, McDonald's, IBM, and Ford. They are viewed as huge transnational firms but none are in the top 20 based on the criteria used to assess transnationality
Source: UNCTAD

TABLE 6.3 — Top 12 companies from developing economies: Index of transnationality 2000

Rank	Company	Home economy	Industry	Index*
1	Guandong Investment	Hong Kong/China	Diversified	88.7
2	First Pacific	Hong Kong/China	Electrical	81.4
3	Orient Overseas	Hong Kong/China	Transport	80.9
4	Neptune Orient Lines	Singapore	Transport	78.6
5	Wbi Corporation	Singapore	Electrical	70.8
6	Savia De CV	Mexico	Diversified	59.3
7	Sappi	South Africa	Paper	57.9
8	Comex	Mexico	Minerals	54.8
9	Hume Industries	Malaysia	Construction	51.6
10	Gruma De CV	Mexico	Food/beverages	51.1
11	Hutchinson Whampoa	Hong Kong/China	Diversified	50.3
12	Fraser and Neave	Singapore	Food/beverages	49.5

Source: UNCTAD

So far, the only examples of product and service offers which have been completely standardised across the world are probably those sold over the Internet in the business-to-business sector. Some of the most widely available products which might be considered to be standardised in fact are substantially adapted. You can taste the Coca-Cola variants from around the world at the museum in Atlanta and try the different McDonald's menus as you travel. IBM and Microsoft use different language options in their service manuals. The concept of globalisation, therefore, is often characterised by contradictions, such as the need to standardise some elements of the marketing mix whilst, at the same time, accepting the need to respond to local needs and tastes. The true nature of **globalisation** is encapsulated in the phrase 'think global, act local' in which there is an acknowledgement of the need to balance standardisation and adaptation according to the particular situation.

Against this background the word globalisation is associated in a very imprecise way with many different aspects of the international marketing strategy process. The term 'globalisation' is frequently used by writers in association with:

- market access
- market opportunities
- industry standards
- sourcing
- products and services
- technology
- customer requirements
- competition
- cooperation
- distribution
- communication
- the company's strategy, business programmes and processes.

ILLUSTRATION 6.1   Nokia: Zero to hypergrowth to maturity in ten years

Twenty years ago the telecommunications industry was composed of largely national monopolies protected by government regulation. Because of the huge investment in infrastructure, governments believed that it was necessary to prevent undesirable competition and duplication. However, digital technology reduced the infrastructure costs and dependence on fixed lines and led to mobile telephones, the Internet and many other information and leisure services that were never part of the old monopoly operations. The old national monopolies, characterised by their high cost structures and poor marketing, could not compete with the new companies, typically with lower cost structures and excellent marketing skills.

Nokia is one of the most successful firms ever. Ten years ago, Nokia was a small, diversified, domestic Finnish conglomerate. Its chief executive had committed suicide and many of its shareholders wanted Ericsson to take it over. But Jorma Ollila had a vision to make Nokia the world's leading maker of mobile phone equipment and in 2003 it shipped 160 million handsets, more than twice the next largest, Motorola. Service providers such as Vodafone helped to sustain this level of sales by being prepared to subsidise the cost of the phone by up to £100 in order to attract subscribers, who were prepared to pay for quite expensive services.

After a good run Nokia now faces some challenges to retain their market leadership. Subscribers are not keen to take additional services based on 3G, such as sending photographs. As the services were not being used, Vodafone cut the subsidy. Microsoft is keen to play a greater role in the mobile market and competition from cheap handsets is expected to increase from Asia.

Question What should Nokia's international marketing strategy be?

Source: Adapted from Woolcock, N., Story Nokia didn't want you to read, *The Sunday Times*, 6 April 2003

Globalisation of market access has increased as the number of inaccessible markets has reduced following the political changes that have opened up markets, for example in Central and Eastern Europe and China, to much greater MNE involvement. Whilst these 'new' markets have become more accessible, firms entering them usually face more difficult problems in viably establishing their global products there because of not only the differences in social and business culture but also the lack of an infrastructure, legal framework and standards of business practice. As a result many global firms have felt unwilling or unable to 'go it alone' in these markets, which are unsophisticated by developed country standards, and have found it necessary to form partnerships with local firms or individuals in order to exploit the new opportunities.

Market access is also being improved by the increasing regionalisation, resulting from the growth of trading blocs. Firms are reinforcing this effect by helping to reduce inter-country barriers and thus improve market access by operating more standardised pan-regional marketing programmes and processes such as product development and advertising.

Globalisation of market opportunities has increased with the continued deregulation of certain sectors, such as financial services, where the traditional barriers between the various parts of an industry, such as banking, insurance, pensions, specialist savings and house loan suppliers are being broken down. This has resulted in mergers of specialist firms to form larger and more powerful groups which can offer a complete range of products or services to their customers in the sector. For such MNEs, the power base may be a large domestic or regional market, as was the case for Citigroup when two companies were from the US merged. As will be discussed later, MNEs from different countries, for example Mercedes Benz (Germany) and Chrysler (USA), have merged to create more comprehensive product ranges in their industry sector.

The largest and most powerful firms from one sector are now aggressively attacking other sectors, for example General Motors is offering credit cards and supermarket groups now routinely offer petrol, banking, pensions and savings plans. The privatisation of government-owned utilities, such as electricity, gas and telephone is leading to industry restructuring where previously there were monopolies with tight operating restrictions. This is allowing firms to compete in geographic areas and industry sectors from which they have previously been excluded.

Globalisation of industry standards is increasing as technical operating standards, professional rules and guidelines are being adopted more widely primarily due to the harmonisation of regulations within trading blocs, but more generally around the world as a result of the increased mobility of experts and advisers, and the wider use of quality standards, such as ISO 9000. Despite this there is a long way to go. For example, fifteen adapters are needed to enable a portable computer to be plugged in locally throughout Europe. It is becoming a precondition of supplying major customers that firms operate to certain product and service standards that can be recognised regionally and globally. In addition, the largest MNEs are expected to work to ethical standards which cover such diverse areas as employment, environmental protection and unfair competition. As a result, MNEs demand that their staff work to exacting company standards. Professional staff are usually also regulated by country bodies but greater regional harmonisation is affecting standards of behaviour and performance.

Globalisation of sourcing has increased as companies search the world for the best and cheapest materials, components and services rather than rely on local suppliers. The benefits of **global sourcing** include:

- **Cheaper labour rates.** Fashion and clothing marketers obtain supplies from low labour rate countries such as China, Indonesia, Costa Rica, Vietnam and Latin America. There can, however, be a problem of product quality and criticism of unethical behavour as these firms resort to 'island hopping' to the new lower labour rate areas resulting from changes in local country economic development.

- **Better or more uniform quality.** Certain countries and companies have competitive advantage as suppliers over others because of the local availability of materials and skills.

- **Better access to the best technology, innovation and ideas.** Firms search the world to identify a particular research or design centre which might offer the specialist expertise they require. For example, Yip (1996) explains that Kodak, IBM and Hewlett Packard have research facilities in Japan and Nissan and Mazda have design facilities in California. Microsoft have established research facilities close to Cambridge University in the UK.

- **Access to local markets.** Developing stronger links with a country through sourcing can help to generate new business in that country. For example, the aircraft maker Boeing has been able to open up the market in China following its decision to purchase components there.

- **Economies of scale advantages.** Where the location of a manufacturing or distribution operation is convenient to supply a whole region it can lead to significant cost advantages.

- **Lower taxes and duties.** Certain countries may offer tax advantages to manufacturers and low rates of duty when shipping goods to the customer. Earth-moving equipment manufacturers Caterpillar and Komatsu have relocated some of their higher added value activities with the benefit of spreading currency risk.

- **Potentially lower logistics costs.** Global transport and warehousing companies use IT more effectively to control product movement and inventory.

- **More consistent supply.** Some foods would be restricted because of seasonality if steps had not been taken to arrange supplies from countries with different growing seasons.

The major risks in global sourcing are in dealing with countries where there might be political, economic and exchange rate risks. There is also a risk of the supplier using its knowledge and power which results from a strong position in the supply chain to become a competitor. An example of this is shown in Dilemma 6.1. What is crucial is that the MNE must retain its competitive advantage and not outsource its supplies to the point where it gives away all its technical and commercial secrets or power in the market. This potential danger needs to be managed by purchasers improving their supplier–purchaser relationships or, perhaps, even forming longer-term strategic alliances. The additional benefit of better supplier–purchaser relationships can be improved communications and the avoidance of some unnecessary supply chain costs resulting from inadequate specifications, misunderstandings about quality and generally poor management.

Using strategic alliances in the supply strategy usually results in a reduction of suppliers and frequently leads to component makers becoming multi-national. For example, Xerox reduced its suppliers from about 5000 to 400 and its lamps for photocopiers are sourced from a single MNE with plants in Europe, Asia and the US.

Globalisation of core products and services. More and more products are reaching the mature phase of their product life cycle and this is leading to greater commoditisation of products and services. Consumers are able to see very little difference between the offerings of many competing suppliers. Also the increased speed at which new innovations can be copied by other competitors means that core benefits can no longer be a point of differentiation between competitors. MNEs are responding to this and gaining competitive advantage over local competition by differentiating their products through such things as the brand image, higher levels of service, or better technical support.

Globalisation of technology. Technology is converging in and between industries, with similar processes and ideas are being used, for example, in telecommunications, information technology hardware and software, entertainment and consumer electronics, so that new products and services cross the traditional boundaries between the industry sectors. New technologies are adopted around the world at ever greater speeds and in many industries this is being driven by a small number of global players that have the market power to change the ways of working and generate sufficient demand from customers to make the wider application of the ideas more cost effective. In this way the globalisation of technology is contributing very significantly to the competitive advantage of the MNEs, who are able to market it in a number of industry sectors because they have developed effective distribution channels and international promotion.

Globalisation of customer requirements is resulting from the identification of worldwide customer segments, such as teenagers with similar worldwide tastes in music, fashion and 'junk' food, and managers, who travel extensively to meet their counterparts in other parts of the world and share common expectations of products and services. Equally, with industries becoming more globalised, the demands placed on the business support services, such as advertising agencies, accountants, law firms and consultants, are converging too. Customers in both the consumer and business-to-business markets are demanding and getting what they perceive to be added value products and services which better meet their changing needs than those they have been used to receiving from national companies.

Globalisation of competition between industry giants tends to result in the same fight being replicated in each corner of the world with MNEs using largely similar competing product or service offers. Traditional national oligopolies are being outmanoeuvred by aggressive fast-growing international competitors who are far better at exploiting technical changes and other globalisation effects. They

---

| DILEMMA 6.1 | How do component makers add value? |

The problem with outsourcing of supplies is that eventually the component makers can become a new power in their own right. The strength of the car component makers comes from a wave of consolidations, leaving three or four makers of parts, such as brakes, transmissions and suspensions, selling to about fifteen worldwide car makers. Suppliers already do three-quarters of the engineering for Toyota and Nissan and account for four-fifths of the added value. As European and US firms follow this trend it is hardly surprising that the car makers are having to look for profits from distribution, service, leasing, finance and insurance.

Despite the over-capacity in the car industry, the component makers have already moved into niche car assembly and could ultimately produce own label products for supermarkets to sell. Finnish parts maker Valmet assembles the Porsche Boxter sports car, Ladas and some Saabs. Steyr Daimler Puch, a manufacturer of transmissions in Austria, assembles Chrysler Jeeps and Voyager minivans and Mercedes off-road vehicles.

Question Where in the supply chain should car companies seek to add brand value? How can they ensure that they maintain control of the intellectual property associated with the car?

are also able to cross-subsidise their activities in different countries, so helping to make the markets more interdependent.

Mature industries, as well as new technology sectors, are being affected by global competition. For example, whilst the majority of the top ten chemical companies are European, there is increasing competition particularly from Asian companies, which have different cost structures and systems of industry regulation. Success in these component and raw material industries has traditionally been dependent upon the product portfolio, the relationship with customers and the levels of technical service and support provided, but increasingly the fact that these are components in the supply chain of branded consumer products means that successful suppliers must carry out more effective marketing to members of the supply chain that are closer to the customer.

Globalisation of cooperation. To compete in all the major world markets it is necessary to make available huge financial resources often outside the scope of individual firms. This is leading to the formation of alliances between major MNEs, members of a supply chain, or between firms with complementary activities. The Japanese '*keiretsu*' go further in that they are formal organisations between banks, manufacturers and trading companies with cross-share ownership and have the huge resources necessary to build businesses in the major world markets. This has enabled them to make investments over a number of years to establish a dominant long-term market position in a particular industry.

Globalisation of distribution is occurring, first, as the supply chain becomes increasingly concentrated on fewer, more powerful channel distributors, retailers and logistics companies and, second, as e-business technology changes revolutionise the exchange and transfer of data and the whole process of product and service transactions, including methods of product and service selling, ordering, customising, progress chasing, payment arrangement and delivery confirmation.

Globalisation of distribution is particularly important for companies such as Amazon that use the Internet for electronic commerce as they must be able to make transaction and logistics arrangements to enable them to provide high levels of service and efficiency to customers wherever they are located.

Globalisation of communication. Major changes in telecommunications and information technology have had two effects. First, global communications, such as satellite and cable TV have made it essential that MNEs develop a consistent worldwide corporate identity and brand image. As consumers travel physically or virtually by way of the media or World Wide Web, they are exposed to communications and advertising originating from an MNE from many parts of the world. Consistency of the communication is vital for reinforcing brand familiarity, quality and values.

Second, digital technology is driving the localisation and individuality of communications, for example through the proliferation of local TV channels and the development of the Internet, which allows greater exposure for individual communications. These developments go further than simply improving the accessibility of the traditional one-way communications with customers by adding a two-way, interactive dimension to the firms' relationships with their global customers. The AOL–Time Warner merger was based upon exploiting this interactivity in the entertainment sector no matter where in the world the customers were situated by customising the marketing mix elements, for example personalising the product, service and promotional communications.

Globalisation of the company's strategy, business programmes and processes. The result of these globalisation effects is to pose challenges to firms to achieve both improved global operational efficiency and greater global market effectiveness. The global firm's response to managing the complexity of international marketing must include developing an all-embracing global strategy supported by effective marketing programmes and processes that will integrate the various disparate activities of the firm's far flung strategic business units.

In considering each of these areas of globalisation in turn it is possible to identify business sector examples in which the globalisation trend is relatively advanced and others in which it is at early stages. For example, until the late 1990s retailing could be regarded as a largely national or, at most, sub-regional activity with few examples of retailers active in more than five or six countries. The challenge for global companies is to lead the development towards globalisation in industry sectors where there is the greatest potential for growth. However, there is no guarantee that by simply being globally active in an industry sector a firm will benefit. Firms must be able to manage the environmental threats and exploit their market opportunities by building global competitive advantage. Illustration 6.2 shows how Gillette is responding to global factors.

ILLUSTRATION 6.2 Gillette planning a close shave

In the late 1970s and 1980s the change to disposable razors by many consumers in the US and Europe meant that shaving products appeared to be turning into a commodity market. For Gillette, which had a 65 per cent share of this market, this was extremely serious. Gillette produced its own disposable razor, but consumers did not differentiate between products and so purchased the cheapest. By the mid-1980s the lower-margin disposable products had captured 50 per cent of the market, considerably reducing profits and forcing Gillette to cut its advertising spend to a quarter of what it was in 1975, so reducing the power of its brand name. It seemed as though Gillette in the US had almost given up on razors.

In Europe, however, Gillette had taken a different approach, starting to spend on a pan-European campaign featuring the slogan 'Gillette – the best a man can get' to emphasise the name Gillette and the top-of-the-range Contour Plus brand, and this had led to both a gain in market share and an increase in margins of 5 per cent.

Gillette's mission statement over the past twenty-five years has been 'There is a better way to shave and we will find it', and Sensor spearheaded Gillette's fightback. Sensor, launched in 1989, had twin blades mounted on tiny springs and was designed to give a closer shave by being able to follow the contours of the face. It had been shown to be significantly better than anything else on the market and user tests showed that 80 per cent of men who tried it kept on using it. Despite some internal opposition Gillette decided to centralise its marketing by combining the

European and US sections into one group, headed by the previous European head, to ensure an effective launch of Sensor under the Gillette umbrella brand. Previously, marketing had been carried out by brand managers in each local country.

Sensor helped Gillette to a 70 per cent share of the world razor market, but by 1997 the double-digit sales growth was flattening, signifying the need for a new product. The new product cost well over US$1bn to develop, including US$750 million on manufacturing systems, US$200 million on R&D and US$350 million on marketing. Gillette had been experimenting with the technology since 1970.

Mach 3 was a three-blade system, protected by patents and designed to give a closer shave. It had a pivoting system held within a cartridge, thinner blades and automatic deposition on to the skin of moisturiser and vitamin E. Rubber fins stretched the skin and held the hairs in place for precision cutting. The product was designed to sell at a premium of 25–35 per cent over the price of Sensor, which Gillette retained as it does not withdraw older products.

But the competition was beginning to fight back. The second largest razor manufacturer, Schick, had been part of the purchase in 2000 of Warner Lambert by Pfizer, but Schick had performed poorly. Its sale by Pfizer could lead to a revival in fortunes. Prompted by advances by Gillette in its South Korean home market, Dorco, the fifth largest razor maker, has decided to fight back. It has developed a Mach 3 competitor with prices 30 per cent cheaper than Gillette. In 2002, 50 per cent of its revenue came from exports to 60 countries, with the US accounting for 40 per cent of its exports.

Question How should Gillette keep its technological lead? Will technology be the only factor in its future success?

Source: Gillette

ALTERNATIVE STRATEGIC RESPONSES

It is against the background of the trend towards globalisation and the need to build a worldwide presence that firms must develop strategic responses which are appropriate to their situation and are feasible to implement. For MNEs, the question may be how to rationalise their activities to gain greater focus and effectiveness. For firms that have progressed through the early stages of expansion into new country markets, as we discussed in the previous chapter, the next stage is to decide whether or not to progress further and, if so, what strategy they might adopt to enable them to manage their involvement in many countries. Underpinning the growth strategy in either case must be some fundamental decisions about, first, how far the firm's marketing activities can and should be standardised and, second, how the firm will develop its product portfolio and geographic coverage.

The level of geographic development and product strength will determine the strategic options available to a company. Gogel and Larreche (1989) argue that the threats of global competition will place higher pressures on the effective use of resources. The two main axes for allocating strategic resources are the development of product strength and of geographic coverage. These two axes have to be managed in a balanced way. Focusing too much attention on product investments at the expense of geographic coverage may result in missed international opportunities. On the other hand, focusing on geographic expansion may result in under-investment in products, weakening the competitive position of the firm.

Gogel and Larreche identify four types of competitors along the two dimensions of product range and geographic coverage as displayed in Figure 6.1. The position of a company on the international competitive posture matrix will determine the strategic options.

Kings. Because these firms have a wide geographic coverage and strong product portfolio they are in a strong competitive position. They have been able to expand geographically and have not dispersed their resources into weak products. They are in the best position to have an effective global strategy.

Barons. These companies have strong products in a limited number of countries. This makes geographic expansion attractive to them. It also makes them attractive to companies wishing to supplement their own product strength and therefore may be takeover targets.

Adventurers. These have been driven to expand geographically, but they lack a strong portfolio. They are vulnerable to an increasing level of global

---

competition. Their challenge is to consolidate their product position by focusing on internal product development, acquisition, or by eliminating products to concentrate on a narrower portfolio.

Commoners. Commoners have a product portfolio with relatively weak international potential and narrow geographic coverage. They may have benefited from legal barriers protecting them from intense competition They are likely acquisition targets, and before any geographical expansion they need to build their product portfolio. A likely international strategy could be one of supplying own-brand products to retailers.

The key issue for firms is that increasing geographic coverage and product strength compete for resources and each quadrant of the matrix reflects the trade-offs that may become necessary. Whilst the position of a firm on the matrix reflects how it has been able to balance its resources between consolidation and expansion of geographic coverage and product strength, the decision it has made will have also been based on its chosen attitude and commitment to achieving a global strategy.

The options for strategic development are shown in Figure 6.2.

The challenge facing firms with aspirations to become truly effective global players appears to be turning widespread international presence into global competitive advantage. The critical success factor in achieving this is to offer added value for global customers by providing them with benefits that are significantly better than those provided by the competitors, particularly local competitors. At the same time they must aggressively seek cost efficiencies that will enable the firm to offer better value for money than their competitors.

In practice, firms manage these apparently incompatible requirements by using strategies that are appropriate to their own situation, and striking a balance between the different degrees of **standardisation** or **adaptation** of the various elements of international marketing.

In general:

■ Marketing objectives and strategies are more readily standardised than operational marketing decisions.

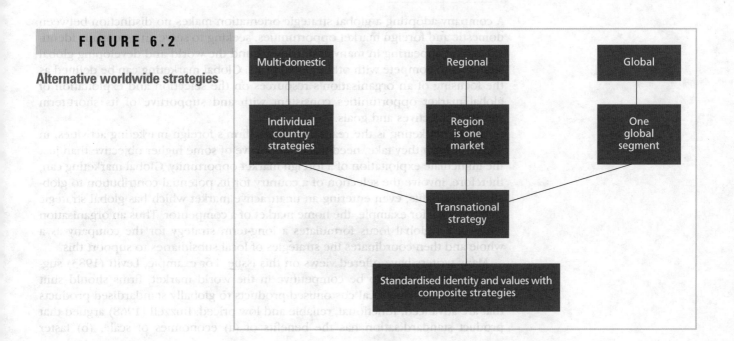

FIGURE 6.2

Alternative worldwide strategies

- Within the marketing mix, products are most easily standardised, promotion less so and distribution and pricing with difficulty.

- The more operational the decision the more likely it is to be differentiated.

Consequently the elements of marketing management should be seen as being at different points of a continuum of standardisation, where the product and service image is generally easier to standardise than individual country pricing.

Pricing	Adaptation
Distribution	
Sales Force	
Sales Promotion	
Product	
Image	
Objective	Standardisation
Strategy	

The standardisation/adaptation discussion leads, at one extreme, to the concept of a multi-domestic approach in which the firm has a completely different strategy for every single market and, at the other extreme, a global approach in which everything in the marketing activity is standardised in all countries. In practice firms adopt a combination of standardisation and adaptation of the various elements of the marketing management programmes and processes by globalising some elements and localising others. In broad terms it is possible to categorise a firm's strategic development as multi-domestic, global or regional, or a third alternative strategy in which separate, but largely standardised marketing strategies are implemented across a region of the world.

The largest, most complex companies in the world use a combination of all these strategies. A transnational approach is one in which the firm has a standardised identity and corporate values throughout the firm but delivers its strategic objectives through composite strategies which contain elements of multi-domestic, regional and global strategies.

Global strategy

A company adopting a global strategic orientation makes no distinction between domestic and foreign market opportunities, seeking to serve an essentially identical market appearing in many countries around the world and developing global strategies to compete with other global firms. Global marketing can be defined as the focusing of an organisation's resources on the selection and exploitation of global market opportunities consistent with and supportive of its short-term strategic objectives and goals.

Global marketing is the realisation that a firm's foreign marketing activities, in whatever form they take, need to be supportive of some higher objective than just the immediate exploitation of a foreign market opportunity. Global marketing can, therefore, involve the selection of a country for its potential contribution to globalisation benefits, even entering an unattractive market which has global strategic significance – for example, the home market of a competitor. Thus an organisation with such a global focus formulates a long-term strategy for the company as a whole and then coordinates the strategies of local subsidiaries to support this.

Many writers have offered views on this issue. For example, Levitt (1983) suggested that in order to be competitive in the world market, firms should shift their emphasis from local customised products to globally standardised products that are advanced, functional, reliable and low priced. Buzzell (1968) argued that product standardisation has the benefits of (a) economies of scale, (b) faster accumulation of learning experience and (c) reduced costs of design modification. Kotabe (1990) concluded that European and Japanese firms that market standardised products have higher levels of product and process innovations and thus greater competitive advantage than those using product adaptation.

In summarising the forces at work in the standardisation debate Meffet and Bolz (1993) describe the globalisation push and pull factors, shown in Figure 6.3, which are driving marketing standardisation, in terms of both the marketing programmes, such as the product portfolio, new product launch and the advertising programme and the marketing processes, for example how the marketing information system and the planning process can be integrated around the world.

In considering this model, it is important to recognise that the global business environment has changed considerably, with many barriers to standardisation being removed or reduced, as has been discussed earlier in this chapter. Some of the globalisation effects, such as economies of scale, the experience effect (or learning curve) explained on page 377 and the high costs of innovation have become more significant drivers of standardisation.

In practice, however, global firms strike an appropriate balance between the relative advantages of standardisation and adaptation to local tastes. There is little point in standardising programmes for marketing products and services if consumers reject them and only buy the products and services that meet their specific needs.

McDonald's, for example, is not only adapting its traditional products to the tastes of different cultures but is also recognising the need for greater variety on its menu.

Multi-domestic strategies

The multi-domestic or multi-national market concept focuses on maximising the company's effectiveness and efficiency in exploiting economies of scale, experience and skill in marketing, production and logistics. A company adopting such an orientation assumes that foreign market opportunities are as important as

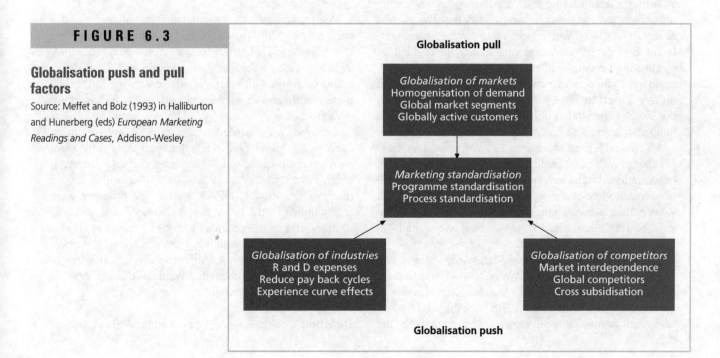

FIGURE 6.3

Globalisation push and pull factors

Source: Meffet and Bolz (1993) in Halliburton and Hunerberg (eds) *European Marketing Readings and Cases*, Addison-Wesley

Globalisation pull

Globalisation of markets
Homogenisation of demand
Global market segments
Globally active customers

Marketing standardisation
Programme standardisation
Process standardisation

Globalisation of industries
R and D expenses
Reduce pay back cycles
Experience curve effects

Globalisation of competitors
Market interdependence
Global competitors
Cross subsidisation

Globalisation push

home market opportunities. However, the company takes the view that the differences between its international markets are so acute that widespread adaptation is necessary to meet market needs and to retain competitive leverage in local markets. Thus the company essentially follows a differentiated marketing strategy with individual marketing mix strategies in many of their world markets.

There has been considerable debate amongst writers about the pros and cons of multi-domestic strategies to achieve a worldwide competitive advantage as opposed to the pursuance of a global strategy through the standardisation of marketing activities. However, it is quite clear that for many major businesses there are few benefits to be obtained from widespread standardisation of their activities. Consequently a well-organised and managed multi-domestic strategy is an effective method for many companies for developing a global business.

An excellent example of an organisation which can be accurately characterised as having a multi-domestic strategy is Asea Brown Boveri (ABB), discussed in Illustration 6.3. The firm used a multi-domestic strategy to gain competitive advantage in its target country markets. A key factor in the strategy is encouraging senior managers to be entrepreneurial in responding to local customer needs, industry standards and different stages of economic development.

Thus whilst there are many forces driving companies towards achieving a global strategy through standardising as many marketing activities as possible, there are also very important prevailing arguments persuading companies that they can also achieve an effective worldwide strategy through a multi-domestic approach. These forces are as follows.

ILLUSTRATION 6.3   ABB: a new model of global entrepreneurialism – good while it lasted?

In 1988 Sweden's ASEA and the Swiss company Brown Boveri merged to form ABB. It had customers in the process industries, manufacturing and consumer industries, and in utilities (oil, gas and petrochemicals). Percy Barnevik as chief executive was faced with merging two companies with different business cultures and operations. He decided to create a fundamentally different model of how a large MNE could be organised and managed. He created the new head office in Zurich to make the merger less like a takeover by the Swedes and started dispersing the two head offices of 6000 staff amongst a number of front-line units.

He created a head office with 135 staff managing 1300 companies with 5000 profit centres. He cut 90 per cent of headquarters staff by moving 30 per cent into the SBUs, 30 per cent into free-standing service centres concerned with value adding activities and eliminating 30 per cent of the jobs. Similar huge cuts in management were made in the headquarters of the subsidiaries.

The management within the SBUs, which usually had fewer than 200 employees, were given a substantially enhanced role in managing their business. ABB was one of the most admired firms of the 1990s. Ghoshall and Bartlett said that Barnevik's achievement was combining the contradictions of big and small, local and global, economies of scale and intimate market knowledge to create a truly global organisation.

ABB employed 160 000 staff in 100 countries and a large part of ABB's manufacturing was moved away from the developed countries to the developing countries, including Eastern Europe. By employing people in developing countries ABB was in a position to sell further expertise and services as they helped build the countries' infrastructure.

Barnevik was succeeded by Jorgen Centremann in October 2000 but he lasted less than two years as the company's share price halved. ABB missed its profit targets, it nearly ran out of cash as its debts mounted, and in 2002 it made its first loss of US$787 million. The problems were compounded by the threat that a US unit would go bankrupt because of the potential liabilities (capped at US$1.3 billion by a US court) resulting from a number of massive lawsuits involving asbestos. Whilst this was still under negotiation ABB could not divest its oil and gas division, which it needed to do to reduce debt.

Question Could the model be blamed for ABB's problems?

Industry standards remain diverse

For many traditional industries such as those based upon engineering and particularly those that involve large investment in plant and equipment the cost of harmonisation of standards is high and the progress to harmonisation is slow. The markets for these industries often involve a country's infrastructure, transport and utilities and, consequently, depend on often protracted government spending decisions. Usually in making decisions such as these governments will give consideration not simply to market factors, but also to the impact on the economy, environment and the electorate's expectations too.

Customers continue to demand locally differentiated products

Cultural heritage and traditions still play a strong role in areas such as food, drink and shopping. Whilst there are increasing moves to accept cross-border products, there is still resistance in many cultures.

Being an insider remains critically important

The perceived country of origin of goods still has a bearing on take-up of products and so local manufacturing of goods is frequently necessary to overcome this scepticism. In business-to-business marketing, there is a definite bias in favour of products sourced from particular areas, such as Silicon Valley in the US, and so IT/electronic firms often decide to set up local manufacture there.

Global organisations are difficult to manage

In finding ways to coordinate far flung operations, firms have to decentralise and replace home country loyalties with a system of corporate values and loyalties. For some companies this proves to be problematic and, in some cases, totally unacceptable to the workforce.

Management myopia

Products and product categories are sometimes candidates for global marketing but managers fail to seize the opportunity. Self-Reference Criterion often makes it difficult for managers to take other than a narrow, country view of international marketing. Companies must see the potential for changing the competitive nature of the industry in their favour by triggering a shift from multi-domestic to a global strategy. Because there are no guarantees that a business can succeed, the firm must be willing to risk the heavy investment that a global strategy requires. For some, the resources required and the risks involved are simply too great.

Regional strategy

Perhaps one of the most significant developments in global marketing strategy is how firms respond to the rise of the regional trading blocs. Even in global industries, company strategies are becoming more of a composite of regionally focused strategies and programmes. For many companies, regionalisation represents a more manageable compromise between the extremes of global standardisation and multi-domestic strategies.

Regional trading blocs tend to favour their own MNEs and so for those companies located outside the region there can be significant tariff and non-tariff barriers. For example, the indigenous manufacturers usually get early warning of new government legislation as they tend to be part of government decision making. Public–private sector committees decide on standards, such as car emissions, safety standards and security. By shifting operations and decision making inside the region an MNE can gain the benefits of insider advantage.

The key to developing effective regional strategies must be in deciding what makes the region distinctive and in what ways the marketing strategy for one region should be differentiated from the others. It is only relatively recently that Japanese car manufacturers are beginning to recognise the importance of modifying their styling for regional tastes. Nissan has found that even the shape of the headlights can give away the origins of the design.

A number of companies are taking the opportunity from the formation of regional trading blocs to build on existing, or form new, trading relationships and are including regional objectives and plans as a significant part of their worldwide strategy. For example, over the past two decades a number of US and Pacific Rim companies have targeted Europe for significant development and now many European and US firms have their sights set on China and Latin America as new growth markets.

The prime motivation in the formation of the regional trading blocs is to enable indigenous companies to build the critical mass of activity within the home region necessary to enable them to compete effectively in global markets. Asian companies have proved to be more effective in developing strategic alliances although now there are some embryo alliances of firms in the European Union that participate in a common supply chain, or offer complementary or competitive products. Where the companies come from different countries, political differences do still arise, particularly if national governments are concerned about the retention of jobs in sensitive industries, such as the defence and airline industries. Airbus is one such consortium.

Transnational strategies

If a firm has sufficient power and resources to exploit all the available opportunities on a worldwide basis, with little need to adapt strategies or involve partners to any great extent, then a simple strategy can be developed. However, many multi-nationals have a wide range of products and services, some of which might be suited to global development and others to multi-domestic development. The successful exploitation of these opportunities might require a much more flexible approach to strategic development. It might involve a number of partners in licensing, joint ventures and strategic alliances as well as wholly owned operations.

Transnational companies integrate diverse assets, resources and people into operating units around the world. Through flexible management processes and networks, transnational companies aim to build three strategic capabilities:

- Global scale efficiency and competitiveness.
- National level responsibilities and flexibility.
- Cross-market capacity to leverage learning on a worldwide basis.

In such organisations the ownership of the operations becomes less clear in terms of where any particular product was made, what the domestic nationality of the manufacturing or service provider was, or which firms manufacture and market the product and services.

Ghoshal and Bartlett (1992) argue that the aim of transnational companies is to further the firm's global scale efficiency and competitiveness in its totality. This task means the firm needs the ability to recognise market opportunities and risks across national borders. The overall goal is to achieve global competitiveness through a fully integrated strategy and operations. Thus a transnational approach is not a particular strategy, but a strategic perspective that evolves as firms and the markets in which they operate increase in complexity. IBM is a transnational organisation because certain of its marketing operations and research and development are centralised and standardised whereas other units operate with a substantial degree of independence. It has a strong corporate identity and some of its promotional themes, for example around e-business, are common throughout the firm. It has also formed strategic alliances with partners in order to carry out certain research and development activities where it is likely to benefit from the participation of partners. In such organisations the implications for strategic development are significant. Any strategy that is to achieve global competitive advantage needs to accommodate some, or all of the following:

- Simple and complex individual product and market policies, which may be independent or interdependent.
- Customer segments that are specific and unique to a cross national niche market and so the resultant segments are transnational and valid across borders.
- Working closely with firms that are customers, suppliers, competitors and partners at the same time, but simultaneously ensuring that the values of the company are maintained and demonstrated to the external stakeholders through establishing clear and unambiguous positioning in all markets.
- Maintaining and building meaningful and added value relationships in the supply chain.

INTERNATIONAL MARKETING MANAGEMENT FOR GLOBAL FIRMS

So far in this chapter we have identified the changing trends in the business environment that are leading to increasing globalisation and the factors that affect the firms' response to this, particularly in the way they standardise or adapt their marketing programmes and processes. We have shown distinct differences in the way global strategies can be developed to meet individual firm situations. Implementing these global strategies, however, poses considerable problems and it is to these that we now turn.

As in the previous chapter, it is useful for the discussion to be based loosely upon the McKinsey 7S framework, which includes the hardware elements of strategy, structure and systems and the software elements of management style, staff, skills and shared values. Again we start with the hardware elements of strategy, systems and organisation structure.

Global strategy implementation

Global firms have the objective of developing effective business operations in all the major markets in the world in order to maximise their performance. Whilst in the past they may well have prioritised the developed economies in North America, Europe and Asia, principally Japan, these firms are now looking to develop a significant presence in many more emerging markets in China, other countries in Asia, Central and Eastern Europe and South America that will offer much higher growth in the future.

Building a **global presence** is hugely expensive and many firms see no value in expanding globally if their home country or region offers sufficient growth prospects without marketing their products and services in what they might perceive to be higher risk areas. US companies have a large domestic market and, despite the rapid growth prospects of other regions of the world, their unfamiliarity often makes them unattractive. However, with growth rates four times as high in Asia as in the rest of the world during the 1990s, almost all the Fortune 500 companies invested heavily in manufacturing in this area.

Asian firms usually take a longer-term view in the way they develop new markets because they usually rely on private capital rather than on shareholders who seek short-term gains. This results in a more conservative, cost conscious and more risk averse approach and this suggests that many, although clearly not all Asian firms, will continue to build their business regionally.

This is especially the case as the predicted medium-term growth rates in the Pacific Rim and particularly in China should provide the strong home market for local Asian companies to build rapidly to become powerful regional players with the prospect of expanding worldwide in the twenty-first century. New competitors have made rapid advances; for example China's Legend group has around 30 per cent of the Chinese personal computer market, compared with the 5 per cent of the global market leader Dell. P T Indofood from Indonesia has a major share of the massive instant noodle market and China Ocean Shipping has overtaken Maersk in the container shipping market.

For firms wishing to build a truly global presence, there are a number of challenges; these include:

■ Responding to the changing basis of **competitive advantage**.

■ Increasing **global appeal** by building the **global brand**.

■ Creating a **global presence** by achieving **global reach**.

■ Managing diverse and complex activities across a range of often similar but often disparate markets and cultures.

Global appeal and the changing basis of competitive advantage

In the past, companies could differentiate their products and services by 'new to the world' innovation that generates new core benefits to customers but genuine new products are getting harder to find. All major firms today should be capable of offering good quality products and service that offer value for customers, and competitors are quickly able to offer a reasonable and usually lower cost alternative. The rapid growth of the Japanese car industry was largely based on value for money criteria, with quality, reliability and performance at a reasonable cost being the basis of the appeal. However, many of their competitors from the emerging economies are now able to offer cheaper and even better value for money cars. Moreover, some of the car makers from the developed countries have substantially improved their quality and reliability and are able to offer designs and brand imagery with better consumer appeal. The focus seems to have moved away from the cheap reliable global car to cars made from global components but with designs and styling which meet the requirements of regional customer segments. Illustration 6.4 shows just how competitive markets that have reached maturity can be. The car market is highly competitive and is characterised by over-capacity and it is becoming harder for major global players to be consistently profitable. This is also the subject of the Chapter 8 case study.

In the information technology industry it is possible to observe similar changes as consumers increasingly expect computer suppliers to offer improved quality and greater reliability as well as becoming more 'user-friendly'. The long-established firms must now offer more intangible benefits, including better styling, higher levels of service support and advice, and more interesting and appealing software and online services. Apple Computers' performance was transformed by the introduction of the i-Mac.

The implications of appealing to less tangible aspects of service are that these are exactly the elements of the total product offer where there are the greatest cultural differences and the greatest need for adaptations. What constitutes an enjoyable fast-food menu, an attractive car design or interesting Web site is clearly affected by local consumer tastes, values and attitudes. In business-to-business situations, whilst the core benefits of the product and service offer may be standardised it will have to be tailored to satisfy specific business requirements. There is no such thing as a standard power station, advertising agency service or mainframe computer.

Increasing global appeal by building the global brand

Branding is usually considered within the marketing strategy as part of the product and service policy and we have addressed the use of brands in international marketing there. Global brands, however, are inextricably tied up with achieving global appeal and building a global presence and so we have included a broader-based discussion of global branding at this point.

Global brand management   The recession of the early 1990s sparked off the first real challenge to the power of the biggest global brands. Before then, apart from a few exceptions, they had seemed to simply increase their dominant position steadily and consistently over decades. Against the threat of unemployment or reduced incomes, however, many consumers sought to restrict their household spending by becoming more cost conscious. In a number of cases they found that the second or minor brands, and especially supermarket own brands,

---

ILLUSTRATION 6.4   Floundering Ford

It is hard to imagine that in 2003 questions could be asked on Wall Street about whether Ford could be in danger of going bankrupt. With annual sales of 7 million cars and a cash mountain of US$11 billion it seems unlikely, but with a loss in 2002 of US$5 billion and forecast loss of US$1 billion in 2003 the cash mountain would not last forever.

At the end of 2000 the problems were most acute for Japanese firms. Only Toyota and Honda of the five major Japanese car makers, Toyota, Nissan, Honda, Mitsubishi and Mazda, were thriving. The others, weakened by declining demand, poor products, bad sales and awful balance sheets, were struggling to survive. Mazda had recorded its fifth year of losses and Mitsubishi and Nissan had recorded substantial losses too. Despite a reduction in sales of Japanese cars from 13.5 million to 11 million, Mazda and Toyota had each opened new factories to give a capacity of 14 million cars in Japan alone.

In 2003, with chronic and increasing over-capacity in the US and Europe, costs rising and prices falling, many

factories were losing money. The weak yen had helped Japanese manufacturers to export to the US, putting the US manufacturers under pressure. For many years Ford had made profits outside the US, but with competition from Japanese and European car makers and a revived GM this was more difficult. Its traditional US profit generator, light trucks, had come under pressure from GM and Japanese products. Already thin margins on car sales in the US had been made worse because Ford had a number of expensive product recalls and it had sought to prop up sales with interest-free loans. In total its debt attributed to loans was a massive US$150 billion. An economic downturn could increase the number of bad debts. With its upmarket cars, Jaguar and Land Rover, losing money and its niche players Volvo and Aston Martin having little effect on the overall figures, the position was bleak.

Question   What could Ford do?

were often indistinguishable from the premium priced brands in perceived quality and so consumers simply traded down. Marlboro, for example, lost substantial market share in the US to own labels before dramatically cutting prices. As a consequence of this, they suffered profit reductions and turned their attention to less developed countries to make up the shortfall.

Khashani (1995) draws attention to changes in a number of factors, which affect the performance of the brands.

- Customers are better educated, better informed, more sceptical, more willing to experiment, less brand loyal, much more media aware and have higher expectations of the total package.

- Competition is more aggressive, with more rapid launches of higher quality 'me-too' products.

- Retailers have installed better electronic point of sale technology and, as a result, have greater awareness of brand performance. In response to better consumer information, they have introduced better quality private labels.

These changes in the brand market environment have been compounded by weaknesses in brand management, including:

- low investment;
- inadequate product development;
- poor consumer communication;
- an emphasis on quick pay-backs rather than long-term brand building;
- too little innovation; and
- an emphasis upon small modifications.

Khashani accuses brand managers of laziness in developing pricing policy, paying insufficient attention to value creation, pricing arrogance, insufficient product differentiation, offering poor value for money and tolerating high cost bases. He summarises much of the present brand management in terms of complacency and acceptance of a comfortable status quo, with little long-term vision, little innovative thinking and insufficient interaction with customers and distributors.

Brand management has typically been bureaucratic, risk averse and taken a short-term view. In short, he feels that brand managers have lost the killer instinct. Khashani's solution is to:

- get lean;
- avoid the temptation to live off past successes;
- cut costs to improve cost structures; and
- provide a basis for aggressive pricing;
- prune weak brands and reallocate resources;
- invest and innovate in the product and service; and
- create more consumer value.

It is essential to listen to the market and get closer to customers. He stresses the need to be bold and think creatively setting new market and performance standards and taking risks. The aim must be to think globally, launch products and services sequentially and rapidly across markets and build world brands. The case study at the end of this chapter shows how the McDonald's brand has been affected by many of these factors.

There are many 'almost great' brands but only a few are truly great. Dilemma 6.2 shows how the management of Shiseido must make some bold decisions if they wish to develop a global brand.

As in the Shiseido illustration, many firms reduce the number of brands they support in order to concentrate their resources. Cutting brands can be risky if the chosen brands fail to perform well in all global markets and the benefit from cutting brands can take some time to appear in results, as happened when Unilever cut a number of brands from its portfolio.

Business-to-business branding So far the discussion has focused on global consumer branding but branding is important in business-to-business marketing too. The reason for this is that purchasers and users value the commitment of suppliers to the product and service and benefit from the added value from dealing with a firm. For example, buyers talk about suppliers such as IBM, Oracle or Microsoft as brands, which lends a sense of authority to the purchasing decision, or users might detail a specific product or service that must be purchased e.g. Hewlett Packard printers. In some situations there may be benefits which can be gained from co-branding or association with globally recognised branded components (e.g. Intel microprocessors in computers and Lycra in garments). This trend is becoming increasingly important as consumers become more influential in the choice of components and services in the supply chain and demand products that contain branded components.

In international business-to-business branding firms use different naming strategies, with some firms concentrating less on corporate brand endorsement and more on the individual brand in the same way as Procter & Gamble and Unilever do in consumer markets. For example, the pharmaceutical product brands Zantac and Tagamet are promoted by GlaxoSmithKline without any obvious association with the manufacturer.

Ultimately, the rationale for the existence of brands in business-to-business marketing is the same as in consumer goods marketing. It is to avoid the commoditisation of products, which leads to decisions being based only on price. As an example, purchasers of capital equipment would expect to pay price premiums for a number of perceived benefits from globally recognised suppliers:

DILEMMA 6.2   **Shiseido transforming from toiletries to cosmetics**

Shiseido of Japan has the ambition to become the world's leading cosmetics company in an industry worth around US$170 billion. Currently the world's fourth largest cosmetics maker, Shiseido's sales are only 40 per cent of those of L'Oréal, the world's cosmetic industry leader. It has some ground to make up before it achieves its objective. With a presence in 59 countries, Shiseido claims that the brand blends Eastern spirituality with Western sophistication and the company has a good reputation in colour make-up and skincare. In Europe and America it has a good name but it is seen in Japan as boring, particularly when compared with new entrants such as Anna Sui from South Korea.

Shiseido made losses in 2001/2 as its home market came under attack from Estee Lauder and L'Oréal and margins reduced as supermarkets adopted low price strategies, following the entry of Carrefour and Wal-Mart, which took a 38 per cent stake in Seiyu. Japan still accounts for 76 per cent of Shiseido's sales.

Shiseido faces a number of dilemmas. Whilst it is aiming to create an exclusive, prestigious image, it has no clear identity. As well as selling cosmetics, it includes toiletries, such as shampoo, soap and sanitary towels within its range. It launches hundreds of new lotions and other products every month. It also has a high-cost distribution system with 25 000 tiny, branded specialist outlets that are losing sales to department stores and mass-market pharmacies, and it still employs 8000 full-time beauty counsellors. It is considering reducing its 160 brands.

Shiseido is seen as expensive and nothing special by young people in Japan and still remains a very traditional Japanese company.

Question What must it do to achieve its ambitions?

- interchangeability of parts;
- short delivery time;
- working with prestigious suppliers;
- full range of spare parts available;
- lower operating costs;
- lower installation costs;
- higher quality materials.

Creating a global presence by achieving global reach

Few firms have the resources to build a strong presence in all the countries in the world. Few others are prepared to wait until they have built the products, services, image and resources through organic growth within the firm. Instead, they use a wide range of growth, market entry and marketing mix strategies to achieve global reach and these are discussed in later chapters. Acquisition and mergers are discussed here because they are being used by MNEs to extend global reach much more quickly and achieve effective marketing worldwide, as Illustration 6.5 shows. Focus is achieved by major restructuring in the form of both acquisition and demergers.

Mergers of equals   In the past, the rationale for acquisitions and mergers has been that a well-managed company should take over a weaker rival marketer of competing or complementary products in order to achieve higher growth and savings in operating, management and marketing costs. As market entry methods, acquisition or mergers are used to facilitate access to particular markets. In some business sectors, however, there appears to be the view that it is only by operating on a very large scale on a worldwide basis that customers can receive the level and quality of service that they need. This seems obvious in the case of aircraft manufacture where there are essentially only two players, Boeing and Airbus, but less so in other sectors. For example, there are not always scale economies in investment banking and accountancy and smaller firms will continue to thrive in these sectors.

ILLUSTRATION 6.5   **Merging for global focus**

The drive for globalisation comes from a firm's desire to dominate the business sector in which it operates. Organic growth takes too long and so a dominant position is created by buying up smaller rivals or merging with equals. Very often businesses are acquired that do not fit the overall portfolio and so it is necessary to sell off the unwanted parts. The £23.8 billion merger between Grand Metropolitan and Guinness created Diageo, the world's largest spirits and wines businesses. It has 12 of the top 100 world spirits brands, including Gordon's Gin, Johnny Walker Scotch and Smirnoff Vodka, as well as Guinness.

To further strengthen its position in 2002, however, Diageo sold off some businesses that might divert it from dominating its sector. Burger King, the second largest fast food chain with 11 000 outlets was sold to a consortium led by Texas Pacific group. Its food division, Pillsbury, was sold to its rival General Mills to form the fifth largest food company in the world. Diageo retained a 33 per cent stake in the merged company. The irony is that Pillsbury and General Mills were both founded in Minneapolis in the 1860s and have been bitter rivals ever since. In practice the negotiations in both these sell-offs took so long that staff became demotivated and performance was hit.

Question   In the short term profits can be increased by being focused on an ever smaller range of brands but the question for Diageo is whether it could also be more risky in the longer term?

In some sectors, however, there have been a number of **mergers of equals** in which firms of similar market power agree to combine, believing that their future success depends upon achieving comprehensive global reach; for example, Citigroup and Travelers group in financial services and Glaxo Wellcome and Smith Kline Beecham in pharmaceuticals.

Cross-border mergers and acquisitions are becoming increasingly common too, for example in telecommunications Vodafone (UK) with Airtouch US and Mannesmann (Germany), and in automobiles Daimler-Benz (Germany) and Chrysler (US).

The merger between Daimler-Benz and Chrysler immediately provided a second brand to Mercedes and avoided the need to expand the Mercedes brand into volume products, which could result in confused positioning. It built upon Mercedes' position as the world's largest makers of trucks. Mercedes had extensive overseas operations, especially in Brazil, and had opened up its first factory in the US to make its M Class sports utility vehicle. Chrysler was mainly a US manufacturer – its strength was in multi-purpose 'people carriers' and the off-road vehicles under its Jeep brand.

Such mergers as these clearly lead to oligopolies which are extremely powerful worldwide players but, so far, the regulators have prevented only a small number taking place. In the pharmaceutical industry the mergers that have already taken place have been allowed because the regulators have taken the view that the combined research and development resources of worldwide operations might be beneficial in developing new and more effective drugs.

Problems do occur if organisations gain too much power and influence. The four largest accounting firms have provided both auditing and consultancy services, so creating potential conflicts of interest. Following the collapse of Enron, the US utilities company, accountancy firm Andersen was forced out of business because they were advising Enron on the use of questionable financial practice and not carrying out the financial audit to an acceptable standard. As a result, three of the remaining accountancy firms have demerged their consultancy business.

One of the implications of mergers, particularly mergers of equals, is the impact upon branding decisions and whether the merged firm will retain two separate brand identities or whether they will merge them. The decision is taken often against a background of whether the senior management believes the brand is important for their particular company or industry sector. Smith (1998) reports research by McKinsey which suggests that there are three routes to brand consolidation:

- Phasing out brands over time, when the strategy is to retain loyal customers who will buy as long as the brand is available.

- Quickly changing some of the branding, which only works well if the firm has control over distribution, advertising and promotion.

- Co-branding to manage the transition, which is the most common approach, used, for example, when Whirlpool bought Philips domestic appliances.

The pitfalls of mergers and acquisitions   There are serious pitfalls associated with mergers and acquisitions, particularly where they involve cross-border ownership and cooperation. Finkelstein (1998) refers to a study of 89 US companies acquired by foreign buyers during the period 1977–90 and found the performance of most of them had not improved within one year. The acquisition of Colombia Pictures by Sony in 1989 is an extreme example of this. Sony's strategy at the time of the acquisition was to develop the ability to market the software of the leisure industry, such as films, videos and CDs, to complement their range of hardware, such as TVs, CD players and video recorders. Sony paid a premium for Colombia and left Columbia's established Hollywood executives largely to run their own show, but it was forced to accept a US$3.2 billion write down in 1994 after considerable problems had emerged in the way the old management had responded to the new ownership.

As well as the obvious organisational challenges that follow from a merger, such as who will be in charge, whose products and services will be offered (or dropped) and where costs savings should be made, particularly if the merger or acquisition was not entirely harmonious, there are the cross-cultural challenges, such as the different ways of doing business in Europe, the US and Asia, different corporate governance, the status and power of different employee and management groups, job security guarantees, government regulations and customer expectations.

Cross-cultural differences are often quite subtle. Upjohn (US) and Pharmacia (Sweden) merged in 1995 but suffered a number of problems. Upjohn executives scheduled meetings in July when Swedes traditionally take holidays. Their direct, detail-oriented style did not fit well with Swedes' preference for discussion and a consensus management style. To avoid the fear of domination by one side the new group opened a head office in London but as the two separate parts retained their old corporate offices in the US and Sweden they simply added another layer of management hierarchy.

Finkelstein (1998) recommends that the integration process should focus on value creation by ensuring employees actually achieve the synergy that is promised before the deal is done, planning in detail how the various cross-border problems will be overcome and developing a clear communication plan to cope with the whole process.

Managing diverse and complex activities across a range of often similar but often disparate markets and cultures

The implications of pursuing a global strategy are that organisations must continually expand into what are likely to be less attractive markets, perhaps tertiary opportunities from Harrell and Keifer's model (page 109) or incipient markets in Gilligan and Hird's model (page 103). Typically these will be the less attractive markets (at least at the present time) because of the associated political and economic risks of entering less developed markets, more difficult trading conditions and barriers to 'free' trade. By comparison with the firms' existing markets, these emerging markets may demand disproportionately high investment in management time and financial resources as well as involving the firm in considerable additional risk.

There are, however, some significant advantages of entering newly emerging markets. Nakata and Sirikumar (1997) give three reasons why emerging markets are becoming attractive:

1 Global companies with good reputations can gain customers relatively quickly in these markets which in the past have been starved of well-known branded products.

2 Eighty per cent of global income comes from the triad of the US, Europe and Japan but there is increased maturation of these developed markets because of low birth-rates and ageing populations. This means that future growth will be ever more difficult to achieve in developed, operationally less risky markets which are also subject to more intense competition.

3 Typically the average rate of growth of the emerging market economies is much higher than in the industrial nations.

These appear to be exactly the reasons for Kodak's entry into China in Illustration 6.6.

The risks associated with specific emerging country market involvement can be substantial, however, and include some or all of the following:

- financial loss associated with inappropriate investment, such as buying unusable assets, being unable to achieve acceptable levels of performance from the purchased assets, losing the assets by misappropriation to the host country government or to partners;

- damage to the firm's reputation through association with the country, its government and intermediaries, especially where they are seen to be corrupt, engage in unacceptable social or business practices, or have close relationships with other countries or organisations which are considered to be corrupt;

- litigation arising from offering an unacceptable product and/or service to the country, or becoming involved in questionable business practices;

- prompting an unexpected international competitor response by attacking a market which it considers to be its home territory;

- initially making arrangements with joint venture partners, distributors, agents or government agencies to secure entry but which become inappropriate in the medium to long term;

- damage to the firm's reputation through insensitivity in its operations in the country, when it might be accused of exploiting local labour, the country's resources or causing environmental damage to the country.

The problem for international strategic management in less developed countries is that the 'rule book' that managers rely on in developed countries does not always apply, because business infrastructure and processes are not well established.

ILLUSTRATION 6.6   **Kodak in China: Smile please**

In the 1980s Fuji Photo Film developed a strategy attacking the global dominance of Kodak by focusing on the American and European markets. They squeezed Kodak's margins and forced them to cut costs. Kodak's share price went down and there was talk of breaking up the conglomerate. Although Kodak struck back against Fuji in Japan, it continually lost market share during the 1990s and was forced to take drastic action.

In 1998 Kodak announced a US$1.1 billion deal to take over and modernise three loss-making Chinese film and photographic product companies. The year previously, Kodak had laid off 20 000 staff. The equipment that Kodak purchased was too old to be of use and so the real value of the purchase was the people, warehouses, distribution system and land. What Kodak really bought was the entry ticket to a potentially massive market. CEO of Kodak, George Fisher, said at the time that if the Chinese could be

persuaded to finish the roll of the film they had bought and have it developed, Kodak would double its global profits. In urban areas Chinese use 0.8 rolls of film per year and in rural areas 0.1, compared with 3.6 in the US and 3.1 in Europe. Despite this, China is Kodak's second biggest market and the firm is continuing to invest heavily.

Fuji is also firmly established in China and the Chinese government is encouraging the local brand Lucky to compete.

Question Given the development of digital photography and Kodak's worldwide business, how can Kodak use its position in China to improve its worldwide performance?

Sources: Adapted from 'Smile Please', *The Economist*, 28 March 1998 and 'Camera Film in China: A market Analysis', *Access Asia*, June 2002

Organisation structure for transnational firms

Having discussed the simple organisation structures that are appropriate for managing the international strategies of SMEs in the previous chapter, we now turn to the **organisation structure** concepts that large firms might use. Transnational strategies, by their very nature, are complex and specific to the firms' context. Organisation structures differ from firm to firm, but it is possible to make some general comments.

Strategic business units and the three management levels

In Figure 6.4 the conceptual framework of a company is illustrated and shows the three management levels, the strategic, management and operational levels. The broad functional areas of the three levels are illustrated in Figure 6.5.

In most companies the strategic level of the firm is typically responsible for formulating the broad aims of the company, setting corporate objectives, identifying resources that can be utilised and selecting broad strategies. These aims, objectives and resources are then broken down into the constituent parts and allocated between the individual subsidiaries or operating units, which are referred to as strategic business units (SBUs).

The management level then breaks down these allocations into departmental objectives, budgets and tasks for which the functional managers (for example, in R&D or marketing) at the operational level are responsible.

The performance of the company in implementing the plans is monitored and controlled by operating the process in reverse. The operational-level managers are responsible for achieving the objectives set by the management level and the management level is expected to achieve the objectives set by the strategic level.

At an early stage in the company's development, the distinctions between levels are unclear as decisions are made in a largely unplanned, reactive way. As the company develops, the separation of management levels and functions becomes clearer and is reinforced by formalised procedures (reports and meetings) to plan and control the business. Whilst we have indicated three broad levels of management, the number of links in the chain between the chief executive and the customer can vary considerably. The recent trend in many companies has been to remove layers of management in order to have a flatter

---

FIGURE 6.4

The conceptual framework of a firm

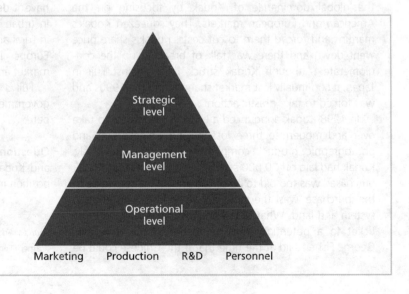

structure to give individual managers far greater responsibility and authority for their part of the company and so replicate the greater flexibility, adaptability and responsiveness of smaller, more entrepreneurial businesses. This has resulted in less distinction between the management activities, with managers at all levels being required to think strategically as well as operationally.

Large firms typically operate matrix management structures with individual members of staff that have international as well as domestic company responsibilities typically having to report to both country and product or brand managers. Majaro (1991) has identified three basic structures in international organisations, the macropyramid, the umbrella and the interglomerate structures (see Figure 6.6), based on the three levels of management within the organisation identified previously: strategic, management and operational.

The macropyramid

The macropyramid is found in multi-national organisations which have a strong nerve centre or headquarters. The organisation is usually highly centralised and the foreign SBUs operate at the management or operational levels of the organisation. Examples of this type of company are McDonald's, IBM, Marks and Spencer and Sony. The individual SBUs have relatively little autonomy and their strategies and tactics are largely determined by the strategic level at the centre. The implications of this structure for marketing are that:

- marketing plans are produced centrally;
- all major decisions regarding the marketing mix are taken centrally and so can be slow and unresponsive to local needs;
- marketing is standardised as much as possible;
- world markets for their products and services are regarded as largely the same;
- local creativity is inhibited;

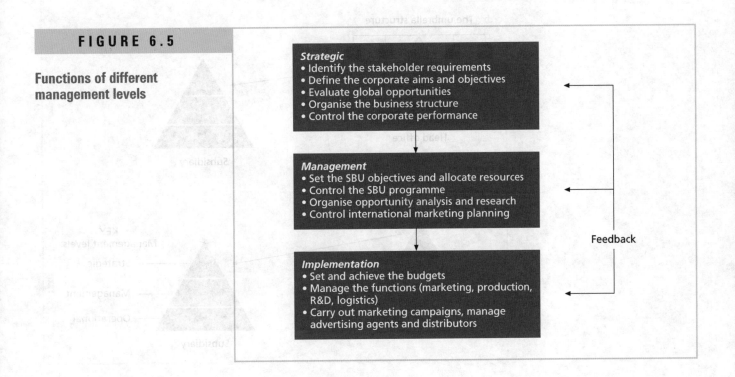

FIGURE 6.5

Functions of different management levels

Strategic
- Identify the stakeholder requirements
- Define the corporate aims and objectives
- Evaluate global opportunities
- Organise the business structure
- Control the corporate performance

Management
- Set the SBU objectives and allocate resources
- Control the SBU programme
- Organise opportunity analysis and research
- Control international marketing planning

Implementation
- Set and achieve the budgets
- Manage the functions (marketing, production, R&D, logistics)
- Carry out marketing campaigns, manage advertising agents and distributors

Feedback

■ communication problems occur as a result of difficulty in interpreting instructions from the centre; and

■ the lack of local autonomy is a disincentive to good managers who must move to the centre for career advancement.

The umbrella structure

Organisations with the umbrella structure take the opposite view to those with the macropyramid. They have fully decentralised planning and control, and give full independence at all levels of management to the foreign subsidiaries. Procter & Gamble and Unilever in the past have operated such a structure. The centre sets only broad corporate objectives, and will provide advice and support, but essentially, each SBU will develop a plan for their area of responsibility.

The implications for the marketing mix of an umbrella structure are:

■ the SBUs can adopt an appropriate marketing mix strategy for the local market;

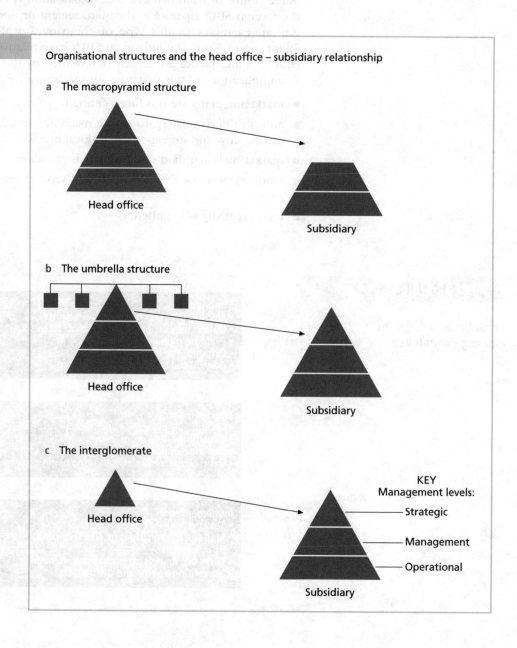

FIGURE 6.6

Development of strategy

Organisational structures and the head office – subsidiary relationship

a The macropyramid structure

Head office

Subsidiary

b The umbrella structure

Head office

Subsidiary

c The interglomerate

Head office

KEY
Management levels:

Strategic

Management

Operational

Subsidiary

- an effective local marketing function can develop local marketing plans;
- market planning can respond to local environmental developments and changes;
- different strategies will be followed for each market and there are implications for usually centralised functions, such as R&D, personnel and finance;
- there is little chance of a global strategy; and
- there can be considerable duplication as different SBUs work on similar strategies and tactics.

This structure, quite obviously, is complex and it is interesting to note that both Procter & Gamble and Unilever have pushed a policy of portfolio rationalisation to address this.

The interglomerate

The interglomerate embraces multi-markets, multi-products and multi-technologies and so no attempt is made by the centre to develop strategies for the individual SBUs which are likely to be international businesses in their own right. Because of the diversity of the firm's activities the centre takes no significant, active management role, and is concerned purely with financial planning and control.

The implications for international marketing are that:

- interglomerates are finance driven;
- the marketing function will not be represented at the strategic level; and
- corporate and marketing strategies are the sole responsibility of the SBU.

Many Western interglomerates of the 1990s, such as Hanson and BTR, have broken up their organisations by demerger and selling off non-core or unprofitable activities. ABB is another example that is under pressure to reconstruct the business. This model remains more common in Asian-owned businesses, such as Hutchinson Whampoa and Guandong Investments, which have significantly different patterns of development.

There is a suggestion that some of the Asian conglomerates are reaching the limits of their founding families to manage them and respond to new competitive pressures. There are suggestions that, in the long term, business methods in Asia will resemble those in the West.

But at the moment the objectives of these Asian interglomerates must be borne in mind when arranging Western–Asian business relationships because they do pose dilemmas, as shown in Illustration 6.7.

Systems, processes and control

Given the complexity of international strategic marketing in global firms it is essential that the organisation operates effective processes for the management of its complex operations, processes and systems to enable managers to be able to share information effectively.

Control

Control is the cornerstone of management. Control provides the means to direct, regulate and manage business operations. A significant amount of interaction is required between the individual areas of marketing (such as market development, advertising and selling) and the other functional areas (such as human resources, finance, production, research and development).

However, for many firms, control means a separate activity through which senior managers are able to keep a check periodically (weekly, monthly or quarterly) on more junior levels of management who often see this in terms of being called upon to justify their actions. Feedback and control systems should be regarded as an integrated part of the whole planning process, and they are essential in ensuring that the marketing plans are not only being implemented worldwide but are still appropriate for the changing environment in each country.

There are a number of benefits of an effective strategic control system. It encourages higher standards of performance, forces greater clarity and realism and permits corporate management to intervene when necessary. Moreover, it ensures that the financial objectives do not overwhelm the strategic objectives, encourages clearer definition of responsibilities making decentralisation work more effectively, and so provides more motivation for managers.

There are three essential elements of the control process:

Setting standards: the standards that are set need to be relevant to the corporate goals such as growth and profits reported by financial measures, such as return on capital employed and on sales, and non-financial indicators, such as market share. Intermediate goals and individual targets can be set by breaking the plan down into measurable parts which, when successfully completed, will lead to the overall objectives being achieved. The standards must be understandable, achievable and relevant to each local country situation.

Measuring performance against standards: to obtain measurements and ensure rapid feedback of information, firms use a variety of techniques, including reports, meetings and special measurements of specific parts of the marketing programme, such as cost benefit analysis of customers, product lines and territories or marketing audits for a thorough examination of every aspect of marketing in a particular country. They also use benchmarking which allows comparisons of various aspects of the business, such as efficiency of distribution, customer response times, service levels and complaints, with other companies that are not necessarily from the same business sector.

ILLUSTRATION 6.7   Conflicting Asian–Western business practices

Western businesses do not understand the way networking plays such a huge role in Asian business. Asian companies generally believe relationships come first, whereas Western firms prefer to decide on the business that interests them and form connections when they are needed. Relationship building is an integral part of Asian business strategy and the opportunities that arise from business connections often result in conglomerates of apparently unrelated businesses. This system of complex conglomerates seems illogical to Western management where building core competencies is common. As regards Asian–Western relationships, many frustrations emerge because of the differences in business practice.

For example, the lack of continuity caused by Western managers moving around from job to job makes it difficult for Asian managers to form the connections necessary for doing business. Moreover, since Asian partners are frequently involved with a number of other firms, conflicts of interest arise. Western managers often complain that their Asian counterparts tend to focus on attaining short-term profits to invest in new ventures with new partners rather than the preferred Western method of building brands or expanding market share.

Question How can Asian and Western firms work effectively together?

Correcting deviations from the plan: perhaps the most difficult decisions that must be made are to determine when performance has deviated sufficiently from the plan to require corrective action to be taken either by changing the plan or the management team charged with the responsibility of carrying out the plan. Evaluation of the performance of a particular management team is particularly difficult in international marketing as the performance of a particular SBU can only be compared with its own plan, a plan determined by the headquarters or with the performance of a 'similar' SBU. There are obvious weaknesses in making any of these comparisons, resulting in considerable difference of opinion between the head office and subsidiary.

A key element in the control process is the input from people, both the directly employed staff of the company but also the staff of the other members of the supply chain. Various quality management models, such as Total Quality Management, Continuous Quality Improvement and Business Excellence, supported by international standards such as ISO 9000, are used by firms to underpin the control process. Consistency across the firm's global operations can be increased and general improvements made using a variety of techniques.

■ Benchmarking against other SBUs within the firm, other firms within the business sector and the 'best in the class' in a particular activity, such as just-in-time operations control, service centre response rates or delivery performance.

■ Identifying good practice, wherever in the world it occurs and applying the lessons either in individual SBUs or across the firm.

■ Encouraging performance improvement through self-assessment (individuals completing questionnaires and improvement plans alone), peer review (evaluation by staff at the same level) and appraisals completed by more senior managers.

Setting standards to achieve consistency and establishing continuous performance improvement projects throughout the global company can, however, be problematic because of cultural barriers, differences in language and ethical standards causing different levels of motivation, communications problems and misinterpretation of instructions and advice. In addition, different measuring techniques, standards and imprecise reporting procedures and processes can create difficulties in achieving a meaningful control process.

Planning systems and processes

The increasingly turbulent environment resulting from more rapid changes in technology, competition, consumer taste and fashion means that the traditional systems and processes for preparing the analysis, strategy development and action plans take too long. Timescales must be reduced to make sure that the plan is still relevant when it is being implemented. Consequently it is necessary to avoid too general and unfocused planning and to improve the quality of implementation and the relevance and responsiveness of the process.

As a result of this, increasing emphasis is being placed by MNEs on scenario and contingency planning to take account of things going wrong because of unexpected changes in the environment. Moreover, greater reliance is being placed on expert systems for understanding market changes, carrying out forecasting, resource planning and gap analysis. The plans prepared tend to be based on the understanding that they will be emergent, and will evolve during the timescale of the plan rather than be decided before the time period of the plan begins. The plans may be designed to be incremental, with the start of each new phase being prompted by a change in the environment or by the successful completion of a previous implementation phase.

Building skills in transnational organisations

Whilst the structures outlined provide some general understanding of the alternative methods of organising the management, they are for most companies an oversimplification. Bartlett and Ghoshal (1987) explain that 'the very act of going international multiplies the firm's organisational complexity'. The domestic organisational variables of product and function are extended by adding the geographic dimension. In a study of nine firms, including ITT, Philips, and Procter & Gamble, they found that the challenge of breaking down biases and building a truly multi-dimensional organisation has proved difficult because there are in-built assumptions within the firm about the roles of the organisational units and the way that they should be managed. The traditional view is that relationships between SBUs should be clear and unambiguous and that the decision-making mechanisms should be clearly understood, but in fact the most successful firms have challenged these assumptions and replaced them with new standards. This has implications for the international marketing manager, as Bartlett and Ghoshal (1992) have concluded. The management of transnational businesses requires highly specialised, closely linked groups of global business managers, country or regional managers, and functional managers who work in networks. They explain the implications for managers in such transnational organisations. Global business or product division managers have the responsibility to further the company's global-scale efficiency and competitiveness. They must combine the strategist skills of recognising opportunities and risks across national and functional boundaries, be the architect for worldwide resource and asset utilisation, and the coordinator of activities and capabilities.

The country manager must play a pivotal role by sensing local customer needs, but also satisfying the host government's requirements and defending the company's market position. The country manager is likely to have objectives that conflict with the business manager and so must be prepared to negotiate to overcome the differences. The functional manager's role is the business environment scanner, cross-pollinator of ideas and champion of specific aspects of the business which are essential for success. The global manager may be required to play a number of roles. The complexity of global operations means that no one person can fulfil the required tasks alone. This manager, therefore, must provide leadership, whilst acting as the talent scout and the developer of the other levels of management.

As a result, patterns of activity in a transnational company will vary considerably in each new situation. Innovations, for example, should be generated at several locations and in several ways throughout the world, so that the company is not restricted to making centralised decisions. For the past ten to twenty years, firms such as Shell, Philips and Unilever have used an integrated network approach, with resources and capabilities concentrated in various locations and accessed through the free flow of knowledge, technology, components, products, resources and people. By developing matrix structures, firms can achieve efficiency, responsiveness and the ability to develop and exploit their knowledge and capability for competitive advantage.

As the international operations of firms increase in diversity and tangible ties between the activities become strained, so the nature of the formal systems and organisational structures must change too. Training programmes, career path planning, job rotation, company-wide accounting, evaluation and data-processing systems become more important as part of the shared value system of the firm.

Staff and the problems of international management

Of the potential sources of problems of planning in international marketing, it is the relationship between headquarters and local subsidiary staff that is likely to be the largest single factor. Headquarters staff, as guardians of the overall company strategies, claim to have a far broader perspective of the company's activities and might expect that subsidiary staff should simply be concerned with implementation of the details of the plan. Subsidiary staff claim that, by being closer to the individual markets, they are in a better position to identify opportunities and should therefore play a large part in developing objectives and strategies. This situation must be resolved if the planning process is to be effective, so that all staff have a clear idea of their own role in setting, developing and implementing policy, and understanding how their individual contributions might be integrated into the corporate objectives and strategies.

The difficulties of planning in international markets are further developed by Brandt *et al.* (1980), in a framework of international planning problems, and Weichmann and Pringle (1979), who identified the key problems experienced by large US and European multi-nationals. Figure 6.7 is a list of problems at head office and in the subsidiary which are the main sources of conflict between headquarters and overseas staff.

Many companies recognise that for strategies to be successful, the managers of all parts of the company must share ownership of them through playing an active part in the development and implementation stages of the process itself. With greater emphasis on staff at all levels in the organisation providing increased levels of service to customers, it is important to involve all staff in the marketing planning process. This is becoming more difficult as MNEs have ever greater numbers of their workers employed outside the head office country. As the company grows, therefore, a company-wide planning culture should be developed, with the following objectives:

■ planning becomes part of the continuous process of management rather than an annual 'event';

FIGURE 6.7

International planning problems

Headquarters	Overseas subsidiary
Management	*Management*
Unclear allocation of responsibilities and authority	Resistance to planning
Lack of multi-national orientation	Lack of qualified personnel
Unrealistic expectations	Inadequate abilities
Lack of awareness of foreign markets	Misinterpretation of information
Unclear guidelines	Misunderstanding requirements and objectives
Insensitivity to local decisions	Resentment of HQ involvement
Insufficient provision of useful information	Lack of strategic thinking
	Lack of marketing expertise
Processes	*Processes*
Lack of standardised bases for evaluation	Lack of control by HQ
Poor IT systems and support	Incomplete or outdated internal and market information
Poor feedback and control systems	Poorly developed procedures
Excessive bureaucratic control procedures	Too little communication with HQ
Excessive marketing and financial constraints	Inaccurate data returns
Insufficient participation of subsidiaries in process	Insufficient use of of multi-national marketing expertise
	Excessive financial and marketing constraints

- strategic thinking becomes the responsibility of every manager rather than being restricted to a separate strategic planning department;
- the planning process becomes standardised, with a format that allows contributions from all parts of the company;
- the plan becomes the working document, updated periodically for all aspects of the company, so allowing performance evaluation to be carried out regularly; and
- the planning process is itself regularly reviewed and refined through the use of new tools and techniques in order to improve its relevance and effectiveness.

What makes a good international manager

For many of the most powerful businesses, increasing globalisation is the future scenario, and the most successful will be managed by people who can best embrace and thrive on the ambiguity and complexity of transnational operations. Despite the rapid internationalisation of businesses, there are still few really international managers – but the creation of cross-cultural managers with genuinely transferable management skills is the goal for the global companies.

A number of researchers have emphasised the need for managers to be able to handle national differences in business, including cultural divergence on hierarchy, humour, assertiveness and working hours. In France, Germany, Italy and a large part of Asia, for example, performance-related pay is seen negatively as revealing the shortcomings of some members of the work group. Feedback sessions are seen positively in the US but German managers see them as 'enforced admissions of failure'.

The **international manager**, therefore, must be more culturally aware and show greater sensitivity but it can be difficult to adapt to the culture and values of a foreign country whilst upholding the culture and values of a parent company. The only way is to give managers experience overseas but the cost of sending people abroad is typically two and a half times that for a local manager, so firms look for alternatives, such as short-term secondments, exchanges and participation in multi-cultural project teams.

Wills and Barham (1994) believe that international managers require four sets of attributes. They must:

1 Be able to cope with cognitive complexity and be able to understand issues from a variety of complicated perspectives.

2 Have cultural empathy, a sense of humility and the power of active listening. Because of their unfamiliarity with different cultural settings international managers cannot be as competent or confident in a foreign environment.

3 Have emotional energy and be capable of adding depth and quality to interactions through their emotional self-awareness, emotional resilience, ability to accept risk. They must be able to rely on the support of the family.

4 Demonstrate psychological maturity by having the curiosity to learn, an orientation to time and a fundamental personal morality that will enable them to cope with the diversity of demands made on them.

Management style and shared values

The different contexts and stages of global development of firms mean that there is no right and wrong management style and shared values for the firm. Indeed the shared values, as we have seen earlier, may be the only common aspect of the firm that binds the various parts together and may be based upon a long tradition in the firm, built up over many years. This is the particularly the case in firms dominated by extended family ownership, such as in many Asian businesses, or where the principles of the founding family of a business are maintained.

What is important to recognise is that although global businesses are complex and diverse, the chief executive can have a major effect on the business. The personality of entrepreneurs such as Bill Gates, Michael Dell and Richard Branson shapes the management style and shared values of the businesses they create from their early days, and influential managers that turn around an ailing business or drive the business in a new direction, such as Jack Welch at GE, Lou Gerstner at IBM and Chris Gent at Vodafone, can create a new 'personality' for the business.

SUMMARY

■ The increase in global business activity has resulted from a number of changes in the environment, such as political and technological developments. Clearly it is communications and information technology that have had the greatest effect.

■ Firms have also accelerated the move towards greater globalisation by developing a worldwide presence and strategy, and offering similar products and services.

■ To exploit global markets firms have developed appropriate strategies for their situation. These range from multi-domestic strategies, in which each market is seen as separate and individual, through to globally standardised strategies in which the firms identify one global segment with similar needs.

■ In practice, the largest firms are too complex for one simple strategy to be appropriate and so they use a combination of different strategies to build global efficiency, local effectiveness and knowledge assets.

■ An increasing feature of transnational strategies is the increasing level of cooperation between firms that could otherwise be competitors, customers or suppliers.

■ To succeed globally firms must build global appeal through globally recognised brands, but also innovate as the basis of competitive advantage in many industries continually changes.

■ To enable managers to set and control the operations of the business an appropriate organisation structure is needed. International managers must also be able to recruit and develop the right staff that will have the skills necessary to deal with the complexity, diversity and conflicting challenges of global business development.

■ Finally, it is often key personalities leading the firm that create a unique style and a set of values that contribute to the distinctiveness of the global marketing strategy.

KEYWORDS

adaptation
competitive advantage
control
global appeal
global brand
global presence
global reach
global sourcing
global strategy
globalisation

international manager
market access
merger of equals
multi-domestic strategy
organisation structure
regional strategy
standardisation
transnational strategy
transnationality

CASE STUDY   McDonald's – repositioning for a global future

Asked to suggest an example of a truly global company, most people would suggest Coca-Cola or McDonald's. McDonald's is a good example as it claims to serve 46 million customers every day in 118 countries, but being global does not guarantee success. In the last quarter of 2002 McDonald's made a loss for the first time in its 48-year history. Where might it be going wrong? Chairman and Chief Executive Jim Cantalupo came out of retirement to shake up the operation. His first response was they should do fewer things but do them better, and concentrate on getting the existing business right. The store-opening programme was cut from 1000 in 2002 to fewer than 400 in 2003.

Early days and dash for growth

McDonald's was started in 1955 on the simple principles of Quality, Speed and Cleanliness and its early competitive edge was speed – the burger was freshly cooked but waiting for you when you ordered. McDonald's became synonymous with the burger in the US.

During the 1980s and based on the highly successful formula, McDonald's increased the programme of new store openings in the US and increased its rate of expansion into overseas markets. But the first rumblings of discontent were beginning. For many years older franchisees had a very lucrative business, but the new stores had to be located closer and closer to older stores and led to cannibalisation and a loss of profitability amongst some older franchisees. Moreover, McDonald's began to 'inflict' promotions on the franchisees rather than through discussion with franchisees. Some, for example the Campaign 55 to celebrate the company's founding, were a disaster.

Competition

With its focus on expansion McDonald's failed to notice that other burger chains that had developed alongside McDonald's were beginning to offer customers alternatives, and in some cases had overtaken McDonald's in customer appeal, quality, speed and cleanliness. An American Customer Satisfaction Index survey in 2001 placed McDonald's almost at the bottom and just above the Inland Revenue Service. McDonald's retaliated by reducing the price of its burger to 99 cents in the US and 99 pence in the UK, but was it a good idea simply to focus on cheapness? Consumers increasingly want variety and are becoming much more health conscious. Firms such as Pizza Hut, KFC, Subway and many more offer alternative fast food menus.

In some country markets local companies, such as Jollibee in the Philippines, which had a similar business model to McDonald's, offered adaptations, such as spicy sauces that appealed to the local markets, and so McDonald's was forced to adapt their offering in different countries to compete, for example the Teriyaki McBurger in Japan and the Maharaja Mac in India.

Litigation and health

For a number of years McDonald's has been the focus of the wrath of campaigners and McSpotlight is a Web site which highlights anti-McDonald's issues around the world. McDonald's itself uses its corporate power to vigorously pursue anyone, no matter how small, it believes has wronged it. McDonald's won a court action in the UK in 1997 but was heavily criticised by the judge. McDonald's more recently has been taken to court over the allegation that the food it serves can lead to obesity in children. More recent research seems to suggest that the speed of eating coupled with high sugar and fat foods can lead to addiction, which in turn can lead to obesity. This, too, could present a problem.

The brand

Clearly, McDonald's recognises the need to reposition, building on its competitive advantage that comes from its competencies, store location and convenience for customers. It must revitalise the brand, so that adults do not just associate it with burgers and their youth. A radical change may not be desirable as it may alienate loyal customers. Although many of their customers are becoming more affluent and health conscious they will not always want to eat 'healthily'. The brand, however, must still be relevant for the next generation of consumers.

Questions

1 Selecting appropriate frameworks for analysis, highlight the key issues that McDonald's must address in the global fast food market. Focus on changes in the environment, in competition and in customer wants and needs.

2 Design an international marketing strategy for the Chief Executive that will address these issues, reposition the McDonald's brand and revive the firm's fortunes.

Robin Lowe, Sheffield Hallam University

Source: Adapted from various public sources, including www.bbc.co.uk, www.theacsi.org

DISCUSSION QUESTIONS

1 What do you consider to be the definition of globalisation? What forces are driving its development?

2 Identify the reasons why global strategies sometimes fail in their objective to achieve a global marketing advantage.

3 What is the rationale behind mega mergers and major acquisitions? How will they lead to global competitive advantage?

4 What are the critical success factors in developing a global brand? What additional factors would you consider to be necessary in developing a successful global e-business brand?

5 What are the main challenges that are faced by international managers in managing and controlling a global marketing strategy? What advice would you give to a manager with this responsibility?

REFERENCES

Bartlett, C.A. and Ghoshal, S. (1987) 'Managing Across Borders', *Sloan Management Review*, Fall.

Brandt, W., Hulbert, J. and Richers, R. (1980) 'Pitfalls in Planning for Multinational Operations', *Long Range Planning*, December.

Buzzell, R.D. (1968) 'Can you standardise multinational marketing?', *Harvard Business Review*, 46 (6): 101–14.

Finkelstein, S. (1998) 'Safe ways to cross the merger minefield', Mastering Global Business Part 4, *Financial Times*, 20 February.

Ghoshal, S. and Bartlett, C.A. (1992) 'What is a Global Manager', *Harvard Business Review*, September–October.

Gogel, R. and Larreche J.C. (1989) 'The battlefield for 1992: Product strength and geograhical coverage', *European Journal of Management*, 17, 289.

Khashani, K. (1995) 'A new future for brands', *Financial Times*, 10 November.

Kotabe, M. (1990) 'Corporate Product Policy and Innovative Behaviour of European and Japanese Multinationals: An Empirical Investigation', *Journal of Marketing*, 54: 19–33.

Levitt, T. (1983) 'The globalisation of markets', *Harvard Business Review*, May/June.

Majaro, S. (1991) *International Marketing*, Routledge.

Meffet, H. and Bolz, J. (1993) in Haliburton, C. and Hunerberg, R. (eds) *European Marketing Readings*, Addison-Wesley.

Nakata, C. and Sivakumar, R. (1997) 'Emerging market conditions and their impact on first mover advantages and integrative review', *International Marketing Review*, 14 June.

Sjobolom, L. (1998) 'Success lies one step ahead of the consumer', Mastering Global Management, *Financial Times*, 6 February.

Smith, A. (1998) 'The conundrum of maintaining image', *Financial Times*, 8 May.

Terpstra, V. and Sarathy, R. (1999) *International Marketing*, 8th edn, Dryden.

Weichmann, U.E. and Pringle, L.G. (1979) 'Problems That Plague Multinational Marketers', *Harvard Business Review*, July/August.

Wills, S. and Barham, K. (1994) 'Being an international manager', *European Management Journal*, 12 (1).

Yip, G. (1996) 'Towards a new global strategy', in Doole, I. and Lowe, R. (eds) *International Marketing Strategy: Contemporary Readings*, Thomson Learning.

MARKET ENTRY STRATEGIES

Introduction

For the majority of companies, the most significant international marketing decision they are likely to take is how they should enter new markets, as the commitments that they make will affect every aspect of their business for many years ahead. Douglas and Craig (1997) suggest that it signals the firm's intent to key competitors and determines the basis for future battles. Having in previous chapters identified potential country, regional and world markets and discussed the development of international marketing strategies in both smaller and global firms, we examine in this chapter the different market entry options open to firms to enable them to select the most appropriate method for their given situation. For most small and medium-sized businesses, this represents a critical first step, but for established companies, the problem is how to exploit opportunities more effectively within the context of their existing network of international operations and, particularly, how to enter new emerging markets.

There are advantages and disadvantages with each market entry method and critical in the decision-making process are the firm's assessment of the cost and risk associated with each method and the level of involvement the company is allowed by the government, or wishes to have in the market. These factors determine the degree of control it can exert over the total product and service offer and the method of distribution.

There is, however, no ideal market entry strategy and different market entry methods might be adopted by different firms entering the same market and/or by the same firm in different markets.

Learning objectives

After reading this chapter you should be able to:

- Identify the alternative market entry options available to firms seeking to develop new country markets
- Compare the different levels of involvement, risk and marketing control of these market entry methods
- Understand the criteria for selecting between the market entry options

■ Appreciate the advantages and disadvantages of the different market entry methods

■ Understand the motivations and challenges of market entry partnership strategies, such as alliances and joint ventures

THE ALTERNATIVE MARKET ENTRY METHODS

The various alternative market entry methods are shown in Figure 7.1, and cover a span of international **involvement** from virtually zero, when the firm merely makes the products available for others to export but effectively does nothing itself to market its products internationally, to total involvement where the firm might operate wholly-owned subsidiaries in all its key markets.

The **market entry** decision is taken within the firm and it is determined to a large extent by the firm's objectives and attitudes to international marketing and the confidence in the capability of its managers to operate in foreign countries. In order to select an appropriate and potentially successful market entry method, it is necessary to consider a number of criteria including:

■ the company objectives and expectations relating to the size and value of anticipated business;

■ the size and financial resources of the company;

■ its existing foreign market involvement;

■ the skill, abilities and attitudes of the company management towards international marketing;

■ the nature and power of the competition within the market;

■ the nature of existing and anticipated tariff and non-tariff barriers;

■ the nature of the product itself, particularly any areas of competitive advantage, such as trademark or patent protection; and

■ the timing of the move in relation to the market and competitive situation.

This list is not exhaustive as the entry method might be influenced by other factors which are very specific to the firm's particular situation. For example, the laws of a host country might prevent a firm from owning 100 per cent of an operation in that country. Trade embargos put in place by the UN may prevent a firm entering the country. Examples include South Africa during the Apartheid years and Iraq more recently.

FIGURE 7.1

Market entry methods and the levels of involvement in international markets

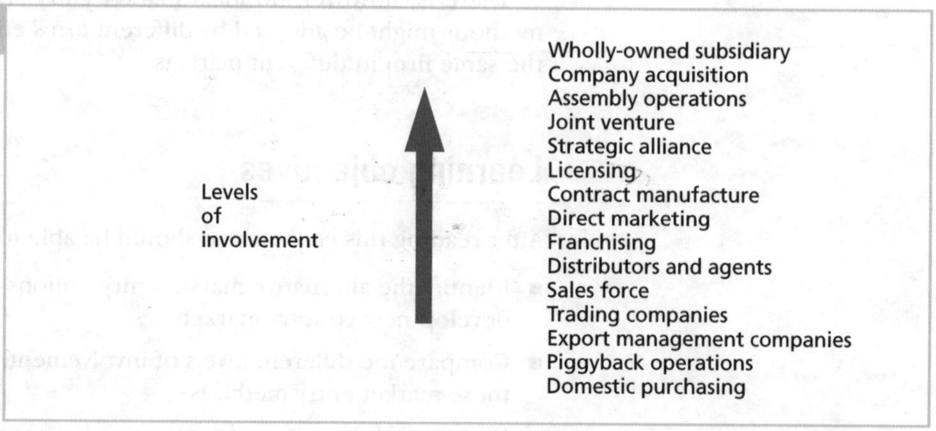

Levels
of
involvement

Wholly-owned subsidiary
Company acquisition
Assembly operations
Joint venture
Strategic alliance
Licensing
Contract manufacture
Direct marketing
Franchising
Distributors and agents
Sales force
Trading companies
Export management companies
Piggyback operations
Domestic purchasing

Timing is another particularly important factor in considering entry. For example, emerging markets typically have bursts of optimism and growth often followed by setbacks caused by political or economic factors, or changing customer expectations. The Asian approach of allocating time and resources in the expectation of improved trading conditions in the future appears to have paid off, as is shown in Illustration 7.1.

Risk and control in market entry

We referred earlier to the fact that one of the most important characteristics of the different market entry methods is the level of involvement of the firm in international operations. The level of involvement has significant implications in terms of levels of **risk and control** and this is shown diagramatically in Figure 7.2. The cost of resourcing the alternative methods usually equates closely to levels of involvement and risk. The diagram does suggest, however, that associated with higher levels of involvement is not only greater potential for control, but also higher potential risk, usually due to the high cost of investment. In practice this is an oversimplification because firms whose products are marketed internationally through domestic purchasing are at risk of losing all their income from international markets without knowing why, because of their total reliance on intermediaries.

Partnerships, in the form of joint ventures and strategic alliances have become increasingly common over the past few years because they are thought to offer the advantage of achieving higher levels of control at lower levels of risk and cost, provided that there is a high degree of cooperation between companies and that their individual objectives are not incompatible.

In making a decision on market entry, therefore, the most fundamental questions that the firm must answer are:

- What level of control over our international business do we require?
- What level of risk are we willing to take?
- What cost can we afford to bear?

ILLUSTRATION 7.1 **Asian first movers**

Asian companies, to a far greater extent than Western companies, recognise the importance of entering new emerging markets at an early stage of development. The rationale for this is the first mover advantage that can be obtained from early entry. They accept that in doing this, mistakes will be made, but they expect to use this experience of customer needs to build competitive advantage. Competitors who wait to see how others fare before making their move into new markets must select the right entry strategy in order to avoid heavy losses.

Chareon Pokhand (CP) in Bangkok have diversified their business activities from chicken feed, to a range which includes petrochemicals and telecommunications. CP began investing in China in 1970 at a time when it was not seen as an attractive market, but early entry enabled CP to overcome

initial difficulties, build expertise and foster long-term relationships with the local authorities before competitors were convinced the environment was stable enough for them to enter.

More recently, Asian firms are again exhibiting a bold approach to investment, focusing on such 'risky' markets as Cambodia and Vietnam.

There is a stark contrast in the attitudes of Western and Asian managers, with the former assessing and minimising the risk associated with every eventuality before they enter a new market as opposed to the latter, who only tend to consider the probability of surviving the worst case scenario.

Question What are the arguments for and against an early first move into emerging markets?

In answering these questions it is important to consider not just the level of control, risk and cost, but also the relative importance that the firm might place upon the different elements of its marketing activity. For example, lack of control over certain aspects of the marketing process such as after-sales servicing, which is often undertaken by third party contractors, may affect the reputation and image of a company or brand because consumers frequently blame the manufacturer rather than a distributor or retailer for the poor quality of after-sales service that they have received.

McDonald's decided to franchise its operation in France, but subsequently found that it was difficult to control and standardise the quality of the product offered in the different restaurants. They had no alternative but to take over the franchises and rebuild their damaged image.

Figure 7.2 shows the four categories of market entry methods, indirect and direct market entry, cooperation and direct investment.

INDIRECT EXPORTING

For firms which have little inclination or few resources for international marketing, the simplest and lowest cost method of market entry is for them to have their products sold overseas by others. The objective of firms which use this method of entry may be to benefit from opportunities which may arise without incurring any expense or simply to sell off excess capacity into foreign markets with the least possible inconvenience. Firms such as these often withdraw from this activity as soon as their sales into the home market improve. Whilst indirect exporting has the advantage of the least cost and risk of any entry method, it allows the firm little control over how, when, where and by whom the products are sold. In some cases the domestic company may even be unaware that its products are being exported.

FIGURE 7.2

Risk and control in market entry

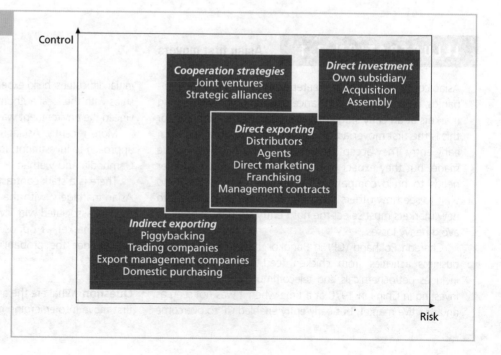

There are four main methods of indirect exporting and these are by using:

- domestic purchasing;
- an export management company (EMC) or export house (EH);
- piggyback operations; and
- trading companies.

Domestic purchasing

Some firms or individuals do not realise that their products or services have potential export value until they are approached by the buyer from a foreign organisation, who might make the initial approach, purchase the product at the factory gate and take on the task of exporting, marketing and distributing the product in one or more overseas market. Anita Roddick used this approach to source naturally occurring ingredients for Body Shop's ranges of toiletries and cosmetics and make domestic purchasing from deprived regions of the world a feature of Body Shop's marketing activity. Taking a moral stance and demonstrating environmental concern, however, can make the firm a target for detractors and suppliers are often difficult to manage.

Local subcontractors to original equipment manufacturers (OEMs) fall into this category as their international market potential is derived totally from being a member of the OEM's supply chain. Whilst for the manufacturer or supplier, **domestic purchasing** could hardly be called an entry strategy, it does provide the firm with access to and limited knowledge of international markets. However, the supplying organisation is able to exert little control over the choice of markets and the strategies adopted in marketing its products. Small firms find that this is the easiest method of obtaining foreign sales but, being totally dependent on the purchaser, they are unlikely to be aware of a change in consumer behaviour and competitor activity or of the purchasing firm's intention to terminate the arrangement. Ben and Jerry's have taken this approach, too, in sourcing ingredients for their ice cream from community-based suppliers but when fashions have changed and certain ingredients are no longer popular, they have been criticised for stopping supply arrangements with community groups. If a company is intent upon seeking longer-term viability for its export business, it must adapt a more proactive approach which will inevitably involve obtaining a greater understanding of the markets in which their products are sold. This can happen if prompted by a change of management or ownership.

Export management companies (EMCs) or export houses

Export houses or export marketing companies (EMCs) are specialist companies set up to act as the export department for a range of companies. They can help small and medium-sized companies to initiate, develop and maintain their international sales. As well as taking orders from foreign buyers, they provide indirect access to international market information and contacts. By offering ranges of products from various companies they provide a more attractive overall 'sales package' to foreign buyers, and by carrying a large range they can spread selling and administration costs over more products and companies, and reduce transport costs because of the economies of making larger shipments of goods from a number of companies.

EMCs deal with the necessary documentation and their knowledge of local purchasing practices and government regulations is particularly useful in markets that might prove difficult to penetrate. The use of EMCs, therefore, allows individual companies to gain far wider exposure of their products in foreign markets at much lower overall costs than they could achieve on their own, but there are a number of disadvantages too. The export house may specialise by geographical area, product or customer type (retail, industrial or institutional) and this may not coincide with the suppliers' objectives. As a result of this, the selection of markets may be made on the basis of what is best for the EMC rather than the manufacturer. As EMCs are paid by commission, they might be tempted to concentrate upon products with immediate sales potential rather than those that might require greater customer education and sustained marketing effort to achieve success in the longer term. EMCs may also be tempted to carry too many product ranges and as a result the manufacturer's products may not be given the necessary attention from sales people. The EMC may also carry competitive products which they may promote preferentially, again to the disadvantage of a particular firm.

Manufacturers should, therefore, take care in selecting a suitable EMC and be prepared to devote resources to managing the relationship and monitoring their performance. The firm must also take the time to learn more about the markets in which their products are being sold in order to ensure that opportunities to sell products into new markets are not being missed by the EMC.

As sales increase, the manufacturer may feel that they could benefit from increased involvement in international markets, by exporting directly themselves. However, the transition may not be very easy. First, the firm is likely to have become very dependent on the export house and unless steps have been taken to build contacts with foreign customers and increase their knowledge of the markets, moving away from using EMCs could prove difficult. Second, the firm could find it difficult to withdraw from its contractual commitments to the export house. This often happens when firms are first setting up the arrangement because they are unable to predict the kind of relationship they would like to have with the EMC some time in the future. Many agreements, therefore, are based only on the current and short-term situation. Third, the EMC may be able to substitute products from an alternative manufacturer and so use their customer contacts as a basis for introducing new competition against the original manufacturer.

Piggybacking

In **piggybacking**, an established international distribution network of one manufacturer might be used to carry the products of a second manufacturer. The second manufacturer is able to ride on the back of the existing reputation, contacts and administration of the carrier with little direct investment themselves. Terpstra and Yu (1990) explain that this makes a particularly effective way for firms from developing countries to break into markets in developed countries.

The carrier is either paid by commission and so acts as an agent, or alternatively, buys the product outright and so acts as an independent distributor. There are also advantages of piggybacking for the carrier as they are able first, to carry a wider product range and so present a more attractive sales package to potential buyers and, second, to benefit from economies of scale by increasing their revenue without incurring additional costs of marketing, selling administration and distribution.

There can, however, be problems as the terms and conditions of the marketing arrangements are often poorly thought out as, frequently, piggybacking starts on a 'try it and see' basis. Either company might become locked into an arrangement that proves unsatisfactory for them, particularly as a firm's strategic objectives change over a period of time. Decisions about such marketing mix issues as branding might not suit both companies and arrangements for providing technical support and service for products often prove to be a source of disagreement and difficulty.

For smaller firms, piggybacking can work when two products are interdependent, or if the second product provides a service for the first. Larger companies, too, have found it successful, particularly when the rider has experienced some kind of barrier to entering particular markets, or the use of an existing distribution network can provide faster market development.

Trading companies

Trading companies are part of the historical legacy from the colonial days and although different in nature now, they are still important trading forces in Africa and Asia. The United Africa Company, part of Unilever, for example, is claimed to be the largest trader in Africa and the *Sogo shosha* have traditionally played an important role in Japanese international business although, as Illustration 7.2 shows, different patterns of business activity could result in them becoming less significant in some sectors.

ILLUSTRATION 7.2   **The future of *Sogo shosha***

In Japan, after the war, the dominant industrial powers that emerged tended to be the *keiretsu* (industrial groups), which grew out of the pre-war conglomerates, and the *zaibatsu* (financial cliques) such as Mitsui, Mitsubishi, Sumimoto and Yasuda. These had evolved from family business empires and government favour and were a key part of the government's expansion abroad. Each *zaibatsu/ keiretsu* has its own *Sogo shosha* (trading company) which in the seventeenth century were simple import–export businesses. Their influence was enormous because their employees, 'shosha-men', spent years overseas developing their expertise. For example, it was suggested that during the Gulf War the Japanese foreign ministry relied on these contacts rather than its own diplomatic sources. The *Sogo shosha* played a major role, for example, in facilitating the relocation of Japanese production facilities by developing industrial parks in Thailand, Indonesia, Philippines, Myanmar and Vietnam with distribution centres for suppliers and finished goods.

At the height of their power the *Sogo shosha* wielded great power. For example, in 1991 they accounted for 43 per cent of Japan's exports and 79 per cent of imports. But now things are changing. The top five, Mitsubishi, Mitsui, Sumimoto, Itochu and Marabeni, are still major players but are having to restructure and embark on joint ventures to maintain their position. Under great pressure from the government and banks they are having to get rid of non-performing assets, to partner with other firms and to cut costs. Some estimates suggest that up to 30 per cent of a *Sogo shosha's* subsidiaries and ventures could be loss-

making at any one time. They suffered in the 1990s due to the long recession in the Japanese economy, where they conduct 50 per cent of their transactions. The need for Japanese companies to adopt global standards in management and more transparent accounting procedures leads to harder decisions being taken on loss-making subsidiaries. The problem is that Japanese employers have been reluctant to sack workers in large numbers, especially when this might lead to sacking staff in other firms with which they are closely tied.

The pressure is greater for the smaller *Sogo shosha*. The sixth and eighth largest, Nissho Iwai and Nichimen, merged with the loss of 4000 jobs. This was a big shock for the shosha-men because a few years ago, like lawyers and doctors, being a shosha-man was a very honourable lifetime career for a university graduate.

The *Sogo shosha* have had a history of reinventing themselves when it has become necessary. However, the main problem they are facing is caused by the change in business practice. For example, Nippon Steel bought from all the *Sogo shosha* to maintain good relations but have now cut suppliers and buy in greater volumes at lower prices. Moreover, e-commerce has the potential to cut out the intermediary's role altogether.

Question What must they do to survive?

Source: Adapted from Kawakami, S. *Goodbye to the Glory Days*, February 2003, www.japaninc.net

The success of trading companies is the result of building long-term relationships over many years. This is the experience in the US where export trading companies have been permitted only since 1982 and have been slow to get off the ground.

One of the major benefits of using trading houses is that their extensive operations and contacts allow them to operate in more difficult trading areas. One important aspect of their operations is to manage countertrade activities, in which sales into one market are paid for by taking other products from that market in exchange. The essential role of the trading company is to quickly find a buyer for the products that have been taken in exchange.

Indirect exporting is often a small company's first experience of international marketing and has the advantages of being a simple and low-cost method of gaining exposure of products in foreign markets without the company first having to gain the necessary expertise in the various aspects of international trading. However, the company has little control over its international marketing activities and is restricted to simply reacting to new situations and opportunities as they arise. It is extremely difficult to build up international marketing knowledge and expertise by marketing at arm's length or to develop any significant long-term product and promotional strategies. Moreover, because of the lack of direct contact between the firm and the market, indirect entry approaches are usually perceived as lacking long-term commitment. As a result, customers and other members of the distribution channels are likely to withhold their full commitment to the firm and its products until the firm becomes more involved in the market, by adopting a more direct approach.

DIRECT EXPORTING

If a company wishes to secure a more permanent long-term place in international markets, it must become more proactive, through becoming directly involved in the process of **exporting**. This requires definite commitment from the company and takes the form of investment in the international operation through allocating time and resources to a number of supporting activities. The key components of the export marketing mix are summarised in Figure 7.3.

The benefits of direct over indirect exporting are that the proactive approach makes it easier to exert more influence over international activities resulting in a number of specific advantages for the exporter such as greater control over the selection of markets, greater control over the elements of the marketing mix, improved feedback about the performance of individual products, changing situations in individual markets and competitor activity, and the opportunity to build up expertise in international marketing.

FIGURE 7.3

The components of the export marketing mix

Product:	selection, development and sourcing
Pricing:	policy, strategies, discount structures and trading terms
Promotion:	corporate promotions and local selling, trade shows and literature
Distribution:	sales force management, agents, distributors and logistics
Services:	market research, training and sales servicing
Finance and administration:	budgets, order processing, insurance and credit control
Technical:	specifications, testing and product quality

The disadvantages of direct exporting are that the direct investment necessary is considerable because the whole of the marketing, distribution and administration costs will now be borne by the company. In taking this decision, the company must be quite sure that the costs can be justified in the light of the market opportunities identified.

Illustration 7.3 shows how an exporter from an emerging market has eliminated competition in a global market.

For those firms wishing to change from indirect to direct exporting or to significantly increase their marketing efforts, the timing can be critical, as the extra costs involved can often place a huge financial burden on the company. The solution to this is, wherever possible, to make the transition gradually and in a well-planned way.

Mahon and Vachani (1992) analyse the role of establishing beachheads, the first 'landings' in overseas markets, as part of an initial exporting strategy and suggest that companies need to address a series of questions:

- What country or geographic area should be chosen for entry, why and when?
- Should the firm enter the main segment of a given market or a smaller niche?
- By what methods should the beachhead be established?

Establishing a beachhead might take the form of finding a country where there is low psychic distance. Also adopting a low profile entry might help to reduce risk; in retailing, for example, by avoiding main city sites, or merely following a major client when providing legal, accounting or advertising services. Komatsu, the Japanese earthmoving equipment manufacturer, for example, initially chose

---

ILLUSTRATION 7.3   High-flying Brazilian exporter

Asked to name the product made by Brazil's top value private sector exporter for three years up to 2001, some readers might suggest soccer players and others brazil nuts! (In fact your brazil nuts are more likely to originate from Bolivia.) The answer is aircraft from Embraer. This is surprising, especially as North American and European manufacturers, such as Boeing and Airbus, dominate the global market for aircraft. Embraer has demolished its opposition to become the fourth largest commercial airline manufacturer.

The origins of the Brazilian aircraft industry, however, go back a long way. Whilst the Wright brothers' flight in 1903 was not witnessed and recorded by the authorities, the powered flight three years later by the Brazilian Alberto Santos Dumont in the Bois de Boulogne near Paris was. Consequently many Brazilians believe that they really invented powered flight.

Inspired by Santos Dumont, the country has become a leader in small, 30 to 50 seat, regional jets that are necessary in a country larger in size than the US. The firm was set up in 1969 as a state industry with a mix of domestic and foreign investment. Despite the scepticism from even Brazilians the firm has thrived. There used to be nine manufacturers in the market but now only Bombadier Aerospace

of Canada is a competitor. A number of well-known producers of small planes have gone out of production including Fairchild Dornier (US–Germany), British Aerospace (UK), Fokker (Netherlands), Saab (Sweden) and Shorts (UK). At the same time Embraer has developed exports worldwide and even sold products to its Canadian rival.

How did Embraer succeed? The company had vision and a degree of luck and ignored turbo-propeller planes, which effectively died in the 1990s. Instead it went straight to producing jets, which were ideal for the growing air travel market in the US, especially since it was deregulated. It employs 12 000 people and invests around US$300 million per year. Its production facilities midway between Rio and São Paulo are probably just as sophisticated as Boeing and Airbus. As part of its growth plans Embraer launched in 2003 a 70-seater plane which would compete with the smaller aircraft in the Airbus range.

Question What makes an exporter from an emerging market successful against worldwide competition?

Source: Adapted from Walters, J. Brazil's winged victory, *The Observer*, 8 December 2002

markets for entry where Caterpillar, the leading US manufacturer, did not have a significant presence. Alternative strategies are to use a specific competitive positioning stance. Ricoh and Nashua offered low price basic products to compete with Xerox in the photocopier market, rather than attack head on. Other firms, however, seek to win a lead customer, usually a market challenger rather than a leader, in order to test their product before committing themselves to full market presence.

As well as deciding which countries to enter, Chryssochoidis (1996) suggests that the selection and subsequent modification of the product portfolio is important and the stages involved in the development of the portfolio are summarised in the adapted model, Figure 7.4.

Factors for success in exporting

A considerable amount of research has been carried out into the barriers and motivations for new exporters and the stages of internationalisation and this was discussed in Chapter 5. Also presented in this chapter were some benchmarks which enable firms to be profiled as being at one of the stages of internationalisation, but Katsikeas *et al.* (1996) explain that the determinants of export performance have not been researched so comprehensively as the barriers, motivations and stages of internationalisation.

In researching Greek exporters, Katsikeas *et al.* concluded that the way exporting performance is assessed is important. The simplest measure is whether firms do or do not export. Measurement of the financial performance of the firm in terms of export sales volume, growth and profitability, and the ratio of export to total sales is useful to measure longitudinal firm performance but is less useful for comparing firm performance between industry sectors because the industry sectors may be structured quite differently. Subjective measurements of the

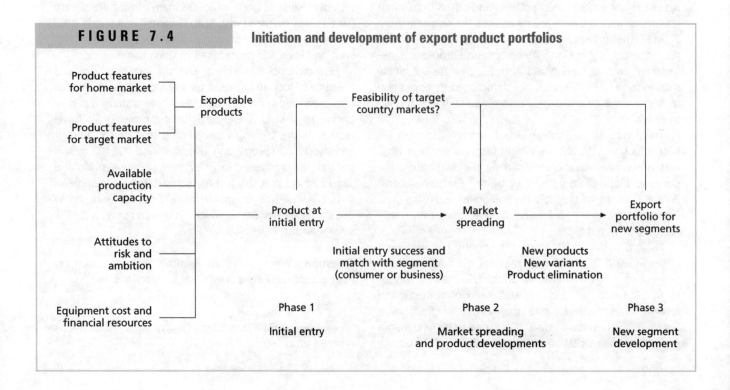

| FIGURE 7.4 | Initiation and development of export product portfolios |

performance of the management of the firm are often helpful but pose a problem, too, in their comparability between firms and sectors.

Katsikeas *et al*. did, however, conclude that a number of factors were important in contributing to successful exporting:

- commitment of the firms' management

- an exporting approach in the firm which emphasised the importance of augmenting and maintaining skills

- a good marketing information and communication system

- sufficient production capacity and capability, product superiority and competitive pricing

- effective market research to reduce the psychic distance between the home country and target country market given that it is knowledge that generates business opportunities and drives the international process

- an effective national export policy which provides support at an individual firm level, and emphasises the need for knowledge-based programmes which prioritise market information about foreign market opportunities.

They found that the cost of export planning incurred by the firm did not correlate with export performance and suggested that this might be explained by the fact that a major source of strength in exporting is flexibility and adaptability to export opportunities and the ability to make an immediate strategic response. Moreover, firm size and the managers' experience were also not critical factors in export success but they did recognise that these factors may be the source of the export stimuli in the first place, and could be major determinants of the firm's commitment to exporting and its ability to solve problems.

It is generally accepted, therefore, that in small business, attitudes and commitment to international expansion are crucial for success, whereas in larger companies other factors can have a bearing on performance. The size of a company can either hinder or encourage international development because of the variations in the capability of the staff for planning, the lack of consistency of information and the degree to which adaptation of the mix is necessary. A number of other factors, such as the types of strategies that are pursued, segmentation, product and pricing can also affect export success.

Selection of exporting method

The choice of the specific individual markets for exporting was discussed in the first section of this book, but it is important to re-emphasise that the more subjective factors, such as a senior executive's existing formal or informal links, particular knowledge of culture or language and perceived attractiveness of markets, may well influence an individual firm's decision.

Once individual markets have been selected and the responsibilities for exporting have been allocated, the decision needs to be taken about precisely how the firm should be represented in the new market. Clearly the nature, size and structure of the market will be significant in determining the method adopted. In a large market, particularly if a high level of market knowledge and customer contact is needed, it may be necessary to have a member of the firm's staff resident in or close to the market. This cannot be justified if the market is small or levels of customer contact need not be so high. Alternatively a home-based sales force may be used to make periodic sales trips in conjunction with follow-up communications by telephone, fax and e-mail.

Many other factors will affect the cost/benefit analysis of maintaining the company's own staff in foreign markets, such as whether the market is likely to be attractive in the long term as well as the short term and whether the high cost of installing a member of the firm's own staff will be offset by the improvements in the quality of contacts, market expertise and communications. The alternative, and usually the first stage in exporting, is to appoint an agent or distributor.

Agents

Agents provide the most common form of low cost direct involvement in foreign markets and are independent individuals or firms who are contracted to act on behalf of exporters to obtain orders on a commission basis. They typically represent a number of manufacturers and will handle non-competitive ranges. As part of their contract they would be expected to agree sales targets and contribute substantially to the preparation of forecasts, development of strategies and tactics using their knowledge of the local market.

The selection of suitable agents or distributors can be a problematic process. The selection criteria might include:

■ The financial strength of the agents.

■ Their contacts with potential customers.

■ The nature and extent of their responsibilities to other organisations.

■ Their premises, equipment and resources, including sales representatives.

Clearly, the nature of the agreement between the firm and its agent is crucial in ensuring the success of the arrangement, particularly in terms of clarifying what is expected of each party, setting out the basis for the relationships that will be built up and ensuring that adequate feedback on the market and product development is provided.

There are various sources for finding a suitable agent at low cost to the exporter:

■ Asking potential customers to suggest a suitable agent.

■ Obtaining recommendations from institutions such as trade associations, chambers of commerce and government trade departments.

■ Using commercial agencies.

■ Using agents for non-competing products.

■ Poaching a competitor's agent.

■ Advertising in suitable trade papers.

Achieving a satisfactory manufacturer–agent relationship

To achieve success the exporter–agent relationship needs to be managed by:

■ Allocating time and resources to finding a suitably qualified agent.

■ Ensuring that both the manufacturer and agent understand what each expects of the other.

■ Ensuring that the agent is motivated to improve performance.

■ Providing adequate support on a continuing basis including training, joint promotion and developing contacts.

■ Ensuring that there is sufficient advice and information transfer in both directions.

Distributors

Agents do not take ownership of the goods but work instead on commission, sometimes as low as 2–3 per cent on large volume and orders. **Distributors** buy the product from the manufacturer and so take the market risk on unsold products as well as the profit. For this reason, they usually expect to take a higher percentage to cover their costs and risk.

Distributors usually seek exclusive rights for a specific sales territory and generally represent the manufacturer in all aspects of sales and servicing in that area. The exclusivity, therefore, is in return for the substantial capital investment that may be required in handling and selling the products. The capital investment can be particularly high if the product requires special handling equipment or transport and storage equipment in the case of perishable goods, chemicals, materials or components.

The issue of agreeing territories is becoming increasingly important, as in many markets, distributors are becoming fewer in number, larger in size and sometimes more specialised in their activity. The trend to regionalisation is leading distributors increasingly to extend their territories through organic growth, mergers and acquisitions. Also within regional trading blocs competition laws are used to avoid exclusive distribution being set up for individual territories. The car industry in the EU was allowed to retain exclusive distribution until Block Exemption was removed in 2002.

Other direct exporting methods

There are three other modes of exporting which are considered to be direct and these are management contracts, franchising and direct marketing.

Management contracts

Management contracts emphasise the growing importance of services, business skills and management expertise as saleable commodities in international trade. Normally the contracts undertaken are concerned with installing management operating and control systems, and training local staff to take over when the contract is completed. Many construction projects such as the rebuilding of Kuwait, Afghanistan and Iraq were undertaken in this way.

Other examples of management contracts may be as part of a deal to sell a processing plant as a *turnkey operation*, in which the capital plant and a management team are provided by the firm to set up and run the plant for the first few months of operation, and then train the local team to take over. With increased privatisation and outsourcing of facilities management by public and private sector organisations there is a substantial growth in management contracts and in firms providing these services.

Franchising

Franchising is a means of marketing goods and services in which the franchiser grants the legal right to use branding, trademarks and products, and the method of operation is transferred to a third party – the franchisee – in return for a franchise fee. The franchiser provides assistance, training and help with sourcing components, and exercises significant control over the franchisee's method of operation. It is considered to be a relatively less risky business start up for the franchisee but still harnesses the motivation, time and energy of the people who are investing their own capital in the business. For the franchiser it has a number of advantages including the opportunity to build greater market coverage and obtain a steady, predictable stream of income without requiring excessive investment.

Chan (1994) identifies two types of franchise. With product/trade franchises, for example car dealerships, petrol service stations and soft drinks bottlers, the franchisees are granted the right to distribute a manufacturer's product in a specified territory. Business format franchise is the growing sector and includes many types of businesses, including restaurants, convenience stores and hotels. This type of franchise includes the licensing of a trademark and the system for operating the business, and the appearance of the location.

Franchising can take the form of single-unit franchising in which the arrangement is made with a single franchisee or multi-unit in which the franchisee operates more than one unit. The multi-unit franchisee may be given the responsibility for developing a territory and opening a specified number of units alone or, as is common in international markets, operating a master franchise, in which the master franchisee can subfranchise to others. In this case the master franchisee is responsible for collecting the fees, enforcing the agreement and providing the necessary services, such as training and advice.

Franchising has grown rapidly during the 1990s (Welch 1992) due to the strong interest in a variety of franchise formats. Trading companies have frequently been appointed as master franchisees and, whilst this has helped to accelerate the growth of franchising, it has also influenced the franchiser's internationalisation process. Because of the global power of these trading companies they are able to challenge the franchiser's decisions in the franchise process and have a considerable say in the strategic development of the business. As competition has increased in franchising so more franchisers, such as Pizza Hut in Australia, have resorted to acquisition of existing chains of similar businesses for conversion to the new franchise.

Welch comments that there is increasing evidence that franchisees, either individually or collectively, are prepared to resort to legal action to control the franchisers' activities when they are considered harmful to their own interests, because they realise that it is not usually in the franchisers' interests to go to court, given the likely adverse publicity. The Arby restaurant chain in the US, Burger King, Benetton, the Italian clothing group, and Body Shop, the UK toiletries retailer, have all experienced problems with franchisees.

One of the main problems for franchisers is deciding to what extent the franchise format should be modified to take account of local demands and expectations; for example, McDonald's have added spaghetti to the menu to compete more effectively with Jollibee in the Philippines, Pizza Hut find that corn and not pepperoni sells well in Japan and KFC find that gravy, peas and pumpkin are popular in Australia.

There are also differences in the way local culture affects franchise operations; for example, Terpstra and Sarathy (1999) explain that Chi-Chi's, a US-based Mexican restaurant operator, faced many problems when they tried to extend their operations into Eastern Europe. They found that there were few entrepreneurs because the current generation had grown up working for the state, were not paid according to performance, and staff were used to treating customers with disdain. By 2003 McDonald's had 30 000 outlets. In some countries franchisees have complained that new outlets have been opened on their doorstep, so cannibalising their business.

Direct marketing

Direct marketing is concerned with marketing and selling activities which do not depend for success on direct face-to-face contact and include mail order, telephone marketing, television marketing, media marketing, direct mail and electronic commerce using the Internet. There is considerable growth in all these areas largely encouraged by the development of information and communication technology, the changing lifestyles and purchasing behaviour of consumers and the increasing cost of more traditional methods of entering new markets. The critical success factors for direct marketing are in the standardisation of the product coupled with the personalisation of the communication. Whilst technical data about the product might be available in one language, often English, the recipients of the direct marketing in international markets expect to receive accurate communications in their domestic language. International direct marketing, therefore, poses considerable challenges, such as the need to build and maintain up-to-date databases, use sophisticated multilingual data processing and personalisation software programs, develop reliable credit control and secure payment systems.

However, it also offers advantages. Whereas American firms have had trouble breaking into the Japanese market, catalogue firms have been highly successful as they are positioned as good value for money for well-known clothing brands compared to Japanese catalogues which are priced higher for similar quality items.

Direct marketing techniques can also be used to support traditional methods of marketing by providing sales leads, maintaining contact or simply providing improved customer service through international call centres. Where multiple channels are used for market entry, especially e-commerce, it is the integration of channels through Customer Relationship Management that is essential to ensure customer satisfaction.

FOREIGN MANUFACTURING STRATEGIES WITHOUT DIRECT INVESTMENT

Having so far considered market entry strategies that have been based upon the development, manufacture and supply of product in the firms' domestic plants, we now turn our attention to strategies which involve production or supply from overseas plants. Before discussing the alternatives available for ownership and control of overseas plants, it is necessary to consider the factors which may lead a firm to start producing in one or more of its international markets.

Reasons for setting up overseas manufacture

The benefits of overseas manufacturing are:

Product. Avoiding problems due to the nature of the product, such as perishability.

Transporting and warehousing. The cost of transporting heavy, bulky components and finished products over long distances is reduced.

Tariff barriers/quotas. Barriers to trade, which make the market inaccessible, are reduced.

Government regulations. Entry to some markets, such as Central and Eastern Europe, are difficult unless accompanied by investment in local operations.

Market. Local manufacture may be viewed more favourably by customers.

Government contacts. Firms are likely to be viewed more favourably if they contribute to the local economy.

Information. A strong local presence improves the quality of market feedback.

International culture. Local manufacture encourages a more international outlook and ensures greater commitment by the firm to international markets.

Delivery. Local manufacture allows faster response and just-in-time delivery.

Labour costs. Production, distribution and service centres can be moved to lower labour cost markets provided there are appropriate skills and adequate information technology infrastructure to maintain satisfactory quality.

For most companies, the cost of setting up an overseas manufacturing operation is initially much higher than expanding the domestic plant by an equivalent amount as we indicated earlier in this chapter in Figure 7.2. Whilst the equipment costs are likely to be similar, and other costs such as labour, land purchase and building may even be cheaper, it is the cost involved in transferring technology, skills and knowledge that normally proves to be expensive and often underestimated.

For many firms, transferring production from a domestic to an overseas plant also immediately reduces the demand on the home plant which might have traditionally supplied all the firm's overseas markets. In response to this reduced demand on the domestic plant, the firm must plan either to reduce the capacity of the domestic plant quickly or find new business to replace the production that has been transferred, otherwise the viability of the domestic plant might be put at risk. Whereas the expansion of existing plants can often be achieved in an incremental way, setting up new plants overseas involves large cash outflows and can put a significant strain on the firms' finances. Poor planning, underestimation of costs or unforeseen problems associated with setting up a plant overseas have frequently caused businesses to fail or be vulnerable to take-over. Moreover, if the overseas plant ultimately fails and the firm finds it necessary to reduce its commitment in the market, it can find that its reputation can be severely damaged.

Whilst the most common reason in the past has related to the nature of the product and been particularly concerned with locating the manufacturing plant close to the market, increasingly it is the costs of manufacture (including labour, raw materials and government support) as well as the costs of transport and being 'close to the market' that are likely to influence the decision about which country location to choose.

Regionalisation is having a significant effect on plant location; for example, the so called 'transplants' of Japanese car manufacturers (Nissan and Toyota) in Europe were not only set up to reduce the cost of transportation, but were also a direct move to avoid the car import quota restrictions of the European Union states. Now location decisions are being based on a variety of factors, such as the participation of the country in monetary union, the different levels of productivity and the need to be closer to the most attractive potential markets. Mexico has expanded its car manufacturing business within NAFTA.

Having emphasised that a move into overseas manufacture involves high cost and risk, firms can choose between different levels of financial commitment. They can, for example, embark upon foreign manufacturing strategies which do not involve direct investment, including: contract manufacture and licensing agreements, or strategies which do involve direct investment albeit at different levels of cost and risk, including: assembly operations, wholly owned subsidiary, company acquisition, joint venture and strategic alliances.

Contract manufacture

A firm which markets and sells products into international markets through its own subsidiary might arrange for a local manufacturer to produce the product for them under contract. The advantage of arranging contract manufacture is that it allows the firm to concentrate upon its sales and marketing activities and, because investment is kept to a minimum, it makes withdrawal relatively easy and less costly if the product proves to be unsuccessful.

Contract manufacture might be necessary in order to overcome trade barriers and sometimes it is the only way to gain entry to a country in which the government attempts to secure local employment by insisting on local production. If political instability makes foreign investment unwise, this may be the best way of achieving a marketing presence without having the risk of a large investment in manufacturing. The disadvantages of contract manufacture as an entry method are that it does not allow the buyer control over the manufacturer's activities. This is the dilemma for breweries with aspirations to go global (see Dilemma 7.1).

Outsourcing from contract manufacturers allows firms, such as Sara Lee, to be very flexible by supplying differentiated food products for different regional markets and adjusting costs more quickly when necessary. It also has financial benefits of lower capital employed, but the risk is that the local contractor may not achieve the desired quality levels or may gain the necessary knowledge to market the product themselves and compete directly with the international marketer. The marketing firm has less control over the conditions in the factory (intentionally or unintentionally). Ikea have had problems in Romania and Nike have had bad publicity with the sweatshop conditions in plants it has used in Asia. As a result Nike have had to sever contracts with plants which refused to comply with company standards for wage levels and working conditions.

Licensing

Licensing also requires relatively low levels of investment. Organisations involved in the film, television and sports industries, as diverse as Disney, the Olympic

---

DILEMMA 7.1   **Beer – global marketing or local heritage?**

The largest brewers of beer aspire to go global but, as Table 7.1 shows, even the largest beer brand, Budweiser, has only a 3.6 per cent share of the market.

Even this is a distortion because nine out of ten cans of Budweiser are sold in the US. Of the beer brands, only Budweiser and Heineken (which claims that its beer is drunk in 170 countries) are in the Interbrand top 75 brands. With 95 per cent of beer being pilsner, some would argue that there is little difference in taste between the brands. Many brewers emphasise the heritage of beer in building the brand image but this tends to be lost in true globalisation. Moreover, beer tends to be uneconomic to transport, heavily taxed at country borders and subject to petty local regulations, and the development of the necessary brewing and distribution infrastructure can be hugely expensive.

In 1999–2000 there were around US$13 billion of international mergers, but they tended to be consolidations within countries. Heineken is seeking to take over brewers in South America but it is still faced with a dilemma. Multinational brewers have so far failed to push their own premium 'international' brands through the new distribution networks that they have acquired, at the same time that they are maintaining distribution of the local brands.

Question Should the international brewers follow a similar model to Coca-Cola and become marketing companies, relying on partnerships with local brewers and bottlers?

Source: 'The big pitcher', The Economist, 20–26 January 2001

Games Committee and Manchester United Football Club have been particularly successful in licensing the use of brands, characters and themes generating huge sales of licensed products. It is a form of management contract in which the licenser confers to the licensee the right to use one or more of the following: patent rights, trademark rights, copyrights and/or product or process know-how. In some situations, the licensor may continue to sell essential components or services to the licensee as part of the agreement.

There are a number of reasons why licensing is a useful entry method. Financial and management commitments can be kept low, the high cost of setting up a manufacturing, retailing or marketing subsidiary can be reduced and tariff and non-tariff barriers can be avoided. Licensing is particularly useful, therefore, to deal with difficult markets, where direct involvement would not be possible, and where the market segments to be targeted may not be sufficiently large for full involvement.

Licensing usually has a number of benefits for the licenser. The licensee pays for the licence normally as a percentage of sales and so, as the sales grow, so does the revenue to the licenser. Considerable control exists as the licensee uses the rights or know-how in an agreed way for an agreed quantity of product, and the licensee markets and purchases products for an agreed fee.

For the licensee, there are a number of advantages. For a relatively low outlay, it is possible to capitalise on established know-how with little risk and avoid the high research and development cost associated with launching a new product. This is particularly important in the industrial market, for example, where licensing of proven technology enables companies to enter markets with products which would be prohibitively expensive to develop.

Problems can occur in licensing if the licensor does not respond to changes in the market or technology, or does not help to develop the market for the licensee. The licensee too, may either be unwilling or unable to develop the market in the way that the licensor would wish. A very capable licensee may have learned so much about the market and product that the licenser is no longer required. These sources of conflict often arise as a result of the environment, competitors and market demand changing over the licensing period.

Terpstra and Sarathy (1999) identify a number of techniques that can be adopted in order to minimise the potential problems of licensing as follows:

TABLE 7.1	Top ten global beer brands 1999		
	Brand	Brewer	Market share
1	Budweiser	Anheuser Busch	3.6
2	Bud Light	Anheuser Busch	2.6
3	Asahi Super Dry	Asahi Breweries	1.8
4	Skol	Ambev	1.8
5	Corona Extra	Grupo Modelo	1.7
6	Heineken	Heineken	1.6
7	Brahma Chopp	Ambev	1.5
8	Miller Lite	Miller Brewing (Philip Morris)	1.4
9	Coors Light	Coors Brewing	1.4
10	Polar	Cervenceria Polar	1.1

Source: Impact Databank

- develop a clear policy and plan
- allocate licensing responsibility to a senior manager
- select licensees carefully
- draft the agreement carefully to include duration, royalties, trade secrets, quality control and performance measures
- supply the critical ingredients
- obtain equity in the licensee
- limit the product and territorial coverage
- retain patents, trademarks, copyrights
- be an important part of the licensee's business.

FOREIGN MANUFACTURING STRATEGIES WITH DIRECT INVESTMENT

At some point in its international development, a stage is reached when the pressure increases upon a firm to make a much more substantial commitment to an individual market or region. The reasons for investment in local operations are:

- **To gain new business.** Local production demonstrates strong commitment and is the best way to persuade customers to change suppliers, particularly in industrial markets where service and reliability are often the main factors when making purchasing decisions.

- **To defend existing business.** Car imports to a number of countries are subject to restrictions and as their sales increase, so they become more vulnerable to locally produced competitive products.

- **To move with an established customer.** Component suppliers often set up their local subsidiaries in order to retain their existing business, compete with local component makers and benefit from increased sales.

- **To save costs.** By locating production facilities overseas, costs can be saved in a variety of areas such as labour, raw materials and transport.

- **To avoid government restrictions** which might be in force to restrict imports of certain goods.

For most multi-nationals operating a global or multi-domestic strategy, there is a strong requirement to demonstrate that they have a permanent presence in all their major markets. The actual form of their operations in each market is likely to vary considerably from country to country, with the largest multi-national companies operating many variants. Companies adopt quite different strategies to a particular situation as Dilemma 7.2 shows.

Increasingly multi-nationals are seeking to reduce manufacturing and operations costs through making the supply chain more cost effective. This takes a number of different forms. Some firms, for example, in the shoe and footwear industries obtain component or finished product supplies from the lowest labour cost areas whereas Ford, for example, locates its component suppliers on a manufacturing campus close to its assembly plants.

Assembly

A foreign owned operation might be set up simply to assemble components which have been manufactured in the domestic market. It has the advantage of reducing the effect of tariff barriers which are normally lower on components than on finished goods. It is also advantageous if the product is large and transport costs are high, for example in the case of cars. There are other benefits for the firm too, as retaining component manufacture in the domestic plant allows development and production skills and investment to be concentrated, thus maintaining the benefit from economies of scale. By contrast, the assembly plant can be made a relatively simple activity requiring low levels of local management, engineering skills and development support.

There is an argument that assembly plants do not contribute significantly to the local economy in the long term. In initially attracting Nissan and Toyota assembly plants, the UK government claimed that many jobs would be created at relatively low cost but critics have claimed that the number of jobs created in the assembly plants was not very significant and, unless the components are made locally, little transfer of technology will be achieved and the assembly plants can relatively easily be moved to a new location. Both to counter this threat and also to generate further employment, countries can take steps to develop the component supply business either by interrupting the component supply chain through imposition of import or foreign exchange rate restrictions or, as in the case of CzechInvest, the inward investment arm of the Czech Republic, by supporting local component manufacturers who can supply 'just in time'. For the international firm, of course, using the assembly option presents an opportunity to move plant from country to country in order to take advantage of lower wage costs and government incentives.

Tait (1997) suggests that one of the considerations of local assembly plants is that costings can be subject to rapid change and global companies investing in them may need to think how quickly they can pull out. Companies typically select a number of regional manufacturing bases which are viewed as longer-term investments useful for testing product innovation, and supplement them with lower skilled assembly plants which can be easily moved between markets. For example, Whirlpool have two microwave plants, one acquired when it took control of Philips European domestic appliance businesses in Sweden, which drives

---

DILEMMA 7.2   The politics of car making in Asia

Currently nine out of ten cars and trucks sold in SE Asia are made by the Japanese but Western firms have planned for the day when the politics and economics of car making in the region change.

ASEAN countries in the past have used import substitution as an economic development strategy and insisted that foreign investors should buy parts locally. This has resulted in firms like Toyota having to create a complete, local supply chain for each of its plants in Thailand, Indonesia, Philippines and Malaysia. In Malaysia the situation has been even worse. A national car manufacturing project was developed and the Proton was protected from foreign competition imports by high tariffs on cars and car parts, especially during the crisis of the late 1990s, when the country tried to conserve hard currency. The result is that Toyota is forced to operate inefficiently and is losing money because it is unable to benefit from pan-regional efficiencies of scale.

The American and European car makers are taking a different approach. They have planned their entry strategy for the time when the Asian Free Trade Area limits tariffs on cars and parts to 5 per cent. General Motors (GM), for example, plans to export up to 90 per cent of the Zafira vans made in its Thai factory to the rest of the region. Ford has designed its plant to be capable of conversion to produce one regional model. BMW's new factory in Thailand sees three phases for its plant: first, to make cars for Thailand, second, to expand production and start exporting and, third, to source from and export to anywhere in the world. The dilemma for the firm is whether to have a long-term regional strategy in the hope that the Free Trade Area will be fully established or adopt a short-term opportunistic market entry strategy.

product development, and the other added later in China, which manufactures competitively for Asian customers and is used for exporting into developed markets.

Virtually all SGS-Thomson Microelectronics exported from Europe to the US and Canada pass through Africa, Asia or Malta. Whilst 60 per cent of the manufacture is located in Europe, testing and assembly is concentrated in low cost areas such as China, Morocco and Malta. It is possible to do this because of the small volume, high value of the products.

Government involvement in foreign direct investment decisions in the early 1990s can be significant. For example, in India Ford, General Motors, Daewoo, Mercedes, Fiat and Peugeot teamed up with local car makers but were blocked out of the low cost segment by Japan's Suzuki which in collaboration with the government has 80 per cent of the Indian passenger car market. As a result the new entrants launched mid-price cars but these were too highly priced for middle-class India where the average annual per capita purchasing power is US$1666 and Ford and GM cars sold for US$22 000.

Wholly owned subsidiary

As we indicated in Figure 7.2 at the start of the chapter, for any firm, the most expensive method of market entry is likely to be the development of its own foreign subsidiary as this requires the greatest commitment in terms of management time and resources. It can only be undertaken when demand for the market appears to be assured, as Illustration 7.4 shows.

This market entry method indicates that the firm is taking a long-term view, especially if full manufacturing facilities are developed rather than simply setting up an assembly plant. Even greater commitment is shown when the R&D facilities are established in local countries too. If the company believes its products have long-term market potential in a relatively politically stable country then only full ownership will provide the level of control necessary to fully meet the firm's strategic objectives. There are considerable risks too, as subsequent withdrawal from the market can be extremely costly, not simply in terms of financial outlay,

ILLUSTRATION 7.4 — Chinese brands building on technology

China is the world's leading exporter and supplies US$70 billion worth of goods to America alone. The pent-up local demand in China coupled with the demand for OEM manufacture, such as for Wal-Mart's Magic Chef refrigerators supplied by Guangdong Kelon, is keeping Chinese manufacturers busy just designing, developing and supplying its products.

Only one Chinese firm, Tsingtao beer, made the Interbrand top fifty non-Japanese Asian brands, but now a few firms have the ambition to be the next Samsung or Hitachi, making the transition from OEM to global brand.

Hai'er's branded refrigeration products already sell alongside Magic Chef in Wal-Mart. The high cost of the advertising necessary to build the brand runs counter to the conservative Chinese business tradition. Zhang Ruimin of

Hai'er has built a factory in South Carolina to serve the US market, emphasising that the selling point is not cheap prices but superior Chinese technology. His motto is 'first hard, then easy'. If Hai'er can survive in the US market, which is more demanding than the other target markets of China's firms, such as Asia, Africa and Latin America, then it will have great advantage over weaker rival competitors. Hai'er is still effectively state owned and, perhaps, has more scope to adopt an ambitious approach than other Chinese white goods manufacturers, such as Kelon which is owned by private shareholders and quoted on the Hong Kong market.

Question What are the critical success factors for Hai'er in developing a global brand?

but also in terms of the firm's reputation in the international and domestic market, particularly with shareholders, customers and staff.

Japanese companies have used this strategy in the past to build a powerful presence in international markets over a long period of time. Their patience has been rewarded with high market shares and substantial profits, but this has not been achieved overnight. They have sometimes spent more than five years gaining an understanding of markets, customers and competition as well as selecting locations for manufacturing, before making a significant move.

Company acquisitions and mergers

In the previous chapters we discussed the role of **acquisitions** and mergers in achieving globalisation. For many Western companies, particularly those from the UK and US, the considerable pressure to produce short-term profits means that speed of market entry is essential and this can be achieved by acquiring an existing company in the market. Amongst other advantages, acquisition gives immediate access to a trained labour force, existing customer and supplier contacts, recognised brands, an established distribution network and an immediate source of revenue.

In certain situations acquisition is the only route into a market. This is the case with previously state owned utilities. By 2003 nine out of 23 water companies in the UK were foreign owned by RWE (Germany), Suez, Vivendi and Bouygues (France), Union Fenosa (Spain) and YTL (Malaysia).

Sometimes the reasons for international business acquisition are, perhaps, not driven by business logic. In 2003 Russian oil tycoon Roman Abramovich bought in-debt and underperforming Chelsea football club (UK) for £59 million and then made over £100 million available for new players.

An acquisition strategy is based upon the assumption that companies for potential acquisition will be available, but if the choice of companies is limited, the decision may be taken on the basis of expediency rather than suitability. The belief that acquisitions will be a time-saving alternative to waiting for organic growth to take effect may not prove to be true in practice. It can take a considerable amount of time to search and evaluate possible acquisition targets, engage in protracted negotiations and then integrate the acquired company into the existing organisation structure.

Another disadvantage of acquisition is that the acquiring company might take over a demotivated labour force, a poor image and reputation, and out-of-date products and processes. All of these problems can prove costly and time consuming to overcome.

However, acquisition can be an extremely effective method of developing a global business. Between 1984 and 1994 the news agency, Reuters, grew from a turnover of £179 million to £1.5 billion, with a market capitalisation of £8 billion, through acquisitions, to become a leading provider of global information services. The recession and structural changes in the industry, however, meant that they had to modify their strategy, when demand for the services reduced, fewer attractive bid targets became available and they began to make losses. Gradually they realigned the business to compete in the knowledge economy.

Takeover of companies which are regarded as part of a country's heritage can raise considerable national resentment if it seems that they are being taken over by foreign firms. A country looking to develop its own technology and manufacturing is likely to believe that acquisition of a domestic company by an MNE is not as desirable as the MNE setting up a local subsidiary. Moreover, acquisition by a large international firm is often associated with job losses and transfer of production facilities overseas. Restructuring of an industry can lead to a stronger global presence. The merger in the wine industry between Australian and American producers could put European producers at a disadvantage, as Illustration 7.5 shows.

Through the past few years there has been considerable debate about acquisition and mergers as a method of achieving rapid expansion. The rationale that is used for acquisition is that an ineffective company can be purchased by a more effective company, which will be able, first, to reduce costs, second, improve performance through applying better management skills and techniques, and third, build upon the synergy between the two companies and so achieve better results. During the late 1980s many takeovers in the UK and US were financed by huge bank loans justified on the basis that an improvement in future profits would be used to pay the high interest charges. In practice few companies were able to realise the true benefits of synergy and the recession of the new millennium reduced demand, and mergers such as AOL–Time Warner underperformed. Other firms focused on their core business and sold off peripheral activities. The Asian crisis also forced cash-starved Asian conglomerates to sell off businesses that did not fit.

COOPERATIVE STRATEGIES

There are a number of situations in which two or more firms might work together to exploit a new opportunity. The methods that are adopted are joint ventures, strategic alliances and reciprocal ownership, in which two firms hold a stake in each other's business.

Joint ventures

Joint ventures are when a company decides that shared ownership of a specially set up new company for marketing and/or manufacturing is the most appropriate

---

ILLUSTRATION 7.5   **A tastier cru?**

Wine producers in Europe have lost their traditional export markets over the past decade because of aggressive producers from Australia and America.

European wine production tends to be very fragmented and dominated by small producers and cooperatives. But the American and Australian industries tend to be made up of larger firms. Now additional pressure is being applied to wine producers as a result of mergers between Australian and American wine producers. In 2000 Beringer Wine Estates of California was taken over by Fosters, a firm better known for beer, but which now earns more from wine. In 2003 BRL Hardy of Australia was taken over by the Constellation Brands Group. American wine producers have grown because of the huge home market but have failed to grow the export business. The smaller Australian market has forced Australian firms to become global earlier. Australian wine outsells French wine in the UK and in 2002 exports to the US increased by 64 per cent.

The mergers are therefore potentially good for both partners. Australian producers get well-developed distribution in the US and the US producers are able to benefit from the Australians' success in difficult markets in Asia and Europe. The Australians have also recognised that wine is increasingly sold through supermarkets, which require a reliable supply chain. American and Australian companies have tried to set up joint ventures with European suppliers, but they are unsuitable because they are too small.

Question Is there anything that European wine producers should be doing to combat the threat?

Source: Adapted from 'Wine industry mergers', *The Economist*, 25 January 2003

method of international market entry. It is usually based on the premise that two or more companies can contribute complementary expertise or resources to the joint company, which, as a result, will have a unique competitive advantage to exploit.

Table 7.2 shows, for example, what was typically contributed in East–West European partnerships in the early 1990s.

Whilst two companies contributing complementary expertise might be a significant feature of other entry methods, such as licensing, the difference with joint ventures is that each company takes an equity stake in the newly formed firm. The stake taken by one company might be as low as 10 per cent but this still gives them a voice in the management of the joint venture.

There are a number of reasons given for setting up joint ventures. These include:

- a number of countries, such as the Philippines, try to restrict foreign ownership
- many firms find that partners in the host country can increase the speed of market entry when good business and government contacts are essential for success
- complementary technology or management skills provided by the partners can lead to new opportunities in existing sectors, such as in multimedia
- global operations in R&D and production are prohibitively expensive, but necessary to achieve competitive advantage.

The main advantages to companies entering joint ventures are that, first, they have more direct participation in the local market, and thus gain a better understanding of how it works, second, they should be better able to finance and profit from their activities, and third, they are able to exert greater control over the operation of the joint venture.

There are, however, some significant disadvantages of joint ventures as a market entry method. As joint venture companies involve joint ownership, there are often differences in the aims and objectives of the participating companies which can cause disagreements over the strategies adopted by the companies. If ownership is evenly divided between the participant firms, these disagreements can

TABLE 7.2	Who provides what in East–West partnerships	
West		**East**
Marketing systems		Land
Financial management		Buildings and equipment
Forecasting		Distribution networks
Planning		Skills
Technology		Low costs
Information systems		Beneficial wage rates
Capital		Tax relief
Know-how		Political connections
Human resources		Neighbouring markets
Financial incentives		

Source: Florescu, I. and Scibor-Rylski, M. (1993) *Making a success of Joint Ventures in Eastern Europe*, CBI Initiative Eastern Europe, London

often lead to delays and failure to develop clear policies. In other joint ventures the greater motivation of one partner rather than another, particularly if they have a greater equity stake, can lead to them becoming dominant and the other partner becoming resentful.

Local partners can turn out to be a liability. The German airline, Lufthansa, teamed up with Modi Group in India, which is engaged in a variety of activities with joint venture partners including Walt Disney, Alcatel, Rank Xerox and Revlon. Lufthansa signed an agreement with one brother to set up a new domestic private airline in 1993 only to find that the five Modi brothers were engaged in bitter feuds. The airline went bust in 1996 and Lufthansa was left seeking US$18.6 million plus the return of three planes whilst Modi has accused Lufthansa of charging too much and delivering defective planes.

The other disadvantages of this form of market entry compared to, for example, licensing or the use of agents is that a substantial commitment of investment of capital and management resources must be made in order to ensure success. Many companies would argue that the demands on management time might be even greater for a joint venture than for a directly owned subsidiary because of the need to educate, negotiate and agree with the partner many of the operational details of the joint venture.

Some experts recommend that a joint venture should be used by companies to *extend their capabilities rather than merely exploit existing advantages* and is not recommended if there are potential conflicts of interest between partners. The role of the government in joint ventures can be particularly influential as it may control access to the domestic market. Moreover, a government may be persuaded to adapt its policy if a firm is bringing in advanced technology or is willing to make a major investment. Most of the major multi-nationals have increased their involvement in joint ventures, but the implications of this are that it leads to increasingly *decentralised management and operations*, more closely aligned to transnational operation rather than to global standardisation in which more centralised control is necessary.

It was anticipated that in Central and Eastern Europe, following the collapse of communist regimes, joint ventures would play a significant part in achieving economic regeneration, but this has not, so far, proved to be the case. The reasons for this include the lack of an adequate legal framework to facilitate joint ventures, the scarcity of supplies of raw materials and components and the lack of suitably qualified people to operate the joint venture, particularly in financial control. There is also the possibility of a conflict of objectives which can occur between the international company, which wishes to develop a new market, and the local company which wishes to develop its own foreign markets or withdraw profits from the joint venture to finance other projects. Finally, companies from developed countries are unable to take out profits because of the lack of hard currency. They are unwilling to wait the ten to fifteen years that it is anticipated that these markets will take to develop.

Illustration 7.6 shows the problems faced by Assi-Domain and their success in their Russian joint ventures.

The problems of running joint ventures in China have been equally disastrous for a number of companies, and increasingly US companies are appealing for help from the US government. Kimberly Clark opened up a joint venture in China, only to find that the joint venture manager who worked for its partner, Xingha Factory Company, had set up a competing factory across the road and was stealing materials.

Although Xingha were not implicated, Kimberly Clark had difficulty getting the local government to take action, and armed security guards were needed to protect the new American manager.

In analysing the results of joint ventures in China, Vankonacker (1997) observes that joint ventures are hard to sustain in stable environments and concludes that more direct investment in China will be wholly owned, offering Johnson and Johnson's oral-care, baby and feminine hygiene products business as a success story.

Strategic alliances

Whilst all market entry methods essentially involve alliances of some kind, during the 1980s the term strategic alliance started to be used, without being precisely defined, to cover a variety of contractual arrangements which are intended to be strategically beneficial to both parties but cannot be defined as clearly as licensing or joint ventures. Bronder and Pritzl (1992) have defined **strategic alliances** in terms of at least two companies combining value chain activities for the purpose of competitive advantage.

Some examples of the bases of alliances are:

- technology swaps
- R&D exchanges
- distribution relationships
- marketing relationships

ILLUSTRATION 7.6   **When joint ventures go wrong**

The Stockholm-based forestry and packaging group Assi was a pioneer in moving into former Soviet bloc markets. The company built or acquired production facilities in Eastern Europe and, later, two in Russia. The Russian market for packaging was growing at 10 per cent a year compared with 4 per cent in Europe.

However, they had mixed fortunes. They were forced to withdraw from a paper-sack joint venture at Segezhabumprom in the province of Karelia in which they acquired a 57 per cent stake for US$45 million in 1996/7. The plant, at 250 000 tonnes, was already Russia's biggest pulp and paper mill and the largest supplier of paper sacks. Assi intended to improve efficiency and· quality but this prompted a local campaign to remove the new bosses as workers feared that job losses would result from this initiative. Threats from powerful interests close to the former management team resulted in the Swedish Chief Executive needing a 24-hour armed guard. Corruption was rife and matters came to a head when Karelia's public prosecutor challenged Assi's ownership of the firm and a Moscow court declared that Assi's takeover was illegal and the company's bank accounts were frozen due to back-dating of the tax liabilities of the previous owners. The company suffered payment problems and Assi had to put in working capital to keep the plant running. The joint venture partners, Upack,

a Russian paper sack distributor, and the Karalenian state property fund, refused to contribute. Assi realised that it had encountered a legal and bureaucratic minefield and the Mafia-style threats against its staff led to it pulling out of its joint venture.

At about the same time, however, the group celebrated the opening of its new US$25 million corrugated board plant at Vsevelzhsk outside St Petersburg. It was built in eighteen months, received tax concessions from the St Petersburg authorities and developed a good relationship with the local politicians. The main difference with this plant was that it was Assi's aim to service MNEs, such as Coca-Cola and Procter & Gamble, rather than compete with Russian companies for a share of the existing local market.

Assi suffered in Karelia because it took on many of the problems associated with the factory and, perhaps, it would have been better to take a longer-term view in making the necessary efficiencies.

Question   What steps can be taken to ensure that joint ventures in emerging markets are successful?

Source: adapted from McIvor, G. (1998) 'Risk and reward in equal measure', *Financial Times*, 3 March

- manufacturer–supplier relationships
- cross-licensing.

Perhaps one of the most significant aspects of strategic alliances has been that it has frequently involved cooperation between partners who might in other circumstances be competitors.

There are a number of driving forces for the formation and operation of strategic alliances.

Insufficient resources: the central argument is that no organisation alone has sufficient resources to realise the full global potential of its existing and particularly its new products. Equally if it fails to satisfy all the markets which demand these products, competitors will exploit the opportunities which arise and become stronger. In order to remain competitive, powerful and independent companies need to cooperate.

Pace of innovation and market diffusion: the rate of change of technology and consequent shorter product life cycles mean that new products must be exploited quickly by effective diffusion out into the market. This requires not only effective promotion and efficient physical distribution but also needs good channel management, especially when other members of the channel are powerful, and so, for example, the strength of alliances within the recorded music industry including artists, recording labels and retailers has a powerful effect on the success of individual hardware products such as the Sony compact disc and Philips digital compact cassette.

High research and development costs: as technology becomes more complex and genuinely new products become rarer, so the costs of R&D become higher. For example, Olivetti and Canon set up an alliance to develop copiers and image processors. In order to recover these costs and still remain competitive, companies need to achieve higher sales levels of the product.

The pharmaceutical company Glaxo's success in marketing Zantac, its antiulcer drug, was achieved by using a network of alliances the most effective of which included Roche in the US.

Concentration of firms in mature industries: many industries have used alliances to manage the problem of excess production capacity in mature markets. There have been a number of alliances in the car and airline business, some of which have led ultimately to full joint ventures or takeovers.

Government cooperation: as the trend towards regionalisation continues, so governments are more prepared to cooperate on high cost projects rather than try to go it alone. There have been a number of alliances in Europe – for example, the European airbus has been developed to challenge Boeing, and the Eurofighter aircraft project has been developed by Britain, Germany, Italy and Spain.

Self-protection: a number of alliances have been formed in the belief that they might afford protection against competition in the form of individual companies or newly formed alliances. This is particularly the case in the emerging global high technology sectors such as information technology, telecommunications, media and entertainment.

Market access: strategic alliances have been used by companies to gain access to difficult markets; for instance, Caterpillar used an alliance with Mitsubishi to enter the Japanese market.

In view of the fact that two thirds of alliances experience severe leadership and financing problems during the first two years, Bronder and Pritzl (1992) emphasise the need to consider carefully the approach adopted for the development of alliances. They have stressed the need to analyse the situation, identify the opportunities for cooperation and evaluate shareholder contributions. Devlin and Blackley (1988) have identified some guidelines for success in forming alliances.

There needs to be a clear understanding of whether the alliance has been formed as a short-term stop gap or as a long-term strategy. It is, therefore, important that each understands the other partner's motivations and objectives, as the alliance might expose a weakness in one partner which the other might later exploit. It is apparent that many strategic alliances are a step towards a more permanent relationship, but the consequences of a potential break-up must always be borne in mind when setting up the alliance.

Glaxo, which was mentioned earlier, appears to have changed its strategy, resulting in the takeover of Wellcome and the merger with Smith Kline Beecham in 2001. At the first attempt the Glaxo–Smith Kline Beecham merger failed, apparently because of a clash of personalities of the top executives.

As with all entry strategies, success with strategic alliances depends on: effective management, good planning, adequate research, accountability and monitoring. It is also important to recognise the limitations of this as an entry method. Companies need to be aware of the dangers of becoming drawn into activities for which they are not designed.

Reciprocal share holdings

In this chapter we have considered many different methods of cooperation between partners. Over the years many firms have taken an equity stake in another firm for a variety of reasons. It might provide the opportunity to influence the strategy of that firm, create a basis upon which to share expertise between the firms or establish a platform that might lead to a more formal business relationship, such as a merger, as well as generating a return on the investment. As shown in Illustration 7.7 Renault took a stake in Nissan to save the company from bankruptcy and succeeded in turning the company around by helping the firm to launch a more attractive and competitive range of cars. Renault then became the recipients of Nissan's expertise in quality and production efficiency.

ILLUSTRATION 7.7   Renault–Nissan: Married or just living together?

When Renault announced in 1999 that it was going to the rescue of Nissan most commentators thought that it was a joke – perhaps the French settling some old scores after their failure to hold back the tide of Japanese imports? After losing money every year since the early 1990s Nissan was on the edge of bankruptcy. Renault took a 40 per cent share but few thought that the cooperation would succeed. Enter Carlos Ghosn, the Brazilian-born French Renault executive drafted in to revive Nissan. In three years Nissan was turned around, making profits in 2001 and 2002. He won the nickname 'Le Cost Killer' as he cut 21 000 jobs and reduced the supplier base by half.

By 2003 Nissan was hiring staff and planning 28 new models. It also transferred Kazumasa Katoh, head of Nissan's powertrain operations, to Renault to help boost quality and manufacturing efficiency, by using Japanese methods. The aim is to get Renault to the same standards

as at Sunderland in the UK, the most efficient plant in Europe. There are some tensions, for example when Katoh noticed Renault assembly workers holding a drill with two hands. Quite reasonably, he showed them how to hold the drill with one hand and the screwdriver with the other! Also Ghosn is tipped to become the next Renault CEO and may want to bring in some Japanese colleagues.

Question Despite the success of their cooperation (Renault now has 44 per cent of Nissan and Nissan 13.5 per cent of Renault) both deny that they will move to a full merger. Should they?

Source: Adapted from Miller, S. and Zaun, T. 'Rescued by Renault, Nissan now works to return the favor', *The Wall Street Journal Europe*, 5 April 2002

What is quite clear is that global firms are adopting a range of market entry partnership arrangements to maximise their global performance and presence. The businesses are becoming increasingly complex as they embark on joint ventures, with the associated formal responsibilities, strategic alliances, with the short-term contractual obligations, and shareholdings, which might be the basis for closer future cooperation.

Inevitably the challenge for management is to maximise the opportunities that come from synergy and the complementary activity of the partners. To do this it is necessary to select partners that are willing and able to contribute at least some of:

- complementary products and services,
- knowledge and expertise in building customer relationships,
- capability in technology and research,
- capacity in manufacturing and logistics,
- power in distribution channels, and
- money and management time.

The management must also deal with the added complexity and potential for conflicts between two quite different partners that arise because of differences in:

- objectives and strategies,
- approach to repatriation of profits and investment in the business,
- social, business and organisation cultures, and
- commitment to partnership and understanding of management responsibilities.

Whilst cooperative strategies promise synergy, the potential for cost saving and faster market entry, it requires considerable management effort to overcome the inherent difficulties and dedication to see the partnerships through to success.

SUMMARY

- For a firm at the start of internationalisation, market entry can be regarded as a critical first step, which is vital not only for financial reasons, but also because it will set a pattern of future international involvement.

- Market entry methods can be seen as a series of alternatives available to international firms. A firm can make individual decisions based on the factors affecting one specific country or the whole region.

- The choice of market entry method should be based on an assessment of the firm's desired involvement and control in the market, set against the financial and marketing risks.

- For large established companies that already have extensive involvement in international markets, the market entry decision is taken against the background of the competitive nature of the market, a global strategy and an existing and substantial network of operations.

- The company's competitive strategy is likely to require simultaneous decisions affecting its arrangements in a number of markets in order to improve its competitive position by entering untapped or emerging markets, or expanding its activities in existing markets.

- In order to achieve these objectives within a very short time scale, companies increasingly need to use a variety of market entry strategies, including joint ventures and alliances.
- This is leading to increasingly complex operations being created in which companies strive to balance the opposing forces of competitiveness and cooperation.

KEYWORDS

acquisition	licensing
contract manufacture	management contracts
cooperative strategies	market entry
direct marketing	market involvement
distributors	piggybacking
domestic purchasing	reciprocal share holding
export houses	risk and control
exporting	*Sogo shosha*
franchising	strategic alliance
indirect exporting	trading companies
joint venture	wholly owned subsidiary

CASE STUDY — Muji – market entry with no brand

Mujirushi Ryohin (meaning no-brand fine goods) started selling a line of generic goods in Japan through a large supermarket chain, Seiyu, in 1980. It now sells a range of homewares, clothing and stationery. The company provides a no-frills, inexpensive, environmentally friendly alternative to the all-pervasive branded offerings enjoying growing popularity. The company offers its own form of minimalist design with products in earth-tone hues of white, brown, beige, slate and silver, with the intention of turning the generic into the stylish. The parent company, Ryohin Keikaku, now has over 290 outlets in Japan plus 16 in the UK, 5 in France and one in Ireland. 'No brand' is becoming a sought-after brand.

However, after an initial period of rapid growth Muji was forced to retrench in 2001 due to over-expansion, the results of slashing prices and poor designs – they replaced half of their designers. The company dropped its plans to open 50 stores throughout Europe and closed five unprofitable units in Belgium and France. Some of the stores were huge – sometimes the size of a football pitch. To fill this size of store required sourcing a huge number of product lines and this led to the dilemma of whether or not to deviate from the core principles of the company. Its experiments with stocking bright coloured clothing were at odds with

Muji's design style of muted tones and it ultimately failed. The management decided to concentrate on expansion in Japan, the Far East and South East Asia for the time being. It has not ruled out future attempts to enlarge its presence in the European and American markets.

One way in which it aims to reach a larger audience without the problems of opening stores is through Muji Online, but online retailing creates its own problems. Physical distribution is required if Muji decides to sell online the items of

Source: Muji

furniture that are stocked in its stores, but at the moment the postal service is sufficient for small items. Certain products are more easily sold online than others. Customers prefer to see and touch clothes and check sizes before purchasing. The main challenge, however, is to increase awareness of the online service. In Japan Muji advertises principally via its catalogue with backup from occasional advertisements on television and in specialist magazines, but of course word of mouth is the best way to create awareness.

Competition

To some, Muji might appear to offer an eclectic mix of products ranging from homewares, where it might compete with Swedish company Ikea, stationery, where in the UK it competes with Paperchase, to health and beauty, where it competes with The Body Shop. Its challenge is to create a unique and distinctive positioning and appeal to customers in a way that sets it apart from competitors. That comes not only from the products that it sells but also from the stores. Much of Muji's appeal is shopping in a calm, ordered environment without brands shouting for attention. The challenge, of course, is whether this can be translated to its Web site.

Customers

The image of Muji is inexpensive, simple and functional but the goods that it sells in Europe can be more expensive than in Japan. This not only presents a problem where customers can easily compare prices online but it also has implications for the customer base and positioning. In Japan the majority of customers are price-conscious younger people, whereas in Europe Muji appeals to a more affluent customer base. In the UK 'no-brand' Muji was one of 50 brands granted Cool Brand Leader status in 2003.

This is in contrast to the initial, poor reaction of European shoppers to Muji, particularly in clothing, because of differences in size and taste. The company responded to this by introducing clothing true to the Muji ethos but with European design, moving from casual to a more tailored look. They now employ European designers for some products.

The future

Without the added value brought by a differentiated brand, Muji would appear always to be in danger of reverting to the status of commodities, becoming trapped in a low margin high turnover cycle. However, the Cool Brand Leader status is confirmation of the Asian influence on style in the West. People are also more concerned about products that are environmentally friendly. The question is whether Muji has developed not only a sufficiently strong design style but also a business model that can be replicated either by a physical store or through online retailing to give it the competitive advantage needed to succeed in different international markets, and especially the US.

Questions

1 Carry out a marketing environment analysis. Which of these factors will be critical for Muji's future success in entering new markets?

2 Prepare an outline international market entry strategy to develop the business in Europe.

Robin Lowe, Sheffield Hallam University
Sources: Adapted from *The Times*, 21 August 2003 and 26 December 2001, *The Nikkei Weekly*, 2 June 2003, *The Scottish Daily Record*, 21 August 2003, various other public sources and the Web sites www.mujionline.com; www.muji.co.uk; www.muji.net

DISCUSSION QUESTIONS

1 Outline the market entry methods and the levels of involvement associated with the development of a company's globalisation process from initial exporting through to becoming a global corporation. Specify what you consider to be the important criteria in deciding the appropriate entry method.

2 Selecting the market entry strategy is the key decision many companies have to take in expanding into overseas markets because it involves both risk and levels of control. Explain how risk and control is affected by different entry methods.

3 When is it appropriate to use contract manufacturing and foreign assembly within an international marketing strategy?

4 Why is acquisition often the preferred way to establish wholly owned operations abroad, and what are its limitations as an entry method?

5 Projects that involve large amounts of development money are sometimes undertaken through a strategic alliance. Explain the rationale behind this form of global partnering and outline the major advantages and disadvantages of the arrangement.

REFERENCES

Bronder, C. and Pritzl, R. (1992) 'Developing Strategic Alliances: A Conceptual Framework for Successful Co-operation', *European Management Journal*, 10 (4), December.

Chan, P.S. (1994) 'Franchising: Key to Global Expansion', *Journal of International Marketing*, 2 (3).

Chryssochoidis, G.M. (1996) 'Successful Exporting: Exploring the Transformation of Export product Portfolios', *Global Marketing*, 10, Part 1: 7–31.

Devlin, G. and Blackley, M. (1988) 'Strategic Alliances – Guidelines for Success', *Long Range Planning*, 21 (5).

Douglas, S.P. and Craig, C.S. (1997) 'Advances in international marketing', *International Journal of Research in Marketing*, 9.

Florescu, I. and Scibor-Rylski, M. (1993) *Making a success of Joint Ventures in Eastern Europe*, CBI Initiative Eastern Europe, London.

Katsikeas, C.S., Piercy, N.F. and Ioannidis, C. (1996) 'Determinants of export performance in a European context', *European Journal of Marketing*, 30 (6).

Mahon, J.F. and Vachani, S. (1992) 'Establishing a Beachhead in International Marketing – A Direct or Indirect Approach', *Long Range Planning*, 25 (3).

Tait, N. (1997) *Financial Times*, 15 October.

Terpstra, V. and Sarathy, R. (1999) *International Marketing*, 8th edn, Dryden Press.

Terpstra, V. and Yu, C.J. (1990) 'Piggybacking: A Quick Road to Internationalisation', *International Marketing Review*, 7 (4).

Vankonacker, W. (1997) 'Entering China: An Unconventional Approach', *Harvard Business Review*, March–April.

Welch, L.S. (1992) 'Developments in International Franchising', *Journal of Global Marketing*, 6 (1/2).

INTERNATIONAL PRODUCT AND SERVICE MANAGEMENT

Introduction

Success in international marketing depends to a large extent upon satisfying the demands of the market and ultimately, on whether the product or service offered is suitable and acceptable for its purpose. More markets are reaching maturity and fewer and fewer products can be differentiated by their core benefits and so are becoming commodities. In defining the term 'product', therefore, we include additional elements such as packaging, warranties, after-sales service and branding that make up the total product offer for the purchaser. Services are taking an increasing share of international trade but managing services internationally poses particular challenges. This is because the delivery of services is so dependent on the context.

In this chapter we focus upon some of the key aspects and recent trends of international product policy by considering the changes in the nature of the products and services offered individually and within the portfolio, their relationship with the market and how new products and services can be developed. Particularly important is the need to provide customers around the world with a satisfactory experience when using the product or service. To achieve this requires a clear understanding of when to meet the similar needs and wants of transnational customer segments and when to adapt to local tastes and requirements.

Learning objectives

After reading this chapter you should be able to:

- Appreciate the elements that make up the product and service offer and the nature of international product and service marketing
- Evaluate the factors affecting international product and service strategy development both external and internal to the firm
- Explain the issues that affect international product and service management across borders
- Identify the implications of the image, branding and positioning of products and services in international markets

■ Understand how new product development contributes to the international
product and service strategy

PRODUCTS, SERVICES AND SERVICE MARKETING

The reason that the majority of companies initially develop international markets
is to generate new market opportunities or increase demand for an existing product or service or to simply off-load excess capacity. However, the product must be
seen as a bundle of satisfactions providing people not just with products but with
satisfying experiences in terms of the benefits they provide rather than the functions the products perform. These concepts are particularly important in international marketing, because, for example, the growth of such global consumer
products as McDonald's and Coca-Cola cannot be attributable solely to a distinctive taste. Much of their success might be attributed to the aspirations of their
international customers to be part of the American way of life, the 'Coca-Cola
Culture', by deriving satisfaction from a close association with the product and
the brand.

In understanding how products can provide satisfying experiences and benefits for people, it is necessary to clearly identify and understand the motivations
of the target consumer and not make assumptions about them. A typical response
to Nike sports shoes, reported in *Sky* magazine was: 'It's kind of like, Nike don't
give a . . . what you do, they don't care where you come from, and they don't
want to hear you talk about it. They just want to see what you can do.'

The term 'product' is used in marketing to refer both to physical goods, such
as a can of baked beans or a refrigerator, and **services** such as insurance or a holiday. In fact few products can be described as pure product with no service element – salt is often suggested as approaching a pure product. Teaching is
probably the closest to a pure service. Before considering the total product 'offer'
in more detail, it is important to consider the specific nature of services and the
challenges they pose in international marketing.

Services are characterised by their:

■ **Intangibility**: air transportation, insurance and education cannot be touched,
smelled or seen. Tangible elements of the service, such as food, drink and
personal video on airline flights, a written policy and a free gift in insurance
and a certificate and a photograph of graduation for success in education, are
used as part of the service in order to confirm the benefit provided and
enhance its perceived value. However, the physical evidence of the service
that is offered may be valued very differently from country to country.

■ **Perishability**: services cannot be stored – for example, the revenues from
unfilled airline seats are lost once the aircraft takes off. This characteristic
causes considerable problems in planning and promotion in order to match
supply and demand at busy and quiet times of the day. Predicting unfamiliar
patterns of demand and managing capacity in distant and varied locations is
particularly difficult.

■ **Heterogeneity**: services are rarely the same, because they involve interactions
between people. For fast food companies this can cause problems in
maintaining consistent quality particularly in international markets where
there are quite different attitudes towards customer service.

■ **Inseparability**: the service is created at the point of sale. This means that
economies of scale and the experience curve benefits can be difficult to
achieve and supplying the service in scattered markets can be expensive,

particularly in the initial setting up phase. Where the service involves some special expertise, such as a pop music artist, the number of consumers is limited by the size and number of venues that can be visited by the performer. If the fans are in a market which is remote, they are unlikely to see the artist and need other tangible forms of communication in order not to feel too separated from the performer.

The three additional marketing mix elements

These differences between product and service offers have certain implications for the international marketing mix and, in addition to the usual four Ps for products (product, price, place and promotion), another **three Ps for services** are added. Because of the importance and nature of service delivery, special emphasis must be placed upon:

- **People**. Consumers must be educated in order for their expectations of the service to be managed and employees must be motivated and well trained in order to ensure that high standards of service are maintained. However, because of cultural differences the staff and customers in different countries often respond differently not only to training and education but also in their attitudes to the speed of service, punctuality, willingness to queue and so on.

- **Process**. As the success of the service is dependent on the total customer experience a well-designed method of delivery is essential. Customer expectations of process standards vary with different cultures and standardisation is difficult in many varied contexts. Frequently the service process is affected by elements for which the service deliverer may be blamed by frustrated customers but over which they have little control. Sports fans might travel to an event at great expense only to experience delays at an airport, excessive policing or bad weather. At its most basic the process of customer management should make it easy for the customer to deal with the firm no matter where they are in the world.

- **Physical aspects**. Many physical reminders including the appearance of the delivery location and the elements provided to make the service more tangible can enhance the overall customer experience. Apart from using appropriate artefacts to generate the right atmosphere, constant reminders of the firm's corporate identity help to build customer awareness and loyalty. For example, the familiar logos of Shell, McDonald's and Nike may give the reassurance necessary for a consumer to make a purchase in a foreign market.

Illustration 8.1 shows how low cost airlines, such as Ryanair and easyJet, have put pressure on the national flag carriers, by changing each element of the marketing mix. There are some specific problems in marketing services internationally. There are particular difficulties in achieving uniformity of standards of the three additional Ps in remote locations where exerting control can be particularly difficult. Pricing, too, can be extremely problematic, because fixed costs can be a very significant part of the total service costs but may vary between locations. As a result the consumer's ability to buy and their perceptions of the service may vary considerably between markets, resulting in significantly different prices being set and profits generated. Increasingly important in service marketing is the need to provide largely standardised services customised to individual requirements. This clearly poses considerable challenges to international service providers. For example, an MNE might employ an international law firm to protect its interests but the scope for offering a standardised service is limited by the fact that every country has a different legal system.

There are a number of generalisations that can be made about international marketing of services. Foreign markets present greater opportunities for gaining market share and long-term profits, partly because local firms are often less experienced and less competitive on quality. Information technology and communications in service delivery, and the development of expert knowledge networks are the sources of competitive advantage for international service marketers. Due to the high initial cost of financing overseas operations, joint ventures and franchising are rapidly growing entry methods, and frequently, the market entry strategy is based on forming alliances or piggybacking as existing clients move into new markets. Whilst government regulations and attitudes to the protection of local suppliers vary considerably from country to country, more new markets are opening up. Most importantly, however, because of the significance of interpersonal relationships in service marketing, it is often cultural empathy in the way services are developed and delivered that is critical for success.

Whilst it might seem appropriate to categorise physical goods as tangible and services as intangible, marketing increasingly appears to be concerned with blurring this distinction. For example, perfume is not promoted as a complex chemical solution, but instead, as one perfume house executive put it, 'dreams in a bottle'. Many services appear to compete over tangible 'add-ons' as we discussed earlier in this chapter.

THE COMPONENTS OF THE INTERNATIONAL PRODUCT OFFER

In creating a suitable and acceptable product offer for international markets, it is necessary to examine first, what contributes to the 'total' product, and second, decide what might make the product acceptable to the international market.

ILLUSTRATION 8.1 **Flying with frills or no frills**

September 11 had a catastrophic effect on air travel and travel to the US in particular. Shortly afterwards, British Airways axed thousands of jobs, American Airlines almost went bust and Sabena, the Belgian airline, did go bankrupt. Many more had similar difficulties.

Despite this, two airline companies, Ryanair and easyJet, prospered. They were following a model pioneered in the US by South West Airlines. The business model of these firms is to offer 'no frills' travel. To do this the company cuts services to the bone. Food on board has to be paid for, there is no seat allocation and around 90 per cent of seat bookings are made on the Internet. The compensation for 'no frills' is low prices. The pricing model is based on yield management software that is designed to maximise the revenue achieved on each flight, by rewarding early customers with low prices and charging high prices to late-

comers. This model contrasts with the full service airlines which have traditionally tried to maintain high ticket prices even when running the plane half-full and have focused on alliances with other airlines to ensure that long-haul passengers have a seamless service.

Ryanair and easyJet have transformed air travel in Europe where distances are short. The model is being tried in other regions of the world but may not work so well. Some suggest that the full services airlines had a business model and marketing mix that was not what customers wanted – September 11 forced them to restructure their business. But now the full service airlines are fighting back with low prices too – sometimes lower than Ryanair and easyJet.

Question What will be the successful marketing mix of the future?

Kotler (2002) suggested three essential aspects of the product offer, which should be considered by marketers in order to meet consumer needs and wants:

■ **Product benefits**: the elements that consumers perceive as meeting their needs and providing satisfaction through performance and image.

■ **Product attributes**: the elements most closely associated with the core product, such as features, specifications, styling, branding and packaging.

■ **The marketing support services**: the additional elements to the core product which contribute to providing satisfaction, and include delivery, after sales service and guarantees.

These elements form the augmented product, an extended version of which is shown in Figure 8.1. Moving down and to the right of the diagram shows the elements that are relatively more difficult to standardise in different country markets.

Having introduced the concept of the total product offer, it is essential to evaluate each aspect of the product in terms of what benefits the consumer might expect to gain and how the value of the offer will be perceived by consumers by answering the following six questions for each market:

1 For what purpose has the product been developed and how would the product be used in that country?

2 What distinctive properties does the product have?

3 What benefits is the consumer expected to gain?

4 How is the product positioned and what image do consumers perceive it to have?

5 Which consumer segments of the total market are expected to buy it, on what occasions and for what purposes?

6 How does the product fit into the total market?

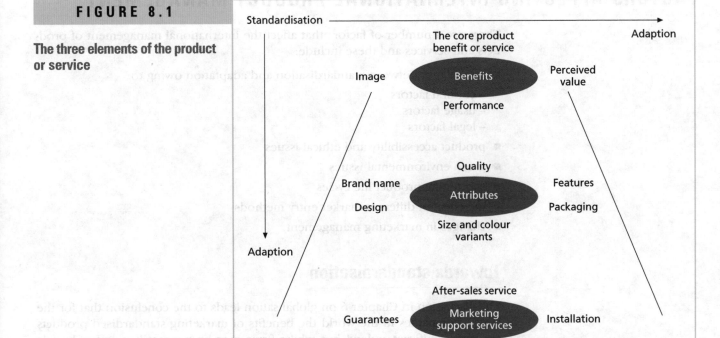

FIGURE 8.1

The three elements of the product or service

The main issue for a company about to commence marketing internationally is to assess the suitability of the existing products for international markets. As a minimum, a purchaser in an overseas market expects to have a clear explanation of how a product should be used, so the instructions on the domestic packaging usually have to be translated for international markets. The question, however, is to what extent the components of the total product offer can and should be adapted for international markets.

In the case of a product where only the packaging needs to be changed, the effect on the overall cost is likely to be minimal, but if more fundamental changes to the product itself are required, because of differences in use or safety regulations, the higher cost might prove prohibitive for a small company. Such problems can be circumvented by taking an alternative market entry approach such as licensing or franchising, but in making strategic decisions of this type, the company must decide exactly what product or aspect of the augmented product will be most valued by customers in the target market. Put simply, the company needs to decide what business it is actually in. The main source of competitive advantage might be in manufacturing, as in the case of Samsung or in promotion and distribution as in the case of Coca-Cola.

The core benefit or main source of competitive advantage can change as, indeed, Samsung has recognised. Samsung can no longer rely on efficient production but recognises the need for a well-known brand and effective promotion. As the market for leisure footwear changed away from white sports shoes Nike's strategy of trying to dominate each sports market by using massive promotional programmes has resulted in considerably reduced margins. In a similar way the clothing retailer Laura Ashley's designs seem to be locked into a particular fashion phase with disastrous consequences for its performance and both companies could be faulted for taking a very myopic view of their markets and competitive advantage.

FACTORS AFFECTING INTERNATIONAL PRODUCT MANAGEMENT

There are a number of factors that affect the international management of products and services and these include:

- the balance between standardisation and adaptation owing to:
  - cultural factors
  - usage factors
  - legal factors
- product accessibility and ethical issues
- green environmental issues
- shortening product life cycles
- the effect of different market entry methods
- changes in marketing management.

Towards standardisation

The discussion in Chapter 6 on globalisation leads to the conclusion that for the largest companies in the world the benefits of marketing standardised products are very significant indeed but whilst firms may be prepared to invest heavily to achieve standardisation, in practice virtually all products must be adapted to some degree. The issue then becomes to what degree their industrial or consumer product or service should be standardised or adapted to the needs of the local market. Even the most obviously global companies achieve only partial standardisation of products. For example, whilst Coca-Cola adopt a global standardised branding strategy, they modify the product for particular customer segments by offering Diet and Caffeine Free Coca-Cola and altering the sweetness for different national tastes. McDonald's, too, alters its menu in different countries to cater for local tastes.

Illustration 8.2 shows how the business-to-business sector can be confronted with the prospect of new technology changing the face of the industry. In responding to this it is important to get the decisions and timing right.

All firms must identify the benefit or satisfaction that the consumer recognises and will purchase. This benefit must provide the basis upon which the company can differentiate its products from those of its competitors. For a product, such as the Sony Walkman, when it was first introduced, the competitive advantage was a

---

ILLUSTRATION 8.2   Cable & Wireless – What a difference two years make

In September 2000 Cable & Wireless (C&W) – led by Chairman Graham Wallace – was being lauded for its focused global strategy and £5 billion of cash on the balance sheet. C&W bucked the trend of the Telecommunications industry – which at the time was about global scale, acquisitions and mergers – by concentrating on one market. 'The value of focus is not just a myth of the financial markets. For fast-growth businesses in rapidly expanding markets, it's essential,' said Graham Wallace, who had been boss of Cable & Wireless for 18 months.

C&W would concentrate solely on the data requirements of global business customers. This involved disposing of assets no longer regarded as 'core' to their strategy: British mobile operator, One 2 One (now T-Mobile), the consumer bit of the cable division (to NTL) and Hong Kong Telecom, Hong Kong's incumbent carrier (to Richard Li's PCCW). The HKT deal netted nearly £10 billion in cash and shares but waving goodbye to the source of 32 per cent of the group's 1999 revenues took some courage, as did getting out of glamour businesses such as wireless and broadband to the home.

It made running this business a great deal simpler. Instead of trying to imagine what television channels elderly women in the north of England might want, or to get into the minds of mobile-phone-toting teenagers, Mr Wallace could eat and sleep the new data services demanded by business customers. Although traditional voice services still represented 60 per cent of C&W Global, by 2010 higher-margin revenues from IP and data that were growing by over 30 per cent a year should make up more than 80 per cent of the total.

But two years later, Moody's, a credit-rating agency, downgraded C&W's debt to junk status. Analysts at Dresdner Kleinwort Wasserstein suggested that investing in the company was 'like buying what appears to be under-valued real estate at the foot of an active volcano'.

What made C&W's implosion so tragic is that it could all have turned out so differently. At the start of the telecoms boom C&W found itself in the unusual position of owning both a worldwide cable network and a collection of local telephone firms in Britain and its former colonies, a hangover from C&W's historical roots as operator of the British Empire's telegraph and telephone networks.

The conventional wisdom in the boom was that the future lay in providing high-speed data connections on a global scale. So C&W duly sold its local-access firms in Britain, Hong Kong and Australia, and invested the proceeds in long-haul data capacity and related services for large companies. It bought an American network, built a European one and beefed up its undersea cable network.

The problem, of course, was that many other firms were doing exactly the same thing, resulting in a capacity glut and tumbling prices. Former national monopolies such as British Telecom and Deutsche Telekom responded to the ensuing crash by retrenching to their home markets, where local-access networks provide reliable revenues. But C&W had lost that option and had no choice but to forge ahead with its global strategy, alongside WorldCom, Global Crossing, 360networks and other troubled operators. It even branched out into the web hosting business just before it collapsed.

Question What implications did the sales of its home-based assets have to Cable & Wireless's strategic choices and what lessons can be learned from the Cable & Wireless experience?

Source: Simon Kelly, Sheffield Hallam University

technical breakthrough, the first easily portable music centre, and so *standardisation of the core benefit* was possible. As products are copied so the firm must find a new source of competitive advantage and this leads to *standardisation of non-core elements* of the augmented product. In the case of Coca-Cola, the core benefit of a specific taste produced from a particular combination of ingredients is no longer a significant source of differentiation, although this might be disputed by cola connoisseurs. Instead competitive advantage is achieved by the standardisation of the imagery associated with the brand and sustained by strong advertising messages.

The decision for most companies to standardise or adapt is based on a cost/benefit analysis of what they believe the implications of adaptation and standardisation might be for revenue, profitability and market share. In normal circumstances, the cost of adaptation would be expected to be greater than the cost of successful standardisation. Only if the needs and tastes identified in the target market segment are significantly different and substantial additional business generated, can the extra cost involved in making and delivering adapted products be justified.

Whilst some companies are tempted to adopt a policy of adaptation in order to satisfy immediate demand, others believe that continual exposure to the standardised products will redefine customer needs and ultimately change their tastes, leading to greater market share in the longer term. It is interesting to contrast the strategies of firms of different nations. American companies have traditionally been very unwilling to adapt products because of the dominance of the home market, whereas Japanese companies, being increasingly dependent on exports, have been prepared to adapt products much more readily. Indeed, product differentiation has become a central part of the strategy of Japanese companies and has led to significant manufacturing process advances, such as production operations being geared to producing small batch sizes and minimum stockholding.

Summarising the advantages of product standardisation, the company benefits from more rapid recovery of investment, easier organisation and control of product management and the possibility to reduce costs through economies of scale and the experience effect throughout most of the firm's operations, such as production, advertising and distribution.

Product standardisation is both encouraging and being encouraged by the globalisation trends in markets, which are emerging because of three factors:

1 markets are becoming more homogeneous;
2 there are more identifiable international consumer segments; and
3 there is an increase in the number of firms moving towards globalisation, so forcing greater standardisation throughout industry sectors.

There are some disadvantages of product standardisation too; for example, market opportunities might be lost when it is impossible to match very specific local requirements. Some managers of local subsidiaries who are only expected to implement global or regional product policies can become de-motivated and miss market opportunities if they are not given the opportunity to innovate.

Greater standardisation of products makes it easier for competitors to copy at ever lower prices, but this leads inevitably to standardisation within a product category so that consumers are unable to differentiate between the core attributes of competing products, with the result that a 'commodity market' is created. To counter this, competition is focusing increasingly upon the augmented product elements. In the family car market, for example, there is very little to choose between the performance, reliability and economy of the main competitors, including Ford, General Motors, Renault, Toyota, Peugeot and Nissan. Against this background, the promotion of individual cars focuses upon design, image, warranties and financing arrangements and rather less on individual performance comparisons.

A more recent trend has been to subdivide particular product categories into smaller niches, such as the Mercedes A Class, the Ford Ka and the new Volkswagen Beetle. The thinking behind this is to appeal to transnational segments whose demands and expectations are more specialised than the mass market. Another recent example of this was the subdivision of 4×4 off-road vehicles into demanding off-road work use, leisure and normal commuting use.

Reasons for adaptation of the product

In some instances, product standardisation may not be possible due to environmental constraints either through mandatory legislation, because of such reasons as differences in electrical systems, legal standards, safety requirements or product liability, or because the firm believes that the product appeal can be increased in a particular market by addressing cultural and usage factors.

Cultural factors

Certain products and services, such as computers and airline flights, are not culturally sensitive – they are international. Here the adaptation is peripheral, for example, translation of instructions into different languages. Other products and services might need to be changed fundamentally. For example, food is a particularly difficult area for standardisation, as the preparation and eating of food are often embedded in the history, religion and/or culture of the country. This presents specific problems for fast food, for example, where the main ingredients of McDonald's and Burger King, beef and pork, prove unacceptable to many potential customers, and the necessary ingredients for fast food, such as the specific type of wheat for pizza bases, suitable chicken and mozzarella cheese are unavailable in certain countries. Indian consumers also prefer a variety of foods and so Pizza Hut and KFC are located under one roof in New Delhi.

A large potential market does not guarantee success. Kellogg's invested US$65 million to launch Corn Flakes in India which has a population of 1 billion people but, after initial success, the sales plummeted. Usually Indians eat a bowl of hot vegetables for breakfast rather than cold cereal. Kellogg's has since introduced other cereals and claims 55 per cent of the cereal market but they have a long way to go before 1 billion people are converted.

Whilst the music tastes of older people from different cultures can be distinctly different, music is becoming increasingly standardised amongst young people, who have much more in common with the same age group around the world than with older people in their own country. There are limitations and sometimes a regional strategy is more effective. The Japanese entertainment industry, having failed to establish itself in the West, has turned to other South East Asian markets which are believed to be some years behind in developing popular music talent. Whilst older generations in South East Asia remember being forced to learn Japanese during World War II, younger generations see Tokyo in the same way as Western youth sees New York.

To the French government, maintaining the traditional culture was politically important, particularly during the GATT discussions (now WTO), and so in 1994 a law was passed that 40 per cent of the output of the music broadcasting stations must be by French musicians.

Changes are taking place in product acceptance, however. For example, fashion is becoming increasingly globalised and the traditional domination of the fashion industry by Western designers is gradually being broken down. Levi jeans are now infiltrating countries like India which have hitherto only accepted traditional dress. Some people believe that the erosion of the country's traditional heritage and culture, particularly by the media and MNE advertising, is unethical and should be resisted but others suggest that larger countries such as India and China simply take those international products which serve a particular need and ignore the rest.

Usage factors

The same product might be used in quite different ways in different markets, partly due to the culture of the country, but also due to the geographical factors of climate and terrain. Unilever and Procter & Gamble have a large variety of products adapted and branded for different markets because of the different ways products are used. For example, French people wash clothes in scalding hot water, whilst the Australians tend to use cold water. Most Europeans use front loading washing machines, whereas the French use top loaders. Honda found that when they first introduced motorcycles into the US they were unreliable and frequently broke down. Whereas Japanese riders were only able to travel short distances, American riders were used to riding the bikes over longer distances and much rougher terrain. Some years ago General Motors of Canada supplied Chevrolet vehicles to Iraq only to find that they were unsuitable for a hot and dusty climate, which led to blocked filters and damaged clutches.

Legal standards

The standardisation of products and services can be significantly affected by legislation. Legal standards are often very country specific – often because obscure laws have been left unchanged for decades. There have been considerable problems for the European Union in attempting to harmonise standards during the creation of the single market and it has taken a number of years to achieve agreement on relatively simple products, such as confectionery, jam and sausage.

Lack of precise, reliable, understandable and universally accepted scientific information, for example in the contamination of beef in Europe, serves only to make it more difficult to achieve a satisfactory industry standard. Pharmaceutical companies experience problems in introducing products into different markets, because individual governments have differing standards of public health and approaches to healthcare. Many countries insist that they carry out their own supervised clinical testing on all drugs prior to the products being available on the market.

Product liability

In the US, over the past few years there has been a considerable increase in litigation, with lawyers seeking clients on a no win–no fee basis. For marketers, particularly those selling potentially life-threatening products such as pharmaceuticals and cars, this demands much greater caution when introducing standard products based on the home country specification into these markets as litigation can lead in extreme circumstances to huge financial settlements, for example in cases related to the tobacco and asbestos industries.

By way of contrast, unscrupulous companies have exploited the different legal controls and lower risks of litigation by sending unchecked lower specification or even hazardous products, such as chemical waste, to less developed countries with lower standards. However, this practice is being increasingly challenged by international pressure groups and is backed up in the US courts which have the power to control the actions of US subsidiaries abroad.

Product acceptability and ethical considerations

Consumers generally are becoming much more discerning and have greater expectations of all the elements of the augmented product. The manufacturer must take responsibility for controlling the pre- and post-purchase servicing and warranties provided by independent distributors and retailers. The packaging, branding and trademark decisions are becoming increasingly important as the global village no longer allows mistakes and failures to go unpublicised.

Consumers, too, have different perceptions of the value and satisfaction of products and so their perceptions of what is acceptable will vary quite considerably from country to country. The product usage and production process may not fit with the culture and environment of the country and the product or service may not be acceptable for its intended use, as was the case with Nestlé powdered milk which was sold in LDCs despite the high cost and lack of clean water to make up the milk. The technology used in the product may not support the country's development policy and the product and production processes may not make use of local resources.

Green environmental issues

Concern for environmental issues is becoming greater in many countries now and has considerable implications for product policies, but the nature, patterns and strength of interest vary considerably from country to country.

Howard (1998) highlights a number of reasons which are making it necessary for firms to pay more attention to global green environmental concerns. These are:

- greater public awareness following the publicity given to environmental disasters, such as floods, fires in Indonesia, Thailand and Mexico, deforestation of the rain forest, water pollution, and reduction in biodiversity
- greater national and local regulation of actions which are likely to affect the environment
- greater stakeholder awareness of MNE activity through better global communications
- greater expectations that MNEs will be more responsive because of their need to preserve a good image of corporate citizenship
- increasing cross-border concerns being shown, with the effect that more powerful countries can exert pressure and influence on MNE activities wherever they are.

Against this background MNEs must respond in an appropriate way to the global and local concerns by taking a more comprehensive approach to dealing with environmental issues by anticipating and, where appropriate, initiating changes. They must also evaluate and proactively manage all the effects on the environment of their operations.

A number of companies are setting corporate strategies which address these issues, for example Sony incorporate environmental considerations into the planning of every product. Ford has adopted the environmental standard, ISO4001, as a worldwide standard.

The goal is to achieve environmental excellence with firms such as The Body Shop, 3M, British Telecom, Johnson Matthey, Merck, Norsk Hydro and Rank Xerox taking a strategic approach rather than making *ad hoc* decisions. There are many problems in building environmental considerations into corporate strategy, including the uncertainties of the science, for example different views on global warming, and the difficulty of deciding on appropriate action because replacement processes or chemicals often give rise to new problems. The problems of adjusting to the scale of the issue have been underestimated as the concerns are increasingly global and cross-border. The precise cause of environmental problems, the effect they have and the best solution are often the source of discussion and controversy. For example, there were significant differences in the scientific evidence offered by Shell and Greenpeace for the disposal either at sea or on land of the Brent Spar North Sea drilling rig. Consumers are much more concerned about the conditions under which products are produced but their concern can be misplaced and ultimately lead to unfortunate consequences, as Dilemma 8.1 shows.

Shortening product life cycles: the merging of markets through increasing globalisation is leading to greater concentration of powerful suppliers who have the resources to rapidly copy a competitor's product or develop their own products to exploit a new market opportunity. The increasing pace of technology means that a technical lead in a product is not likely to be held for very long as competitors catch up quickly. This means that product life cycles are becoming shorter and improvements are introduced more frequently. To this must be added the much higher cost of research, development and commercialisation of new products which places much greater pressures on the firm to distribute the new product throughout world markets as quickly and widely as possible in order to achieve a high return on research and development investment before new products are introduced.

Franchising, joint ventures and alliances: the pressure to exploit new technology and products as quickly and widely as possible has encouraged the rapid

---

DILEMMA 8.1   The football stitching game

A poster in the Chamber of Commerce building in Sialkot, a village in Pakistan, reads 'A child employed is a future destroyed'. Sialkot is a major centre for producing footballs and it received bad publicity when a journalist exposed local manufacturers who were employing child labour to stitch the balls. In 1997, the Atlanta Agreement was signed and 66 local manufacturers volunteered to stop child labour and allow monitors to check on their production. Now Save the Children believe that there is almost zero child labour in that area.

Before the agreement, most of the cutting and laminate printing was done in factories whereas stitching was outsourced to families around the villages. Now stitching is done by full-time adults in centres. This has had a number of beneficial effects. Saga Sports, which makes 4–5 million balls a year for Nike and other brands, now has better control systems, shorter delivery times and lower inventory.

However, the balls are now costly to make and consumers are not willing to pay extra for adult-only certified products. Chinese machine-stitched balls are cheaper and their machine stitching is now suitable for more expensive balls. Indeed, Saga are setting up a factory there. Pakistan's share of the football market dropped from 65 to 45 per cent between 1996 and 1998. Some smaller producers went out of business and family incomes fell by about 20 per cent.

Save the Children supports the Atlanta Agreement but makes a distinction between child labour and child work, which they believe can give children income, skills and self-confidence without damaging schooling. Before the agreement 80–90 per cent of children who were stitching footballs at home already went to school. Of greater concern are child workers in industries, such as brick and surgical-instrument making, which are less publicised and controlled.

The dilemma is: how can the ethical concerns of consumers buying products be balanced with the needs of local communities producing them?

expansion of more creative and cost-effective ways of achieving cooperation in research, development and distribution, such as franchising, joint ventures and strategic alliances. As was discussed in the previous chapter, whilst these market entry methods allow less control than total ownership, they do enable firms to develop a wider sphere of activity than they could do alone. Of course, the challenge is to find partners with truly complementary expertise, knowledge and capability.

Marketing management: these trends have led to significant changes in the way that marketing management operates, allowing a more creative approach to be adopted in developing product policy. First, there are a wider range of options available in international marketing management, particularly by using the marketing mix elements which will be discussed later in this book. Second, there have been significant improvements in the tools available for marketing research, performance measurement and planning. Third, there are more accurate and widely available sources of information which allow greater power for global brand management. It must be pointed out that success in using them depends upon managers being more flexible in redefining niche segments and creative in innovating in all areas of the marketing mix. Fourth, with improved internal and external networking, new product development can become much more integrated within the firm's strategies and be capable of more satisfactorily meeting customer needs through the management of supply chain relationships.

PRODUCT POLICY

Having considered the factors which affect the starting point in developing an **international product portfolio** the next steps are to look first at the suitability of the existing products before embarking on the development of new or modified products. The decision about which products should be included in the range to be marketed internationally is determined by several factors:

- the company's overall objectives in terms of growth and profits;
- the experience, philosophies and attitude of the company to international development, and which of the company's financial and managerial resources will be allocated to international marketing;
- the characteristics of the markets, such as the economic development and the barriers to trade of the firm's domestic and host countries;
- the requirements, expectations and attitudes of the consumers in the market, for example as in Dilemma 8.2;
- the products and services themselves, their attributes, appeal and perceived values (their positioning), the stage that they are at in the life cycle and economies of scale;
- the ease of distributing and selling them;
- the support the products require from other elements of the marketing mix and after-sales services;
- environmental constraints (such as legal or political factors) which must be overcome;
- the level of risk that the company is prepared to take.

Dilemma 8.2 shows that threats can be posed to products that seem to have the most secure future.

Product strategies

Against the background of so many variables, it is inevitable that companies adopt a very wide range of **product strategies** in international markets. In formulating product policies, Mesdag (1985) postulated that a company has three basic choices:

SWYG	Sell What You have Got.
SWAB	Sell What people Actually Buy.
GLOB	Sell the same thing GLOBally disregarding national frontiers.

All three strategies have been used for a long time. Heinz, Mars, Heineken and Johnnie Walker have been international brands for decades using global product and brand strategies to enable them to clearly position their products as global brands. The Danes have long dominated the UK bacon market by following a SWAB strategy as have the French in their marketing of cheddar cheese in the UK. The disadvantage of the SWAB strategy is that it is only possible to penetrate one market at a time. It may be also difficult to compete with local firms on their own terms. Furthermore, it is sometimes difficult for a foreign company to establish credibility as a supplier of products which have a strong domestic demand; for example, Suntory of Japan made good whisky but could not attempt to market it in the UK and so it acquired Morrison Boxmore Distillers, which produces distinctively Scottish single malt whisky brands.

The SWAB approach is the classic differentiated approach, but whilst it is responsive to market needs it does make considerable demands on the firm's development, manufacturing, logistics and financial resources and is often impractical for these reasons. The first Fiat Palio, launched in Brazil in 1996, was designed specifically for the emerging markets and sold 250 000 within 18 months whilst Ford decided to make its Western European Fiesta in Brazil and suffered delays, product recalls and very poor results after launch.

SWYG are the most common form of export strategies, but they are also the most common reason for failure. The key objective for most firms following such strategies is to fill production lines at home rather than meet a market need, but by concentrating only on a few markets, many companies do successfully implement this kind of strategy. Mesdag argues also that some of the most successful global products started off as domestic products with a SWYG strategy, for example pizza, hamburgers and yoghurt. Success has been the result of the companys' ability to meet new international emerging demand for the convenience of fast foods. The products may not necessarily be formulated identically across markets

---

DILEMMA 8.2   **Trying to ensure that diamonds are forever**

Consumers are concerned about the source of products, the conditions under which they are produced and any adverse implications of production for host countries. De Beers, the South African diamond cartel, was accused by non-governmental organisations (NGOs) of buying diamonds from war zones, thus allegedly providing rebels with the cash to buy arms. As a result, De Beers wound down its business in Angola, withdrew its buyers from Congo and Guinea and promised to refuse supplies from Sierra Leone. De Beers says that only 4 per cent of diamonds come from

war zones and other less scrupulous diamond traders will step in to trade in these countries. Moreover, De Beers argues that the damage that could be done to the industry's image could be similar to that done by animal rights protesters in the fur trade. Loss of sales of diamonds could put at risk the livelihoods of miners in more peaceful countries, such as Botswana, Namibia and India.

The dilemma for the legitimate diamond trade is: how can it protect its image and yet compete effectively in the industry?

but they appeal to a pan-regional or global need and can therefore be positioned as cross-frontier brands. The success of the strategy has been based on identifying and meeting the needs of transnational customer segments. Heineken, the Dutch brewing firm, took over Egypt's only brewery, Al Harham Beverages, in 2002 and in doing so acquired Fayrouz, a fruit flavoured non-alcoholic malt drink popular in Egypt and certified halal by Al Azhar, a leading Sunni Islam religious institution. Heineken then had the opportunity to market Fayrouz in the Indian subcontinent and to Muslims in the UK, Germany, Netherlands and France.

Keegan (1989) has highlighted the key aspects of international marketing strategy as a combination of standardisation or adaptation of product and promotion elements of the mix and offers five alternative and more specific approaches to product policy.

One product, one message worldwide

Since the 1920s, Coca-Cola have adopted a global approach, which has allowed them to make enormous cost savings and benefit from continual *reinforcement of the same message*. Whilst a number of writers have argued that this will be the strategy adopted for many products in the future, in practice only a handful of products might claim to have achieved this already. A number of firms have tried this and failed. Campbell's soups, for example, found that consumers' taste in soup was by no means international.

Product extension, promotion adaptation

Whilst the product stays the same, this strategy allows for the *adaptation of the promotional effort to target either new customer segments* or appeal to the particular tastes of individual countries; for example, Yoplait yoghurt attempts to capture the mood of the country in its various television advertising.

Product adaptation, promotion extension

This strategy is used if a *promotional campaign has achieved international appeal*, but the product needs to be adapted because of the local needs. Many suppliers of capital goods promote the idea of providing technical solutions rather than selling industrial plants; Exxon used the 'tiger in the tank' campaign around the world and IBM have used 'Solutions for a small planet'.

Dual adaptation

By adapting both products and promotion for each market, the firm is adopting a *totally differentiated approach*. This strategy is often adopted by firms when one of the previous three strategies has failed, but particularly if the firm is not in a leadership position and, instead, must react to the market or follow the competitors.

Product invention

Product invention is adopted by firms usually from advanced nations who are supplying products to less well-developed countries. Products are *specifically developed* to meet the needs of the individual markets. After watching a programme on TV about AIDS in Africa at his home on Eel Pie Island in the middle of the Thames in London, Trevor Bayliss invented the clockwork radio to help the news to be spread to areas which did not have electricity and could not afford batteries. Despite rejections by major MNEs, Bayliss persevered and 50 000 radios per month are made by disabled staff by BayGen in South Africa. BayGen is now worth in excess of £100 million.

MANAGING PRODUCTS ACROSS BORDERS

The product life cycle

In the domestic market models such as the product life cycle and Boston Consulting Group's portfolio matrix are used to manage a portfolio of products. The concepts can be applied in international markets to the management of a product, brand or product range across a portfolio of countries.

The life cycle concept is used as a model for considering the implications for marketing management of a product passing through the stages of introduction, growth, maturity and decline and can be applied to international marketing. The British popular music industry was outstandingly successful as a major exporter during the 1960s, 1970s and early 1980s, all starting, perhaps, with the era of the Beatles and the Rolling Stones, when British artists rapidly gained global recognition. The market share of the industry declined during the early 1990s from 23 per cent to 18 per cent of the world market and this share resulted largely from re-releases and new offerings from ageing rock stars such as Eric Clapton, Elton John and Sting. The mid-1990s saw the emergence of new groups such as the Spice Girls and Oasis, but shortening product life cycles appear to affect this industry too, with new stars staying at the top for much shorter periods.

Stars such as Kylie Minogue that have maintained their success over a long time have periodically repositioned themselves to 'rejuvenate' their product life cycle and brand.

The **international product life cycle** suggests that products in international markets can have consecutive 'lives' in different countries; this is illustrated in Figure 8.2. Soon after the product was launched in its domestic market it was

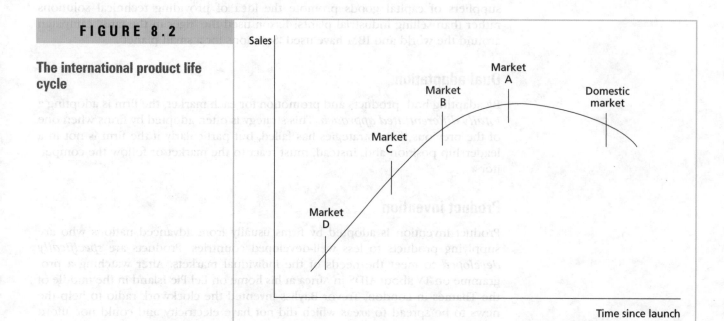

FIGURE 8.2

The international product life cycle

introduced into another developed country, A. Later it was introduced to other developed and newly industrialised countries, B and C, and only recently to a less developed country, D. In the domestic market and country A, a replacement product is required, whilst considerable growth is still possible in the other countries.

In the past the length of the total product life cycle from birth to death has been unpredictable, but in some high technology markets it is now possible to accurately predict when new technology will force a new product's introduction. As a result it is now necessary for the product to be project managed for a limited and specific lifetime to ensure that by the end of its life the product has been profitable.

The most significant change for both life cycle models is that the international communication revolution has led to more frequent *simultaneous product introductions*, particularly of consumer products, by global companies into different world markets backed by global branding and promotion, and so the sequential approach to marketing and manufacturing that is encapsulated in the original model applies less frequently. However, as we established earlier, not all companies operating internationally are global corporations, and it is therefore important not to ignore the model altogether. The concept of phases in the life cycle is still useful for a company that is simply exporting specialist engineering components and tools or agricultural equipment from an advanced economy.

On balance, therefore, although the validity of the product life cycle has at various times been attacked by a variety of writers, it does have a role to play for certain types of company insofar as it is a model that provides a framework for thinking in detail about product policy, new product development, product introduction and product elimination. Because life cycles generally are shortening, there is an increased need for a well-developed policy of new product development or repositioning for new markets in order to replace or extend the life cycle, as Tiger Balm has achieved, shown in Illustration 8.3.

ILLUSTRATION 8.3   Tiger Balm: Relieving the pains of warlords and sports stars

Tiger Balm is a herbal ointment remedy that was developed to relieve the aches and pains of the warlords and emperors in the imperial courts of China. The patriarch of the Aw family, Aw Chu Kin, passed his knowledge of Chinese medicine to his sons Boon Par (meaning gentle leopard) and Boon Haw (meaning gentle tiger), who was the marketing pioneer. The company name Haw Par comes from the names of both brothers.

Control of Haw Par has passed from the family to a large corporate group based in Singapore and now has sales in excess of US$100 million. The product sells into 70 countries on the basis of its strong Asian heritage. The packaging is unique, with its springing tiger logo. It still retains the old reproduction photographs of the brothers with their names in Chinese and English and has an imitation official-looking seal as the cover round the small hexagonal jars and round cans. The original recipe has been enhanced with Chinese and Western additives to increase its effectiveness. It is now used by young and old and endorsement by sports stars has increased its appeal.

Question What strategies could be used to further grow the brand?

Source: Haw Par Healthcare Ltd

Source: Adapted from Temporal, P. Tiger Balm: www.brandingasia.com/cases/tigerbalm.html

Product portfolio analysis

The use of portfolio approaches in international product management centres around the Boston Consulting Group's Growth–Share Matrix, the General Electric/McKinsey Screen, and the Arthur D. Little Business Profile Matrix. They are designed primarily to clarify the *current strategic position* of a company and its competitors, and to help identify any future strategic options.

The complexities and dimensions of the analysis increase considerably when applied to the firm's international portfolio, since the competitive positions occupied by a product are likely to differ significantly from one market to another, as indeed will the nature and intensity of competition. Comparing the strength of a portfolio across a variety of markets becomes difficult as the analytical base constantly changes. For these reasons, the BCG matrix, for example, might be based on one product range with the circles in the matrices representing country sales instead of product sales, as shown in Figure 8.3. This then provides a basis for analysing the current international product portfolio, assessing competitors' product/market strengths and forecasting the likely development of future portfolios both for itself and its competitors.

Introduction and elimination activities

Whilst the major focus of product policy is upon new product development, the increased pace of the activity has a number of consequences for product management at both ends of the product life cycle. The factors that need to be taken into account in managing the product portfolio are:

■ the firm's objectives;

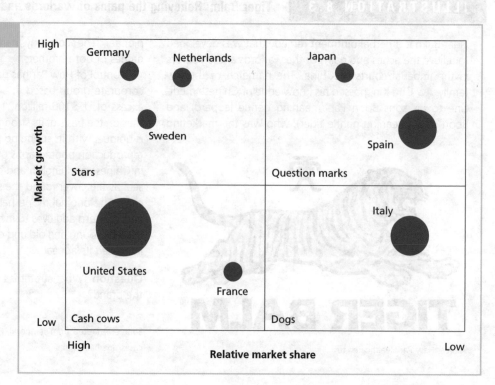

FIGURE 8.3

The portfolio approach to strategic analysis (BCG matrix)

- the company's existing range of products and degree of overlap in the positioning of products in the range;
- the stage in the life cycle that the products have reached;
- the manufacturing capacity available;
- the likely receptiveness of the market to the new product; and
- the competitive structure of the market.

These factors have a number of implications for the product policy. Too many product introductions can risk overburdening the firm's marketing system. There is a constant need therefore for a regular review of the range and for elimination decisions to be made where a product is either in its decline stage or simply failing to generate sufficient profit. The international perspective, however, means that decision making is more difficult, since a product may be manufactured principally in a plant in one country, be a 'cash cow' in one market and a 'dog' in another. Careful analysis is therefore needed before the product elimination decision is taken. The identification of overlaps or gaps in the product range may necessitate elimination of products if they are in the declining stage of the product life cycle, have been duplicated or have been replaced by a newer product.

The complexity of managing a wide portfolio of products at Nestlé, Unilever and Heinz is shown in Illustration 8.4 and it raises some fundamental issues about the product strategy alternatives.

ILLUSTRATION 8.4   Portfolio management Unilever, Nestlé and Heinz style

The marketing of many food products is culturally sensitive as many customers want local, traditional products and brand names. But some foods are accepted globally and there are strong arguments for standardisation of these. Unilever, Nestlé and Heinz clearly demonstrate contrasting approaches to portfolio and brand management in the global food market.

Unilever in the late 1980s and early 1990s was aiming for responsiveness to local markets whilst striving for unity within its complex and diverse activities but by the late 1990s Unilever was in a mature market with few new opportunities appearing and so the emphasis was on adding value. In response to this, Unilever undertook product rationalisation from 1600 to 500 major international brands, such as Magnum. Because of the difficulty of generating new products internally it acquired Ben and Jerry's, the socially aware ice-cream company, and Slim-Fast, the diet food manufacturer. Its whole approach is to focus on major brands that are capable of global development.

Swiss food manufacturer Nestlé has a vast range of products, many of which are products that sell in just a few countries. These include Gales honey, Sun Pat peanut butter, Buitoni pasta and Sarsons vinegar. Nestlé continues to support the large portfolio and is not currently rationalising its range, but at the same time it is applying its corporate brand more obviously across its products. For example, the chocolate bar, Kit Kat, part of its acquisition of Rowntree (UK), now carries the Nestlé brand. Nestlé has two top products capable of becoming at least regional, ice-cream and pet food, but both lag well behind the market leaders, Unilever in ice-cream and Mars in pet food.

With the exception of a few products, such as its famous tomato sauce – eaten everywhere with burgers and hot dogs – Heinz (US) applies effectively a multi-domestic strategy, making only a small effort to force a global or even pan-regional strategy. For example in 2001 it took over Honig (Holland) which makes very local traditional delicacies, such as chocolate sprinkles topping.

Question Which strategy is most effective in maximising the companies' return on investment given that brand and product managers have the problem of managing their time between their responsibilities for global or regional and local products?

IMAGE, BRANDING AND POSITIONING

Of all the elements of the product or service offer, it is the image of the brand which is the most visible and it is the perceived value which consumers attach to this that is the central factor in positioning the products in the various markets.

The image of products, companies and countries can confer different values to consumers in different countries. Research by a number of writers has shown that products from particular countries have a stereotyped national image for such attributes as quality, price and reliability. Individual corporate brands either benefit from positive country of origin perceptions or must overcome negative perceptions to succeed in international markets.

Country of origin effects

Buyers evaluate the products that they may wish to purchase, based on their assessment of intrinsic cues (taste, design, performance and quality) and extrinsic cues (brand names, packaging and country of origin).

Where the buyers' knowledge about the product is limited, for example because they do not understand the technology, country of origin perceptions influence their buying decisions. The consumers' perceptions of companies are usually based on national stereotypes, for example Japanese products tend to be regarded as high quality, reliable and 'miniaturised' whereas US products are big and 'brash'.

By contrast, products from developing countries are often seen by Western consumers as low quality, unreliable and usually copies of products from developed countries. This was the perception of Japanese products too some decades ago and shows that it is possible to change consumer attitudes.

There are significant differences between countries in the willingness of consumers to buy locally produced products. Usually this appears to be related to the feeling of nationalism that exists in the country at the particular time the assessment is made. In developing countries, such as China, Ho (1997) found that nationally produced goods are often seen to be inferior to foreign goods.

The **country of origin effect** does extend further. For example, the stereotyping relates just as much to developed countries. For example, there are strong associations between countries and the products that they are known for, for example Italy and pizza and Germany and machine tools. Agarwal and Sikri (1996) found positive correlations between the best-known product categories from a country and the expectations that buyers have of new products from that country. Overcoming these stereotypes is often the first challenge for international marketers who must prove that their product does not reinforce negative stereotypes.

Increasingly, of course, the MNE's headquarters, the brand's perceived 'home', the location of product design and places of manufacture may all be in different countries. Research is carried out into these effects on consumer purchasing habits, for example, by Haefer (1997) and Thakor and Kohli (1996).

An interesting case is that of British cars such as Jaguar, Rover and Rolls-Royce which have not succeeded internationally as well as they might have, perhaps because of negative perceptions and experiences of the cars during the 1960s and 1970s. Foreign ownership by Ford, BMW and Volkswagen, respectively, has achieved different levels of success. BMW sold Rover in 1999 but Jaguar has regained some of its former glory within the Ford group. Some broader conclusions about the country of origin effects in the car industry are shown in Illustration 8.5.

Product image: as we have already emphasised, product image is one of the most powerful points of differentiation for consumers. The aspirational and achiever groups of purchasers wish to belong to particular worldwide customer segments and are keen to purchase products which are associated with that group. An interesting example of this is that the sales of luxury goods remained buoyant during recent recessions due to increased sales to emerging countries as the 'new' rich sought to buy similar products and services to the 'old' rich.

Company image is becoming increasingly important in creating a central theme running through diverse product ranges that reinforces the vision and the values of the company which can be recognised by employees and customers alike. For this reason many companies have spent considerable effort and

---

ILLUSTRATION 8.5   **Our best selling car is made here**

In the UK in 2002 less than one in four of the cars sold were made in the UK. Despite the EU wanting to see more cross-border buying, typical French customers buy French, Swedes buy Swedish and German customers buy German. Most of the major car markets follow the same pattern. Russians buy Russian and Americans buy American.

The reasons are often price and tax but there does seem to be loyalty to local brands too, which is not always replicated in other product sectors. In the UK there has been strong loyalty to Ford since 1911 when a factory was set up in Manchester to produce the Model T, the earliest mass produced car which sold 15.5 million between 1908 and 1927.

Perhaps locally produced cars have the right look and feel for the local market. In developing countries the best-sellers are often local versions of foreign models. The best selling cars are made in the country even if the brand is foreign. The VW Gol, built in Brazil since the 1980s, is a special VW sized between the Polo and Golf. The Citroen Xsara is made in Spain, the Toyota Tazz is a local version of a 1987 Corolla and the Maruti 800 is an old Suzuki-based model made in India.

Worldwide, the Toyota Corolla was the world's favourite car in 2002, selling 1 million in 140 countries with the Ford Focus second. Twenty-nine million Corollas have been made over 36 years from 9 iterations of the brand. Twenty-two million VW Golfs have been produced over five generations and 21 million VW Beetles were built. The Fiat 124, launched in 1967 and still built in Russia as the Lada Riva, has sold 14 million.

Question How does the country of origin influence car purchasing behaviour?

Source: Adapted from Hutton, R. 'Local heroes take top prizes in world sales', *Sunday Times*, 30 March 2003

Best sellers in 2002

Country	Best seller	Second place	Third place
Australia	Holden Commodore (GM)	Ford Falcon	Toyota Corolla
Brazil	VW Gol	Ford Falcon	Toyota Corolla
France	Renault Clio	Peugeot 206	Renault Mégane
Germany	VW Golf	BMW 3 series	Mercedes C class
India	Maruti 800	Hyundai Santro	Tata Indica
Italy	Fiat Punto	Fiat Panda	Ford Focus
Japan	Honda Fit	Toyota Corolla	Suzuki Wagon R+
Russia	Lada 2107	Lada 2110	Lada 2109
South Africa	Toyota Tazz	Toyota Corolla	BMW 3 series
Spain	Citroen Xsara	Renault Mégane	Ford Focus
Sweden	Volvo V70	Saab 9-5	Saab 9-3
UK	Ford Focus	Vauxhall Corsa	Vauxhall Astra
US	Ford F Series	Chevrolet Silverado	Toyota Camry

resources on controlling and enhancing the corporate identity through consistent style and communications, discussed in more detail in Chapter 9.

Image can be equally important at the other end of the product spectrum to luxury goods. Aldi (Germany), Netto (Denmark) and Lidl (Sweden) use a no-frills approach to retailing by reinforcing their message of low prices with simple decor, warehouse-type displays and single colour understated packaging.

The image of a company also plays a vital role in business-to-business marketing, for example, when quoting for international capital projects. Decisions are likely to be made on the grounds of the perceived reputation of the company as, without a strong international presence, it can be quite difficult to break into a small elite circle of international companies, even if very low prices are quoted.

The Carlyle Group is a highly profitable but low profile investment firm based in the US but with activities in 12 countries. Its personnel include former US president George Bush, former UK prime minister John Major, former Philippines president Fidel Ramos and past US secretary of state, James Baker, all of whom presumably have powerful and influential business contacts.

International branding

Closely linked with the image of the product is the issue of branding. The role of branding, important as it is in domestic markets, takes on an additional dimension in international markets as it is the most visible of the firm's activities, particularly for global companies as we have discussed in Chapter 6. Brands allow customers to identify products or services which will promise specific benefits, such as performance, price, quality or image. For the firm, brands provide a point of differentiation from their competitors' products and are a way of adding value to the product. For these reasons, brands are extremely valuable in providing access to markets.

In 1988 brand values reached a peak, with Kohlberg Kravis Roberts paying US$25 billion for RJR Nabisco with the brands valued at US$18 billion, and Nestlé paying US$4.5 billion for Rowntree with the brands valued at US$4 billion.

Rather than discuss the definitions of branding, which are covered widely in the business journals it is, perhaps, more useful to consider a different approach which enables a range of consumer and business-to-business brand issues to be considered together. Underpinning the concept of branding is that the company owning the brand and its customers must both obtain benefit. De Chernatony (1989) suggests that there are nine themes which help to define the brand over a wide range of situations:

- a legal instrument
- a differentiating device
- a company
- an identity system
- an image in consumers' minds
- a personality
- a relationship
- added value
- an evolving entity.

These themes suggest that the constituents of the brand can include both tangible benefits, such as quality and reliability, and intangible benefits which may bring out a whole range of feelings, such as status, being fashionable or possessing good judgement by purchasing a particular brand. Very young children are now fully aware of which fashion label is 'in' at the moment and advertisers are well aware of the effects of 'pester power'.

The brand value equation (Figure 8.4) draws attention to the offer to consumers of the intangible benefits that the brand adds over and above the tangible, functional benefits of a commoditised product or service. The challenge for international branding, of course, is to what extent the intangible benefits from branded products and services vary between countries, cultures and individuals. During the late 1990s, wearing Nike trainers in some countries was the price of peer pressure, measured in terms of the cost of belonging to a particular reference group, whereas elsewhere it set the wearer apart as the leader of the group, as having status and style to which the other members of the group must aspire. But, of course, Nike trainers in these terms were a fashion item and the test of a truly global brand is its ability to achieve durable brand strength by responding to, or indeed, driving market changes and this will only be established over a period of many years.

These tangible and intangible benefits must also be valued against the background of the total cost of ownership of the branded product by the customer. The total cost of ownership and the tangible and intangible benefits are accrued over the lifetime of the product. For example, car ownership offers different benefits and costs in different markets, especially when considering the longer-term implications of, for example, warranty and servicing costs, car resale value and changing car fashions. Brand strength for cars is, to some extent, determined by the second-hand car values, with car marques such as BMW and Mercedes holding their value exceptionally well and some cars, such as Ferrari, even increasing in value.

Brand value

It has been suggested that the strongest brands convey a core value to all their customers by the associations that are made with their name. By adding '-ness' to the brand names consumers instantly associate values which are globally recognised – for example, 'IBMness' is distinguishable from 'Microsoftness'. The great brands (Figure 8.5) have achieved their global status through high levels of investment and consistent management across their country markets of the dimensions used to value the brand over a long period of time. Usually the investment includes a large commitment to advertising but other factors, such as understanding their customers' needs and wants, totally consistent quality, reliability and continuous innovation are just as important to achieve widespread customer loyalty and recommendations.

FIGURE 8.4

The brand value equation

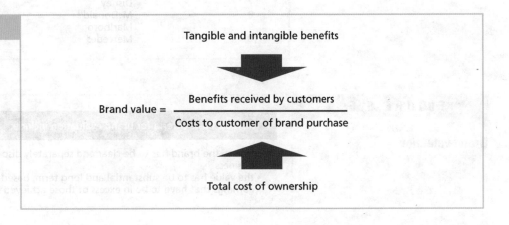

Brand valuation is to some degree inevitably subjective but the dimensions indicated in Figure 8.6 show that building the brand requires dedicated management of the complete marketing mix across the various markets and there is evidence of this in all the successful brands. Brands can, of course, also decline in value from time to time due, for example, to a failure to understand customer expectations (Marks and Spencer), to inappropriate brand stretching (a number of the top fashion brands), to a failure to reposition in response to market decline (manufacturers of tractors and other agricultural machinery) or failure to respond to new competition (Pan Am, formerly state-owned telecoms businesses and many of the European and American car manufacturers at some point in their recent history).

Branding strategies

There are four recognised branding strategies:

Corporate umbrella branding is used by firms such as Heinz, Kellogg's and Cadbury's. The corporate name is used as the lead name for all their products, for example Kellogg's Healthwise, Kellogg's Frosties, Kellogg's Corn Flakes.

Family umbrella names are used to cover a range of products in a variety of markets. For example Marks and Spencer use their St Michael brand for clothing, food, household goods and toiletries.

Range branding is used for a range of products with a particular link in a specific market such as Lean Cuisine for low-calorie foods.

Individual brand names are used with individual products in a particular market, with different weights, colours, flavours and pack sizes. Procter & Gamble and Unilever use individual brand names such as Daz, Ariel and Omo with no reference to the corporate name.

FIGURE 8.5

The world's most valuable brands 2002

Source: Interbrand

	Brand	Brand value (US$bn)
1	Coca-Cola	69.64
2	Microsoft	64.09
3	IBM	51.19
4	GE	41.13
5	Intel	30.86
6	Nokia	29.97
7	Disney	29.26
8	McDonald's	26.38
9	Marlboro	24.15
10	Mercedes	21.01

FIGURE 8.6

Brand valuation

The most basic criteria for brand evaluation include:

- title to the brand has to be clear and separately disposable from the rest of the business
- the value has to be substantial and long term, based on separately identifiable earnings that have to be in excess of those achieved by unbranded products

A further branding strategy, *private branding*, is the practice of supplying products to a third party for sale under their brand name. Ricoh gained a 9 per cent market share for its small plain paper copiers by acting as an *Original Equipment Manufacturer* (*OEM*) for a number of suppliers including Nashua for Canada and Europe, Kalle of West Germany for Europe and Savin for the US. The two South Korean companies, Samsung and LG, have rapidly developed internationally to the point now where they have high shares of certain product categories. They have achieved this largely by being an OEM manufacturer but it is interesting to note that these companies over the past few years have increasingly prioritised their own Samsung and Goldstar brands.

Private branding is used widely in retailing and as the major retailers have become more powerful, so the private brand share of the market has increased significantly, especially during times of recession. This is because the consumers perceive private brands as providing 'value for money', and this has been encouraged as retailers have continually improved the quality of their own label products.

Quelch and Harding (1996) suggest that supermarket brands increase profits; in the US just over 19 per cent of supermarket volume is from store brands whereas 54 per cent of Sainsbury (UK) and 41 per cent of Tesco (UK) sales are from private labels and they return 5 per cent higher pre-tax profits than the US firms. By being part of a stable oligopoly international retailers have the size and resources to invest in high-quality own label development.

There are significant implications of these strategies in international markets, and an example of this was Nestlé, which was selling Camembert cheese throughout Europe using several different national brands in different styles of packaging. Having redesigned and standardised the packaging, they placed the Nestlé brand logo alongside the local brand logo on the packaging and then gradually increased the size of the Nestlé brand and reduced the size of the local brand.

Much of what has been said so far about product standardisation and adaptation applies to branding. De Chernatony *et al.* (1995) identify two components of brand planning: the core concept (the essence of what the brand stands for in terms of its added value positioning) and its execution (the detailed implementation through packaging, product contents, tactical promotions and media policy). In a demand–supply model (Figure 8.7) they emphasise the most important con-

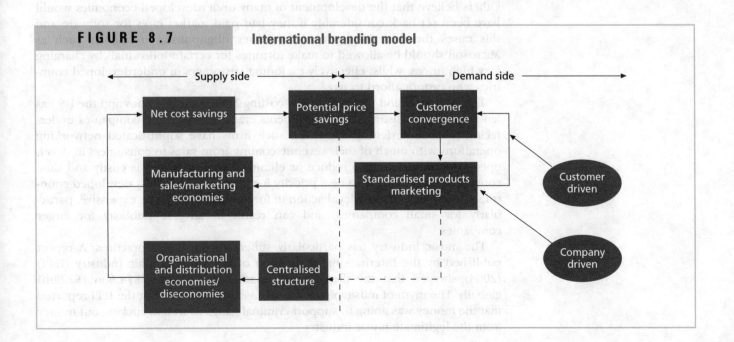

FIGURE 8.7   International branding model

siderations to be the extent of customer convergence in the demand side and the cost savings from the supply side.

Brand piracy

One of the most difficult challenges for brand management is dealing with **brand piracy**. Research suggests that the problem of forgery of famous brand names is increasing and many but by no means all of the fake products have been found to originate in developing countries and in Asia. It is important to recognise the differences between the ways in which forgery takes place. Kaitiki (1981) identifies:

- Outright piracy in which a product is in the same form and uses the same trademark as the original but is false.

- Reverse engineering in which the original product is stripped down, copied then undersold to the original manufacturer, particularly in the electronics industry.

- Counterfeiting in which the product quality has been altered but the same trademark appears on the label. Benetton, Levi Strauss and LaCoste have all been victims.

- Passing off involves modifying the product but retaining a trademark which is similar in appearance, phonetic quality or meaning – for example Coalgate for Colgate and Del Mundo for Del Monte.

- Wholesale infringement is the questionable registration of the names of famous brands overseas rather than the introduction of fake products. This might be considered brand piracy but is entirely within the law. This has been very prevalent in e-business with the registration of dotcom sites by individuals hoping to sell the site later, at substantial profit, to the famous name.

There is a vast trade in pirated brands and copied products. It has been estimated that 90 per cent of the software used in India is counterfeit and the problem is likely to be as severe in China. However, some cultures do not accept that individuals should gain from ideas which should benefit everyone and so there can be substantial differences of the perception of the importance of counterfeiting. Others believe that the development of many underdeveloped economies would have been set back considerably if they had paid market rates for software and this raises the ethical question of whether oligopolistic companies such as Microsoft should be allowed to make fortunes for certain individuals by charging very high prices, whilst effectively excluding customers in underdeveloped countries who cannot afford to pay.

The issue of brand piracy clearly is costing MNEs vast revenues and the US has led the way in insisting that governments crack down on the companies undertaking the counterfeiting. However, such firms have sophisticated networking operations with much of their revenue coming from sales to consumers in developed countries. Trying to reduce or eliminate their activities is costly and time consuming and unlikely to be a priority for governments in less developed countries. Moreover, pursuing legal action in foreign markets can be expensive, particularly for small companies, and can result in adverse publicity for larger companies.

The music industry has particularly suffered from illegal practices. A report published by the International Federation of the Phonographic Industry (IFPI) (2003) showed that the illegal music market was worth US$4.6bn (£2.8bn) globally. The myth of music piracy was of a victimless crime but the IFPI reported that the money was going to support criminal gangs as well as sucking out money from the legitimate music industry.

Two out of five CDs were illegal and the top ten countries for piracy were Brazil, China, Mexico, Paraguay, Poland, Russia, Spain, Taiwan, Thailand and Ukraine. Forty per cent came from factories that produced professional-looking products but did not pay royalties. There was a growing problem of CD-burning software which allowed mass production cheaply and discretely. Sanctions had been applied by the US against Ukraine but the illegal trade had simply moved across the border into Russia.

Illustration 8.6 shows that it is not only Western but also Chinese brands that are suffering from counterfeiters in China.

Positioning

Closely related to brand strategy and at the heart of the implementation of brand strategy is positioning. Positioning is largely concerned with how a product or service might be differentiated from the competition. However, it is important to stress that *it is the customers' perceptions of the product or service* offer that will indirectly confirm the positioning and so determine its success. Firms can only seek to establish and confirm the positioning in the consumers' minds through their management of the marketing mix. In countries at different stages of economic development the customer segments that are likely to be able to purchase the product and the occasions on which it is bought may be significantly different. For example, whilst KFC and McDonald's restaurants aim at everyday eating for the mass market in the developed countries, in less developed countries they are perceived as places for special occasion eating, and out of reach of the poorest segments of the population. A Mercedes car may be perceived as a luxury car in many countries but as an 'everyday' taxi in Germany.

Unilever has a different approach. It introduced a new logo for its ice cream, so that whilst the familiar names stay the same, for example Wall's in the UK and

---

ILLUSTRATION 8.6   **Counterfeiting in China**

Heinkel, the German food and chemical group, believes that 20 per cent of the sector products are counterfeit and found 300 versions of its fifteen brands on the shelves in China. They suspected that some of the counterfeiting had been done with the cooperation of local employees. The consequences of counterfeiting may not just affect financial performance. They can be life threatening. Mercedes found counterfeit wheels, some of which had fractured and collapsed.

Levi Strauss claims to have eliminated its problems after cracking down on piracy networks but others suggest that temporary closure of factories is not a permanent solution as the network will set up again. As a condition of joining the WTO, China is signing an agreement on trade-related intellectual property rights but it could take three to five years to comply.

Less publicised is the fact that Chinese firms have suffered too. Feng Xiogang, a top film director, claimed that

pirated discs of his film *Called Sigh*, about adultery, had taken half his box office receipts. Wang Zhentao is president of the China Aokang Group, a shoe brand with over 700 outlets in China. He is carrying out a publicity campaign and using security technology in the form of shoe tags in an effort to stop piracy putting at risk his ambitious plans for an international brand.

The problem is so great that it is estimated that counterfeited goods account for a quarter of Chinese manufacturing. Local protectionism makes it dangerous to carry out investigations and local officials often consider counterfeiting to be a normal part of business practice. Fifty-four multi-nationals in China, even direct competitors, have joined a united front to press the Chinese government into action.

Question What are the implications of counterfeiting for businesses in developed and developing economies?

Ola in the Netherlands, the background design and font are being standardised around the world.

The perceptions of the product positioning are likely to vary in some dimensions. However, there appears to be an increasing demand for standardised products, particularly in the developed countries, amongst market segments that are mobile and susceptible to influence by the media and through travel, and clearly there is a strongly emerging demand for the same products amongst consumers in the less developed countries. Achieving unique positioning for a product or service must come from the creative dimensions of positioning rather than resorting to simple price positioning.

In confirming the positioning of a product or service in a specific market or region, it is necessary, therefore, to establish in the consumers' perception exactly what the product stands for and how it differs from existing and potential competition by designing an identity which will clarify the value of the product. In doing this it is necessary to emphasise the basis of the positioning strategy, which might focus upon one or more elements of the total product offer. The differentiation might be based upon price and quality, one or more product or service attributes, a specific application, a target consumer or direct comparison with one competitor.

NEW PRODUCT DEVELOPMENT

A recurring theme of discussions of international marketing issues is the increasing need for companies to have a dynamic and proactive policy for developing new products in order to satisfy the apparently insatiable demand of consumers for new experiences and to reinforce and, where necessary, renew their source of competitive advantage. 3M, for example, sets itself the target that 10 per cent of its sales must come from brand new product introductions and 25 per cent of sales from products less than four years old.

The nature of new product development

It is important to recognise at the outset, however, that few new products are actually revolutionary products. Figure 8.8 shows the various categories of new products in terms of their newness to the market and company. The implications of this are that firms need to innovate in every aspect of their business through a process of continual improvement rather than wait for the next breakthrough invention.

Many of the products are largely intended to refresh and reinforce the product range by complementing the existing company and brand image rather than causing a change of direction. In the famous New Coke fiasco, the new recipe, preferred in taste tests and intended to improve the product, was resisted in the US in favour of retaining a traditional image because it was seen to pose a threat to the American culture.

Major invention breakthroughs still occur, although significantly less frequently than before, but there are exceptions. Usually, developing new technologies is hugely expensive. For example, it is estimated that the cost of developing a new drug is now in excess of US$300 million and takes over fifteen years. In order to recover the research and development costs it is necessary to market new ideas simultaneously in all developed countries, as the time taken by competitors to copy or improve products and circumvent patents is shortening. Even the largest companies do not have sufficient resources on their own to achieve rapid distribution of the product into all world markets and so the diffusion of new products into world markets is at least as important a part of the process as the initial idea. This leads to the use of different market entry methods, such as licensing, franchising and strategic alliances, to secure cost-effective diffusion.

The new product development process

In its simplest form developing products follows a similar process for international markets to that in domestic situations:

- idea generation
- initial screening
- business analysis
- development
- market testing
- commercialisation and launch.

Where the process does differ in international markets, however, is in the level of analysis, coordination and communication that becomes necessary when assessing the new product's suitability for a variety of markets. Particular emphasis must be placed upon the quality of the information system since it is essential that the product or service meets the needs of the customers and is positioned accurately in each market from the outset. With this in mind the international development process should incorporate the following elements.

Idea generation must ensure that ideas worldwide are accessed so that duplication is avoided and synergy is optimised by effectively using all available internal and external resources to generate new ideas, including employees, R&D departments, competitors, sales people, customers, distributors and external experts.

Initial screening involves establishing rigorous international screening criteria, including both production and marketing factors to test the ideas for suitability in all world regions so that opportunities and limitations are not overlooked. Ideas that may, for example, be inappropriate for Western Europe might be appropriate for South America. In doing this an assessment should be made of the degree of adaptation that will be necessary for individual markets.

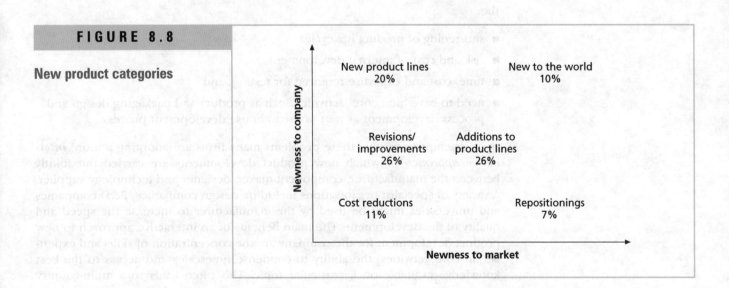

FIGURE 8.8

New product categories

Business analysis must involve establishing criteria for potential success or failure of the product and linking the criteria with regions and/or markets. It must make provision for contingencies such as environmental and competitive situations and unexpected events which might adversely affect the business case.

Product development must include ensuring that all relevant functions such as production, design and packaging become involved in the process. The most appropriate R&D centres for the development process should be selected, with particular attention being paid to such factors as access to technological expertise and location near prime target and lead markets.

Market testing must involve ensuring the test area is representative of the prime target markets, an adequate infrastructure in terms of the necessary services such as advertising and market research agencies, and an appropriate distribution network. It should also take account of potential competitor response both in the test market and globally.

The launch must be planned either to be sequential, with an initial concentration upon prime markets or lead markets, or to be a simultaneous launch. Allowance must be made for aggressive competitive responses as few competitors will give up market share without a fight.

To protect the firm's competitive advantage the company needs to pay particular attention to the ability of competitors to copy a new product and launch it in a separate market. There are a number of actions that companies might take to protect their intellectual property, such as taking strong patent protection, or entering into licensing arrangements to ensure fast, widespread penetration of the world or regional markets.

Timing is perhaps the most critical element of the process, not only in terms of exploiting an opportunity or competitive weakness at the right moment but also minimising the time to market – how long it takes from when the idea was first generated to making it available commercially and the time it takes to achieve the desired level of diffusion.

Approaches to technology transfer and the benefits for marketing

The traditional, sequential and largely internal approach to new product development has considerable disadvantages because of a number of factors, including the:

- shortening of product life cycles;
- risk and cost of internal development;
- time, cost and expertise required for testing; and
- need to have 'non-core' activities such as product and packaging design and process development as part of the in-house development process.

In an attempt to resolve these problems many firms are adopting a more *interactive approach* in which new product developments are carried out jointly between the manufacturer, component maker, designer and technology supplier. A variety of specialist organisations including design companies, R&D companies and universities might be used by the manufacturer to increase the speed and quality of the development. The main benefits of an interactive approach to new product development for the company are the concentration of skills and expertise on core activities, the ability to condense timescales and access to the best knowledge available on a particular topic. This often leads to a multi-country membership of a project team and with it the difficulties of coordination and management that have already been discussed.

The 747 design for Boeing was developed by engineers, the components put out to competitive tender and then sold to airlines with little customisation. By contrast the initial design for the 747 was created using virtual reality software that allowed easy access and participation by suppliers from around the world who could make contributions as the design evolved and helped in the process to optimise the design for manufacture, assembly, efficiency, safety and quality. At the same time the airlines could also have an input, from purchasers to baggage handlers, flight attendants and even passengers, as well as Boeing's accountants, assembly workers and marketing experts.

Research and development strategies

No matter which approach is adopted, major international companies must still decide upon the aims of their own R&D, the exact nature of the activities undertaken and where they should be located. They must take decisions on:

■ the location of their own internal R&D facilities;

■ the extent to which they contract out certain parts of their research and development programme;

■ whether or not they might acquire a company which can provide either the required new technology or a new product;

■ licensing the technology and process from another company; or

■ funding joint ventures or strategic alliances with companies that have complementary technology.

Smaller companies, with low-key international operations which amount to little more than *ad hoc* exporting, are rarely involved in genuine considerations of international new product development and concentrate their R&D activities in the domestic country, but as they grow, pressures emerge to establish R&D facilities in other locations and it becomes necessary to balance the arguments for and against centralisation. As the operations of transnational companies and the diversity of sources of supply become increasingly complex, different patterns of involvement in R&D investments emerge such as:

■ units to transfer technology from the parent company to foreign subsidiaries;

■ local technology units to specifically develop new and improved products in the local markets;

■ global technology units, not necessarily based at the head office, to develop and launch products simultaneously into the major world markets; and

■ corporate technology units, which concentrate upon the generation of new technology of a long-term/exploratory nature.

In general, the R&D activities of international companies tend to follow an evolutionary path, but for many the major question is whether or not they should move away from the dominance of their domestic country R&D location and if so, where should their R&D facilities be located.

Many companies still concentrate a large proportion of R&D activity in their country of origin, but as they move increasingly towards transnational operations, so the concept of the 'home country' becomes increasingly meaningless. It is, however, useful to consider the arguments for and against the centralisation of R&D activities and these are shown in Figure 8.9.

Illustration 8.7 addresses the alternative approaches to managing innovation locally, and how this relates to international marketing.

Success and failure in new product development

One of the most difficult aspects of NPD is to reduce the risk (and therefore the cost) of new product failure. The classic studies of success and failure of new products in developed countries, particularly the US and UK, emphasise that for success it is necessary to place greater emphasis upon marketing rather than technical factors. Cooper (1994) suggests that the NPD success factors include the need for a well-defined, unique and superior product; a market driven, customer focused new product development process; the importance of screening, market studies, feasibility studies and preparation of the business case and a cross-functional team approach.

The reasons for the failure of new product developments in international markets include:

- tariff barriers and non-tariff barriers;
- local competitor subsidies;
- cultural insensitivity;
- poor planning;
- poor timing;
- lack of a unique selling proposition in the international market;
- product deficiencies in the market; and
- misguided enthusiasm of top management.

The impact of process development on international marketing

In highlighting the role of research and development, it is important to emphasise not just product development, but also the ways in which process developments have an impact upon international marketing. A good example of this is included in the illustration of Whirlpool (Illustration 8.8).

The importance of process development is argued by Kotabe (1990) who points out that, today, product innovations are easily 'reverse engineered',

---

FIGURE 8.9

The arguments for and against centralisation of R&D

Arguments for centralisation	Arguments against centralisation
• economies of scale	• pressure from subsidiaries
• easier and faster communication	• pressure from governments
• better coordination	• benefits of public relations
• greater control over outflow of information with implications for secrecy	• use of wider range of skills and abilities
• greater synergy	• benefits from comparative advantage
• avoiding duplication	• greater sensitivity to local tastes
• overcoming problems of ownership	• better monitoring of local competitive activity
	• closeness to possible acquisitions
	• access new technology wherever it is located

improved upon and invented around by competitors without violating patents and other proprietary protections. In contrast, manufacturing processes are more difficult to copy because they are built on not only tangible machinery but also intangible knowledge and skills hidden away in the firm. Continual improvement of processes is essential as the rate of technological change in the marketplace accelerates and he draws attention to the fact that many US companies that are extensively sourcing products and components externally could, in the long run, lose touch with technology and lose the ability to manufacture effectively.

Kotabe and Murray (1989) draw attention to the links between process and product innovations, and modes of sourcing in international firms. They found, in a study of European and Japanese firms, that continual process improvements lead to new products, whereas low product or process development activity within the company coupled with high levels of outsourcing tends to equate to lower market performance.

Information technology and communications are central to process development but are also closing the gap between R&D, manufacturing and international marketing.

ILLUSTRATION 8.7   Managing new product innovation

Fast-moving consumer goods (FMCG) suppliers require a flow of new ideas being developed, produced and taken through to successful commercialisation. However, success rates for new product launches tend not to be high. In the 1970s NPD was handled in R&D laboratories and was more concerned with what could be produced rather than what customers wanted. The concept of marketing became much more embedded in the 1980s and, often, the responsibility for NPD was passed to marketing departments. Brand teams had a tendency to concentrate on building the brand and gaining more shelf space and so the NPD tended to be focused on short-term adaptations. This is referred to as the 'low hanging fruit' strategy. Alternatively, cross-functional teams are set up to allow many parts of the organisation, such as R&D, manufacturing, supply chain, to become involved but this can result in the process becoming too bureaucratic and the NPD process is likely to stall.

Increasingly there is a tendency to create separate innovation departments for medium-term projects so that day-to-day problems do not swamp staff. There appear to be five models of innovation:

Brand marketing manager is responsible for new products: Examples include Kraft, Unilever Bestfoods, Procter & Gamble Foods.

Innovation team reports to marketing director: Examples include McVities, Diageo and Nestlé.

Innovation department reports to the board: Coca-Cola Great Britain is using this approach to relaunch brands and develop more UK-originated brands.

Global companies hand responsibility to one country: Unilever has a focus on its global brands and gives country responsibility for their development. For *Lever Fabergé*, the UK handles deodorants, such as Lynx, while France handles the shampoo sector, such as Sunsilk. Products are developed and then handed over to the local country operation to be launched.

Skunkworks: A number of companies have set up 'skunkworks' as entirely separate units physically outside their offices to maximise creativity. Unilever set up Unilever Ventures to encourage employees, scientists and entrepreneurs by giving one-off payments or the opportunity to work with brand teams to develop their idea.

The question is how separate should the products be from the parent company. The first product of GlaxoSmithKline's (GSK) thefuturesgroup was Plenty, a juice drink. The question for GSK was whether to launch under a new brand, The Ealing Juice Company, or the GSK brand, which it ultimately did.

Question What are the arguments for and against the different management models for innovation in international markets?

Source: Adapted from Murphy, C. 'Innovation masterminds', *Marketing*, 15 May 2003

Computer aided design (*CAD*) allows engineers and designers to generate new product designs far more quickly and to transfer them using the Internet, so allowing rapid feedback from distant customers.

Virtual reality allows the design concept to be converted to a three-dimensional image of how the product might look and work. It is useful for eliciting ideas and comments from customers and non-design functions in the company.

Flexible manufacturing systems (*FMS*) are groups of machines that can easily be programmed to switch from manufacturing one product to another.

Computer aided manufacturing (*CAM*) allows the integration of FMS with design, manufacture and component and resource planning in order to provide *Just In Time* (*JIT*) manufacturing, a concept which is based upon providing rapid response to orders and minimising stockholding. The major benefit which becomes apparent from this is that the coordination and integration of all operations can be used for competitive advantage in international marketing. JIT as a concept is increasingly being used in retailing, too, through linking *electronic point of sale* (*EPOS*) sales recording systems and Web-based systems into a direct ordering facility.

There is little doubt that the integration of information transfer, communications technology, robotics and computerisation will further enhance product and process development. These technologies have the capability to intelligently communicate with customers around the world and it is for this reason that it will be the integration of design, operations and marketing that will be vital in achieving the accuracy and speed of response in product and process development necessary to gain competitive advantage in international product management in the future.

ILLUSTRATION 8.8   Whirlpool and the world cooker

Whirlpool (US) is developing the 'world cooker'. Taking an idea from the car industry, Whirlpool believes that it can innovate quicker and at lower cost by globalising the development of new products. Its range, which includes microwave ovens, air conditioners, dishwashers, laundry products, refrigerators and conventional cookers, is manufactured in 35 countries. Whirlpool has 10 per cent of the US$85 billion world market.

Although the appliances outwardly differ significantly from market to market, when the product engineers from different Whirlpool plants got together they found that the technological differences were much smaller than they had originally thought. The idea is to develop a platform which is the technological heart for each appliance all over the world. The parts of the products which consumers see will then be modified to suit different market requirements.

In the case of a refrigerator the platform includes the casing, compressor, evaporator and sealant system. The features that provide the appearance include the door, the layout of the shelves, the position of the freezing compartment, the controls and the air-blowing system which makes it frost-free. In practice the refrigerators differ significantly; for example, Americans want larder sized, frost-free cabinets, Germans want lots of space for meat, Italians want more vegetable compartments and Indians, with their high proportion of vegetarians within families, want internal compartments sealed to prevent odours circulating.

In this way Whirlpool expects to reduce the current 135 platforms down to 65. To support this, Whirlpool has developed a special Web site with product specifications for its 2000 product engineers worldwide so that, for example, a Brazilian engineer could borrow an idea from elsewhere in the company to solve a new design problem.

Question List the benefits and disadvantages of using a shared platform for the development of 'global' products.

Source: Adapted from Marsh, P. and Tait, N. (1998) 'Whirlpool's global clean up', *Financial Times*, 24 March

SUMMARY

- In many business sectors product and service strategies are being affected by the increased globalisation of consumer tastes, communications, technology and the concentration of business activity.

- Product managers are balancing the efficiency benefits of standardisation with the need to adapt products and services to meet the needs of local customers, regulations and usage conditions.

- As more products are reaching the mature phase of the life cycle they are becoming commodities, and there is a need to use services to differentiate them from competitor offerings. However, services are often difficult to standardise globally because they are affected significantly by the different expectations of service that exist in different cultures.

- The product or service strategy is usually at the centre of international marketing operations. Branding is a key part of product and service management, particularly in international markets, but it is difficult to establish truly global brands that are truly distinctive and have images that appeal to cross-cultural customer segments.

- Innovation, new product and service development are essential for growth and the renewal of the international portfolio and it is essential to obtain input from the different stakeholders in order to ensure that they will be successful.

KEYWORDS

adaptation	international product offer
brand piracy	international product portfolio
branding strategies	new product development
country of origin effect	perishability
heterogeneity	product platform
inseparability	product strategies
intangibility	service 3Ps
international branding	services
international product life cycle	standardisation

CASE STUDY   The world car or cars for the world?

Originally car manufacturers owned one brand and supplied a distinct niche. Porsche made powerful sports cars and Land Rover off-road vehicles. But consolidation has taken place in the industry with five major car manufacturing groups (see Table 1) created through mergers, acquisition and joint ventures. Apart from Toyota, which uses just two names, the car groups own many brands.

New car segments have emerged (see Table 2) and to maximise sales, offer choice and build brands the car groups try to offer many products for each segment.

The cost of developing new cars, setting up and running production plant, promoting and distributing cars is hugely expensive. Therefore the groups are looking for efficiency from global-scale operations and the efficiency of using the

Table 1   Major global car groups

General Motors	Ford	Volkswagen	DaimlerChrysler	Toyota
Cadillac	Ford	Volkswagen	Mercedes-Benz	Toyota
Chevrolet	Lincoln-Mercury	Skoda	Chrysler	Lexus
Pontiac	Jaguar	Seat	Plymouth	
Buick	Mazda	Bentley	Dodge	
Oldsmobile	Volvo	Audi	Jeep	
Saturn	Aston-Martin	Bugatti	Smart	
Opel	Land Rover	Lamborghini		
Vauxhall				
Saab				
Holden				
Isuzu				
Fiat (part)				

Some other large but not global players:

Renault-Nissan
Peugeot-Citroen
Fiat, Alfa Romeo, Ferrari, Maserati and Lancia

Source: Automotive empires, BBC News Online, 28 February, 2002

same components. However, Illustration 8.5 shows that customers do not seem to want a global car that is the same everywhere. They also want brands to be distinctive and differentiated with different designs, driving characteristics and image.

Car groups are managing this by basing different products and brands on a common 'platform'. Originally the 'platform' was the steel structure that formed the floor and frame for the car. The VW Golf platform is shared between the Audi TT, Skoda Octavia, VW Beetle, Audi A3, Seat Leon,

Table 2   Some car segments

Segments	Examples
City cars	Ford Ka, Smart, Daewoo Matiz
Superminis	Mini, Nissan Micra, Skoda Fabia
Small cars	Honda Civic, Toyota Corolla, Ford Focus
Family cars	Vauxhall Vectra, Ford Mondeo, Renault Laguna
MPVs	Renault Espace, Toyota Previa, Seat Alhambra
Executives	BMW 5, Mercedes E, Jaguar S
Luxury cars	Lexus LS, Rolls Royce, Mercedes S
4 × 4s	Volvo Xc90, BMW X5, Range Rover
Supercars	Porsche 911, Ferrari 360, Lamborghini Murcielago

Seat Toledo and VW Bora. The idea of a common platform has now been extended to include similar component sets wherever possible, and there are fewer differences between individual cars. This is reaching extremes with cars such as the CityRover, which is a rebadged Tata Indica (India).

Sharing platforms is now occurring between car groups; for example, the Saab 9-2 for the US is based on a Subaru Impreza Turbo platform and the Smart ForFour (Mercedes) is based on a Mitsubishi Colt platform. GM have introduced a small 4 × 4 with partners. It was designed and made by Suzuki using a Fiat diesel engine. It carries the badges of Vauxhall, Opel, Suzuki and Fiat. The first example of platform sharing between groups was when Ford, VW, Fiat and Peugeot got together to produce MPVs, not sure whether there would be sufficient volume to support individual development. Variants were also produced within the car groups, by VW with the VW Sharan and Seat Alhambra, by Fiat with the Fiat Ulysse and Lancia Phedra, and by Peugeot with the Peugeot 806 and Citroen C8.

Car manufacturers seem to accept that customers are now more knowledgeable about the platform systems, common component sets and the modular construction of cars. Of course, customers who are less concerned with image and status can pay much less for a car that is made from similar components. The price for a Skoda Octavia is less than half the price of an Audi TT and much less than a VW Golf.

Mercedes say that platforms should be shared only between cars of similar price but others, such as Ford, have not taken this view. The Jaguar S-type shared a platform with Ford's Lincoln LS, which is sold at a lower price. But there was early criticism of the obvious cost-saving measures on the Jaguar and Jaguar was forced to make some expensive modifications to the car. The design might also be compromised. There has been criticism of the Porsche Cayenne's rather awkward appearance. It is based on the VW Touareg, which is two-thirds of the price.

As development of the platform takes place a shared component, such as a more efficient engine, might be put into the next car to be launched, which could be a lower priced car. In this case the lower priced car may have more advanced components than its more expensive 'sister', as has happened with Skoda. Some commentators have suggested that the advancement of the 'value for money' Skoda cars has been at the expense of the VW brand.

Ford claims that platform sharing can save 15 per cent of the development cost of a new car and doubling the volume can save 5 per cent of the costs of a component. GM seems set to take the use of this approach to car design and development to the next level. The vehicle architecture used to develop the Vectra has been applied to the Saab 9-3

and will ultimately encompass 7 brands, 13 body styles in 6 different sizes and dozens of engines.

Many of the car groups, such as Nissan, have been in financial trouble and reports in 2003 suggested that Ford was facing bankruptcy. Further consolidation seems inevitable because of the huge overcapacity in car production. The question is whether platform sharing will support or further undermine the sustainability of the companies.

Questions

1 What do you consider to be the key factors that the car industry will face over the next three to four years? You should consider issues relating to the environment, customer requirements and competition.

2 Choose one of the five major groups highlighted in Table 1. Against the background of the analysis carried out, develop a product strategy for the group that includes new product development, supply chain considerations and brand development.

Robin Lowe, Sheffield Hallam University
Source: Adapted from Hutton, R. 'I've seen you somewhere before . . .', *Sunday Times*, 13 July 2003 and other public sources

DISCUSSION QUESTIONS

1 How do environmental trends affect product portfolio management across international markets?

2 In an ideal world companies would like to manufacture a standardised product. What are the factors that support the case for a standardised product and what are the circumstances that are likely to prevent its implementation?

3 Examine the ways in which a major company operating in many countries around the world can use new product development and commercialisation to enhance its ambitions to become a global company.

4 What differences, if any, are there in marketing products and/or services for:

(a) A developed to another developed country?

(b) A developed to a less developed country?

How might these differences be overcome? Illustrate your answer by choosing a product or service of your choice.

5 International services marketing is a major growth area. Using as an example one service sector, explain what are the main barriers to success and what strategies might be used to overcome them.

REFERENCES

Agarwal, S. and Sikri, S. (1996) 'Country Image: Consumer evaluation of product category extension', *International Marketing Review*, 13 (4).

Cooper, R.G. (1994) 'New products: the factors that drive success', *International Marketing Review*, 11 (1).

De Chernatony, L. (1989) *Branding in an era of retailer dominance*, Cranfield School of Management.

De Chernatony, L., Halliburton, C. and Bernath, R. (1995) 'International Branding: demand or supply-drive opportunity?' *Harvard Business Review*, 12 (2): 9–21.

Haefer, S.A. (1997) 'Consumer knowledge of country of origin effects', *European Journal of Marketing*, 31 (1): 56–72.

Ho, S. (1997) 'The emergence of consumer power in China', *Business Horizons*, September–October.

Howard, E. (1998) 'Keeping ahead of the green regulators', Mastering Global Management, Part 10, *Financial Times*.

IFPI (2003) Commercial Piracy Report, July, London, available at www.ifpi.org.

Kaitiki, S. (1981) 'How multinationals cope with the international trade mark forgery', *Journal of International Marketing*, 1, (2): 69–80.

Keegan, W.J. (1989) *Multinational Marketing Management*, Prentice Hall.

Kotabe, M. (1990) 'Corporate Product Policy and Innovative Behaviour of European and Japanese Multinationals: An Empirical Investigation', *Journal of Marketing*, 54: 19–33.

Kotabe, M. and Murray, J.Y. (1989) 'Linking product and Process Innovations and Models of International Sourcing in Global Competition: A Case of Foreign Multinational Firms', *Journal of International Business Studies*, Third Quarter: 383–408.

Kotler, P. (2002) *Marketing Management: Analysis, Planning, Implementation and Control*, Prentice Hall.

Mesdag, M. van (1985) 'The Frontiers of Choice', *Marketing*, 10 October.

Quelch, J. and Harding, D. (1996) 'Brand versus product labels – fighting to win', *Harvard Business Review*, January–February.

Thakor, M.V. and Kohli, C.S. (1996) 'Brand origin: conceptualisation and review', *Journal of Consumer Marketing*, 13 (3): 27–42.

International marketing planning: strategy development

Introduction

In the Li-Ning activity, against the background of information on the market structure and customer needs, a segmentation approach was developed. In this activity we focus on possible strategic alternatives and the development of a global marketing strategy in a market which is highly competitive and where environmental trends signal potential changes in the strategic options the firms in the market should consider in order to sustain their future competitive advantage.

Arguably the most significant change in international marketing over recent years has been the growth of multi-national, global and, recently, transnational approaches to strategic development. In this activity we consider a market which has become truly global and highly competitive. The basis of the competitive advantage of the firms involved has changed due to shifts in market structures and product innovations as well as advances in marketing weaponry. This has had the impact of altering the competitive landscape of the global beauty market and changing the way companies now struggle for a competitive advantage. It is these issues and how the companies should resolve them that are explored in this activity.

Learning objectives

After completing this unit the reader should be able to:

- Critically appraise the alternative global marketing strategies that companies follow and evaluate the reasons for their success or failure
- Understand the role and value of global marketing planning and its implications for the organisation structure
- Understand the concept of globalisation and how it affects the strategies of organisations

The scenario: the global beauty market

The global beauty market has seen exponential growth over the past two decades across the globe. It is now estimated to be worth in the region of US$160 billion a year, if make-up, skin and hair care, fragrances, cosmetic surgery, health clubs and diet pills are included. Americans spend more each year on beauty than they do on education. It is an industry where there has been a high rate of product innovation, sweeping changes in the marketing environment in which it operates, and, as the market has become more competitive, evidence of intense rivalry as the key global players jostle for the number one position. All of this makes it an interesting industry to examine in terms of the varying global strategies pursued by the different competitors.

The beauty business took off in the early part of the twentieth century when Eugène Schueller founded the French Harmless Hair Colouring Co, which later became L'Oréal – today's industry leader. Nivea was next when a Hamburg pharmacist developed the first cream to bind oil and water. Today, Nivea sells in 150 countries, the biggest personal-care brand in the world. The other major development was in Japan when Arinobu Fukuhara produced a eudermine lotion – the first Japanese cosmetic based on a scientific formula, and the first product for the Shiseido company.

In America, Elizabeth Arden opened the first modern beauty salon in 1910, followed a few years later by Helena Rubinstein, a Polish immigrant. The two took cosmetics out of household pots and pans and into the modern era and established the competitive rivalry that characterises today's global market place.

It is now estimated by Goldman Sachs that the global beauty industry – consisting of skin care worth US$24 billion; make-up, US$18 billion; US$38 billion of hair-care products; and US$15 billion of perfumes – is growing at up to 7 per cent a year, more than twice the rate of the developed world's Gross National Income (GNI).

Isobel Doole, Sheffield Hallam University (From various sources)

The market leader, L'Oréal, has had compound annual profits growth of 14 per cent for 13 years. Sales of Nivea have grown at 14 per cent a year over the same period.

However, the major global growth is not coming from cosmetics for the youth market but is being driven by richer, ageing baby-boomers and increased discretionary income in the West, and by the growing middle classes in developing countries. China, Russia and South Korea are turning into huge markets. In India, sales of anti-ageing creams are growing by 40 per cent a year, while Brazil has more 'Avon Ladies' (900 000) than it has men and women in its army and navy. Although the industry's customers are predominantly women, it is increasingly marketing itself to men too.

The household-goods giants Unilever and Procter & Gamble (P&G), facing maturity in many of their traditional businesses, are devoting more resources to their beauty divisions. Unilever has created a new company, *Unilever Cosmetics International*, to extend its global portfolio of prestige beauty and fragrance brands. P&G has recently purchased Germany's Wella, a hair-care company, as well as Clairol. P&G now markets a range of well-known beauty and healthcare brands including: Pantene, Head & Shoulders, Olay, Clairol Nice'n' Easy, Herbal Essences, Cover Girl, Max Factor, Noxzema, Old Spice, Hugo Boss, Crest, Vicks, Actonel, Clearasil, PUR and more. P&G employs nearly 98 000 people in more than 80 countries. They are now, however, planning to offload smaller parochial brands to allow them to concentrate on the brands they identify as having true global potential, such as Olay and Clearasil.

Luxury-goods manufacturers such as Dior, Chanel and Yves St Laurent are also competing in the market with perfumes, make-up and creams. LVMH, the biggest luxury-goods group of all, has moved into retailing with its Bliss spas and Sephora shops (which sell make-up).

At the same time the industry is consolidating. Many innovative younger brands have been swallowed up by the giants. Japan's Kao bought John Frieda to tap into the hair-dye business, one of the fastest-growing segments of the market. And in the past five years, LVMH has bought Hard Candy and Urban Decay, while Estée Lauder has acquired Stila, MAC and Bobbi Brown, another collection of up-and-coming names in make-up.

Six multinationals account for 80 per cent of American make-up sales, while eight brands control 70 per cent of the skin-care market. With its Nivea brand, Beiersdorf is one of the few large independents left, desired by everyone from P&G and Unilever to L'Oréal.

This competition has left casualties. Revlon, once one of the biggest make-up brands, has been tottering on the edge of bankruptcy and is fighting to get the business back on track. Unilever is facing slowing growth overall, and has made a number of tactical errors. For example, it sold the Elizabeth Arden brand and missed out on the boom in hair colour. Meanwhile, P&G, seen as the first serious threat to L'Oréal for decades, is struggling with its US$5 billion acquisition of Clairol. It has been losing market share at an alarming rate to both L'Oréal and to Kao's John Frieda.

However, keeping the competitive edge is becoming increasingly expensive. L'Oréal generates more than 80 per cent of its sales outside France, with operations in every major trading region. They have made North America a particular focus of attention, wrong-footing domestic rivals with a series of smart launches, clever acquisitions, and dynamic marketing. However this has come at a huge cost. *Advertising Age* estimate L'Oréal spend approximately US$1.5 billion per annum on advertising worldwide. This is putting pressure on their rivals to do the same. Elizabeth Arden's marketing budget grew by 40 per cent this year on top of a previous growth of 25 per cent last year. Avon is also increasing its advertising budget by 50 per cent.

Changes in distribution are also helping to separate the winners from the losers. The only real growth is coming through huge grocery chains such as Wal-Mart that want to deal with just a handful of big suppliers. That is good news for P&G and L'Oréal (which already gains two-thirds of its revenues from mass retailers). But Estée Lauder and Revlon are more dependent on unfashionable department stores where sales are declining and selling costs are high.

The beauty industry is also facing a number of changes in the environment which may affect its future prospects. There is some evidence that changing social attitudes may ferment into a growing consumer backlash as we have seen in the tobacco and food industries. Consumers are now questioning the truth in increasingly extravagant marketing claims. So far, women have been willing to buy into the illusion. Should that change (and there are signs it might), then manufacturers expose themselves to the rush for litigation that such global brands as McDonald's and the tobacco companies have had to face.

There is also growing concern at the power of the beauty industry to permanently change a person's looks. Given advances in genetic engineering and the competitive drive, a race for beauty is conceivable in which people will strive to model themselves on some form of idealised human being. The industry may find itself roundly condemned and subject to legislation.

Then there is the threat of the lobbyists pushing through tighter regulations. Europe recently passed new labelling and animal-testing laws on cosmetics and will soon give the public the right to probe how firms create cosmetics. This is sure to raise costs for the industry worldwide. Non-compliance also leaves the cosmetics open to attack from lobby groups as is evidenced by the recent campaign of Nature Watch to boycott L'Oréal products because of their belief that their products are being tested on animals.

L'Oréal dominates the global industry at the moment, but the question is how long they can hold on to this position in face of the concerted attack on their market share by global giants such as P&G and Unilever and the changing global marketing environment in which they operate.

Sources: Adapted from various sources: 'Pots of promise' *The Economist*, 22 May 2003; 'The colour of money', *The Economist*, 6 March 2003; http://www.unilever.com; http://www.aallwebwire.com; http://www.adbrands.net

The task

1 Critically analyse the global marketing environment for the beauty business, paying particular attention to the key international trends impacting on the development of the market and the competitive positioning of the key global players.

2 Choose one of the companies identified in the readings supplied. In light of the above analysis, critically evaluate the global/international marketing strategy of the specified company.

3 Choose one particular trading region where future potential for growth in the beauty business has been identified (e.g. South America, Eastern Europe, East Asia, China etc.).

   For the company you have chosen in Q2, assess the attractiveness of this region in helping the company address the issues identified in Question 2. You will be expected to fully justify your choice of region.

4 Develop an outline international marketing strategy for the region chosen. Your strategy will be expected to show how your recommendations contribute to the development of a long-term global competitive advantage across the region.

Useful Web sites

www.mmc.com
www.britishchambers.org.uk
www.ce.cei.gov.cn
www.gbrands.com
www.accenture.com
www.Unilever.com
www.p&g.com
www.L'Oréal.com
www.Nivea.com

www.elizabetharden.com
www.helenarubinstein.com
www.esteelauder.com
www.Revlon.com
www.maxfactor.com
www.businessweek.com
www.brandchannel.com

Getting started

In this section the case study focuses on the global beauty business. You should use this case study to obtain an understanding of the industry and the competitive positions of the global players as well as for general background information. To complete the learning activity, however, you will need to access a range of research material from libraries and web-based sources as well as perhaps external sources of information.

In task 1 we build on the skills developed in activity one. However, in this task it is important to pay particular attention to the key trends affecting the development of the global beauty market, the competitive positioning of the global players and how the changes occurring impact on the way the market is structured.

The starting point for tasks 2, 3 and 4 is articulating an overall vision and setting appropriate corporate objectives for the firm. If they do not already exist, to do this you need to fully assess the strengths and weaknesses of the company. The International marketing strategy that is developed should be based on a relevant segmentation approach such as you devised in Part 1. Against the background of the firm's capabilities, existing and potential future competition the firm should consider the strategic options it has and develop a positioning statement that will ensure the firm and its products and services are clearly differentiated from the competition.

Key decisions in the strategy development will relate to the degree to which the firm wishes, and is able, to standardise its product and service offerings or needs to adapt them to the requirements of the local markets. Market entry methods need to be selected if it is to enter new markets and the products and services that will be the portfolio need to be chosen. You also need to consider how the recommendations made contribute to the development of a long-term global competitive advantage across the region and the implications your recommendations have for resource allocation and portfolio management for the specified company. In summary, in completing the task you need to ensure you consider the key factors listed in Figure II.

FIGURE II

Key factors to consider in evaluating the global beauty market

The element of the plan	Some concepts, models and issues to be addressed
Analysis	• The key international trends impacting on the development of the market • An assessment of the structure of the global market • An evaluation of how the global market is segmented • The competitive positioning of the key global players
Company evaluation	• An assessment of the strengths and weaknesses of specified company • In light of question 1, the opportunities and threats relevant to them • Identification of the key strategic marketing issues the company needs to address to compete effectively in the global market
Trading region analysis	• Evaluation of the trading region • Coherent cross-country analysis to make decisions • Identification of the strategic issues for the company in the chosen region
Strategic recommendations	• Clear long-term marketing objectives • Realistic long-term marketing strategy • Clear and logical link between analysis and response • Innovation and creativity in the response • Coherence and justification of recommendation • The contribution to a long-term global competitive advantage • The implications for resource allocation and portfolio management for the specified company

The way forward

The task in this activity shows how the diversity encountered in global marketing makes planning and controls a difficult activity to carry out satisfactorily. After studying Part 3 of the text you may wish to revisit the solutions you have recommended in this activity and consider how your recommendations could be successfully implemented.

In doing so you may wish to consider such aspects as: what is an appropriate organisation management structure for delivering your strategy? How can you ensure a systematic planning system throughout the globe that will enable the company to satisfactorily implement the strategy, organise the diverse operations and ensure the managers around the globe respond to the challenges you have identified? All of this is hard to achieve in a global marketing strategy. For senior managers, the problem is how to maintain cohesion between all staff in order to ensure uniform standards, a coherent worldwide strategy, retain a unique vision and purpose, and yet at the same time create an operation which has empathy with consumers in each host country.

For most firms the international planning process is concerned with managing a number of tensions and ambiguities. It is how you would resolve such tensions that you may wish to consider on completion of Part 3. There is a need to adopt a regular, thorough and systematic sequence, but at the same time provide the flexibility which allows more junior managers to realise opportunities and address problems when and where they occur. Whilst detailed analysis is necessary to fully appreciate the complexities of a situation at the host country level, there is also a need for a clear uncluttered vision, shared by all staff, of where the company intends to go.

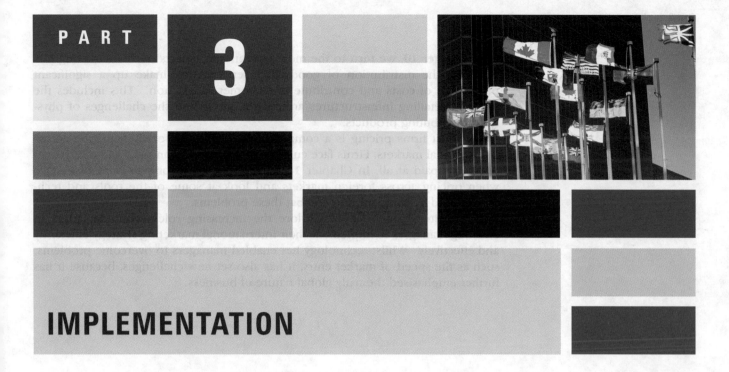

PART 3

IMPLEMENTATION

9 International communications

10 The management of international distribution and logistics

11 Pricing for international markets

12 International marketing implementation through enabling technologies

Introduction

Having defined the international marketing strategy and determined the market entry and product policy in Part 2 we now turn to implementation. The aim of this, Part 3 of *International Marketing Strategy*, is to examine the implementation issues and determine the activities that will ensure that the strategies, products and services are effective in meeting the needs of the customers. Whilst we address the elements of the marketing mix in turn, throughout the section we emphasise the need to integrate the various elements of marketing activity as they are mutually reinforcing. Where possible, many firms seek to standardise their marketing activities but recognise too that they need to be adapted to the needs of the specific markets in which they are operating. In this respect market entry and product and service management are also considerations in both strategic development and implementation.

In the first chapter in Part 3, Chapter 9, we examine the importance of communications, quite broadly. International communications is not only concerned with the promotion of products and services and differentiating them from those of competitors. It is also about achieving effective communications internally, establishing a corporate identity that is understood worldwide and building long-term relationships with customers.

In Chapter 10, we turn to the more operational aspects of the marketing mix involving the distribution of goods and services that make up a significant proportion of costs and contribute to customer satisfaction. This includes the different retailing infrastructures around the globe and the challenges of physically distributing products.

For most firms pricing is a complex area, especially so when pricing across international markets. Firms face currency risks, transaction risks and the risks of not being paid at all. In Chapter 11 we examine the problems companies face when pricing across foreign markets and look at some of the tools and techniques used by companies to combat these problems.

Finally, in Chapter 12 we explore the increasing role technology plays in enabling managers to implement their international marketing strategy efficiently and effectively. Whilst technology has enabled managers to overcome problems, such as the speed of market entry, it has also set new challenges, because it has further emphasised the truly global nature of business.

INTERNATIONAL COMMUNICATIONS

Introduction

The geographical and cultural separation of the company from its marketplaces causes great difficulty in communicating effectively with its stakeholders. In this chapter we take a broad view of communications and include not just the traditional promotional mix of personal selling, advertising, sponsorship, sales and public relations but also other methods of communications which have the objective of developing better and more personalised relationships with global customers. In our discussions we acknowledge the fact that the target audience extends beyond existing and potential customers and includes other stakeholder groups that have a potential impact on the global development of firms and their international reputation.

In doing this, the development of internal relationships between staff from different strategic business units within the global organisation is vital in influencing overall performance. Some remote strategic business units often appear to have a closer relationship with their customers than they have with the parent organisation and this seems to be particularly important as firms embark on joint ventures and strategic alliances.

Achieving cost effectiveness requires the integration of the supply chain in order to add value and remove unnecessary costs. Success depends upon building good relationships with all these interested parties.

Learning objectives

After reading this chapter you will:

- Appreciate the nature and role of communications in implementing international marketing strategies

- Understand the challenges faced in the successful management of international marketing communications

- Be able to explain the use of the elements of an international communications strategy, including corporate identity, products and services promotion and the development of relationships with customers

- Identify the use and the limitations of the communications tools in international marketing
- Recognise the value of integrating the communications by standardising programmes and processes, where possible, and adapting to local needs, where necessary

THE ROLE OF MARKETING COMMUNICATIONS

Marketing communications are concerned with presenting and exchanging information with various individuals and organisations to achieve specific results. This means not only that the information must be understood accurately but that, often, elements of persuasion are also required. In a domestic environment the process is difficult enough but the management of international marketing communications is made particularly challenging by a number of factors including the complexity of different market conditions, differences in media availability, languages, cultural sensitivities, regulations controlling advertising and sales promotions, and the challenge of providing adequate resourcing levels.

A variety of approaches have been taken to define and describe the marketing mix area which is concerned with persuasive communications. Some writers refer to the 'communications mix', others to the 'promotional mix' and others, for example Kotler (2002), use the communications mix and promotions mix to mean the same thing. Communications, embracing as it does the ideas of conveying information, is the most helpful term in implying the need for a two-way process in international marketing. It also implies including internal communications between the organisation's staff, especially as organisations become larger, more diverse and complex. In addition, the boundaries are becoming less distinct between what should be considered as internal and external, as organisations participate in alliances and supply chains. Here too, difficulties are experienced with managing communications.

Figure 9.1 shows the external and internal marketing communication flows and emphasises the need to consider three dimensions: external, internal and interactive or relationship marketing.

Internal marketing

For a large diverse multi-national firm a key task is to ensure that all staff employed in its business units around the world are aware of the strategies, tactics, priorities and procedures to achieve the firm's mission and objectives. As partnerships between supply chain members become closer it becomes necessary to include external firms within the internal communications network.

Staff in remote locations are often overlooked in communications or receive messages that become unclear as they cross cultural and language boundaries, in the same way that external audiences may misunderstand the firm's external communications. Staff in remote locations can become closer to the staff of local customers and even competitors, making it vital that they regularly receive information about the strategy as well as being reminded of the standards and values.

Interactive marketing

Because many customers of MNEs are MNEs themselves it is essential for staff around the world to deliver consistent service to customers. This includes call centre operators, service engineers and salespersons in each location. Staff are trained in how to communicate, take appropriate decisions that fit with the strategy and coordinate communications throughout the firm. The consequences of poor coordination of communications are discussed later in this chapter.

External marketing

The traditional role of international marketing communications is largely concerned with providing a mechanism by which the features and benefits of the product or service could be promoted as inexpensively as possible to existing and potential customers in different countries using the promotion mix (personal selling, advertising, sales promotion and public relations) with the ultimate purpose of persuading customers to buy specific products and services. International marketing communications, however, have now become much more important within the marketing mix and the purposes for which marketing communications might be used externally in international markets are now more diverse. They include the need to communicate with a more diverse range of stakeholders and build higher levels of customer service through interactive or relationship marketing. International marketing communications might now be considered to include the three distinct strategic elements shown in Figure 9.2.

Communicating product and service differentiation

As we have discussed in Chapters 6 and 8, increased competition and the maturation of markets have led to many firms offering largely similar core product and service specifications with the result that, in addition to its traditional role of promoting products and services, international marketing communications is increasingly used to provide the firm with an important source of differentiation,

FIGURE 9.1

External, internal and interactive marketing

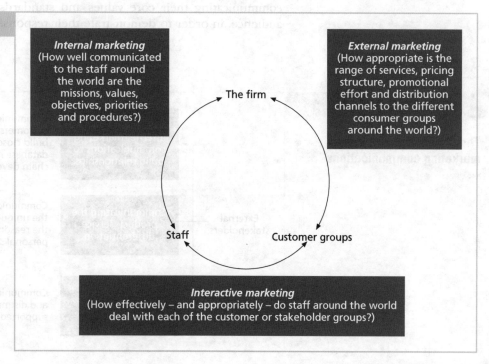

for example by providing customers with an easily recognisable and distinctive brand image, and by explaining the unique positioning of the product. Koranteng (1998) suggests that while Nike has relied on sexy, provocative ads of top athletes and Adidas has associated itself with European soccer stars, Reebok has confused the market. It is known as a running shoe in the UK, a fashion statement in the US and more generally as a women's fitness and aerobics shoe, with little consequent appeal for men.

In contrast to this, the Volkswagen Beetle was conceived as the people's car in 1938 to suit the functional needs of the German mass market (Meenagham 1995). By the 1960s it came to represent a particular type of person and lifestyle – not into materialism and status symbols. He or she wanted to make a statement by driving an ugly funky car thereby demonstrating independence – a willingness to go against the grain, irreverence for convention, being young in spirit, admiring a sense of humour and a logical and practical mind. The new Beetle was aiming to build very precisely on those values. However, it was by no means priced for the 'people's market'.

With the vast increase in the range and volume of communications to which consumers are exposed as they go about their normal work and leisure, making one product or service distinctive becomes an increasing challenge. There are a wide variety of promotional tools that might be used to persuade customers to buy the firm's products and services and the newer information and communications technologies are increasing this choice all the time. The challenge for the firm is to use these tools as cost effectively as possible to reach out to consumers wherever they are in the world.

Communicating the corporate identity to international stakeholders

As stakeholders in general have become more aware of how they are affected by international organisations, both good and bad, companies have found it necessary to justify their international activities by constantly and more widely communicating their core values and standards to their internal and external audience, in order to demonstrate their responsibility to shareholders, trustwor-

---

FIGURE 9.2

The dimensions of external marketing communications

External stakeholders

Using traditional and internet marketing communications to build relationships	Communication with existing and potential customers regularly and systematically to build close relationships, supported by database management, e-business and supply chain development
Communicating the product, service differentiation	Communication of a distinctive brand image, the unique positioning of the product and the reasons to buy, supported by advertising, personal selling and sales promotion
Communicating the corporate identity	Communication to all stakeholders of a clear and distinctive corporate identity for the firm supported by sponsorship and public relations

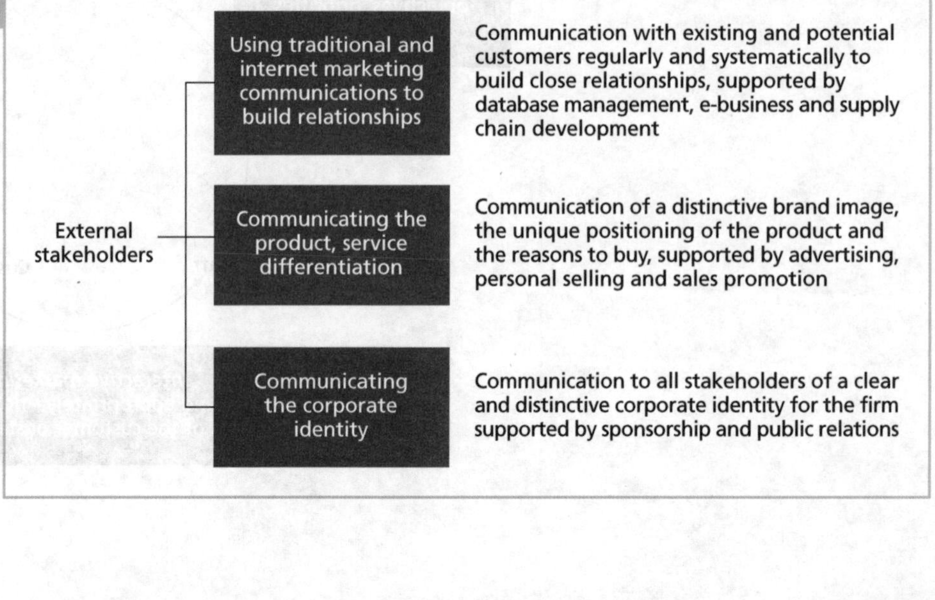

thiness to customers and care and concern for the local community, environment and local employees. The corporate image or logo is the most visible part of the identity and, in some firms, is the only standardised element of the marketing mix. The **corporate identity** of the firm should be deeper and more pervasive and should be reflected in a clear and distinctive message supported by appropriate sponsorship and proactive public relations activity. Illustration 9.1 shows the importance of a corporate identity and sponsorship in the international marketing of the host city for the Olympic Games.

Using communications to build relationships

More intense global competition has provided consumers with greater choice of products and services which they perceive to be capable of satisfying their needs and providing new experiences. Customers also feel that there is less risk of dissatisfaction in switching to alternative products and services, and so are becoming less likely to stay loyal to one supplier or brand.

With the increasing cost of marketing communications and the need to reach an ever wider international audience, organisations are becoming much more aware of the high costs of winning new customers and the relatively lower costs of retaining existing customers. Attention has been drawn to how much a single customer might purchase of one product over his or her lifetime. Readers might like to calculate how much they buy from a food retailer, car manufacturer or a travel company if they stay loyal to that supplier for five, ten or twenty years.

ILLUSTRATION 9.1   **Corporate identity and the Olympic Games**

Arguably the most expensive and prestigious sponsorship event in the world is the Olympic Games. It reaches a huge audience in just about every corner of the world. Some would suggest that the five rings of the Olympic committee is the most recognised symbol (as against company name) in the world. The elite group of sponsors, such as Coca-Cola, McDonald's, Kodak, IBM, Xerox, Samsung and Panasonic, pay very large sums to have their logos projected around the world through their association with the Games. For the very short duration of the winter Olympics in Nagano, Japan, in 1998, each paid around US$30 million.

To the host city the effectiveness of their international marketing, too, is vital. Montreal's 1976 summer Games left the city in debt and the Atlanta 1996 Games will be remembered, at least in part, for some poor organisation and questionable commercial activities. By contrast, Los Angeles in 1984 was deemed a complete success and the winter Games at Lillehammer in Norway and Whistler in Canada have put both venues on the winter sports map. In 1992 Barcelona used the event to rebrand and transform the city by emphasising both the elegance and excitement of the city. Sydney 2000 was heralded as the most successful

Games ever. A key part of the international marketing of the Games is to maximise sponsorship by creating a corporate identity but also enhance the reputation and image of the city so that it will live on after the Games.

The logos, such as Sam the eagle in LA, Kobi the dog in Barcelona and Izzy the computer character in Atlanta, are the source of income through franchising on merchandise, such as stamps, toys, souvenirs and T-shirts. Sydney in 2000 used a stylised athlete that featured Aboriginal boomerang shapes.

In 2004 the Olympic Games are 'coming home' to Greece but Wolff Olins, the corporate identity consultants, have developed the brand idea of Athens 2004 Games as not just about Greece. The vision is to 'embrace the world', recognising the need to re-emphasise the Olympic ideals and also help to move them into the future. The logo is a stylised olive branch, symbolising the spirit of the original Games and a universal message. The vibrant blue and white colours echo the colours of the national flag.

Question Can a logo be effective in communicating internationally the complex messages that might come from an event such as the Games?

Food retailers now offer incentives for customer loyalty, such as bonus cards and money-off vouchers for other products and services they offer, such as petrol and banking services. They routinely communicate with consumers using direct mail to inform them of new product offers.

Firms are now much more willing to invest resources in Customer Relationship Management to retain existing customers.

The concept of **relationship marketing** has taken on an increased level of significance as improvements in information and communications technology enable firms to communicate in a much more intelligent way by basing their messages on a better knowledge of the characteristics and responses of their existing and potential customers and a better understanding of what they might wish to hear. In this way firms are able to develop better relationships with their customers and other influential stakeholders irrespective of their location in the world.

THE FUNDAMENTAL CHALLENGES FOR INTERNATIONAL MARKETING COMMUNICATIONS

All forms of international marketing communication have a fundamental purpose which is to ensure that the intended messages (those which are part of the firm's international strategy) are conveyed accurately between the sender and the receiver, and that the impact of unintentional messages (those which are likely to have an adverse effect on the firm's market performance and reputation) are kept to a minimum. The communications process should be two-way and the sender should always make provision for feedback to ensure that the receiver has understood the message as it was intended and has responded positively to it.

In practice this apparently simple process poses considerable challenges for firms trying to manage their international marketing communications as can often be seen from the business press which contains many serious but frequently amusing anecdotes about the failed attempts of major firms to communicate in international markets. Cadbury caused offence in India and Pakistan with an advertisement to promote Temptations chocolates. It showed Kashmir with the strap-line 'too good to share'. Mistakes in the use of language, particularly using messages which do not translate or are mistranslated are a particular problem but more serious is a lack of sensitivity to different cultures amongst international communicators.

Many of the **failures of communications** are unintentional, of course. Following negotiations with the Council on America–Islamic Relations, Nike had to scrap almost 40 000 pairs of sports shoes because the flame design which was used bore a resemblance to the Arabic for Allah. Two years earlier Nike was forced to withdraw a billboard showing a basketball player above the caption 'They Called him Allah' when it caused an outcry amongst Muslims.

Besides the often highly visible failures which make firms appear to be incompetent and insensitive there are many examples of wasted effort and resources which are not so widely publicised. There are a number of reasons for international marketing communications failure including, for example:

- inconsistency in the messages conveyed to customers by staff at different levels and from different countries and cultures
- different styles of presentation of corporate identity, brand and product image from different departments and country business units which can leave customers confused

- a lack of coordination of messages, such as press releases, advertising campaigns, and changes in product specification or pricing across the various country markets
- failure to appreciate the differences in the fields of perception (the way the message is understood) of the sender and receiver. The field of perception tends to be affected significantly by the self-reference criteria of both parties. This is, perhaps, where the greatest problems arise because, as we have already discussed, avoiding this requires knowledge of different market environments, cultural empathy and the willingness to adapt the communications programmes and processes to local requirements.

Illustration 9.2 shows the importance of appreciating the subtlety of language and tone in communications.

Whilst this last area is influenced by knowledge, attitudes and empathy the other three areas of potential communications failure are concerned with the effectiveness of the firm's strategy and planning, and the degree to which the staff within the organisation understand and are involved in the communications planning process. It is almost inevitable that some communication failures occur from time to time and it is vital that firms learn from their mistakes. To ensure success in these areas it is important to have in place an effective control process.

Whilst it can be argued that the majority of these failures are ultimately within the control of the company, a number of situations arise where the firm's communications can be affected by factors which are outside the firm's control or are extremely difficult to control. Examples of these situations are where:

- **counterfeiting** or other infringements of patents or copyright as discussed in Chapter 8 take place. Not only does the firm lose revenue but it may also suffer damage to its image if consumers believe the low-quality goods supplied by the counterfeiter are genuine;

ILLUSTRATION 9.2   **Negativity in advertising**

Global firms see the cost benefits and brand building benefits of standardisation of creative work. However, to understand the reason why advertisements might or might not cross borders requires more subtlety, particularly in Asian markets.

There are many reasons. One is the issue of negativity. If a person in some western countries is asked, 'How are you?', the answer might be 'Good' or 'Fine'. It also might be 'Not bad', which really also means good. For many on the Indian subcontinent, 'Not bad' is more precise and often means neutrality – neither this nor that. They place great significance on negative expressions, such as non-violence, non-greed and non-hatred, which are embedded in the culture and convey important personal values. In Western advertising, the appeal might be based on an unacceptable or annoying situation that can occur if a particular product is not bought. A Western advertisement for a TV set might emphasise the picture is 'free from distortion', whereas in Asian markets a TV that has a clear picture might communicate a clearer message. A western food

product ad might emphasise 'not lacking in goodness, refreshment or nourishment' whereas an ad that emphasises 'full of goodness and nourishment' might be more understandable in Asia.

In Western advertising, there is little distinction between praise and flattery, whereas in Sinhala and Tamil languages, spoken in Sri Lanka, flattery becomes something deceitful and false. In this case, care needs to be taken with over-positive expressions in advertising.

In the West, emphasis is placed on logic and rationality in advertising, whereas the Asian view is that the truth will emerge.

Question How can managers responsible for cross-border campaigns ensure that they will convey the message effectively?

Source: Adapted from *Marketing Business*, 2000

- **parallel importing**, which is discussed in greater detail in Chapter 11, communicates contradictory messages that do not reflect the image of the brand and thus confuse consumers. This can be particularly problematic if the parallel importer seriously undercuts the prices charged by the official channel;

- **competitors, governments or pressure groups** attack the standards and values of the MNE by alleging, fairly or unfairly, bad business practice. Perhaps surprisingly, despite their huge resources, some of the largest firms are not very effective in responding to allegations from relatively less powerful stakeholders. For example, companies such as Shell, Exxon and McDonald's have suffered following criticism of their lack of concern for the environment. The lack of standards and controls on the Internet has made the problem worse. For example, anti Coca-Cola Web sites can post negative communications without the need to substantiate the messages.

International marketing communications, standardisation and adaptation

The most obvious tactic for reducing instances of international communications failure might appear to be to adopt a strict policy of standardisation in the implementation of communications plans. Firms adopt this principle, for example, in their use of corporate identity and global advertising campaigns. However, given the need also to demonstrate cultural sensitivity and empathy with a wide range of international customers and to avoid the type of mistakes referred to earlier it becomes necessary to adapt the international communications to local market needs. In this section therefore we address the factors both inside and outside the control of the firm that affect the degree to which international marketing communications can be standardised or should be adapted.

Towards standardisation

The drivers for **standardisation of international marketing communications** come, first, from the organisation's desire to improve efficiency. Cost-saving activity in marketing communications includes benefits from economies of scale, for example, in advertising creative work, media buying, more economic use of staff time, and from the experience effect, by replicating successful marketing communications programmes and processes in different countries.

Second, standardisation of communications provides customers with perceived added value, particularly in the intangible elements of the product/service offer. Customers believe that they gain additional benefit and value from a consistent and widely recognised image; for example, teenagers (as well as rather more elderly sports enthusiasts too) gain peer recognition, credibility and prestige from wearing branded sports wear which has a powerful image from its associations with sports stars. A company may use a top international business consultancy or advertising agency just as much for the way that the association is perceived by the company's suppliers and customers as for the cost effectiveness of the work that is carried out.

Consistency in the corporate identity and branding, too, reinforces awareness in stakeholders' minds and provides the familiarity with the company which leads to a feeling of confidence, trust and loyalty. For example, it may be reassuring for a visitor to see the familiar logo and appearance of a fast food outlet, hotel chain or bank in a foreign country that they are visiting.

Over the years changes in the political and economic environment have led to greater prosperity and thus greater buying power at least for some people and a greater acceptance of imported products. Consumers and business-to-business customers often prefer internationally available products, with which they have become familiar through increased travel, radio and television communications and the written media. This familiarity has increased further because of the greater impact of telecommunications and IT. Satellite and cable television, for example, have assisted considerably in creating worldwide customer segments for many more globally standardised products and services.

The Internet, too, allows customers to access products from organisations from very distant locations. Moreover, it not only allows specialist suppliers to make their standard products and services globally available to customers, but also enables smaller companies to compete essentially on equal terms with their much larger counterparts so 'punching above their weight'. Of course, companies that only communicate using the Internet are limiting their customer base to those customer segments that can access the Internet.

At an operational level advertising standardisation can be used when a number of conditions apply:

- visual messages form the main content of the advertisement
- well-known international film stars, popular celebrities and sports personalities are featured
- music is an important part of the communication
- well-known symbols and trademarks are featured. For example, the Grand Canyon in the US can be used to symbolise certain types of outdoor American values.

Even then the real impact of the promotion may be restricted to a particular region. For example, advertisements do not travel well to other countries:

- when the use of spoken and written language forms an important part of the communication
- if humour is used – humour is often very specific to certain cultures
- if they use personalities who are well known in one country but are not known internationally
- if campaigns are used that rely on specific knowledge of previous advertising.

Towards adaptation

The principal drivers of international marketing **communications adaptation** are the cultural differences that must be managed when communicating with customers in different countries. As we have already seen in this book there are some fundamental differences in the ways that consumers from different cultures respond to different communication approaches. More specifically, however, in a comparison between the US and Chinese responses to advertising Zhang and Neelankavil (1997) observe that, overall, US subjects preferred the individualistic appeal (self-orientation, self-sufficiency and control, the pursuit of individual gains) whereas Chinese subjects favoured the collective appeal (subordination of personal interests to the goals of the group, with emphasis on sharing, cooperation and harmony, and a concern for the group welfare). It is these differences which must be recognised, but there is also likely to be continuing convergence and moves toward standardisation.

Neelankavil et al. (1996) studied the contents of advertisements for language, customs and values in local language magazines in Hong Kong, Japan, Korea and Taiwan, countries which they considered to be steeped in ancient Asian culture but also major forces in the global marketplace. They found that the use of Western language and models was affected by the product type, customer countries, countries of origin, and countries of manufacture. They observe that with greater liberalisation, there is likely to be a convergence of ideas, cultures, values and even language in advertising but they comment that insufficient is known about the effects of the benefits of such standardisation.

Advertisers believe that advertising is most effective when it is relevant to the target audience and one area where there are significant differences is in the portrayal of women in advertising.

Siu and Au (1997) report that research studies of advertising suggest that:

- over 80 per cent of voice-overs are male
- women are depicted as housewives, mothers and/or sex objects
- females are shown as product users whereas males are shown in the roles of authority.

However, the role of women is changing rapidly with many more women entering the workforce. In research carried out in China and Singapore, they found that sex-role stereotyping was more apparent in China where women were depicted as product users and men as having product authority whereas in Singapore, women generally appeared as the spokesperson for the product, to have product authority and be the providers of help and advice.

Other environmental factors also make it necessary for the communications strategy to be adapted for local situations. There are political and legal constraints; for example, Wentz (1997) argues that rather than pricing itself out of the world markets the EU has regulated itself out, restricting promotional activity, offering examples such as the French ban on alcohol advertising and a Danish attack on loyalty programmes. Certain countries, too, prohibit comparative advertising, advertising alcohol, tobacco and products for children.

There are many local reasons why firms may need to adapt their communications strategy. Many companies have to change their brand names because of different meanings they have when they move to new markets. The New Zealand Dairy Board, a large exporter of dairy foods, uses the brand name Fern for its butter in Malaysia although Anchor is the flagship brand well known in Western Europe. In Malaysia, Anchor is a widely advertised local beer and Malaysian housewives are unlikely to buy dairy products for their children which they would subconsciously associate with alcohol.

Johnson & Johnson on entering the Hong Kong market used the name zhuang-cheng which means 'an official or lord during feudal times', but this upper-class association was seen as inappropriate for China and so the more upbeat modern tone of 'qiang-sheng', meaning 'active life', was used instead to better reflect the drive for modernisation.

The fundamental differences in appeal between Western and Asian communications are more fundamental than simply changing brand names. Chan and Huang (1997) suggest that brands can be enhanced if names and/or symbols of favourite animals and flowers and lucky numbers are used. In Asia written figures may be perceived as potent symbols; thus, as Schmitt and Pan (1994) point out, in Asian countries the emphasis may be heavier on the distinctive writing and logo of the brand than on the jingles that Western marketing communications favour.

Firms use a variety of ways of becoming more sensitive to cultural differences. Unilever has set up innovation centres in Asia in order to bring together research, production and marketing staff to speed up developments of international brands which have a local appeal. In Bangkok there are innovation centres responsible for ice-cream, laundry detergents and hair care. Asian Delight is a regional brand of ice-cream – between the Magnum brand and local brands – and uses English and Thai on its packaging in Thailand, English only in Malaysia, Singapore and Indonesia. It is sold from Wall's mobile units and cabinets in convenience stores and supermarkets. The flavours have a local appeal and include coconut milk based ice-cream mixed with fruits and vegetables traditionally used in desserts or chewy strings of green flour, black beans and sago.

Illustration 9.3 shows how Pepsi is taking some lessons from international marketing to develop multi-cultural marketing in the US. What is significant here is that the segmentation approach that is driving the promotion strategy is moving beyond traditional language and culture to tribalism based on popular culture.

Adaptation taken to its limits means customisation, one-to-one marketing and interactivity and this is dealt with more fully in chapter 12.

INTERNATIONAL MARKETING COMMUNICATIONS STRATEGY

So far in this chapter we have highlighted the need to consider the nature and role of international marketing communications more broadly than was the case in the past, by focusing upon both internal and external communications and a wider range of communications tools. In thinking about developing strategy there are two significant issues to address. First, the need to state clear and precise objectives for the international marketing communications strategy and, second, how the various communications activities might be coordinated to maximise their cost effectiveness.

The promotional objectives (Wilson and Gilligan 2003) can be categorised as sales-related and brand/product communications-related which might be stated in terms of *increasing sales by*:

- increasing market share at the expense of local and/or international competitors

---

ILLUSTRATION 9.3   Pepsi – promoting to tribes

Pepsi did its first African-American ad in 1948. Many firms use ethnic segmentation for advertising and this underpins the advertising strategy but Pepsi realises that this is over-simplistic, particularly for its young ethnic consumers. Pepsi believe that race and whether you are African-American or Latino is not the unifier, but interests, such as music, are. In the US Pepsi see their market as 20 per cent Latino, 15 per cent African-American and 6 per cent Asian-American. Forty per cent of Pepsi's market is in major urban centres, such as New York, Los Angeles and Miami, where the youth minorities can be the majorities. For them popular culture is at the heart of their lives.

Pepsi aims to be multicultural throughout. It targets specialist local media to carry targeted campaigns. A typical music ad, therefore, has two versions, one sung in Spanish and one in English. Pepsi can combine promotion of its cola with Doritos, its tortilla snack, but promotes it in different ways for Latins, who love a fiesta, and for Afro-Americans who are mellow and cool – and love barbecue flavour! Products have been specifically developed and promoted to other ethnic groups too.

However, Pepsi realises that much of its youth market, such as bicultural Hispanics, read more English media than Spanish, so language is not the key to unlock the market. What is important is culture, but more importantly, popular culture and appealing to the popular culture 'tribes'.

Question   Do multicultural campaigns have a role in domestic marketing? If so what are the main drivers of multicultural campaigns?

Source: Adapted from Wentz, L. 'Pepsi's new multicultural campaigns go tribal', AdAge.com, 7 July 2003

- identifying new potential customers
- obtaining a specific number of responses to a promotional campaign
- reducing the impact of competitors in the market

and brand/product communications related by:

- increasing the value of the corporate brand and product image
- helping to establish the position or to reposition the product or brand
- increasing awareness levels especially in new country markets
- changing consumers' perceptions of products, brands or the firm.

The options that are available for a generic marketing communications strategy centre around the extent to which a **push or pull strategy** could and should be adopted (Figure 9.3). A push strategy means promoting the product or service to retailers and wholesalers in order to force the product or service down the distribution channel by using promotional methods, such as personal selling, discounts and special deals. A pull strategy means communicating with the final consumer to attract them to the retailer or distributor to purchase the product. In this case mass advertising, sales promotions and point of sales promotions are the most obvious promotional methods. In domestic markets firms realise the need to have a combination of push and pull strategies including both encouraging the intermediaries to stock the products and attracting end users to buy.

In domestic markets the nature of the market structure that already exists may well affect the degree to which push and pull strategies are used; for example, how well the distribution channel is established, how powerful the retailers or distributors are, how well established the competitors are and whether the firm marketing its products or services wishes to, or has the power to challenge the existing 'route to market' by setting up a new channel.

Frequently, the international marketing communications strategy of a firm has to be adapted because of the variation in the market structures and distribution channels from country to country (for example, some are highly fragmented, whilst others are very concentrated). More often than not, however, it is the weakness of the marketing firm in the target country markets that limits its strategic choice. It may well not have sufficient resources to implement a successful domestic strategy in the new market and yet there may be a need for quick success. As a result the firm may be forced into making use of and relying heavily

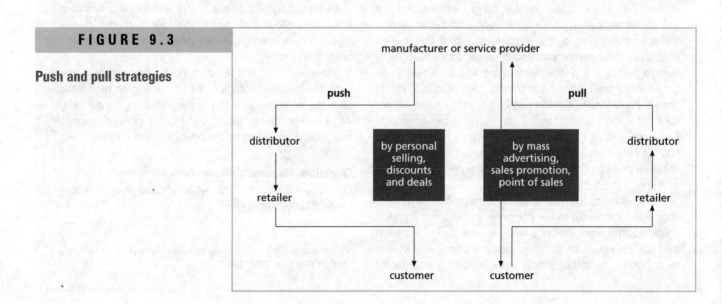

FIGURE 9.3

Push and pull strategies

upon established intermediaries to do the promotion through existing channels. For this reason it is possible to find organisations that have a pull strategy in their domestic or other established markets and a push strategy in their newer markets. Because of this the firm's promotional and communications mix may be significantly different in different markets.

Having determined the objectives and decided upon the degree to which a push and pull strategy might be used, the following dimensions of the international marketing communications implementation strategy can be defined. These are:

- the message to be communicated
- the target audience to which the message will be directed
- the media that will be used to carry the message
- the ways in which the impact of the communications will be measured.

As we said at the start of this chapter, continually evaluating the impact of the communications is vital in not only improving the effectiveness of the communication but also assessing the degree to which each of these dimensions can be standardised across international markets.

Communicating with existing and potential customers

Given that the primary objective of international marketing communications is to persuade customers to buy products and services which will meet their requirements, it is appropriate to consider how international marketing communications are used strategically to influence each of the stages of the buying process and to help customers to complete their purchase.

A number of writers have developed models of buying behaviour which tend to vary according to the context of the study, but all acknowledge that there are a number of stages in the buying process. A simplified version of these stages (AIDA) includes:

- **Awareness** of the firm, its products and services, and their reputation
- **Interest** in the products and services, because they may be suited to the consumers' needs and worthy of consideration for potential purchase
- **Desire** to buy the product or service, in preference to that of the competitor, after consumers have become better informed about its performance
- **Action** by the customer in overcoming any remaining reservations or barriers and purchasing the product or service.

Different messages must be prepared and the most appropriate promotional tool selected for each part of the buying process in order to persuade customers to move to the next stage. At each stage in this process the marketing firm faces particular problems in international markets. For example, in fast moving consumer goods marketing, advertising can be used to raise awareness, create interest and encourage consumers to purchase, but only if the messages are sensitive and appealing to the international customers and the customers have access to the media used for advertising. Other tools such as point of sale promotion can be used to support the strategy provided it is possible for the firm to maintain some level of control over the displays used by local retailers. At the final stage and having been entirely convinced about the firm's offer, customers may still have reservations about buying from a foreign supplier.

There are significant differences between consumer markets, business-to-business and institutional market purchasing. Selling capital equipment usually depends more on personal selling and providing technical service to a buying committee. This would typically be supported by awareness raising in the trade press, using PR and corporate advertising. Here the need for monitoring the consistency of approach and ensuring good communications with the manufacturing operation must be balanced against the need for sensitivity to the way that business is done in that particular country.

Coordination and planning of the international marketing communications strategy

To achieve its objectives, the communications strategy almost certainly will include a variety of promotional tools. The key to success in international promotion is integrating the various promotion elements in a cost-efficient way and adding value through choosing the communications methods which will have the most impact on the customers. The actual mix chosen will depend upon a number of issues surrounding the context of the purchasing situation, including:

- the market area and industry sector
- whether it is consumer, institutional or business-to-business marketing
- the customer segment to be targeted
- the participants in the purchasing process, their requirements and the best methods to reach and influence them
- the country or region, the culture, the communications infrastructure and the preferred methods of communicating
- the resources made available by the organisation and the implications for the level of involvement and control it wishes to exert over the communications process.

Smith *et al*. (1997) suggest that the value of different promotional methods varies according to the context in which the marketing communications are being used and the degree to which they are integrated within a marketing communications strategy, as shown in Figure 9.4.

The critical issue is to what extent they must be adapted so that they can be effective in international markets. Dilemma 9.1 shows how difficult it is for managers to make decisions that require them to go against their instincts and self-reference criteria.

THE MARKETING COMMUNICATIONS TOOLS

There are a number of marketing communications tools for the external market and it is to these that we now turn. For convenience we have grouped these tools within broad categories. In practice there is some flexibility in the way the tools are used within a coordinated strategy but the tools are listed as follows:

Communicating product and service differentiation. This group includes personal selling and word of mouth communications, exhibitions and trade fairs, trade missions, advertising and the use of agencies, sales promotion and direct marketing.

Communicating with a wider range of stakeholders. This includes the corporate identity, sponsorship and public relations.

The use of technology is becoming a key tool in enabling effective communication and is dealt with in Chapter 12.

Personal selling and word of mouth

For many companies the first use of the communications mix to promote exports is personal selling. Selling is often used to gain the first few orders in a new market and as the main component of a push strategy to persuade distribution channel members, such as agents, distributors or retailers to stock the product. It is expensive, however.

The use of personal selling tends to be limited to situations in which benefits can be derived from two-way information flows and ones in which the revenue from the sale is sufficiently high to justify the costs. This is typically the case with business-to-business marketing and in consumer markets where the purchase price justifies the high cost of personal selling, for example for cars, holidays, homes and for consumer durable products. Even here the need for personal selling is being challenged as direct marketing, particularly using the Internet, is now being used routinely to purchase these products.

In countries where labour costs are very low, personal selling is used to a greater extent than in high cost countries. This ranges from street and market

FIGURE 9.4

Internal and external international communications programmes

Marketing programmes influencing communications	International communication aims
Internally focused programmes	
Corporate identity	Consistency in all aspects of company logo, signs and image
Internal marketing communications	Reinforce motivation through telling staff what is happening
Salesforce, dealer and distributor training and development	Training through conferences, manuals and brochures
Retailing merchandising	Point of sale persuasion through displays and shelf facings
First contact customer service	Welcoming first contact through telephonist and receptionist training
After sales service	Customer retention and satisfaction through staff training and brochures
Quality management	Assuring a continuous quality approach in all programmes
Brand management	Achieving common brand standards and values
Externally focused programmes (marketing mix)	
Product attributes	Offering innovative, high quality products
Distribution channel	Ensuring easy access to products and frequent customer encounters with the products
Price	Messages about quality and status
Product/service promotion	Managing customer expectations through the integration of the marketing mix communications
People	Using staff–customer interactions to reinforce the aims, standards and values of the firm
Customer service process	Providing a satisfactory total experience through the service offer
Physical evidence for the service delivery	All contacts with the facilities reinforce the firm's messages

trading to quite sophisticated multi-level distribution chains for business-to-business products. In high labour cost countries personal selling of low unit cost products is used rarely, except for illegal trading, for example, of drugs. It is of course a successful method of selling niche products, such as Avon cosmetics, Tupperware and Amway household products. The basis of the appeal of these products is to make shopping a more social event, by selling to friends or family, and introducing a 'party' atmosphere into the selling process.

Effective selling in international business-to-business and consumer markets involves a wide range of tasks and skills, including product and market knowledge, and listening and questioning skills. However, it is in the core selling activities of negotiation and persuasion discussed in Chapter 3 that higher order expertise is required. It is likely that local people will be more effective than home-based representatives in understanding the subtleties of the negotiation process as they apply within the local business culture. They will have fluent language skills and an intimate knowledge of the culture of the country. However, where the negotiations relate to high value contracts they may well require high levels of specialist technical knowledge, an understanding of the processes and systems and strict adherence to the firm's standards and values. For these reasons the company may well prefer to use staff from its head office to ensure that the sales people are well informed about the firm's capabilities and that their activities can be controlled.

This is particularly the case if the opportunities to make a sale are very infrequent (e.g. with capital goods) when high levels of technical skill and an understanding of the company's systems are needed but not easily learnt by new people. For example, Rolls-Royce use a complete team of UK-based engineers, accountants, and sales people to sell aero engines to customers in the US. Some of the team will make frequent visits to the US, others will be based in close con-

---

DILEMMA 9.1   SRC in advertising decisions

Advertising managers who are involved in cross-border campaigns face the problem of self-reference criteria. A European brand manager for Heinz, based in the UK, was responsible for approving advertising campaigns that had been developed by local agencies for the local country subsidiary as part of a pan-European campaign. In Germany the local agency produced a television advertising campaign. The European brand manager, his boss and his boss's boss, all English, turned down the agency's creative work.

The advertisement was meant to be humorous but they did not find it at all funny and they were concerned that it would devalue the brand and the campaign. The agency insisted that they had tested the ad on consumers and the humour would work in Germany. After various delays the manager had to make the decision whether or not the ad should go ahead on the following Monday. However, it was the weekend and he could not reach his bosses for help with the decision. The campaign would cost £1 million and this would be lost if the campaign did not go ahead. If the campaign adversely affected the campaign it would be a greater disaster. His job could be on the line! Against

his better judgement, and overcoming his self-reference criteria, he decided the advert should be broadcast. The campaign was a great success!

Western firms also realise that it is important to appreciate the levels of intelligence and sophistication of emerging markets. When Heinz first launched tomato ketchup in Russia they used an existing TV ad from the UK with minor modifications. Now that would be unacceptable as the Russian audience is more sophisticated. Russian actors would be needed on the advertisement. Heinz is particularly sensitive to the need to adapt to local markets and this is part of their strategy.

Consumers are very knowledgeable and well aware when some big brands are behaving in an arrogant manner and telling them what to buy. They can become annoyed when firms insult their intelligence. A number of firms have seen their reputation and share price suffer because of insensitive promotion and PR. The dilemma for firms is when should they insist on standardisation and consistency, and when should they trust partners with local knowledge.

tact with the customer for a period of many months. The sheer complexity of the contracts means that only Rolls-Royce employees could understand the detail sufficiently to handle the negotiations. The high contract price provides sufficient revenue, if the contract is won, to pay for the costs of the UK-based sales team.

An alternative compromise arrangement to the two extremes of employing local or head-office sales staff (both have their advantages and disadvantages) is to employ expatriates, staff from the domestic country to work for extended periods in the host country in order to bridge the culture and company standards gap.

In practice the expatriate is likely to experience a culture shock, caused by living in a foreign culture, where the familiar symbols, cues and everyday reassurances are missing, often causing feelings of frustration, stress and anxiety. The expatriate can respond to the situation in one of three ways. At one extreme, adjustment is made to the expatriate culture only. In effect the expatriate only adjusts to the way of life of a ready made cultural island within the host country and makes little attempt to adjust to the host culture. At the other extreme the expatriate's reaction is to completely embrace the host culture and actively minimise contact with the expatriate community and the firm too. Ideally the expatriate adjusts to both the local culture and the expatriate culture. In this way the expatriate retains the home country's and firm's system of values and beliefs, but is considerate and respectful towards the people of his or her host country and to their culture. It is this last option that is usually most beneficial for the firm's sales effort.

Whichever approach to selling is adopted, it is through relevant training that firms aim to manage their sales staff's involvement with the firm and the market, and maintain their enthusiasm for selling. As the cost of personal selling is increasing, so firms are seeking ways of improving their cost effectiveness by using more systematic ways of analysing customer requirements and carrying out the sales role rather than relying on a good firm handshake for closing the deal.

Exhibitions and trade fairs

Exhibitions and trade fairs are an effective method of meeting many existing and potential customers from different countries. The cost of exhibiting at international trade fairs is very high, when the cost of the stand, space rental, sales staff time and travelling expenses are taken into account. It is for this reason that the selection of the most appropriate fairs for the industry is critical. Also important are the creative work for the stand, preparation of sales literature and selection of suitable personnel for the stand, bearing in mind the need for cultural and language empathy.

Trade missions

Trade missions are organised visits to a country or region of a group of senior business managers from a number of firms perhaps from the same geographic region or from the same industry. They are often subsidised by national or local government. Discussions with potential customers are arranged in advance in the host country.

Trade missions are usually associated with exporting and may be used both to carry out introductory talks with prospective clients or to negotiate a contract. As with trade fairs, good preparation work before the visit is essential to ensure that meetings are arranged with appropriate customers where there is a genuine possibility of business being generated. Usually the home country's local embassy staff will provide support for trade missions and often, too, depending on the importance of the mission, there will be discussions with the host government, civil servants and politicians about how trade between the two countries can be developed.

Advertising

Advertising is one of the most visible forms of communication and is often the most important part of the whole strategy for consumer products in countries with a well-developed media industry. It has disadvantages because it is essentially a one-way method of communication and in international marketing it can be difficult to control in terms of its reach (the geographic area in which consumers are exposed to the messages). The objective is to obtain the maximum exposure of the product or brand to the largest possible target audience. Clearly the opportunities for precise targeting are limited in some advertising media, especially television, and this presents problems in international marketing in terms of targeting specific user segments or even specific countries.

However, cross-border transmission can be problematic too (Hu and Griffith 1997). When Radion was promoted in Germany, demand was stimulated in neighbouring Austria through spread of print and commercial television adverts. Although unintended, Unilever's advertising reach stretched across national borders.

In most business-to-business markets advertising tends to be used as a supporting activity, for example to increase awareness or interest in the company as a whole or in a new concept such as IBM's focus on electronic business in 1998. In business-to-business markets the number of important customers is often comparatively small and it is essential that advertising is precisely targeted, using appropriate specialist trade media.

Together with the increased harmonisation of consumer demands for some products and the benefits of standardised products and services to firms, there is a strong move to pan-regional advertising campaigns (Smith 1998).

Advertising agency Young and Rubican say that pan-European campaigns make up 40 per cent of their business, twice the amount of five years ago. Reckitt and Benckiser, the household goods and pharmaceutical products group, find that 90 per cent of media spending is on regional campaigns. Consumers increasingly share common values and characteristics but there are differences as, for example, Central and Eastern European people are still developing their habits as consumers. There are few differences in purchasing between European countries for home and personal-care products, such as deodorants and disinfectants. New products, too, can often use common advertising programmes. PepsiCo's Frito-Lay created a single campaign for Doritos, the tortilla chip brand introduced within the past decade, whereas more established snack foods tend to require specific local advertising. As Illustration 9.3 shows, it is now adopting more targeted campaigns, too.

There are considerable differences in the availability and usefulness of other advertising media such as radio, cinema, outdoor and transport posters. These differences make it essential to obtain data about media effectiveness in order to make informed decisions about international media schedules. For instance, in remote regions exposure to certain media is prevented because of the poor transmission output quality from radio stations, the target audience having insufficient disposable income to afford television or radio and low adult literacy levels preventing significant numbers of adults reading printed advertising.

The opportunity to use mass-communications media to reach the target market is therefore severely limited in some countries. Even in developed countries it may not be possible to reach the majority of the market because of the absence of truly national press or national television. In these situations it may be necessary to develop a campaign based upon a multitude of individual media activities but this means that the measurement of the cost effectiveness of the campaign is extremely difficult given that individual components of the campaign may produce different effects.

Advertising is shown to work in emerging countries, with increased spending by Coca-Cola leading to them becoming the best-selling soft drink in China and overtaking Pepsi in a number of Central and Eastern European republics. There is also an apparent trend towards advertising amongst conglomerates from emerging countries that appears to recognise the value of moving from product orientation to marketing orientation. In 1996 Daewoo increased advertising spending outside the US by 66 per cent, Hyundai by 22 per cent and LG by 29 per cent (Fannin 1997).

In Shanghai, advertising multiplied 16 times between 1990 and 1994 and Soames Hines, MD of J Walter Thompson in Shanghai, said in 1997 that it was a chaotic outdoor media environment with essentially everything up for sale – every lamppost, bus, hoarding, bus shelter and rooftop.

The appeal of advertising in China is based on young people who are optimistic rather than cynical – they expect to be better off than their parents. Despite this modernism, Chinese traditions still prevail and family values have a powerful selling appeal even with the young. The Chinese know that foreign brands may be better at the moment but do not like to have this overemphasised. In the past, JWT used expatriates, but have realised that this cultivates only international clients and deters the growing numbers of Chinese clients. As a consequence JWT have appointed a Taiwanese manager (Harding 1997).

Figure 9.5 shows the top 15 advertising spenders in 2001 worldwide and inside the US and shows the changes that a number of firms have made to their advertising budget compared with 2000. The information is collected from 77 countries.

Television advertising

The main influence on television advertising expenditure is the size of the economy in gross domestic product per capita, but the regulatory environment also

FIGURE 9.5

The top 15 advertising spenders in 2001

Source: Adapted from *Advertising Age*, 11 November 2002

Rank	Advertiser	HQ country	Worldwide US$bn	% Change on 2000	US$bn
1	Procter & Gamble	US	3.82	6.6	1.70
2	General Motors	US	3.03	−20.1	2.21
3	Unilever	UK/Netherlands	3.00	2.6	0.57
4	Ford	US	2.31	3.0	1.27
5	Toyota	Japan	2.21	−3.1	0.77
6	AOL Time Warner	US	2.10	9.5	1.56
7	Philip Morris	US	1.93	−19.0	1.33
8	Daimler-Chrysler	Germany	1.84	−12.4	1.40
9	Nestlé	Switzerland	1.80	3.2	0.50
10	Volkswagen	Germany	1.57	−2.0	0.46
11	Honda	Tokyo	1.43	5.6	0.68
12	McDonald's	US	1.41	−3.6	0.67
13	Coca-Cola	US	1.40	6.5	0.41
14	L'Oréal	France	1.35	−2.1	0.50
15	Walt Disney	US	1.26	−1.6	1.05

affects spending, particularly television which tends to be more closely regulated than other media. As a result not all advertisers who wish to use television advertising are able to gain access. Broadcasting liberalisation has occurred in Europe over the past 15 years. Howard (1997) notes, for example, that following the launch of new commercial television, advertising spending increased substantially. Since 1980 European television advertising spending has increased by 200 per cent in real terms whilst newspapers and magazines have grown by only 53 per cent and 21 per cent respectively. During this period television's share has almost doubled to just over 31 per cent.

Cable and satellite television have contributed to a proliferation of television channels so that viewers can receive a rapidly increasing number of programmes. This means that there is a greater capacity for television advertising but, of course, there is greater competition for prime television advertising spots (and much higher costs) if there is likely to be a large audience. Both satellite and cable television have the potential to cross country borders and attract large audiences for programmes of common international interest, for example major sporting events.

It is not only overt television advertising in large amounts that sells. The prominent placing of products on television shows that are likely to be transmitted in other countries can also become an important part of the advertising campaign as Illustration 9.4 shows.

Shannon (1997) suggests that in future television will focus more on local targeting. The introduction of digital television technology enables the output to be tailored to local culture and preferences, and provides the opportunity for hundreds of local niche channels to be set up. The established television industry has had to pre-empt this by targeting its output more precisely. MTV has established four European services for the UK, pan-northern, central and southern areas each

---

ILLUSTRATION 9.4   The power of television

Television is a powerful medium for changing attitudes. It can have a significant effect in preparing the way for international product launches. New television channels using satellite technology are having an effect on viewing habits and, again, are preparing the way for international brands.

An example of how TV has spread the American culture can be seen in how Israel has absorbed the influence of the US. More than 20 per cent of Jews travel abroad each year and a significant number visit the US, so when US firms enter Israel they usually receive a warm reception. When Dunkin' Donuts were introduced into Israel Steven Esses, the local licensee, found it was not necessary to use the all-encompassing advertising campaign developed with the ad agency because Jews watch US TV shows such as *ER* in which products are prominently placed and so the awareness levels of Dunkin' Donuts was already very high. He has spent only US$60 000 on marketing and public relations and yet the first two operating stores have triple the turnover of US stores. Perhaps all the aspects of the American culture have not yet permeated across to Israel because the main difference is that in Israel the customers eat in store whilst in the US they take out.

On the other hand, for Palestinians, who number 2.5 million, labelling in Hebrew on the packaging of products is a sign of quality, whereas English labelling is a sign of low quality, largely because inferior quality products with English labelling were supplied in the past from countries like Greece, Turkey and Egypt. The Palestinians, however, do visit Tel Aviv and other big Israeli cities and are exposed to many American brands and are also exposed to dozens of Arabic TV channels via cable and satellite. Palestinians are getting used to American products and already use 'Pampers' as the generic name for disposable nappies.

Question   Product placement can be expensive – is it possible to measure the benefit to the firms across diverse markets?

Source: Adapted from Sugarman, M. (1997) 'New Israel embraces cachet of US brands', *Ad Age International*, April

reflecting distinctive local tastes, Eurosport is now available in 14 languages and CNN has four separate services for different regions of the world.

Press advertising

Media availability and effectiveness are particularly important in deciding the nature of campaigns because they can vary from country to country. High levels of readership of the press in a country are still unusual. The more usual situation is that the press is available but with only token readership outside certain usually urban regions.

In some countries, in Africa and Asia, adult literacy levels might restrict newspaper and magazine sales opportunities but the lack of mass-circulation national titles might cause distribution difficulties, too, as it is easier to distribute quickly in small compact countries than in much larger countries such as France or Spain. Vast countries like the USA are much more likely to develop a distinctive regional press. Newer publishing and printing technology has allowed many more local newspapers and specialist magazines to be introduced to both consumer and business-to-business markets. By their very nature they tend to be highly targeted at specific market segments and can be useful to niche marketers. However, for mass marketers the resulting fragmentation of readership that comes from very localised media titles means that national campaigns are more difficult to coordinate.

The use of agencies and consultancies

Most companies in which marketing communications are an important part of the marketing mix will use agencies and consultancies. The reasons why this is so can be explained by financial considerations, specialist knowledge, creative input and external perspective.

Financial. Advertising agents that are recognised by the media are eligible for a commission based on booked advertising space. The agency can therefore perform the advertising services of creation, media planning and booking more economically than the client.

Agencies and consultancies can use specialist people and resources, such as a database for media planning, with a number of clients. This helps spread costs for both the agency and clients.

Specialist knowledge. By concentrating on one particular area, agencies and consultancies can become experts in specialised techniques, for example international database marketing or training sales people. Client companies might have an infrequent need for these services and so find it more cost effective to subcontract the work.

Creative input. Creativity is very important in marketing communications. The organisation culture of client companies is unlikely to encourage true creativity in external communications. The challenge of new and different projects for different clients contributes to the creativity of agencies.

External perspective. The external view of agencies reduces some of the myopia of the client company. This might be particularly valuable at times of major transition in international marketing, for example in moving towards global marketing.

The selection of agencies and consultants is an important business decision. If the agency is going to be involved over a long period and be trusted with large expenditures of time and money the decision process will be significant. A dilemma (see Dilemma 9.2) for global marketers, such as Microsoft, is whether they should select one central agency or many local agencies.

Sales promotions

Sales promotions can be used in a variety of ways to add value to the sale and are particularly effective if they are part of an integrated communications strategy.

DILEMMA 9.2 — Xbox: Agency centralisation or decentralisation

A key question for multi-nationals is how to structure their relationships with advertising agencies – whether to centralise or decentralise to their autonomous business units.

Microsoft's Xbox was launched to compete with Playstation 2 in 16 European countries over the Christmas 2002 period. Universal McCann were the media agency with the responsibility of establishing a clearly differentiated brand position for Xbox, achieving high sales over the Christmas period and connecting with the gaming youth of Europe, by penetrating youth culture.

Microsoft's structure is centralised for Europe with headquarters for EMEA (Europe, Middle East and Africa) in London. It has marketing departments in all key markets with the responsibility of implementing the communication plans. To get 'buy-in' from all markets briefings were attended by all clients, the European creative agency and Universal McCann. Focus groups were held in each key market to understand how the media and the gaming and youth culture interacts with the target audience. From this the marketing and communications objectives could be set, and the target audience profile, consumer brand and media insights, the strategic driver for media placement, guidelines for the campaign execution and measurement established.

The regional strategy could then be shared with the local client and agency teams. In this way the intention was to encourage local creativity and build on local insights, but achieve consistency of thinking and strategic direction. Xbox sold 17 per cent more consoles than Playstation 2 over the Christmas period and passed 1 million consoles in the UK, France and Germany alone.

Centralisation achieves more control, can reduce creative costs and achieve cost savings because of increased media buying power. However, sometimes this may not be as good as it might seem. Europe-wide media groups, such as MTV, offer pan-European coverage but their impact in different countries may differ considerably, and more appropriate local media might be available. Consequently local knowledge is needed from local agencies. Local knowledge also provides knowledge about media availability, regulations, lifestyles and customer insights.

Source: Microsoft

Large agencies set up local offices to reflect the structure of the client and offer a seamless service. But this is not always possible or desirable and independent local agencies are used in conjunction with the lead agency. The problem then arises how much data and expertise should the lead agency share with the independent agencies. The dilemma for the firm is, first, should they centralise or decentralise and, second, if a combination of both centralisation and devolved responsibility is used, how best can the conflicting demands be balanced?

Sales promotions can be used within the promotions mix for fast-moving consumer goods and business-to-business markets. Consumer goods sales promotions might include coupons or money-off vouchers, 'special offer' price reductions and competitions. As well as these, business-to-business sales promotions might also include database and direct marketing, exhibitions and trade fairs, bundled sales deals, in which extra product features might be added, such as trade-ins on old products, extra warranty and service cover and operative training.

Sales promotions are usually used close to the purchase decision and have the objective of offering better value to the customer at the most influential moment in the purchase process. In some markets there may be no meaningful differences between a number of companies or brands, except for the degree of attractiveness of the sales promotion offer. The customers' perception of the relative value of the alternative promotions depends to a great extent on their cultural values. Citing a recent Turkish craze for collection-based promotions which were not replicated in other neighbouring countries, Read (1997) suggests that cultural differences lead to certain types of sales promotion being very successful in one country but failing in another.

Legal restrictions also affect the opportunity for firms to standardise sales promotion across country borders. There are limitations on the amount of cash discounts and special sales promotions in some coutries allowed in Europe. Different legal definitions of the rules for lotteries, too, prevent some competition-based promotions being operated across borders.

Direct marketing

In the past, direct marketing has usually taken the form of direct mail or telephone selling and these are still, perhaps, the main routes to the market but the Internet is becoming an important alternative method. The key elements of direct marketing are an accurate up-to-date database, the ability to purge the database of incorrect data and to merge the database with a firm's promotional message. Usually it is important to offer a telephone (toll-free) number and, of course, the customers need to have a telephone if telephone marketing is to be used. Usually firms subcontract direct marketing to specialist agencies which provide the various services, such as list broking, purging and merging. Latin America offers considerable opportunities for direct mailing although the infrastructure in some countries will pose problems as shown in Illustration 9.5.

Communicating with the wider range of stakeholders

At the outset we said that the principal objective of the international marketing communications strategy was to sell products and services. However, before messages are communicated with the specific purpose of encouraging consumers to buy it is necessary to make them more broadly aware of the company and its products. In the early stages of the buying process it is the reputation which the international firm has in the wider community that is important. Quite simply customers in a host country are unlikely to even contemplate buying from a foreign firm that is perceived to be exploiting its local workers, bribing government officials, showing little regard to environmental protection issues, offering poor or variable product quality or is likely to pull out from the country at any moment and thus be unable to fulfil its guarantees and obligations. By contrast a foreign firm can build increased loyalty amongst its customers at the expense of local firms if it is perceived to offer better quality and value for money, to be a more reliable supplier, more caring about the local community (see Illustration 9.6) and, in some cases, through association, to be respected by world personalities.

These objectives can be achieved through the effective use of a number of communications elements under the following general headings:

- Corporate identity
- Sponsorship
- Public relations and lobbying.

Corporate identity

Corporate identity is concerned with consistently communicating not just what business the firm is in and what image it wishes to project in the market, but also how it does its business. It must reflect the standards and values it aims to uphold in its dealings with all its stakeholders. For this reason there are two distinct elements. For many MNEs the focus is upon the image it wishes to create, which is reinforced by consistency in the way the company name and logo is presented and applied to the vast range of physical outputs and assets of the company including signs, staff uniforms, letterheads, visiting cards, gifts, annual reports, packaging specification and promotional literature.

As we have already discussed in principle, whilst these can all be controlled by the firm, there are many challenges in applying them consistently in all the countries where the firm operates especially where it develops alliances with

---

ILLUSTRATION 9.5   **Direct marketing in Latin America**

Latin America has a population of 650 million and, given the largely democratic governments, the increasing affluence and its proximity to North America, offers considerable opportunities for direct marketers. The size of the market is impossible to estimate but both consumer and business-to-business markets are expected to grow at 40–50 per cent a year in most countries.

Five to ten years ago companies were predominantly state owned but the privatisation industries, such as telecommunications, transportation, utilities, water, propane distribution, highways and roads are offering new opportunities. The differences between the markets are considerable.

Direct marketing is, therefore, at different stages of development compared to the US, with the possible exception of Brazil. However, Latin American countries are likely to catch up fast, but by using a different route – the Internet. Direct marketers face some problems in moving forward because different dialects of Spanish are spoken and Portuguese is spoken in Brazil. Long-distance telephone calls are expensive, so the direct marketers will have to set up local operations. There are few reliable lists of potential customers and few public sources of data. Whilst consumer data is being collected, business-to-business marketers usually have to collect their own information.

Question How can direct marketing be used most effectively in emerging markets?

Source: Adapted from Loro, L. (1998) 'Direct Marketing', *Advertising Age*, January

	Argentina	Brazil	Chile	Peru
Direct marketing agencies	10	72	10	1
Telemarketing firms	25	36	15	3
List brokers	5	16	3	1
Merge/purge companies	2	27	1	0
Toll free free service	yes	yes	yes	soon
Phone penetration	65%	n/a	45%	18%

partners who might also wish to maintain their corporate identity in joint communications.

Arguably, of more importance is the underlying identity of the firm, its beliefs, standards and values which will show through in everything the firm does. These may pose more difficulties to the firm's attempts to achieve consistency and a favourable impact throughout the world because of the different cultural values of its staff and stakeholders in different countries.

Sponsorship

Sponsorship involves a firm (the sponsor) providing finance, resources or other support for an event, activity, firm, person, product or service. In return the sponsor would expect to gain some advantage, such as the exposure of its brand, logo or advertising message. Sponsorship of music, performing arts and sporting events provides opportunities for:

- brand exposure and publicity
- opportunities to entertain customers and employees
- association between brands and events, with the events often reinforcing the brand positioning, for example Dunhill's golf sponsorship and BMW's sponsorship of classical music concerts
- improving community relations by supporting community-based projects
- creating the opportunity to promote the brands at the event, either through providing free products or gifts such as T-shirts carrying the brand logo.

Expenditure on global sponsorship has expanded rapidly over the past two decades and it is being used much more for the following reasons identified by Meenahan (1991):

ILLUSTRATION 9.6   **Coca-Cola's global multi-local strategy**

For years Coca-Cola's historical strength came from its appeal to global commonalities coupled with its local market awareness gained by working closely with its bottling partners. Control, however, had to be centralised in order for its global expansion to be effectively managed. Consolidation of the bottlers was encouraged by Coca-Cola as an effective response to the consolidation of retailers, and to give the bottlers strength to survive market and economic turbulence.

The company suffered poorer performance in the late 1990s. There was a view that it was being run by bureaucrats and accountants, who developed a highly efficient distribution system, but at the cost of innovation, flexibility and a willingness to take risks. The company recognised that the world (and Coca-Cola) had moved towards globalisation, but that national and local leaders were seeking to secure their own country's sovereignty over their political, economic and cultural future.

Its response was to cut costs at its Atlanta, US headquarters and restructure to become a multi-local company. It recognised that it must not lose the benefits of being global but must make it happen by giving authority and responsibility to those closest to the individual sales. Local management must be allowed to be innovative so long as they stayed within the company's values, policies and standards of integrity and quality.

In building brand strength the company must be the world's best marketer. This meant that the company must be model citizens, understand the difference between doing business in societies rather than in markets and so be responsive to the desire of communities to retain their individuality.

Question What international marketing action should Coca-Cola take in order to achieve this outcome?

- restrictive government policies on tobacco and alcohol advertising leaving sponsorship as the most effective way of communicating the brand imagery to a mass market, for example in Formula 1 car racing
- the escalating costs of media advertising
- increased leisure activities and sporting events
- the proven records of sponsorship
- greater media coverage of sponsored events
- the reduced efficiencies of traditional media advertising because of clutter and zapping between television programmes, especially during advertising breaks.

There is an increase in the amount of broadcast sponsorship where a film, television or radio programme is sponsored. This can result in the benefit of the event sponsorship being reduced. For example, Heinz sponsored a Rugby World Cup only to find that Sony sponsored the national commercial television coverage in the UK resulting in most viewers thinking that Sony had sponsored the whole event.

For the James Bond film *Die Another Day* twenty companies contributed US$70 million sponsorship in exchange for product placement. As a result Bond turned his back on BMW and renewed his love affair with his Aston Martin, changed vodka brands and threw away his Rolex watch. The reason that the firms were prepared to pay so much is that the traditional advertising routes for TV are less effective as TV viewing is shared between more channels. By comparison cinema has global appeal, especially in the case of the Bond films, given the last three grossed US$1 billion. In the future, interactivity will make it possible to buy the watch off Bond's wrist, so further clouding the distinction between the film content and advertising.

Public relations

Public relations is concerned with communicating news stories about the firm, its people, products and services through the media without charge in order to develop relationships, goodwill and mutual understanding between the firm and its stakeholders.

The purposes of PR are as follows:

- helping to foster the prestige and reputation of the firm, through its public image
- raising awareness and creating interest in the firm's products
- dealing with social and environmental issues and opportunities
- improving goodwill with customers through presenting useful information and dealing effectively with complaints
- promoting the sense of identification of employees with the firm through newsletters, social activities and recognition
- discovering and eliminating rumours and other sources of misunderstanding and misconceptions
- building a reputation as a good customer and reliable supplier
- influencing the opinions of public officials and politicians, especially in explaining the responsible operation of the business and the importance of its activities to the community
- dealing promptly, accurately and effectively with unfavourable negative publicity, especially where it is perceived to be a crisis which might damage the firm's reputation

- attracting and keeping good employees.

Public relations is concerned with a wide variety of activities in order to deliver these objectives, including:

- dealing with press relations
- arranging facility visits
- publishing house journals and newsletters
- preparing videos, audio visual presentations, printed reports and publications describing the firm's activities
- training courses
- arranging community projects
- lobbying governments.

From a communications perspective the effect of public relations generated stories in the media is different from advertising. The viewer, listener or reader will perceive the information differently. Editorial material in the media is perceived by consumers to be factual and comparatively neutral whereas advertising material is expected to be persuasive and present a positive statement for the advertisers' products. Whereas the firm controls every aspect of advertising, a press release covering a firm's news story will be interpreted by the journalist who writes the story for the press or edits the videotape for television. Therefore the value of the same amount of media space used in editorial or in advertising is quite different. Customers from developed countries treat advertising with greater cynicism than customers from less developed countries and on occasions a negative story can result from PR designed to enhance the firm's image, particularly where language translations and cultural misunderstandings might have shown the foreign firm as having little empathy or understanding of the host country.

Stakeholders

MNEs have a larger number of stakeholders than those firms limited to domestic markets. These stakeholders or target groups have varying degrees of connection with such organisations. Some will be part of the value system of a firm and some will be part of the environment surrounding the firm both domestically and internationally. Some may be supportive, others may have a controlling role and yet others may have the intention of being destructive. Even though the firm may want to achieve the same objectives in different country markets its patterns of engagement with stakeholders can be quite different as Illustration 9.7 shows.

One of the main roles of international public relations is to try to manage the often substantially different and often conflicting expectations of stakeholders. Frequently the problem is one of when to disclose information that could prove damaging to the company's image and reputation.

In international marketing one of the most important responsibilities of public relations is to manage unexpected crises which occur from time to time. Over the past few years there have been a number of examples of good and bad practice in managing information when dealing with a crisis within the company. Crises of this type have included environmental pollution, unethical promotion, exploitation of labour and health scares, caused by food contamination. The golden rule is that the firm should be seen to act, before the media or government forces it to do so, in order to show that it is sorry that an incident has occurred. However, it should neither accept responsibility nor apportion blame until the evidence is investigated and the real cause of the problem identified.

Many MNEs consider government lobbying an essential part of international marketing with the aim of influencing foreign governments both directly and indirectly through asking the home country government to help. The most obvious example of lobbying has been by US firms seeking greater access to Japanese markets over the past two decades and the main objectives of the strategy have been to convince both governments that allowing market access is in both their interests.

As government lobbying becomes increasingly important it raises issues for the company about how high profile the company should be in pressing its case and how much effort should be expended on persuading the home country government to put pressure on the host country government. Some firms go one stage further by making donations to political parties. This, of course, can have the effect of alienating other stakeholders. There is little doubt that firms are increasingly making lobbying a major responsibility of senior management given the pivotal role of governments in making decisions which might affect the MNE.

RELATIONSHIP MARKETING

So far in this chapter we have focused upon the communications strategies that might be used to ensure that the firm's broad base of stakeholders around the

---

ILLUSTRATION 9.7   Charity begins in the neighbourhood

When National Westminster Bank (now the Royal Bank of Scotland) expanded into New England, US they found it necessary to adapt their approach to corporate charitable giving. The logic of this may not at first be apparent. Being East Coast, English speaking and attuned culturally to giving (sometimes more than one per cent of profit), Natwest America, in a similar way to its parent organisation, appreciated the need to demonstrate corporate citizenship and cement relationships with its customers, employees, the media and shareholders by giving. Furthermore, patterns of donation were alike, with roughly 60 per cent going to social and community affairs and the balance split fairly equally between the arts and sport. The whole approach practised by the community relations managers converged and on both sides of the Atlantic a blend of altruism and high impact giving, matched closely to corporate identity, prevailed. What then was the difference requiring different working practices?

Divergence originated not in cultural differences, though Natwest America probably looked a little harder for value and donated alongside a more established network of personal philanthropy. It derived largely from structural environmental barriers associated with geography and the legal/political make-up of the US banking industry. At the time the US banking system was highly fragmented by legislation, which inhibited the development of multi-state banks. In addition, conditions of New York State banking

licences involved a quota system requiring prescribed levels of business within narrow 'blue lined' geographic communities. Natwest UK faced no such restrictions and, although they gave locally, they were able to maintain a much more regional and narrow focus.

Corporate benevolence in the US banking sector was much more highly localised and even individual, for example support for students from the Hispanic community. The US was also simply so large that the key stakeholders associated little with corporate activity outside their own state. Because their media, such as the New York Times, was regional, they were unlikely to hear about 'good works' elsewhere, rendering such giving unattractive to an organisation altogether. In contrast, the UK is small and has a particularly developed national media network. The corporate quotas for Natwest America meant it had to maintain and build relationships and attract new business from various groups within the local community and this drove the different charitable profile from the UK approach. Corporate communications were divided by more than just a common language!

Question What should drive the strategy for corporate giving?

Source: Rod Radford, Sheffield Hallam University

world are aware of the company's standards and values, the distinctiveness and quality of its brands, products and services and that customers are exposed to the messages that will encourage them to buy the firm's products and services rather than the competitor's. Once customers have been won over, usually at a considerable cost, firms increasingly realise that it is less costly if they can persuade them to stay loyal to the firm rather than lose them to a competitor and so face the cost of winning them over again. The potential cost of failing to satisfy customers can be high. For example, Nissan did not immediately produce a successor to a very successful sports coupe, which had sales of approximately 40 000 in Europe, because the car was perceived not to be a success in Japan and not to be worth launching in the US. The loss of potential sales of the replacement was substantial but, in addition, a considerable number of disappointed customers were forced to buy from Nissan's competitors.

Keeping customers is particularly important for B2B marketing, where the number of opportunities to win over new customers may be very limited and the loss of a major customer could have a disastrous effect on the firm. The lifetime value of the customer is considerable. In response to this the importance of relationship marketing began to be recognised in the 1970s and relationship marketing was explained as a new theory and practice in the 1990s (Groonroos 1996). Of course marketers have always recognised, albeit informally, that building relationships was a key part of supplier–customer transactions, especially when supply exceeds demand. Relationship marketing is concerned with developing and maintaining mutually advantageous relationships between two firms in a supply chain and using their combined capability and resources to deliver the maximum added value for the ultimate customer. It involves a more holistic approach to understanding the market dynamics and developing implementation strategies to respond to the changes in the market needs that have been identified.

The concept is very broadly applied and Illustration 9.8 shows how partnerships can be used in the media for non-profit purposes too.

The concept of relationship marketing

There are significant differences between adopting a traditional marketing approach based on individual transactions, in which the emphasis is placed on the 4Ps of the product marketing mix, and an approach based upon building relationships in the form of the services marketing mix, in which there is an emphasis on the three extra Ps of the service mix (people, physical aspects and process), referred to in Chapter 8. Some of the differences are illustrated in Figure 9.6. At the core of relationship marketing is the idea that rather than simply trying to add customer service onto a predetermined product offer, based on a rigid marketing mix, as shown in Figure 9.7, the firm should provide customer satisfaction by offering a flexible marketing mix to meet individual needs, as shown in Figure 9.8.

In the customer service model of Figure 9.7 the focus is a total product and service offer that can be marketed to customers using a predetermined marketing mix designed by the firm prior to it being offered to customers. The customer service department will deal with problems that occur when the product offer does not meet customer expectations. The relationship marketing concept is based upon a 'no compromise' approach to the delivery of customer satisfaction. The customer relationship is managed to ensure individual customer satisfaction by making the marketing mix as flexible as possible, for example by tailoring promotion, product and price to meet customer needs. In practice, of course, the marketing mix may not be infinitely variable but rather be composed of different mixes of standard elements, managed using appropriate business processes on a standard business platform. Horovitz (2000) suggests that in relationship marketing the 4Ps of the traditional marketing mix are changed altogether and replaced by the 4Cs of relationship marketing: customer needs and wants; costs; convenience; and communication.

There is some discussion about whether the concept of relationship marketing can and should be applied to all marketing contexts and Groonroos (1996)

ILLUSTRATION 9.8   **Media partnering to educate Africa about AIDS**

Partnerships are being used in communications for many purposes. For example, BBC Online reported in 2003 that the BBC, Viacom and the Henry J Kaiser Family Foundation had joined together to try to raise awareness and educate people in Africa about the danger of HIV/AIDS, by using a series of broadcasting innovations. Seventy per cent of the people suffering from HIV/AIDS come from sub-Saharan Africa.

The BBC World Service claims to be the world's leading international broadcaster, reaching audiences of 150 million listeners each week in 43 languages by using services via

the Internet and radio. It reaches 50 million in sub-Saharan Africa and in certain countries its reach is 30 per cent of the radio audience. Viacom is a global media company that includes MTV. It has huge audiences in Europe and the US. The Henry J Kaiser Family Foundation is a philanthropic organisation focused on health policy, public education and health and development in South Africa. Funding is from Kaiser, Viacom and other charitable organisations.

Question   What are the benefits of this partnership action for the BBC and Viacom?

FIGURE 9.6

The dimensions of transaction and relationship marketing

Transaction	Relationship
• Purchaser–marketer interaction	• Team-based, integrated interactions
• Features–benefits offer	• Value added
• Discrete interactions	• Continuous interactions
• Competitive	• Cooperation
• Winning new customers	• Retaining customers
• Top down directives	• Same level interactions
• Quality, value and service	• Customer satisfaction

FIGURE 9.7

Transactional marketing based on customer service

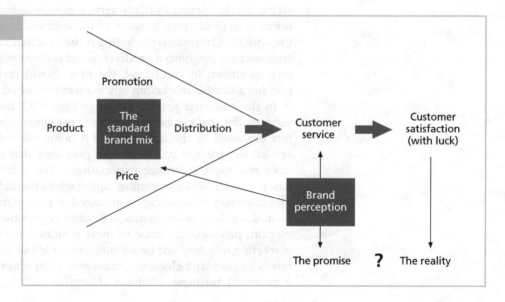

suggested that relationship marketing becomes more relevant when moving to the right on the continuum illustrated in Figure 9.9.

In practice relationship marketing has most relevance in business-to-business marketing. Both supplier and customer have something to gain from the relationship marketing concept which is based on the ideology of achieving a 'win-win' and mutual benefit, and the practical benefit of customer retention. As we shall consider later, consumers of fast moving consumer goods (fmcg) may not see much benefit from being involved in a relationship with a major company.

Relationship marketing strategy

Changing the focus from winning to retaining customers, therefore, has considerable implications for the marketing strategy in general and the communications strategy in particular. Instead of the communications being relatively simple, one-directional, with a single point of contact as they are in traditional marketing, shown in Figure 9.10, they become much more interactive and complex, with the communications being multi-level and multi-directional as shown in Figure 9.11. In Figure 9.10 the sales person from the marketing company and the buyer from the customer firm are the only points of contact, whereas in Figure 9.11 there are many points of contact between the firms. The salesperson's role then becomes one of key account management and the effective coordination of all the interactions that the firm has with the customer. An example might be the negotiation of price for products and services offered to an MNE customer that might purchase in many locations around the world. Achieving this level of integration in

---

FIGURE 9.8

Relationship marketing based on customer satisfaction

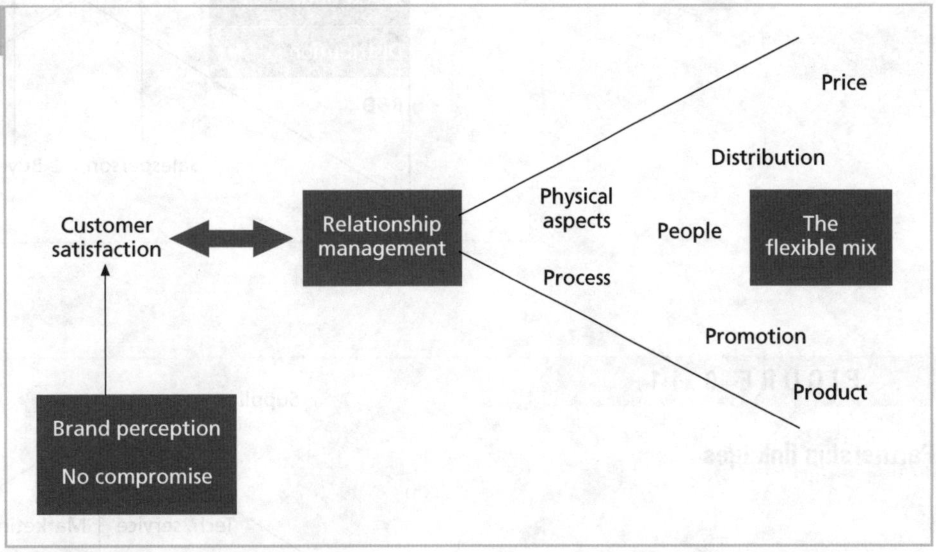

FIGURE 9.9

The transaction–relationship marketing continuum

Source: Adapted from Groonroos (1996)

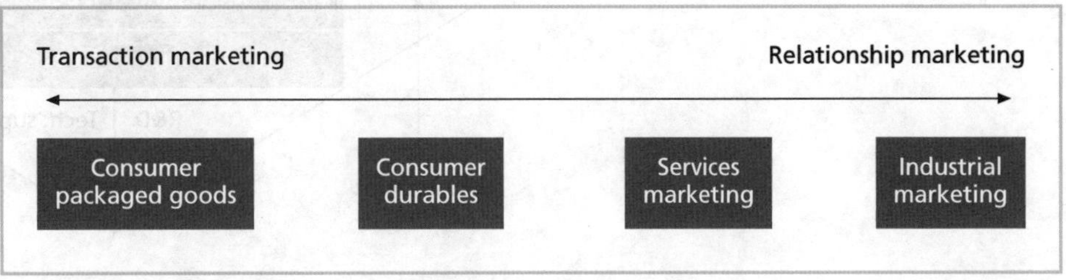

international marketing can be particularly challenging, given the different stakeholder perceptions of internal and external communication. It is at this point that effective internal marketing and a good company communication system are needed to ensure that all staff adopt a consistent approach, for example to customer service, no matter where they are in the world.

Throughout the firm the objectives of relationship marketing are to:

■ Maintain and build existing MNE customers by offering more tailored and cost effective business solutions

■ Use existing MNE relationships to obtain referral to business units and other supply chain members that are perhaps in different parts of the world and not currently customers

■ Increase the revenue from customers by offering solutions that are a combination of products and services

■ Reduce the operational and communications cost of servicing the customers.

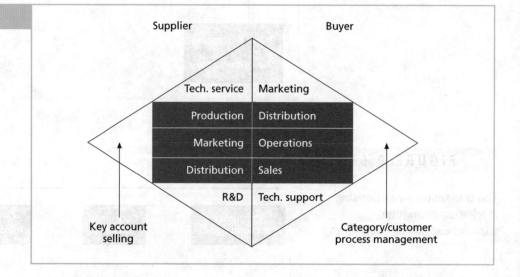

FIGURE 9.10

Traditional relationship

Supplier   Buyer

Tech. service   Tech. support

Production   Marketing

Marketing   Operations

Distribution   Sales

R&D   Distribution

                                Salesperson   Buyer

FIGURE 9.11

Partnership linkages

                        Supplier   Buyer

                    Tech. service | Marketing
                        Production | Distribution
                        Marketing | Operations
                       Distribution | Sales
                           R&D | Tech. support

Key account   Category/customer
selling   process management

The challenges of implementing a relationship marketing strategy on a worldwide basis

Inevitably relationship marketing requires a different philosophy in the firm and changes in the marketing and communications strategy objectives, budgets and performance measurements. Groonroos (1996) suggests that relationship marketing has two distinct dimensions: strategic relationship marketing and tactical relationship marketing.

The strategic issues of relationship marketing are identified as:

■ Defining the business as a service business
■ Recognising that the key competitive elements are concerned with offering a total service rather than simply selling a product
■ Managing the firm with a process management perspective and not from a functional perspective (the process of creating value for customers rather than managing operations and marketing purely for efficiency)
■ Developing partnerships and networks to be able to handle the whole service process, for example by making close contacts with well-known suppliers and intermediaries.

The tactical or operational issues are concerned with the following:

■ Seeking direct contacts with customers and other stakeholders
■ Building a database covering the necessary information about customers and other stakeholders
■ Developing a **customer relationship management (CRM)** system to manage the processes of customer information, product and service ordering and delivery and after-sales service.

Seeking direct contacts

The further implications of relationship marketing are that it is necessary to build relationships not only with the final customers but also with those other stakeholders that might influence the final purchase. Payne *et al.* (1995) suggest that typically there are up to six markets, shown in Figure 9.12, that must be targeted for relationship marketing to be used effectively. However, the power and influence of these markets vary considerably around the world and the relative importance of them depends upon the specific context of the firm's activity. In the tech-

---

FIGURE 9.12

Focusing on the six markets

- **Internal markets** The actions and beliefs of individuals and groups in the organisation determine the style and ethos of its marketing and operational activity.
- **Referral markets** Professionals and satisfied customers help the firm to build relationships by encouraging word of mouth recommendations.
- **Influence markets** Organisations and individuals influence the marketing environment in which the firm is operating using PR.
- **Employee markets** Recruiting and retaining good people makes the firm attractive not only to good potential employees, but also to help it gain respect in the wider community.
- **Supplier markets** Close and effective relationships improve quality, innovation, lower inventory and enable a faster time to market for the firm.
- **Customer markets** The main driver for relationship marketing is to satisfy customers by providing excellent service for external purchasers.

nology sector, for example, key influencers and high-profile lead customers may be located in a particular country market but their decisions might influence purchasing decisions in the whole industry.

Database development

The starting point is to build a database that will identify those customers with which it is worthwhile developing a relationship. The database can best be built from the company records of its interactions with customers and then supplemented with purchased lists of possible customers. By collecting details about the customer along with their purchasing behaviour, promotion and communications can be effectively targeted. Shrimp (2003) explains how recency, frequency and monetary value of purchases can be used to identify the priority customers, which in relationship marketing terms are likely to be the most valuable to the firm.

Marriott Hotels, with 3.5 million people on their honoured guest programme, claim to have the most popular incentive programme in the hotel industry. Bonus points are awarded and discounts or free gifts are offered to the best customers. The air miles programme in which frequent flyers collect points until they have enough for a free flight is, perhaps, one of the best known loyalty programmes. Frequent flyer programmes offer customers high perceived added value but are based on the low additional cost of carrying extra passengers in what would otherwise be empty seats. Customer information stored on a firm's database can be extremely useful not only for giving high added value service to customers but also for more precise targeting. General Motors have developed a database to identify and accurately target their most loyal and creditworthy customers enabling them to offer generous financial rebates for card users. Jaya Jusco is one of the main shopping centres in Malaysia. It uses loyalty cards not only to retain customers but also to help its Japanese parent Jusco to adapt and improve its services for the Malaysian market.

Customer relationship management

International consumer markets are characterised by their sheer size and relative anonymity of their customers. Even small retailers cannot possibly know their customers' individual behaviour and attitudes, whereas an industrial marketer with only a few customers possibly can. As we have discussed in the section on databases, technology has been developed to try to manage the vast amounts of information. Customer relationship management (CRM) is effectively computer software coupled with defined management processes and procedures to enable staff throughout organisations to capture and use information about their customers to maintain and build relationships. Companies such as Siebel (US) have built their business around such concepts.

However, these systems are often a quick fix to try to manage vast amounts of data and they make broad generalisations about customer segments and are often too insensitive to different consumer cultures and concerns. Indeed, O'Malley (2003) suggests that often the technology is used, but not understood, for a process of customer management that staff are unfamiliar with. Too often the CRM systems are driven by the IT requirements and are therefore technology driven. As a consequence they may track and respond to behaviour but fail to take into account the differing customer attitudes, which are at the heart of international marketing. Too often CRM is not adopted on an organisation-wide basis and instead is adopted by individual departments for very specific reasons. It also gets modified because of the need to interface it with existing legacy systems and so becomes fragmented and, rather than reducing cost, actually increases it. The introduction of CRM leads to raised expectations of service levels amongst customers and staff and if this is not delivered then CRM can have a detrimental effect on the business.

O'Malley suggests that improving customer relationships requires a systematic approach:

■ Evaluate the nature of existing relationships with all stakeholders.

■ Consider what level of relationship is necessary and appropriate, given the specific business context, product and service and resources available.

■ Develop the strategy, taking into account the need for staff development, the necessary changes to organisation systems, such as customer service and billing, and the impact on marketing strategies, such as advertising or direct marketing.

■ Assess the need for additional technology to support CRM.

■ Calculate the costs to implement the strategy.

The opportunities for relationship marketing to offer benefits are increasing because of improvements in communications, IT and increased cross-border purchasing. However, Christy *et al*. (1996) suggest that the successful establishment of relationship marketing depends on the extent to which each player understands the potential rewards and also the reciprocal duties necessary to make it work. Moreover, Fournier *et al*. (1998) emphasise that the consumer is not necessarily a willing participant in the relationship mission, and unless this is recognised, relationship marketing will prove to be of limited value. Indeed the question must be asked whether the majority of consumers will derive any benefit from a relationship with a MNE – the benefits will be mainly with the firm.

For relatively low purchase price items there is a danger that the costs to the firm of building customer loyalty might outweigh the costs of a more traditional approach to marketing products and services. It is difficult to measure the relative merits of short-term costs against longer-term revenues and few companies are willing to take a long-term view based upon their assumptions of what might happen in the future.

In practice the methods of relationship marketing in the consumer markets are diverging from relationship marketing in the business sector. In consumer markets relationship marketing will become more concerned with making one-to-one connections with customers through interactivity and promoting and placing products and services in the appropriate media at just the right moment. Business relationship marketing is leading to ever-closer relationships and partnerships for essential supply chain supplies but also more transient purchasing relationships for commodity items, and this is discussed in Chapter 12.

SUMMARY

- External international marketing communications are driven by the need for a consistent corporate identity, the promotion and differentiation of products and services, and marketing to build long-term customer relationships.

- Firms also need to focus on internal and interactive communications and ensure that staff in remote locations deliver consistent and integrated international marketing communications.

- A consistent corporate identity should communicate an instantly recognisable identity worldwide. It should be distinctive and differentiate the firm from other firms in the sector.

- There are benefits to the firm of standardising the promotion processes and programmes, wherever possible, but communications are extremely sensitive to local culture and conditions and, without attention to detail, they can be the source of many problems for firms offering their products and services throughout the world.

- Customer perceptions can be damaged by poor communications management within the firm and by external factors too. The international firm must concentrate on communicating consistency in its image, standards and values to a diverse range of stakeholders as well as making its direct appeal to existing and potential customers.

- The communication tools must be used appropriately to suit the context of the markets being served, different customer needs and the firm's objectives. Media availability, cultural and legislation differences and the nature of the products and services being marketed will influence the communications strategy and choice of tools.

- Because of the high cost of winning and losing customers, firms must build relationships to retain their most valuable customers in the long term.

- Customers in future will want the traditional communications discussed in this chapter integrated with the enabling technologies, discussed in Chapter 12, to further develop interactive, one-to-one customer relationships.

KEYWORDS

communication adaptation	interactive marketing
communication standardisation	internal marketing
communications failure	product and service differentiation
communications mix	promotional mix
communications tools	push and pull strategies
corporate identity	relationship marketing
customer relationship management	transactions
external marketing	

CASE STUDY   Harley Davidson – rockers' idol

For four days in August 2003, 250 000 fans converged on Milwaukee, US, the birthplace of the star, to celebrate a 100th birthday. Similar events had been held, albeit on a smaller scale, all around the world. Surely no rock star had reached 100! No, the reason they were going to the party was to see a procession of 10 000 Harley Davidson motorcycles. Whereas other brands have customers and can claim to have built relationships, Harley Davidson goes further and has fans, or devotees, some of whom are so much in love with the brand that they have the name tattooed on their body. It is claimed that 45 per cent of Harley Davidson's customers have bought a Harley before and the only reason that many would defect from the brand would be death or bankruptcy. In its 100th year Harley was looking to sell 290 000 bikes, up by 10 per cent on 2002. It reported in 2002 a gross profit of US$1.4 bn on US$4 billion sales.

In the first 50 years Harley had steadily destroyed the local competition in the US but in the early 1960s Honda entered the market. Initially the tiny motorcycles were ridiculed but sales increased to provide Honda with a platform to launch larger bikes. By the 1970s Japanese competition had increased to the point where Harley had only 30 per cent share of its traditional US market. Harley had been a long-time exporter of products and, curiously, Japan had been one of the earliest markets following US occupation and the end of the war. However, faced with a deteriorating domestic market position Harley virtually abandoned its overseas markets. It was facing extinction but was saved in 1981 by a management buyout by 13 of its managers from the American conglomerate, AMF, which had little interest in motorcycles.

To get out of trouble the management team, perhaps surprisingly, focused not on cutting costs, staff and dealers, but instead concentrated on making the product better by creating customer value. They created Harley Owners' Group to encourage customer loyalty. It has 800 000 members worldwide, who spend holidays and weekends together, sometimes with up to 25 000 riders at a time. In markets such as the US, Australia, Japan, Spain and Denmark, Harley has high market share and focuses on advertising widely to find new potential owners. In the rest of Europe there is a fiercely competitive heavyweight bike sector (over 650 cc) and Harley's share is relatively small. The market is dominated by Japanese competition (see Table 1).

Harley is generating less than 15 per cent of its sales from outside North America with only 8 per cent of its sales from Europe (see Table 2), even though Europe represents 35 per cent of the worldwide large motorcycle market.

In countries such as the UK, Harley sells only about 10 000 motorcycles per year and focuses on building profit,

Table 1   Market share of 650 cc plus motorcycle registrations

	North America	Europe	Asia-Pacific
Harley Davidson	46.4	6.6	21.3
BMW	2.5	15.1	7.3
Kawasaki	7.1	8.5	15.8
Yamaha	9.3	17.7	13.6
Suzuki	9.8	14.8	10.1
Honda	20.2	21.0	19.1
Other	4.6	16.2	12.8

Source: Harley Davidson

Table 2   Harley net revenue by region 2002

	US$000,000
US	3416
Europe	337
Japan	143
Canada	121
Other countries	72
Total	4091

Source: Harley Davidson

not volume. Its promotion is more concerned with developing the owners' groups and promoting in specialist magazines, rather than widespread advertising. It has, however, shown its commitment to developing profitable business in Europe by opening a new headquarters in Oxford, UK.

Harley's customers

Harley concentrates on building bikes to meet the expectations of its niche market. Its customers have moved away from being 'metal bikers' towards a new stereotype – the affluent, professional, rather elderly rocker, such as lawyers, doctors and captains of industry. The median age of Harley riders is 45.6 years and median income is US$78 300. In the decision to buy a Harley price is not a factor, but more important is whether the money would be better spent on a conservatory, swimming pool or a luxury cruise. Harley's appeal is based on the dream and legendary mystique of owning an American classic. Customers buy the dream of escaping work and the boredom of everyday life for the freedom of the road. To encourage those dreaming of becoming a wild child again Harley has opened a brand experience centre called Riders Edge In Wales, where visitors can ride a Harley, even if it is only for 100 metres, before (as Harley hope) going down to their local dealer to consider a purchase.

Brand stretching

One area where Harley Davidson has been less successful has been in brand stretching. The Harley wine cooler did not catch on and, after selling 6 million products per annum in the early years after the launch, sales of cosmetic products, made through a licensing partnership with L'Oréal, are now considerably down. Cosmetic products are still sold in France, Germany, Spain and Greece but have been withdrawn in the UK. The intention was to let younger potential bikers own some of the brand. More successful licensing agreements on biker gear, leisurewear and fashion ranges now account for 5 per cent of revenue and more recently Harley Davidson Financial Services have grown rapidly to contribute 12 per cent of company income.

Harley is a niche international marketer, very much associated with the American dream. It has one of the best-known brands in the world and yet is still a relatively small organisation with quite limited international marketing experience.

Questions

1 Carry out a marketing environmental analysis to determine the basis of Harley's success in developing relationships with its customers.

2 What are the major strategic issues Harley Davidson has to face in planning a three-year international development strategy?

3 Select either Europe or South East Asia (including Japan) as your chosen area for overseas development. Do not write about both. Having identified your chosen area, outline the options Harley Davidson might consider in developing a market entry strategy. Make a recommendation and justify it. Then explain (again in outline) how Harley Davidson might implement its strategy, including marketing mix considerations.

Robin Lowe, Sheffield Hallam University
Source: Adapted from Hiscock, J. '100 years on the road', *Marketing*, May 2003, and a CIM examination case study

DISCUSSION QUESTIONS

1 Communications are central to effective marketing planning. What are the key issues in planning, executing and controlling an international communications strategy?

2 Critically examine the case for using one advertising agency to create and implement an international advertising campaign.

3 What factors would constrain the use of standardised sales promotion campaigns for a multi-national enterprise in international markets?

4 Select an economic region. Identify the advantages and disadvantages of pan-regional advertising. How would you manage a pan-regional campaign for a product or service of your choice?

5 Select (1) a business-to-business and (2) a business-to-consumer purchasing situation. Explain the role of relationship marketing in each of these situations.

REFERENCES

Chan, A.K. and Huang, Y. (1997) 'Brand naming in China: a linguistic approach', *Marketing Intelligence and Planning*, 5 (15): 227–34.

Christy, R., Oliver, G. and Penn, J. (1996) 'Relationship marketing in consumer markets', *Journal of Marketing Management*, 12 (1–3).

Fannin, R.A. (1997) 'Top global marketers', *Advertising Age International*, November.

Fournier, S., Dobscha, S. and Divid, G.M. (1998) 'Preventing the premature death of relationship marketing', *Harvard Business Review*, January–February: 43–51.

Groonroos, C. (1996) 'Relationship marketing strategic and tactical implications', *Management Decision*, 34 (3).

Harding, J. (1997) 'Consumer revolution: the risks and rewards of marketing western goods in China', *Financial Times*, 14 July.

Horovitz, J. (2000) 'Using information to bond customers', in Marchand, D. (ed.) *Competing With Information*, Wiley.

Howard (1997) 'Survey of European advertising expenditure 1980–1996', *International Journal of Advertising*, 17.

Hu, M.Y. and Griffith, D. (1997) 'Conceptualising the global marketplace: marketing strategy implications', *Marketing Intelligence and Planning*, 15 (3).

Koranteng, J. (1998) 'Reebok finds its second wind as it pursues global presence', *Advertising Age International*, January.

Kotler, P. (2002) *Marketing Management*, Prentice Hall.

Meenagham, T. (1995) 'The Volkswagen Beetle: the role of advertising in brand image development', *Journal of Product and Brand Management*, 4 (4).

Meenahan, T. (1991) 'Sponsorship: legitimising the medium european', *Journal of Marketing*, 25 (11).

Neelankavil, J.P., Mummalaneni, V. and Sessions, D. (1996) 'Use of foreign language and models in print advertisements in East Asian countries: a logit modelling approach', *European Journal of Management*, 29 (4): 24–38.

O'Malley, L. (2003) 'Relationship marketing', in Hart, S. *Marketing Changes*, Thomson Learning.

Payne, A., Christopher, M., Clark, M. and Peck, H. (1995) *Relationship Marketing for Competitive Advantage*, Butterworth-Heinnemann.

Read, D. (1997) 'Country Practice', *Marketing Week*, 3 July.

Schmitt, B.H. and Pan, Y. (1994) 'Managing corporate and brand identities in the Asia Pacific Region', *Californian Business Review*, Summer.

Shannon, J. (1997) 'TV focuses on local targeting', *Marketing Week*, 21 August.

Shrimp, T.A. (2003) *Advertising, Promotion*, 6th edn, Thomson South-Western.

Siu, W. and Au, A.K. (1997) 'Women in advertising: a comparison of television advertisements in China and Singapore', *Marketing Intelligence and Planning*, 15 (5).

Smith, A. (1998) 'Ads across the oceans', *Financial Times*, 24 April.

Smith, P., Berry, C. and Pulford, A. (1997) *Strategic Marketing Communications*, Kogan Page.

Wentz, H. (1997) 'A single Europe: reality or mirage', *Advertising Age International*, May.

Wilson, R. and Gilligan, C. (1997) *Strategic Marketing Management: Planning, Implementation and Control*, Butterworth-Heinemann.

Zhang, Y. and Neelankavil, J.P. (1997) 'The influence of culture on advertising effectiveness in China and the USA: a cross cultural study', *European Journal of Management*, 31 (2): 134–49.

THE MANAGEMENT OF INTERNATIONAL DISTRIBUTION AND LOGISTICS

Introduction

In Chapter 7, we examined strategies for international expansion and the options available for firms entering foreign markets. In this chapter we will build on the issues discussed in Chapter 7 but focus on managing the distribution and logistics within foreign markets.

The management of foreign channels of distribution is a key area in a firm's efforts to gain competitive advantage. As products become more standardised across the world, the ability to compete on customer service becomes more vital. In order to be effective in this area, a firm must have a well-managed **integrated supply chain** within foreign markets and across international boundaries.

In this chapter, we will examine the strategic issues in managing distribution channels and discuss the issues of selecting intermediaries and how to build long-term effective relationships in international markets. We will also examine the developments in retailing and the differences in retailing across markets at different levels of economic development.

Finally, we will examine the logistics of physically moving goods across national boundaries and the importance of efficient distribution management to minimise costs in international markets.

Learning objectives

After reading this chapter you should be able to:

- Strategically evaluate potential foreign distribution options for a given situation
- Discuss the complexities of efficiently managing intermediaries in an international marketing context
- Appreciate the difference in retailing infrastructures across the globe
- Advise and recommend potential solutions to developing a logistics strategy in foreign markets
- Understand the export documentation process

THE CHALLENGES IN MANAGING AN INTERNATIONAL DISTRIBUTION STRATEGY

Distribution channels are the means by which goods are distributed from the manufacturer to the end user. Some companies own their own means of distribution, some companies only deal directly with the most important customers but many companies rely on other companies to perform distribution services for them. These services include:

- the purchase of goods
- the assembly of an attractive assortment of goods
- holding stocks or inventory
- promoting the sale of goods to the end customer
- the physical movement of goods.

In international marketing, companies usually take advantage of a wide number of different organisations to facilitate the distribution of their products. The large number is explained by considerable differences between countries both in their distribution systems and in the expected level of product sales. The physical movement of goods usually includes several modes of transport – for example, by road to a port, by boat to the country of destination and by road to the customer's premises. The selection of the appropriate distribution strategy is a significant decision. Whilst the marketing mix decisions of product and marketing communications are often more glamorous, they are usually dependent upon the chosen distribution channel. The actual distribution channel decision is a fundamental decision as it affects all aspects of the international marketing strategy.

The key objective in building an effective distribution strategy is to build a supply chain to your markets that is, as Kotler (2003) said, 'a planned and professionally managed vertically integrated marketing system that incorporates both the needs of the manufacturer and the distributors'.

To achieve this across international markets is a daunting task and will mean the international marketing manager has to meet a number of important challenges in order to ensure they develop a distribution strategy which delivers the effective distribution of products and services across international markets. The major areas they will need to consider are as follows:

- *Selection of foreign country intermediaries.* Should the firm use indirect or direct channels? What type of intermediaries will best serve their needs in the marketplace?

- *How to build a relationship with intermediaries.* The management and motivation of intermediaries in foreign country markets is especially important to firms endeavouring to build a long-term presence, competing on offering quality services.

- *How to deal with the varying types of retailing infrastructure across international markets.* Achieving a coordinated strategy across markets where retailing is at varying stages of development and the impact of the growth of retailers themselves globalising are important considerations in the distribution strategies of firms competing in consumer goods markets.

- *How to maximise new and innovative forms of distribution*, particularly opportunities arising through the Internet and electronic forms of distribution.

■ *How to manage the logistics of physically distributing products across foreign markets*. Firms need to evaluate the options available and develop a well-managed logistics system.

In the following sections of the chapter, we will examine the issues in each of these areas of international distribution and logistics.

SELECTING FOREIGN COUNTRY MARKET INTERMEDIARIES

A distribution decision is a long-term decision, as once established it can be difficult to extract a company from existing agreements. This means that channels chosen have to be appropriate for today and flexible enough to adapt to long-term market developments.

In some instances, difficulties may arise because of legal contracts as in the case of the termination of an agency; in other situations they result from relationships that need to be initiated and then nurtured. For example, the development of sales through wholesalers and distributors might be substantially influenced by the past trading pattern and the expectation of future profitable sales. Therefore a long-term relationship needs to be developed before a firm is willing to invest significantly in an intermediary.

The long-term nature of distribution decisions forces a careful analysis of future developments in the distribution channel. If new forms of distribution are emerging (for example, mass merchandise retailing or Internet retailing), this has to be considered early in the planning stage of the distribution channel.

Another important challenge is the comparative inexperience of managers in the channel selection process in international markets. In domestic marketing, most marketing managers develop marketing plans which will usually be implemented within the existing arrangement of the company's distribution channels. This is quite a different proposition to the pioneering process of establishing a distribution channel in the first place and then achieving a well-supported availability through channel members in different country markets.

Furthermore, if **foreign market channels** are being managed from the home market, there maybe preconceived notions and preferences that home market systems can operate elsewhere. Because they are unfamiliar with the market, managers may underestimate the barriers to entry erected by local competitors and even government regulations. For instance, in both France and Japan there are restrictive laws which inhibit the growth of large retailers. In Japan no one can open a store larger than 5382 square feet without permission from the community store owners. Thus it can take eight to ten years for a store to win approval.

Indirect and direct channels

One of the first decisions to make in selecting intermediaries for international markets is, should the product be distributed indirectly? In other words, using outside sales agents and distributors in the country or should the product be distributed directly, using the company's sales force, company-owned distribution channel or other intermediaries in a foreign country? The former option is an independent channel which is non-integrated and provides very little or no control over its international distribution and affords virtually no links with the end users. On the other hand, direct distribution, which is an integrated channel, generally affords the manufacturer more control and, at the same time, brings responsibility, commitment and attendant risks. As we have discussed, distribution decisions are difficult to change and so it is important for firms to consider the alternatives available and the differing degrees of commitment and risk, evaluate the alternatives and select the most appropriate type of distribution.

Integrated (direct) channels of distribution are seen to be beneficial when a firm's marketing strategy requires a high level of service before or after the sale. Integrated channels will be more helpful than independent channels in ensuring that high levels of customer service will be achieved.

Indirect channels on the other hand require less investment in terms of both money and management time. Indirect channels also are seen to be beneficial in overcoming freight rate, negotiating disadvantages, lowering the cost of exporting and allowing higher margins and profits for the manufacturer. An independent channel, therefore, allows the international firm to tap the benefits of a distribution specialist within a foreign market such as economies of scale and pooling the demand for the distribution services of several manufacturers.

The advantages and disadvantages of indirect exporting were discussed in Chapter 7. In this section we will focus on issues facing firms who have made the decision to involve themselves with intermediaries in foreign country markets, either through the use of agents or distributors or using their own company-owned sales force. These intermediaries offer a wide range of services which are as follows:

- **Export distributors** – usually perform a variety of functions including: stock inventories, handling promotion, extending customer credit, processing orders, arranging shipping, product maintenance and repair.

- **Export agents** – responsibilities often include: buyer/seller introductions, host market information, trade fair exhibitions, general promotional activities.

- **Cooperative organisations** – carry on exporting activities on behalf of several producers and are partly under their administrative control (often used by producers of primary products – e.g. bananas, coffee, sugar).

A company-owned sales force may be one of three types:

1 **Travelling export sales representatives.** The company can begin by sending home-based sales people abroad to gather important information, to make the necessary customer contacts and to conduct the negotiating and selling process.

2 **Domestic-based export department or division.** An export sales manager carries on the actual selling and draws on market assistance as needed. It might evolve into a self-contained export department performing all the activities in export and operating as a profit centre.

3 **Foreign-based sales branch or subsidiary.** A foreign-based sales branch allows the company to achieve greater presence and programme control in the foreign market. The sales branch handles sales and distribution and may also handle warehousing and promotion. It often serves as a display centre and customer service centre as well.

The choices available to a firm may well be determined by whether they are operating in the business-to-business or consumer goods sector. Figure 10.1 illustrates the choices for a manufacturer of business goods.

The main channels for business goods, therefore, tend to be agents, distributors and companies' wholly owned sales force. The main distribution channels for consumer goods are shown in Figure 10.2.

Over the past few years there have been considerable developments in retailing across national boundaries. In a later section in this chapter, we will examine these trends and other new forms of retailing. First, however, we will look at the factors to consider in selecting channels of distribution and then building effective relationships with intermediaries.

Channel selection

In selecting appropriate channel intermediaries, a firm has to consider many factors. Czinkota and Ronkainen (2004) suggested the *11c model* to explain the factors a firm should consider in their selection process. The eleven elements to consider are:

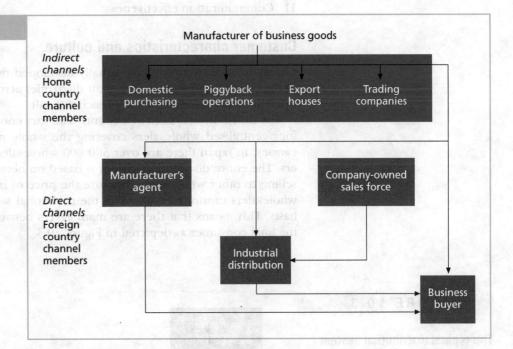

FIGURE 10.1

Distribution channels for business goods

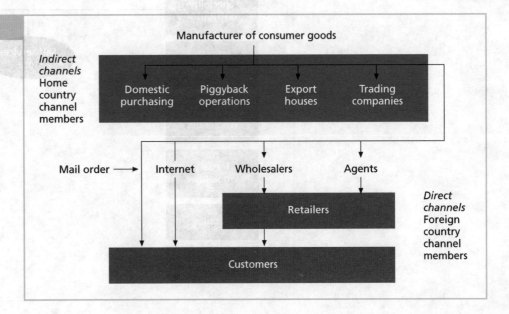

FIGURE 10.2

Distribution channels for consumer goods

1 Customer characteristics
2 Culture
3 Competition
4 Company objectives
5 Character of the market
6 Cost
7 Capital required
8 Coverage needed
9 Control issues
10 Continuity provided
11 Communication effectiveness

Customer characteristics and culture

Channels of distribution have usually developed through the cultural traditions of the country and so there are great disparities across nations, making the development of any standardised approach difficult.

The distribution system of a country can vary enormously. In Finland, there are four centralised wholesalers covering the whole market for most product categories. In Japan there are over 300 000 wholesalers and over 1.6 million retailers. The entire distribution system is based on networks with lots of wholesalers selling to other wholesalers. Because the price of land is so high in Japan, many wholesalers cannot carry stock in the traditional sense, so may order on a daily basis. This means that there are many layers between the foreign company and the final consumer as depicted in Figure 10.3.

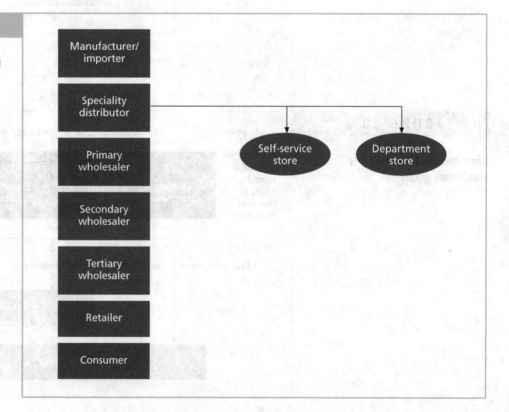

FIGURE 10.3

The typical distribution system in Japan

The Japanese system centres on distributor linkages to *dainyo* manufacturers, where the distributor accepts a subservient social status in return for economic security. From this interaction emerges the *ryatsu-keiretsu*, a political hierarchy in which units are arrayed in hierarchical layers and power resides at the 'commanding heights' of large *keiretsu*.

Distributors at 'lower' layers in the vertical structure are tied to the *keiretsu* system by bonds of loyalty, mutual obligation, trust and power that extend throughout existing distribution structures. Whilst this arrangement guarantees members some degree of security it also deprives them of economic freedom. Thus, distributors that choose to deal with firms outside of the established group risk severing their ties with the group.

Whilst distributors lack the freedom to transact with whomever they wish, they are also relieved of many costs associated with being independent – for example, smaller distributors in the system need not shoulder the risk of carrying inventories of products that will not sell and can depend on reliable delivery and financial help where necessary. A number of companies have tried to circumvent the system as can be seen in Illustration 10.1

Thus the characteristics of the customer and the cultural traditions of the country have a major impact on the choices available to a firm. A Belgian shopper may buy groceries from huge hypermarkets, concentrating on purchases which have long shelf lives and are easy to store in their spacious apartments and houses. The Japanese customers on the other hand can be characterised by their logistical imperatives, as confined living space makes storage of goods very difficult. Therefore, customers make frequent visits to shops and rely on stores to keep their inventories. Moreover, Japan's narrow roads and lack of parking space (except for suburbs) predispose most of its population to do its shopping on foot.

Company objectives and competitive activity

The channel choice will also be determined by the company's objectives and what the firm's competitors are doing in a particular market. The distribution policy is part of a firm's international direction. Therefore, the distribution system developed will depend on the company's objective, i.e. whether their strategic objective is long term or short term and how quickly they need to realise their investment.

Most firms operating in international markets will endeavour to maintain a cost-effective balance between direct and indirect channels of distribution. Firms will use **direct channels**, perhaps their own sales force, in foreign country

---

ILLUSTRATION 10.1 **Changing the Japanese distribution system**

Japan has traditionally had a multi-tiered distribution system but marketers are now looking to innovative new methods which avoid the existing channels. Discounters are a relatively new breed of retailer that operate outside of the *ryatsu-keiretsu* hierarchy. Toys 'R' Us, the American toy retailing giant, was the first large US discount store to open in Japan. The company teamed up with McDonald's Japan to operate toy stores and fast food outlets on the same site. By purchasing directly from manufacturers with low-cost,

direct supply contracts, the multiple layers of wholesalers are eliminated. The inflow of foreign retailers is being aided by the Japanese government's push for deregulation in retail markets, but is proving to be a huge threat to traditional, small family-owned stores which have previously been protected by the rigid relationships in the distribution system.

Question What can companies do to overcome such rigid distribution systems in foreign countries?

markets where their company's objective is to deliver high value solutions to buying problems in order to maximise customer satisfaction. Thus, the firm is practising 'interaction' marketing as opposed to 'transaction' marketing. A firm whose objective is to build long-term, stable relationships with its foreign customers will have quite different objectives in the building of relationships throughout the supply chain than a firm with relatively short-term objectives in foreign country markets who purely wishes to complete the transaction before moving on to the next customer.

Character of the market

The characteristics of the market will also determine the choice available. Products often are introduced later into international markets than to the home domestic market; the company's image and awareness is normally lower, in many cases much lower, than in the domestic market and the market share attainable in the market is lower, at least initially. This makes it a much less profitable business proposition for distribution channel intermediaries. Furthermore, distribution channels are already being used by other companies who will have built up relationships with the intermediaries. This provides less space and opportunity for firms newly entering the market.

Developing countries are characterised by distribution systems consisting of a myriad of intermediaries and retail outlets. Such fragmentation results in cost inefficiencies as large volumes of product cannot be centralised and moved quickly from manufacturers to wholesalers to retailers.

Fragmented and circuitous channels also diminish possible competitive advantage by reducing the abilities of firms to get their products and services quickly and efficiently to masses of buyers. This is particularly the case for time-sensitive products. For example, overnight package couriers in some markets have failed in some cases to live up to delivery promises due to flight cancellations, poor road conditions and insufficient phone lines (Nakata and Sivakumar 1997).

Often in emerging markets, the problems of fragmented distribution are compounded by legal restrictions as to which channels of distribution can be used by foreign imported products.

The World Trade Organisation is working towards the opening up of participation in distribution systems by foreign firms in a number of countries. Recently, Indonesia has eased restrictions as is discussed in Illustration 10.2.

ILLUSTRATION 10.2   Jakarta eases distribution restrictions

In 1998, Indonesia cut trade tariffs and opened up its distribution and wholesale sector for foreign investors. Foreign companies will now be allowed to set up their own distribution and wholesale companies and will be allowed to retail as well.

The ban on foreign participation in distribution, set up to defend traditional marketplaces and small shop owners, has kept out many producers of consumer goods and limited profits of existing projects.

Previously foreign companies were forced to rely on well-connected but often inefficient wholesale and retail agents, often little more than front companies, to market their goods.

Hopefully, this will make it much easier for international marketers to develop more sophisticated distribution strategies in this emerging market.

Question Explore what distribution strategies are suitable for countries such as Indonesia for foreign companies entering the market.

Source: Adapted from Thoener, S. (1999) *Financial Times*, 4 November

Capital required and costings

In assessing the financial implications of channel selection, a firm needs to assess the relative cost of each channel, the consequences on cash flow and the capital required.

The relative costs of each channel. It is generally considered that it may be cheaper to use agents than setting up a firm's own sales force in international markets. However, the firm has little control and may have little commitment from the agent. Also, if the company has long-term objectives in the market, then as sales develop the use of agents may be more expensive than employing the company's own sales force. A break-even analysis is necessary to evaluate the relative cost of each channel alternative over time.

Consequences on cashflow. If a firm uses wholesalers or distributors then traditionally they take ownership of the goods and the risks. This has a positive impact on cash flow.

If the firm wishes to circumvent such channels and deal direct with the retailer or even the consumer, it means they have to be prepared to take on some of the traditional wholesaler services e.g. offering of credit, breaking bulk, small orders. This means the firm will have capital and resources tied up in managing the distribution chain rather than developing the market.

Capital required. Direct distribution systems need capital injected to establish them. Non-recurring capital costs, as well as the recurring running costs when evaluating expected return in the long term, have to be taken into account.

A company also needs to evaluate whether it can raise the finance locally or whether borrowing restrictions are placed on foreign companies, what grants are available and what the regulations on earnings capital repatriation will be.

The coverage needed

Required coverage will also be a determining factor. In some markets, to get 100 per cent coverage of a market, the costs of using the company's own sales force may be too high and so indirect channels are more appropriate, especially in countries which are characterised by large rural populations. However, firms who rely on sparse retail outlets can maximise the opportunities that fragmented distribution channels afford. Avon has recruited and groomed armies of sales representatives to sell its cosmetics directly to millions in all reaches of Brazil, Mexico, Poland, China and Argentina. Altogether Avon is successfully operating in 26 emerging economies and targeting more (e.g. India, South Africa, Russia and Vietnam).

Control, continuity and communication

If a firm is building an international competitive advantage in providing a quality service throughout the world then channels that enable the firm to achieve rapid response in foreign markets will be important as will the development of a distribution system which gives them total control in the marketplace and effective direct communication to their customer.

It is the drive to achieve high levels of quality of service that, to some extent, has led to the breakdown of conventional barriers between manufacturers, agents, distributors and retailers, as firms strive to develop effective vertical marketing systems. To achieve this, some manufacturers have bought themselves into retailing and other parts of the supply chain, whilst others, such as Benetton, have pursued similar results by franchising.

Such firms will be selecting intermediaries which will enable them to be solution-oriented service providers operating on high margins across a multitude of international markets.

The selection and contracting process

Having evaluated the criteria discussed above, a firm must select intermediaries capable of helping the firm achieve its goals and objectives. The intermediaries chosen must provide the geographic coverage needed and the services required in the particular international market(s). It is often desirable to select intermediaries that are native to the country where they will be doing business as this will enhance their ability to build and maintain customer relationships.

The selection process for channel members will be based upon an assessment of their sales volume potential, geographic and customer coverage, financial strength (which will be checked through credit rating services and references), managerial capabilities and the size and quality of the sales force and any marketing communications services and the nature and reputation of the business. In some countries, religious or ethnic differences might make an agent suitable for part of the market coverage but unsuitable in another. This can result in more channel members being required to give an adequate market coverage.

Before final contractual arrangements are made, it is thought wise to make personal visits to the prospective channel member. The long-term commitment involved in distribution channels can become particularly difficult if the contract between the company and the channel member is not carefully drafted. It is normal to prescribe a time limit and a minimum sales level to be achieved in addition to the particular responsibilities for each party. If this is not carried out satisfactorily, the company may be stuck with a weak performer that either cannot be removed or is very costly to buy out from their contract. The difficulties that can arise when contracts in international markets are interpreted differently by the parties concerned are illustrated in the Merry case at the end of the chapter.

BUILDING RELATIONSHIPS IN FOREIGN MARKET CHANNELS

Management of sales activities and business relationships across international boundaries is a particularly complex and often overwhelming task. The combination of diverse languages, dissimilar cultural heritages and remote geographic locations can create strong barriers to building and maintaining effective **buyer–seller relationships**. Further, in international settings, communications are often complicated by a lack of trust – a critical dimension in any business relationship. Non-verbal cues, product origin biases, sales force nationality issues and differences in inter-cultural negotiation styles add even more complexity to the international business environment. Added to the traditional responsibilities of a sales manager, these factors make managing international relationships in distribution channels a unique and challenging task. Thus it is crucial for firms and their sales managers to both understand and be able to work within various international markets throughout the world (Lewin and Johnston 1997).

Motivating international marketing intermediaries

International marketing intermediaries can pick and choose the products they will promote to their customers. Therefore, they need to be motivated to emphasise the firm's products. But as difficult as it is for manufacturers to motivate their domestic distributors or dealers, it is even more difficult in the international arena. The environment, culture and customs affecting seller–intermediary relationships can be complicating factors for the uninitiated.

Motivation, whether in the context of domestic or international channels, is the process through which the manufacturer seeks to gain the support of the marketing intermediary in carrying out the manufacturer's marketing objectives. Three basic elements are involved in this process (Rosenbloom 1999):

1 finding out the needs and problems of marketing intermediaries
2 offering support that is consistent with their needs and problems
3 building continuing relationships.

First, the needs and problems of international marketing intermediaries can be dramatically different from those at home. One of the most common differences is in the size of the intermediary. This is particularly true in some of the less-developed countries in Asia, Africa, Latin America and Eastern Europe. However, it also holds even for some highly developed countries such as Japan and Italy. Many of these dealers have little desire to grow larger. Thus, they may not aggressively promote a manufacturer's product.

Second, the specific support programme provided by the manufacturer to its international intermediaries should be based on a careful analysis of their needs and problems. Factors to be included are:

■ the adequacy of the profit margins available
■ the guarantee of exclusive territories
■ the adequacy and availability of advertising assistance
■ the offer of needed financial assistance.

In light of the cost structures faced by many foreign distributors and dealers, the need to provide them with good margin potentials on the foreign products they handle is even more important. Doing so, however, may force manufacturers to change their ideas of what constitutes a 'fair' or 'reasonable' margin for foreign distributors.

Territorial protection or even the guarantee of exclusive territories sought by many distributors in the domestic market can be even more desirable in foreign markets. Overseas distributors, many of whom have quite limited financial resources, will not want to assume the risk of handling and promoting the manufacturer's product line if other distributors will be competing in the same territory for the same customers.

Advertising assistance for foreign distributors and dealers is another vital form of support. A foreign manufacturer, especially a large one, can have an advantage over indigenous firms in providing advertising support because of its often greater financial resources and experience in the use of advertising. For example, firms such as Johnson Wax (with extensive distribution in Europe) and 3M (in Asia) have used their considerable resources and advertising expertise to support distributors to very good advantage in those markets.

Financial assistance in countries where intermediaries are small and fragmented is essential. Levi-Strauss found in Russia they needed to give a six month credit period to persuade intermediaries to stock their products. Their usual credit period was 30 to 60 days. Such constraints do not mean that manufacturers selling through international intermediaries cannot build strong relationships with them; it is certainly possible to do so. However, the approach used may have to be quite different from that taken with domestic intermediaries. For example, for thousands of years agents and distributors in the Middle East have been influenced by bazaar trading. Marketing to them means to 'sit on the product' and wait for the customer to come to them. A common attitude amongst merchants is that they do not sell, but people buy. The 'carrot and stick' philosophy of motivating distributors in the US and Europe fails in the Middle East.

Financial incentives may not motivate them to push the product aggressively if the process is complex and long.

It is important to keep in regular contact with intermediaries. A consistent flow of all relevant types of communications will stimulate interest and sales performance. The cultural interface between the company and the channel member is the essence of corporate rapport. Business people from low context cultures may be thought to be insensitive and disrespectful by agents in high context culture countries. The problem can be compounded if sales performance is discussed too personally. According to Usunier (2000), precise measurement of sales people's performance, for example of the agent or the distributors, may be considered as almost evil in some countries. In South East Asia the ethic of non-confrontation clearly clashes with an objective to review performance. Various types of motivation need to be considered. In some cultures, intrinsic and group-related rewards work best. In the US, a country in which individualism and rationalism are the foundations of its society, individual and extrinsic rewards work best.

Controlling intermediaries in international markets

The process of control is difficult. Control problems are substantially reduced if channel members are selected carefully, have appropriately drafted contracts which have been mutually understood and agreed and are motivated in a culturally empathetic way.

Control attempts are often exercised through other companies and sometimes through several layers of distribution intermediaries. Control should be sought through the development of written plans with clearly expressed performance objectives. These performance objectives would include some of the following: sales turnover per year, number of accounts, market share, growth rate, introduction of new products, price charged and marketing communications support.

ILLUSTRATION 10.3   Kodak's distribution strategy in China

As discussed in Illustration 6.6, in 1998 Kodak invested US$1.1 billion to take over and modernise three loss-making Chinese film and photographic product companies and will pay US$380 million for the assets. The deal not only trounces Fuji, it sets a new pattern in big foreign involvement in China.

Kodak's executive vice-president reckons the main assets of value he has bought are people, warehouses, a distribution system and land.

Beyond the sheer size of the market, Kodak is keen on China because it is the one place in the world where it is clearly trouncing Fuji. By manufacturing and distributing locally, Kodak hopes to turn the battle into a rout. As part of the deal, no other foreign film company will be allowed to manufacture in China for four years.

Three years ago China was solid Fuji territory. The Japanese film maker had been an early and energetic entrant to the market. Its green banners could be seen above photo shops everywhere. But Kodak attacked with force.

Offering help including 'marketing assistance' of US$2000 or more to corner shops in exchange for becoming a Kodak Express and evicting competing film brands, Kodak expanded its Chinese sales by 30 per cent a year. They now amount to 7 per cent of the firm's global business.

Last year, Kodak says it overtook Fuji to become the market leader in China for film and film products. (Fuji claims it still has a lead of a few percentage points for film itself.) Kodak now has 3700 stores to Fuji's 2000. Between them the two companies have more than 90 per cent of the US$800 million market, the world's third largest.

Question Evaluate the effectiveness of Kodak's distribution strategy as a means of gaining a competitive advantage over other potential foreign investors.

Source: Adapted from *The Economist* (1998) 'Kodak in China', 28 March

Control should be exercised through a regular report programme and periodic personal meetings.

Evaluation of performance and control against agreed plans has to be interpreted against the changing environment. In some situations, economic recession or fierce competition activity prevent the possibility of objectives being met. However, if poor performance is established, the contract between the company and the channel member will have to be reconsidered and, perhaps, terminated. In an age in which relationship marketing is becoming more important in the Western world, the long-term building of suitable distribution relationships provides something of the Eastern flavour of obligation and working together.

Channel updating

In managing distribution channels, firms need to ensure that as they increase their involvement in the market, they are able to adapt and update their channel strategy accordingly. Thus, the management monitoring and control mechanisms a firm puts in place should give them the ability to develop their presence in the marketplace. In China, Kodak (see Illustration 10.3) ensured this capability was in place in their early negotiations.

Developing a company-owned international salesforce

Firms with expansion plans and an interest in becoming more involved in global markets will eventually take control of implementing their own marketing strategies and establish and manage their own international salesforce. Generally, the firms begin to gradually move from indirect exporting to direct exporting via marketing intermediaries to a company-owned sales force (Kotler 2003). The company can do this in several ways, including: travelling export sales reps, domestic-based export department or division and foreign-based sales branch or subsidiary.

The advantages of using a company-owned sales force include:

- it provides far greater control over the sales and marketing effort since the sales force is now directly employed by the company
- it facilitates formation of closer manufacturer–customer relationships
- once established, the company-owned sales force can be helpful in identifying and exploiting new international marketing opportunities

The disadvantages of developing a company-owned sales force include:

- a relatively larger resource commitment
- somewhat higher exit costs should the firm decide to no longer serve a particular market
- increased exposure to unexpected changes in the political/social environment of the host country.

One common strategy is to begin export operations by establishing a domestic-based export department and/or using home-based travelling salespeople. Then, as sales reach a certain volume in the new market, the decision is made to set up a foreign-based sales branch or subsidiary in the country.

The new unit may be strictly a marketing/sales arm or may also involve a production or warehouse facility. In either event, the firm must make a commitment of resources to develop its own direct sales force to sell the firm's offerings and build relationships with the firm's customers in that market.

It may well be that a firm uses its own sales force for key accounts and agents and distributors for small accounts. Equally, its own sales force may work in conjunction with international intermediaries, building links directly with customers but always with and through the intermediaries. This has the advantage of enabling the firm to build relationships with the customer and the intermediaries whilst not having to make the capital investment required to run a wholly owned subsidiary.

However, for many multi-nationals, managing international operations is an issue of 'does the company control operations centrally or allow sales subsidiaries around the world a high degree of autonomy?' In some countries they may have little choice not only due to the strength of local competition but the loyalty of local distributors to locally made brands. This is the challenge facing Interbrew, the Belgian brewer, in China (see Dilemma 10.1).

TRENDS IN RETAILING IN INTERNATIONAL MARKETS

Retailing structures differ across countries, reflecting their different histories, geography and politics. **Retailing** varies across the different levels of economic development and is influenced by cultural variations. The cultural importance attached to food in France provides the opportunity for small specialist food retailers to survive and prosper. In other developed countries, for example the US, the trend is towards very large superstores which incorporate a wide range of speciality foods. The French approach relies on small-scale production by the retail proprietor. The US approach encourages mass production, branding and sophisticated distribution systems to handle inventory and freshness issues.

In this section, our discussion will be concerned with three important issues for international marketers. First, the differences in the patterns of retailing around the world with particular reference to emerging markets and developing countries. Second, the internationalisation of retailers and its impact on **distribution channel structures** and, third, the emergence of new forms of retailing which are particularly relevant to firms competing on international markets.

DILEMMA 10.1   Local distributors vs the global operators

A number of Western brewers have entered the Chinese beer market with varying success, despite market growth being estimated at 6 per cent per annum. Anheuser-Busch makes Budweiser in its own brewery in Wuhan, an inland city, and last year took a stake in Tsingtao, China's largest brewery. SAB Miller, the world's second largest brewer, has a joint venture with a Chinese firm. However, several Western brewers have failed to break into the market, including Bass (now part of Interbrew), Fosters and Carlsberg. All these firms marketed their own global brand names, the latter ones finding they could not compete against the local distribution networks pushing the local brands.

Interbrew, the Belgian brewer, has now entered the market. It has bought 70 per cent of K.K. Brewery, the leading beer maker in Zhejiang Province, in China's Yangtze delta. This is in addition to their purchase of the biggest-selling brewery in the Pearl river delta.

Interbrew do not want to repeat the mistakes of the other global players and so face the dilemma as to how they should develop the market without coming under attack from local distribution networks.

Question   What recommendations would you make to them?

The differing patterns of retailing around the world

The concentration of the retailing industry varies significantly between markets. Low concentration ratios of retailer ownership give more power to the manufacturer. A 'no' decision from any one retailer does not make a big impact on total sales. Whilst the low concentration ratios to be found in Japan and Italy and in many lesser developed countries increase the relative power of the manufacturer, there are problems. First, low concentration ratios in retailers might be counterbalanced by powerful wholesalers. Second, the costs of the sales force in calling on a multiplicity of very small retailers and the logistics of delivering products to them can reduce the manufacturer's profitability. If economies are sought by using wholesalers, the power balance might tilt away from the manufacturer to the wholesaler.

The main differences between traditional retailing structures found in lesser developed countries and the advanced retailing structures in more developed economies are illustrated in Table 10.1.

Retailing in developing countries is characterised by low levels of capital investment. The large size, purpose-built retail outlet, full of specialist display shelving and electronic point of sale equipment, is rarely found in LDCs. The more likely picture is of a very small space with goods sold by the counter service method and technology limited to a cash register or a pocket calculator.

Retail stores are often managed by the owner/proprietor and staffed by the extended family. The lack of capital input is partially offset by large quantities of low-cost labour. The management style is usually based on limiting risks. The retailer will seek to stock goods with a proven demand pattern. In addition, the retailer will try to obtain interest-free credit from the interface channel partners: the wholesaler and the manufacturer.

TABLE 10.1	Retailers – typical differences between developing and developed countries	
Retailing issues	Traditional retailers in developing countries	Advanced retailing structures in mature economies
Concentration of retail power	Low	Often high
Site selection and retail location	Limited to the immediate locality	Very important, often sophisticated techniques to pin-point the most valuable sites
Size of outlet	Limited	Large and tending to get larger
Retailer initiation of product assortment	Limited to the buy/no buy decision	Wide range of stock possible. Use of own-label and store-specific sales promotions
Retail concepts, images and corporate identity	Rarely used	Very important – examples: Toys 'R' Us, Laura Ashley, Boots, Benetton
Retailer-initiated sales promotion	Rarely used. Reliance on manufacturer and wholesaler-developed sales promotion and point of sale material	Very important
Use of retail technology	Limited	Vital e.g. EDI, EPOS
Service	Mainly counter-service	Efficient customer response systems

Distribution channels in developing countries depend on manufacturers and wholesalers for their sales promotion ideas and materials. In developed countries retailers often take the initiative regarding sales promotions and will develop their own sales promotions. The opportunities for the manufacturer to influence the retailer in advanced countries are becoming fewer and fewer.

Small-scale retailing limits the opportunities to follow own-label strategies. The minimum economies of scale cannot be reached by the small urban and rural retailer in developing countries. The balance of power lies with the manufacturer to innovate and adapt products.

The proliferation of very many small-scale retailers means that the retail market is widely dispersed. The levels of concentration of ownership are much lower than are found in mature economies with relatively structured levels of retailing.

Illustration 10.4 compares the retailing patterns across culturally and geographically dispersed countries.

These differences give rise to principally four stages of retailing around the world: traditional, intermediary, structured and advanced (McGoldrick 2002).

Traditional retailing

'Traditional retailers' are typically found in Southern Europe, Latin America and Japan. The concentration of operators is weak, segmentation is non-existent and the level of integration of new technology is very low. These are often small-scale family retailing businesses employing few people and with a low turnover.

Intermediary retailing

Retailing in Italy, Spain and Eastern Europe is in the process of transformation, being both modern and traditional and so examples of intermediary retailing. Most businesses are independent with a turnover lower than the European average. However, there is a marked tendency towards concentration, particularly in the food sector, where the number of food retailing outlets per 1000 people is dropping. The importance of wholesalers and voluntary chains is still very strong, particularly in Italy (192 000 wholesale businesses).

ILLUSTRATION 10.4   Comparative retailing traditions

In the UK consumers are used to shops being open 7 days a week and in the US 24-7. In Germany, however, it is only recently that shops have been allowed to open on Saturday afternoons. A recent new federal law allows city centre shops to open until 8 pm. However outside the city most still close at 4 pm for the weekend and Sunday opening is still highly restricted. This is much the same as New Zealand where stores close at 5.30 pm except for one night each week when they are open until 9.00 pm. Stores are also closed on Sundays and many are closed on Saturday afternoons.

In India opening hours are unrestricted but most retail stores are family owned and are much smaller in size. With the exception of a few (small) super bazaars, consumers are not allowed to walk freely inside the stores, examine and compare labels of different brands before making the selection. Instead, consumers approach shops with a predetermined list of items to purchase, which are then pulled out of the bins by the salesperson.

Retailing in Greece on the other hand has until recently been small scale and highly traditional. The majority of stores are family owned and small in size and shopping for pleasure is less popular. Most purchases are made in cash, although credit cards are becoming more popular. However, the entry into the country of some of the big global retailers is starting to change the face of retailing there.

Question How can a company achieve a global distribution strategy when retailing infrastructures vary so much?

In the major cities of China there have been huge developments in the retail structure of the country, taking retailing in the major cities to intermediary status. One of the most aggressive foreign investors has been Yaohan, a Japanese retailer which plans to open more than 1000 supermarkets and stores there by 2005. To show its zeal, Yaohan even moved its group headquarters to Shanghai where it now operates one of the world's largest department stores. But it has found it harder to set up shop in China than it expected. Faced with mounting debts, it has put further expansion on hold. The problem, in a nutshell, is that most of the Chinese trooping through its smart new stores are only window shopping!

Countries with intermediary retailing structures have been attractive locations for retailers expanding internationally. Spain and Central European countries have been attractive markets for retail expansion. The level of economic development and the intermediary structure of retailing have meant that these countries are not host to large domestic retailers, making entry into the market relatively easy.

Over the course of the past five years, the entry of foreign operators into areas like Latin America has altered the retailing landscape. There are now hypermarkets, variety stores and non-food specialists which have stimulated competition and greatly modernised retailing across the continent.

Structured retailing

Retailing in the north of Europe tends to be fairly structured, reflecting the level of economic development. Denmark, Luxembourg, the Netherlands and France have enterprises larger in size, have a higher level of concentration and a greater level of productivity per employee than Southern European retailers.

In these markets, retail competition is fairly well developed and there is a mature relationship between suppliers and retailers.

Retailers also have introduced fairly sophisticated technologies facilitating more elaborate competitive strategies. They are also, themselves, finding growth through opportunities overseas and new retailing formats.

Advanced retailing

The US, Germany and the UK are all examples of countries in which retailing is the most advanced in terms of concentration, segmentation, capitalisation and integration. In Germany and the UK there are about 60 retailing businesses per 10 000 inhabitants, 98 being the European average. Retailer strategies are advanced and are becoming much more marketing focused and generally incorporate five important dimensions.

Interactive customer marketing. Targeting of customers as individuals, developing strategies to improve retention and increase sales per shop visit.

Mass customisation. Retailers are looking for improved margins through higher volumes, reduced costs and achieving low levels of returns.

Data mining. Retailers are using technology and electronic point of sale (EPOS) information to improve knowledge of customers, ensure the ability to make targeted offers which are timely and clearly differentiated. Data mining is beginning to be used by retailers in emerging and developing markets where there has been little reliable data on which to previously base decisions.

Category management. Retailers are aiming to achieve improved levels of customer satisfaction through reducing costs, reducing mark downs and optimising product assortment.

Effective consumer response. Retailers are establishing permanent links with manufacturers, establishing electronic data interchange (EDI) systems for efficient inventory replenishment and ensuring a continuous just in time delivery of supplies.

In these markets the balance of power in the supply chain, for the present at least, seems to lie firmly with these large retailers who are increasingly dictating the trends in their home markets and as these reach maturity are seeking growth opportunities by expanding internationally.

The globalisation of retailing

One of the key trends in international distribution over the past few years has been the aggressive strategies pursued by many major retailers as they have pursued global marketing objectives. Tesco, J. Sainsbury, the French hypermarket groups Auchan, Carrefour and Promodes, and the German discount food retailers Aldi, Lidl and Swartz have all expanded globally. The food retailing sector especially is now dominated by huge global retailers. Table 10.2 gives the top ten in the world. However it is not just in food that retailers are going global; the US retailer Wal-Mart and specialists Toys 'R' Us, Home Depot, Staples, Benetton, Body Shop and Hertz are all now global retailers. Hong Kong retailers A S Watson and Dairy Farm entered neighbouring countries with supermarkets and pharmaceutical chains and Japanese department stores Takashimaya and Isetan have established outlets across Asia. More recently this trend has accelerated, with German retailers Metro, Rewe and Tengelmann expanding into the Czech Republic, Hungary and Poland often using joint ventures with former socialist cooperatives. Three Western European retailers, Tengelmann (Germany), Ahold (Netherlands) and Delhaizae Le Lion (Belgium), now generate more sales and profit from their foreign activities, which include the US, Central Europe and Asia, than they do in their home markets. Tesco, already strong in Ireland, Central Europe and Asia have recently announced plans to move into Japan (see Illustration 10.5).

The expansion of international activity of retailers around the world has given rise to four different types of international retailers: the hypermarket, the power retailers, the niche retailer and the designer flagship stores who target particular global cities for their stores. Examples of these are given in Figure 10.4.

TABLE 10.2	Top ten global food retailers by sales (US$bn)
Wal-Mart (US)	147
Carrefour (France)	39
Ahold (Netherlands)	36
Kroger (US)	31
Metro (Germany)	29
Target (US)	26
Tesco (UK)	24
Costco (US)	23
Albertsons (US)	21
Rewe (Germany)	21

Source: M+M Planet Retail

Besides the growing sophistication of the industry and the opening up of new markets around the world, the globalisation of retailers can be attributed to a number of 'pull' and 'push' factors.

The 'push' factors are:

- saturation of the home market or over-competition
- economic recession or limited growth in spending
- a declining or ageing population
- strict planning policies on store development
- high operating costs – labour, rents, taxation
- shareholder pressure to maintain profit growth
- the 'me too' syndrome in retailing.

The 'pull' factors are:

- the underdevelopment of some markets or weak competition
- strong economic growth or rising standards of living

ILLUSTRATION 10.5   Tesco goes for global growth

The UK food retailer Tesco has been following an aggressive internationalisation strategy in its bid to compete on a global scale. Its early international growth was into Central and Eastern Europe. It has established 66 stores in Poland, 53 in Hungary, 17 in the Czech Republic and 17 in Slovakia. Its recent focus has been on South East Asia where it has opened stores in Thailand, Malaysia, Taiwan and South Korea.

Tesco have now decided to break into one of the world's toughest retail markets and have bought a chain of convenience stores in Japan. The interesting dimension of their strategy is that whereas in other countries, Tesco have opened their own hypermarket-sized stores, in Japan they entered the market by acquiring a chain of 78 small stores.

Tesco argue that this strategy will enable them to learn about the market and get to know the Japanese consumer and so avoid the mistakes of other global retailers such as Carrefour who have encountered a number of setbacks in their attempt to introduce hypermarket-sized stores in the country.

Question What are the difficulties for global retailers in entering Japan? Do you think Tesco have made the correct decision?

Source: Adapted from *The Sunday Times*, 15 June 2003

FIGURE 10.4

Global retailer categories

Hypermarkets	Niche retailers
Carrefour	Body Shop
Promodes	Tie Rack
Auchan	HMV
Metro	Hertz
Ahold	Amazon

Power retailers	Flagship designer stores
Ikea	Donna Karen
Wal-Mart	Ralph Lauren
Toys 'R' Us	Gap
Costco	Rockport
Target	Jaeger

- high population growth or a high concentration of young adults
- a relaxed regulatory framework
- favourable operating costs – labour, rents, taxation
- the geographical spread of trading risks
- the opportunity to innovate under new market conditions.

Marketing implications for development of international distribution strategies

The internationalisation of retailing has meant a new era of distribution is developing. This new competitive landscape in distribution has a number of implications for the development of the distribution strategies of international firms. The most important of these are:

- power shifts in supply chains towards retailers
- intense concentrated competition with significant buyer power across country markets
- rapidly advancing technology facilitating global sourcing and global electronic transactions
- unrelenting performance measures being demanded of suppliers by international retailers
- smart, demanding consumers expecting high levels of customer service.

Thus power in many international markets is moving from the supplier down the supply chain to the consumer. This means effective management is critical to suppliers competing in international markets. It again highlights the importance of ensuring the distribution strategy across international markets is driven by an understanding of the target market segments both within each foreign country market and across national market boundaries.

This intensive growth in the size and power of retailers in countries with advanced retailing structures and retailers internationalising means there is now tremendous pressure on suppliers to improve the quality of service to them. Retailers are demanding:

- streamlined and flexible supply chains
- suppliers who can guarantee quality and reliability across global markets
- the ability to supply high volumes and close relationships with intermediaries in the supply chain
- suppliers who can meet the global sourcing requirements of large-scale retailers who wish to buy centrally across the globe.

It could mean, therefore, that the firms who are successful are the firms who develop the capability to compete effectively in the supply chain activities compared to their international competitors. It is for this reason that the distribution strategy of the international company has taken on such an important dimension in recent times.

Internet retailing

Multi-media technology has provided a number of opportunities for interactive shopping which offer particular opportunities in international markets. Teleshopping and the Internet offer suppliers the retailing opportunities for direct contact with consumers throughout the globe without the problems and expense of having to establish infrastructures in foreign country markets. For example, Amazon.com, the bookshop which sells purely over the Internet, carries no books as they are directly shipped from the publishers' or distributors' warehouses. This means Amazon have few inventory or real estate costs. They offer 2.5 million titles including every English language book in print whereas even the largest book-store would only stock 170 000. EToys, the Internet competitor to Toys 'R' Us, has no retail outlets but a higher market capitalisation than Toys 'R' Us. EToys pro-actively trap individual information on consumer purchases and then flash messages back telling consumers of other products bought by consumers making similar purchases. The diffusion of the Internet, and with it electronic commerce, increasingly is challenging the traditional channels of distribution as the World Wide Web (WWW) brings together buyers and sellers through the creation of an online marketplace. However, despite exponential growth in access to the Internet, consumers are still limiting their purchases to relatively few product lines. It is estimated that nearly 40 per cent of all Internet purchases are for travel, another 26 per cent for the purchase of tickets for events and concerts and 25 per cent is spent on books and CDs.

In international marketing the major impact, as we will discuss in Chapter 12, has been the ability of the Internet to enable small and medium-sized companies to access niche markets around the globe that were previously too logistically dif-ficult for them to access. By simply setting setting up their own sites, a company in effect becomes global and can sell goods and services throughout the world. However, there has also been the development of market sites which have impacted on the way business transactions take place internationally, such as:

- *Auctions*. Online marketplaces where negotiations of price between independent buyers and sellers is implemented through a standard auction open to all participants (e.g. eBay, Dabs exchange, On Sale).

- *Single buyer markets*. Where a large buyer establishes an online intranet market for its own suppliers (e.g. GE Trade Web), usually for them to gain access to the site, the suppliers will have achieved the status of *approved supplier*.

- *Pure exchanges*. Where individual buyers and sellers are matched according to product offers and needs.

The most promising products are often those where existing intermediaries do not perform many of the traditional 'wholesaler' functions for a broad market owing to the high cost of servicing small diverse and geographically or function-ally dispersed players. Klein and Quelch (1997) identify several market character-istics which favour the development of electronic channels of distribution:

- *Inefficiencies in traditional distribution channels*. Buyers cannot find all possible sellers or vice versa (see Illustration 10.6).

- *Market fragmentation*. Markets with many geographically dispersed buyers and sellers across the globe.

- *Minimum scale barriers*. In traditional markets, smaller manufacturers may be boxed out of regular channels by larger players who reap economies of scale and exploit distribution relationships.

- *Commodity-type products*. Products with well-known technical specifications, or manufacturer brands that can easily be price-compared and those products that do not require substantial after-sales service.

- *Short life-cycle products*. Product-markets with short life cycles create large quantities of obsolete and discontinued items. Customers may experience difficulty finding spare parts or compatible accessories for earlier generations of product.

- *Trade association involvement*. Industries where trade associations play an active role in organising members, e.g. TRADEex's partnership with the Australian Chamber of Manufacturers.

THE MANAGEMENT OF THE PHYSICAL DISTRIBUTION OF GOODS

Physical distribution management (PDM) is concerned with the planning, implementing and control of physical flows of materials and final goods from points of origin to points of use to meet customer needs at a profit (Kotler 2003).

In international physical distribution of goods the total distribution costs will be higher than domestic distribution. The extra activities, increased time taken and the need to adapt to special country requirements will all increase costs. The extra costs centre around three areas:

Increased distance; this means, in terms of costs, increased transport time, inventory, cash flow and insurance.

New variables to consider; new modes of transport (air, sea, rail, road), new types of documentation, packaging for long transit times.

Greater market complexity; language differences requires the translation of documents, the extra costs of bureaucracy and longer lines of communication.

It is important for the firm to take full account of all these extra costs when evaluating alternative distribution strategies. In taking the **total distribution cost** approach firms will include the costs of transport, warehousing, inventory, order-processing, documentation, packaging and the total cost of lost sales if delays occur. Companies find that changes to one element of distribution influence the performance and the costs of other elements, as Cisco found to its advantage in Dilemma 10.2.

ILLUSTRATION 10.6   **Internet helps Western countries penetrate Japan**

The impact of the Internet on growth is proving to be more powerful in the more restricted economies of Japan and Europe than the more open economy of the US. This is because by increasing price transparency and competition the Internet is having its greatest impact on those economies that have built-in structural inefficiencies in their economies.

Japan, with high distribution margins, is starting to see considerable price erosion and big gains in efficiency. By exposing firms to more intense global competition in order to compete effectively, businesses are having to rethink old inefficient habits and seek new ways to eliminate market rigidities that have previously protected them from international predators.

In Japan the Internet strikes at the heart of the archaic and expensive distribution system that holds prices artificially high. Suppliers and retailers tend to be tied to manufacturers. This allows manufacturers to control prices by restricting distribution to their own retailers. The Internet, by giving more power to the consumer through price transparency, is allowing Western companies to bypass the many layers of middlemen that in the past have proved to be such a formidable barrier to them. Companies that have failed to penetrate the market previously are finally being able to reach potential consumers in the Japanese market.

Question What are the other benefits of using Internet marketing in countries with high operational barriers?

The logistics approach to physical distribution

Many writers on physical distribution use logistics and physical distribution as terms meaning the same thing. Kotler makes the distinction between physical distribution as a more traditional activity and logistics as being more market-oriented. In this way, physical distribution thinking starts with the finished product at the end of the production line and then attempts to find low-cost solutions to get the product to the customer. Logistics thinking, on the other hand, considers the customer and then works back to the factory. In this section we will use the market-oriented view. We will use the term logistics to mean an integrated view of physical distribution management in which customer demand influences are at least as important as cost-cutting forces. More and more companies are integrating their physical distribution strategies and linking their operations in different countries with more common processes and so rationalising their manufacturing and distribution infrastructure to make more effective use of business resources and so taking a logistical view of their distribution operations.

In Europe 75 per cent of businesses operating across European markets have a pan-European **logistics or distribution strategy** in place. McKinsey Consultants estimate the European logistics market to be worth about US$200 billion. The logistics function is having an increasing influence in many parts of the business, especially in inventory planning, information technology, purchasing and manufacturing.

There are a number of factors influencing this change:

- Customers demanding improved levels of customer service.
- **Electronic Data Interchange** (EDI) becoming the all-pervading technology for firms to build links with customers, suppliers and distribution providers.
- Companies restructuring their physical distribution operations in response to the formation of regional trading blocs.

In the following sections, we will briefly examine the developments in each of the above areas.

Customer service

The main elements of customer service will revolve around:

- order to delivery time
- consistency and reliability of delivery
- inventory availability
- order, size constraints
- ordering convenience
- delivery time and flexibility

DILEMMA 10.2 **Cisco Systems**

Cisco Systems enforces very high quality control standards on all its suppliers. This has always involved the company in lengthy and cumbersome processes of certification which proved very costly to the company. Furthermore, whenever the company put anything out to tender evaluation of tenders was very time-consuming. In order to maintain their competitive advantage internationally the company prioritised this area as one where significant cost savings could be made.

The dilemma is how can this be achieved without compromising standards?

- invoicing procedures, documentation and accuracy
- claims procedure
- condition of goods
- salesperson's visits
- order status information
- after-sales support.

In developing customer service levels it is essential to use the elements of service that the customer regards as important. Delivery reliability might be more important than a quick order to delivery time that is unreliable in meeting delivery schedules. Understanding the way in which the international customer perceives service is important. There will be considerable differences. Customers who are distant might be more concerned about the guarantees of reliable rapid availability than customers much closer to the production source. The ability and corporate capability to meet widely differing customer requirements in different countries needs to be managed.

In all countries, customers are becoming increasingly demanding. Partnership arrangements are becoming significant in many sectors as supply chains become more integrated. These developments are usually customer-led demands for improved service.

Consumers are demanding ever quicker delivery and ever more added value from their products that increasingly require 'just-in-time' distribution. The product cycle from manufacture to payment is becoming shorter, a trend that is likely to accelerate. Moreover, a global manufacturer operates a **globally integrated supply chain**. If it is to effectively benefit from cheap labour costs at one side of the globe, it will need an efficient global logistics strategy if it is to effectively service the rich consumers at the other side of the globe.

Information technology

Developments in information technology are critical. It is estimated that more than three in four companies actively involved in international markets have introduced multi-national computer systems for logistics processes and international electronic data interchange (EDI).

The 'old silk road' has been replaced by the 'new silc road' with optical fibre systems making direct links between Europe, East Asia and Australia. Much of the new SDH-based silc road (SDH or syndchronoms digital hierarchy which is an enabling technology that increases the speed and volume of traffic using optical fibre networks) has been laid. The network stretches 2500 miles across the former Soviet Union into China through countries such as Uzbekistan, regenerating their economies.

Optic fibre cables have been routed through Japan, South East Asia and through to Australia. Thus there are significant developments in electronic links between companies and distributors and producers around the world.

In regional trading blocs, such as the European Union and NAFTA, there has been the development of common systems for customer order processing, demand forecasting and inventory planning.

Foreign companies are increasingly using the Internet to track the progress of products through the distribution system. DHL have Web sites which allow customers to track the progress of their packages and is attracting 400 000 hits a day. The other major area of IT involvement is in stock control and buying. Despite having 600 stores in 14 countries and using 12 different own labels, C&A is still able to deliver nine times a day to its stores due to its efficient centralised buying operation for menswear and childrenswear in Brussels and womenswear in Dusseldorf.

The restructuring of physical distribution operations

In mature trading regions such as the US and Europe, a large number of firms have restructured their distribution networks in response to changes in the trading structures in the region. Cross-border deliveries have increased and the number of factories and warehouses has decreased. The number of distribution centres serving more than one country has increased whereas there has been a decrease in the number of warehouses dedicated to within-country movements.

Lucent Technology dispatches all its products from its factory in Spain to a test and assembly centre in Singapore before final delivery. It might go back to a customer sitting 10 kilometres away from the factory in Spain but it will still go to Singapore. The company gives a 48-hour delivery guarantee to customers anywhere in the world, posing demanding logistical challenges.

The physical movement of goods is a high cost activity. Companies often incur 10 to 35 per cent of their expenditure on physical distribution. Because distribution is such a high cost activity, it is now receiving close attention from general management and from marketing management.

The logistics approach is to analyse customer requirements and to review what competitors are providing. Customers are interested in a number of things: deliveries to meet agreed time schedules, zero defect delivery, supplier willingness to meet emergency needs, supplier willingness to replace damaged goods quickly and supplier willingness to engage in just in time (JIT) delivery and inventory holding.

If a company is to achieve a logistically effective system of distribution it will become involved in a highly complex and sophisticated system and will, therefore, need to:

- clearly define areas of responsibility across foreign country markets
- have a highly developed planning system
- have an up-to-date and comprehensive information support system
- develop expertise in distribution management
- have a centralised planning body to coordinate activities and exercise overall control.

Thus, a logistical system helps the company not only pay attention to inventory levels but think through market relationships to minimise costs of stock out and maximise distribution efficiency across a large number of markets.

In developing an efficient logistical system of physical distribution across international markets there are a number of important considerations:

- how intermediaries such as freight forwarders can enhance our service
- what modes of transportation should be used
- how the firm can make effective use of export processing zones
- what documentation is required
- what are the packaging requirements for transit and the market
- how should the export sales contract be organised.

In the following sections, we will briefly discuss some of the important issues in each of these areas.

The use of intermediaries

Traditionally, intermediaries such as forwarders and freight companies simply offered transportation by land, sea and air. However, now there are many types of intermediaries which offer global logistical services. FedEx, UPS and DPWN (Deutsche Post World Net, which absorbed DHL) have global networks to offer express-delivery services which they also use to offer customised logistics solutions. Broking houses such as Kuehne & Nagel offer their skills in tying together different modes of transport. Other companies offer specialised services, for instance transport and warehouse-management firms which organise the physical movement and storage of goods. Still others are dedicated contract carriers and freight forwarders, who buy capacity on ships and cargo planes, and put together loads from different companies to fill them. Most freight forwarders will offer services such as preparation and processing of international transport documents, coordination of transport services and the provision of warehousing.

However, as we have seen in the above section, recent trends such as just in time delivery, outsourcing of non-core activities, cutting inventories and the trend to **build to order** (BTO) have meant international firms have had to build a comprehensive but flexible logistical operation to ensure goods reach their customers around the world in the right place at the right time. This is such a challenging task that companies are no longer able to do it all themselves. So more of them are using intermediaries and outsourcing the logistical functions. This has meant the global freight-transport industry itself has had to reshape, as manufacturers seek service suppliers with global reach. Manufacturers want custom-designed delivery systems, using all types of transport – land, sea and air. Many of the larger firms now offer a whole range of functions beyond their original specific function. This has meant that distinctions between the various intermediaries, such as freight forwarders, transport companies, express couriers and logistics services, are blurring.

All intermediaries deal with three parallel flows: physical goods, information and finance (leasing, lending, brokerage). What is happening now is that whilst previously intermediaries specialised in one of the flows they are now offering the full range of services. Even global manufacturers are entering the logistics business. Caterpillar, which makes construction equipment, uses the global distribution network it has already developed as a channel for the products of other manufacturers.

There have been two driving forces for this. First, global competition has meant a downward pressure on costs. This has spawned the phenomenon that began in the logistics sector with outsourcing but has extended to the whole range of other services now regarded as legitimate logistics tasks. Indeed, many of the multi-national logistics companies such as DPWN, FedEx, UPS and TNT, the so-called integrators, themselves outsource the functions they take-on to small specialist suppliers.

Second, the technological advances discussed earlier means that logistics specialists are able to offer increasingly sophisticated services to exporters that firms cannot provide in-house. For example, a firm's products might once have passed from factory to national warehouse and then on to a foreign regional warehouse, then to a local depot, before delivery to the end consumer: a wasteful process in terms of time and cost. Today, using state-of-the-art systems, a logistics specialist taking responsibility for the warehouse function will deliver to the customer direct from the main warehouse, cutting out three of four links in the chain.

At the more advanced end of the logistics services spectrum, companies are handing control of more and more roles to their logistics partners. This is partly driven by the sheer geographical complexity of many exporters' operations where, for example, head office, factory and customer may be separated by thousands of miles.

As more companies attempt to develop the newly opened emerging markets where they have little knowledge or understanding of the distribution system, the use of third party intermediaries to organise logistics is becoming an essential part of a global marketing strategy.

Transportation

The physical handling and movement of goods over long distances will practically always have to be performed by third parties.

Transportation is the most visible part of the physical distribution strategy. The main options are:

- **Ocean transport**: capacity for large loads of differentiated products, raw materials, semi-finished goods, finished goods. Handling of goods in bulk, in packaged or unitised form, pallets, containers.

- **Inland waterway transport**: heavy and bulk products. Growing container transport. Restrictions because of need for suitable loading/unloading terminals.

- **Air transport**: urgent shipments, perishables, low-density light/high value, relatively small shipments.

- **Road transport**: most flexible door-to-door transport for all kinds of products but mostly finished goods. Container transport.

- **Rail transport**: long distance heavy and bulk products. Container transport.

Ocean and inland waterways

Sea and inland waterways provide a very low-cost way to transport bulky, low value or non-perishable products such as coal and oil. Water transport is slow and is subject to difficulties caused by the weather; for example, some ports are iced over for part of the winter. Water transport usually needs to be used with other modes of transport to achieve door-to-door delivery.

One of the policies used to encourage growth in South Korea, a newly industrialised country, has been the stimulation of its shipping and shipbuilding industry.

Ocean shipping can be *open market*, i.e. *free ocean* where there are very few restrictions, or it can be organised in *conferences* which are essentially cartels that regulate rates and capacities available on routes.

As in other areas of distribution, the containerisation of ports and the impact of information technology have meant sea transport has become a capital intensive industry where there is high pressure to achieve full capacity utilisation.

The costs of ocean freight, as a result, have declined over the past decade and so it is still the most cost-effective method of transporting goods to distant markets.

The average cost for a 6 metre dry cargo container to be shipped from the UK to Shanghai in China will be £750–£950 and the approximate transit time would be 30–35 days.

However, a number of hidden costs can arise in overseas shipping:

- overseas warehousing costs due to having to send large inventories in container loads

- inventory losses from handling spoilage, theft, obsolescence and exchange rate charges in manual time

- cost of time in transit
- lost sales from late arrival.

Inland waterways are very important in countries with poor infrastructures. In Vietnam the most popular mode of transportation is by water. A dense network of waterways exists although even this system will suffer the vagaries of both flood and drought conditions.

Air

Air freight is considerably more expensive per tonne/kilometre than the other modes of transport. Air freight is particularly appropriate for the movement of high-value low-bulk and perishable items. For example, diamonds, computer software, specialist component parts and cut flowers use air freight. Air freight is extending its market through promoting its advantages. The higher freight charges can often be off-set. Packing costs and insurance rates are significantly less by air. Storage en route, overseas warehousing, inventory losses may all be less by air as will the actual cost of the time in transit. In addition, the development of larger and more flexible aeroplanes for air freight has helped reduce costs.

Road

Very flexible in route and time. Schedules can deliver direct to customers' premises. Very efficient for short hauls of high-value goods. Restrictions at border controls can be time consuming, however, and long distances and the need for sea crossings reduce the attractiveness of freight transport by road. In some parts of the world, particularly in LDCs, road surfaces are poor and the distribution infrastructure poor. In Vietnam, an attractive emerging market for many international firms, the majority of the road network is beaten track which, during the wet

---

ILLUSTRATION 10.7   Nightmare logistics in Cameroon

Douala, Cameroon's major port, is one of Africa's busiest ports, handling 95 per cent of Cameroon's international trade. It also serves Cameroon's neighbours, Chad and the Central African Republic.

Douala was once considered one of the worst ports in the world; however, since borrowing money from the World Bank and investment by the government in the port infrastructure things have improved somewhat. The main problem now is, once the goods have landed in the port, to safely transport them to their destination. The only viable route is by road and that can be very problematic.

The city suffers from horrendous traffic problems and once outside the city, roads have been built on soft soil with little foundations. The heat and the rain soon cause wide potholes and huge cracks. Besides the potholes, motorists must dodge the wrecks of cars that have smashed. Under Cameroon law, these cannot be moved until the police have given permission.

In 1980 there were 7.2 km of roads per 1000 people; now the figure has shrunk to only 2.6 km per 1000. One estimate suggests less than a tenth of them are paved and most of these are in a very poor condition.

Companies like Coca-Cola and Guinness transporting drinks face nightmare problems. On a journey through Cameroon they may lose up to a third of a truckload. The cost of distribution alone can be as much as 15 per cent higher than in a country with decent roads. This is besides the traumas of police controls, local government bureaucracy and the longer length of time it takes for a truck to make a simple journey.

Question What can companies do to minimise logistical problems in countries like Cameroon?

Source: Adapted from *The Economist*, 19 December 2002

season (six months of the year), make transporting anything by road very difficult. The problems of transporting goods across African countries due to poor road infrastructure can be seen in Illustration 10.7.

Rail

Rail services provide a very good method of transporting bulky goods over long land distances. The increasing use of containers provides a flexible means to use rail and road modes with minimal load transfer times and costs.

In Europe, we are seeing the development of the use of 'Bloc Trains' as a highly efficient means of rail transport. In the US they use 'Double Bloc' trains to transport goods across the vast plains. In a number of markets, rail transport is fraught with difficulties. In China, a shipment from Shanghai to Guangzhou, a distance of approximately 2000 kilometres, can take 25 days. Across the interior it is even slower. Shanghai to Xian, 1500 kilometres, can take 45 days. Much of the rail capacity is antiquated and many of the rail lines are old, leading to frequent derailments.

The final decision on transport

The decision concerning which transport mode to use is discussed by Branch (2000). He identifies four factors as decisive in choosing transport: the terms of the export contract, the commodity specification, freight and overall transit time.

In the terms of the export contract, the customer can specify the mode(s) of transport and can insist on the country's national shipping line or airline being used. In considering different modes of transport, the specification of the commodity will have a strong influence on modal choice. For example, transport of fresh food will have requirements to prevent spoilage and contamination. The cost of transport is of major importance. It creates extra costs above the normal domestic cost. It is important, therefore, that transport options are researched thoroughly so that the best value arrangements can be made for both the buyer and the supplier.

Export processing zones

The principle of **export processing zones** (EPZs) started with the opening of the world's first EPZ at Shannon in the Republic of Ireland. Since then there has been a proliferation in the establishment of EPZs worldwide, with notable examples being Jebel Ali at Dubai in the UAE and Subic Bay in the Philippines. The principle of the EPZ has been embraced as a worldwide instrument for national economic development by the United Nations.

The concept of the EPZ concerns the duty-free and tax-free manufacture or processing of products for export purposes within a customs-controlled ('offshore') environment. Components may be imported into the zone duty-free and tax-free to be processed or manufactured into the finished product or stored for onward distribution and are then re-exported without any liability of import duties or other taxes. The purpose of the EPZ is to ensure that at least 70 per cent of the zone-produced articles are re-exported. The remaining percentage of items produced within the zone may be imported into domestic territory upon payment of the appropriate import duty and tax for the finished article.

Companies trading from within the export processing zone can be wholly owned by foreign-based enterprises and, in most cases, all profits may be repatriated to the home country. Foreign direct investment by overseas-based companies is encouraged in zone operations, since normal national rules regarding profits or ownership do not apply. It is also possible for locally based companies to engage in zone operations as long as they are involved in import and export operations.

It is also likely that the workforce used will cost the zone company less than for home-based operations, since the majority of the EPZs are located in developing countries, especially East and South East Asia and Central America.

The advantages for companies in taking advantage of EPZs are:

- All goods entering the EPZ are exempted from customs duties and import permits.
- Firms can use foreign currency to settle transactions.
- EPZs can be used for assembly of products and so help reduce transportation costs.
- EPZs give a company much more flexibility and help avoid unwanted bureaucracy of customs and excise.

China has developed a number of export processing zones in the coastal regions and special economic zones (SEZs) in the interior of China to help develop export sea trade. Examples of EPZs in China are Hong Kong, Shenzen, Shanghai and Tianjin.

Documentation

A number of different documents are required in cross-border marketing. These include invoices, consignment notes and customs documents. SITRO, the Simpler Trade Procedures Board, has been involved in developing simpler documentation and export procedures with the aim of encouraging international trade. Electronic data interchange (EDI) is expanding and now providing a fast integrated system which is reducing documentation preparation time and errors.

The process of documentation has more importance than its rather mechanistic and bureaucratic nature would suggest. Errors made in documents can result in laws being broken, customs regulations being violated or, in financial institutions, refusing to honour demands for payment. Country variations are considerable with regard to export documentation procedures. Different documents are required in different formats. Figure 10.5 shows a typical export order process.

Documentation problems have five main causes: complexity, culture, change, cost and error. Complexity arises from the number of different parties requiring precise documents delivered at the correct time. In addition to the customer, banks, chambers of commerce, consulates, international carriers, domestic carriers, customs, port/terminal/customs clearance areas, insurance companies and the exporting company or freight forwarding company are being used by the exporter.

Different countries require different numbers of copies of documents, sometimes in their own language and sometimes open to official scrutiny that is strongly influenced by the culture of that country. Document clearance can, therefore, be slow and subject to bureaucratic delays.

Errors in documentation can have serious consequences. The definition of an 'error' is open to interpretation. Errors can result in goods being held in customs or in a port. Clearance delays cause failure to meet customer service objectives. In extreme cases, errors result in goods being confiscated or not being paid for.

The development of regional trading blocs is reducing some of the complexity of documentation. Previous to the single European market, a firm transporting goods from Manchester (UK) to Milan (Italy) would require 38 different documents. Now, theoretically, none are required! Some companies seek to minimise their exposure to documentation problems by using freight forwarders to handle freight and documentation. Other companies develop their own expertise and handle documentation in-house.

Packaging

Packaging for international markets needs to reflect climatic, geographical, economic, cultural and distribution channel considerations. In this section we will concentrate on the specific requirements that particularly relate to transport and warehousing.

The main packaging issues of interest for the exporter are: loss, damage and the provision of handling points to cope with the range of transport modes and the levels of handling sophistication and types of equipment used throughout the entire transit.

■ **Loss**. The main concerns of loss of goods relate to misdirection and to theft (pilferage). The use of containers has reduced some of the opportunities for theft. Misdirection can be minimised by the appropriate use of shipping marks and labelling. High-value consignments need to be marked in such a way as to avoid drawing them to the attention of potential thieves. Marking needs to be simple, security-conscious and readily understandable by different people in different countries.

FIGURE 10.5

The export order and physical distribution process

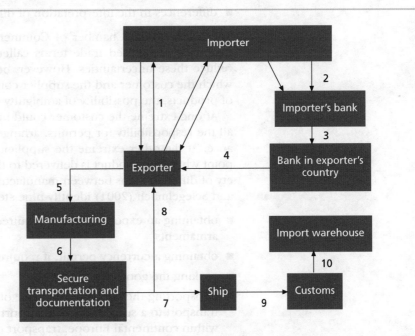

Note: I Importer makes enquiry to potential supplier; Exporter sends catalogues and price list; Importer requests samples; Importer requests pro-forma invoice (price quote); Exporter sends pro-forma invoice; Importer sends purchase order; Exporter receives purchase order. 2 Importer arranges financing through his bank. 3 Importer's bank sends letter of credit (most frequently used form of payment). 4 Exporter's bank notifies exporter that letter of credit is received. 5 Exporter produces or acquires goods. 6 Exporter arranges transportation and documentation (obtained by exporter or through freight forwarding company). Space reserved on ship or aircraft. Documents acquired or produced, as required: Exporter's licence; Shipper's export declaration; Commercial invoice; Bills of lading; Marine insurance certificate; Consular invoice; Certificate of origin, Inspection certificates; Dock receipts. 7 Exporter ships goods to importer. 8 Exporter presents documents to bank for payment. 9 Importer has goods cleared through customs 10 and delivered to his warehouse.

■ **Damage**. The length of transit and variations in climate and physical movement give rise to many opportunities for damage to occur. Goods stowed in large ships might be contaminated by chemical odours or corroding machinery. Goods might be left out in the open air in equatorial or severe winter conditions. Wal-Mart found that local Brazilian suppliers could not meet their standards for packaging and quality control.

A good balance needs to be achieved between the high costs of the substantial export packing required to eliminate all or almost all damage and the price and profit implications that this has for the customer and the exporter.

Over the years, export packaging has been modified from wooden crates and straw, etc., towards fibreboard and cardboard cartons. Different countries have different regulations about what materials are acceptable. In addition, export packaging influences customer satisfaction through its appearance and in its appropriateness to minimise handling costs for the customer.

The export sales contract

The export sales contract covers important terms for the delivery of products in international trade. There are three main areas of uncertainty in international trade contracts which Branch (2000) identifies as:

■ uncertainty about which legal system will be used to adjudicate the contract

■ difficulties resulting from inadequate and unreliable information

■ differences in the interpretation of different trade terms.

The International Chamber of Commerce (ICC) has formulated a set of internationally recognised trade terms called *Incoterms*. The use of Incoterms will reduce these uncertainties. However, because there are many different ways in which the customer and the supplier could contract for the international delivery of products, the possibility of ambiguity can exist unless care is taken.

At one extreme the customer could buy the product at the factory gate, taking all the responsibility for permits, arrangements and costs of transport and insurance. At the other extreme the supplier can arrange and pay for all costs to the point where the product is delivered to the customer's premises. There are a variety of different steps between manufacture and delivery to the customer. Keegan and Sclegelmilch (2001) identify nine steps:

■ obtaining an export permit, if required. For example, for the sale of armaments

■ obtaining a currency permit, if required

■ packing the goods for export

■ transporting the goods to the place of departure. This is usually road transport to a seaport or to an airport. For some countries, for example within continental Europe, transport could be entirely by road transport

■ preparing a bill of lading

■ completing necessary customs export papers

■ preparing customs or consular invoices as required in the country of destination

■ arranging for ocean freight and preparation

■ obtaining marine insurance and certificate of the policy.

There are many Incoterms specifying many variations of responsibility for the required steps in the delivery process. The main terms are defined below:

- **Ex-works (EXW).** In this contract the exporter makes goods available at a specified time at the exporter's factory or warehouse. The advantage to the buyer in this arrangement is that of obtaining the goods at the lowest possible price.

- **Free on board (FOB).** In this contract the exporter is responsible for the costs and risks of moving the goods up to the point of passing them over the ship's rail. The FOB contract will specify the name of the ship and the name of the port. The benefit to the buyer in this arrangement is that the goods can be transported in the national shipping line of the buyer and can be insured using a national insurance company. In this way the amount of foreign currency needed to finance the contract is reduced.

- **Cost, insurance, freight (CIF).** This contract specifies that the exporter is responsible for all costs and risks to a specified destination port indicated by the buyer. The buyer benefits from receiving the goods in the home country and is, therefore, spared the costs, risks and management of the goods in transit. The exporter can benefit from a higher price for the contract. Whether the contract is more profitable will depend on the extra total distribution costs associated with the CIF contract. From a national point of view, the use of CIF contracts by a country's exporters is preferred as invisible earnings through extra freight and insurance services are increased when CIF contracts are used rather than FOB contracts.

Governments of all types of political and economic persuasion sometimes develop policies to favour their own national companies, and they can try to influence the availability of transport modes. In addition, the extra incentive to increase foreign currency earnings can change the export sales contract and with it the specification of the Incoterms.

SUMMARY

- The management of international distribution channels and logistics is challenging because, frequently, it is determined more by the available infrastructure and host country channel structure than by what the firm would like to do.

- Marketers experienced in domestic marketing often find that the first time that they have to make decisions about which distribution channel options to use is when they are assigned to international duties.

- The lack of experience in distribution decision-making is exposed further by explicit and implicit cultural differences. It is important to understand and manage cultural differences amongst different members of the variety of distribution channel arrangements in different country markets.

- Cultural differences add to control difficulties. Typically, companies have less control over international channels than they have in their domestic market. The usual pattern is to have a smaller market share and to use longer distribution channels, that is, using more layers of distribution intermediaries. Both of these factors reduce the power of the manufacturer. Less channel power usually results in less control over other channel members.

■ The changing nature of retailing patterns influences distribution planning. The long-term commitments that form the basis of successful distribution need to be nurtured. However, change also implies some adapting of distribution channel arrangements. It is a considerable challenge to add new types of distribution intermediaries whilst holding on to long-established accounts.

■ Successful management of international distribution channels and logistics represents a significant challenge to the international marketer. The proximity of the company, the distribution intermediaries and the customer make cultural interactions an important influence on success.

■ Success in international distribution channel and logistics management has to be based on high-quality strategic decisions and consistent and efficient tactical implementation.

KEYWORDS

build to order	globally integrated supply chain
buyer–seller relationships	interactive customer marketing
category management	interactive shopping
data mining	just in time
distribution channel structures	logistics or distribution strategy
effective consumer response	mass customisation
electronic data interchange	multi-media technology
export processing zone	open market
foreign market channels	retailing
indirect/direct channels	total distribution cost

DISCUSSION QUESTIONS

1 Explain the role played by the freight forwarder in the international physical distribution industry. Evaluate three factors which might influence the future role for the freight forwarder.

2 How might the analysis of the retailer infrastructure and retailer marketing practices in advanced economies influence the development of marketing plans for retailers based in less-developed countries?

3 In terms of potential market and channel development, what are the implications for organisations intending to market their products and services in countries which are experiencing World Bank inspired change from a command to a market economy?

4 The arrival of the global village has had a major impact on companies' distribution methods. Identify four factors involved and explain how each has influenced distribution.

5 Fully evaluate the statement: 'Distribution and logistics are increasingly becoming the battleground in international markets as companies seek to gain global competitive advantage.'

CASE STUDY   Merry Management Training

Merry was a training consultancy producing a range of management training courses. Their own staff delivered the courses. They also marketed a range of distance learning management courses which they marketed internationally through agents. A client that successfully completed a training course would receive a Merry certificate.

In the mid-1990s John Razor of Merry investigated the possibility of entering the Middle East. Research had shown that there were potential opportunities for distance learning management programmes, particularly in the Gulf States. By chance he met Yabmob Nig, the managing director of a small management consultancy firm based in Dubai called Ala-Meer Ltd. Ala-Meer was owned by two partners, Yabmob Nig and a silent partner who took no part in the management of the business. The silent partner, a local Dubai businessman, was necessary because Yabmob Nig was an expatriate from India and so could not be sole director of the business.

Yabmob and John had a series of meetings and developed a good rapport. It was not thought necessary to draw up a detailed contract at this stage and so a brief memorandum of understanding (MOU) was signed. The main terms of the MOU were as follows:

1 Ala-Meer had exclusive rights to market and recruit clients throughout the Middle East.

2 Ala-Meer would receive 20 per cent of the fee income.

3 Ala-Meer would charge for other services as agreed.

4 All fees would be made payable to Merry but collected by Ala-Meer.

Ala-Meer were very effective marketers. They very easily got potential clients to sign up for a course but were finding it hard to get clients to make the payments direct to Merry.

Yabmob Nig persuaded John Razor to change the method of payment. The new method of payment allowed clients to pay Ala-Meer in the local currency who would then pass on the payments to Merry. Ala-Meer were then able to market the courses much more easily and were soon recruiting clients from most of the countries in the Middle East. They did this by newspaper advertising, mail shots, Web advertising and subscribing to a number of search engines on the Internet.

Client numbers grew rapidly and everyone was pleased with the market development. Merry was dispatching a large volume of material to the Middle East and Merry staff were conducting seminars in the region on a regular basis.

This was the honeymoon period for the business relationship, as both parties had a common objective – to grow sales. A high degree of trust existed between the parties at this stage.

At the end of the first two years of operations Merry undertook a financial audit of the partnership. However, this was quite difficult to do, as there were no proper audited accounts. Under Dubai law firms do not have to publish audited accounts. Even so, the auditors found evidence to indicate that the business could be a profitable partnership. However, the cash flow was poor. They found that few clients were making payments directly to Merry; most were making payments to Ala-Meer. The audit also showed there was a substantial sum of money that should have been paid to Merry by Ala-Meer which had not been paid.

Yabmob Nig was holding back payment as he and John Razor disagreed on the amount of fees that were outstanding. Ala-Meer were claiming a large amount of expenses that Merry argued had not been agreed in the contract. Ala-Meer saw the 20 per cent margin as pure profit whereas Merry had assumed costs would be defrayed from this percentage. Ala-Meer were also aggrieved that Merry had started marketing their courses in Turkey; they thought they had exclusive rights to the whole of the Middle East, and, to them, that included Turkey.

After long negotiations Merry found it almost impossible to agree the sum that Ala-Meer should pay as a result of the fees they had collected. Ala-Meer were constantly claiming 'additional costs' and reporting lower recruitment figures than Merry had delivered material for. In the end Merry had to send out its own accounting staff to audit Ala-Meer records and agree how much Ala-Meer had to pay to Merry. The relationship between the two parties deteriorated rapidly from this point on and Merry terminated the relationship.

Questions

1 Why did this promising business relationship go so badly wrong?

2 How could Merry have protected their business in the Middle East more effectively?

3 What lessons can be drawn from this case regarding cross-cultural negotiations?

Source: Nick Payne, Sheffield Hallam University

REFERENCES

Albaum, G., Strandskow, J., Duerr, E. and Dowd, L. (1998) *International Marketing and Export Management*, 3rd edn, Addison-Wesley.

Branch, A.E. (2000) *Export Practice and Management*, 4th edn, Thomson Learning.

Cateora, P.R. and Graham, J.L. (1999) *International Marketing*, 10th edn, Irwin.

Czinkota, M.E. and Ronkainen, I.A. (2004) *International Marketing,* 7th edn, Thomson Learning.

Davies, R. and Finney, M. (1998) 'Retailers rush to capture new markets', Mastering Global Business, Part 7, *Financial Times,* 13 March.

Horovitz, J. and Kumar, N. (1998) 'Reaching the global consumer', Mastering Global Business, *Financial Times*, Week 7.

Keegan, W.J. and Sclegelmilch, B. (2001) *Global Marketing Management – A European Perspective*, FT Prentice-Hall.

Klein, L.A. and Quelch, J.A. (1997) 'Business to Business Market Making on the Internet', *International Marketing Review*, 14 (5).

Kotler, P. (2003) *Marketing Management*, 11th edn, Pearson Education Intn.

Lewin, J.E. and Johnston W.J. (1997) 'International sales force management: a relationship perspective', *Journal of Business and Industrial Marketing*, 12 (3/4).

McGoldrick, P.J. (2002) *Retail Marketing*, McGraw-Hill.

Nakata, C. and Sirakumar, R. (1997) 'Emerging market conditions and their impact on first mover advantages: an integrative review', *International Marketing Review*, 14 June.

Rosenbloom, B. (1999) *Marketing Channels, A Management View,* 6th edn, Dryden Press.

Stern, L. and El-Ansary, A.I. (1992) *Marketing Channels*, Prentice-Hall.

Usunier, J.C. (2000) *Marketing Across Cultures*, 3rd edn, Prentice-Hall.

PRICING FOR INTERNATIONAL MARKETS

Introduction

Many organisations believe that pricing is the most flexible, independent and controllable element of the marketing mix and that it plays a major role in international marketing management. This is largely based on the fact that pricing changes appear to prompt an immediate response in the market. However, despite the apparent simplicity of using pricing as a major marketing tool, many managers find pricing decisions difficult to make. This is in part due to the fact that whilst most firms recognise the importance of pricing at a tactical level in stimulating short-term demand, far fewer recognise the importance of the strategic role of pricing in international marketing.

In this chapter, we focus upon both the internal and external factors that affect international pricing decisions, the role that pricing plays in developing strategies to meet corporate objectives, and the relationship between pricing and other aspects of the firm's activities. In addition to considering the stages involved in developing a comprehensive international pricing policy, we discuss the specific problems associated with pricing in international marketing which do not affect the domestic business. We then go on to explore the financial issues in managing risk in pricing and of nonpayment of debts.

Learning objectives

After reading this chapter you should be able to:

- Discuss the issues that affect international pricing decisions
- Evaluate different strategic options for pricing across international markets
- Differentiate between the problems facing companies engaged in foreign market pricing and those faced by companies trying to coordinate strategies across a range of global markets
- Find solutions to the problems of pricing in high-risk markets

DOMESTIC VS INTERNATIONAL PRICING

For many companies operating in domestic markets, pricing decisions are based on the relatively straightforward process of allocating the total estimated cost of producing, managing and marketing a product or service between the forecast total volume of sales, and adding an appropriate profit margin. Problems for these firms arise when costs increase, sales do not materialise or competitors undercut the prices. In international markets, however, pricing decisions are much more complex, because they are affected by a number of additional external factors, such as fluctuations in exchange rates, accelerating inflation in certain countries and the use of alternative payment methods such as leasing, barter and counter-trade.

In recent years, too, it has become more apparent that customer tastes have become much more sophisticated, and so purchase decisions are made less frequently on the basis of price consideration, but are increasingly influenced by wider expectations of product performance and perceptions of value. This has particular implications for international products, which are often perceived to be of significantly different value – higher or lower – than locally produced products. Pricing strategies are also strongly influenced by the nature and intensity of the competition which exists in the various local markets.

For these reasons, it is important to recognise at the outset that the development and implementation of pricing strategies in international markets should follow the following stages:

1 **Analysing the factors** which influence international pricing, such as the cost structures, the value of the product, the market structure, competitor pricing levels and a variety of environmental constraints.

2 Confirming what impact the **corporate strategies** should have on pricing policy.

3 **Evaluating the various strategic pricing options** and selecting the most appropriate approach.

4 **Implementing the strategy** through the use of a variety of tactics and procedures to set prices at SBU level.

5 **Managing prices and financing** international transactions.

THE FACTORS AFFECTING INTERNATIONAL PRICING DECISIONS

A firm exporting speculatively for the first time, with little knowledge of the market environment that it is entering, is likely to set a price based largely on company and product factors. Because of its restricted resources, the firm places particular emphasis on ensuring that sales revenue generated at least covers the costs incurred. However, whilst it is important that firms recognise that the cost structures for production, marketing and distribution of products and services are of vital importance, they should not be regarded as the sole determinants when setting prices. Terpstra and Sarathy (2000) identify many other factors that firms should take into consideration, such as environmental factors, market factors, company factors and specific product factors; these are summarised below. It is by giving full recognition to the effect of these factors on pricing decisions that the company can develop a strategic rather than a purely tactical approach to pricing.

Factors influencing the pricing strategy

Company and product factors

- corporate and marketing objectives
- firm and product positioning
- product range, life cycle, substitutes, product differentiation and unique selling propositions
- cost structures, manufacturing, experience effect and economies of scale
- marketing, product development
- available resources
- inventory
- shipping costs.

Market factors

- consumers' perceptions, expectations and ability to pay
- need for product adaptation, market servicing
- market structure, distribution channels, discounting pressures
- market growth, demand elasticities
- need for credit
- competition objectives, strategies and strength.

Environmental factors

- government influences and constraints
- currency fluctuations
- business cycle stage, level of inflation
- use of non-money payment and leasing.

Companies operating internationally must consider all the above factors detailed for each specific country market. However, as with all the other marketing mix factors, the individual country pricing policies need to be integrated and co-ordinated within a wider regional or global strategy in order to enable corporate objectives to be met.

Whilst it is important that companies consider all the factors listed, some of them, such as corporate objectives, market and product factors, consumer perceptions, competitor responses and cost structures are of particular significance.

Company and product factors

Corporate objectives

The short-term tactical use of pricing such as discounts, product offers and seasonal reductions is often emphasised by managers, at the expense of its strategic role. Firms will use export markets if they have excess production capacity to dump excess products. This means they use marginal pricing strategies, pricing at really low prices so they cover only the variable costs. Yet pricing over the past few years has played a very significant part in the restructuring of many industries, resulting in the growth of some businesses and the decline of others. A number of authors have explained how Japanese firms, in particular, have approached a new market for a specific product with the intention of building market share over a period of years, through maintaining or even reducing pricing levels, establishing the product, the brand name, and setting up effective distribution and servicing networks. As a result of this strategy, Japanese companies have come to dominate a whole range of industries, from consumer electronics to zip fasteners. This has usually been accomplished at the expense of short-term profits as Japanese international companies have consistently taken a long-term perspective on profits. The Japanese banks, which are usually part of the same loose groups of companies linked through mutual shareholding, have played a significant part in this process, seeing themselves as being more closely involved with the company rather than simply being external providers of finance. Consequently, they are prepared to wait much longer for returns on investments than some of their Western banking counterparts.

By contrast, US firms have relied in the past more on international corporate strategies with greater emphasis on factors such as advertising and selling, believing that these reduce the need to compete on price. The reason for this is that the cost base of US manufacturing is usually much higher than that of its foreign competitors. However, the rapid growth of the South East Asian economies has led to a change in the priorities of US firms. In a recent survey US firms ranked pricing as more important than any other element of the marketing mix, whereas South East Asian firms, which have been aggressively reducing their cost base for years, now place greater emphasis upon other factors, such as continually upgrading their products, through research and development, in order to reduce the risk of their being substituted by me-too copies.

The international nature of competition leads to the question of whether firms should aim for a broadly standardised price structure, or whether prices should be adapted in each country.

Product factors

Whilst in theory, standardisation in pricing might appear easier to manage and therefore be preferable, in practice the different local economic, legal and competitive factors in each market make it rarely achievable. The occasions when **price standardisation** is achievable are more usually related to the nature of the product and its stage in the life cycle – for example, standardised pricing can be adopted for certain high-tech products where limited competition exists. Mueller and Cavusgil (1996), however, note that when the technology becomes more freely available, the marketers adopt more market-led pricing. Aircraft makers, for example, because of the relative uniqueness and complexity of the technology, tend to charge the same price regardless of where the customer is based. However, in contrast, shipbuilders, with products in the mature phase of the product life cycle, adapt prices to meet each particular purchase situation.

In developing pricing strategies, a company needs to be aware of the price dynamics of specific products in the various markets. Five characteristics of the product are important in pricing:

- **Frequency of purchase.** Frequently purchased products, for example baby food, petrol, tea and bread, tend to be very price-sensitive in all international markets, whereas occasional purchases are not.
- **Degree of necessity**. If a product is essential for its users, price changes are unlikely to affect the market size, except in countries where extreme poverty exists and people cannot afford even the most basic necessities.

- **Unit price.** High-priced products such as holidays and cars are evaluated in greater detail in terms of the consumer's perceptions of value for money, and so, for example, reliability, style and features of cars are extremely important to consumers besides price.

- **Degree of comparability.** Consumers are less price-conscious about insurance policies than grocery products, because the alternatives are more difficult to compare. Price-setting is particularly difficult in certain services, such as advertising, consultancy and accountancy, which have a different perceived value from country to country.

- **Degree of fashion or status.** The high prices of luxury goods are seen as establishing their quality and it is usually the goods that have a prestige image, often created in other countries, which are not price-sensitive.

Price positioning and value for money

The characteristics of the product or service, particularly the high unit price items, lead international marketers to adopt local pricing strategies which are broadly similar for individual markets, so that the positioning of specific products remains consistent from country to country. Marks and Spencer sell basic foods at higher prices than other food retailers in the UK, by guaranteeing extremely high consistency of quality. This difference is not perceived to be so great in other countries, however, where consumers feel that the general quality is not significantly different to justify a substantially higher price.

Price plays an important role in product differentiation by enhancing the perceived value of the product and helping consumers to distinguish between offers from different competitors in order that their needs can be met. Watch prices, for example, range from very little for a child's watch, to a high premium price for a Rolex. Within this range, individual manufacturers normally confine specific brands within particular pricing bands which are linked to the positioning of the brand and the profile of the watches within the range, and to the characteristics of the target segment.

The key role of price in differentiating products within a category and within a particular market can be used as an offensive strategy. This is demonstrated by the South Korean car manufacturer, Kia, which entered the US car market knowing that its brand name had little credibility there and that the market was already saturated with broadly equivalent products. It targeted its Japanese equivalents, the Honda Civic and Toyota Corolla, by offering a similar car at a 25 per cent lower price.

The influence of cost structures on pricing

There is a close relationship between prices, costs and sales volume of a product, because the price charged affects sales volume by increasing or decreasing the overall demand. As a result of producing or marketing larger volumes, the unit cost of an individual product reduces, and so, of all the factors, often this becomes the initial stimulus for firms taking the decision to export.

The relationship between demand and sales volume

The way in which price affects demand is influenced by many factors. Some products are characterised by having **elastic demand** and being extremely price sensitive, so that sales volumes increase significantly as prices are reduced. In underdeveloped markets, where there is low penetration but considerable desire for Western products such as soft drinks or fast food, sales will increase rapidly if the price is reduced relative to consumers' ability to pay.

By contrast, other products are characterised by **inelastic demand**. For example, suppliers of power generation equipment cannot significantly stimulate demand in individual markets by reducing the price. For such firms, an increase in business revenue is largely determined by changes in external factors, such as an improvement in the economy. The potential market for the European power generation equipment suppliers National Power and ABB was increased by the political decision in Malaysia to partially privatise state utilities.

The relationship between cost and sales volume

A second situation of inelastic demand occurs if a firm finds that it has reached saturation in its home market, so that even if prices were reduced, there would not be significant extra sales to off-set the loss of profit. The firm might conclude that exporting would provide an alternative method of increasing sales and thereby generate additional profit.

This is especially so when firms can increase sales by entering an export market and they can make use of existing spare production capacity and so price purely to cover their variable costs. Consider the situation shown in Table 11.1 where all the fixed costs are absorbed by the sales in the domestic market, but in addition, 10 per cent extra sales are obtained in export markets at the same prices. Provided there are no increases in fixed costs, there would be recovery of the fixed costs because of the additional 10 per cent export business. This recovery of fixed costs by the export business would be shown as an additional contribution to the general overheads of the business. The contribution from the export business would be all additional profit.

The fixed **production cost** of the product includes depreciation of equipment, building rental and business rates. General overheads include advertising, selling, distribution and administration.

The example shows that in practice the additional £100 000 sales have generated an additional £40 000 profit (6.3 per cent on total sales) – far greater than the £30 000 profit generated on the £1 million domestic sales (3 per cent profit on total sales). The firm could therefore afford to reduce its export price considerably and still make a profit, provided that no extra general overhead costs were

TABLE 11.1	The effect of additional export sales on contribution		
	Domestic sales (100 000 units) £000	+ 10% Export sales	Domestic + 10% export sales (110 000 units) £000
Sales	1000	100	1100
Fixed production costs	300		300
Variable production costs	500	50	550
Total costs	800	50	850
Contribution to general overheads	200	50	250
General overheads	170	10	180*
Profit	30	40	70

Note: *General overheads are higher due to additional exporting costs.

incurred, as long as there was spare production capacity and no extra investment had to be made.

In export markets, the firm might choose one of the following four alternatives, setting the selling price at:

■ **Production cost** plus general overhead plus added profit (this would normally be the list price).

■ **Production cost**, but without general overhead or profit added.

■ **Below production** cost.

■ **Production cost** with specific export costs added.

The choice of alternatives will depend on the firm's objectives in entering international markets. The first leads to the safest, albeit least competitive, price and is frequently the approach adopted by new exporters who are unwilling to take any significant risk. The firm might even take the list price, including the domestic gross margin, and add to it all the costs of exporting such as marketing, distribution and administration, resulting in the export price being far greater than the domestic price. In most international markets, however, a list price calculated in this way is unlikely to gain significant market share, and so a lower selling price is required.

The arguments for using the second opinion, to set a lower export selling price, are based on the belief that export costs should not include domestic sales costs such as advertising, marketing research, domestic and administration costs. Whilst this option has some merit, it might well fail to take account of high specific export costs.

The third option is clearly quite risky as it is designed to substantially increase volume. The danger, of course, is that if the increased volume generated does not absorb the fixed and general overhead costs, the product will be unprofitable and losses will result. This approach is often used in overseas markets and is based on **marginal costing**, whereby unused production capacity or extended production runs can provide extra goods for sale with little or no change in fixed costs, so that the extra production can effectively be produced at a lower cost than the original production schedule. Another risk with this strategy is that the firm could be accused of **dumping excess capacity** in foreign markets. This sometimes is exacerbated as a result of government policy, particularly in declining industries. For example, in the European steel industry, certain governments, including those of Germany, Italy and Spain, have continued to subsidise their own inefficient steel industries by providing various incentives such as subsidised, low-cost energy, which has had the effect of maintaining unwanted capacity. When the European Union Commission's plan for steel restructuring was presented, the more efficient private sector companies were unwilling to cut their capacity until the state-owned sector did the same.

The fourth option begs the question of whether or not export pricing should reflect all the costs specific to export sales, and if so, which costs can be directly attributable to exports. It can be argued that, particularly if a firm intends ultimately to commence manufacture in foreign markets, it is vital to know exactly what are the realistic costs for foreign markets. Allocating costs such as research and development accurately and appropriately, however, can be difficult.

Specific export costs

Whilst export volumes are small in comparison to the domestic market, some experimentation in export pricing is possible, but as exporting becomes a more significant part of the activities of the company, perhaps requiring the allocation of dedicated equipment or staff, it is necessary to reflect all costs that are specific to export sales. These costs include tariffs, special packaging, insurance, tax liabilities, extra transport, warehousing costs and export selling.

The most immediate and obvious result of all these costs being passed on is that the price to the consumer in an export market is likely to be much greater than the price to a domestic consumer. An example of this is shown in Table 11.2.

This raises the question of whether foreign consumers will be prepared to pay a higher price for imported rather than locally produced goods. Justifying the cost of the product on the basis of its added value might be possible in the short term, but is unlikely to provide the international marketer with a basis for long-term viability in each local market. A strategy must be developed to deal with this situation in which the cost to the ultimate consumer is reduced. The main options available to the exporter include:

- *aggressively reducing production costs*, modifying the product if necessary and sourcing overseas
- *shortening the distribution channel*, for example, by selling direct to retailers
- *selecting a different market entry strategy*, such as foreign manufacture, assembly or licensing to avoid the additional costs of exporting.

The implications of changing the market entry and distribution strategy have been dealt with in earlier chapters of this book; here we discuss strategies for reducing cost.

Cost reduction

The rationale behind any firm's decision to enter international markets is usually to increase profitability, and this is based upon a recognition of the fact that the size of the firm's actual market share is a primary determinant of profitability. This is supported by PIMS (Profit Impact of Market Strategy) research findings. This shows that firms with a larger market share normally have lower unit costs, and they are perceived by customers to market higher-quality products, leading to relatively higher market prices. Both of these factors result in higher profits for the firm.

TABLE 11.2	Escalation of costs through exporting		
		Export price (£)	Domestic price (£)
Manufacturer's FOB price		10.00	10.00
Sea freight and insurance		1.20	
Landed cost (CIF)		11.20	
Import tariff: 8 per cent on CIF value		0.90	
CIF plus tariff		12.10	
17.5 per cent VAT		2.12	1.75
Distributor purchase price		14.32	11.75
Distributor mark-up (15 per cent)		2.15	1.75
Retailer purchase price		16.47	13.50
Retail margin 40 per cent		10.98	9.00
Consumer purchase price		27.45	22.50

Most companies in international markets have the potential to benefit from driving down costs through achieving **economies of scale**, exploiting the benefits of the **learning curve** and making strategic decisions on the location or relocation of manufacturing plants within the context of worldwide operations.

Economies of scale

Economies of scale are obtained as a result of manufacturing additional products with the same or only slightly higher fixed costs, so that, in practice, for every additional product produced, the unit cost reduces. This is a slight over-simplification of the situation as, for example, installation of new plant might in the short term increase unit costs during the period when the plant is running at below its economic capacity. Whilst in domestic markets the benefits from economies of scale follow directly, in international markets these economies must more than off-set savings achieved by having local plants, which result in reduced transport costs and the avoidance of import tariffs.

Learning curve

Some authors have suggested that, although it is less well known than economies of scale, the learning curve has potentially greater benefit for cost reduction. Its origins lie in the production of aircraft in World War II. The observation that the time needed to perform a specific task reduced as the operatives become more familiar with it was made. Since then a series of studies by the Boston Consulting Group have found evidence that the effect was much more widespread than this, however, and covered all aspects of business, including high and low technology, products and services, and consumer and industrial products. They point out that there is a direct relationship between the cumulative volume of production and the costs incurred in producing the same product benefits. The major sources of savings from the experience gained through the learning curve are:

- greater labour efficiency
- task specialisation and method improvement
- new production processes
- better performance of existing equipment
- changes to the mix of resources
- greater product standardisation
- improved product designs.

Thus the learning curve provides an opportunity for cost reductions, although if managers do not make a concerted effort, costs will rise.

The combined effects of economies of scale and the learning curve were seen in the electronics market, where aggressive firms slashed prices to gain market share, knowing that cost reductions would follow. For example, Sony set the price of its mini-disc players in the US market at a third of the actual manufacturing cost, on the basis that the volume generated by increased demand would force component and assembly costs down, through a combination of these two effects. A key issue in international marketing is how best these effects can be exploited, particularly as the skills and experience are spread throughout the world. The efficient transfer of these skills and knowledge between different strategic business units then becomes paramount.

Location of production facility

Driven by the continual need to reduce costs, companies have increasingly considered selective location or relocation of production facilities. As firms increasingly market their products globally, so their choice of manufacturing locations is determined by many other considerations than simply being close to particular markets. They might choose to locate a factory in a less developed country in order to take advantage of lower labour costs, but also they may well develop specific skills and areas of specialisation in those locations. For example, a large proportion of televisions, radios, calculators, and jeans are manufactured in South East Asia.

India, with 1 billion inhabitants, 100 million of whom are considered to represent a financially aware middle class, presents the attractive opportunity of an emerging market as well as a huge skilled but cheap workforce for multinationals seeking low-cost manufacturing bases. Thomson-CSF (France), Coca-Cola, Motorola, IBM and Hewlett Packard have all decided to set up there, as did Rolfe and Nolan in resolving their dilemma (see Dilemma 11.1).

Problems associated with manufacturing in Western countries have helped to accelerate this transfer of manufacturing. Lagging productivity, reluctance to source materials and parts globally, strong unions and high standards of living were the causes of the decline in the US manufacturing base. Many regions and countries are responding to this opportunity for inward investment by marketing a variety of incentives and attractions to companies wishing to relocate.

It is not only in manufacturing that relocation of activities can benefit from lower labour costs. For instance, the introduction of fibre optic cables allows considerably more information to be transferred quickly and accurately by telecommunications, and so can lead to high labour-content jobs such as data input, order processing and invoicing being carried out in other countries. This has considerable implications for services such as insurance and banking.

Market factors

Consumers' response

Perhaps the most critical factor to be considered when developing a pricing strategy in international markets, however, is how the customers and competitors will respond.

There are nine factors which influence the sensitivity of customers to prices and all have implications for the international marketer. Price sensitivity reduces:

- the more distinctive the product is
- the greater the perceived quality
- the less aware consumers are of substitutes in the market
- if it is difficult to make comparisons, for example in the quality of services such as consultancy or accountancy

---

DILEMMA 11.1   **The cost of servicing global customers**

Rolfe and Nolan PLC market software solutions within the finance and commodity trading industries. They have over 300 international customers. In the early 1990s they had a large number of offices globally to service their international markets. In the mid-1990s Rolfe and Nolan came under increasing pressure to cut costs and increase efficiency when new firms entered the market. Equipped with the latest technology, such firms were able to compete by offering a similar service at a much lower cost. Rolfe and Nolan had to respond to the competitive threat. They wanted to maintain their market share without sacrificing healthy profit margins.

- if the price of a product represents a small proportion of total expenditure of the customer
- as the perceived benefit increases
- if the product is used in association with a product bought previously so that, for example, components and replacements are usually extremely highly priced
- if costs are shared with other parties
- if the product or service cannot be stored.

The issue with all these factors is that it is customer perceptions and purchasing behaviour which are most important in setting prices. In France, EuroDisney suffered considerably from weaknesses in its financial structure. The fundamental problems were that customer perceptions and demand for EuroDisney were out of step with forecasts. The explanation for the weaknesses in their offer was found to be in the factors affecting price sensitivity. High interest rates and high labour costs were underestimated and the availability of disposable income of potential consumers overestimated. After a five-year major effort EuroDisney became profitable. Customers' perception of credit can also influence purchasing behaviour. In Central Europe and Asia, consumers have been reluctant to borrow money to buy goods. However, as we can see from Illustration 11.1, this is now changing.

Competitors' response

As competition increases in virtually every product and market, the likely response of the competitors to a firm's pricing strategy becomes increasingly important. An attempt should be made to forecast how competitors might react to a change in pricing strategy by analysing the market and product factors which affect them, consumer perceptions of their product offers and *their* internal cost

---

ILLUSTRATION 11.1 **Consumer credit fuels consumer purchases**

Central and Eastern European countries are seen as high growth markets and many retailers in recent years have moved into the region. However, until recently, retailers have had difficulties in persuading consumers to take on credit and so buy more of their goods. Hampering their efforts until recently has been the lack of credit agencies to carry out credit ratings on potential borrowers. There also has been no reliable court procedures through which creditors could recover bad debts. This is now changing; both Poland and the Czech Republic have set up Western-style credit bureaus and whilst court procedures are still slow, lenders have been investing heavily in systems to spot and chase late payments.

Such efforts could reap rich rewards, as it is the view of many that Central and Eastern Europeans are fast developing the spending habits of their Western neighbours and in so doing are starting to accept credit as a necessary cost if they are to realise their aspirations. Lending to households is now growing at 26 per cent per annum. In the Western-

owned shops, customers are offered not only groceries and consumer goods but also credit cards and personal loans.

In East Asia it is a similar story. Until recently banks have only been interested in lending to corporate clients but that too is changing. In China banks are actively encouraged to lend to Chinese consumers by the China Central Bank. East Asia is seen by Visa as its fastest-growing market in the world.

However, this growth does come with a risk. The southern province of Guandong is seen as a hotbed of piracy in the production of fake credit cards as pirates shift from designer brands to consumer credit. In one raid alone police seized over 17 000 fake credit cards.

Question How do you account for the changing attitudes across Central Europe and East Asia?

Source: Adapted from *The Economist*, 27 February 2003 and 2 June 2003

structures. Competitors' pricing strategies will be affected by such issues as their commitment to particular products and markets, and the stance that they might have adopted in the past during periods of fierce competition.

Before implementing pricing strategies and tactics, therefore, it is essential to estimate the likely consumer and competitor response by evaluating similar situations which have arisen in other international markets or countries. The responses of competitors who adopt a global strategic approach are likely to be more easily predicted than a competitor adopting a multi-domestic strategy.

It is useful to consider how these factors have affected the competitive responses of a number of companies such as Gillette, Kodak and Philip Morris.

DEVELOPING PRICING STRATEGIES

Having discussed the factors which firms should consider in the pricing process, we now turn to the development of international pricing strategies. The first question to be addressed is to what extent prices should be standardised across the markets. There are three approaches to international pricing strategies:

Standardisation, or ethnocentric pricing, based on setting a price for the product as it leaves the factory, irrespective of its final destination. Whilst each customer pays the same price for the product at the factory gate, they are expected to pay transport and import duties themselves, either directly or indirectly, and this leads to considerable differences in the price to the final consumer.

For the firm, this is a low-risk strategy as a fixed return is guaranteed and the international buyer takes all the exchange rate risk. However, no attempt is made to respond to local conditions in each national market and so no effort is made to maximise either profits or sales volume. This type of pricing strategy is often used when selling highly specialised manufacturing plant.

Adaptation, or polycentric pricing, allows each local subsidiary or partner to set a price which is considered to be the most appropriate for local conditions, and no attempt is made to coordinate prices from country to country. The only constraints that are applied when using this strategy relate to transfer pricing within the corporate structure.

The weakness with this policy is the lack of control that the headquarters have over the prices set by the subsidiary operations. Significantly different prices must be set in adjacent markets, and this can reflect badly on the image of multi-national firms. It also encourages the creation of grey markets (which are dealt with in greater detail later in this chapter), whereby products can be purchased in one market and sold in another, undercutting the established market prices in the process. Firms marketing on the Internet of course find it very difficult to pursue such strategies because of the free flow of information across markets. Gap customers soon discovered they could save up to 40 per cent of the price of a garment by buying online rather than in their local store.

Invention, or geocentric pricing, involves neither fixing a single price, nor allowing local subsidiaries total freedom for setting prices either, but attempts to take the best of both approaches. Whilst the need to take account of local factors is recognised, particularly in the short term, the firm still expects local pricing strategies to be integrated into a company-wide long-term strategy. The benefits of this approach are shown in the following example. A firm which intends to establish a manufacturing base within a particular region may need to rapidly increase market share in order to generate the additional sales necessary for a viable production plant. In the short term, the local subsidiary may be required to sell at what for them is an uneconomic price, so that by the time the new plant comes on stream, sufficient sales have built up to make the plant and the individual subsidiaries profitable.

The objectives of pricing

The objectives of the firm's pricing strategy are directly related to the various factors which have been discussed, but it should be emphasised that they will be affected as much by the prevailing company culture and attitudes to international marketing as by market and environmental conditions. The most common pricing objectives for companies are listed below, but it must be recognised that firms also adapt or add other specific objectives according to their own specific and changing circumstances. The alternative approaches are:

Rate of return. Cost-oriented companies set prices to achieve a specific level of return on investment, and may quote the same ex-works price for both domestic and international markets.

Market stabilisation. A firm may choose not to provoke retaliation from the leader, so that market shares are not significantly changed.

Demand-led pricing. Prices are adjusted according to an assessment of demand, so that high prices are charged when demand is buoyant and low prices are charged when demand is weak.

Competition-led pricing. In commodity markets such as coffee and wheat, world market prices are established through continual interaction between buyers and sellers. Selling outside the narrow band of prices that have been mutually agreed will either reduce sales or unnecessarily reduce profits.

Pricing to reflect product differentiation. Individual products are used to emphasise differences between products targeted at various market segments. Car makers, for example, charge prices for the top of the range models which are far higher than is justified by the cost of the additional features which distinguish them from the basic models but problems arise in different international markets, as consumers' perceptions vary as to what is considered to be a basic model.

Market skimming. The objective of market skimming is for the firm to enter the market at a high price and lower the price only gradually, or even abandon the market as competition increases. It is often used by companies in recovering high research and development costs.

Market penetration. Low prices can be used by a firm to rapidly increase sales by stimulating growth and increasing market share, but at the same time discouraging competition. Japanese companies have used this strategy extensively to gain leadership in a number of markets, such as cars, home entertainment products and electronic components.

Early cash recovery. Faced with liquidity problems, products in the mature or declining phase of the product life cycle, or products with an uncertain future in the market because of changes in government policy, a firm may aim for early cash recovery, to increase sales and generate cash rapidly. A variety of mechanisms are used, including special offers, discounts for prompt payment and rigorous credit control; all this type of pricing is a form of **marginal cost pricing**.

Prevent new entry. Competitors can be discouraged from entering a market by establishing low prices which will indicate to potential competitors the prospect of low returns and price wars. Domestic firms have used this strategy to attempt to prevent entry by international competitors; however, the danger is that the other firm might successfully enter the market with a quite different positioning, such as higher specification or quality, or with improved service levels. The defending firm, due to its low-price strategy, may not have the income to make the necessary investment to compete with the new entrant.

Setting a price

Having determined suitable strategies for pricing in international markets, a company must then consider the options available in setting individual prices. Companies can decide on the basis of their knowledge, objectives and situation to take either a cost, market or competition-oriented approach.

Cost-oriented approaches are intended to either:

- achieve a specific return on investment; or
- ensure an early recovery of either cash, or investments made to enter the market.

Market-oriented pricing approaches give the company the opportunity to:

- stabilise competitive positions within the market;
- skim the most profitable business; or
- penetrate the market by adopting an aggressive strategy to increase market share.

Competition-oriented approaches are designed to:

- maintain and improve market position;
- meet and follow competition;
- reflect differences in the perceived value and performance of competitive products; or
- prevent or discourage new entrants in the market.

No matter which of these broad strategies are adopted, the process for determining export pricing is essentially the same:

- determine export market potential
- estimate the price range and target price
- calculate sales potential at the target price
- evaluate tariff and non-tariff barriers
- select suitable pricing strategy in line with company objectives
- consider likely competitor response
- select pricing tactics, set distributor and end-user prices
- monitor performance and take necessary corrective action.

PROBLEMS OF PRICING AND FINANCING INTERNATIONAL TRANSACTIONS

There are a number of specific problems which arise in setting and managing prices in international markets. Problems arise in four main areas:

Problems in multi-national pricing. Companies find difficulty in coordinating and controlling prices across their activities sufficiently to enable them to achieve effective financial performance and their desired price positioning:

- How can prices be coordinated by the company across the various markets?
- How can a company retain uniform price positioning in different market situations?
- At what price should a company transfer products or services from a subsidiary in one country to a subsidiary in another?
- How can a firm deal with importation and sale of its products by an unauthorised dealer?

Problems in managing foreign currency and fluctuating exchange rates. Considerable problems arise in foreign transactions because of the need to buy and sell products in different currencies:

- In what currency should a company price its products in international markets?
- How should the company deal with fluctuating exchange rates?
- How can a company minimise exchange rate risk over the longer-term transactions?

Problems of obtaining suitable payment in high-risk markets. Obtaining payment promptly and in a suitable currency from the less developed countries can cause expense and additional difficulties:

- How might/should a company deal with selling to countries where there is a risk of non-payment?
- How should a company approach selling to countries which have a shortage of hard currency or high inflation?
- How can a company obtain payment upfront on long-term transactions?

Administrative problems of cross-border transfer of goods. Problems of bureaucracy and delays arise as a result of simply moving goods physically across borders:

- At what point should an exporter release control and responsibility for goods?
- What steps can be taken in the export order process to minimise delays?

These four major problem areas will now be dealt with in the following four sections.

PROBLEMS IN MULTI-NATIONAL PRICING

Coordination of prices across markets

The pressure on companies to market truly global products backed by globally standardised advertising campaigns is caused by three major trends: the homogenisation of customer demand, the lowering of trade barriers and the emergence of international competitors. At the same time these largely undifferentiated global products can be sold at very different prices in different countries, based on factors such as purchasing power, **exchange rate** changes and competition and consumer preferences.

Until recently this has been a perfectly acceptable practice. However, in the past decade it has become increasingly difficult for companies to maintain a differentiated pricing strategy across international markets when they are marketing similar if not standardised products. Readily available information on worldwide prices through modern data transfer and the Internet have greatly increased price transparency. Advances in telecommunications systems have also greatly reduced international transaction costs. Global companies who obviously follow differentiated pricing policies are often threatened, first by an erosion of consumer confidence as customers learn of the more attractive pricing policies in other markets and second by *grey marketing* which can result in the cannibalisation of sales in countries with relatively high prices and damaging relationships with authorised distributors.

The issue of achieving **price coordination** across markets has become particularly pertinent in the European Union (EU) since the inauguration of the European Monetary Union and the launch of the Euro.

National price levels across the EU are far from uniform. Amongst the inaugural group of countries joining the EMU, Austria and Finland were significantly high-priced markets, France, Belgium, Portugal and Germany were seen as average and Spain as the bargain basement of Europe. In Denmark, which did not join the EMU, price levels were on average 40 per cent higher than Spain.

Differences in taxation and excise duties as well as disparities in production costs and wage levels lead to price differentials. Firms in the past have tended to adapt their prices to the buying power, income levels and consumer preferences of national markets. Despite the formation of the Single European Market these differences have been largely concealed from the European consumer. The formation of the EMU and the introduction of the euro has changed all that.

Now prices are no longer distorted by fluctuating exchange rates. This means companies competing on the European market need to consider the implications of the transparent euro dominated prices that are now emerging across Europe. Many firms are now operating a euro pricing policy (see Illustration 11.2).

ILLUSTRATION 11.2   Competing in Europe against the euro

In the first years after the euro was launched it was viewed by the markets as a weak currency and soon lost value. At its low point, it had lost more than a fifth of its value against the dollar. This, however, was good for exporters in the eurozone who were able to compete effectively on international markets. European suppliers trying to establish pan-euro pricing using the euro as opposed to sterling or the US dollar had a competitive advantage over suppliers from outside the eurozone not only because of the currency advantage but also because of the extra benefits they were able to offer to the customer by the use of a single currency across their markets, including reduced costs of handling transactions and reduced currency risks. However, in the

years since the launch of the euro consumers have increasingly demanded that the cost savings associated with the wider use of the euro be passed on to them. Cost savings have had to be reflected in prices, whether or not the suppliers in question have achieved such cost savings.

Now of course the euro's fortunes have been reversed and the euro has dramatically increased in strength. This is good for the euro economy but not so good for the exporters in the eurozone already facing tremendous competition in international markets.

Question What are the implications for exporters marketing to Europe from outside the eurozone?

The on-set of **price transparency** will impact on firms in different ways. Highly specialised products with few direct rivals could be largely immune to the risk of price transparency generating more intense competition. However, companies marketing goods that are supplied direct to the consumer could come under pressure from retailers to reduce margins if retailers themselves have had to cut prices to meet new price points set in euros. Furthermore, as more retailers and businesses move to a policy of European-wide sourcing it will soon become impossible for companies to operate on the European market without a sophisticated strategy to effectively coordinate prices across the EU. As a result of this a number of firms have revamped their European marketing strategies.

Firms who fail to meet this challenge will leave themselves open to the threat of grey market goods cannibalising their sales in high-priced national markets.

What is grey marketing?

Grey marketing is a business phenomenon that has seen unprecedented growth in the past few years as information on prices has flowed across countries and consumers have discovered how varying prices can be when companies try to pursue highly differentiated pricing strategies across markets that can no longer be kept separate.

Grey marketing occurs when trademarked goods are sold through channels of distribution that have not been given authority to sell the goods by the trademark holder. This could occur within a country but more and more it is becoming common across countries. This becomes problematic, especially for global marketers trying to manage a coordinated marketing strategy across different markets. Coca-Cola had to bring forward the European launch of Vanilla Coke after it found the product was already being sold in the UK by a distributor who had imported it directly from Canada, where it had been launched several months previously. Typically, however, grey market goods are international brands with high price differentials and low costs of arbitrage. The costs connected with the arbitrage are transportation costs, tariffs, taxes and the costs of modifying the product, i.e. changing the language of instructions.

It is perhaps important to point out that there is nothing illegal about grey market goods; it is purely the practice of buying a product in one market and selling it in other markets in order to benefit from the prevailing price differential. Grey markets tend to develop in markets where information on prices for basically the same product in different countries is cheap and easy to obtain (e.g. cars, designer goods, consumer durables). The Anti Grey Marketing Alliance estimates the revenue generated by international grey marketing activities to be about US$20 billion a year. Whilst grey marketing is seen by its critics as a *free-riding* strategy, it is being increasingly seen as a viable international strategy by smaller firms who, with limited resources, can use it to compete against larger firms in international markets. This is the case of the Malaysian company cited in the case study at the end of Chapter 11.

There are three types of grey markets (see Figure 11.1).

Parallel importing, when the product is priced lower in the home market where it is produced than the export market. The grey marketer in the export market will parallel import directly from the home market rather than source from within their own country; for example, there is a strong parallel import trade in Levi jeans between the USA and Europe. Levi Strauss recently took out a lawsuit against the retail chain Tesco for selling Levi jeans they have sourced directly from outside the EU (see Illustration

11.3). Levi are insisting that jeans in Europe should only be sourced from authorised dealers within the EU.

Re-importing, when the product is priced cheaper in an export market than in the home market where it was produced; re-importation in this case can be profitable to the grey marketer.

Lateral importing. When there is a price difference between export markets, products are sold from one country to another through unauthorised channels.

A disturbing example of this can be found in the pharmaceutical industry where it is estimated that US$18 million of reduced price HIV drugs intended for African markets were diverted back to Europe to be sold at much higher prices on the grey market.

Price coordination strategies

Typically firms try to defend themselves against grey market activities by calling for government intervention or legal protection. As seen in the previous section, companies may resort to imposing restrictions or even threats to retailers. Wal-Mart in the US sourced products through grey markets and suffered the resultant threats from firms such as Adidas and Levi jeans. Other reactive measures have included the refusal to issue warranties in certain markets or even buying out the grey marketer.

Companies competing in international markets who wish to develop more effective strategies to deal with the problem of price coordination across increasingly interdependent markets and the threat of grey market goods have four options open to them.

Economic measures. The company can influence the country manager's pricing decision by controlling the input into those decisions. A multinational can do this through transfer pricing (see later section in this chapter). By raising the price by which it transfers products to the low priced country the headquarters essentially imposes a tax on that market. Closely related to transfer pricing is rationing the product quantities allocated to each country or region and so limiting the number of units sold in the diverting country.

FIGURE 11.1

Three types of grey market

Source: Assmus and Weisse (1995)

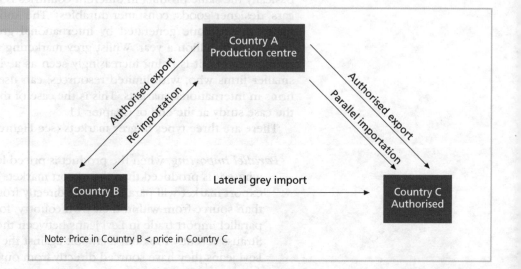

Note: Price in Country B < price in Country C

Centralisation. The company can move towards more centralisation in the setting of prices. Traditionally many multi-national companies have given country managers a high degree of decision-making autonomy. Usually they are in the best position to assess consumer response to any given pricing decisions and they are able to react swiftly to competitor activity. A centralised approach, however, could overcome difficulties with grey market goods although it does usually result in dissatisfaction amongst country managers. A compromise approach is to shift the decision-making authority in pricing from a country to a regional level; however, increasingly grey market goods are becoming a global issue.

Formalisation. The company can standardise the process of planning and implementing pricing decisions. Thus the company influences prices at the local level by prescribing a process that is followed by country managers when establishing pricing policy.

Informal coordination. A number of companies have moved towards a more informal system of coordination without either a high degree of centralisation or formalisation. This thinking is usual in the transnational company where international subsidiaries make differentiated and innovative contributions to an integrated worldwide operation. Whilst this approach may incorporate a variety of techniques the essential asset is that there are common shared business values across the subsidiaries that are backed by compatible incentive systems.

In a proactive approach to coordinating its pricing decision across international markets, a company has to select the appropriate strategy which will in effect be determined, first, by the level of local resources available, and then by the level of environmental complexity, as illustrated in Figure 11.2.

ILLUSTRATION 11.3 Grey clouds cause black anger

Not so long ago Levi Strauss took the retail chain Tesco to court over its sale of Levi jeans. Tesco had bought the jeans from outside the European Union and then sold the jeans within the EU well below the price that the authorised dealers were charging. The judgment by the court, which shocked consumer rights groups everywhere, was that Tesco should not be allowed to import jeans made by Levi Strauss from outside the EU and sell them at cut-down prices without first getting permission from the jeans maker. The ruling was based on a directive which had been designed to protect EU manufacturers from price dumping but was used very effectively by the US multi-national to control its brand positioning in a foreign market.

Levi persuaded the court that Tesco was destroying the image and the brand value of Levi, which could ultimately lead to less brand innovation which would have an adverse effect on the consumer. Tesco said such an argument was specious and that they were purely arbitraging the price

differential between Levis sold in the US and Europe – something, as a global retailer sourcing around the globe, they should be free to do.

Critics of the Levi victory suggest it may prove in the long run to be a rather unsatisfactory, pyrrhic victory. Tesco was freely given huge amounts of sympathetic publicity, whilst Levi's stance was viewed as anti-consumer. Levi has been losing market share in Europe in recent years and is seen by brand experts as no longer strong enough to command premium prices in the market. Its court victory may help it hold on for a while but market forces may in the long run dictate otherwise.

Question Was Levi right to take the action against Tesco? What other options could they have considered?

Source: Adapted from *The Economist*, 24 November 2001 and *Marketing Week*, 20 February 2003

Transfer pricing in international markets

Transfer pricing is an area that has created complications for many international marketing firms. It is concerned with the pricing of goods sold within a corporate family, when the transactions involved are from division to division, to a foreign subsidiary, or to a partner in a joint venture agreement. Whilst these transfer prices are internal to the company, they are important externally because goods being transferred from country to country must have a value for cross-border taxation purposes.

The objective of the corporation in this situation is to ensure that the transfer price paid optimises corporate rather than divisional objectives. This can prove difficult when a company internationally is organised into profit centres. For profit centres to work effectively, a price must be set for everything that is transferred, be it working materials, components, finished goods or services. A high transfer price, for example from the domestic division to a foreign subsidiary, is reflected in an apparently poor performance by the foreign subsidiary, whereas a low price would not be acceptable to the domestic division providing the goods. This issue alone can be the cause of much mistrust between subsidiaries – at best leading to fierce arguments, and at worst leading to loss of business through overpricing.

There tend to be three bases for transfer pricing:

Transfer at cost, in which the transfer price is set at the level of the production cost, and the international division is credited with the entire profit that the firm makes. This means that the production centre is evaluated on efficiency parameters rather than profitability.

Transfer at arm's length, when the international division is charged the same as any buyer outside the firm. Problems occur if the overseas division is allowed to buy elsewhere when the price is uncompetitive or the product quality is inferior, and further difficulties arise if there are no external buyers, making it difficult to establish a relevant price. This is the strategy most preferred by national governments.

Transfer at cost plus is the usual compromise, where profits are split between the production and international divisions. The actual formula used for assessing the transfer price can vary, but usually it is this method which has the greatest chance of minimising executive time spent on transfer price disagreements, optimising corporate profits and motivating the home and international divisions. Often a senior executive is appointed to rule on disputes.

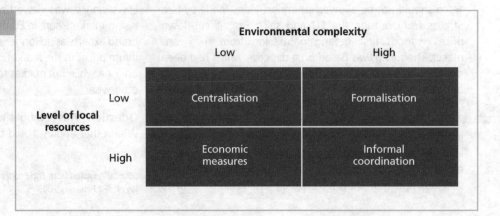

FIGURE 11.2

A framework for selecting a coordination method

Source: Assmus and Weisse (1995)

		Environmental complexity	
		Low	High
Level of local resources	Low	Centralisation	Formalisation
	High	Economic measures	Informal coordination

However, the real interest of transfer pricing is how it is used strategically by companies either to act as a barrier to entry, or to marshal resources around the world.

To create barriers to entry

Most oil companies are vertically integrated, from oil exploration right through to selling petrol at the pumps, and use transfer pricing as part of their strategy to maintain barriers to entry. The major cost for oil companies is at the exploration and refining stage and so, by charging high transfer prices for crude oil, profits are generated at the refining stage of the process, rather than in distribution, where it is relatively easy to enter the market. Oil companies therefore attempt by the use of transfer pricing to make petrol distribution unattractive to potential competitors. Supermarkets and hypermarkets, however, with their huge purchasing power, are increasingly challenging the dominance of the oil companies by using low-priced petrol as a loss leader to entice customers to stores.

To avoid domestic tax liabilities

When countries have different levels of taxation on corporate profits, firms try to ensure that profits are accumulated at the most advantageous point. Companies operating in countries with high corporation tax may be tempted to sell at low transfer prices to their subsidiaries in countries with lower corporate taxation.

To avoid foreign tax

Foreign tax authorities wish to maximise the taxable income within their jurisdiction, and there are a number of strategies a company might use to avoid tax – for example, by charging lower transfer prices if there is high customs duty on goods. The impact of such avoidance strategies is diminishing, as customs authorities become more aware of this practice. Recently the US government demanded huge taxes from Sony when it discovered that it generated 60 per cent of its global sales in the USA but very little profit due to Sony's management of transfer pricing. Japan then retaliated by doing the same to Coca-Cola. However, it can be argued that as the general level of import duties is reducing as international trade agreements come into effect, so the need to take avoiding action is declining.

To manage the level of involvement in markets

If a firm has both a fully owned subsidiary and a joint venture in a particular country, it will wish to sell at a higher price to a company with which it has a joint venture than one that is a fully owned subsidiary. Selling at a low price to foreign partnerships or licensees has the effect of sharing more of the profit with the partner.

Transfer pricing is an area where profit objectives, managerial motivations and government regulation interact and so the expertise of many people – accountants, legal counsel, tax advisors and division managers – is needed to achieve an agreement. The international marketing manager's contribution is primarily concerned with two aspects of the problem:

- achieving an effective distribution of goods to world markets
- ensuring that the impact of the transfer price does not affect foreign market opportunities.

PROBLEMS IN MANAGING FOREIGN CURRENCY TRANSACTIONS

Perhaps the most critical issue for managers is how to deal with the various problems involved in managing transactions which involve currency exchange; a second difficulty is what action to take when selling to countries where there is high inflation.

What currency should the price be quoted in?

In any international marketing transaction, the exporter has the option of quoting in either the domestic or the local currency. If the exporter quotes in the domestic currency, then not only is it administratively much easier, but also the risks associated with changes in the exchange rate are borne by the customer, whereas by quoting prices in the **foreign currency** the exporter bears the **exchange rate risk**. However, there are benefits to the exporter in quoting in foreign currency:

- it could provide access to finance abroad at lower interest rates
- good currency management may be a means of gaining additional profits
- quoting in foreign currency could be a condition of the contract
- customers normally prefer to be quoted in their own currency in order to be able to make competitive comparisons and to know exactly what the eventual price will be.

Furthermore, customers in export markets often prefer quotations in their own currency to enable them to more easily compare the tenders of competitors from a range of countries.

Often the choice of currency for the price quotation depends partly on the trade practices in the export market and the industry concerned. Suppliers competing for business in the oil industry, wherever in the world they may be supplying, may well find they are asked to quote in US dollars.

UK exporters have recently experienced a period of strong sterling, reducing their competitiveness on international markets and subjecting them to price-cutting pressures from overseas customers as was experienced by MDL (see Dilemma 11.2).

Thus as well as the decision as to what currency to quote in, the main worry for both suppliers and customers on international markets is fluctuating exchange rates and how to deal with them. (See Illustration 11.4.)

The introduction of the euro will effectively eliminate exchange rate risk in the countries that enter the **European Monetary Union**. Even countries like the UK, who have decided to delay their decision to enter the EMU, increasingly find that companies selling goods into Europe are pressurised to quote prices in the euro.

Should prices be raised/ lowered as exchange rates fluctuate?

One of the most difficult problems that exporters face is caused by fluctuating exchange rates. The major trading nations appear to have differing strategies to deal with exchange rate appreciation – for example, UK, French and Canadian firms all tend to increase their prices by more than the exchange rate appreciation, whereas Japanese firms only passed on about half the appreciation of the yen in the form of a price rise. Japanese exporters have, therefore, preferred to retain market share by absorbing some of the impact of yen appreciation, at the expense of short-term profits.

Terpstra and Sarathy (2000) identified three types of risk affecting firms, arising from exchange rate fluctuations:

1 **Transaction risk** occurs when the exporter quotes in a foreign currency, which then appreciates, diminishing the financial return to the firm. US hoteliers in Hawaii experienced a very noticeable decline in Japanese tourism when the dollar rose in value from Yen 90 to Yen 120 in just over a year.

2 **Competitive risk** arises because the geographic pattern of a firm's manufacturing and sales puts them at a disadvantage compared to their competition. If, for instance, the firm is manufacturing in a country with an appreciating currency but trying to compete in a marketplace where currencies are depreciating, it could lose out to a local manufacturer.

3 **Market portfolio risk** occurs because a company with a narrow market portfolio will be influenced to a much greater extent by changes in exchange rates than a diversified firm that is better able to balance changes in exchange rates through operating in many countries.

DILEMMA 11.2　　　**Can we avoid the currency risk without losing our customers?**

Management Development Ltd (MDL) is a small firm specialising in management training and development. The firm delivers training programmes using a combination of self-study material and study weekends. The firm operates in the UK, Middle East and the Far East.

In 1996 the firm took a strategic decision to enter the Malaysian market. The firm appointed an agent in Malaysia to market the courses and recruit students. To encourage students to join training courses payment could be made in stages.

The majority of the firm's costs, developing study material, tutoring etc. were incurred in sterling. The income from selling in Malaysia would normally be in ringgits.

Income in ringgits and costs in sterling meant MDL faced a currency risk. A fall in the sterling/ringgit exchange rate could quickly result in a profitable activity generating significant losses for the firm. This in fact happened in the late 1990s when the ringgit/sterling exchange deteriorated.

MDL were unwilling to incur any currency risk. Traditional methods for avoiding currency exposure (hedging) were not considered appropriate due to the small scale of the operation.

Question How should MDL resolve their dilemma?

Source: Fiona Elspeth

ILLUSTRATION 11.4　　　**Dealing with stormy currencies**

After a period of relative calm, exporters are yet again facing the stormy sea of volatile currencies which makes planning and budgeting as well as pricing for international markets very difficult. In early 2003 the euro rose 25 per cent against the dollar and the dollar has lost more than 15 per cent of its value. In Britain, after a long period of strong sterling, the pound has slumped to its lowest level for six years against the euro. This was welcomed by UK exporters and the pro-euro lobby who saw the over-valued sterling as a major barrier to the UK joining the euro. The appreciation of the yen, meanwhile, is causing consternation for the

Japanese government. In Japan, prices have been falling for three consecutive years. Now the government is worried that the rising yen will make exporting for Japanese firms even more difficult and recession even more likely.

Question What can Japanese firms do to remain competitive in their export markets when their own currency is very strong against other world currencies?

Source: Adapted from *The Economist*, 12 May 2003

Various tactics can be adopted to deal with currency fluctuations. When the domestic currency is weak, the firm should:

- compete on price
- introduce new products with additional features
- source and manufacture in the domestic country
- fully exploit export opportunities
- obtain payment in cash
- use a full-cost approach for existing markets, but use marginal costs for new more competitive markets
- repatriate foreign-earned income quickly
- reduce expenditure and buy services (advertising, transport etc.) locally
- minimise overseas borrowing
- invoice in domestic currency.

When the domestic currency is strong, the firm should:

- compete on non-price factors (quality, delivery, service)
- improve productivity and reduce costs
- prioritise strong currency countries for exports
- use counter-trade for weak currency countries
- reduce profit margins and use marginal costs for pricing
- keep the foreign-earned income in the local country
- maximise expenditures in local country currency
- buy services abroad in local currencies
- borrow money for expansion in local markets
- invoice foreign customers in their own currency.

PROBLEMS IN MINIMISING THE RISK OF NON-PAYMENT IN HIGH-RISK COUNTRIES

The international marketing manager increasingly needs to be knowledgeable about the various complexities of financing international marketing transactions and sources of finance to support international marketing strategies, especially when trading with markets seen to be high risk due to adverse economic and political conditions, high inflation or perhaps lack of hard currency. For a company exporting goods to such markets there is a considerable risk of non-payment, for a variety of reasons, such as:

- the buyer failing or refusing to pay for the goods
- insolvency of the buyer
- a general moratorium on external debt by the host
- government political and legal decisions
- war
- failure to fulfil the conditions of the contract
- lack of hard currency
- high inflation.

Traditionally managers will seek financial support to help reduce the risk of non-payment due to the above factors through home governments, commercial banks or some kind of cooperation agreement.

Government-sponsored finance. Governments are often willing to financially support companies in financing international trade transactions in the hope that increased exports will generate economic growth at home and boost employment. National governments approach such support in a variety of ways but in most countries there is an Export–Import bank or perhaps Export Bank or, as in the UK, a government department (Trade Partners UK) who fund a variety of support packages to help companies finance export strategies. Governments will also provide low-cost export guarantee insurance to protect their exporters against non-payment by foreign buyers. However, such protection may not be available in particularly high-risk markets.

Commercial banks compete intensively to offer international trade services to companies operating in international markets. However, they tend only to be willing to support low-risk activities, which sometimes makes it difficult for companies expanding into emerging markets. Commercial banks may also be more interested in short-term financing and so potentially not such a good source for companies making a long-term investment decision in incipient markets where it may be several years before a full return on investment can be achieved. Many banks who made long-term loans to developing markets have suffered losses when countries not experiencing the growth rates expected have been unable to meet debt repayments. This has led to a number of banks being less willing to expose themselves in long-term high-risk markets.

One of the ways banks can help against the risk of non-payment is by forfaiting.

Forfaiting. This is a way of financing without recourse. This means that companies selling products essentially transfer the transaction risk to a forfaiting house. A bill of exchange is drawn up to the value of the contract and the seller transfers the claim resulting from the transaction to the forfaiting house. The seller immediately receives the full amount of the contract minus the discount agreed for the period of the contract. This discount will vary depending on the length of the contract, the level of country risk and whether the invoice is guaranteed by a commercial bank. For the company it provides a source of finance to support medium-term contracts in a market and a means of reducing the risk of non-payment.

Cooperation agreements. These agreements are special kinds of counter-trade deals (see section below) that extend over long periods of time and may have government involvement. They may be called product purchase transactions, buyback deals or pay as you earn deals. For instance, a company may obtain finance to help set up a factory in a particular country if they then agree to buy back the output of the plant.

Counter-trade and leasing

So far in this chapter we have focused upon largely conventional approaches to international pricing; however, over the past two decades there has been a dramatic increase in the use of leasing and counter-trade deals, which are used as a response to the lack of hard currency, particularly amongst less developed countries.

Counter trade deals are more prevalent when companies are trying to enter emerging or less developed markets. The reason for this is threefold.

- It is sometimes difficult to obtain finance commercially to enter such markets.
- The markets themselves may have limited access to hard currency which means the finance of joint ventures or strategic alliances has to be sought through less traditional means.
- Emerging markets may see such deals as a way of encouraging job creation in their own countries and so actively encourage such financing deals.

What is counter-trade?

Counter-trade covers various forms of trading arrangements where part or all of the payment for goods is in the form of other goods or services, and price-setting and financing are dealt with together in one transaction. The original and simple barter system has been developed in order to accommodate modern trading situations. Estimates of counter-trade activity range from 20 to 30 per cent of world trade, and it is predicted to grow further due to its ability, first, to overcome market imperfections and, second, to provide opportunities for extraordinary profits to be made.

There are many variants of counter-trade, resulting from the need to adapt arrangements to meet the needs of individual transactions. The following are the basic forms:

Barter. This is a single exchange of goods with no direct use of money, and does not require intermediaries. It is the simplest form, but has become unpopular because, first, if the goods are not exchanged simultaneously then one participant is effectively financing the other, and second, one of the parties may well receive unwanted goods as part of the deal.

Compensation trading. This involves an agreement in which payment for goods is accepted in a combination of goods and cash.

Counter-purchase. This involves the negotiation of two contracts. In the first, the international marketer agrees to sell the product at an established price in local currency. In the second, simultaneous, contract the international firm buys goods or services for an equivalent or proportionate cash payment from another local supplier.

Off-set. This is similar to counter-purchase, but in this case national governments cooperate to support the deal. Sometimes called a product purchase transaction, it is a way in which the international firm is able to obtain more saleable goods from the country in exchange. For example, Boeing sold AWACS aircraft to the British Ministry of Defence on the basis that the purchase price would be spent on British goods (see Illustration 11.5).

Switch deals involve a third party (usually a merchant house), which specialises in barter trading, disposing of the goods. For example, if an Eastern European company importing Western products can only provide in return heavily discounted relatively low-quality products, which may not be saleable in the West, a third country will need to be found in order that a switch deal can be set up in which these lower-quality goods can be exchanged for other products that are more suitable for the original Western markets.

Cooperation agreements. These can cover buyback deals, pay as you earn deals or a range of other beneficial arrangements made between two parties. It is an arrangement whereby part or all of the cost of purchase of capital equipment might be paid for in the form of production from the equipment supplied, either over time or in the form of some other benefit. Illustration 11.6 gives the example of Ikea who, in one such agreement, leased machinery and equipment to a plant in Poland to upgrade production in exchange for an export contract.

In Japan and South East Asia compensation and off-set are the most frequently used forms of counter-trade. Barter and counter-purchase tend to be more common in lesser developed countries.

So far, the examples of counter-trade have involved deals of products, but many other less tangible elements such as know-how, software and information can be included in agreements. Many of the deals set up are complicated and in some cases have stretched over many years.

Leasing

Leasing is used as an alternative to outright purchase in countries where there is a shortage of capital available to purchase high-priced capital and industrial

---

| ILLUSTRATION 11.5 | Counter-trade deals for GEC |

GEC – the Marconi electronics subsidiary – became involved in three 'off-set' counter-trade deals to entitle them to trade in the Middle East. The contribution to the local economy, in the form of investment in a furniture factory in Abu Dhabi, was made in return for an arms contract. In the deal, local craftsmen assemble furniture and fittings for palaces, hotels etc. in UAE. GEC is in partnership with local sheikhs and a Birmingham company for the venture, who agreed to export at least 50 per cent of the output to Europe and the Far East.

Other off-set counter-trade projects include the formation of a local company to charter ships for an Emirate group and a joint venture to provide geological and topographical information to help evaluate water, oil and gas and other natural resources.

Question What are the advantages and disadvantages of such deals?

| ILLUSTRATION 11.6 | Ikea competes on its supply route |

Ikea's UK profit amounted to £522m last year, and with 130 million people visiting 150 branches in 28 countries, it has been viewed as a highly successful global retailer. Central to its marketing strategy is the standardisation of its core concept of *Swedish democratic designs*. Its democratic stance includes its view of its staff. Employees are referred to as co-workers, some of the stores are run as franchises and last October a day's profits were split among its 4000 staff in the UK.

However, its competitive prices are the mainstay of its competitive edge, and Ikea manages its supply route specifically to ensure it can keep prices down. It sees suppliers in Eastern Europe as playing a key role in its strategy. An essential part of the process is buyback, a form of counter-trade in which machinery and equipment for increasing and upgrading production is leased to Eastern European

companies in exchange for an export contract. In this way the suppliers are able to meet Ikea's high-quality standards and specifications. The repayment period is between three and five years, and in return, Ikea usually buys three to four times the value of the equipment supplied.

In this way drilling and planing equipment has been supplied to a firm in Poland and sewing machines and leather and fabric cutting machines have been supplied to a firm in the Czech Republic, both on a buyback agreement.

Question Evaluate the pros and cons of such a strategy in helping Ikea to sustain low prices in their international markets over the longer term.

Source: Adapted from *The Guardian*, 2 March 2000

goods. Usually the rental fee will cover servicing and the costs of spares too, and so the problem of poor levels of maintenance, which is often associated with high technology and capital equipment in LDCs, can be overcome. Leasing arrangements can be attractive, too, in countries where investment grants and tax incentives are offered for new plant and machinery, in which case the leaser can take advantage of the tax provisions in a way that the lessee cannot, and share some of the savings. It is estimated that leased aircraft account for about 20 per cent of the world's aircraft fleet.

Advantages and limitations of counter-trade

The advantages of counter-trade are as follows:

- New markets can be developed for a country's products, as marketing and quality control skills are often 'imported' with the deal, and it can lead to gaining experience in Western markets.

- Surplus and poorer quality products can be sold through counter-trade whereas they could not be sold for cash. Moreover, dumping and heavy discounting can be disguised.

- Counter-trade through bilateral and multilateral trade agreement can strengthen political ties.

- Counter-trade and contract manufacture can be used to enter high-risk areas.

- Counter-trade can provide extraordinary profits as it allows companies to circumvent government restrictions.

However, there are disadvantages and limitations in using counter-trade:

- There is a lack of flexibility, as the transactions are often dependent on product availability, and counter-traded products are often of poor quality, overpriced or are available due to a surplus.

- Products taken in exchange may not fit with the firm's trading objectives, or may be difficult to sell.

- Dealing with companies and government organisations may be difficult, particularly in locating and organising counter-trade products.

- Negotiations may be difficult, as there are no guide market prices.

- Counter-trade deals are difficult to evaluate in terms of profitability and companies can, through counter-trade, create new competition.

It is likely that in the future, counter-trading will develop further in the form of longer-term rather than shorter-term partnerships as multi-nationals seek permanent foreign sources for incorporation in their global sourcing strategy. LDCs offer the benefits of low-cost labour and materials, as well as relatively untapped markets for goods. This has resulted in multi-nationals reversing the traditional counter-trade process by first seeking opportunities, and then identifying potential counter-trade partners with which to exploit the opportunities.

ADMINISTRATIVE PROBLEMS RESULTING FROM THE CROSS-BORDER TRANSFER OF GOODS

For many companies, particularly those that are infrequent exporters or that have insufficient resources for effective export administration, the process of ensuring that goods reach their ultimate destination is beset with difficulties: goods held in customs warehouses without apparent reason, confusing paperwork, high and apparently arbitrary duties, levies and surcharges, and the need to make exorbitant payments to expedite the release of goods. The UN Conference on Trade and Development (UNCTAD) believe these additional costs to world trade could be as much as 10 per cent of the US$7 trillion taken a year in total world trade. UNCTAD also believes that those costs could be cut by US$100 billion by customs computerisation. It is unlikely, however, that such changes as these will happen quickly, and so companies face a series of decisions about how to manage their own risks and costs, whilst still providing an effective service to their customers.

Deciding at what stage of the export sales process the price should be quoted

Export price quotations are important, because they spell out the legal and cost responsibilities of the buyer and seller. Sellers, as previously mentioned, favour a quote that gives them the least liability and responsibility, such as FOB (free on board), or ex-works, which means the exporter's liability finishes when the goods are loaded on to the buyer's carrier. Buyers, on the other hand, would prefer either *franco domicile*, where responsibility is borne by the supplier all the way to the customer's warehouse, or CIF port of discharge, which means the buyer's responsibility begins only when the goods are in their own country.

Generally, the more **market-oriented pricing** policies are based on CIF, which indicates a strong commitment to the market. By pricing ex-works, an exporter is not taking any steps to build relations with the market and so may be indicating only short-term commitment. The major stages at which export prices might be quoted are as follows:

- Ex (point of origin), such as ex-factory, ex-mine, ex-warehouse.
- FOB: free on board.
- FAS: free alongside.
- FAS: vessel (named port of shipment).
- C. & F.: cost and freight.
- C. & F.: (named point of destination).
- CIF: cost, insurance freight.
- CIF: (named point of destination).
- DDP: direct to destination point.

The export order process

To further emphasise the complexity of managing international pricing, a major task of the marketer is to choose payment terms that will satisfy importers and at the same time safeguard the interests of the exporter. The export process for handling transactions is illustrated in Figure 11.3.

In the process, the customer agrees to payment by a confirmed letter of credit. The customer begins the process (1) by sending an enquiry for the goods. The price and terms are confirmed by a pro-forma invoice (2) by the supplier, so that the customer knows for what amount (3) to instruct its bank (the issuing bank) to open a letter of credit (L/C)(4). The L/C is confirmed by a bank (5) in the supplier's country.

When the goods are shipped (6) the shipping documents are returned to the supplier (7), so that shipment is confirmed by their presentation (8) together with the L/C and all other stipulated documents and certificates for payment (9). The moneys are automatically transmitted from the customer's account via the issuing bank. The customer may only collect the goods (10) when all the documents have been returned to them.

Whilst letters of credit and drafts are the most common payment method, there are also several other methods:

- **A draft.** Drawn by the exporter on the importer, who makes it into a trade acceptance by writing on it the word 'accepted'.

- **A letter of credit.** Similar to a draft, except it is drawn on the bank and becomes a bank acceptance rather than a trade acceptance. There is greater assurance of payment, as an unconditional undertaking is given by the bank that the debts of the buyer will be paid to the seller.

- **Open account.** Sales terms are agreed between buyer and seller, but without documents specifying clearly the importer's payment obligations. There is less paperwork but greater risk of non-payment, so it is only used when a trusting relationship has been developed between the trading parties. In countries where foreign exchange is difficult to obtain, drafts and letters of credit will be given priority in any currency allocation.

- **Consignment.** The exporter retains title of the goods until the importer sells them. Exporters own the goods longer in this method than any other, and so the financial burden and risks are at their greatest. In addition, the recovery

---

FIGURE 11.3

The export order process

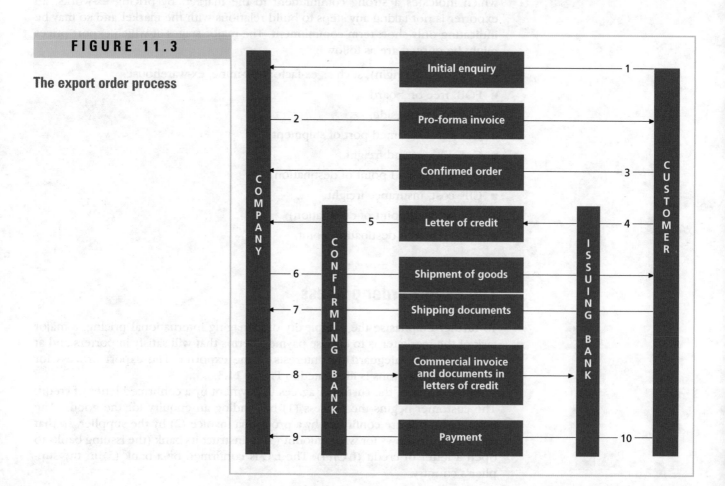

of either goods or debt could be very difficult, and so it is for this reason that consignments tend to be limited to companies trading with their subsidiaries.

- **Bill of exchange**. An unconditional order in writing is signed by one person and requires the person to whom it is addressed to pay a certain sum of money on instruction at a specified time.

The credit terms given are also important in determining the final price to the buyer. When products from international competitors are perceived to be similar, the purchaser may choose the supplier that offers the best credit terms, in order to effect a greater discount. In effect the supplier is offering a source of finance to the buyer, and in some countries – for example Brazil – government support is given to firms to help them gain a competitive advantage through this method. There has been a variety of international agreements to try and stop such practices, but it is still quite prevalent in some countries.

SUMMARY

- The management of pricing in international marketing is significantly different from domestic marketing because it is necessary to manage cost, price and finance.

- Many factors and problems contribute to making effective pricing management one of the most difficult aspects of international marketing to achieve. As well as the market factors associated with pricing decisions in each country it is necessary to deal with the complexities of financing deals based in different currencies and trying to maintain cross-border consistency of pricing.

- Whilst there are cost benefits in standardising products, services and processes, local factors affect the cost base in individual countries and make it difficult to maintain similar prices in different markets.

- In addition to this strategic role, there are a number of issues relating to the detailed operational management of international transactions. These particularly relate to the reduction of risk in carrying out international trade transactions, especially when trading in high-risk countries.

- There are also areas of specific management expertise in pricing that exist in international marketing. These include, for example, the management of transfer pricing between business units within an MNE, grey marketing and counter-trade and the administration of cross-border transfers of goods.

- What becomes quite clear in developing international pricing is that there is a need not only to use pricing in a key role in achieving a company's financial objectives, but also as part of an integrated strategy, for example along with other marketing mix elements, to respond positively to the opportunities and threats of the various markets in which it operates.

KEYWORDS

counter-trade	grey marketing
dumping excess capacity	internal cost structures
economies of scale	learning curve
elastic/inelastic demand	marginal cost pricing
ethnocentric	market-oriented pricing
European Monetary Union	polycentric
exchange rate risk	price coordination
export administration	price standardisation
fixed production costs	price transparency
foreign currency	transfer pricing
geocentric	

CASE STUDY   Beta Automotive

Beta Automotive is an owner-managed firm dealing with the import, export and wholesale of genuine Japanese automotive parts in Singapore.

The managing director, Mr Sing, is a Chinese Singaporean. The firm has eight employees; four of the employees have at least eight years of experience in handling Japanese automotive parts. Most of the employees are able to speak and understand Malay as well as Chinese and the managing director also speaks English.

Beta competes by selling genuine automotive parts at a much lower price than the authorised distributor. They also offer technical expertise and ensure all customers are given all the technical information required to make an accurate and informed buying decision. The 'integrity' of the technical information is also personally guaranteed by Beta and all products are sold with a full warranty. Mr Sing believes that even when competing on the grey market a firm must not only be competitive in pricing but should also be able to solve customers' automotive parts problems satisfactorily.

The firm sources the automotive parts from within Singapore and Japan and is able to supply a deep assortment of genuine automotive parts to car models from a number of manufacturers such as Toyota, Nissan and Isuzu. Besides being a parallel importer, the firm is also the authorised genuine parts dealer of two franchised companies in Singapore.

Sales turnover of the firm is approximately US$3 million. Sixty per cent of the sales are generated by exports to South East Asia, principally Malaysia, Indonesia, The Philippines and Pakistan, although since the crisis in Indonesia very little business has been transacted. Beta's export customers

can purchase on an (Ident) order basis (delivery time is about 90 to 120 days) or through ex-stock sales (for fast-moving items only). There is a minimum transaction value for any sea shipment and Beta price Free On Board (FOB). The main transaction costs to Beta are local transportation charges, documentation fees, port charges etc. However, to date all the export sales have been indirect export transactions, through agents in Singapore acting on the behalf of buyers in the export market. These agents acted as guarantors and so ensured Beta were paid for the parts and for the services rendered.

Mr Sing is now developing his international marketing strategy and wishes to expand his business further in South East Asia by directly exporting into the markets himself. His main priorities are to spread the firm's existing business and financial risks and to maximise on sales opportunities identified in other South East Asian markets. However, he is concerned that by directly exporting to the country he will need to become involved in many activities previously not undertaken, such as negotiating and liasing with freight forwarders and banks and insurance companies on terms of engagement. This is all besides the complexities of the processing of export documentation to facilitate the transactions. Furthermore, the firm will need to consider how to mitigate its foreign business and financial risks exposures since payment will no longer be guaranteed by an agent.

The main strengths of the firm have been assessed by a consultant as being:

- Access to multiple supply sources which enable Beta to compete effectively on price and give them the flexibility to meet changing parts requirements and demand patterns in both domestic and overseas markets.

- Order fulfilment flexibility. Depending on the nature of the required item, Beta's customers have the options to purchase ex-stock supplies or (Ident) order.

- The range of genuine Japanese automotive parts handled by the firm (e.g. Nissan, Toyota and Isuzu) matches with the major brands of vehicles in circulation in South East Asia.

- Staff at Beta are all highly self-motivated and technically knowledgeable.

- Strong customer-orientation and the commitment and a determination to be successful in overseas markets.

- Little internal bureaucracy compared to authorised distributors.

- Flexible and adaptive staff.

- Short lead-time.

- Language skills.

Their key weaknesses were viewed as being:

- The firm has limited knowledge and exposure to direct export marketing.

- Lack of strategy and marketing planning in the firm.

- No current relationships with direct automotive parts importers or other useful contacts in export markets that can be exploited.

- Limited company resources.

- Inadequate and poor management information.

- The firm does not effectively make use of available external resources to support its foreign market development efforts.

- Contacts with relevant logistical (e.g. freight forwarders) and trade services providers (e.g. banks, insurance companies) are still not well developed.

- Choice of target market segment is limited to those foreign buyers who are able to import more than the minimum transaction value.

Questions

1 What are the financial risks that Beta will have to face as a direct exporter that they have not had to deal with to date?

2 Fully evaluate the viability of achieving a long-term competitive advantage in international markets as a grey marketer.

3 What advice would you give to Beta?

Christopher Tan Hak Heng, Sheffield Hallam University

DISCUSSION QUESTIONS

1 What are the arguments for and against using price and non-price factors when competing in international markets?

2 What pricing problems might a multi-national company face in marketing to less developed countries, and how might they be overcome?

3 How can exporting companies reduce financial risk?

4 Why should a domestic supplier invoice export goods in a foreign currency? What are the advantages and disadvantages of foreign currency invoicing?

5 The Internet is increasing price transparency across international markets. Fully evaluate the problems and opportunities this brings to the company trying to build a global competitive advantage.

REFERENCES

Assmus, G. and Wiesse, C. (1995), 'How to address the gray market threat using price coordination', in Doole, I. and Lowe, R., *International Marketing Strategy: contemporary readings*, International Thomson Business Press.

Carter, J. and Gagne, J. (1988) 'The Do's and Don'ts of International Countertrade', *Sloan Management Review,* Spring: 31–38.

Dicken, P. (2003) *Global Shift: Reshaping the Global Economic Map in the 21st century*, 4th edn, Sage Publications.

Keegan, W.J. & Sclegelmilch, B. (2001) *Global Marketing Management – A European Perspective*, FT Prentice-Hall.

Kotler, P. (2003) *Marketing Management*, 11th edn, Pearson Education Intn.

Mueller, B. and Cavusgil, S.T. (1996) 'Unraveling the mystique of export pricing', *Business Horizons*, 31 (3).

Terpstra, V. and Sarathy, R. (2000) *International Marketing,* Dryden Press.

Usunier, J.C. (2000) *Marketing Across Cultures*, 2nd edn, Prentice Hall.

INTERNATIONAL MARKETING IMPLEMENTATION THROUGH ENABLING TECHNOLOGIES

Introduction

International marketing is evolving as the marketplace becomes increasingly global. It can be argued that many of the changes taking place, such as the greater homogenisation of consumer demand and the increasing speed and intensity of competition, have been accelerated because of advances in technology.

As we saw in the first section of the book, technology is a major driver of both the pace and magnitude of change in international marketing. It provides more immediate methods of gathering marketing information from around the world and quicker and more effective methods of analysis and prediction of future customer needs and wants.

It also provides the enabling mechanism by which effective and integrated strategic responses can be made to the changes and is therefore an essential element in the development of the international marketing strategy. Technology both influences and underpins the choice of implementation strategies of the marketing mix, facilitates the process of learning and sharing best practice and enables the more effective control of a firm's diverse international activities.

In this chapter, therefore, we focus upon the impact of recent technologies on the nature of international marketing, the role of technology in providing solutions to international marketing problems and the mechanisms to exploit opportunities. The technology tools that are available to develop appropriate strategic responses will be identified and, as we shall see, this often involves integrating separate elements of international marketing into a cohesive approach, for example through supply chain and customer relationship management. Finally, we focus on the challenges and opportunities faced in international markets in the future and consider the role enabling technologies will play in them.

Learning objectives

After reading this chapter you should be able to:

- Understand how technology has changed the nature of international marketing strategy

- Appreciate the role of the enabling technologies in the international marketing strategy process
- Identify the technology enabling tools and their use in the international marketing strategy
- Understand the integration of solutions to international marketing strategy problems through the use of enabling technologies
- Identify the challenges posed by the use of enabling technologies now and in the future

THE ENABLING TECHNOLOGIES

Down the centuries, advances in technology have provided solutions for business problems, such as in design, manufacturing, operations, internal and external communications, inventory control, managing finances and so on. Technological advances have enabled innovative firms to make product and service developments. The technology is either industry sector specific or generic in nature. Of course, a specific industry technology may sometimes start off being used in one sector and over time be transferred to other sectors. For example, the Internet was initially developed for use in the defence industry.

Other technologies, particularly communications technologies, such as telephone, radio and television, have provided solutions to generic business problems in many industry sectors and have had the effect of 'shrinking the world'. However, it is the IT and communications technologies of the past three decades that have been all-pervasive and have grown at a phenomenal rate and had a major impact on the way business is done. In particular, the Internet has facilitated the worldwide integration of the different technologies, systems and processes that are being used locally by different parts of the organisation and its partners. It enables experts around the world to be accessed virtually and instantly. When some advanced GE medical equipment being used to treat a child broke down in the middle of the night in the US the customer was not able to get hold of a local engineer. However, it was normal working hours for the call-centre in France. The problem could be diagnosed online and expert help provided from France to solve the problem.

We refer here to enabling technologies, because there is no single technology. The major steps forward in recent years have been associated with the integration of many technologies, such as those that support e-commerce, information management, telecommunications, computer aided design, process, inventory and logistics management. So, enabling technologies in international marketing provide the solutions to old problems, such as how can customers in remote locations around the world contribute to the design of a new global product as much as the customer next door and how can a ten-person business market its products or services to its potential customers in forty or fifty countries? Managing market entry in so many countries through agents and distributors would probably be beyond the resources of most small businesses.

Technology does not change the elements, challenges and dilemmas associated with the international marketing process, such as the impact of culture on international marketing and the need to achieve a balance between the standardisation and adaptation of the international marketing process and programmes, but it does have a major impact on the nature of the international marketing strategy that is used and the solutions that are developed.

Whilst we have discussed these challenges in previous chapters it is useful to focus specifically upon how technology helps firms and their managers to address these challenges. Technology both drives change and provides a means of responding to change. The development of new and existing technology allows things to be done better and faster than before. At the outset, however, it is important to emphasise that technology is of no value until it has a practical application. As illustrated in Figure 12.1, those firms that are first to embrace a new technology and find a practical application, for example in creating a new product or service or a new route to market, will gain a new source of competitive advantage. However, this might well set new standards for the industry sector that will mean that competitors will also have to achieve those standards if they wish to compete in the future. So all competitors in the sector will have to catch up by embracing the new technology. Consequently, the innovative firm again has to find a new technological advance that allows them to get ahead again. This is the situation for many firms, including Dell, which is discussed later.

Communications technology helps people around the world to become more aware of changes in the market environment and to the response of companies to those changes in the form of products and services. Customers are more easily bored with their existing products and services and are always looking for innovative new products and services that will regain their interest. They are less brand-loyal and if one firm does not meet the needs of international customers then a competitor will. Customers find out about the development of new products or new ways to reach the market and they want to benefit from the changes. Customers want it and they want it now!

Businesses must respond to the changes in order to retain and develop their customers. With technology changing so quickly it is necessary to make choices about where to focus the business activity. It is sometimes difficult to decide where to place the emphasis, and a good decision at one point could prove to be a bad decision with the benefit of two years' hindsight, as Illustration 12.1 shows. The other problem raised in the illustration is that it is difficult to know what the next technology will be and, indeed, when it will be needed. The illustration highlights the problems for a business but whole communities can be affected too. The crash in the economy caused by the technology bubble bursting resulted in 313 000 jobs being lost in the San Francisco area alone in 2001–2003 and led to the State of California being US$38 billion in debt.

FIGURE 12.1

The vicious circle of technology and competitive advantage

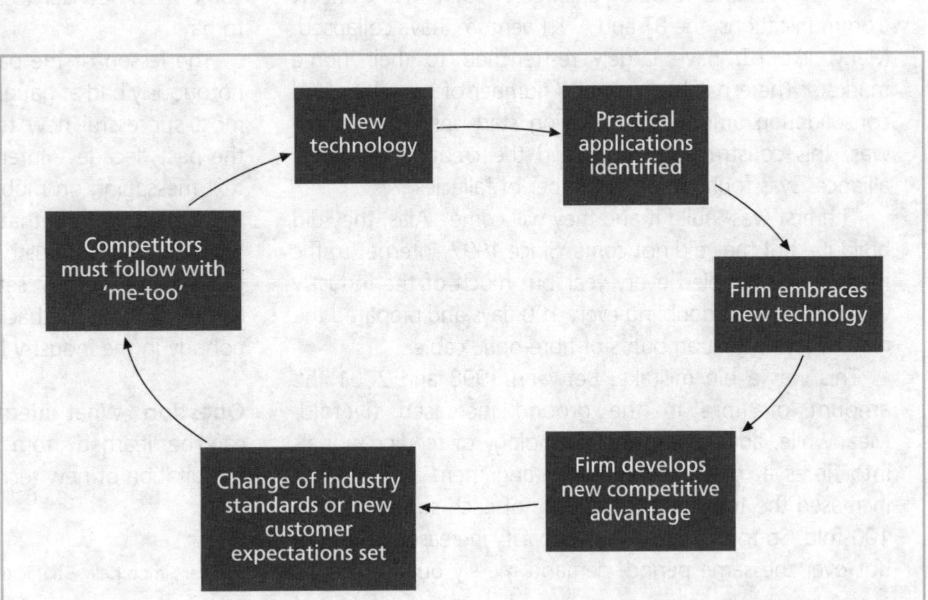

The rate of growth of the Internet has outstripped the rate of growth in the early years of other communications technologies such as telephone, radio and television. However, it is important to recognise that many people in emerging economies do not have access to these old technologies, let alone the latest information and **telecommunications** technology, and so the division between rich and poor nations will further increase. Little is being currently done by the rich nations to reduce the imbalance. For example, it has been calculated that half the world's population still have never made a phone call.

Whilst there seems to be a lack of real concern and understanding of the situation by MNEs and governments from developed nations, clever adaptations of quite advanced technology by individual entrepreneurs sometimes make a huge impact on emerging economies. Examples include the development of the wind-

---

ILLUSTRATION 12.1 — Growth based on shaky foundations

Since the late 1990s things have changed dramatically in the global telecoms market. The start of this period was characterised by Internet mania and the assumption of astronomic rates of global telephone traffic growth. This was spurred on by bullish investors and led to the creation of a number of start-up firms who spent vast sums on infrastructure investments. The former national monopolies in Europe, AT&T in America and NTT in Japan followed suit and tried to transform themselves into global operators. They built new networks and bought stakes in foreign operators. European companies gambled that the predicted surge in demand for fixed communications capacity would be followed by a similar leap in demand for mobile capacity, and they paid over US$90 billion for licences to run 'third-generation' (3G) mobile networks. In the process, they ran up huge debts.

Many of the global alliances, such as Concert Communications, the BT and AT&T venture, have collapsed. Many, like BT, have largely re-trenched to their home markets. There has been a huge number of casualties and consolidation among the surviving start-ups. The trouble was, this construction boom and the creation of global alliances was founded on a number of fallacies.

The first was 'build it and they will come'. Alas, they did build it – but they did not come. Since 1997, Internet traffic has roughly doubled every year but much of the industry was betting on it doubling every 100 days and prepared the way by laying vast amounts of fibre-optic cable.

This was a big mistake. Between 1998 and 2001 the amount of fibre in the ground increased fivefold. Meanwhile, advances in the technology of feeding signals into fibres at one end and extracting them at the other increased the transmission capacity of each strand of fibre 100-fold. So total transmission capacity increased 500-fold. But over the same period, demand merely quadrupled. In the United States, more than a dozen national fibre backbones were constructed; a similar duplication happened in Western Europe.

When it became clear that the industry had bet on an increase in demand that was not likely to materialise in the near future, ferocious competition and frantic price-cutting ensued. Equipment vendors' sales dried up. And some firms resorted to concealing the lack of revenue in the accounts.

Internet traffic is (reliably) said to be doubling every year, and voice traffic on both fixed and mobile networks is rising, but traffic growth does not translate into revenue growth for telecoms firms. Moreover, in the rich world at least, markets are saturated, so new revenue cannot come from new subscribers either, which is what has recently fuelled the mobile-phone industry. Instead, it will have to come from new services for which customers are prepared to pay.

The lesson of the past few years is that the industry is notoriously bad at gauging demand for its services. The two most successful new telecommunications technologies of the past decade – Internet access on fixed networks, and text messaging on mobile networks – were both unexpected breakthroughs that emerged in spite of, rather than because of, the industry's best efforts. Once the smoke has cleared and the dust settled, expect the telecoms revival to come riding on the back of an unexpected technology that nobody in the industry has yet heard of.

Question What international marketing strategy lessons can be learned from this example of the commercial exploitation of new technology?

Source: Simon Kelly, Sheffield Hallam University

up radio by Trevor Bayliss, discussed earlier in the book, and the software development example discussed in Illustration 12.2.

Some of the technology that is now available could enable some countries to leapfrog existing technology. For example, the cost of a fixed line telecommunications structure would be prohibitively expensive in some largely rural countries but mobile telephony and satellite systems could be more cost effective. Many isolated communities will not be linked to electricity supply systems, but local solar energy systems could be used to power communications equipment. The challenge, of course, is to find a way of reducing the cost of these advanced technical solutions in emerging economies.

An advanced infrastructure is needed to support e-business, but it should be for maintaining relationships rather than creating them in the first place. The UK Department for International Development in Research in Bangladesh, Kenya and South Africa claimed that a number of software sellers have sold expensive software in emerging economies which is inappropriate. Except in a few cases business has not accelerated for firms from poor countries that have gone online. The reason given is that buyers from developed countries, such as the US, need to build a personal relationship with suppliers from emerging economies before they are prepared to take the risk of doing business online.

Global growth of e-business

The United Nations Conference on Trade and Development (UNCTAD) estimated that the number of Internet users reached 655 million in 2003, one-tenth of the world's population. The US had 143 million and China 56.6 million online. UNCTAD estimate that the US accounted for 45 per cent, Europe 25 per cent and Japan 15 per cent of e-commerce revenues, with 6.7 per cent from developing countries, mainly Asia Pacific. Of interest is the fact that IT products contributed a larger share of exports from developing countries than exports of agricultural, textiles and clothing products combined.

The prevalence and use of the Internet varies considerably. By 2003, 58 per cent of Americans had Internet access at home, whereas in Europe the figure was

ILLUSTRATION 12.2	Soft in Ghana

On holiday in his home country, Ghana, UK-based Hermann Chinnery-Hesse accepted a schoolfriend's bet that he could not make a fortune in West Africa. His business idea was rather surprising! He would take on Microsoft. Using his old computer in his bedroom he developed Soft, a software designed for the local Ghanaian market. It needed to be simple and cheap, 'tropically tolerant' to the frequent power cuts and it needed to be ultra secure to stop people fiddling the books.

The company started with software for micro-finance and the timber industry and is now developing partnerships with companies in Nigeria, The Gambia, Senegal and Kenya. It employs 70 staff, including 20 developers. In 2003, 40 per cent of the business was sold to international investors, the first time a technology firm in West Africa has gained such investment. The firm has the potential to develop in many ways, because it understands local problems. India's largest software firm, Infosys, will use Soft for marketing and support in the West African market.

Hesse has won his bet but he realises that Africa must not be left behind in technology as it was with industrialisation. West Africa, for example, simply cannot compete with countries from Asia in manufacturing.

Question How can technology be used to bridge the gap for emerging economies?

Source: Adapted from Hale, B. 'Ghana trumps mighty Microsoft', BBC News Online, 3 June 2003

only 38 per cent. In Europe there was great disparity, with Sweden and the Netherlands over 60 per cent and Germany and the UK just below 50 per cent, whereas in Greece the figure was around 10 per cent. In India 1 in 147 of the population were online. On the African continent 1 in 118 people were online but outside South Africa, Egypt, Kenya, Morocco and Tunisia the figure dropped to 1 in 440.

In China, CNNIC, the official data collector, estimate that only 2 per cent of Web users have bought online. Eachnet, the online auction site (see Illustration 12.4, page 414), have found that 40 per cent of sellers find a customer in their own home town so that they can swap goods for cash face-to-face. Consumers are suspicious of the banking sector and only about 20 million out of 1300 million Chinese have a credit card, as getting a credit card requires a friend to guarantee repayment. Cards are issued by individual banks without coordination and the banking sector lacks a clearing system. As a result, cards have limited value for Chinese people travelling within the country.

In the business-to-business sector in China, sales volumes are also small but the prospects seem better. E-commerce is still mainly used, however, for sourcing products from a database of manufacturers, with most payments made off-line.

THE INTERNET AND WEB SITES

Inevitably our discussion on enabling technologies has at its core the Internet. The Internet, from its origins in 1969, has developed into an unstructured network of computers linking private and business users around the world, allowing them to communicate and transfer data instantly and relatively inexpensively. The computer networks are linked by telephone lines, fibre optic cables, microwave relays and satellite. Individual users gain access to the Internet from their computer through portals that provide powerful search engines to find the information and services they need. Internet Service Providers (ISPs), such as America Online (AOL) and CompuServe, facilitate access for consumers for a fee.

The main Internet services are e-mail (individual electronic messaging), the World Wide Web (the collection of electronic files that provide the information content that is read using a Web browser, such as Microsoft Internet Explorer) and Usenet (the network of discussion newsgroups). The Internet also supports extranets, which are private networks that make connections between organisations, and intranets, which are the networks that make connections within organisations.

The Internet has had a profound effect on the way that individuals and organisations from developed countries now communicate around the world. Words, both stationary and moving images, sound, and complex data can be transferred instantly to the most remote parts of the world. The effect has been dramatic on the way that firms carry out their international trade. No longer is international marketing limited by the physical boundaries of the media footprint or the salesperson's or distribution company's territory. Moreover, new developments in Wireless Application Protocol (WAP) allow Web pages to be viewed on hand-held devices, such as mobile phones and organisers whilst travelling.

The provision of this virtual infrastructure for electronic communication has created huge business opportunities for firms supplying information technology hardware and software, consultancy, business support services and telecommunications businesses, such as IBM, Cisco, Deloitte Consulting and Vodafone. However, for many firms the dotcom boom did not exist for very long. A few innovative and well-run start-up firms that we refer to in this chapter have, however, built successful businesses.

For e-businesses the role of the Internet is to provide a global marketplace that is open to everyone, and particularly:

- a method of collecting and exchanging marketing and business information;
- an alternative route to market to traditional distribution channels;
- a means of building customer relationships;
- a device for the digital delivery of certain information services;
- a networked system for managing the supply chain; and
- a virtual marketplace, trading floor and auction house.

The purpose of Web sites

Web sites are created by individuals and organisations as a shop window for the activities they wish to communicate. Whilst they are used for many purposes, their relevance for international marketing falls into four main categories:

- Organisation sites
- Service online
- Information online
- Business transactions online.

Organisation sites

Many organisations use their Web site to provide information to their stake-holders about the organisation, ranging from its origins, business mission and areas of activity, standards and values, brands, financial performance, job opportunities and contact points through to quite specific information about products and their applications. Firms appealing to global customers must consider the degree to which their Web site should be offered in several languages. For a university offering courses taught in English, a greeting in a local language is probably enough. Indeed, if students cannot read the rest of the site in English, they are unlikely to be suitable candidates! However, other organisation sites need to develop much more empathy and build much closer relationships with customers by providing a site in the local language. There are, of course, dangers too in just translating Web content without addressing the need for it to be sensitive to cultural needs.

Essentially, Web sites can be set up for any individual or on behalf of any organisation. Illustration 12.3 shows consumers successfully using an information Web site to raise an important issue and demanding a response, Ford using their Web site effectively to respond and Bridgestone Firestone failing to use their Web site to manage criticism.

As well as providing information about products, some sites take customers through the purchasing process. For example, BMW help customers to design their new car from a range of options, such as whether to have cruise control, petrol or diesel, metallic paint and alloy wheels, but when the customer has designed the car they are then referred to their local dealer to complete the purchase.

Service online

Before the 1980s banks operated a service based on physical transactions but, for example, in the UK they opened only from 10 am to 3 pm, five days per week. It was not possible for customers to obtain cash from the bank outside these times.

The introduction of automatic teller machines (ATM) meant that customers could then withdraw cash 24 hours per day, seven days per week, but the service was incomplete because only limited information about accounts was available to customers at ATMs. Also, the provision of ATMs at convenient locations was very costly for banks.

It took telephone banking to enable customers to transfer money between accounts, make payments and receive help and advice on their accounts 24 hours per day, seven days per week. Online banking, however, puts customers more in control of their accounts and enables them to obtain information from anywhere in the world and make transactions any time of the day or night. The saving to the bank is being able to reduce the resourcing of bank branches and service centres and cut the cost of individual banking transactions.

Firms delivering packages, such as Federal Express, have been able to make huge savings on staff employed to answer queries from customers about where their package is, by providing an online tracking service around the world. The system involves applying a bar code to the package, which is then scanned each time it progresses past a key point on its journey. This information can then be transferred to the Web site and accessed by customers worldwide. Another example is real-time in-flight information that can be accessed online by those that are going to meet a flight, letting them know if the plane is going to be late.

Information online

Organisations in the business of providing information, such as the Financial Times, provide Web sites that enable customers to access current and archived past files of news, data and images. Often, such sites provide one level of access free, but may charge a subscription for heavier users or may require payment for more valuable information. As this information is in digital form it can be accessed and delivered online anywhere in the world.

Sites of media organisations are used to maintain and build the relationship with their consumers considerably beyond the scheduled content. The BBC site is one of the most popular and best presented sites in the UK and provides background and supporting material for programmes, a searchable database of their own stories and files from the World Wide Web, news for a broad range of inter-

---

ILLUSTRATION 12.3   Firestone shoulders the blame

The Internet is a powerful tool for communicating information and this can be either positive or negative. In 2000 Bridgestone Firestone issued a massive recall of 6.5 million tyres following reports that Firestone tyres had contributed, at least in part, to hundreds of rollovers by the Ford Explorer SUV. Ford denied that they were responsible and blamed Firestone. A number of consumer groups, such as the Tire Action Group, used the Internet to intensively debate the accidents and the contribution of Ford and Firestone to the problem. The speed of negative information could not be controlled by Ford or Firestone and so consumer concern increased around the world. However, the two firms responded in quite different ways.

Firestone was very slow to do anything but Ford realised that it must respond very fast and placed banner ads on 200 Web sites to click through to Ford for more information about the problem. The Ford Web site provided information about which products were being recalled and a statement by the Ford CEO expressing concern. Clearly Ford could not be absolved of blame as the vehicles carried the Ford badge, but with the Web PR they succeeded in ensuring that the public blamed Firestone.

Question How should Firestone have reacted?

national consumers and the ability to access programmes online around the world.

Business transactions online

In the above types of sites, business is not transacted online but information is provided and exchanged that allows the traditional business transaction to be conducted more effectively. Business transactions online is the most significant development in international marketing and it is to this that we now turn.

E-MARKETS AND E-MARKETING

There are a number of e-marketing models and e-marketplaces and these originally started as digital extensions of physical marketing models. For many businesses the first stage in the e-marketing revolution was simply to put their sales brochure on the Web site and wait for customers to order, but the Internet is interactive and so capable of supporting much more sophisticated business models and these are discussed later in the next section. The main models are consumer marketing, usually referred to as **business to consumer** (B2C), and industrial marketing, referred to as **business to business (B2B)**, but other business model variants are emerging and we also refer to these.

Business to consumer (B2C)

In the B2C sector, the Internet has allowed individuals or businesses of any size to set up a Web site as a virtual shop – an online showcase for their products and services. The best Web sites offer potential customers the choice of which language they wish to communicate in and are sensitive to the local culture and legal frameworks. Existing and potential customers are able to browse through the information that is available about the products and services they are seeking to buy and, at their leisure, compare an online product 'offer' with other offers from competitive Web sites or from the local shop. Having selected the product they wish to buy customers can purchase and pay for the product online, using credit cards to make payment. In practice, many more customers are prepared to use the Internet to carry out their information search on companies, products and services but are unwilling to pay online because of fears about the security of online payment and the potential for fraud. Firms that have both virtual and physical stores allow customers to find out information and then choose whether to buy online or go round to the store. For example, Argos (UK) allow customers to buy online or check if a product is in a physical store, in which case the customer can reserve the product and collect it later.

In principle, buyers that have access to a computer almost anywhere in the world can purchase any product or service but, in practice, certain products and services lend themselves to online retailing more than others. Products that sold on the basis of their design or quality of manufacture may not be s their best effect without allowing customers to feel them and touch th

Some services can be supplied as digital services online over th example, information, software, financial advice, ticketless tra be downloaded direct to the customer's computer. CDs, boo sampled digitally prior to purchase. The case at the end online travel distribution.

For physical products, however, the supplier still needs a suitable distribution method to deliver the goods to the consumer. Fulfilment of the order depends on more traditional distribution, with its associated limitations of the existing infrastructure and the availability of appropriate logistics in each customer's country. Small items such as CDs and books can be posted but delivering valuable goods, very bulky goods such as furniture (see the case of Muji at the end of Chapter 7) or goods that require special storage conditions, such as food, directly to the door also requires arrangements to be made for the customer to receive them. This frequently presents difficulties for Internet marketing companies and is leading to a number of innovations designed to overcome the problem. Clearly certain products better lend themselves to buying online than others.

Making money from the Internet

Using the Internet to transact business in this way grossly underutilises its potential, however. This rather basic form of e-commerce improves the speed and flexibility of the purchasing process and increases the geographical reach of communications compared to the physical media. Having just a Web site, however, does little to build competitive advantage, nor improve the overall effectiveness of the operation in winning global customers and developing their loyalty. Many so-called 'dotcom' businesses that have been selling products and services over the Internet have spent large amounts of money in building sophisticated, entertaining, interactive Web sites, providing useful information for their customers and attracting advertising and sponsorship from other firms. Without building sufficient sales quickly enough to become viable, however, they have subsequently failed. Moreover, without building competitive advantage and unique selling propositions firms using the Internet to sell their products are vulnerable to lower priced offers from competitors, because sophisticated search engines can now be used to identify the cheapest offers of commodities supplied from anywhere in the world.

Many companies believed they could survive and grow by offering the lowest priced products direct to customers, thus cutting out retailers and distributors, but inevitably new entrants will always offer lower prices, even if they are not sustainable in the longer term. Whilst the cost of setting up a Web site is quite modest, the cost of establishing an e-business typically involves substantial outlay for information technology, systems, management and Web site development. The challenge for a business is therefore to maximise its income. Moreover, e-commerce firms require sophisticated systems and need to innovate constantly to fulfil orders promptly and accurately to retain customer interest and loyalty.

As a consequence of the difficulty of achieving viability quickly enough, Web-based marketing companies seek additional ways of generating income. These depend upon the nature of the business but include:

- Subscription fees: members of a club pay a fee. ISPs, for example, use this approach.

- Licence fee: a fee is paid on a one-off or regular basis to have access, for example, to software.

- Activation fee: a fee is paid to activate the software or business service but after that the service is free.

- Sponsor fee: a second firm might obtain benefit from the Web site and might be persuaded to pay a sponsorship fee to support the business.

- Transaction fee: a fee might be paid to the firm owning the Web site for every direct or indirect sale that results from customers accessing the Web site.

- Per use fee: a fee might be paid every time a customer obtains information or research data from the site.

- Invisible fee: if a second firm has a banner advert and a direct link to the home page to another Web site it might expect to pay a small 'click through' fee.

- Advertiser fee: a firm advertising on another's Web site might be charged a fee for occupying advertising space.

Generating income through these different methods has significant implications for the firm's cash flow, especially since the costs and timing of resourcing the service might be significantly different from when the revenue is generated. Other models of exchange between supplier and customer are emerging.

Consumer to consumer (C2C)

The concept that underpins this model is that consumers sell to each other through an online auction. eBay is the most successful site for trading between individuals who buy and sell antiques, collectable items and memorabilia by virtual bidding. This type of buying and selling tends to become almost a hobby in itself for customers. eBay takes a fee to insert the advertisement and a fee based on the final value. eBay has competitors, such as QXL, but is taking the lead internationally and demonstrating fast growth, as Illustration 12.4 shows.

Consumer to business (C2B)

This works in reverse to the normal type of auction as consumers join together to reduce the prices they pay through bulk buying. A final date is set and the price falls as more customers join the buying group. While this is an established model in the business-to-business sector, it is less well established in C2B. Sites such as Letsbuyit.com facilitate the process but have struggled to develop a viable business model. Priceline.com is similar but provides a mechanism for consumers to say what they are prepared to pay for a product or service, such as an airline flight as in the end-of-chapter case. Suppliers decide whether they are prepared to accept the offer.

It is increasingly recognised that, whilst online retailing has many benefits as a route to market for international development, a combination of virtual and physical routes to market might deliver the best results for many businesses. Amazon.com has developed an alliance with Toys'R'Us and has increased its own warehousing capacity to increase the speed and quality of its service. Barnes and Noble has 1000 bookstores in the US and has joined with Bertelsmann (Germany) to provide online retailing.

Business to business (B2B)

Whereas B2C is primarily based on pre-priced products made to a standard specification, albeit with some exceptions, the interactions in B2B are much more complex. Interactions involve the exchange of significant amounts of information between the seller and customer before, during and after any transaction. The information includes such things as specifications, designs and drawings, purchase contracts, manufacturing and delivery schedules, inventory control, negotiation of price and delivery. The information comes from different departments within the firms and is exchanged between the firms. Clearly firms for many years have been using information technology to improve the efficiency and effectiveness of the internal firm processes, for example demand forecasting, inventory control, computer aided design and computer aided manufacturing, but the Internet enables this to be linked with external organisations.

Twenty years ago Electronic Data Interchange (EDI) first enabled quite complex information to be exchanged digitally between organisations – in fact the first rudimentary extranet. Supply chain members, such as suppliers, manufacturers, distributors and retailers were able to exchange inventory information, for example, sending orders and invoices electronically, and EDI has grown during the intervening period. Merrill Lynch estimated EDI to account for US$250 billion in 1999. However, EDI requires information to be sent in a particular format and, of course, this restricts the type of information that can be sent and so limits its usefulness. EDI systems are essentially private networks that are also expensive to implement and to expand.

The Internet has enabled a far wider range of data to be exchanged without restriction on the number of participant organisations. The mechanisms by which the exchanges take place and business can be transacted are Web portals. These

---

ILLUSTRATION 12.4   **The growth of eBay**

Whilst many firms suffered after the dotcom boom, eBay, the online auctioneer from the US, maintained very rapid growth. In March 2003 it reported quarter revenues up 29 per cent in the US and 164 per cent in international markets (especially Britain, Germany and Australia) when compared to a year previously. In the UK it overtook Amazon in terms of audience (6 million, up 160 per cent in a year compared to Amazon, 5.2 million, up 40 per cent).

It has, however, had mixed success in Asia. In March 2002 it closed its company in Japan because it was failing to compete with Yahoo Japan, which had the advantage of being first mover into the market. Yahoo had 3.5 million products whilst eBay offered only 25 000.

At the same time, however, it was buying NeoCom Technology, a Taiwanese online auction company, and buying a 33 per cent stake in the Shanghai-based EachNet, which was founded by two Chinese Harvard graduates, Shao Yibo and Tan Haiyin, who modelled EachNet on eBay.

A year later in April 2003, eBay bought out the remaining two-thirds of EachNet. eBay president Meg Whitman gave the reason that EachNet had built up a strong business, which could take a significant share of the US$16 billion online sales in China predicted by 2005. Online sales in China in 2003 were low but analysts expected that the outbreak of SARS in China might encourage more Chinese to buy online during the outbreak and keep the habit afterwards.

Question What criteria should eBay use to select market entry targets?

Source: www.ebay.co.uk

are 'hubs' where all the interested participants congregate. Typically there are two types of hubs:

- industry-specific hubs, such as automobile or aerospace manufacturing; and
- function-specific hubs, such as advertising or human resource management.

Using e-hubs, firms improve the efficiency of the processes of transactions and thereby lower costs. The hubs can reduce the transaction cost by bringing together all the purchasing requirements of many hundreds of customers worldwide (Kaplan and Sawhney 2000). E-hubs attract many buyers who are able to negotiate bulk discounts on behalf of a range of smaller, individual buyers.

If the products are commodities with no need to negotiate specifications then dynamic pricing enables buyers and sellers to negotiate prices and volumes in real time. In sectors such as energy purchasing the peaks and troughs of supply and demand can be smoothed.

The US still dominates B2B and much of the innovation in B2B has come in the US but firms around the world recognise that the potential savings can be quite significant and a number of countries, particularly in Europe, are catching up. This will accelerate with the increasing internationalisation of sourcing and supply chain management. A culture change in the attitude of firms is needed as firms that may normally be competing (as in the case of Illustration 12.5) can cooperate for the mutual benefit of reducing costs. Increasingly these are cross-border cooperations as the case shows.

The benefits of e-procurement, such as convenience and cost saving through group purchasing, appeal to governments for public sector and private–public sector purchasing but often progress is much slower than in private business. The European healthcare sector has been slow to migrate to e-procurement and a

---

ILLUSTRATION 12.5   The B2B marketplace for steel

In 2001 Europe's four leading steel producers established two B2B marketplaces for the industry to bring buyers and sellers together. Steel is sold on Steel24-7.com and BuyforMetals.com is an e-procurement site for steel businesses to buy raw materials, services, repairs, logistics and other goods. There are other marketplaces for metals, including steelscreen.com, spectronmetals.com, copper-net.com and materialnet.com, and there are also some Web sites set up by individual metal producers. Other buying sites, such as Covisint for the car industry, are also of interest to steel producers. Covisint was originally set up by car makers Daimler-Chrysler, Ford, General Motors, Nissan and Renault together with Commerce One and Oracle to enable the manufacturers to source cost effectively from thousands of component suppliers. Peugeot-Citroen have also joined the alliance.

The purpose of the steel sites is to increase liquidity in the industry and facilitate freer trading by cutting costs and increasing price transparency. It is also intended to take out the middlemen and their mark-ups from the traditional metal exchanges. Major players see these steps as essential to help them become more competitive, especially against

Asian and Latin American producers. The steel industry has gone through periods when demand has been catastrophically low, forcing steel producers to merge. Indeed the four producers setting up these sites have gone through a number of mergers and acquisitions themselves. Krupp and Thyssen (Germany) merged; British Steel and Koninklijke Hoogovens (Netherland) merged to form Corus; France's Usinor merged with Sacilor in 1987 and acquired Cockerill Sambre of Belgium; and Arbed of Luxembourg took over Aceralia of Spain.

Some people think that alliances such as this will lead to price fixing, with little opportunity for industry bargaining, and, in the US, the Federal Trade Commission is investigating whether these sites will have a detrimental effect on competition.

Question What benefits might be expected for suppliers and customers?

Source: Adapted from 'Steel moves to the Internet', BBC News Online, 22 June 2000

Frost and Sullivan report in 2003 estimated that e-procurement in Europe was worth only around €0.4 billion in 2002. Only the UK and Germany are moving ahead. The main problems are that healthcare authorities are conservative, have a very prescriptive approach to purchasing and are unwilling to change processes. There are fears among healthcare professionals about data security and hospitals are driven by clinical need, not profit. Moreover, their funding is usually insufficient and so procurement is more concerned with 'buy while you can' rather than efficiency.

The Global Healthcare Exchange was set up by vendors to facilitate e-procurement. It is clear that products routinely used, such as disposables and pharmaceuticals, will increasingly be bought this way, but online buying of other products and services may take longer.

INTERNATIONAL MARKETING SOLUTION INTEGRATION

The most significant international marketing strategy development that is facilitated by technology is business solution integration. As competition increases, so firms must seek to find new sources of competitive advantage, secure ever-lower costs, increase their speed of action and offer new innovative products and services perceived by customers to be valuable. They must also develop better relationships with their customers and business partners in order to retain their business. The strategy to achieve these outcomes is based on the effective integration of the elements of the marketing and business processes.

Knowledge management

The move to an increasingly global market served by e-business has prompted firms to redefine their sources of competitive advantage. In a global market the traditional sources of competitive advantage can be easily challenged. A company that operates in a small number of countries or within a restricted business sector may believe that its competitive advantage comes from low-cost manufacturing, design capability, sales expertise and distribution efficiency. However, when exposed to global competition it may find that its own competitive advantage cannot be transported to new countries and discover, instead, that regional or global competitors have even greater competitive advantage in its own domestic market as well as in the target country market.

By contrast, knowledge, expertise and experience have the potential to be transferable if they can be effectively collected, stored, accessed and communicated around the world (hence the term knowledge management). Below we discuss the processes for managing knowledge to support the customer–client interface but knowledge management is essential to maximise added value throughout the supply chain. There is a danger in building competitive advantage through knowledge management, of course, because the knowledge assets of a firm are locked into their staff and their records, typically contained in their computers. Staff are becoming increasingly mobile, computer systems are still notoriously insecure and the potential loss of knowledge to a competitor is still a problem for firms.

Supply chain management

Technology-enabled supply chain management has helped firms to grow through exploiting market development opportunities, reducing investment by buying rather than manufacturing components, and enabling small firms to have similar costs to large firms through e-procurement. It is vital that each part of the supply chain of the product must maximise the added value and this is made possible by integrating the activities. A supply chain for a complex product might typically involve such distinctly different activities as design, manufacture of raw materials, component assembly, advertising, logistics and local servicing. It is highly unlikely that one company could be the leader in each of these areas of activity, particularly when the most efficient members of the supply chain will increasingly be located around the world.

During the late 1990s electronic commerce was seen very much as providing the opportunity for business growth but the recession at the start of the new century has placed the focus much more on cost saving. As a result e-commerce is continuing to grow at very substantial rates. The drive is to change from paper or person-based transactions to digital transactions. This enables firms to have a much better picture worldwide of who supplies goods and services to the whole organisation, a better understanding of where their costs are incurred and therefore where cost savings can be made. The other change of emphasis has been from the peripheral, non-core parts of the supply chain, such as buying stationery, office equipment and travel, to the core activities of buying raw materials and key components and services of the manufacturing operation. Whereas the e-commerce purchase of non-core activities could make some cost savings, greater savings can be made on the cost of core elements. For example, British Airways claims to have reduced its suppliers from 14 000 to 2000 and made savings in excess of £210m.

The implications, of course, are that through using e-commerce for procurement partnerships can be set up and dissolved instantly. Of course, suppliers need to have huge flexibility and excellent systems to manage the rapid changes that are necessary to survive in this type of market. Suppliers are in completely open competition with other firms around the world.

Cost savings can be made in all areas of the supply chain, such as inventory reduction and just-in-time sourcing. Amazon is able to offer 4.7 million books and music titles by quickly obtaining stocks held anywhere in the world whereas an average bookstore might hold only 170 000 titles physically. Savings can be made in evaluating suppliers, specifications and delivery times and arranging scheduling. Marketing costs can be reduced because it is easier, quicker and cheaper to make alterations to Web content than incur the design and printing costs of a new brochure. For small firms, using e-procurement can have similar costs to large firms and so increase their competitiveness.

Advantest America Inc. supplies measuring instruments, semiconductor test systems and related equipment. It outsourced its delivery of its replacement parts, e-commerce and supply chain management services to FedEx Corporation, which provides transport. Using FedEx's sophisticated, integrated systems it was able to reduce its delivery times by more than 50 per cent, to 48 hours in Asia and 24 hours for customers in America and Europe. Previously, starting from the time the order was taken, it could take between 25 and 42 hours even to get through customs and on to a commercial aeroplane. Extending the system to the firm's customised printed circuit boards would avoid the need for the customer to hold stock on site, thus considerably reducing their inventory.

Every element in the logistics process must be tackled in order to improve performance. For example, a British firm, Kewill, is working with FedEx to develop a system to effectively manage returns from anywhere in the world.

In service call-centres the cost of employing a person capable of dealing with service calls in India is about one-tenth of the cost of employing a person in the UK for an equivalent level of performance. Very often service centre calls are routine and technology can be used to make further savings by replacing people-based transactions with 'intelligent' computer-based responses.

Value chain integration

The key question is how effectively the individual supply chain members around the world work in partnership to maximise the effectiveness of their contributions towards improving efficiency and adding value across the entire value chain, so-called value chain integration. Success is then likely to be dependent on the effectiveness of the working relationship between the members of the supply chain, the speed and openness of information sharing and the degree of collaboration between each company, its suppliers and customers, with the objective of adding value and removing transaction costs.

So, for example, a supermarket chain will allow its hundreds of suppliers to have access to its data warehouse, so they will know how their particular product is selling in each individual store, and to the inventory system to ensure that the supermarket never runs out of stock. This system makes it easier for additional suppliers to be included and managed at low additional cost, allowing consumers more choice and more competitive prices. Dell is at the forefront of using technology to provide business solutions throughout the firm (see Illustration 12.6).

| ILLUSTRATION 12.6 | Dell online |

Michael Dell enjoyed tinkering with computers but in 1983, in his first year at college, it became a business. He purchased out-of-date IBM machines from local retailers, upgraded them and sold them on to students and local firms, door-to-door, bypassing distributors. He sold US$180 000 worth of PCs in the first month of his summer holiday at the end of his first year. He then began to purchase the components and assemble PCs, offering them at 15 per cent below the market price. By 1992, by the time he was 26, his turnover had reached US$2 billion.

Dell did try traditional retailing but it was not a success. He could not afford the retailer margins as there was now fierce price competition between retailers. Because the firm had sold principally to businesses, Dell had a brand recognition problem, too.

Virtually all Dell orders are now placed over the telephone, to a company sales representative, or through the Web site. Almost all Dell PCs are made to order, in Austin, Texas, Penang, Malaysia or Limerick, Ireland to eliminate inventory,. Within 36 hours of the order being placed the PC can be loaded for delivery. Larger customers can have their computers shipped in as little as 12 hours from receipt of order. Components must be delivered to the factories within one hour of the request and, on arrival, trucks take the components immediately to the assembly lines. Order processing accounts for only 10 per cent of Dell's costs.

Technology continues to be the key to Dell's vision of virtual integration between supply chain members as real-time data sharing, just-in-time manufacturing and the Internet change traditional relationships and structures.

The Internet has provided Dell with an instantaneous global sales network and Dell would like all customers ultimately to buy through the Web site. However, competitors are now following the Dell model, also cutting costs from the supply chain and challenging Dell's position. With the downturn in the business environment and 35 per cent of its business with the large corporate businesses, Dell is continually looking for new global opportunities to sustain the business. It has increased its efforts in the consumer market and began offering low-price, off-the-shelf computers, made in Taiwan.

Question Which strategies will be best for the future global market – to continue to give priority to the web strategy, to build to order or pre-make or should Dell concentrate on the consumer market?

Customer relationship management

Customer relationship management (CRM) is the process of identifying, attracting, differentiating and retaining customers (Hoffman 2003). It allows a firm to focus its efforts on its most lucrative customers, no matter where they are from, and is based on the 'rule' that 80 per cent of a firm's profits come from 20 per cent of its customers. It also is designed to achieve efficient and effective customer management. As pressures increase on costs and prices firms must manage customers as inexpensively as they can without losing customer loyalty. To answer a customer query with an automatic Web-based service can be less than a tenth of the cost of a person handling it by telephone through a service call-centre but the question is whether it can be as responsive to customer queries.

CRM allows customers to be *categorised* on the basis of their past profitability. The most profitable customers will be recognised and will be *routed* to the area that will handle calls fastest. For example, this can be done automatically by transferring telephone calls with a particular number. The profitable customers can then be *targeted* with attractive deals. The information is *shared* throughout the company to ensure integration of the firm's activities so that profitable customers get priority service throughout the firm and also from partner firms.

To deliver a CRM strategy the key component is the database of customer information. Techniques and systems are used to manage and extract data (data mining) to identify trends and analyse customer characteristics that enable the targeting to be carried out.

There are some limitations with CRM. Customers may well find out that they are not a priority customer and may resent not receiving 'first class' treatment. The system involves the retention of large amounts of detailed information about individual customers in a firm database. Customers often resent firms holding information about them and in some countries it would infringe privacy laws. Companies analyse the data that they have but only past behaviour has been recorded and so this data may not be an accurate predictor of future behaviour. Finally, there is an assumption that customers want a 'relationship' with suppliers and that in some way they will benefit from it. If the benefit is not clear, then customers will not remain loyal.

Customisation

As we have suggested on a number of occasions, customers increasingly want to be treated as individuals and not simply be the unwilling targets of mass market advertising. The Internet allows companies to mass customise their offering and a variety of firms are exploiting the flexibility of online communication. A number of firms are providing software applications that are designed to personalise or more individually target the firm's interactions. For example, Lindgren (2003) explains how Poindexter (US) uses statistical analysis to identify the shared characteristics of online advertising viewers, and be able to cluster those customers who respond to Web sites and online advertisements in a similar way. The clusters can then be offered a customised marketing mix and customised promotions and product offers. For example, an online shopper who puts products in an online basket but does not go through with the purchase might be offered a discount by the online retailer, as an incentive to go through with the purchase. As more viewers are analysed the system learns the best response and so delivers better performance. A potential customer of insurance group Norwich Union (UK) might complete an online application for car insurance but not buy online. The customer might receive a cash-back offer by e-mail and, if this does not work, a further cash-back offer by post with a prompt to phone the call-centre to confirm the service.

Customers can be targeted and made aware of special deals being offered in their own neighbourhood, perhaps on travel, at a restaurant or at the wine shop. Global positioning systems coupled with mobile telephony, enable firms to text consumers about deals available in the shop that they are just passing.

THE IMPACT ON INTERNATIONAL MARKETING STRATEGY

Having discussed the central role of the Internet as a technology enabler of international marketing and highlighted the various elements of the electronic marketplace, we now turn to how these can both influence and support the much more dynamic approach to international marketing strategy development that we mentioned at the start of this chapter.

Impact of technology on analysis

Demand patterns are now changing more quickly because of changes in the environment, customer needs and wants and competition, and so it is increasingly vital for firms to be able to track changes through an effective marketing information system. Much of the data that must be gathered from around the world can be more effectively collected, managed and communicated through integrated Web-based systems. Firms can track political, economic and legal changes and new product launches by competitors as they are announced by using search engines and sites that provide up-to-date expert analysis. Point of sale information can be collected and analysed on a daily basis to provide information about what products are selling and not selling so that appropriate action can be taken to avoid unnecessary inventory, and develop a supply chain that is flexible and responsive. For example, for clothing products sourced from Asia to sell in the US, the fabric production, garment making and logistics must be fast, flexible and quickly adaptable to changing needs to avoid stock write-offs or write-downs.

The Internet provides not only general information about the firm's products but also information that can be used for promotion and product development by providing direct and indirect indications of consumer behaviour. It is easier and faster to apply questionnaires to existing and potential customers around the world by using the Internet. Procter & Gamble has developed a database of observed behaviour accessible to staff worldwide through an intranet. Customer behaviour can be monitored on Web sites to provide new insights.

The impact of technology on strategy development

For some firms their international marketing strategy is inextricably linked to enabling technologies either because of the nature of the business in the case of firms such as IBM, Microsoft and Acer or because it is the route to market in the case of Expedia, Dell and CDWow. For firms in many other industries technology is changing the source of international competitive advantage from manufacturing and operations to knowledge management, emphasising the importance of supply chain management and integration for enhancing value.

For these reasons technological competence and capability become a key criterion for segmenting and targeting customers. Firms using e-marketing as a key element of their strategy will prioritise customers that are willing and able to do business over the Internet. Similarly, they will segment suppliers in the same way because of the lower cost of doing business with firms that use e-business. Of course, this puts at a severe disadvantage firms from emerging economies that are competing to be a member of a major MNE's supply chain if their local country infrastructure does not support e-business. This was highlighted in Illustration 12.2 and is further reinforced in Dilemma 12.1 that follows.

Market entry

Web-based services will be successful if firms develop a global strategy based upon the integrated value chain. As this is a pervasive method of entry, based on global communications, it can facilitate lower-risk access to difficult markets. By building online delivery capability it is possible to serve markets profitably where there might be limited demand. Of course, an e-commerce strategy is limited in scope simply because it appeals to a very specific segment – those that are able to gain access to the firm's Web site.

The impact of technology on strategy implementation and control

Product and service management

Technology supports the delivery and control of all the elements of the augmented product and service offer (Figure 8.1) and integrates the worldwide members of the supply chain as has been discussed earlier in this chapter. It is also used to speed up innovation and facilitate worldwide contributions to product and service development activity.

DILEMMA 12.1	Will e-commerce exclude or enhance businesses from emerging economies?

For twenty years Cordelia Salter-Nour was an IT expert for development projects in Africa and became frustrated by the fact that technology was not benefiting the most disadvantaged members of African society. So she set up eShopAfrica.com, which retails online African art and craftsmanship.

Quite deliberately, the site is targeting the 'snobbery market' – those that want to show off their original artefacts at dinner parties, and to cater for this the site is providing detailed information about each product. For US$1000 it is possible to purchase a coffin in the shape of a fish, aeroplane or beer bottle. These coffins originate from Ghana where the coffin has traditionally reflected how the deceased earned a living.

One of the biggest problems for the site is taking credit card payment as local banks cannot yet cope with this and international credit card service providers require a bank account to be held in the West. In eShopAfrica.com's case Ms Salter-Nour has solved the problem because she has a

personal credit card with a bank account held in the West, but this is unsatisfactory in the longer term.

The US market was expected to be large because of African-Americans keen to find out about their roots but the US market is rather disappointing at the moment because it is flooded by mass importers, who are often accused of paying unfair wage rates. Moreover, many Chinese products made to look like African products are imported to the US.

The site is operating fair trade and tries to ensure that a price is paid that will provide reasonable wages for the craft workers. Its goals are modest at this stage – to help five African craft businesses a year to become sustainable.

Question What are the main benefits and challenges of developing an online strategy in emerging economies?

Source: Adapted from Briony Hale, 'African crafts go online', BBC News Online, 3 February 2003

In doing this, technology is increasingly supporting, on the one hand, the standardisation of the components of the product, and creating worldwide product 'platforms' as was discussed in Illustration 8.8. On the other hand, however, it is enabling firms to offer increased customisation of products and services and one-to-one marketing.

Pricing

As we have discussed earlier in the chapter, technology is driving down costs and therefore prices through supply chain efficiencies, economies of scale, the experience curve effect and greater price transparency. Price transparency for customers and other stakeholders is created because of the ease with which it is now possible to compare prices offered by competing potential suppliers across borders by searching through the information on their Web sites. Some sites such as Expedia in travel and Kelkoo on a range of products in B2C markets and the sector and function e-hubs in B2B provide the opportunity for customers to compare prices on one site. The sophistication and usefulness of Web search activity is improving.

The Internet facilitates grey marketing and makes it much more difficult for many firms to operate specific geographic territories and different price differentials across country borders, so grey marketing may become less of an issue in international markets as firms give up hope of trying to control it. Other factors such as the euro in the EU also encourages price transparency by making it much easier for customers to compare prices on- or off-line by removing the need to make exchange rate calculations.

Price transparency has the effect of driving mature products towards commoditisation as products become less differentiated and competition is based largely on price. When there are many competitors, price transparency forces down prices as suppliers have to respond by cutting the costs of their products and services. This usually forces them to find ever-lower cost sources. The alternative is to innovate and develop new products and services or add additional services. However, these strategies will only work if customers perceive them to be valuable and of additional benefit over the commodity product alternative.

Customisation is clearly the opposite of commoditisation and therefore can be used partially to counter price transparency. Because international pricing embraces both pricing and financing the transaction, technology allows pricing to be customised. It can enable complex calculations to be made to facilitate the negotiation of mutually beneficial deals between supplier and customer with flexible pricing and financing and also control non-standard repayment schedules that ensure that the transaction is ultimately profitable. An example of this from personal finance is that it is possible to off-set longer-term loans, such as a mortgage to buy a house, against a current account and pay interest daily on the balance outstanding.

Channel management

Electronic marketing has encouraged disintermediation, or the removal of intermediaries from the supply chain, as suppliers market directly to customers. Technology now enables firms to efficiently manage thousands of small transactions that previously would have been left for an intermediary to undertake. This is possible now because e-marketing has typically lower transaction costs and is capable of managing large inventories, logistics, ordering and payments but also allows the virtual bundling of products that might be sourced from different partner suppliers. Disintermediation provides the manufacturer with stronger control of its activities in the market and avoids being so reliant on third parties. It also enables the distribution channels to be customised to the specific needs of the customers.

For those firms that are maintaining intermediaries within their distribution channel, technology allows much closer cooperation through sharing of market information but also greater control of intermediaries by making it easier to check on a daily basis that they are fulfilling their commitments to the supplier.

Communications

The main advantage of e-marketing communications is that they are targeted and are often based on one-to-one communications. The most important aspect is that they are based on being interactive. Customers are required to do something rather than being passive recipients of untargeted advertising or other promotion. As customers become more involved, so they are more likely to buy. The increase in eBay's business referred to earlier is quite probably due to customers spending a lot of time on the site and becoming 'hooked'.

Clearly the attractiveness and functionality of Web sites is key to success but the Web site must make it easy for customers to buy. Siegel (1999) explains that many firms build 'introvert Web sites' from the inside. They reflect how the firm or an existing product range is organised in the firm rather than 'extrovert Web sites' which reflect the customer groups that the firm intends to attract. This is particularly important in international markets where customers must feel that the Web site is built for them.

Marketing through even interactive Web sites is reactive, because potential customers must take the initiative and locate the Web site first. Word of mouth referral is important in building traffic to the Web site, but to gain a large market in unexciting business sectors it is not enough just to have a Web site. It is also necessary to proactively market and promote the brand and Web site in the traditional media. The fundamental questions of marketing need to be asked, such as who are we targeting, where will we find the target customers on the Internet and how will we get them directed to our site? How best can we then communicate our message to them globally and at low cost? The key is to deliver the right message to the right people at the right time in the right place using the right e-based communication channel.

Control, evaluation and learning

Technology enables firms to collect, transfer and analyse vast amounts of data from anywhere in the world. Using Enterprise Resource Planning (ERP) software they are able to control the use of resources and improve the efficiency of their operations. Financial management and control can be more immediate and more detailed. Firms use other processes and systems to control the supporting operations to ensure quality and efficiency of the manufacturing, distribution operations, and the effectiveness of the marketing processes and programmes.

These techniques can be applied in worldwide operations because they can be supported by information technology and systems. Underpinning all these techniques is the need to develop a learning organisation that develops good practice, shares new ideas and develops greater confidence in the abilities of its staff so that they can be empowered to take decisions in their own area of expertise and knowledge. Whilst many MNEs would claim to have developed a learning organisation within a country, few have yet genuinely achieved cross-border learning that enables them to evaluate and improve their programmes and processes based on knowledge shared worldwide.

Some limitations of e-commerce for international marketing strategy

There are some disadvantages in operating e-business globally, including the high cost of providing a global Web site with 24-hour service for customers who expect interactive capability, wherever possible, in their own language and culture and adapted to their own environment. There are also some significant perceived and real dangers associated with e-commerce. Customers are concerned with data security and the risks, for example, of their credit card number being stolen and used. Customers are also concerned with data protection and the use, storage and passing on to third parties of personal information to firms anywhere in the world. Of course technology is being continually developed and improved to try to overcome these difficulties.

Firms basing their business on e-commerce must recognise that there are typically low entry barriers and competitors have greater and easier access to information that can be used to challenge the existing supplier. Computer systems are still prone to system failure and corruption and it is still alarmingly easy for computer hackers and computer viruses to cause severe damage to multinational enterprises. Often MNEs do not publicise such difficulties as it may well deter customers. There is also a proliferation of anti-MNE Web sites that can publicise damaging stories – true or not – virtually without challenge. This is possible, of course, simply because of the relatively uncontrolled nature of the Internet.

Of course, the decisions of customers in e-commerce are strongly affected by cultural issues and the patterns of growth in different cultures will continue to be different.

International e-business marketing businesses face some challenges:

1 Customers from some countries, typically low context countries, are likely to embrace the Internet much more readily than those in high context cultures, because of the lower emphasis placed on implicit interactions when building relationships and purchasing products.

2 Brand values often depend on a number of communication methods, both explicit and implicit, such as image, reputation, word of mouth and continual exposure whilst travelling or shopping. This emphasises the need for an integrated communications approach involving virtual and physical media.

3 By being global, e-commerce favours global players. Consumers expect high quality of performance and image but these can be severely tarnished by a low-cost, poorly performing Web site and slow or inaccurate order fulfilment. One of the most important issues facing Internet advertisers is the degree to which customers will purchase from an international company rather than a domestic company.

4 The effectiveness of Web sites includes factors such as the ease of Web-site navigation, company and products information, shipping details and overall rating. US research suggested that if a Web site had negative ratings the likelihood of purchase from a domestic company was reduced by 42 per cent but from an international company by 87 per cent.

5 The barriers to entry must be significant if the defenders of domestic or limited country niches wish to retain their market share. It must be recognised by marketers that the marketing skills to ensure success in e-business are different from traditional skills in that success depends on attracting consumers to sites and this is typically more difficult because of the increased media 'noise'.

6 The development of intelligent agents that search for specific pieces of information on markets and potential suppliers means that marketers cannot base their appeal to customers on traditional marketing-mix factors but must find new sustainable competitive advantage.

Legislation

The aspect of the Internet that seems to raise most concern is the fact that there is very little control exerted and consequently the Internet is used for unethical and illegal purposes and to circumvent the law. The Internet has grown extremely rapidly and the application of existing law and introduction of legislation to control activities has lagged behind. Governments do not want to stifle development and so legislation is being developed not in anticipation but only as problems arise.

Problems of application of existing law to the Internet

The Internet removes traditional geographic boundaries, so that virtually anyone anywhere in the world can access a Web site. Zugelder, Flaherty and Johnson (2000) explain that a particular difficulty, of course, is the fact that Web sites are subject to the laws of individual countries, both home and host country where customers are based. Web sites are also subject to regional trade agreements (e.g. EU and NAFTA) and regulations of organisations such as the WTO, the World International Property Organisation (WIPO) and the Berne Convention on copyright law. Of course the situation is made worse because countries either do not recognise or interpret differently many conventions. For example, half the world nations (including China, India, Brazil and Taiwan) do not recognise the Berne Convention.

The result is a chaotic situation in which multiple and contradictory laws apply to the same transaction, leaving a marketer open to the possibility of unintentionally violating the laws of a foreign country. A whole series of issues arise in e-marketing, including what constitutes a contract in cyberspace, how international tax can be harmonised and how tax should be collected for online transactions.

There are many issues of intellectual property protection, including copyright infringement, inappropriate linking to information from another Web site and trademark infringement, such as the registering of existing trademarks as domain names for the Web site. Because of the demand for domain names, second-level (for example .co, .org and .com) and third-level country names (.uk and .de) have been added. Countries, including the UK, Mexico and Russia, have taken a 'first come, first served' approach to this, and companies such as Nike, Chrysler and Sony have failed to register as widely as they should have and have suffered as a consequence.

For e-marketing to succeed it is necessary to provide consumer protection for international consumer clients to avoid unfair and deceptive trading practices, such as unsubstantiated advertising claims and false endorsements. Relationship marketing is based, especially for small firms, on building substantial data on customers in order to retain their loyalty, but in a number of countries gathering such information is illegal as laws exist to protect consumer privacy.

Marketers must also know the difference between what is considered free speech and what is defamation and disparagement. In 1997 McDonald's won a court case against two self-proclaimed anarchists who had published leaflets defaming McDonald's but the case cost McDonald's US$15 million. At the time a rogue Web site, McSpotlight, run by volunteers in 22 countries added further derogatory material about McDonald's. Hundreds of rogue Web sites have been set up, such as I Hate McDonald's page and ToysRUs Sucks, and firms have considerable difficulty controlling the negative publicity that these sites create.

The new problems of the Internet

The problems discussed so far have related to the application of largely existing legislation to the new medium and the fact that the Internet crosses country borders indiscriminately. Other issues are the ease of access and lack of control of illegal activity. It has been estimated that a large percentage of international consumer e-commerce is devoted to pornography and a worrying part of this traffic is illegal and supporting paedophilia. It requires close cooperation between country law enforcement agencies to catch the culprits.

The ease of communicating with many recipients makes it easy to send out 'junk mail'. Millions of messages can be sent out worldwide in the hope of getting just a few responses. Many firms sell to potential customers through e-mails and text messages. However, if this is overused it degenerates into spam. Spam is the intrusive, offensive and often pornographic junk e-mail that fills up the inboxes of e-mail systems. It threatens to create gridlock on the Internet if it is not controlled. The US has proposed opt-out legislation so that spam would be legal unless the receiver has opted out of receiving it. The EU legislation is opt-in – spam could not be sent unless the receiver had given consent to receive it – and would be more effective in controlling spam.

In the UK, in May 2003, spam accounted for 55 per cent of all e-mails compared to 2–3 per cent in the previous year. It was estimated by the EU Spamhaus project that a third of unwanted e-mails received by children were hardcore pornography. The team had identified 200 of the worst spammers who were responsible for 90 per cent of all unsolicited e-mails. The 200 were typically fraudsters and habitual criminals exploiting cross-border opportunities.

MOVING TO A CUSTOMER-LED STRATEGY

Towards the turn of the millennium a major debate was taking place, with certain writers suggesting that technology and, in particular, e-business was going to revolutionise business and change the fundamental principles of marketing for ever by allowing anyone anywhere in the world to buy online from anyone else. The technology would level the playing field between small and large firms and the most innovative firms, small or large, would become the winners. The technologists rather than the marketers would be in control. As a result of this, money poured into start-up 'dotcom' businesses and their share prices went through the roof on predictions of astronomical growth, but of course the bubble burst.

Seybold (1998) provides an answer to the question of why many e-businesses failed, 'What's the secret of a successful e-business initiative? What's the winning formula? You've guessed it. It starts by focusing on your existing customers, figuring out what they want and need and how you can make life easier for them.' Peppers and Rogers (1997) explain that every day, all around the world, managers worry about the declining loyalty of their customers. Customers are being wooed ever more feverishly by competitors offering better prices, better deals – a process that has dramatically accelerated with the growth of the Internet. As customers become more interactive with the companies they buy from, business success hinges increasingly on creating long-term, profitable, 'one-to-one' customer relationships.

At the start of the chapter we emphasised the idea that technology is an enabler, and Hamill and Stevenson (2003) suggest that technology facilitates cost-effective relationship building, but does not automatically achieve a customer-focused approach. Technology has shifted the balance of power from suppliers to customers. Consequently, customer dominance must be accepted and those arrogant firms that take customers for granted will suffer. Organisations must adopt a **customer led** approach. This means that they must develop innovative approaches to sales, marketing and overall corporate strategy that are driven by what customers need and want.

The objective of being customer led is to identify, acquire, retain and grow 'quality' customers. Nykamp (2001) suggests that organisations must achieve competitive differentiation by building impermeable customer relationships and the challenge is to use the interactive power of the Internet to facilitate this by helping the organisation to build close one-to-one relationships with their most valuable and growable customers.

Many firms have recognised the need to be customer led and have responded by implementing sophisticated and expensive Customer Relationship Management systems. Hamill and Stevenson suggest that many of these systems have failed to produce the expected return because they have been technology driven rather than customer led. The term CRM has been hijacked by software vendors promising 'out-of-the-box' solutions to complex strategic, organisational and human resources problems. They claim that technology has a part to play but customer-led is not about software, database marketing, loyalty programmes, customer bribes or hard selling. It is about building strong one-to-one relationships with quality customers, achieving customer loyalty and maximising customer lifetime earnings and re-engineering the firm towards satisfying the needs of 'quality' customers on a customised and personalised basis. The most convincing reason for a customer to buy from any company in the world is that they are totally satisfied, have no reason to complain about the service they receive and are surprised and delighted by some of the firm's innovative actions.

To deliver this requires a more fundamental reinvention of the firm if it wishes to really succeed in the future. A new mindset is needed together with an innovative approach to the strategy. In practice firms will need to:

- *Focus not on markets but on quality customers from anywhere in the world*. By quality customers it is the strategically significant, most valuable and 'growable' customers that should be given the highest priority. The suggestion is that, over time, firms have moved from supplying markets to serving market segments, and are now focusing on serving individual customers one at a time.

- *Focus on one-to-one relationships*. To do this firms must learn about customers and deliver personalised and customised products, services and support in order to maximise the up- and cross-selling opportunities. The implications of this are that at one level firms must be sensitive to the customer's business and social culture and the customer's business dynamics. At another level the firm must be able to form supply and value chain alliances that enable the up- and cross-selling to be developed for the customer's benefit

- *Increasing both lifetime and short-term revenue from customers*. Firms must focus on the delivery of exceptional value by developing an effective worldwide supply chain, building ever-closer relationships both with customers and partners and finding ways to erect barriers to entry by competitor firms.

- *Win-win*. The long-term business relationships must be valuable for both supplier and provider and so long-term value for the customer and firm must be maximised. This could require some compromises by both parties to achieve this.

■ *Integrated and coordinated approach*. The success of a customer-led relationship building approach is that it requires commitment at all levels, creating, communicating and delivering value. For all businesses, but particularly global businesses, this is clearly a major challenge.

Most firms would claim to be customer led but the real test for them is whether they would be willing to change their strategy radically because of the trends that are being perceived in the marketplace. Lindstrom (2003) reports on research that suggests that marketing strategies in the future may need to be changed radically in order to be customer led. Dilemma 12.2 asks just how far firms should change their international marketing strategy.

Technology enabling

It is evident that information technology and management systems are critical to the successful implementation of such an approach and the key challenge is to manage and integrate the customer-facing systems with the operational and management systems internal to the firm and its supply chain. Even here, however, the major challenge is not that of setting up the systems and processes but rather obtaining total commitment from staff, no matter what their cultural background, to implement the systems.

Technology provides the mechanisms by which strategic planning of a customer-led approach can be effectively managed. The elements include customer mapping and developing an integrated, coordinated, multi-channel approach to planning in order to answer the questions on a worldwide basis: who should we serve, what should we serve to them and how should we serve them?

| DILEMMA 12.2 | Should international marketing be led by the tweenagers? |

The next generation of consumers will have a dramatic effect on promotion and communications. This group is the tweens who are now aged 8–14. Lindstrom (2003) paints a picture of their behaviour and communication now and suggests ways in which they will change marketing. He maintains that they are already influencing 80 per cent of the brands purchased by their parents and affect 67 per cent of their families' car purchases.

Thirty per cent of tweens text each other several times a day, 15 per cent prefer to communicate with their friends via the net or mobile phone rather than face-to-face and one-fifth communicate regularly with tweens in other countries. They adapt their language while texting because it is perceived as cool. Grammatically correct sentences in advertising are considered by them to be outdated. They spend an average of 2.5 hours a day in front of the computer and prefer surfing the net to watching the TV and half would rather play a computer game than watch a TV show.

This group is the first generation to be truly interactive and Lindstrom suggests that traditional TV advertising and Internet banner ads will not win business. What will be necessary will be product placement or situation placement – getting the right message in front of the right audience at the right time. Brands will need to be interactive.

The dilemma for customer-led firms is: to what degree should they change their international marketing strategies in order to be a first mover, or should they wait to see how the next technological revolution will affect consumer behaviour?

Source: Lindstrom, M. and Seybold, P. (2003)

SUMMARY

- Technology is changing the way business is done in international markets. New technology provides new possible solutions to solve old problems but also sets new challenges for international marketing management.

- Firms will underperform or even fail if they are not able to exploit the global opportunities offered by the new technology or if they take the wrong decisions about how new technology might change their industry sector.

- Consumer e-marketing, and especially innovative business models, such as online auctions, attract the interest of global consumers and facilitate new routes to market.

- Business-to-business e-commerce models, however, are having the greatest effect on international marketing. For example, e-procurement through e-hubs enables purchasing to be more efficiently managed worldwide.

- Although the Internet and advances in telecommunications have had the most dramatic effect on international marketing other technologies and software to support integrated marketing solutions have been part of this change.

- Greater cooperation because of improvements in communication and the ease of information sharing make supply chains more effective. Excess capacity and increased competition mean that the power in the supply chain is increasingly favouring the customer.

- Because of this, firms will need to work ever harder to find new customers and retain the loyalty of existing customers. To achieve this their international marketing strategies will have to be customer led. But technology must be embraced to make this happen.

KEYWORDS

B2B	industry hubs
B2C	information technology
customer led	Internet
customer relationship management	knowledge management
customisation	legislation
e-commerce	online auctions
e-procurement	supply chain management
enabling technologies	telecommunications
function hubs	Web site

CASE STUDY   Travel distribution

Background

According to the World Tourism Organisation, international tourism generated US$463.6 billion in receipts worldwide in 2001. Despite the economic slowdown, terrorism and conflict the tourism sector continues to expand. In 2002 the number of international tourist arrivals exceeded 700 million for the first time in history.

However, tourists now search for better value and increasingly book at the last minute – all of which affects revenue levels. As a result, many tourism-related businesses are struggling for survival but online travel distribution continues to grow in volume and revenue, with many online travel Web sites growing at over 100 per cent. Forester Research shows that of the B2C e-commerce revenue of US$48 billion in 2001, over US$14 billion was spent on travel products. This may understate the e-commerce contribution as the Travel Industry Association of America (TIA) estimates that in that year around 64 million Americans researched their travel options online but only 39 million booked online.

Efficient and effective distribution is particularly important in the tourism sector, as travel products are highly perishable and so every airline seat, hotel room or cruise-berth needs to be sold for every day at an optimum price in order to maximise profitability. Travel agents and tour operators have traditionally been the core of the distribution system, helping balance supply and demand by filling seats for the suppliers (airlines, hotels etc.) and helping consumers make choices and seize bargains.

Suppliers, intermediaries and end-consumers are dependent on comprehensive, accurate and timely information to aid their travel-related decisions and advances in information and communications technologies have superseded the traditional paper-based systems.

Global distribution systems

During the 1960s the major airlines used electronic systems to help control their growing number of flights and fares. Designed initially to be used by each airline's own reservations staff, these central reservations systems (CRS) were gradually made available to travel agents to help them make reservations directly. Gradually the systems were expanded from airline seats to hotels, car hire and cruises. The resulting 'one-stop travel shop' information systems are now called Global Distribution Systems (GDS). Four main companies (Amadeus, Galileo, WorldSpan and Sabre) dominate the sector along with several smaller regional GDSs, including Infini (Japan), Axess (Japan), Tapas (Korea), Fantasia (South Pacific), and Abacus (Asia/Pacific).

The GDSs were developed primarily for air flights and so many other travel businesses developed their own computerised reservations system (CRS) and linked them electronically to the GDS to gain access to the powerful travel agent market. They pay a transaction fee to the GDS owners for each booking processed.

In 1994 the Internet revolutionised travel distribution. The GDS-based electronic distribution system enabled certain firms to control the supply chain, whereas Web-based distribution encourages both competition and cooperation in a very open way. Consequently, most participants in the travel distribution chain now compete with each other using Web sites with booking facilities and freely available information. The providers, such as airlines, are re-engineering their travel systems to bypass both the GDS and the travel agent and create a Web site with direct links with the customer.

Online travel agencies

However, as well as more competition, there is also more cooperation. Many online travel sites were set up around 1997 but a small number now dominate the market. Expedia, Travelocity and Priceline were set up in the US; Ebookers and Lastminute.com were set up in the UK and have a European focus. Hotels.com specialises in hotel booking but, following takeover, is now a sister company of Expedia. Interesting new business models have emerged with the aim of matching supply and demand. Priceline asks customers to name the price they are prepared to pay and invites suppliers to bid for the sale, and Lastminute.com disposes of short lead-time products.

The key attraction to customers of online travel agencies is that they offer multiple products (air, hotel, car etc.) from multiple vendors and the facility for customers to make comparisons. To be successful, they need to be full-service and provide the ability to research and purchase an entire trip online. In order to do this, they need the detailed content and access to reservation facilities that they can only get by cooperating with other distribution providers. As a result of this, non-exclusive virtual alliances are being formed, with companies combining to develop new synergistic relationships.

For example, the GDS, in addition to facilitating travel agent bookings, also provides the reservation engine behind many of the online travel agency Web sites – in effect to its own competitors. However, each partner benefits – the GDS by leveraging its investment in developing and maintaining its reservation engine and its virtual partners by having access to an efficient service without having to develop one for themselves.

Online travel distribution is increasing in Europe, particularly in the UK, France and Germany and, as Internet use grows in Asia-Pacific, the 2003 level of 3 per cent online bookings was set to grow. Expedia and Hotels.com have entered this region too.

But the online agencies realise they must change their model too. Three-quarters of online travel items purchased are air tickets, but US airlines are reducing online commissions as ticket prices fall, and many airlines are encouraging customers to buy directly from their own Web site, thus avoiding them altogether. Online agencies must look to complementary products, such as insurance, which offer higher commissions. They are also resorting to more traditional methods of generating income, albeit with the online angle, as the way to prosper in the future. The *merchant model* involves the bulk purchase of inventory at discount prices and resale to the consumers, for example the 'Expedia Special Rate' programme. The *packaging model* involves the online agency packaging travel products for customers rather like tour operators do.

The changing balance of power

Power has changed in the travel business. Consolidation amongst the online agencies means that the top five controlled 59 per cent of the entire online travel market in 2001. There appear to be few opportunities for small firms or individual travel suppliers, such as a hotel chain, to secure a significant share of the market.

The online agencies exert considerable power over the airlines now because of the number of bookings they control and, for example, they have resisted the airlines' attempts to restrict commissions. Aware of the potential threat to their power base, a number of major US airlines established Orbitz as their own online distributor. It grew quickly because the airlines channelled their cheapest seats through Orbitz rather than through competitor online agencies. Hotwire and Opodo, both set up by airlines, and Travelweb, set up by a number of hotel groups are similar online businesses set up to challenge the power of the online agencies. Legal claims relating to uncompetitive and monopolistic practices inevitably followed in the US.

Clearly online purchase of travel will continue to grow, but consumer research suggests that there appears to be little differentiation of online brands. Moreover, there are likely to be some major battles between the big players in the travel supply distribution market in the future.

Questions

1 Identify the key issues affecting the travel distribution market, including the competitor, customer and environment factors. Explain the role of technology in driving and responding to changes in these factors.

2 Develop an international marketing strategy for an online travel agency that focuses on being customer led.

3 Explain the action that should be taken to ensure that technology enables this customer-led strategy.

Robin Lowe, Sheffield Hallam University
Source: Adapted from Mintel reports on Travel Distribution, sourced February 2003, and other public sources

DISCUSSION QUESTIONS

1 Choose a service firm. Write a report to the management of the firm on the factors that should be considered when developing an e-based international marketing strategy.

2 As a consultant to an electronics component supplier from a Central European country, explain how the development of e-hubs to facilitate global business-to-business transactions will affect their business. What do you consider to be the critical success factors in their survival and growth?

3 Write a report to the Chief Executive of an insurance company critically analysing the effects of the growth of e-commerce on the global channels of distribution.

4 A small firm which provides consultancy in engineering is seeking to develop an e-commerce strategy to enable them to grow substantially

from their current base of customers in eight export markets. Develop an international marketing strategy that would enable them to do this.

5 A Chinese manufacturer of speciality foods is setting up a Web site to support an online retailing operation in Europe. What advice would you give them?

REFERENCES

Hamill, J. and Stevenson, A. (2003) 'Customer-led strategic Internet marketing', in Hart, S. (ed.) *Marketing Changes*, Thomson Learning.

Hoffman, K.D. (2003) 'Services Marketing', in *Marketing Best Practice*, Thomson Learning.

Kaplan, S. and Dawney, M. (2000) 'E-Hubs: The new B2B marketplaces', *Harvard Business Review*, 78 (3), May–June: 97–103.

Lindgren, J.H.E. (2003) 'Marketing', in *Marketing Best Practice*, Thomson Learning.

Lindstrom, M. and Seybold, P. (2003) *BRANDchild*, Kogan Page.

Nykamp, M. (2001) *The Customer Differential*, AMACOM.

Peppers, D. and Rogers, M. (1997) *Enterprise One to One: Tools for competing in the Interactive Age*, London: Piatkus.

Seigel, D. (1999) *Futurize your enterprise*, John Wiley & Sons.

Seybold, P. (1998) *Customers.com: How to Create a Profitable Business strategy for the Internet and Beyond*, London: Century Business.

Zugelder, M.T., Flaherty, T.B. and Johnson, J.P. (2000) 'Legal issues associated with international Internet marketing', *International Marketing Review*, 17 (3).

3

International marketing planning: implementation, control and evaluation

Introduction

In the previous two special focus sections on planning we explored the dimensions of analysis and strategy development. We now turn to the implementation of the plan through the application of the marketing mix that has been covered in the Part 3 chapters. In practice, of course, some of the content of the previous chapters needs to be revisited because there is no clear distinction between what might be considered strategy development and implementation. This is especially true of product and service strategy, where many decisions can be regarded as operational, and market entry, where many decisions are closely associated with distribution.

The starting point for implementation is planning the international marketing mix. This includes completing the product and service plan, preparing communications, distribution and pricing plans. The plan should explain how relationships with key partners can be built and managed within the supply chain, how customer relationships can be developed and how technology can be use to facilitate the firm's international marketing plan implementation.

The success of the implementation plan is also dependent on the planning ability, management capability and the motivation and effectiveness of the firm's staff. Management need to anticipate and plan for potential problems that might arise in managing the implementation stage.

We also consider how to establish appropriate performance standards and measurement techniques that can be used to maintain control over the plan and the evaluation that will enable corrective action to be taken whenever the firm's performance deviates from the plan (as it surely will).

In this activity the focus is on developing the skills of decision making in a local business unit at an operational level, whilst still keeping in mind the implication of these local decisions within the firm's global strategy.

Learning objectives

On completing this activity the reader should be able to:

- Appreciate the opportunities for growth in an international service sector
- Use appropriate concepts and an analysis of local factors to develop marketing mix implementation strategies
- Appreciate the benefit of developing better customer relationship management
- Identify the methods that should be used for the management and control of the business

ISS cleaning up the world

The company is based in Denmark. It operates in 38 countries in the EU, Asia and Latin America with 300 000 staff. It is in the top ten employers in Europe and has aspirations to dominate its sector in Asia. Would you guess the company is a contract cleaner and the company is ISS Group? Most people think that cleaning is done by small local operators, using unskilled, part-time, casual, low-paid and largely unmotivated staff. ISS are proof that it can be done another way.

Market environment changes

ISS's growth strategy has been built upon the opportunities that have resulted from the changes in the macro- and micro-environment. ISS spotted the

Robin Lowe, Sheffield Hallam University (from various sources)

opportunity to rejuvenate and restructure the cleaning business, which traditionally was characterised by having a negative external image, many small-scale, local and rather unprofessional operations and poor management. It has grown rapidly on the back of the move by both private and public sector organisations to focus on their core activities and outsource support services and facilities management. ISS actually offers a very wide range of facilities management services, ranging from property or IT management, landscaping and waste collection through to pest control. Clients such as hospitals, travel and transport, and computer firms increasingly outsource specialised as well as general facilities management services.

The trend to outsource facilities management has gradually spread from a few countries and particular business sectors. The concept is gaining ground much more widely – more parts of the world, more business sectors and all sizes of business. As we shall see, the company is building its competitive advantage on the changing aspirations and needs of its international employees and customers.

The ISS competitive advantage and strategy

The rapid growth of ISS is in part due to its expertise in contract tendering and project management but the key to success is the contribution of its own people. It invests heavily in the training of all staff, not just managers, to maintain quality, avoid accidents, ensure the correct cleaning agents are applied, and time and supplies are managed cost effectively. It supports the promotion of staff from 'shop floor' to management and recognises that not all good staff will have the ability to be managers. So it appoints team leaders who have the responsibility for profit and performance on individual cleaning contracts and managing a small team of people. It believes in peer pressure and so even for contracts with small and medium-sized enterprises, where normally one person would do the work, ISS provides a two- or three-person 'hit squad'. This ensures that even a huge multi-national has a local 'face'.

An ISS objective is low staff turnover and so it gains from its investment in training. Its pay rates are a little higher, but most of all ISS wants motivated staff who are proud to work for the company. In Denmark it achieves 20 per cent staff turnover against an industry average around 80–90 per cent. It is also aiming at achieving the target of 80 per cent full-time staff, again very different from industry averages. It will take some time to achieve this worldwide, because the firm has grown through takeovers and many of the employment policies of the acquired firms have to be changed.

ISS has therefore identified a distinctive transnational segment that it can serve. Its positioning is determined by the whole ethos of the company, exemplified by the way it manages its staff. Essentially this means that it targets those customers and sectors that can benefit from a very professional service that focuses on quality. Conversely it is unlikely to appeal, at least initially, to those organisations that are only interested in a very low-cost supplier.

Growth strategy

The firm clearly sees growth opportunities in all regions of the world. These growth aspirations can be justified because the firm is offering a more innovative approach to cleaning at the service delivery level. It is a professional operator with considerable resources and so can handle large complex contracts. Only multinational service providers will appeal to multi-national customers wishing to outsource facilities management and yet maintain standards and control across borders and cultures.

ISS's business growth comes partly from winning new contracts where its existing staff or new recruits work for a new customer, partly from taking over the management of a customer's existing department and existing staff and partly from taking over existing cleaning companies that already have a customer base, staff, contacts and a recognised presence in the market.

After its initial growth phase in its home market the firm's growth has accelerated because of its expansion into international markets, particularly through the acquisition of existing businesses.

Implementation

The critical factor for success for ISS and, therefore, the subject of the series of tasks here, is developing an international marketing implementation strategy. The key is to recognise that success in international services is based on achieving good people relationships at all levels.

The key task is to consistently deliver service at the local level. Every interaction between the cleaner and the customer is vital to the success of the contract. Office workers do not like or expect to be interrupted by the cleaners but ISS realise that some contact – say half an hour overlap between the cleaning hours and office hours – can provide useful feedback on customer satisfaction. The successful delivery of the services is arguably more important than offering low prices for a service that the customer may not be able to rely on.

Relationship management is vital as customers are often reluctant to change a service provider without good reason. Often contracts will be renewed for years. But if there are complaints the contract will be terminated very quickly and the news very rapidly goes through the industry, damaging the firm's reputation.

Good techniques, management systems and human resource processes are essential for dealing with people. However, service expectations and service delivery are affected very much by cultural considerations, so this is often an important consideration in maintaining service delivery consistency.

One of the main considerations in effective implementation for ISS is that frequently they must take over not just firms and contracts but the management of the people that are currently working there along with their existing employment rights. Changing people's conditions of work, contracts and payment to bring them into line with those prevalent in the facilities management sector and the new company's conditions is often difficult. For example, when ISS won a contract for cleaning police stations in Leicestershire, UK, staff were offered the option of leaving with a compensation package or agreeing to fewer paid holidays, revised working hours, different arrangements for sick pay and a cut in the number of hours worked. The negotiations ended up at an employment tribunal.

In taking over contracts and companies ISS inevitably must deal with the employment rights, health and safety laws and other legislation that is often specific to the local country. Moreover, they often have to manage the different working conditions applied by different companies and the different cultures associated with employment in different countries.

Finally, monitoring and control of a large people-based service industry is critical, as ISS has found to its cost. Failure to monitor and control its operation can lead to disastrous consequences. It was in the 'back office' where the problem occurred in ISS. In the mid-1990s poor control in the US failed to spot accounting errors in a key division and this almost drove the firm into bankruptcy.

Sources: Adapted from *The Financial Times*, 3 September 2001, *The Bangkok Post*, 16 December 2000, *The Guardian*, 27 August 2001, *The Economist*, 25 April 1998, *The Leicester Mercury*, 15 September 1998 and other sources

The task

1 Critically analyse the global marketing environment for ISS, paying particular attention to the changing nature of business-to-business buying by large domestic and global clients.

2 Choose one region of the world, and develop a marketing strategy in outline. Focus on the marketing mix implementation issues, including an assessment of the key brand, product, service and communications issues. Identify, too, the factors that will influence pricing.

3 Develop a relationship marketing approach that will build necessary partnerships with key customers and stakeholders to obtain long-term business.

4 Prepare a plan for the control, management and continuous improvement of the operations, including the organisation structure, measures and processes that are required to achieve sustained success.

Useful Web sites

www.issworld.com; www.ifma.org; www.bifm.org and online newspapers which provide details of local contracts and takeovers.

Getting started

This section focuses on the business-to-business sector and a service business too. You should use this case study not only to focus on the implementation issues of the strategy process but also to study in greater depth the particular issues involved in the B2B sector and the service sector. Facilities management as an outsourced service is a relatively recent growth sector but it is now a very significant sector in terms of revenue, staff employment and now international activity. Clearly the effective delivery of people-based services requires an appreciation of staff motivation and management, service expectation, customer relationship building and the cultural issues that underpin much of this.

Task 1 requires an analysis of the factors that have led to this growth in facilities management in international markets and of the factors that will determine the nature of purchasing in the future – the degree to which it will be in the form of competitive tenders or relationship building with long-term clients. By now you should have a very good understanding of how you can access and analyse research material from libraries and online sources to complete this task. ISS have focused on Asia for growth, whilst not losing sight of the growth possibilities in its existing markets. You should focus on one region in order to complete task 2. You require an understanding of the facilities management services that must be provided, how the services are bought and managed and the nature of outsourcing relationships. Again you will find

FIGURE III

Key factors to consider in evaluating the business-to-business market for facilities management

The element of the plan	Some concepts, models and issues to be addressed
Environmental analysis	• Identify the global trends that have provided the opportunity for growth in the facilities management sector • Analyse the nature of customer needs and the nature of competition in the sector • Evaluate the ISS strategy and its regional focus
Marketing mix	• Building the corporate identity and managing the brand • Product differentiation and the three service Ps • Communication to customers and other stakeholders and negotiating new contracts • Managing the delivery to achieve customer satisfaction • Managing costs and the pricing strategy • The use of technology to improve the operation
Relationship marketing	• The methods of identifying current and potential high value customers • Knowledge and database management • Customer relationship management
Control and management	• The organisation and management structure using the 7S framework • Internal communications with its own staff • Financial and marketing measures and controls • Performance management and improvement processes, including benchmarking, balanced scorecard and self-assessment and improvement • Technology-enabled systems

substantial amounts of material online which will give you an appreciation of how this is done, what leads to success and also what leads to failure and the termination of contracts.

Customer satisfaction is very dependent on the customers' perception of the delivery by the individual staff doing the jobs. Consequently, setting realistic customer expectations, motivating and training staff, solving problems effectively and managing a cost-effective service are all critical for success. Task 4 requires you to think about how you would organise and manage this on a global basis.

In completing the tasks you need to consider the issues highlighted in the following framework shown in Figure III.

The way forward

Strategy development and planning is a continuous process. Having completed the tasks in this section, you will have gained a better understanding of the facilities management business sector and the strategy of ISS on both a strategic and operational (implementation)

level. You should now be well informed to revisit the strategy development process.

You should return to the Part 1 planning framework on page 138 to review the current market environment for ISS as the basis for their ongoing strategy. The most important issue is to decide where and how the firm can maintain its international expansion, using an assessment of the market environment, customer demands and competitor activity. Given the firm's ambitions in Asia, you might focus on the market factors in the countries of this region and use the market information and research framework to identify further growth opportunities or you may return to their more established regional markets to assess the opportunities to increase market share. Finally, you might reassess the company capability and expertise that will be expected to underpin its continued expansion.

You should then return to Part 2 and, using the framework on page 290, review the firm's vision and objectives as stated on the Web site and decide if they are still appropriate. You should re-evaluate and restate the firm's competitive advantage and assess how this informs the international positioning of the ISS brand. Using the recent data available online you should assess the market entry methods used and the effectiveness of these methods in delivering the strategy.

Checklist for success

Having completed the integrative learning activities you should think about how comprehensive your work is and whether you really have addressed the fundamental issues that could well make the difference between a failing and a successful strategy. To help you do this we have identified some of the issues you should consider. Clearly you may not be able to answer these in detail because you will not have sufficient detail about the firms' operations but you should have thought about how you would address the issues given access to the information.

Does the plan contain:

- Assumptions about the world economy and the environmental trends in the principal markets?

- Details of historical performance (sales, costs, profitability)?

- Forecasts of future performance based on (a) an extrapolation of the past, (b) alternative scenarios?

- Identified opportunities and threats?

- Analysis of the company strengths, weaknesses and future capabilities in comparison with local and international competition?

- Long-term aims and objectives and the strategies to achieve them?

- One-year marketing objectives and individual strategies (for example, budgets, brand objectives and development of personnel)?

- Country-by-country forecasts and targets?

- Country-by-country plans for all marketing activities and coordination with other functions (for example, manufacturing)?

- An explanation of how country plans will be integrated regionally or globally if appropriate?

- A summary of the critical factors for success?

- An assessment of the likely competitor response? If your objective is to increase market share, your competitors will not simply lie down and let you without fighting back!

- A contingency component for when the unexpected happens and things do not go to plan?

- A control process for feedback, evaluation and taking corrective action?

Index